THE RATIONALITY OF DICTATORS

Series Supranational Criminal Law: Capita Selecta, Volume 22

Recently published in the series:

6. *Supranational Criminology: Towards a Criminology of International Crimes*, Alette Smeulers and Roelof Haveman (eds.)
7. *Individual Criminal Liability for the International Crime of Aggression*, Gerhard Kemp
8. *Collective Violence and International Criminal Justice – An Interdisciplinary Approach*, Alette Smeulers (ed.)
9. *International Criminal Law from a Swedish Perspective*, Iain Cameron, Malin Thunberg Schunke, Karin Påle Bartes, Christoffer Wong and Petter Asp
10. *The Implementation of the European Arrest Warrant in the European Union: Law, Policy and Practice*, Massimo Fichera
11. *The Principle of Mutual Recognition in Cooperation in Criminal Matters*, Annika Suominen
12. *The European Public Prosecutor's Office*, Martijn Willem Zwiers
13. *Victimological Approaches to International Crimes: Africa*, Rianne Letschert, Roelof Haveman, Anne-Marie de Brouwer, Antony Pemberton (eds.)
14. *The United States and International Criminal Tribunals*, Harry M. Rhea
15. *EU Sanctions: Law and Policy Issues Concerning Restrictive Measures*, Iain Cameron (ed.)
16. *Whose Responsibility?* Malin Thunberg Schunke
17. *Genocidal Gender and Sexual Violence*, Usta Kaitesi
18. *Addressing the Intentional Destruction of the Environment during Warfare under the Rome Statute of the International Criminal Court*, Steven Freeland
19. *Individual Criminal Liability for the International Crime of Aggression*, Gerhard Kemp
20. *Selective Enforcement and International Criminal Law: The International Criminal Court and Africa*, James Nyawo
21. *The Governance of Complementary Global Regimes and the Pursuit of Human Security: The interaction between the United Nations and the International Criminal Court*, Andrea Marrone

THE RATIONALITY OF DICTATORS

Towards a more effective implementation of the responsibility to protect

Maartje WEERDESTEIJN

intersentia
Cambridge – Antwerp – Portland

Intersentia Ltd
Sheraton House | Castle Park
Cambridge | CB3 0AX | United Kingdom
Tel.: +44 1223 370 170 | Fax: +44 1223 370 169
Email: mail@intersentia.co.uk
www.intersentia.com | www.intersentia.co.uk

Distribution for the UK and Ireland:
NBN International
Airport Business Centre, 10 Thornbury Road
Plymouth, PL6 7 PP
United Kingdom
Tel.: +44 1752 202 301 | Fax: +44 1752 202 331
Email: orders@nbninternational.com

Distribution for Europe and all other countries:
Intersentia Publishing nv
Groenstraat 31
2640 Mortsel
Belgium
Tel.: +32 3 680 15 50 | Fax: +32 3 658 71 21
Email: mail@intersentia.be

Distribution for the USA and Canada:
International Specialized Book Services
920 NE 58th Ave. Suite 300
Portland, OR 97213
USA
Tel.: +1 800 944 6190 (toll free) | Fax: +1 503 280 8832
Email: info@isbs.com

The Rationality of Dictators. Towards a more effective implementation of the responsibility to protect

Cover image: Francisco DE GOYA (1746-1828), Etching, Plate 40 from 'Los desastres de la guerra'

ISBN 978-1-78038-443-7
D/2016/7849/103
NUR 828

British Library Cataloguing in Publication Data. A catalogue record for this book is available from the British Library.

ACKNOWLEDGEMENTS

Having the opportunity to write this book has been a privilege and I would like to express my appreciation to Tilburg Law School for making this research possible.

Furthermore, I would like to thank my supervisors. There have been many people who have influenced and inspired me academically, but none more so than Alette Smeulers. I feel fortunate to have had such a phenomenal researcher, gifted lecturer and above all kind and compassionate person as my supervisor. You always believed in me, you allowed me to believe in myself and I cannot tell you how much this meant to me. Thank you for only strengthening my love and enthusiasm for the field, for your invaluable comments on my research and for all the advice you have given me throughout the years.

Tijs Kooijmans once famously said in his inaugural lecture '*Dit is mijn zaak*' (2011). Thank you for making it your *zaak*, task at hand, to provide me with insights and guidance. Your involvement enhanced the quality of my PhD and opened my eyes repeatedly to a new perspective. I am very appreciative of the fact that you always made time for me, and thankful for all the questions you posed, and answers you gave.

I looked forward to each and every day I worked at Tilburg University and this is also due to the lovely colleagues I have had the pleasure to work with. Thank you for all the laughter and support.

I would also like to thank my former colleagues at Griffith University, Australia who graciously welcomed me in their midst as a visiting scholar. From the day I started there, I felt as though I was part of your team and am so grateful for all your comments and feedback on my work. Stephen, I cannot thank you enough for providing me with the opportunity to come to Australia and thoroughly enjoyed working with you on our article.

In addition, I would like to thank everyone who has made the time to comment on my work, whether it be in a brainstorm session, by reading a chapter or through feedback when I presented my research. Of course, I would like to thank the reading committee in particular: professors Alex Bellamy, Marc

Groenhuijsen, Stephan Parmentier, Nikolas Raijkovic and Wouter Werner. The comments I received have truly enhanced the quality of the book.

My dear *paranimfen*: thank you so much for everything. Barbora, you are an amazing scholar, and above all, a great friend. Thank you for always being there for me and for all our discussions that stem from a love and passion for the field that, considering its gruesome nature, not everyone can relate to. Marlijn, we have come a long way from our shared office at the VU. This is what we always wanted, and now, here we are, published authors. Throughout it all, I came to admire you for the beautiful person that you are and feel blessed for being able to share this journey with you.

I would also like to thank my friends and family. Thank you for all the faith you had in me, and all the love you gave me.

Last but not least: Martijn thank you for always being supportive. For encouraging me to realize my dreams and to pursue my passion. I love you now and always.

To the next generation, to Daniël who has my heart, may the world you grow up in be a safer and more peaceful one.

Tilburg, September 2016

CONTENTS

CHAPTER 1
INTRODUCTION

1.1. INTRODUCTION AND RESEARCH QUESTION

On January 7 1979, Pol Pot was forced to flee from Phnom Penh as Vietnamese forces enter the city. After years of having inflicted death and destruction on his own country and the contested border region with Vietnam, Pol Pot was finally removed from power. During his reign, the people of Cambodia[1] were subjected to constant starvation, torture and were worked to death (Chandler, 1999). After just four years in power, between one and two million people had died – up to a quarter of the population (Chandler, 1999, p. 4; Kiernan, 2003, p. 587). Because Vietnam's invasion violated international law, it initially denied its involvement and placed the responsibility on an army of refugees that were trained by Vietnam (Bazyler, 1987, pp. 608-609; Morris, 1999, p. 109; Power, 2013, p. 141). Despite the fact that the invasion probably saved thousands of lives, it was harshly condemned by most countries (Hanlon, 2006b, pp. 60-61). Vietnam became a pariah state and the old regime of Pol Pot continued to be recognized as the legitimate government of the country, retaining its seat at the UN (Morris, 1999, pp. 221-222). Sovereignty, at this point in time, meant leaders were free to do as they pleased within the borders of their countries (Evans, 2008, p. 21).

Twenty years later, another intervention without explicit Security Council authorization, forced a different dictator to compromise in order to stay in power. During the war in Kosovo, Milosevic had initiated a brutal ethnic cleansing campaign that had displaced thousands of people. The violence was reminiscent of the horrible crimes that had been perpetrated just several years before when Yugoslavia fell apart, and NATO decided it was time for more decisive action. After Milosevic refused to sign the peace agreement at Rambouillet, they decided to start bombing Serbia proper in order to persuade Milosevic to return to the negotiating table (Power, 2013, pp. 444-451). While the war in Kosovo also

1 For reasons of mere consistency and continuity, the region that has become known under various names, most notably Cambodia and Democratic Kampuchea, will be referred to throughout the book as Cambodia. Similarly, the territory that has existed under different names between 1918 and 1991 will be referred to throughout as Yugoslavia. After Yugoslavia fell apart the subregions become more important and in those instances they will be referred to by their respective names, e.g. Serbia and Kosovo.

angered many world leaders, a resolution to demand a cessation of the bombing campaign never made it through the Security Council (SC/6659, 1999).

The war in Kosovo led to difficult questions about the responsibility of the international community to protect populations from mass atrocities. The conflict, however, also highlighted how much the world, and the idea of sovereignty, had changed since the 1970s (Bellamy, 2009, p. 171; Cronin, 2007; Power, 2013, p. 467). Over the years, the continuous mass violence that affected so many countries and the inability or unwillingness of the United Nations and individual states to stop it, ensured that the concept of sovereignty and the notion of what constituted a threat to international peace and security, slowly evolved and became more comprehensive (Cronin, 2007, p. 298; Grünfeld, 1998). The UN Security Council increasingly acknowledged that gross human rights violations could constitute a threat to international peace and security (Grünfeld, 1998). Although countries promised 'never again' after World War II (WWII), this promise was continuously broken, first during the Cold War when the UN Security Council was deadlocked, and thereafter in the 1990s when the international community failed to prevent, *inter alia*, the genocides in Srebrenica and Rwanda (Askin, 2005; Cronin, 2007, p. 297).[2]

The tension between intervening forcefully, even when the Security Council is deadlocked, and standing by as civilians were killed, led Secretary General Kofi Annan to ask the General Assembly the following question

> '… if humanitarian intervention is, indeed, an unacceptable assault on sovereignty, how should we respond to a Rwanda, to a Srebrenica – to gross and systematic violations of human rights that affect every precept of our common humanity?' (cited in International Commission on Intervention and State Sovereignty, 2001, p. vii).

The Canadian government took it upon itself, together with several major foundations, to find an answer to this question, and announced in 2000 the establishment of the International Commission on Intervention and State Sovereignty (ICISS). In their report, they reshaped the concept sovereignty in terms of responsibility. According to the Commission, state sovereignty brings with it responsibility for the protection of citizens. This responsibility to protect citizens only falls upon the international community when the state is unable or unwilling to protect its population and the latter is suffering serious harm. It encompasses the elements to prevent, react and rebuild, and points to guiding

[2] This was also greatly influenced by the manner in which peace operations were conducted. Reports like *An Agenda for Peace* and the *Report of the Panel on United Nations Peace Operations (Brahimi Report)* and more recently, the report of the High-Level Panel on Threats, Challenges and Change, *A More Secure World: Our Shared Responsibility* and the report of the High-Level Independent Panel on Peace Operations, *Uniting Our Strengths for Peace: Politics, Partnership and People*, have been influential in this process. For an overview see Smith (2016).

principles for military intervention (International Commission on Intervention and State Sovereignty, 2001).

At the 2005 UN World Summit the countries reached agreement on the responsibility to protect (R2P), simplifying the concept significantly. While the concept has become increasingly important in international politics over the years, its operationalisation, and the determination how the international community should achieve their goal of protecting the population against the worst atrocities, leaves much to be desired (Bellamy, 2015; Havel & Tutu, 2012).[3] It remains unclear how one should realize the goals of the responsibility to protect, or interpret the few criteria for interventions that are still present in the 2005 formulation.

The responsibility to protect, as formulated in 2005, specifies that states have the responsibility to protect their population from mass atrocities, more specifically genocide, crimes against humanity, war crimes and ethnic cleansing. These crimes are most often perpetrated in non-democratic regimes. There continues to be a discussion about whether the worst atrocities are perpetrated in the most repressive regimes or whether there is, in the words of Helen Fein, 'more murder in the middle', but there is consensus that they are least likely to occur in established democracies (Bellamy & McLoughlin, 2009; Fein, 1995; Rummel, 1994). There are situations in which dictators are unable to protect their citizens from mass atrocities perpetrated by other factions, but very often, too, the dictatorial regime is involved in its perpetration with the leader orchestrating and legitimizing the violence through destructive ideologies (Woolf & Hulsizer, 2005, pp. 106-107).

The present research will focus on how the international community can make foreign policy measures that aim to persuade dictators to mitigate – or preferably stop – the perpetration of mass atrocities more effective and, in doing so, further the implementation of the responsibility to protect. Considering the important role the dictator frequently plays in orchestrating the perpetration of atrocities, and bearing in mind that he often exercises significant influence over policy choices, his responsiveness should be considered an important determinant for the success of foreign policy measures.

This research therefore seeks to answer the **question** to what extent and why dictatorial leaders differ in their responsiveness to measures from other countries and the international community that are aimed to stop them from committing mass atrocities. In addition, it seeks to ascertain what consequences this has for the implementation of the responsibility to protect.

---

3 MARO (Mass Atrocity Response Operations) is a step towards closing that gap (Hiebert, 2011) but is more concerned with technical details of a military intervention rather than comprehensive guidelines as to which foreign policy mechanisms would be effective in a particular situation (Kuperman, 2011, pp. 60-61).

In doing so it will challenge popular conceptions of dictators that typically assume dictators are crazy and power hungry individuals. Importantly, it also advocates reconsidering some of the most important assumptions underlying the work of many scholars who have studied dictators and their regimes. The dominant approaches either assume that the dictator's primary motivation is retaining his position of power, or assumes he is in fact not a rational actor, and investigates possible psychological defects which may explain the behaviour (Bruce Bueno De Mesquita & Smith, 2011, p. xviii; Escribà-Folch, 2012; Ezrow & Frantz, 2011, p. 84; Glad, 2002; Kinne, 2005, p. 118; Post, 2004; Wintrobe, 2009).[4]

1.2. THE RATIONAL DICTATOR AS A DECISION MAKER

Focusing on the individual when studying foreign policy decisions is controversial in and of itself. Even though increasingly scholars are asserting that the individual should not be overlooked as an important determinant that influences policy, the dominant approaches within international relations (IR) still focus on the state as the primary actor (Hudson, 2005, pp. 1-2; S. Smith, Hadfield, & Dunne, 2012a, pp. 4-5). It has been frequently argued that decision makers are limited in the choices they can make because the international balance of power dictates the options they have (Hermann & Hagan, 1998, p. 124; Tetlock, 1983, p. 45). Even when scholars acknowledge that individuals impact the formulation of some of the goals states pursue, personal factors are dismissed with the idea that the primary goals, such as safeguarding the nation's national security, are similar to all states regardless of the influence of individuals on some secondary goals (Byman & Pollack, 2001, p. 113). In short, states and their elites are more or less viewed as 'rational actors in pursuit of a few basic goals and interests while overwhelmingly constrained by their structural environment' (Rosati, 2000, p. 48).

However, increasingly, scholars have warned against viewing the state as a black box. As Hermann *et al.* explain, especially in many dictatorships the decision-making process is dictated by the 'predominant leader' (2001, p. 84). In those circumstances, a single individual stands at the top of the hierarchy and has such power that his decisions 'cannot be readily reversed' (Hermann *et al.*, 2001, p. 84). Hermann *et al.* argue that when the leader makes use of his position of power to dictate a policy outcome, he should be studied as an important determinant in the decision-making process (Hermann *et al.*, 2001, pp. 84-85). Within non-democratic regimes, the leader tends to be much more important in determining the course of action than a leader is in democratic regimes.

[4] Throughout the book dictators are referred to as 'he' due to the fact that overwhelmingly, they have been men.

Ultimately, many individual, domestic and international factors will influence the outcome of a state's foreign policy (Tetlock, 1983, p. 46). It is not argued here that the individual leader, rather than the state, should be viewed as the more important homogeneous entity from which decisions flow. However, the individual may be an important piece of the puzzle and there is now increasingly a renewed interest in when, and the manner in which, the individual may play a decisive role in determining the foreign policy of a state (Byman & Pollack, 2001). Especially in times of great change or during times of crisis and when power is concentrated in the hands of one person, the individual may be an important factor to take into account (Byman & Pollack, 2001, p. 109).

Yet even when scholars take the individual as the unit of analysis, rather than the state, the role rationality plays in their decision-making process remains a controversial issue in the field. As modern psychology started questioning the notion of a rational self, the role of reason in foreign policy decision-making was re-examined (Kahler, 1998, p. 919). The findings show that cognitive limitations prevent people from acting perfectly rationally and this has led to a wide array of literature that shows how these human imperfections impact the decision-making process (Rosati, 2000). A comprehensive study of differences in the cost-benefit assessment between individuals is lacking, however, resulting in the assumption that all leaders are equally and similarly rational (Razi, 1988).

Since rationality has a central place in foreign policy analysis (FPA) and international relations (IR) literature in relation to the role the individual plays, and considering dictators are sometimes portrayed as raging mad men, rationality will be at the heart of the present study. Weber's work on rationality is particularly insightful because it highlights how different kinds of rationality can influence the decision-making process which may cause some behaviour to appear irrational while in fact it is not.

The first type of rational social action that was described by Weber, instrumental rationality, most closely resembles what is commonly understood to constitute rational action. According to Weber, instrumental rationality is oriented towards a 'system of discrete individual ends' (Weber, 1964, p. 115). The decision maker in this case takes the expectations of the actions of others and possibly changing circumstances into consideration. He weighs the pros and cons of alternative means and the relative importance of different goals in the decision-making process (Blokland, 2006, p. 30). Weber, however, also identified a second type of rationality, which is largely neglected in the literature on foreign policy and international relations. The person who acts from a value rational orientation feels obligated to act to fulfil certain 'demands' which he feels are required by 'duty, honour, the pursuit of beauty, a religious call, personal loyalty, or the importance of some "cause" no matter in what it consists' (Weber, 1964, p. 116). It allows the individual to pursue its goal regardless of the chances of success or the high personal costs involved (Varshney, 2003, pp. 86-87; Weber,

1964, p. 116). A person with a value rational orientation consequently shows a high level of commitment and a disregard for the consequences of his actions (Weber, 1964, p. 117).

Weber notes that a person's behaviour is seldom characterized by only one type of social action (1964, p. 117) and next to the two types that deal with conscious, rational decision-making, Weber also identified two other types from which he says action originates but which lie on the border of what can be considered 'meaningfully' oriented action (Weber, 1964, p. 116). Action that stems from these types is often uncontrolled and automatic. He identified one type of social action that has an affectual orientation and another which is traditionally oriented (Weber, 1964, p. 115). The latter may shade into value rationality when habitual practice is upheld by varying degrees of consciousness (Weber, 1964, pp. 115-116). Similarly, affectual oriented action may become rationalised when it concerns a conscious release of emotional tension (Weber, 1964, p. 116). It is only when this happens that the action would fall within the scope of this research, which is concerned with the conscious decision-making process of dictators and the role rationality plays therein. In this sense, the present work will look at the types of rationality rather than to the degree rationality is bounded by emotional responses or habits. In addition, Weber is careful to point out that the types of rationality are not mutually exclusive. It is possible, for instance, for a person to try to achieve a value rational goal through instrumental rational means (Weber, 1964, p. 117).

Weber's categorization lends itself particularly well to studying instances of mass violence since ideology plays a particularly important role in the perpetration of atrocity crimes, and a rigid ideological outlook can be an important motivator for some dictators (Alvarez, 2008; Chirot, 1994, pp. 167-168; 171; Maynard, 2015). On those occasions, they may want to impose their vision on society and create what they would consider to be a utopian society, a goal that may be looked upon as sacred and does not allow for compromise. While there are certainly also irrational dictators, and moments where otherwise rational dictators will unthinkingly make irrational decisions, many dictators can, and should, be seen as rational individuals. It just needs to be acknowledged that different types of rationality may be dominating the decision-making process.

1.3. METHODOLOGY AND SCOPE OF THE RESEARCH

The typology of rational social action of Weber is used as an ideal type and is in this manner primarily an analytical tool that allows for an assessment of the extent to which the actual occurrence approximates the theoretical description.

The ideal type typology, which differentiates between instrumental- and value rational action, will be used to analyse which type of rationality predominated in the decision-making processes of Pol Pot and Slobodan Milosevic by analysing the decisions they made throughout their lives. Thereafter, the impact of the type of rationality which dominated their decision-making processes, on the choices they made during a crucial moment in their time in power will be investigated. The decision of Pol Pot and Milosevic whether or not to succumb to pressure from Vietnam and NATO respectively to stop perpetrating mass atrocities will be analysed through a most similar comparative case study design. The underlying presumption is that when a person is, or is not, committed to a particular ideology, this will not change on a moment's notice. As D'Avray explains, values and convictions are not easily changed and tend to be enduring since they are generally not very vulnerable to counter-arguments (D'Avray, 2010, pp. 70-71).

1.3.1. IDEAL TYPE TYPOLOGY BASED ON THE WORK OF MAX WEBER

There is much academic discussion on the precise methodological functions of ideal types. There is debate amongst others about whether it is a model, a theory, or derived from theory, but the fundamental concept is relatively clear at its core (Bailey, 1994, p. 17). Two characteristics define the essence of the ideal type, namely that the ideal type is not found empirically and that it may be used to study the extent to which an empirical occurrence diverges from the ideal type (Bailey, 1994, p. 17). Weber formulated it as follows:

> 'an ideal type is formed by the one-sided *accentuation* of one or more points of view … In its conceptual purity, this mental construct (Gedankenbild) cannot be found anywhere in reality. It is a utopia. Historical research faces the task of determining in each individual case the extent to which the ideal-construct approximates to or diverges from reality' (Weber cited in Bailey, 1994, p. 17. Italics in the original).

Ideal types thus serve as an analytical tool and a unit of comparison. They cannot readily be found anywhere in reality, not as a perfect reflection of the theoretical construct. This, however, does not make the ideal type hypothetical or non-empirical. It, rather, should be seen as the clearest, most complete example of the type (Bailey, 1994, pp. 21-22). It does exist in reality, but will not be found in its purest form (Bailey, 1994, pp. 19-20). The ideal type has the merit of clear

> 'understandability and lack of ambiguity. By comparison with this it is possible to understand the ways in which actual action is influenced by irrational factors of all sorts, such as affects and errors, in that they account for the deviation from the line

of conduct which would be expected on the hypothesis that the action were purely rational' (Weber, 1964, p. 92).

It should be kept in mind that proposing that ideal types of rational social action are valuable as analytical tools does not signify the belief that rationality predominates in human life in general (Weber, 1964, pp. 92-93). Accepting that there are different types of rational behaviour out of which some behaviour may stem will help us to understand the actual occurrences by analysing the extent to which the actions approximate the ideal type. Although not a single social action will perfectly fit the ideal type, it will be argued that value or instrumental rationality is more dominant in the behaviour of some individuals in comparison to others. In doing so it will thus primarily look at the conscious decision-making processes and will follow Weber in believing that for the 'purposes of a typological scientific analysis it is convenient' to look upon irrational elements as deviations from a rational ideal type (Weber, 1964, p. 92).

The study will therefore not neglect cognitive limitations or emotions when it becomes evident that this influenced the dictator's decision-making processes but will treat them as deviations from the conscious more rational decision-making process. The latter will form the main subject of inquiry, whereas cognitive limitations, habits and emotions, will be studied as inhibitors to the rational decision-making process rather than independent topics of study. As Weber also points out, ideally one, of course, would like to actually test our interpretation of events by comparing it with the actual course of events. However, Weber also admits this type of verification is only very rarely possible through psychological experimentation. He suggests the alternative is to compare 'the largest possible number of historical or contemporary processes which, while otherwise similar, differ in the one decisive point of their relation to the particular motive or factor the role of which is being investigated.' (Weber, 1964, p. 97).

1.3.2. MOST SIMILAR CASE STUDY DESIGN

This research will rely on a comparative case study with a most similar case study design to establish why Pol Pot and Milosevic made very different choices when they were threatened with military intervention even though the situations they were in were remarkably similar. Both dictators faced military intervention because of atrocities they perpetrated in contested border regions[5], both faced intervention by forces that were much stronger than they were, and both were offered peace deals (Burchett, 1981, p. 160; Daalder & O'Hanlon, 2000, pp. 103; 164-165; Morris, 1999, p. 103). While conventional wisdom would have us think

5 The motivation of both intervening powers, however, certainly was not entirely humanitarian (Bazyler, 1987, p. 608; Morris, 1999, p. 16; Power, 2013, p. 448).

it would be wise for each to come to a peace agreement, neither did initially, and eventually only Milosevic decided to settle while Pol Pot was removed from power.

The most similar research design, sometimes also called the method of difference entails 'comparing instances in which the phenomenon does occur with instances in other respects similar in which it does not' (Mill cited in Odell, 2001, p. 167). When there is only one difference in an otherwise similar case study, it can be concluded that it can only be the feature which differs which can account for the difference in outcome (Odell, 2001, p. 167). Paired comparison, especially the most similar research design, thus has more parallels to experimentation as it allows, to the greatest extent possible, an assessment to be made of the influence of one particular variable on the outcome (Tarrow, 2010, p. 244).

Even though this method thus has a better chance of actually lending support for a possible causal relationship than a single case study is able to, there are limitations to what can be achieved. As Tarrow explains

> 'an experimenter has the ability to randomly assign subjects to treatment and control groups, making both groups probabilistically equal on all variables other than the experimental one' (Tarrow, 2010, p. 244).

This is impossible in most case studies, including the present one. The causal relationship can never be established beyond any doubt, since all other factors are never completely identical. Consequently, there are almost always other differences which could potentially have been relevant to account for the difference in outcome (Odell, 2001, p. 167). According to Torrow, the underlying idea is that

> 'observable variables will exhaust all the possible causes of an outcome of interest and that a single difference among those variables can be identified as the sole cause of the outcome. But this assumes that all relevant variables can be observed, that there is only one difference among these variables, and that the correlation between this difference and differences in the outcome can confidently be regarded as causal' (Tarrow, 2010, p. 247).

It is of course questionable whether these assumptions always hold true. Another major concern can be the non-representativeness of the case selection or the selection of cases out of convenience, for instance because of their geographic proximity, rather than because of their usefulness for the development of the theory (Tarrow, 2010, pp. 246-247). Care, therefore, has been taken to extensively list, and explain, the similarities and differences between the cases. Differences that can potentially account for the difference in outcome, like the era in which the conflicts took place, and the role that the great powers played, are closely scrutinized to determine the extent to which they actually have explanatory value.[6]

Two cases were carefully selected in which the dictator was faced with the most extreme form of foreign pressure that can be placed on another country, namely military intervention. In addition, the intervening force needed to be much stronger but was not determined to use violence from the start of the conflict and had attempted to negotiate a more peaceful solution, with one of the dictators actually deciding to do so. The overwhelming strength of the intervening force ensured that the objectively rational course of action was to come to a peaceful resolution of the conflict and there was a willingness of the intervening force to try to work towards a negotiated solution, making this option an actual possibility. That being said, the availability of data for practical reasons was an important factor to take into consideration. While both cases have been extensively researched, the extremely secretive nature of Pol Pot's regime nevertheless posed challenges. More details are known about the decision-making process of Milosevic than Pol Pot which accounts for the greater detail in the analysis of the former. More recent cases were not deemed as suitable for the present research because they have not been subjected yet to such extensive research and the lack of information would be even more problematic.

1.3.3. GENERALIZABILITY

It is usually problematic to generalize the findings of qualitative case studies across other situations or cases. Generalizing qualitative research in a similar sense as can be done with quantitative research, meaning generalizing from sample to population, is impossible (Merriam, 1995, p. 57). This, however, should not be taken to mean that case study research does not have general implications that may go beyond a single case (Merriam, 1995, pp. 57-58). Case study generalizability may be conceptualized as generating workable hypotheses rather than definite conclusions that can be applied across a wide variety of situations (Merriam, 1995, p. 58). In addition, it is often possible to uncover insights that are likely to apply in other situations as well. Merriam explains, case study research can lead someone to apply 'what is learned in a particular situation ... to similar situations subsequently encountered' (Merriam, 1995, p. 58). This, however, does not necessarily need to be done by the researcher but can also be done by those using the research (Merriam, p. 58). In this manner, it is possible to speak of a 'continuum of usefulness' which begins with the actual case studies that have been investigated and decreases in usefulness as the cases or situations become more dissimilar (Wilson, cited in Merriam, 1995, p. 58).

6 See chapter 11.

While in theory, there is no reason why the results of this research are not applicable to many leaders, a few preconditions need to be mentioned. Not every leader of a dictatorial regime can be studied under this framework. Only leaders who possess sufficient unilateral power over the government institutions to warrant an individualist approach will fall in the purview of the present research. Such leaders must be able to impose their personal preferences on the formulation and implementation of both domestic and foreign policy, which is in general more likely to be the case in dictatorships than in mature democracies where leaders are constrained by parliament and their constituents. In addition, these leaders must not only possess such power but actually exercise their power in the foreign policy arena (Hermann *et al.*, 2001, p. 85). The terms used for such leaders in the literature differs, depending on the author and focus of the research. Hermann *et al.* would use the term predominant leader, although the term does not exclusively apply to authoritarian leaders (Hermann *et al.*, 2001).

1.4. TERMINOLOGY

When the responsibility to protect was adopted in 2005, the international community decided to accept responsibility only for genocide, war crimes, crimes against humanity and ethnic cleansing. Combined, these categories have become known as mass atrocities, or mass atrocity crimes (Evans, 2008, p. 11). It is not uncommon for atrocity crimes to be equated with international crimes. Botte, for instance, noted

> 'genocide, war crimes, ethnic cleansing and crimes against humanity are often referred to as core international crimes because there is widespread consensus among all States on the fact that particular crimes are the most serious international crimes.' (Botte, 2015, pp. 1030-1031).

In fact, while the acts that constitute atrocity crimes and international crimes will overlap, they consist of different categories. International crimes in fact encompass genocide, war crimes, crimes against humanity, and are defined in the statutes of the different international criminal courts and tribunals. Ethnic cleansing is not listed as a separate crime under the Rome Statute but can be prosecuted as a crime against humanity or a war crime.[7]

Both categories therefore encompass similar behaviour and the different categories that are used, and consequently the different terminology that was developed, is unfortunate. It creates an unnecessary gap between international

[7] For a more elaborate explanation of the crimes that fall within the scope of R2P, see Chhabra and Zucker (2012).

criminal justice and R2P as a political commitment. For the purposes of the present research it meant a choice needed to be made between these competing discourses. Because R2P is the most important focus of the research, the decision was taken to use the terminology 'atrocity crimes' or 'mass atrocities'. It is, nevertheless important to emphasise that because both terms cover similar behaviour to a large extent this is a question of semantics and when atrocity crimes are perpetrated in a country, the acts of the perpetrators are likely to fall within the scope of the core crimes as defined by the Rome Statute.

1.5. TOWARDS A MORE EFFECTIVE IMPLEMENTATION OF THE RESPONSIBILITY TO PROTECT

Ultimately, the aim of this research is to contribute to a more effective implementation of the responsibility to protect. Considering the role of many dictators in inciting and legitimizing the crimes, and the enormous influence they potentially wield over policy, the dictator should play an important part in efforts to bring the crimes to a halt. How they respond to measures from the international community or other countries that aim to bring mass atrocities to an end, or at least mitigate them, is an important determinant for the success of these foreign policy initiatives.

In order to analyse their responsiveness to foreign policy, the type of rationality that predominated their decision-making process and the choices they made throughout their lives, up to the moment they are faced with the threat of military intervention, are investigated. Their childhood and formative years will be looked at first, after which their rise to power and reign will be scrutinised. Finally, the extent to which their type of rationality influenced the decision-making processes of Pol Pot and Slobodan Milosevic during the intervention of Vietnam and NATO will be investigated and the research will delve into the question of what lessons can be drawn from this for the responsibility to protect.

1.6. CONCLUSION: OUTLINE OF THE BOOK

The present research will include a wide array of disciplines, each with its own focus and contribution to make to the overall field. Most of these disciplines have developed in isolation while they have much to learn from each other. From an overarching criminological perspective the disciplines will be combined, the common ground between them will be highlighted and it will be argued that combining these disciplines will be beneficial. When a broader multi- and interdisciplinary approach is taken, it becomes apparent that they can contribute to filling each other's blind spots.[8]

The book will be subdivided into two parts. In Part I the different disciplines will be combined for a theoretical overview of the role of the dictator in the perpetration of mass atrocities and the responsibility of the international community to protect populations from these crimes. In addition, Part I will discuss why the dictator and his type of rationality are important variables for the success of foreign policy measures that are targeted to stop or mitigate mass atrocities.

The next chapter will draw mainly from political science to describe the world of the dictator. It will analyse the important definitions, how much it actually differs from democracy, how dictatorships function, the strategies dictators use to stay in power, and the challenges they face in determining what their policies should be. The third chapter will mainly use literature from genocide studies[9] to analyse how dictators foster environments that are conducive to mass atrocities. The fourth chapter will use law to assess to what extent countries have a responsibility to protect populations in other countries from mass atrocities. The fifth chapter will focus on international relations and foreign policy analysis literature to analyse to what extent the individual leader of a country, with a particular focus on dictatorships, is relevant when trying to analyse interstate relations and the success of foreign policy measures. The sixth and final chapter of this part will use the sociological work of Max Weber to argue how the debate on rationality that currently dominates the international relations and foreign policy analysis literature should be nuanced to include different types of rationality.

In Part II the comparative case study will be discussed. Before delving into the lives of the dictators to uncover what type of rationality predominated their decision-making processes throughout their lives, the research will firstly ascertain, in Chapter 7 and 8 what role Pol Pot and Milosevic played in the perpetration of the crimes and importantly the extent to which they were predominant leaders within their regimes. In Chapters 9 and 10, the question of what type of rationality they were most oriented towards throughout their

8 For a more elaborate argument that interdisciplinary research is necessary to study mass atrocities, see Weerdesteijn (2016 – in press), and for an argument in favour of an interdisciplinary approach to study international law more generally, see Rajkovic (2016).

9 The distinction between genocide studies and international criminology is somewhat blurred as both are interdisciplinary and look at instances of mass violence from different perspectives and angles. For a state of the art on genocide studies, see A. Jones (2011), and for a criminological approach to international crimes see (Haveman & Smeulers, 2008; Haveman, Smeulers, Parmentier, & Poot, 2011; Parmentier, 2013; Smeulers & Grünfeld, 2011).

lives, will be analysed. Chapter 11 will investigate what the impact of this was when they faced the threat of military intervention of a much stronger power while Chapter 12 will analyse the implications this has for a more effective implementation of the responsibility to protect. Thereafter, the findings of the research will be summarised in a concluding chapter.[10]

---

10 This research was concluded in May 2016 and any developments that occurred thereafter have for this reason not been included.

PART I
THE THEORY

CHAPTER 2
THE WORLD OF THE DICTATOR

2.1. INTRODUCTION

Dictatorships and dictators are shrouded in secrecy, making them difficult to study. Government sources are usually unreliable and independent media is usually hampered or censured. Studying dictatorial regimes, and how they function, is therefore an extremely difficult task. Unsurprisingly political science has traditionally paid much more attention to democratic countries than their dictatorial counterparts (Ezrow & Frantz, 2011, p. xiv). Interest in the topic, however, has increased and, an impressive body of work has emerged in which dictatorship and democracy are usually treated as each other's counterpart. In the literature, dictatorships are commonly defined negatively as non-democratic regimes (Lidén, 2014, pp. 50-51), but how clearly can we delineate one from the other, and to what extent do dictatorships actually function differently than democracies? Scholars increasingly see the distinction between dictatorships and democracies as a rather fluid one. Democracy and dictatorial rule are now regarded in this approach as either ends of a spectrum, with some regimes being more or less democratic. The distinction is no longer seen as being either black or white, but many regimes are now conceptualised as semi-authoritarian, the so-called 'hybrid regime', to denote the different shades of grey (Bogaards, 2009). While this adds to the sophistication of contemporary research, it is important to gain more understanding of what characterizes a dictatorial regime, and how it works. What does the concept 'dictatorship' entail and how does it function? To what extent can the dictator actually determine the policies of a country, how influential is he and how does he obtain and maintain such power? These are some of the questions the present chapter seeks to answer in order to explain the dictator's role in determining the policies of his regime, both within his country, as well as the foreign policy of his country.

A factor that complicates answering these questions is the extent to which dictatorships may differ from one another. They may differ, for instance, in the extent to which power is concentrated in the hands of one individual or a small clique, the role the military plays, and the extent to which the regime tries to infiltrate every aspect of people's lives. The leaders of these regimes likewise differ enormously from one another. The common perception is that dictators are irrational, eccentric, self-centred, and brutal (Kelder, 2010). Saddam Hussein became known as the 'madman of the Middle East' and Slobodan Milosevic was called 'Butcher of the Balkans' (Post, 2004, p. 179; 211). Some dictators have indeed been exceptionally brutal, sadistic even. Idi Amin, for instance, had an estimated 250,000 people killed and issued explicit instructions to mutilate many of them (Decalo, 1989, p. 99; Kyemba, 1997, p. 108). Not all dictators are as cruel, however. Kenneth Kaunda of Zambia stopped short of perpetrating mass atrocities and propagated an inclusive ideology in order to balance ethnic tensions in the country (McLoughlin & Weerdesteijn, 2016). Recognizing the differences between dictators has, moreover, been complicated by the fact that the same dictators might be judged differently depending on the approach taken. While some scholars have unquestioningly assumed that the dictator is a rational actor whose primary goal is to maintain his position of power (e.g. Tullock, 1987, pp. 11-12; Wintrobe, 2009), others have analysed possible personality disorders in different dictators (e.g. Glad, 2002). This caused Stalin, for instance, to be analysed as a rational actor in one study, while he was judged to have a personality disorder in another (Glad, 2002; Gregory, Schröder, & Sonin, 2011).

The present chapter will delve into this contradictory and complex body of literature to try to clarify some central concepts, to analyse the dictator in the context of his surroundings and synthesise the conclusions from different studies. Firstly, the different terminology and types of dictators and dictatorship will be explored. Thereafter, an analysis will follow of their *modus operandi*, differentiating between their domestic and foreign policy. Subsequently, pitfalls in deciding on particular policy measures will be highlighted. The conclusion will reflect on what this means for the present research.

2.2. TERMINOLOGY AND TYPES

There are many different terms denoting undemocratic rule and some have been favoured over others in different periods in history. Frequently, the different concepts are used interchangeably, with or without acknowledging the discussion on their subtle differences (e.g. Ayittey, 2011, p. 7). Potentially, the reason behind this may be the large and confusing body of work that focuses solely on the terminology and different types of dictatorial regimes that exist. Some have even referred to it as a 'terminological Babel' (Bogaards, 2009, p. 415). While it should be acknowledged that the large variety of terms and typologies may stand in the way of research building on previous work, all too often the large variety between dictatorships and their leaders is neglected all together, which seems undesirable due to the large differences in the manner in which they function. The present paragraph will aim to find the middle ground by systematizing the literature by highlighting the common ground and fundamental differences between the different types and terms.

2.2.1. CONCEPTUAL CONFUSION: DICTATORS AND DICTATORSHIPS

The terms that have been used to describe states that are ruled by one individual or a small group of people, and the meaning that is attached to them, have changed over time. Dictatorship, tyranny and despotism have often been used interchangeably, even though at times the use of one term was favoured over another. Where distinctions between the terms are made, subtle but important nuances in relation to the legality of the institution as well as its reprehensibility can, and should, be recognized. In order to understand the conceptual minefield it is important to discuss these in turn.

While today, the term dictatorship carries with it moral condemnation, this has not always been the case (Lidén, 2014, p. 51; Linz, 2000, p. 61). In Rome, *dictator rei gerundae causa* denoted an emergency provision in the constitution that was to last for no more than six months, and as such did not carry the negative connotation that it does today (Linz, 2000, p. 61). Authoritarian rule only became a more permanent form of political organization when Sulla became *dictator legibus faciendis et rei publicae constituendae causa* in 82 B.C., and Caesar later on became a dictatorial leader for longer periods of time (Arato, 2016, p. 271; Linz, 2000, p. 63). Sulla and Caesar tested the concept to its limits and it later caused the institution to be described not merely in terms of being a dictatorship, but as being tyrannical, which carried a much more negative undertone (Kalyvas, 2007, pp. 413-415). The two concepts originally carried a very distinct meaning, with dictatorial rule being legal and an occasional necessity to protect the society in times of emergency and with tyranny being inherently unjust, brutal, going against the common good and illegal (Kalyvas, 2007, pp. 415-416). Kalyvas' description of the crucial distinction, which was reflected in the goals as well as duration of each phenomenon, is worth quoting at length:

> 'the dictator had a concrete task, the elimination of threats during a crisis and a return to the *status quo ante bellum*. Although the salvation and re-establishment of the constitution was the strict commission of the dictator, no such authorization existed for a tyrant whose acts were arbitrary and indeterminate, directed toward the satisfaction of his selfish desires and private interests. The dictator's actions were generally considered to be inspired by a strong civic commitment to the public good, a real manifestation of the patriotic attachment of the republic citizen. He was the guardian of the republican order; the tyrant is its usurper. In short, the dictator was a servant who defended what the tyrant aspired to acquire and destroy' (Kalyvas, 2007, p. 416).

The other important distinction of course was the notion that dictatorial rule was only to last for a few short months while tyranny could potentially be relatively permanent (Kalyvas, 2007, pp. 416-417).

Richter explains that throughout the Middle Ages, Renaissance and Reformation, tyranny was the dominant concept to denote abusive rule (Richter, 2007, p. 13). In the 18th century, however, the focus shifted to despotism, which was at times conflated with tyranny (Linz, 2000, p. 51; Turchetti, 2008, p. 171). Aristotle described both concepts and is frequently cited when tracing back the original meaning of the terms (Richter, 2007, p. 12; Turchetti, 2008, pp. 161-162). According to Turchetti, Aristotle used tyranny to describe a regime which is only concerned about its own interests, rather than that of its population, governs against the will of its subjects, and finally violates the law and justice (Turchetti, 2008, p. 162). Despotism by contrast, was referred to as a form of rule that is grounded in law and tradition where the subjects willingly subjugated themselves to their ruler (Turchetti, 2008, p. 162). Aristotle used the example of Asian barbarians whom, he reasoned, subjected themselves voluntarily to their ruler because they were born slaves (Richter, 2005, p. 228). Turchetti summarised the distinction between tyranny and despotism as follows:

> 'Despotism is a form of government which, while being authoritarian and arbitrary, is legitimate if not legal, in some countries, whereas tyranny, in the most rigorous sense, is a form of government which is authoritarian and arbitrary and which is illegitimate and illegal, because exercised not only without, but against the will of the citizens, and also scorns fundamental human rights' (Turchetti, 2008, p. 160).

Also basing himself on the work of Aristotle, for Richter a crucial distinction lies in the role of the leader, as opposed to the regime overall. According to Richter, where despotism referred to a corrupt regime, tyranny referred to a situation in which an otherwise good regime has been corrupted by an abusive leader (Richter, 2007, p. 12). The two interpretations of Aristotle's work meet, however, in their argument that tyranny distinguishes itself because of the manner in which it becomes abusive and violates laws and rights (Richter, 2007, p. 12; Turchetti, 2008, p. 162). The importance of differentiating the two lies in the idea of tyrannicide, a right to resist a tyrant when he comes to power, and the fact that there is no such equivalent in the history of political thought for despots (Turchetti, 2008, p. 160).

Montesquieu blurred the boundary between the concepts, making despotism the dominant term, and argued its power rested on instilling fear in the population (Richter, 2007, pp. 15-16; Turchetti, 2008, p. 172). Turchetti explains that the ambiguity between the words has led many to prefer the term dictatorship (Turchetti, 2008, p. 159). While there are some remarkable similarities between despotism and dictatorship, both being formal, even legal, institutionalized forms of rule, they are certainly not the same. While dictatorial rule was meant to be temporary (Kalyvas, 2007, p. 416; Linz, 2000, p. 61), despotism can be a rather permanent state of governing, potentially outlasting even the individual leader (Richter, 2007, p. 12).

The three central concepts that have been discussed so far coexist in a complex and unclear fashion since there are differing opinions about how each of the concepts should be defined, depending on the time period and the observer. However, when the concepts are not used interchangeably, it is nevertheless possible to distinguish some meaningful differences that distinguish each concept from the other two. In the literature three dominant elements, or parameters, are discernible in the history and evolution of the concepts. Firstly, for each of the concepts, mention is made of the timeframe; how lasting is the phenomenon? The second parameter that is discussed in relation with each of the concepts is the legality of the regime; can it operate within the legal or constitutional bounds that the society knows? The last important aspect that separates the concepts is the manner in which each concept is either positively or negatively evaluated. The central differences between the concepts can thus be summarised in the following table.

Simplification of the most important parameters of the central concepts

	Timeframe	**Legality**	Normative
Dictatorship	Originally 6 months, but in contemporary definitions such a time restriction is absent	Originally it had a constitutional provision	In early definitions, it had a positive connotation but in contemporary definitions, it carries a negative connotation.
Despotism	Long lasting; can outlast the individual leader	Accepted by the people	Differs; carries some legitimacy because it is accepted by the people but is generally seen as an undesirable system (Richter, 2005, p. 228)
Tyranny	Potentially lasts at least as long as the individual leader	Illegal abuse of power against the will of the people	Negative connotation

The three most important concepts that have been discussed so far, thus changed over time in terms of content and use. While dictatorship is now the favoured term, Turchetti explains, it is a problematic concept because over time its meaning has in essence been entirely reversed from something positive, the legitimate authority that was placed upon an individual by the Roman Senate, to something inherently reprehensible in contemporary discourse (Turchetti, 2008, p. 159). Dictatorship as a concept lost its temporary and positive character and became a heavily condemned alternative to democratic rule (Lidén, 2014, p. 51). Turchetti is therefore particularly sceptical about the term, explaining that 'dictatorship has added no clarity to our thinking, since it is even more ambiguous than the other terms [despotism and tyranny, mw]' (Turchetti, 2008,

p. 159). The term tyranny, in the meantime, fell out of fashion almost entirely, although there has been renewed interest in the concept (Richter, 2005, p. 222; Turchetti, 2008). Tyrannicide has likewise received more attention in the last few decades and seems to have been used to legitimize military intervention (Richter, 2005, pp. 223-225).

Some scholars prefer to use the term 'autocracy', which Burnell admits is 'rather poorly defined' (Burnell, 2006; Tullock, 1987). Tullock, however, does shed some light on what distinguishes autocracy from dictatorship. Autocracy, according to Tullock, explicitly includes hereditary rule of the kind that is common in Kingdoms or Empires. This criterion, however, is less straightforward than it seems since many successions are contested (Tullock, 1987, p. 1). In practice both autocracy and dictatorship seem to function in a very similar manner, and while some scholars are inclined to subsume dictatorship within the term autocracy, others study monarchs as obvious examples of dictatorial regimes (Ezrow & Frantz, 2011; Tullock, 1987, p. 1). Tullock, therefore rightfully emphasizes that 'they clearly belong to the same family of governments' (Tullock, 1987, p. 1). The similarity of the two concepts is also underscored by the definition of Burnell:

> 'autocracies can be understood as political regimes where competitive political participation is sharply restricted or suppressed and the power holders reserve a right to determine the rights and freedoms everyone else enjoys, while being largely free from institutional constraints themselves' (2006, p. 546).

The definition does not include the hereditary element but consists of a number of factors that hold true for most non-democratic regimes. The concepts are therefore not seen to differ so much that it is worthwhile including autocracy in the abovementioned categorization.

Less well known have been characterizations of dictatorial regimes as Caesarism and Bonapartism. These concepts have been created in order to understand and denote the regimes that were created by Caesar and Napoleon and Louis Bonaparte respectively (Linz, 2000, p. 63; Richter, 2005, p. 237). Both terms were used to denote a situation in which a powerful leader takes charge of society, while supported by the masses, in order to act decisively to save it (R. H. Jackson & Rosberg, 1982, pp. 167-168; Richter, 2005, p. 240). Caesarism and Bonapartism sometimes carried a negative connotation but were also seen as positive phenomena by those who believed military rule was sometimes necessary when parliaments were ineffective and indecisive (Richter, 2005, pp. 239-240). Since these terms largely fell out of use, they will not be subject to more in depth analysis in the present research.[11]

---

[11] Another term that arguably belongs in this category, 'sultanism', will be dealt with in section 2.2.2. when discussing Weber's types of legitimate domination.

Particularly after democracy came to be regarded as the ideal form of rule in the late 19th and early 20th centuries, dictatorship became the preferred term for non-democratic regimes (Linz, 2000, p. 51). The primary focus of political science has since been on democracies, and consequently dictatorships were negatively defined as everything that is not democratic. It has been argued, however, that seeing dictatorships solely as something they are not, rather than attempting to delineate what they are, can inhibit a deeper understanding of the phenomenon (Ezrow & Frantz, 2011, p. xiv; Lidén, 2014, p. 51; Linz, 2000, p. 51). Moving beyond the term non-democratic regime and defining dictatorships positively, however, frequently still reflects that democracy is used as a starting point. Lidén, for instance, uses the following definition:

> 'In dictatorships there are methods *other than competitive elections* used for distributing political power, and in such societies the political and civil rights of individuals are frequently violated' (emphasis my own Lidén, 2014, p. 53).

The definition that is cited by Richter (2005) to emphasizes how dictatorship received a negative connotation in the first half of the 20th century, focuses on how in dictatorships democratic processes are completely undone

> 'a highly oppressive and arbitrary form of rule, established by force or intimidation, enabling a person or group to monopolize political power without any constitutional limits, thus destroying representative government, political rights and any organized opposition' (Richter, 2005, p. 243).

Moghaddam emphasizes the relative open nature of democracies whereas dictatorships should be characterized as relatively closed (2013, p. 13). He defines dictatorship as 'rule by a single leader or clique' that was not chosen in free and fair elections, cannot be removed from power by the population and has control over the security forces which allows him to repress the opposition. He underscores that there is no independent judiciary nor are there other legislative checks that limit the decisions of the dictator. Its policies are characterized by a high degree of control of the individual and 'reflect the wishes and whims' of the leader or clique (Moghaddam, 2013, p. 18).

According to Bueno de Mesquita & Smith 'dictatorship really means a government based on a particularly small number of essentials, drawn from a very large group of interchangeables and, usually, a relatively small batch of influentials' (Bruce Bueno De Mesquita & Smith, 2011, p. 8). Their definition stresses that much of the population does not really matter with citizens being interchangeable, that there are only a few people that can influence politics, and that the leader's hold on power only depends on a very small number of individuals that are essential to his rule (Bruce Bueno De Mesquita & Smith, 2011, p. 5; 8).

There are important similarities between the definitions mentioned above. Most of the definitions stress the role of the individual or small group or clique, the power the individual has over policy and the violation of political and civil rights. For the present research, these elements are the most important characteristics that define a dictatorial regime although the focus leans heavily towards the decision-making process of the individual leader, with his closest advisors only coming in to play to the extent that they influence the decisions of the leader at the top. Yet despite these overlapping elements in the different definitions, that give some sense of agreement on what a dictatorial regime entails today, some conceptual confusion remains.

Less useful is the manner in which Ayittey goes about the definitional minefield. On the one hand, Ayittey points out that he uses the terms despot, autocrat, tyrant and dictator interchangeably, but on the other hand he does acknowledge that the terms denote subtle differences. He sees despot as being 'more reminiscent of medieval monarchs' who believed they were destined to rule and therefore became highly narcissistic. The autocrat, according to Ayettey, lacks this self-aggrandisement but is tremendously powerful. The tyrant is excessively oppressive and the dictator is a 'ruler with a military background who barks orders, issues diktats or edicts and expects full compliance and obedience' (Ayittey, 2011, p. 7). While interesting, his characterization of the different terms seems largely devoid of their historical background, and it remains unclear on what else Ayittey bases the differences he identifies.

Further complicating the research on democracy and dictatorship has been the emergence of regimes that are neither fully democratic nor completely authoritarian, and where the democratic process has not been completely undone.[12] While frequently the umbrella term 'hybrid' regimes is used, here, too, a panoply of different terms has been used, signalling subtle differences between these regimes (Bogaards, 2009, pp. 399-400). A useful subdivision can be made between those definitions that define hybrid regimes with democracy as a starting point and see them as 'flawed democracies', and those that rather see them as 'weak authoritarian, regimes, using the other end of the spectrum as the point of departure (Bogaards, 2009, pp. 399-400).

The present research acknowledges that there is an enormous variety in the extent to which a regime relies on democratic processes, with varying degrees to which the population actually can influence who rules and how their leader rules. In addition, it should be emphasized that there is likewise much variance in the extent to which human rights are violated in dictatorships, which is, as explained, another important element in many of the definitions of dictatorships. While gross violations of human rights are not a prerequisite *per se* to define a regime as dictatorial, the focus of this research will be on those dictatorships that

12 While some scholars have challenged the idea that this is a new phenomenon, it seems to have become much more prevalent (Bogaards, 2009, p. 406).

are violating human rights on a large scale and are committing mass atrocities. In deciding which terminology matches the focus of this research best, it is therefore possible to argue that since there is always an abuse of power at play, the concept of tyranny is perhaps most applicable. This temptation, however, needs to be resisted because even though all leaders that are covered in this present research are brutal, using tyranny as the favoured term risks opening the door to the use of the term tyrannicide, which evokes immediate questions about the legitimacy of overthrowing regimes (Richter, 2005, p. 223). Tyrannicide and the legitimacy thereof is an important and contentious topic. Richter explains, for instance, that political theorists continue to disagree

> 'about whether resistance to tyrants, including putting them to death, could be justified and, if so, under which conditions, and on what grounds. It is worth noting that none of the other regime types designating oppressive rule or illegitimate domination generated terms analogous to tyrannicide.' (Richter, 2005, p. 225).

While these questions continue to be highly relevant (Witteveen, 2011) they form the other side of the coin; asking not how the dictator may respond to intervention, but whether the intervention should even take place. As such, it falls outside of the scope of the present research.

For the purposes of this research, therefore, the currently much more common concepts dictator and dictatorships are used. While it is acknowledged that it is indeed important for dictatorship to transcend beyond a negative conceptualization of what democracy is, for the present research a broad and inclusive definition is desirable because it is relevant to all regimes who have a predominant leader who can influence policy. Dictatorships shall therefore be defined as non-democratic regimes that are characterized by the absence of free and fair elections, with dictators being the leaders of these regimes.

The focus of the research within this overarching category will be on dictatorial leaders who incite, legitimize and otherwise create the circumstances in which mass atrocities can be perpetrated.[13] The explicit distinction that is made between dictators and dictatorship, is both crucial and often neglected. Ezrow and Frantz are the exception and make a point to emphasize how important it is to differentiate between the two (Ezrow & Frantz, 2011, p. xv). They explain:

> 'The overthrow of the dictator is not synonymous with the overthrow of the dictatorship. Authoritarian regimes, in fact, often last well beyond the fall of any particular ruler. Conflating dictators with dictatorships can lead to misunderstandings of not only leadership survival and regime survival, but also a variety of other political outcomes' (Ezrow & Frantz, 2011, p. xv).

[13] How they are able to do so will be the topic of the next chapter.

This chapter will cover literature related to both dictators and dictatorships simultaneous because ultimately the dictator has to operate in the dictatorial regime that he created, or inherited from his predecessor. Ultimately the central focus lies with the dictator and his decision-making process.

The broad definitions that are provided in the present chapter, however, need to be nuanced further because they disregard the major differences between dictatorships (Lidén, 2014, p. 53) and their leaders. Literature that has acknowledged the differences between the different regimes, usually divided them into typologies.

2.2.2. TYPOLOGIES OF DICTATORSHIPS

Within dictatorial regimes as an overarching category, several sub-types have been distinguished. Perhaps the most profound and seminal distinction is between authoritarian and totalitarian regimes (Linz, 2000). The regimes of Stalinist Russia, Nazi Germany, and possibly Italy under Mussolini, appeared to form an unfamiliar type of regime that scholars subsequently decided to characterize as totalitarian (Tucker, 1965, p. 555). Friedrich and Brzezinski argued that 'totalitarian regimes are historically novel' and continued to explain that the most important features are 'a single party typically led by one man, a terroristic police, a communications monopoly, a weapons monopoly, and a centrally directed economy' (Friedrich & Brzezinski, 1965, p. 21). Arendt, in her work on totalitarianism, emphasizes the role that terror plays, which she calls 'the essence of totalitarian government' which incapacitates the population since fear is no longer useful as a guiding force as it has become impossible to deliberately evade being subjected to the terror (Arendt, 1962, pp. 466-467). What makes terror in a totalitarian government unique is that 'terror is no longer used as a means to exterminate and frighten opponents, but as an instrument to rule masses of people who are perfectly obedient' (Arendt, 1962, p. 6). While in most dictatorships it is to be expected that violence lessens when it is no longer necessary to maintain political control, Arendt observed it actually increases in totalitarian regimes because it aims to achieve ideological, rather than political goals (Boesche, 1996, pp. 447-448). Tucker likewise points out that terror in totalitarian regimes is unprecedented and the state maintains control over society through modern technology and an extensive bureaucratic system (Tucker, 1965, pp. 560-561). The ideology is imprinted on society through a sophisticated propaganda campaign and 'every pore' of the society is infiltrated (Tucker, 1965, p. 560). Mass participation in society generated this particular type of regime with apparent popular support and at times these regimes have been described as residing in a permanent state of revolution (Tucker, 1965, p. 599; 561). While many of these features might be found in different regimes that cannot be considered totalitarian, it is their combined presence that signals the totalitarian nature of a particular regime (Linz, 2000, p. 67).

Its counterpart, authoritarianism was most prominently defined by Linz, who argued authoritarianism distinguished itself as

> 'political systems with limited, not responsible, political pluralism, without elaborate and guiding ideology, but with distinctive mentalities, without extensive nor intensive political mobilization, except at some points in their development, and in which a leader or occasionally a small group exercises power within formally ill-defined limits but actually quite predictable ones' (Linz, 2000, p. 159).

Linz acknowledged that not all non-democratic regimes could be identified as either totalitarian or authoritarian. The residual category, where arbitrary rule is exercised without attempts to legitimize or institutionalise such rule, Linz called 'sultanistic' and where a part of society imposes its will on another part, Linz uses the term 'racial democracy' (Linz, 2000, p. 54). The regimes that emerged after the Cold War in eastern Europe, he called 'post-totalitarian' (Linz, 2000, p. 54). In addition, there are a number of authoritarian subtypes, namely the 'bureaucratic authoritarian regimes', 'organic sultanism', 'postindependence mobilizational authoritarian regimes and the 'post-totalitarian authoritarian regimes' (Linz, 2000, p. 54). Eventually, the typology was refined and emphasized democracy, authoritarianism, totalitarianism, post-totalitarianism and sultanism as the main types (Linz & Stepan, 2004).

Hadenius and Teorell explain that the subcategorization was a response to the criticism that very few regimes matched the totalitarian type while the authoritarian category covered a wide range of regimes (Hadenius & Teorell, 2007, p. 144; Linz & Stepan, 2004, pp. 154-155). The advances made with the subcategorization, however, according to Hadenius and Teorell, are insufficient to safeguard the usefulness of the distinction. They argue

> 'that the payoff of this typological strategy is limited. The criteria entering the classification are questionable, and no attempt is made to apply the model systematically over time, or to a broad range of cases.' (Hadenius & Teorell, 2007, p. 144).

A second problem with the distinction between authoritarian and totalitarian regimes is that it frequently leads to a blurred distinction between regimes and its leader. While the different types of dictatorial leaders that have been identified will be more elaborately listed below, it is important to highlight that the authoritarian and totalitarian regime types have led some scholars to link, or even conflate, these specific regime types with types of leaders. Sondrol compares both authoritarian and totalitarian leaders and looks at the regime they put in place. He focuses on three features that highlight the differences between the regimes and their leaders. The first element he focuses on is charisma. Charismatic appeal, he argues, is generally high for totalitarian regimes and low for authoritarian leaders. This quality actually blends the leader and the state, since the leader becomes the personification of the state allowing charisma to become institutionalized (Sondrol, 1991, pp. 602-603). They purposefully create a 'prophetic image' and corresponding personality cult (Sondrol, 1991, pp. 600-604; 610). Secondly, he argues that the role that the leaders envision for themselves within these regimes differs. According to Sondrol, the self-conceptions of totalitarian leaders 'are typically teleological. The tyrant is less a person than an indispensable "function" to guide and reshape the universe' (Sondrol, 1991, p. 600).[14] Authoritarian leaders, on the other hand, are more individualistic and content with the status quo. Lastly, as a result of these differences, authoritarians need to rule by instilling fear and buying loyalty because they lack the legitimacy that an ideology can provide (Sondrol, 1991, p. 600).

A possible explanation for the fact that leader and regime have become meshed together can possibly be found in the fact that many of the most influential scholars have emphasized the role of the leader in totalitarian regimes. Linz links the regime to the individual by focusing on the role that ideology plays (Linz, 2000, p. 70; 76). According to Linz

> 'There can be no doubt that totalitarian leaders, individuals or groups, in contrast to other nondemocratic rulers, derive much of their sense of mission, their legitimation, and often very specific policies from their commitment to some holistic conception of man and society' (Linz, 2000, p. 76).

In this sense the regime type, whether it be totalitarian or authoritarian, is often associated with an implicit or explicit type of leadership. Within totalitarian regimes it is then argued that leaders are motivated by their dedication to the ideological cause (Linz, 2000, p. 76) while authoritarian leaders, on the other hand, have their continued rule as a primary goal and utilize their power to predominantly serve private ends (Sondrol, 1991, pp. 604-605). There is no denying that ideology is very important in totalitarian regimes, as a source of legitimacy and guiding principle that allows society to be mobilized (Linz, 2000, pp. 77-78), but it seems presumptuous to assume that the leader of a totalitarian regime is genuinely committed to the ideology. It can even be argued that arguments such as these actually highlight the importance of distinguishing between the regime and its leader.

---

14 Tucker also describes the totalitarian leader's role is primarily described as serving a function but disagrees with the leader's role being confined to that of a 'function' because the personalities of Stalin and Hitler were crucial to explain the decisions of their governments (Tucker, 1965, pp. 564-566).

The literature on totalitarianism has nevertheless proved informative in examining the totalitarian dictator 'as a personality type' as well, moving beyond analysing merely the function of the leader (Tucker, 1965, p. 555). Tucker argued that totalitarianism as a concept did not leave enough room to analyse the importance of the personality of the totalitarian leader, despite the fact that Hitler and Stalin 'at many crucial points individually dominated the decision-making process and behavior of their governments' (Tucker, 1965, p. 566). He therefore built on the existing literature to analyse Stalin and Hitler further as leaders of the most important totalitarian regimes. They were successful in their organizations because they were able to present their enemy as society's enemy and, according to Tucker, as such the dictator 'carries conviction because he has conviction' (Tucker, 1965, pp. 578-579). Both individuals were influential in establishing the totalitarian terror that was inflicted on the population, as becomes especially obvious in Stalin's case, since the nature of the terror changed after Stalin's death becoming more 'dictatorial' and less specifically 'totalitarian' (Tucker, 1965, pp. 570-571).

Another approach, frequently associated with totalitarian leaders, is a focus on the charisma totalitarian leaders are frequently argued to possess (Linz, 2000, p. 77; Sondrol, 1991, pp. 602-603). The concept is most famously analysed in the work of Max Weber who described charisma 'a gift of grace' and 'a certain quality of an individual personality by virtue of which he is set apart from ordinary men and treated as endowed with supernatural, superhuman, or at least specifically exceptional powers or qualities' (Weber, 1964, p. 358; 360). According to Weber, charisma rests on the relationship with his followers who have a '*duty* ... to recognize its quality and to act accordingly' (emphasis in original Weber, 1964, p. 359). Post therefore rightfully speaks of 'the charismatic leader-follower relationship' (Post, 2004). Adair-Toteff explains that Weber emphasized that the relationship between the leader and the led is very personal and based on the devotion of the latter for his or her leader with the follower perceiving the leader as a hero who can make miracles happen (Adair-Toteff, 2005, p. 194). Central to this conception of charismatic leadership is the sense

> 'that the leader has been chosen, that he (or she) belongs to God's grace (1976:140). So it seems as if the charismatic leader possess the power and holds sway over his followers. However, Weber insists that the charismatic leader is dependent upon the followers for recognition' (Adair-Toteff, 2005, p. 195).

Max Weber saw charismatic authority as being derived from a calling, religious or otherwise (Friedrich, 1961, p. 12). The concept was borrowed from its original meaning that had a religious context. According to Friedrich, originally charisma denoted 'leadership based upon a transcendent call by a divine being, believed in by both the person called and those with whom he has to deal in exercising his calling.' (Friedrich, 1961, p. 14). Weber opened the concept to include secular even demagogical callings and he suggested that charisma also can become 'routinized' or stabilized and institutionalized (Friedrich, 1961, p. 13;15;22).

Charismatic leadership is part of Weber's three-pronged typology on *Herrschaft*. *Herrschaft* has proven difficult to translate and can be considered to mean either 'rule', 'dominion', 'control', 'power', 'sway' or 'authority' (Adair-Toteff, 2005, p. 191; Roth, 1968, p. 195). The other types include the traditional and the legal rational subtype (Weber, 1964, p. 328). The latter subtype dictates rule that is in conformity with the laws and rules that govern the office of the individual, making the person hardly of any importance. The legitimacy stems from the office, not the person (Weber, 1964, p. 328). With traditional authority, the person who holds the position is obeyed. In the legal rational subtype, the leader is bound by the rules of the office, in the traditional subtype the limits stem from the customs and tradition (Weber, 1964, p. 328).

Weber listed several subtypes of traditional authority, namely gerontocracy, patriarchalism and patrimonialism. In the first two subtypes, the leaders act to further the collective interests of his group, with patriarchalism being based on kinship, while with gerontocracy one of the 'elders' is in control (Weber, 1964, p. 346). Weber explains that when there is a personal administrative staff, 'especially a military force under the control of the chief, traditional authority tends to develop into "patrimonialism"'(Weber, 1964, p. 347).[15] In patrimonial systems the leader is 'entitled to exploit' his position for his own benefit and that of his staff. He will try to extend the power beyond the limitations placed on him by tradition by granting favours. When the leader is able to impose his will arbitrarily, Weber called it sultanism (Weber, 1964, p. 347).

Patrimonialism has provided an important basis on which scholars have built their knowledge on personal rule (Guliyev, 2011, p. 577).[16] Roth, whose seminal article gave new meaning to the concept, identified two forms of patrimonialism. The traditional patrimonial regimes as analysed by Weber are less common today, but he identified a second type which entails 'personal rulership on the basis of loyalties that do not require any belief in the ruler's unique personal qualifications, but are inextricably linked to material incentives and rewards' (Roth, 1968, p. 196). Roth furthermore argues that patrimonialism should not be linked too closely to the concept of authoritarianism which he sees as merely a demarcation point somewhere on the scale between pluralism and

15 Weber adds 'where absolute authority is maximized, it may be called sultanism' (Weber, 1964, p. 347).

16 Note that there is a disagreement here between on the one hand, Roth, and on the other, Linz. Linz sees sultanism, the extreme form of patrimonialism, as closely related to authoritarianism, although it is nevertheless treated as a separate type, while Roth finds this ill-advised (Linz, 2000; Linz & Stepan, 2004). Roth believes that the characteristics of patrimonialism can be found anywhere along the continuum of democracy and totalitarianism (Roth, 1968, pp. 196-197).

totalitarianism (Roth, 1968, p. 197). It is difficult to see, however, how many of the characteristics that are frequently associated with patrimonialism, including corruption for instance (Roth, 1968, p. 196) in its purest form, are easily reconcilable with pluralist, or democratic standards. At the same time, of course, Roth is right in noting that other elements, such as the importance of personal networks, are also important, albeit to a lesser extent, in democratic regimes today (Roth, 1968, p. 199).

Neopatrimonialism was subsequently developed and updated to describe more modern regimes that combine elements of Weber's traditional and legal rational types. In these regimes, informal institutions are more important than the formal ones (Brooker, 2014, p. 138; Guliyev, 2011, p. 578). Guliyev explains:

> 'the traditional patrimonial apparatus in Weber's scheme is a personal administrative staff, [while] a modern neopatrimonial administration is based on personal (non-ideological) loyalty/dependence and some form of merit based personnel recruitment of lower levels of bureaucracy' (Guliyev, 2011, p. 584).

Personalist regimes, of which (neo)patrimonialism is an example, have become part of the most influential typologies of nondemocratic regimes. These include Huntington's typology who identified personal dictatorship, one party rule and military regimes as the most important modern forms of authoritarian regimes (Huntington, 1991, pp. 580-581). Geddes further developed the influential typology by including amalgams of these types (Geddes, 1999, p. 121). This overarching division has been the springboard for many who have elaborated upon, worked with or nuanced the typology (e.g. Brooker, 2014; Escribà-Folch, 2012; Ezrow & Frantz, 2011; Hadenius & Teorell, 2007; Kailitz, 2013). Hadenius and Teorell criticize the typology because Geddes omitted monarchies and electoral autocracies. In addition, they believe personalism to be inappropriate as a separate category but advocate seeing the other types as being more or less personal (Hadenius & Teorell, 2007, p. 145). Others have added sub-types to Geddes' categories, adding, for instance, no-party, one party, multi-party regimes (Lidén, 2014, p. 54).

Kailitz takes Geddes' and Weber's typology as a starting point to create a typology that is based on the form of legitimation. He argues that the legitimacy that a government claims 'is usually not merely window-dressing' (Kailitz, 2013, pp. 40-41). Kailitz argues that in order for any justification to be credible, the leader must believe it (Kailitz, 2013, p. 41) but leaders can put forward an ideology which is credible but to which the leader is not personally devoted.[17] Despite this important caveat, Kailitz develops an interesting typology that brings together several strands of the previous literature. First of all, he distinguishes between liberal democracy and electoral autocracy, with the latter

[17] As will be explained in the chapters that follow.

either denying rights are curtailed or claiming it is not possible to have those rights enforced at that time (Kailitz, 2013, p. 46). Furthermore, he also identifies communist ideocracy, although he points out this type may also include national socialist/fascist and Islamist ideolocracies which all claim to guide the nation to a utopian future (Kailitz, 2013, p. 47). This should be distinguished from one-party autocracy where there is often 'a vague political vision justifying the exclusion of all political alternatives' (Kailitz, 2013, p. 47). There are also military regimes which claim only intervention of the military can save society from a particular crisis or threat; monarchies where the claim to legitimacy usually entails a 'God-given, natural or at least established historical right to rule'; and personalist autocracies, which are negatively defined as '(almost) "institutionless polities"' (Kailitz, 2013, pp. 48-49).

Rather than asking who rules, there have also been scholars who differentiated between regimes on the basis of the strategies they use (Ezrow & Frantz, 2011, pp. 12-15). Wintrobe, for instance, uses economic theory to develop a typology of dictatorial leaders and their regimes that is based on the dictator's motivations and strategies (Wintrobe, 1990). His starting point is the classic differentiation between totalitarian regimes and authoritarian regimes, which he calls tin-pot dictatorships (Wintrobe, 1990, p. 849). Wintrobe conceptualizes dictatorial regimes as a marketplace in which 'political exchanges' take place in which the dictator seeks to increase his power. He can garner support by providing 'individuals or interest groups with public services or patronage' or he can use repression to increase his power (Wintrobe, 1990, p. 851). Wintrobe's model predicts that when performance increases, for instance when its economy performs well, it will reduce the amount of repression in tin pot dictatorships, simply because it does not need to use it to stay in power, while totalitarian governments are likely to actually increase repression in an attempt to eliminate opposition completely (Wintrobe, 1990, p. 859; 863; 870).

As was mentioned before, more recently scholars have tended to view dictatorial and democratic regimes not as complete opposites but as either ends of a scale. (Moghaddam, 2013, p. 7; 18). Naturally, when conceived of like this, there will be many regimes who will find themselves in between either of these extremes (Bogaards, 2009; Ezrow & Frantz, 2011, p. 8). This trend is exemplary of the development of dictatorship as a phenomenon. While a few decades ago totalitarianism and authoritarianism were the dominant terms used to denote the differences among dictatorships, as Lintz now argues, this hardly seems appropriate anymore since totalitarianism turned out to be a phenomenon with only a few occurrences (Linz & Stepan, 2004, pp. 154-155). Differences therefore need to be distinguished within the authoritarian type and an important consideration is that dictatorships increasingly take the form of a 'democratically disguised dictatorship' (Brooker, 2014, p. 8).

2.2.3. TYPOLOGIES OF DICTATORS

Dictatorial leaders and their regimes are intertwined but should not be confused with one-another. As will be elaborated on in the next paragraph, the dictator is embedded in his regime, he has to function within the confines of the state and the institutions that are present, that either he created or inherited from a predecessor (Ezrow & Frantz, 2011, p. xv). When one conflates the regime type and the dictator type, misperceptions may emerge because it is very well possible that while ideology plays an important role in a particular regime, and is perhaps even important to the population, ideology does not necessarily have to be important to the leader of the regime. It does not automatically mean that the dictator is personally devoted to the ideology. While North Korea, for instance, might best be described as an 'eroding totalitarian' regime, the ideology that remains an important characteristic of the regime and was important to Kim Jong Sung, no longer seems to carry the same meaning for his successors (Chirot, 1994, p. 171; Post, 2004, pp. 249-250; Scobell, 2005).

The role that ideology plays for the non-democratic leader is an important factor for Chirot's typological map of tyrants. He developed a scale that ranges from extreme ideological certitude to pragmatism on the one hand and corruption *versus* honesty on the other and proceeded to place dictators along this fourfold spectrum (Chirot, 1994, pp. 170-171). Hitler, Stalin, Mao, Pol Pot and Kim Il Sung are mentioned as examples of leaders who act on the basis of extreme ideological certitude (Chirot, 1994, p. 167). Other regimes were not at all ideologically motivated, like Idi Amin, for instance, and there were regimes who should be classified somewhere in between these two extremes, such as Nicolae Ceaucescu and Saddam Hussein (Chirot, 1994, pp. 167-168).

Jackson and Rosberg focus specifically on a subset of dictators, namely those that have established personal rule in Africa. Personal rule refers to the 'system' of rule (R. H. Jackson & Rosberg, 1982, p. 4), but most of the book focuses on the leaders who were in charge of the regimes. They developed a fourfold ideal type typology in which they differentiate the prince, the autocrat, the prophet and the tyrant (R. H. Jackson & Rosberg, 1982, pp. 77-80). The first two types, the prince and the autocrat, have in common that 'they are practical and circumspect builders generally without heroic socioeconomic goals or a master plan' (R. H. Jackson & Rosberg, 1982, p. 77). The prince is gifted in forging alliances and gaining loyalty and rule through the 'politics of accommodation' (R. H. Jackson & Rosberg, 1982, p. 78). The autocrat is more dominant, he has all the power and the only limitations on his rule stem from the amount of resources that are at his disposal (R. H. Jackson & Rosberg, 1982, p. 78). Prophets rather base their rule on a vision, or ideology which in the case of African rulers has most often been socialism (R. H. Jackson & Rosberg, 1982, p. 79). These leaders tend to be very charismatic and it is 'his charm, mystique, and personality – that counts most in a prophetic regime' (R. H. Jackson & Rosberg, 1982, p. 79). Finally, the tyrant does not only rule without any legal restraint, but also acts without being hampered by moral scruples (R. H. Jackson & Rosberg, 1982, p. 80). They have no respect for human life and rule through fear while ensuring enough rewards and incentives are provided to followers, making them dependent on the tyrant's continued rule (R. H. Jackson & Rosberg, 1982, p. 80). Jackson and Rosberg warn that leaders may possess characteristics of each type and can potentially change over time (R. H. Jackson & Rosberg, 1982, p. 81).

They acknowledge being influenced by the research that was described above by Max Weber on charismatic and patrimonial domination (R. H. Jackson & Rosberg, 1982, p. 9). Jackson and Rosberg point out that Weber's conception of traditional and charismatic domination are closely related to their conceptualisation of autocratic or princely rule and prophetic rule (R. H. Jackson & Rosberg, 1982, p. 73). At the same time, however, they also emphasize that there are important differences. The concepts patrimonialism or sultanism, as developed by Weber, assumed that the traditional rules imposed restraints on the leaders. Jackson and Rosberg argue, rather, that in the African cases they studied, there have been very few political traditions that could have such a restraining effect (R. H. Jackson & Rosberg, 1982, p. 74). They also added the type tyrant, which obviously was not part of Weber's description of legitimate domination (R. H. Jackson & Rosberg, 1982, p. 74).

Most of the literature on dictatorial leaders, however, is less interested in creating typologies and has rather studied individual leaders. Studying the personality of a particular leader came to be seen as an important explanatory variable (Moghaddam, 2013, p. 13; 81). Moghaddam is sceptical about research which focuses solely on the character traits of the individuals, arguing they are constrained by their surroundings and the situation in which they find themselves (Moghaddam, 2013, p. 36). Contemporary research that focuses on individual leaders and their personality, nevertheless continues to be important and dictators are often studied within the context the leader finds himself. Sometimes several dictators are studied and compared (Overy, 2004; Post, 2004), but frequently scholars investigate them as a single case study (e.g. Chandler, 1999; LeBor, 2003). The latter category usually concerns political biographies or historical case studies where the leader is examined in the context of a particular conflict or era. When leaders are studied from a comparative perspective, broader lessons are frequently drawn. Post analyses, for instance, the effect of illness, old age or stress on foreign policy decisions of destructive leaders and how hateful and narcissistic leaders relate to their followers (Post, 2004).

A recurring question in the literature on dictators is whether dictatorial leaders are mad or crazy individuals. Glad argues that the self-defeating behaviour of the five tyrants she analysed is mainly due to narcissism and 'severe superego deficiencies' (Glad, 2002). Post too emphasized the role that narcisissism can play by focusing on the leader-follower relationship, where both leader and follower can come to believe in the unique qualities of the destructive leader (Post, 2004, p. 193). Tucker, rather, focuses on the paranoid characteristics that Hitler and Stalin had and which formed part of their 'warfare personality'. They saw themselves bound up in an endless struggle against enemies that not only threatened themselves but also their organizations and societies (Tucker, 1965, pp. 577-578).

There are also those who explicitly warn against seeing dictatorial leaders as having mental deficiencies. Chirot argues that while there may be an obvious appeal into thinking that the dictators are crazy and nothing like us, and while this may be true in a few cases, 'on the whole' Chirot explains 'the truly insane are unable to keep themselves in power long enough to do much harm'. (Chirot, 1994, p. 12). Mandel explicitly argues that dictators should be studied as normal human beings using the same social psychological theories (2002). In addition, there seems to be a trend to draw parallels between dictators and other types of leaders making dictatorship merely an extreme form of destructive leadership, milder versions of which can be found in any political system or business (Bruce Bueno De Mesquita & Smith, 2011; Kellerman, 2004).

In the discussion that follows the differences among the different kinds of dictators and regimes needs to be kept in mind. At the same time, while these differences should not go unnoticed there are also important similarities in the tactics used by each regime (Ayittey, 2011, p. 15). Therefore, although it is acknowledged that differences between dictators and regimes are important for how they work, it is deemed appropriate and necessary to emphasize where the literature converges, and paint a general picture of how dictators maintain power and make policy choices. Whenever relevant important differences between the dictators and their regimes will of course be emphasized.

2.3. THEIR DOMESTIC POLICY: HOW THEY MAINTAIN POWER

Dictators maintain power through a large array of measures but they can be classified overall into three overarching categories: maintaining some legitimacy, buying loyalty and the use of force, which will be discussed in turn in the paragraphs that follow. Some of these work contradictorily. When a government lacks legitimacy, it needs to use force in order to stay in power, and the more force is used, the more its authority fades, requiring the regime to consequently use more force in order to maintain power (Hoefnagels, 1977, pp. 30-35). Dictators therefore constantly seek to strike a balance between the three mechanisms to stay in power.

Dictators also likely differ in the extent to which they rely on either of these measures. Some scholars have argued, usually on the basis of Geddes' typology, that this differs per regime type or type of leader (Ezrow & Frantz, 2011). Others have treated dictators and their regime as a uniform phenomenon (Ayittey, 2011; Moghaddam, 2013). Bueno de Mesquita and Smith do not even differentiate between democratic or dictatorial regimes. They argue regimes only differ in the extent to which they rely on others to stay in power. No leader can rule completely alone or is all-powerful, but the amount of people a leader needs to keep satisfied to stay in power differs enormously across regimes (Bruce Bueno De Mesquita & Smith, 2011, pp. 1-8). They simply argue that how many people are essential to the leader's rule and how many can influence his policy, matters for the choices the leader will make (Bruce Bueno De Mesquita & Smith, 2011, pp. 8-9).

What the literature generally has in common is the underlying assumption that the primary motivation of the leader is to maintain power (e.g Bruce Bueno De Mesquita & Smith, 2011, p. xviii; Escribà-Folch, 2012; Ezrow & Frantz, 2011, p. 84; Kinne, 2005, p. 118). Bueno de Mesquita and Smith even go as far as to argue that 'where politics are concerned, ideology, nationality, and culture don't matter all that much', and believe that 'the self-interested calculations and actions of rulers are the driving force of all politics' (Bruce Bueno De Mesquita & Smith, 2011, p. xix; xxiii). Such an approach is problematic for those leaders who do not act out of self-interest, but are ideologically driven and have as a primary purpose the realization of an utopian future[18], but it is nevertheless important to cover this strand of literature since it is insightful for those leaders that first and foremost want to safeguard their position of power.

Who threatens the dictator's position of power most is a contentious issue. While Dobson argues that dictators predominantly fear their own population, Ezrow and Frantz and Moghaddam note that the population in fact does not threaten the dictator's position of power very often (Dobson, 2013; Ezrow & Frantz, 2011, pp. 81-83; Moghaddam, 2013, pp. 24-25). Others have argued that the nature of the threat varies per type of leader and regime. Overall personalist dictators are least likely to be overthrown, single party dictators face more risk, and military leaders are most likely to be overthrown. This is due to the fact that the elite can easily coordinate their efforts to remove the dictator in the latter two regime types, and the elite in military regimes, in addition have access to troops and weaponry (Ezrow & Frantz, 2011, pp. 85-86; 93). They also differ in the manner in which they are removed. Most assassinations occur in personalist dictatorships, while expulsions or institutionalized turnovers that do not necessitate the death of the leader are more common for military, and to a lesser extent, single party dictators (Ezrow & Frantz, 2011, pp. 88-90).

These findings show the importance of mechanisms that allow the dictator to deal with opposition, in the population, and especially also within the group of elites on which his rule predominantly depends. It has been suggested that dictators always have to contend with one major problem – they never know who

[18] This will be more elaborately addressed in Chapters 5 and 6.

is genuinely loyal and whom merely pretends to be – which leaves them eternally insecure as to their position (Haber, 2014, p. 694). The insecurity is a product of the repression dictators use to stay in power and has been called 'the Dictator's Dilemma' (Wintrobe, 2009, p. 366). It essentially means that the dictator who relies on repression to rule will never know how much support he has among the elite or the population because they are most likely too scared to voice any criticism (Wintrobe, 2009, p. 366). The uncertainty of the intentions of his followers will subsequently be a source of fear and anxiety for the dictator who will have to rely on more policy mechanisms than just repression to break the cycle (Wintrobe, 2009, p. 366).

Several scholars have argued that non-democratic regimes rely predominantly on legitimacy, loyalty and force (e.g. Brooker, 2014, p. 107; Escribà-Folch, 2012, p. 685). Ultimately, each regime also needs the tacit support of a subset of the population; the support does not have to be genuine and may be the product of coercion, but should be such as to prevent widespread opposition to the regime from materialising (Ezrow & Frantz, 2011, p. 55). Force, legitimacy and ensuring loyalty to the leader and his regime thus go hand in hand for the dictatorial leader in maintaining his position in power. Overall it seems dictatorial regimes have become more sophisticated in the manner in which these mechanisms are utilized, bearing greater resemblance to democratic regimes (Brooker, 2014, p. 8; Dobson, 2013, pp. 4-5).

2.3.1. A FAÇADE OF LEGITIMACY

The extent to which legitimacy plays a role in dictatorships is highly debated. Moghaddam explicitly rejects the idea that dictators would want to establish legitimacy in their respective societies (2013, p. 4) while other scholars argue it plays an important role. According to Wintrobe, 'dictators have the same incentive to build loyal bases of support as democratic politicians' (1990, p. 854) and Jackson and Rosberg contend on the basis of their study of African personalist rulers, that while there are some regimes which rely exclusively on state terror to stay in power, for most, legitimacy plays some role (1982, p. 38). In separate studies Kailitz and Burnell take the debate a step further by arguing that there are different kinds of legitimacy that different dictators tend to rely on and Burnell also emphasizes that the legitimacy dictators enjoy often varies among different parts of the population (Burnell, 2006; Kailitz, 2013).

Many dictatorships have institutionalized non-competitive, or only marginally competitive elections that are used to enhance the legitimacy of their regime (Brooker, 2014, p. 110). They have the added benefit of serving as a powerful tool to signal to potential rivals that anyone is expendable and can be replaced (Bruce Bueno De Mesquita & Smith, 2011, p. 61). Elections in this manner can secure the position of the dictator in power both with respect to the population and with respect to the elite. Elections in non-democratic regimes are not there to give the people a choice, but they are often there to give the dictator more options. Stalin reportedly said 'The people who cast the vote decide nothing. The people who count the votes decide everything' (Ayittey, 2011, p. 101).

Particularly when elections are non-competitive, ideological legitimacy also plays an important role (Brooker, 2014, p. 113). According to Brooker, this is the 'modern equivalent of the now largely extinct religious claims to legitimacy' (Brooker, 2014, p. 114). Exceptions are perhaps non-democratic regimes where the leadership legitimizes its rule on the basis of their 'status as clerics', examples of which include Iran and Saudi Arabia (Burnell, 2006, p. 548). A personality cult may also enhance the legitimacy of the dictator's rule. The dictator is then portrayed in a matter that is similar to the way prophets or saints would otherwise be depicted (Moghaddam, 2013, p. 144), p. 144). The personality cult usually includes an over the top or even fabricated story about the leader's history, accomplishments and personality, and the leader can become a symbol for the ideology he represents (Brooker, 2014, p. 132; Moghaddam, 2013, p. 145).

Moghaddam argues that ideologies are mainly formulated to justify the policies towards the elite and keep them united (2013, p. 4; 26). He explains that while

> 'the masses are kept in place by force and only at a secondary level by false ideologies, it is the dictatorial leadership and the power elite who need the crutch of strong legitimizing ideologues justifying their rule in dictatorships within the group and for themselves. Thus, the role of ideology in dictatorships is to enable the ruling elite to achieve a high level of cohesion and unity within their own group so that they feel justified in using brute force to maintain control over the masses' (Moghaddam, 2013, p. 4).

Ayittey, on the other hand, argues that the elite could not care less about the ideologies and only care about the money (Ayittey, 2011, p. 88). Both authors neglect the possibility that the extent to which legitimacy and ideology play a role in influencing the masses might differ per regime. Ayittey's book has a strong focus on Africa (2011, p. 6), where corrupt neo-patrimonial regimes have been very prevalent, while Moghaddam's book is largely inspired by Iran as a case study, where religion played a much more important role in the decision of the elites to support Khomeini (Moghaddam, 2013, pp. 97-98).

Other types of legitimacy that dictators can rely on are hereditary legitimacy and performance legitimacy (Burnell, 2006, pp. 548-549). In case of the latter, the dictator is either judged on the basis of how many goods he can distribute in society or among his cronies (Burnell, 2006, p. 549). According to Brooker, this type of legitimacy is always complementary to other types of legitimacy (Brooker, 2014, p. 110).

On the one hand, the international community can increase the level of legitimacy of a particular regime, but on the other hand, depending on the regime, portraying the country as battling the rest of the world can also enhance the domestic support they receive (Ayittey, 2011, p. 107; Burnell, 2006, p. 549). Of course, none of the above mentioned forms of legitimacy are mutually exclusive (Burnell, 2006, p. 549).

Some of these types of legitimacy can also be vulnerabilities of the dictators and their regimes (Burnell, 2006, p. 546). When a dictator overwhelmingly loses an election, it can be very difficult to cover up the loss, at times sparking mass protests (Bruce Bueno De Mesquita & Smith, 2011, pp. 203-204). There are also numerous ways in which performance legitimacy, and the risk of being unable to maintain it, can actually make a regime very vulnerable. Firstly, there is the risk that competitors will claim to be able to provide more goods. Secondly, it can make the regime very vulnerable to factors that influence its performance that are outside of its control. Thirdly, when the expectations of the population rises, so too must its overall performance to maintain its legitimacy. Fourthly, the growth might take several years to materialise and lastly, the involvement of the military in politics and society might seem less urgent or warranted as society becomes more stable and economic growth materialises (Brooker, 2014, p. 109). In general, though, providing cronies with material rewards in exchange for loyalty is an important tool for maintaining control of most dictators.

2.3.2. CO-OPTATION AND BUYING LOYALTY

There are several ways in which the dictator is able to subdue opposition without using extreme violence. Leaders can, for instance, co-opt them or buy their loyalty through the distribution of goods to particular groups or elite in society (Escribà-Folch, 2012, p. 685; Haber, 2014, p. 701). Who the most important individuals are for a dictator, depends on the type of leader or regime. Personalist dictators compete with rivals for the support of a limited number of crucial members of the elite, while single party regimes have much larger winning coalitions and military regimes predominantly seek the support of the military (Escribà-Folch, 2012, p. 687).

Bueno de Mesquita and Smith argue that when leaders are dependent on just a few powerful individuals, providing them with material rewards for their backing is an effective manner of ensuring continued rule (Bruce Bueno De Mesquita & Smith, 2011, p. xviii). When there are only a few people the leader needs to keep satisfied to cling to power, the leader will only spend the revenues of his country on these individuals, rather than on policies that will benefit the entire population (Bruce Bueno De Mesquita & Smith, 2011, pp. 11-12). According to Bueno de Mesquita and Smith, it all comes down to five general rules. Firstly, the leader needs to keep the amount of people he needs to stay in power as small as possible, secondly, he needs to ensure that he can replace anyone who may be able to influence his policies, decisions or continued rule. Thirdly, he needs to control where the money goes to and ideally this means dividing the money to keep a few important people wealthy, while the unimportant majority is allowed to be poor. Fourthly, those who support the leader need to be dependent on him, and it is important to pay them just enough to keep them loyal but no more; and finally, do not improve the welfare of the people overall if this is at the expense of loyalists (Bruce Bueno De Mesquita & Smith, 2011, pp. 17-18).

Regarding personalist regimes, Jackson and Rosberg argue that the relationship between the ruler and his high-placed followers and immediate subordinates is important to guarantee some stability. The ruler therefore needs to set up a system of clientelism which Jackson and Rosberg refer to as 'a system of patron-client ties that bind leaders and followers in relationships not only of mutual assistance and support, but also of recognized and accepted inequality between big men and lesser men' (R. H. Jackson & Rosberg, 1982, p. 39). Gaining resources can be an important motivation for such a relationship, but beyond that the leader must also win a degree of loyalty, built on devotion, to survive any setbacks in their ability to provide the resources (R. H. Jackson & Rosberg, 1982, pp. 40-41). This loyalty can be partly based on ethnic or clan bonds, but must also be earned by being a strong and decisive leader (R. H. Jackson & Rosberg, 1982, p. 41). The downside is, of course, that the state apparatus tends to grow enormously, since being part of the government becomes a way to secure wealth (Ayittey, 2011, p. 91). All state institutions will be vulnerable and affected by this trend. Whether it be the state media or judiciary, professionalism will be tarnished and traded in for sycophancy (Ayittey, 2011, pp. 91-92).

Yet it is not always the dictator who will distribute the wealth – he may also allow his subordinates to gather it themselves. Corruption can in this sense be an important policy tool to reward loyalists and sanctioning corruption by officials can subsequently be a manner to enforce loyalty (Bruce Bueno De Mesquita & Smith, 2011, p. 88; 158). The dictator can also buy loyalty by allowing cronies to benefit from private enterprises that can take advantage of the limits that the dictatorial regime places on competition (Haber, 2014, p. 701).

Next to distributing spoils, the dictator can also make policy concessions to increase loyalty. While spoils can be handed out directly to important individuals by the dictator and do not always need to portray an image that this is done lawfully, when policy concessions are made, these do require a semblance of legality in order to avoid more widespread rebellion (Gandhi & Przeworski, 2007, pp. 1281-1282). Having formal institutions can therefore be very useful (Gandhi & Przeworski, 2007, p. 1282). These can take the form of partisan legislators but might also more simply be a consultative council, junta, or political bureau (Gandhi & Przeworski, 2007, pp. 1280-1282). With monarchs, the institutional setting revolves around the royal family and with military regimes, the army plays an important role. Non-royal civilians need to create institutions (Gandhi & Przeworski, 2007, p. 1284). The extent to which this is necessary for regime survival differs. When there is an abundance of natural resources, many spoils can be distributed directly, making the institutional setting less important. When revenue needs to be created through a functional economy, they need to acquire cooperation from a large portion of society (Gandhi & Przeworski, 2007, p. 1281; 1285).

Buying support for authoritarian rule is sometimes presented as an 'authoritarian bargain' which Desai, Olofsgård and Yousef explain entails 'an implicit arrangement between ruling elites and citizens whereby citizens relinquish political influence in exchange for public spending' (Desai, Olofsgård, & Yousef, 2009). Examples include several oil rich states in the Middle East and several Sub-Saharan African states where ethno linguistic differences influence how resources are spent (Desai *et al.*, 2009, p. 95).

Sometimes co-optation of the opposition can give the regime an almost democratic appearance, especially in combination with multiparty elections. While costly, and while occasionally it might result in outcomes that are unfavourable to the dictator, ultimately having institutions in place that are familiar to most democratic systems can actually lengthen their rule (Ezrow & Frantz, 2011, p. 68; Gandhi & Przeworski, 2007, pp. 1283-1284). Elections create a system in which competitors need to operate and when they acquire functions in that system, they will also be discouraged from eliminating it (Ezrow & Frantz, 2011, p. 69). They also provide an institutional framework in which elite can compete for resources and disputes can be resolved (Ezrow & Frantz, 2011, p. 70; 76).

It is a delicate balance that needs to be struck because it is in the best interest of the dictatorial regime that opposition movements remain fractured and weak and are not given any opportunity to organize themselves (Ezrow & Frantz, 2011, p. 56). Yet Ezrow and Frantz also acknowledge that '[w]hen members of the opposition are given opportunities to participate in the system (primarily via political posts), they have fewer incentives to coalesce and challenge the regime' (Ezrow & Frantz, 2011, p. 57). An important risk is that autocrats may err in their assessment of the amount of opposition there is in society or their direct surroundings, either because of personal ideosyncracies or because they are surrounded by 'yes men' (Gandhi & Przeworski, 2007, p. 1289).

2.3.3. REPRESSION AND VIOLENCE

Dictators will also make sure that their inner circle knows that they are expendable and can be purged, often with fatal consequences, and that therefore they should maintain loyalty to their leader (Bruce Bueno De Mesquita & Smith, 2011, pp. 62-63). The other mechanisms are thus supplemented by a certain amount of repression and violence, which is used to keep elite and security forces in line when buying loyalty is not enough but it can also be used to control the population (Ayittey, 2011, p. 92).

Using violence to control the elite, is a risky strategy because it means that other influential individuals will be highly motivated to remove the dictator from power if this allows them to save their skin. In addition, it requires the creation of an organization which can implement the violent policy but which can potentially also turn against the dictator (Haber, 2014, p. 699). Parallel institutions are therefore often built, particularly in the security forces, oftentimes in combination with the creation of a presidential guard to secure his own safety (Ayittey, 2011, p. 92).

Dictatorships prefer to keep their population content and elicit their support, but do not shy away from other means when they fail to do so (Dobson, 2013, p. 6). When the dictators feel cornered they may very well risk whatever little legitimacy they have and opt for brutal force (Dobson, 2013, pp. 288-289). The level of repression obviously varies enormously across regimes. For the most repressive regimes this will include torture, show trials, imprisonment and possibly disappearances and executions or concentration camps (Brooker, 2014, p. 118; Haber, 2014, p. 698). In addition, in nearly all dictatorial regimes the free press is also curtailed, and people risk dismissal (Ayittey, 2011, pp. 94-95).

In regimes which have more democratic pretensions, oppression tends to be done in a less obvious manner (Dobson, 2013, p. 5). As Dobson explains,

> 'today's dictators understand that in a globalised world the more brutal forms of intimidation – mass arrests, firing squads, and violent crackdowns – are best replaced with more subtle forms of coercion. Rather than forcibly arrest members of a human rights group, today's most effective despots deploy tax collectors or health inspectors to shut down dissident groups. Laws are written broadly then used like a scalpel to target the groups the government deems a threat … Rather than shutter all media, modern day despots make exceptions for small outlets – usually newspapers – that allow for a limited public discussion. Today's dictators pepper their speeches with references to liberty, justice and the rule of law' (Dobson, 2013, p. 5).

Elections can be useful to signal how strong the opposition is and harassment and violence will be used, alongside numerous other forms of electoral fraud, to win (Ezrow & Frantz, 2011, pp. 71-73). In Zimbabwe, for instance, a second round was necessary in the contested elections of 2008 because no candidate managed to secure the absolute majority of the votes. Mugabe unleashed a reign of terror in the period leading up to the second round which was so vicious his competitor Tsvangirai decided to withdraw his candidacy (Bratton & Masunungure, 2008, p. 41).

For regimes that take on a democratic appearance, law, too, forms a powerful weapon. The regime can use defamation or libel suits to discipline the opposition

(Ayittey, 2011, p. 96). The judiciary is no longer independent and judges can be reprimanded as well if they rule against the state (Ayittey, 2011, p. 100). The emphasis is often on less invasive punishments which may include dismissal or other means to disadvantage a person's standing in society and economic well-being (Brooker, 2014, p. 119). When more extreme measures are taken, they occur outside of the public gaze. Moghaddam notes torture used to be public in a time when dictatorships got their right to rule from their power, now opposition groups are repressed behind closed doors (Moghaddam, 2013, p. 137).

When the population rises up, the dictator can either increase democracy or become even more repressive (Bruce Bueno De Mesquita & Smith, 2011, p. 198). Moghaddan argues that when a regime feels more threatened, whether it be from external or internal sources, repression and state violence increase and when a regime is extremely repressive, uprisings and rebellion become less likely (Bruce Bueno De Mesquita & Smith, 2011, p. 196; Moghaddam, 2013, p. 147).

2.4. THEIR FOREIGN POLICY: DICTATORS IN THE WORLD

Dictators often have a complex relationship with democratic countries. The latter have always gone back and forth between attempts to improve the human rights situation in non-democratic regimes and supporting them to further their own strategic interests (Ayittey, 2011, pp. 107-108; 219). Jeane Kirkpatrick's argument, which was developed in the midst of the Cold War, is perhaps most well-known. She argued that the US should continue its support for friendly authoritarian regimes because their downfall could mean the emergence of a totalitarian regime that would adopt policies that were even more cruel for its population, and harmful to US strategic interests (Kirkpatrick, 1979). Adesnik and McFaul believe that the underlying question that Kirkpatrick grappled with: how to promote change in autocracies without harming the strategic interests of – in this case – the US, outlived its Cold War context (Adesnik & McFaul, 2006, p. 12). Moral concerns with such an approach abound and countries have grappled with the question of whether to use positive engagement or punitive measures. The rationale behind punitive measures is eloquently explained by Nincic:

> 'The thought is that, although basic incentives behind the objectionable behaviour are fixed and cannot easily be changed, they can be offset by counterincentives in the form of externally imposed fears and hardships. Governments care especially about their domestic position, whereas those who, within the country, most acutely experience the punishment may threaten to withdraw their support of the government or engage in active opposition, leading it, in a spirit of self-preservation, to revise its policies in the desired direction' (Nincic, 2006, p. 323).

In other words, it is assumed that the predominant goal of those who rule is the preservation of their position of power and when such a position can be undermined with punitive measures, the costs of the behaviour may start to outweigh its benefits and it may choose to bow to pressure. Escribà-Folch, who investigates the responses of dictators to the imposition of sanctions, in a similar vein assumes 'that dictators are rational and self-interested actors who want to maximize their probability of remaining in power' (Escribà-Folch, 2012, p. 689). As will be explained more in depth in the upcoming chapters, this assumption does not always hold true, but the existing literature is nevertheless valuable and highly relevant for those dictators who do want to maximize the chances of retaining their position of power.[19] Instead of focusing on coercive diplomacy, compellance and deterrence more generally, the measures on which these strategies rely will be discussed separately. This is seen as more desirable because, although a large and sophisticated body of work has been developed it has also been associated with '(i) vague and unclear definitions of key concepts and variables, (ii) limited systematic and rigorous empirical analysis, and (iii) a reluctance to address known policy problems' (Jakobsen, 2011, p. 157). In addition, because of the focus of the present research, the overview below will predominantly analyse policy mechanisms when they are targeting dictators to improve their adherence to human rights standards.

2.4.1. DIPLOMACY

In comparison to the foreign policy mechanisms discussed below, relatively little is written about the manner in which dictators respond to diplomatic initiatives or about diplomatic policies within dictatorial regimes more generally. Considering the limited information that is available on the manner in which dictators engage in, and respond to, diplomatic initiatives, the reaction of states that are accused of human rights violations more generally is gauged as well.

It is deemed important to divide the many mechanisms that fall under the overarching concept of diplomacy into two categories.[20] The first concerns the manner in which states engage with each other openly and the other; quiet diplomacy involves more subtle forms of communication behind the scenes.

[19] See Chapters 3, 5 and 6.

[20] The focus, here, is on communication between leaders and regimes. Coercive diplomacy, which was defined by Craig & George as the use of 'threats or limited force to persuade an opponent to call off or undo an encroachment' (Craig & George, 1995, p. 196) entails not only communication, but also the threat, or actual use, of other measures such as sanctions or military intervention which will be discussed seperatly.
Preventative diplomacy is more tied to the moment in which foreign policy mechanisms are utilized rather than a separate form of interactions between states and as such is not dealt with separately (see for an overarching typology of different forms of diplomacy and the moment in which they are initiated, Jentleson (1996)).

Quiet diplomacy entails the traditional mechanism in which states 'deal unobtrusively with each other in private meetings, bringing matters of mutual concern to each other's attention' (Baehr, 2009). Neither form is necessarily more effective than the other. As Baehr explains 'Sometimes a government can be more easily persuaded to make certain concessions if there is no threat of loss of face involved. On other occasions, publicity, or the threat of such publicity, may force a government into action.' (Baehr, 2009).

Critics have stated that quiet diplomacy is flawed and have argued it is largely ineffectual (Graham, 2006, p. 116). Its success is often difficult to determine, considering the secrecy that surrounds the policy (Graham, 2006, p. 116). The policy of quiet diplomacy that South Africa engaged in for a long time to try to improve the human rights situation in Zimbabwe has been highly criticized on that basis (Graham, 2006).

Condemning another nation can be perceived as a sanction in international politics, and especially in the field of human rights, the policy of naming and shaming can be of tremendous importance (Grünfeld, 1999, p. 113). Naming and shaming is done not only by other governments, but also by NGOs and international organizations (S. Cohen, 1996, p. 517). The evidence that diplomatic sanctions and naming and shaming are effective in counteracting human rights abuses is contradictory (DeMeritt, 2012; Franklin, 2008; Hafner-Burton, 2008; Krain, 2012, 2014), but there is reason to be more opitimistic when it concerns dictatorships. Investigating the impact of naming and shaming by international Non-Governmental Organisations, Hendrix and Wong (2013) come to the counter-intuitive conclusion that it increases the respect for human rights more in autocratic regimes than it does in democracies or hybrid regimes. Because democracies and hybrid regimes have organized political opposition and comparatively independent press, they are likely to have already taken the costs of the abuses becoming public into account when they decided on the policy and consequently information about abuses which is distributed by INGOs have a greater impact in autocracies (Hendrix & Wong, 2013, pp. 660-661).

The research stands in marked contrast with the work of Cohen, who assumes that highly repressive regimes are unconcerned with the domestic impact of such reports because they do not have to deal with internal dissent and are unconcerned with maintaining a positive image internationally (S. Cohen, 1996, p. 521; 523). When countries do respond, several forms of denial are used. The first is literal denial, meaning a simple claim that 'nothing is happening' (S. Cohen, 1996, p. 523). This reaction is common among authoritarian regimes when they do not decide to ignore the matter altogether. Cohen explains, 'such countries have no need to elaborate any response. Their control over internal information, the absence of free media, and the ban on human rights monitoring does not allow their denials to be countered' (S. Cohen, 1996, p. 523). The second way in which countries may respond is through interpretive denial, by claiming that 'what is happening is really something else' (S. Cohen, 1996, p. 525). This response has become more likely since literal denial is more difficult to sustain in the world today. In this scenario, the facts themselves are acknowledged but the meaning is changed. While the deaths of individuals might be recognized, the reprehensible nature of such facts is denied by stating their deaths were not the result of genocide or extra-judicial killings, for instance (S. Cohen, 1996, p. 525). A third response can be to claim that whatever happened was justified, a reaction which Cohen has called implicatory denial (S. Cohen, 1996, p. 529). As an alternative strategy a country may also decide to commence a counter-offensive to discredit the report and the organization that produced it, and on occasion a government will respond with a partial acknowledgement of the maltreatment of its citizens (S. Cohen, 1996, pp. 534-537).

The extent to which a dictatorial leader will be personally involved in the diplomatic process, is likely to differ across regime and across different moments in time and issue areas. There is, however, reason to think that the dictatorial leader can play a very important role. Sofer, using the 1930s as an example, has argued that in dictatorial regimes the dictator has frequently acted as his own diplomat, curtailing 'the diplomat's room for manoeuvre' (2001, p. 111). In addition, there seems to be agreement overall that diplomacy is likely to be more successful when conducted among leaders, or their immediate representatives, directly in a personal meeting which therefore tends to happen quite regularly (Graham, 2006, p. 115). Adesnik and McFaul also recognized that the dictator plays an important role. They warned dictators will 'bend over backward to find evidence that the US is willing to tolerate their regime' and because the dictator will search for indications that a country might not be adamant to bring about change stressed the importance of the consistency of any message that is communicated to them (2006, p. 20).

Diplomacy in itself is not likely to have any major impact[21] on a country's policy, yet they can influence a government in the long term and can contribute to change indirectly. Some argue this was the case in South Africa, where Apartheid was subject to many diplomatic initiatives that have eventually contributed to its end (Baehr, 2009, p. 166; Donnelly, 2003).

2.4.2. ECONOMIC SANCTIONS

Where lawyers tend to see sanctions as a punitive measure, which addresses past conduct, political scientists often focus on the manner in which sanctions could potentially change future behaviour (Grünfeld, 1999, p. 113). Esciba Folch for instance characterizes sanctions in the following manner:

21 The impact of INGO reports on autocracies was also rather small, according to Hendrix and Wong (Hendrix & Wong, 2013, p. 671).

> '[e]conomic sanctions consist of the imposition of coercive measures with the aim of bringing about a policy or institutional change in the target country or of destabilizing the incumbent regime' (Escribà-Folch, 2012, pp. 687-688).

Most often these measures are employed against non-democratic regimes (Escribà-Folch, 2012, p. 688), but these are at the same time also the most difficult to influence (Drezner, 2011, p. 99). Grünfeld argues they are neither receptive to internal nor external pressure and unlikely to conform to the wishes of the international community (Grünfeld, 1999, p. 121).

Escribà-Folch, however, finds that sanctions often have an impact on the domestic policy in dictatorships because sanctions can have a destabilizing effect on the continued rule of the dictatorial leader (Escribà-Folch, 2012, p. 684). Using Geddes' typology, Escribà Folch has found that personalist dictatorial regimes are most likely to increase their levels of repression when sanctions are imposed. Military and single party regimes in contrast will respond by diverting funds to groups whose backing they require in order to maintain their position of power (Escribà-Folch, 2012, p. 684). The costs of these measures tends to increase after sanctions have been imposed (Escribà-Folch, 2012, p. 689). Loyalty might become more expensive because the sanctions may harm interests of the elite, potentially making other potential leaders more attractive and doubts may arise as to the stability of the regime (Escribà-Folch, 2012, p. 689). Sanctions can also strengthen the position of the opposition and raise their morale and potentially act as a catalyst when grievances cause a population to become restless (Escribà-Folch, 2012, p. 692).

Despite potentially weakening the power position of the dictator, there are, however, several reasons that Nincic highlights which may explain why frequently punitive measures are unlikely to be successful. The first reason is that domestic support is not always weakened when sanctions are imposed. The population may rally around the flag and the support of the regime may thus actually be strengthened. In a similar vein, the population and political actors may rally around the political agenda that caused the sanctions to be imposed (Nincic, 2006, pp. 323-324). The harm sanctions may impose on the population is also likely to weaken the sympathy for the demands of the international community (Grünfeld, 1999, p. 114; 124). In addition, sanctions may weaken some sectors of the economy but often benefit others as the grey and black economy may thrive and new economic actors may benefit from the sanctions that were imposed. They may seek out an alliance with politicians causing politicians to have a stake in keeping the sanctions regime in place (Nincic, 2006, pp. 323-324). Some scholars have suggested that sanctions can even be beneficial for a dictator and strengthen his power position, although others have argued this varies per regime type (Drezner, 2011, p. 100; Escribà-Folch & Wright, 2010).

The use of comprehensive sanctions was heavily criticized after the human toll of the sanctions regime that was imposed on Iraq in the 1990s became apparent (Drezner, 2011, p. 97). Smart sanctions were developed to make sanctions more effective by targeting the elite in the hope that they will consequently put pressure on the dictator to change his policy, while reducing the costs to the population (Drezner, 2011, p. 100). The measures included financial sanctions, travel bans, often aiming to impact individuals rather than the whole country (Drezner, 2011, p. 100). Several studies suggest that human suffering is less when smart sanctions are employed, partly because authoritarian regimes were less likely to increase repression when smart sanctions were used, but overall smart sanctions seem to be somewhat less effective (Drezner, 2011, p. 102).

Regardless of the type, sanctions are frequently used as a last attempt to prevent war (Grünfeld, 1999, p. 113). The threat of war, or the decision to intervene militarily, therefore is a step closer when sanctions fail. Although some scholars have doubted whether war is always more destructive than economic sanctions (Aloyo, 2015, p. 197), military intervention and the threat thereof is an extremely coercive measure with potentially disastrous consequences.

2.4.3. MILITARY INTERVENTION AND WAR

The democratic peace theory, the idea that democratic states never go to war with another democracy, is one of the most well substantiated claims in international relations (Ezrow & Frantz, 2011, p. 143). There does not seem to be a similar trend for dictators. Their behaviour is quite disparate; some have fought other dictatorships, some fought democracies and others have been rather peaceful (Brooker, 2014, p. 141). Peceney *et al*, however, have found that, using Geddes' distinction, no personalist or military regimes have fought a similar counterpart. While single party regimes have fought each other, they were still more peaceful than mixed dyads (Peceny, Beer, & Shannon, 2002).

In general, there is reason to believe that democracies are less inclined to go to war (Ezrow & Frantz, 2011, p. 144). Bueno de Mesquita and Smith, for instance, argue that while democrats will only decide to go to war when their chances of winning are promising, dictators are willing to take more risks (Bruce Bueno De Mesquita & Smith, 2011, pp. 228-229; 144). Democrats are likely to lose their position in power when they lose a war, but such an outcome is less likely for a dictator who retains enough resources (Bruce Bueno De Mesquita & Smith, 2011, pp. 240-241; 244). Resources will not be diverted from paying off cronies to protecting soldiers on the battlefield since they cannot be voted out of office by the relatives of those who die (Bruce Bueno De Mesquita & Smith, 2011, p. 230; Ezrow & Frantz, 2011, p. 144). Consequently, Bueno de Mesquita and Smith argue that 'democrats more often than autocrats fight when all other means of gaining policy concessions from foreign foes fail. In contrast, autocrats are more likely to fight casually, in the pursuit of land, slaves, and treasure' (2011,

p. 237). Jackson & Rosberg likewise argue that foreign policy in many personalist African states can be very irregular due to the freedom that the leader has to initiate it, and is frequently decided on the basis of what is likely to be good for the leader in power (R. H. Jackson & Rosberg, 1982, p. 30). Peceney *et al* suggest democracies might purposefully target weak personalist regimes, but Ezrow and Frants doubt this (Peceny *et al.*, 2002, p. 25). They cite more recent research that suggest that the frequency with which democracies and personalist regimes fight each other is because personalist regimes provoke war with democracies (Ezrow & Frantz, 2011, pp. 143-144).

International relations scholars have suggested that an important reason why war emerges between states is that there is so much uncertainty regarding the other's intentions and commitment to promises or threats. This line of research suggests that democrats can signal their determination more easily than dictators can. When democrats make threats, they have obvious costs for reneging on them because they can be held accountable for foreign policy failures by domestic audiences (Ezrow & Frantz, 2011, pp. 146-148). Dictators can therefore much more easily make threatening statements and not follow through on them (Ezrow & Frantz, 2011, p. 148). This may also explain why there is so little war between democracies. As Frantz and Ezrow explain,

> 'crises are averted when there is complete information about resolve. The outcome can be anticipated and ahead of time, and the state that would have eventually have been defeated backs down' (2011, p. 148).

Most dictatorships are to some extent accountable to the elite but again, the extent to which the elite can hold dictators accountable and potentially unseat them, differs per regime type. Dictators of military regimes are much more likely to be held accountable for their actions by the elite than the dictators of single party dictatorships or personalist regimes who are least likely to be held to account (Ezrow & Frantz, 2011, p. 149). Dictators of military regimes are therefore much more capable of signalling their commitment than leaders of personalist regimes and crises that are started by personalist dictators are therefore most likely to escalate (Ezrow & Frantz, 2011, pp. 148-149). Some scholars have therefore argued that only personalist dictatorships are less capable than democracies of signalling their determination (Ezrow & Frantz, 2011, p. 148).

2.4.4. POSITIVE ENGAGEMENT

Positive engagement can occur through diplomatic initiatives, and as such overlaps with the earlier analysis of diplomacy as an important foreign policy tool, but it encompasses much more. According to Resnick, engagement should be defined as 'the attempt to influence the political behavior of a target state through the comprehensive establishment and enhancement of contacts with that state across multiple issue areas (i.e. diplomatic, military, economic, cultural' (Resnick, 2001, p. 559). While there has been much less focus on positive inducements as a way to change behaviour than there has been on the more coercive counterpart, some contemporary scholars have advocated combining sticks and carrots, or have argued that positive behaviour should be further stimulated immediately by adopting a tit-for-tat strategy (Adesnik & McFaul, 2006; Nincic, 2006, p. 322).

Nincic specifies two ways in which positive engagement might be effective. Firstly, when enough is offered, the regime might be bribed in exhibiting desirable behaviour, and secondly, by undermining the position of those who thrive because of bad behaviour, the motivation for the regime to exhibit the undesirable behaviour may lessen (Nincic, 2006, pp. 325-326). The latter is most likely when the regime has difficulty to secure the support of groups who would like to see the undesirable policy continue, and therefore needs to secure the support of other groups in order to maintain its position of power (Nincic, 2006, p. 326). In addition, foreign support may lessen the economic hardships that often follow when policies are liberalized and can potentially prevent a regime from sliding back in old behaviour (Nincic, 2006, pp. 326-327).

At the same time, however, there are also many concerns relating to positive engagement. There have been fears, for instance, that benefits will simply be claimed by those in office without any changes being made. In addition, as Nincic explains, there are concerns 'about the moral hazard of appearing to recompense badness, a concern that evil must not go unpunished, and a discomfort with the historical connotations of appeasement' (2006, p. 322).[22]

In addition, Wintrobe points out that unrestricted aid could have the effect of keeping a tin-pot dictator in office (Wintrobe, 1990, p. 868). When the aid is tied to improvements to human rights, this may be a source of destabilization (Wintrobe, 1990, p. 868). Only if the aid would force the dictator to increase his human rights situation over a longer period of time which would allow him to use the money to buy loyalty, without having to cut back on his personal winnings, then potentially aid could be an incentive to cut back on repression (Wintrobe, 1990, p. 869).

Bueno de Mesquita and Smith argue against supplying foreign aid to non-democratic regimes because the leader can abuse the aid for policies that might harm the population or keep him in power (Bruce Bueno De Mesquita & Smith, 2011, pp. 162-167). They explain that it allows the dictator to pay his loyalists and may increase repression because he becomes less dependent on money being

22 Resnick explicitly warns against conflating the concepts of engagement and appeasement, with the latter meaning 'the cession of territory and/or spheres of influence to a target state' (Resnick, 2001, p. 564).

generated within a well-functioning economic system and because the aid can force him to make policy concessions that might be unpopular, causing him to have to rely more on repression to quell the dissent (Bruce Bueno De Mesquita & Smith, 2011, p. 180). In sum, while some scholars have argued in favour of positive engagement, there are also many legitimate concerns with such a strategy.

2.5. PITFALLS OF POLICY

In non-democratic regimes the leader is crucial for the decision-making process but he frequently is unable to make well informed decisions and is therefore more likely to make mistakes. According to Ayittey, 'dictators insist on making all important decisions themselves' (2011, p. 88). The extent to which this holds true, however, differs somewhat per regime type. Particularly in very personalised regimes the dictator might consult with a small group of confidants but the final decision will be taken by the leader (Ayittey, 2011, p. 88). The policies will reflect the idiosyncrasies of the dictator most in personalist dictatorial regimes while the policies of military regimes and single party dictatorships are less likely to overlap completely with the whims of the leader because they need to forge agreement (Ezrow & Frantz, 2011, pp. 114-115). This is especially so because in personalist regimes, the dictator is able to exert more power and influence over his inner circle. They can select the elite on the basis of whether or not they are supportive of their policies and can replace them if they want to. As a result, Ezrow and Frantz claim, 'elite policy preferences are essentially the leader's policy preferences' (Ezrow & Frantz, 2011, p. 114). Their changes in policy can therefore also be quite erratic (Ezrow, Frantz, p. 115). Having such extensive control over the country's policies allows dictators to realize any utopian plans they have for their country more easily, as Brooker points out, the 'degree of autonomy enjoyed by a personal dictator enables him to indulge his ideological preferences, demons and fantasies' (Brooker, 2014, p. 164).

Ayittey argues that 'for parrots, sycophants, and "followers," it is not dedication to the despot's ideology but the expectation of sharing in the spoils of office that keeps them faithful' (p. 88). This, however, seems a bit too simplistic. Self-interest, adoration and fear of the leader can all play important roles (Chirot, 1994, p. 164). Which emotion will dominate among his cronies, is also likely to depend on the dictator. In personalist regimes the leader is largely able to personally control who is in his inner circle. This also means that the information he receives from them tends to be rather poor for two important reasons. Firstly, the elite may fear the consequences of aggravating the dictator and secondly, the elite do not tend to be very capable individuals because they can become potential rivals (Bruce Bueno De Mesquita & Smith, 2011, p. 58;

Ezrow & Frantz, 2011, pp. 156-157). In addition, when a dictator purges the few competent individuals around him, the regime can be crippled even more (R. H. Jackson & Rosberg, 1982, p. 54). Ultimately, having a dictator at the top of the hierarchy compromises the ability of the regime to come to an optimal policy.

2.6. CONCLUSION

Despite the fact that political science has overwhelmingly focused on the workings of democracies, there is now an abundance of literature that also examines the world of the dictator. Great strides have been made to define dictatorship beyond the absence of democracy and a great number of regime and leadership types have been delineated. While this research is extremely valuable, for the purposes of this research a rather simple definition of dictatorship suffices. What matters is that it needs to be established that the individual leader is crucial in the decision-making process. Since the research focuses on the individual and his decision-making process, the more important the individual leader, the more relevant the findings of the present research. It is therefore important that the leader that is studied actually has control over the policy choices of the regime which is always more likely to be the case in dictatorships than in democracies.

Distinguishing beyond the democratic-dictatorial divide, it can be argued that the present research is most likely to be relevant for a personal dictator, where the line between dictator and dictatorship is not as clear (Ezrow & Frantz, 2011, p. 82). At the same time, it is in no way precluded that its findings are equally relevant in other regimes, especially because personalism is a difficult category. One party or military dictatorships can also have a strong, dominant leader, which is why Hadanius and Teorell rejected personalism as an overall category, and rather studied it as a factor which was more or less present across regime types (Hadenius & Teorell, 2007, p. 145). It is therefore ultimately important that in each case that is being analysed, to assess to what extent the individual is important for the decision-making process.

A major problem that occurs in these types of regimes, where there is such a strong leader, most notably in dictatorships, is that there is a distortion of the rational decision-making process. Dictators rely in varying degrees on legitimacy, buying loyalty and co-optation and repression that often includes violent purges of the elite. Depending on the dictator, his most important followers can be full of adoration, fear and highly dependent for their own wellbeing on the dictator's perception of them. This inhibits information from reaching the dictator and will negatively impact the decision-making process.

Despite the wealth of information that has been gathered by scholars over the years, there remain also serious limitations. The overwhelming amount of the research assumes that maintaining a position of power is the overarching motivation for *all* dictators. While this will be true for many dictators, this assumption is problematic for ideological dictators.[23] This is particularly problematic when looking at dictators that incite mass atrocities, since ideology is incredibly important in the perpetration of mass atrocities (Alvarez, 2008; Maynard, 2015). The role of the dictator in inciting and legitimizing mass atrocities and the manner in which he can orchestrate their perpetration will be the focus of the next chapter.

23 See for a more elaborate analysis Chapters 3, 5 and 6.

CHAPTER 3
MASS ATROCITIES AND THE ROLE OF THE DICTATOR

3.1. INTRODUCTION

In order to understand the causes of mass atrocities, a wide array of risk factors have been identified which are said to heighten the potential for mass violence. These factors range from structural societal factors like episodes of previous conflict and schisms in society to more immediate factors such as periods of economic or political crises and the level of democracy, or lack thereof (e.g. Harff, 2003; Staub, 2000, pp. 369-370; Woolf & Hulsizer, 2005). The latter point is of particular relevance to the present research. Many scholars have argued that dictatorial regimes and their leaders, especially if they profess an exclusionary ideology, are important for the perpetration of mass atrocities (Mandel, 2002, p. 262; Staub, 2000, p. 372; 2010, p. 174; Valentino, 2004; Woolf & Hulsizer, 2005, pp. 106-108). Surprisingly little research exists, however, on why this is so and how the dictator relates to the other factors that have been identified as important risk factors which enhance the possibility that mass atrocities occur (an exception is McLoughlin & Weerdesteijn, 2016). The current research on leaders who perpetrate mass atrocities therefore remains underdeveloped (McLoughlin & Weerdesteijn, 2016, p. 118; Padilla, Hogan, & Kaiser, 2007, p. 177; Woolf & Hulsizer, 2005, p. 107).

Mass atrocities are not only perpetrated in dictatorships, nor do all dictatorial regimes perpetrate atrocities, but the absence of an established democratic system of government heightens the risk mass atrocities will be perpetrated. Although some of these regimes will be merely unable to stop the perpetration of atrocities, frequently the dictatorial regime is orchestrating its perpetration.[24] Dictatorial rule has led to horrible suffering and as Chirot notes, '[i]n some cases, it was error, the mistaken policies of rulers that produced such horrors. But more often than not, killing and suffering on a gigantic scale was started on purpose, to carry out specific political goals' (Chirot, 1994, p. 9). These included either obtaining or solidifying power, or executing particular policy goals, once

[24] Such abuse of power by a government against its citizens has rightfully been characterized as 'the most fundamental perversion of the legal order that can be imagined' (translated from Dutch, Groenhuijsen, 2011, pp. 1011-1012).

in power (Chirot, 1994, pp. 7-9; Woolf & Hulsizer, 2005, pp. 106-107). Valentino even goes as far as saying that generally,

> 'mass killing will be best understood when the phenomenon is studied from what I call a strategic perspective. The strategic perspective suggests that mass killing is most accurately viewed as an instrumental policy – a brutal strategy designed to accomplish leaders' most important ideological or political objectives and counter what they see as their most dangerous threats' (Valentino, 2004, p. 3).

The dictator may thus use the atrocities to attain ideological or political goals.

The question therefore emerges as to how dictatorial regimes create circumstances that are conducive for the perpetration of mass atrocities. How do these risk factors relate to each other, and what is the role of the dictator in catalysing these crimes? In order to be able to answer these questions, it is important to look at the long term risk factors for mass violence that have been identified in the literature, and to analyse how dictatorial regimes and their leaders relate to these other factors. It becomes important to analyse the extent to which leaders can manipulate the risk factors and are able to turn a country's vulnerability to collective violence into actual atrocities. This chapter therefore aims to create a synthesis in the literature that identifies risk factors and the research that analyses the role of the leader in the perpetration of mass atrocities.

Firstly, the literature on the causes and risk factors of mass atrocities will be discussed. Thereafter, the role of the dictator will be analysed by investigating how the dictator can use existing pre-conditions and create new ones to foster a climate in which mass atrocities become more likely. In the section thereafter, it will be discussed how the dictator takes a final step into ensuring that the mass atrocities are actually perpetrated, by building the institutions that will actually commit the crimes.

3.2. CAUSES OF MASS ATROCITIES

The literature thus far has identified a number of factors that together form an elaborate but fragmented picture of the causes of mass atrocities. Scholars have focused on different levels of analysis and looked into many features that influence the occurrence of atrocity crimes at different periods in time. Structural factors tend to stem from long-term causes, such as a country's history, or are related to its institutional design, while more immediate factors trigger the outbursts of violence (McLoughlin, 2014, p. 30; Straus, 2015; Valentino, 2004, pp. 1-2).

Trigger factors have not been extensively researched. Straus argued that for many episodes of mass atrocities there was a turning point, which can usefully be described as a 'trigger', that escalated the violence (Straus, 2015, p. 13), but at the same time cautioned that

> 'the effects of triggering events cannot be separated from their context or from the influential decision-makers who respond to the events. The same event often has quite different ramifications in different countries, which suggest that underlying risk conditions are most determinative for the outbreak of atrocities. Moreover, elites have some autonomy in setting in motion violence ... Reactions to the events rather than only the events themselves are crucial' (Straus, 2015, p. 6).

This research will therefore not discuss trigger factors as isolated events. Any relevant turning points will be covered when analysing the comparative case study but such a discussion will take place while considering the context of the more structural risk factors and the reaction of the leader to them.

Structural factors have received more comprehensive scholarly attention. A history of colonialism, recent conflict or previous genocides establish the backdrop against which violence can be initiated (Harff, 2003, p. 66; Staub, 2000, p. 370). In some societies a 'culture of violence' may be created where aggression is often seen as a mechanism to solve problems, where a society perceives itself as being constantly under threat, and where an ideology of supremacy is incorporated into the fabric of society (Woolf & Hulsizer, 2005, p. 102). Difficult life conditions may be caused by an economic or political crisis or due to a war that is being fought, but especially when these factors coincide and there is a non-democratic leader to further push the country towards violence, the threat of mass violence becomes particularly grave (Woolf & Hulsizer, 2005, pp. 105-106). How the dictatorial leader is able to do that and how he is able to compel people to commit these atrocities will be explicated later on in the chapter. First, a closer look will be taken at each of the abovementioned risk factors.

At the outset though, it should be noted that while some of the research cited focuses explicitly on genocide and politicide (Harff, 2003), or on state-sponsored mass murder which also encompasses both genocide and politicide (Krain, 2000), other literature rather focuses on broader categories of personal integrity rights and life integrity violations (Fein, 1995; Regan & Henderson, 2002), or related concepts such as one-sided violence (Kreutz, 2006). Since many of the causes overlap, the commonalities rather than the differences between these different types of violence will be emphasized.

3.2.1. A NON-DEMOCRATIC SYSTEM OF GOVERNMENT

Since dictators are the primary focus of the research, and the absence of democracy an important risk factor for the perpetration of mass atrocities, this will be the starting point. It is important to note that the link between dictatorship and mass violence has been long established, although it has of course been contested and subject to refinements throughout the years. Already in 1995, Rummel showed with his large quantitative research that a link existed between dictatorship on the one hand, and genocide and mass murder, on the other. Rummel reaches the conclusion that 'the less democratic and more totalitarian the world's regimes, the more the world's battle-dead and the more sharply increased its overall democide' (Rummel, 1994, p. 6). He found democracies killed less than authoritarian regimes and the latter less than totalitarian regimes (Rummel, 1994, pp. 7-8). Although democratic regimes also killed, they behaved in a more authoritarian manner when they did, covering their tracks with lies, deceit and censorship. Rummel, therefore, argued that this finding underscores his overall conclusion that unrestrained power is most deadly (Rummel, 1994, p. 5). With his research, Rummel made dictatorship a risk factor for the perpetration of mass atrocities. Presently, Rummel's research is part of a substantial body of work that reaffirms the age-old adagium that 'power kills [and], absolute power kills absolutely' (Davenport, 1999; Rummel, 1994, p. 1). Woolf and Hulsizer even go as far as to state that they believe that 'one key characteristic of genocidal states is the presence of a totalitarian ruler and an authoritarian form of government' (2005, p. 106).

Like Rummel, Davenport's research also supports what he calls the 'democratic proposition' and finds that generally democratization brings less repressive governance (Davenport, 1999, p. 108). The reverse holds equally true, autocratization brings forth more repressiveness, but after several years the regime lessens its grip, possibly because once power is consolidated, the necessity for stringent sanctions to keep the population in check is reduced (Davenport, 1999, pp. 107-108). Within democracies, or countries undergoing democratization, it was believed that the elite increased respect for its citizens' rights and would lessen repression because these characteristics were deemed incompatible with democratic governance (Davenport, 1999, p. 92). There is a significant body of work, however, from other scholars, which suggests the relationship is not that simple (e.g. Fein, 1995).

While fully-fledged democracies do not tend to bring forth mass violence, more fragile, newer democracies, that just made the transition from autocracy to democracy, are actually more at risk (Krain, 2000, pp. 44-46; Kreutz, 2006, p. 188; Mann, 2005, p. 4; Regan & Henderson, 2002).[25] As Fein explains, there is 'more murder in the middle' (Fein, 1995). Harff's quantitative analysis corroborates these observations. Harff finds that state failures in authoritarian regimes are more likely to lead to genocide and politicide, especially when the elite are committed to an exclusionary ideology as 'elite ideologies are crucial determinants of their choices' (Harff, 2003, p. 62; 66).

---

25 While failed states can also lead to instability and violence, surveying the literature on failed states goes beyond the present research. See François and Sud for an analysis of the role the international community should have in stabilizing failed states (2006).

Yet, a third strand of literature posits that it is not the regime type but the perception of threat that determines the level of repression. Ultimately, however, these scholars, too, conclude that democracies repress less. The main difference lies in the explanation offered (Regan & Henderson, 2002, pp. 119-120). In the latter line of reasoning it is posited that it is the nature of the opposition, and the extent to which they challenge the ruling elite and desire reform, which shapes the response (Gartner & Regan, 1996; Regan & Henderson, 2002). Gartner & Regan, for instance, argue from a rational choice perspective that highly democratic societies generally repress less only because the extent of the challenges to the regime are generally not of such a nature that the benefits of repressing them would outweigh the costs (1996, p. 278). Regan & Henderson create a synthesis of the different perspectives and reach the conclusion that

> 'threats increase when the ruling coalition is unable to cater to the demands of its citizens. Demands in a highly autocratic society will in effect be muted by fear of retribution, while demands in a highly democratic society will be channelled politically. In the middle (ie [sic] in semidemocracies), where demands are high yet mechanisms for addressing these demands are inadequate, repression will be greater' (Regan & Henderson, 2002, p. 133).

Mann also acknowledges that 'stable institutionalized democracies are less likely than either democratizing or authoritarian regimes to commit murderous cleansing' because they have 'constitutional guarantees for minorities' (Mann, 2005, p. 4). He, however, nevertheless sees ethnic cleansing to be the product of the dark side of democracy and emphasizes democratizing countries are more at risk of mass violence than stable authoritarian regimes. According to Mann, democracies can potentially conflate the demos and the ethnos. Ethnicity in this process becomes intertwined with a sense of exploitation and overlapping class resentment (Mann, 2005, pp. 3-6). Because mass violence is inherently incompatible with democracy, the regime will become less democratic as ethnic cleansing becomes the favoured policy choice. He therefore sees the dark side of democracy as entailing the 'perversion' of the ideals of democracy as a country slides further towards the perpetration of mass murder (Mann, 2005, pp. 3-4).

Ultimately, the findings are therefore more consistent than they initially appear to be. Scholars seem to agree that fully-fledged democracy is always preferable, as in well-established democracies there are the least grave human rights violations. Pinker even calls democracy 'one of the greatest violence reduction technologies since the appearance of government itself' (Pinker, 2011, p. 161). Yet even if the concentration of power is important, it is unable to explain the timing of periods of mass atrocities (Krain, 1997, p. 355; 2000, p. 44). In addition, the non-democratic nature of a regime on its own it is not a sufficient predictor of whether mass violence will ensue (Krain, 1997, p. 355).

3.2.2. CULTURAL ENEMIES: HAVING A HISTORY OF VIOLENCE

Long lasting hostility between certain groups within society has often been linked with a heightened risk of mass violence (Harff, 2003, p. 63; 66; Staub, 2000, pp. 370-372). Not only individuals, but societies are said to be harbingers of emotions. In this instance one is speaking of collective emotions, which can be defined as 'emotions that are shared by large numbers of individuals in a certain society' or alternatively, of group based emotions that 'are felt by individuals as a result of their membership in a certain group or society' (Bar-Tal, Halperin, & De Rivera, 2007, p. 442). They result from 'particular societal conditions, common experiences, shared norms, and socialization in a society' (Bar-Tal *et al.*, 2007, p. 442). Individuals thus experience emotions not solely because of what happened to them personally, but also because of the experiences of the group with which they identify (Bar-Tal *et al.*, 2007, p. 442).

In times of conflict, fear can be an overwhelming emotion which may emerge after conscious consideration but is often triggered automatically (Bar-Tal *et al.*, 2007, p. 448). The great difficulty with fear as a collective emotion, is that it may continue to exist even when the reasons to be afraid have subsided (Bar-Tal *et al.*, 2007, p. 448). It may lead to mistrust, deligitmation of the enemy and violence (Bar-Tal *et al.*, 2007, p. 448).

Next to fear, hatred also forms an important emotion that may lead to group conflict and mass atrocities (Bar-Tal *et al.*, 2007; Kressel, 2002; Sternberg, 2003, p. 448). Nevertheless, although intuitively the level of violence with which genocidal campaigns are initiated suggests hatred subsumes the perpetrators, such a conclusion would be too simplistic (Moshman, 2007, p. 117). A substantial body of research has established that ordinary people, for a variety of reasons, not necessarily immediately related to fomenting hatred, may come to commit mass atrocities. Browning suggests conformity plays a crucial role (Browning, 1992); Milgram obedience to authority (Milgram, 1974); and Arendt argued that Eichmann represented the banality of evil, and was not a fanatical zealot (Arendt, 1963). Staub explains that society descends along a continuum of destruction where mistreatment slowly escalates and slowly becomes mass killing. The initial maltreatment of the victim makes subsequent harm more likely because of the changes this brings about in perpetrators and bystanders who start to come up with reasons for their behaviour (Staub, 1989, pp. 80; 116-127). However, these other factors do not exclude the possibility hatred does not also play a role. Conformity and obedience often mesh with rationalisations based on ideological commitments that stem from the hate propaganda to convince 'themselves that they were right and that what they were doing was justified' (Smeulers & Werner, 2010, p. 37).

Feelings of hatred and resentment thus often do play a role, but it would be too simplistic to pose, as the media has frequently done, that genocide is perpetrated because of 'ancient hatreds' (e.g. Kaplan, 1991). Harff, in her empirical analysis on the causes of genocide and politicide found that ethnic cleavages, although predisposing the country to conflict, only evolved into genocide or politicide when there is active ethnic discrimination or when the elite stems from one particular ethnic minority (Harff, 2003, p. 68).[26] Although ethnic or other cleavages in society between groups may be ingrained in cultural traditions, the image of an enemy may actually be created through propaganda, which will be discussed in more detail below. At the same time, however, this enemy is more easily created when the targeted group is already marginalised. A particular ideology resonates more when people have an affinity with the prejudice based on a shared history (Tindale, Munier, Wasserman, & Smith, 2002, pp. 149-150; 157). Ideology does not really resonate with the population unless it is made to fit within the already existing culture and myths (Sémelin, 2003, p. 196). Because 'individuals with a hostile attributional bias or perceived threat orientation are more prone to perceive aggressive intent in other's actions', there is a risk that negative stereotypes escalate into an image of the out-group as an enemy (Woolf & Hulsizer, 2005, p. 102). The danger thus stems from the *perceived*, rather than *actual* threat that a group supposedly formed to another group. Chirot and McCauley explain that 'memory and historical reconstruction, often invented but nevertheless sincerely believed, are important contributors to demands for vengeance of past wrongs that in turn can lead to a new series of mass killings' (Chirot & McCauley, 2010, p. 91). This in turn can be manipulated by destructive leaders (Woolf & Hulsizer, 2005, p. 103), as will be explained further below.

3.2.3. DIFFICULT LIFE CONDITIONS: ECONOMIC OR POLITICAL CRISES AND WAR

Several scholars have made the link between difficult life conditions or crisis situations and the instigation of mass atrocities (Shaw, 2007a; Staub, 2000, pp. 369-370; Woolf & Hulsizer, 2005, pp. 104-105). War is one of the gravest sources of stress on a society, but of course war, economically difficult times and political crises are in no way mutually exclusive and often go hand in hand (Wayne Nafziger & Auvinen, 2002, p. 154). Woolf and Hulsizer, however, point out that there are many people living in extreme poverty who do not resort to mass violence (2005, pp. 104-105). Difficult life conditions, therefore, should be understood not as objective poverty *per se*, but it is rather the loss of prosperity, frustration and relative deprivation which may act as a trigger for

[26] Although Harff also notes that once ethnic strife or civil war has started, active discrimination does not predict which conflict results in genocide or politicide (Harff, 2003, p. 70).

violence (Staub, 2000, p. 372). The greatest danger should therefore be sought in 'situations that result in unanticipated difficult life conditions in populations unaccustomed to such difficulty' (Woolf & Hulsizer, 2005, p. 105). These crises may be caused by an economic downturn, a political crisis or due to the effects of war, for instance (Woolf & Hulsizer, 2005, p. 105).

Harff, in her research, investigated whether political upheaval may lead to genocide or politicide. She defines this particular pre-condition as entailing 'an abrupt change in the political community caused by the formation of a state or regime through violent conflict, redrawing of state boundaries or defeat in international war'. Harff finds that this, indeed, is a strong indicator that genocide will reoccur when there is a situation of state failure (Harff, 2003, p. 62; 66).

In addition to political crisis, there is a strong relationship between war and mass atrocities. War often generates severe social upheaval and can destabilize a society (Fein, 2000, p. 49). While war crimes by definition have a nexus with war, there are strong linkages between war and crimes against humanity and genocide as well. Several studies indicate that wars, especially civil wars, are an important indicator that there is great risk for state-sponsored mass murder (Alvarez, 2001, pp. 68-71; Krain, 1997).

Scholars have mentioned several reasons why there may be such a strong relationship. Both can be conceptualized as entailing the destruction of a particular group (Shaw, 2007a, p. 464). In the case of war, this entails military destruction to the extent that there no longer is any resistance from the enemy. During a genocide, its aim is also its social and cultural destruction (Shaw, 2007a, pp. 464-465). Alvarez points out war brutalizes a population, making them less sensitive to violence and, therefore, also less likely to resist when genocidal violence commences. This is compounded by the fact that people struggling to survive will create scapegoats out of particular minority groups, who therefore become much more vulnerable during times of war (Alvarez, 2001, pp. 69-71). Fein, likewise, argues that war is always accompanied by aggression and allows the perpetrator to blame the victim (2000, p. 49). In addition, during times of war the state already acts more secretively and can conveniently rely on the police and army, who are already up in arms, to carry out a genocide (Alvarez, 2001, pp. 70-71). Wars strengthen the security apparatus of the state, thus also enhancing a culture among the elite that favours forceful solutions to problems and often allows non democratic leaders to be installed into power (Krain, 2000, p. 42). Wars may, subsequently, also serve as a pretext to hide the criminal nature of violent behaviour (Fein, 2000, p. 49; Krain, 2000, p. 42). A military victory that allows the majority to impose its will upon a minority is simultaneously also a factor which enhances the opportunities to violently repress or eliminate certain groups in the population (Krain, 2000, p. 43). The more intense a conflict has been, the greater the risk for mass violence. According to Harff this is due to two factors. Firstly, authorities are likely to be more threatened when the fighting has been severe and secondly, there are more opportunities for authorities to rely on a 'final solution' to fence of challenges to its regime (Harff, 2003, p. 62; 66).

As has been explained in the previous chapter, many scholars have suggested that a democratic peace exits. Democracies rarely fight each other and more often than not at least one of the warring parties is a dictatorship (Kreutz, 2006, p. 175). Some have suggested that for intra-state conflicts, this relationship is rather shaped like an inverted U-shaped curve. Partly free states are most likely to become involved in an intra-state war (Kreutz, 2006, pp. 175-176). Intermediate states are less stable than autocracies, which are less stable again to full-fledged democracies (Hegre, Ellingsen, Gates, & Gleditsch, 2001). Kreutz also emphasizes non-democratic countries (weak and powerful authoritarian regimes) are additionally much more likely to engage in one sided violence against its population than democratic regimes (Kreutz, 2006, p. 182).

It thus seems to be the case that the factors mentioned thus far, war and dictatorship, which are likely to bring about mass violence, are mutually reinforcing and intertwined. When combined with the earlier mentioned discrimination of certain groups in society, Fein argues that 'we can infer a chain of linkage; ethnic discrimination triggers conflict in the state provoking high levels of violations leading to a prolonged internal war' and has found that 'war increases violations among free, partly free, and authoritarian states but free states are much less likely to go to war' (Fein, 1995, p. 180; 185).

3.3. THE ROLE OF THE DICTATOR: MANIPULATING THE PRECONDITIONS

The leader needs a favourable environment in order to rise to power, but this alone is not enough: to bring forth a movement, a strong leader is indispensable (Hoffer, 1951, pp. 111-113). There is thus an interplay between dictators and their environment. They may use particular societal conditions to rise to power, and once in power, he can use them to further contribute to an environment in which atrocities become more likely. A population is prone to turn to powerful individuals who they believe might save them from the threatening situation, especially when they feel like their collective identity is threatened (Moghaddam, 2013, p. 65; 72). Threats make people more ethnocentric and intolerant of dissent, and as Moghaddam explains, 'difficult, uncertain societal conditions are associated with gravitation toward ideologies that provide certainty' (Moghaddam, 2013, pp. 61-62). People tend to cope with the uncertainty by trying to enhance their identification with a particular group, and it can make people particularly susceptible to extremist groups (Moghaddam, 2013, pp. 61-62).

Once in power, the dictator can use the risk factors to implement his violent policies. When there is a non-democratic system of government, the leader can be a decisive factor in whether mass atrocities actually occur when risk factors are present in a particular society (McLoughlin & Weerdesteijn, 2016). The dictator inherits some of these risk factors from predecessors but they may also emerge because of a deliberate policy of the dictator. An economic downturn, for instance, may be the result of mismanagement, but economic crises can also emerge because of extreme weather conditions or the prices of certain goods on the international market. The dictator is unable to change the history of the country but can reinterpret the history and give it new meaning. In the upcoming paragraphs, the manner in which the dictator can use the abovementioned factors to facilitate the perpetration of mass atrocities is explained.

3.3.1. TRANSFORMING HISTORY: CREATING ENEMIES

As mentioned previously, it is not merely the actual events of a country's history that influence the present, but it is, rather, the way in which this past is remembered that matters most. History may be rewritten and given a new meaning at the hands of a dictator. Moghaddan stresses that it is crucial to understand

> 'the processes through which meaning making comes to be monopolized throughout society by the dictator and his henchmen ... [after coming to power the dictator can use] his power monopoly to shape the normative system in society, ascribing meaning to things and behaviors. Of course, many people will attempt to resist this new normative system but sheer force and intimidation is used to crush the opposition' (Moghaddam, 2013, p. 51).

Dictators can use their power over the normative system to enhance in-group, out-group schisms and devalue the inferior out groups further through state propaganda tools (Smeulers & Grünfeld, 2011, pp. 248-249; 265; Woolf & Hulsizer, 2005, pp. 106-109). It is through defining the 'other' that the self is also defined and cohesion between members of the in-group can be created (Sternberg, 2003, p. 310; 315; 320). Cohesion brings forth three subsequent effects: leaders tend to be more respected in a cohesive group, the values of the in-group are increasingly idealized and there is an increased readiness to punish those who do not conform to the group (Chirot & McCauley, 2010, p. 65). The extent to which the in-group feels threatened by the out-group, influences not only the degree of cohesion within the group but also the punishment that is meted out for those who deviate from the group norms (Chirot & McCauley, 2010, p. 65).

Moshman suggests that it is the dichotomization of identity which causes a separation between 'us' and 'them', where the grey areas are removed and individuals are forced to choose sides, that is crucial to understand why genocide is perpetrated (Moshman, 2007, pp. 118-120). Waller calls this the 'obliteration of a common ground between perpetrators and victims' (Waller, 2010, p. 28). It forms part of an absolutist worldview, where neutrality, finding the middle ground and compromise are no longer possible (Alvarez, 2008, p. 226). According to Moshman, this process may lead to dehumanization of the out-group and ultimately to its destruction when they are placed outside the moral universe of obligation (Fein, 1993, p. 82; Moshman, 2007, pp. 120-123). The out-group is often not only portrayed as the enemy but dehumanised, as animals, vermin or diseases (Alvarez, 2008, p. 224).

When groups create their own identity in contrast to those of others in order to boost their own self-esteem, they tend to devalue the other group (Smeulers & Grünfeld, 2011, p. 248). In-group bias may emerge where the favouritism for one's own group extends beyond what the situation or evidence would warrant and stereotyping and prejudices may take over (Smeulers & Grünfeld, 2011, p. 248; J. C. Turner, Brown, & Tajfel, 1979, pp. 187-188). A myth of pure evil is created in which the out-group is qualified as pure evil and their own group as only good (Baumeister, 2001, p. 91). The population will then identify with the group they belong to and tie their own welfare to that of their group (Chirot & McCauley, 2010, p. 75). Generally, the perpetrator groups tend to see themselves as the victims, and believe they are the ones who are threatened (Alvarez, 2008, p. 222; Baumeister, 2001, pp. 88-89).

The likelihood that the dichotomy between 'us' and 'them' becomes more pronounced is greatly facilitated by the presence of difficult life conditions, as will also be explained in the next paragraph. As people fear for their own security, and that of their family, a search to comprehend the insecurities commences (Staub, 1989, pp. 4-5). The 'others' are blamed for society's woes; they are scapegoated. Stereotypes do not have to be reinforced with personal experiences. Research suggests that in fact stereotypes are stronger when based on information from others. As Sternberg emphasizes 'the strongest stereotypes can be those that have the least basis in personal experience!' (Sternberg, 2003, p. 310). The scapegoated group can be subjected to misplaced aggression (Woolf & Hulsizer, 2005, pp. 112-113). Anger is redirected and feelings of threat and frustration result in the desire to hurt others. The belief that victims are deserving of their fate becomes ever more prevalent and they become more and more devalued (Staub, 1989, pp. 16-17).

Usually a group is chosen that is 'distinctive, powerless and socially stigmatised' particularly when targeting the group is 'authorized by social norms' (Baron & Kerr, 2003, p. 157). When there is a history of enmity between the two groups, even when not personally experienced by the perpetrators, collective memories of such periods are easily evoked. In order for propaganda to work, people need to be susceptible to it (Smeulers & Grünfeld, 2011, p. 265).

Therefore, people need to be at least ambiguous about the topic or face massive exposure to it (Woolf & Hulsizer, 2005, p. 111).

The need to vilify that particular group is often embedded in an elaborate ideology that provides hope for a better future and a utopian vision of what this should look like. Ideology should be understood to mean shared beliefs and belief systems which not only allows people to make sense of the world but also provides them with a sense of identity and purpose (Alvarez, 2008, p. 216). A given ideology finds its origin in the culture of the society but the belief system can be manipulated. Alvarez explains that

> 'to marginalise, disenfranchise, and persecute a group of people requires many citizens to accept the necessity and morality of policies of destruction and this is largely done through the manipulation of belief systems by politicians and others in order to dissimulate, persuade, and mobilize populations in a cause' (Alvarez, 2008, p. 217).

The extent to which a dictator shapes or even creates the ideological narrative will vary but more often than not the ideology is built upon already existing prejudices stemming from the nation's history. The history can then subsequently be transformed by the dictator and reshaped through an ideological narrative in which a particular group is identified as the enemy. Especially the ideologies which emphasize the in-groups superiority and mythologize and glorify past wrongs, and portray the violence as redeeming and necessary to prevent renewed victimization, are likely to lead to mass violence (Alvarez, 2008, p. 222).

There is a tendency of human beings to remember negative encounters longer than positive ones, which is called the negativity bias (Chirot & McCauley, 2010, p. 64). According to Chirot and McCauley this bias explains 'how leaders manipulate their groups' emotions by stressing negative images and acts by the enemy group, and why this so often works even though groups may have coexisted for long periods of time with only occasional problems and with relatively little past violence' (2010, p. 65).

When mass violence occurs in a war, the argument is frequently heard that these are mere ethnic hatreds which manifest itself in violence back and forth. Yet the mere fact that ethnic hatreds may have played some role, or that the victims themselves have also used violence, does not have to mean that the violence is the inevitable result of ethnic hatreds. Ethnic conflict, research shows, is often exacerbated by 'ethnic entrepreneurs' who polarise the societies and further reinforce the image of the victim as 'the Other' (Fein, 2000, p. 51).

The propaganda functions ultimately to rationalize and justify the crimes. In a classic criminological study Sykes and Matza identified neutralization techniques which were used before and after the crimes by juvenile delinquents in order to be able to commit the crime without damaging their self-image (Sykes & Matza, 1957, pp. 666-667). Sykes and Matza pointed out that, these techniques were to neutralize 'disapproval flowing from internalised norms and conforming others in the social environment' (Sykes & Matza, 1957, pp. 666-667). They consist of the denial of responsibility, the denial of injury, the denial of the victim, the condemnation of the condemners and appeal to higher loyalties (Sykes & Matza, 1957).

Several scholars have more recently pointed out these techniques also play a role when mass atrocities are being perpetrated and are often present in the state's propaganda (Alvarez, 2001, pp. 112-125; Day & Vandiver, 2000, pp. 45-47; Smeulers & Grünfeld, 2011, pp. 308-312; Weerdesteijn & Smeulers, 2011, p. 335). The denial of responsibility, first of all relates to the actual perpetrator, who oftentimes can reason away his own responsibility by arguing that he was just following orders (Alvarez, 2001, pp. 115-117). Secondly, the denial of injury often comes into play through the use of euphemisms, which may hide the gruesome nature of the acts that are being perpetrated. These euphemisms could be initiated by the government or could be developed by the units who perpetrated the atrocities in order to make it easier on themselves to carry out the acts (Alvarez, 2001, pp. 117-120). Thirdly, the denial of the victim occurred, as explained earlier, by portraying the victim as deserving of the atrocities that were perpetrated. The victim is not seen as an actual victim but as an enemy. The pervasive ideology put forward by the regime plays a tremendous role in this neutralization technique. The same holds true, for our fourth neutralization technique, the appeal to higher loyalties. It is the ideology itself that defines the higher purpose behind the acts of the individual, the ideology defines the act as good rather than evil, and allows it to be carried out for a higher purpose (Alvarez, 2001, pp. 120-125). Finally, and fifthly, the neutralization technique condemning the condemners is often directed to the countries that condemn the atrocity crimes. The critical nations may themselves be demonized for their own blemished past in order to deflect attention (Alvarez, 2001, pp. 123-124).

It is particularly the power of the leader to control the manner in which the population thinks and interacts that makes him so influential (Woolf & Hulsizer, 2005, p. 108). Woolf and Hulsizer describe the dual challenges of the leader of having to promote a slow escalation of violence while at the same time ensuring that the group maintains its positive self-image and sense of superiority (Woolf & Hulsizer, 2005, p. 113). One way of doing so is by giving violence a different meaning, reinterpreting it as a positive, heroic feat and removing its negative connotation. The government can thus provide a sense of authorization for the violence (Kelman, 2005), allowing for the disengagement of self-sanctions (Bandura, 1999). The dictatorial regime, through the control it has over the media and other aspects of society, including often popular culture, can normalize the violence which has become ingrained in society (Weerdesteijn & Smeulers, 2011). The dictator, therefore, creates the context in which these crimes are perpetrated and propagates the ideological narrative that legitimizes the crimes.

3.3.2. SEIZING THE MOMENT: DIFFICULT LIFE CONDITIONS

Although difficult life conditions are important in order for a period of collective crimes to commence it is not enough in and of itself. Harff, for instance, finds that political upheaval 'is a necessary but not sufficient condition for geno-/politicide' (Harff, 2003, p. 62). According to Harff the level of democratic constraint and whether the elite is committed to exclusionary ideologies, are important variables that determine whether mass violence will actually take place (Harff, 2003, pp. 62-63). Chirot and McCauley reach a similar conclusion, and find that while economic frustrations are relatively common, large scale violence and genocide remains quite rare. They explain this predicament by proposing that actual violence requires 'a moral construction' (Chirot & McCauley, 2010, p. 67). They argue that human beings are

> 'moralising animals who need to justify their acts. Poverty, disaster, political turmoil, or other painful experiences may anger us, but we will not kill unless we have a specific target, and we must justify our anger toward that target by making its behaviour morally repugnant.' (Chirot & McCauley, 2010, p. 67).

According to Staub, people especially turn to new leaders with a destructive ideology when there are difficult life conditions as people start looking for ways to understand their new reality (Staub, 1989, p. 15; 2000, p. 370). Therefore, it seems that especially in times when people suffer under difficult life conditions such as war or economic troubles, the above-mentioned construction of an enemy becomes more influential and more likely.

Not only the population, but the leader, too, is impacted by the societal conditions. It is this knowledge that they are able to use to their own advantage. Staub argues that 'both their awareness of what is happening to the population and the shared experience enables leaders to speak to people's concerns and psychological needs' (Staub, 2010, p. 174). When a country emerges from a period of war, for example, this may not only become a risk factor for mass atrocities because it easily allows enemies to be identified, but in addition, because the collective self-esteem may be harmed when a war is lost. In such situations, the elite may exploit the sense of loss and this may aid the rise of revolutionary elites with destructive ideologies (Fein, 2000, p. 49). Difficult life conditions may result into loss of group pride, frustration and can result in a hostile attitude towards some groups that are blamed for the problems (Staub, 1989, pp. 15-17). Therefore, when difficult life conditions emerge a useful strategy may be to scapegoat, as it protects one's own identity and strengthens bonds within the in group, as described above (Staub, 2000, p. 370).

Even when groups are competing for scarce resources or status, it would only turn truly violent when it is believed the victim group deserves the harm which is inflicted on them (Chirot & McCauley, 2010, p. 71). In addition, when people start competing for scarce resources the leader of a country can exert influence over this process (Woolf & Hulsizer, 2005, p. 113). Not only because it can influence the manner in which the victim is portrayed, but as Woolf and Hulsizer explain 'the authoritarian elite can make the aforementioned resources more salient to the populace in response to a perceived threat' (2005, p. 113).

Furthermore, it can be the mismanagement of the dictator that caused the scarcity and economic downturn in the first place. Rather than providing incentives for growth, the ruling elite may extract resources from the economy in order to enhance their own personal well-being (Ayittey, 2011, pp. 18-19; Wayne Nafziger & Auvinen, 2002, p. 154). This may lead to relative deprivation, which as has been explained, may lead to public discontent and can be mobilized by the elite to pave the way for collective violence (Wayne Nafziger & Auvinen, 2002, p. 154).

Since non-democratic leaders often need economic resources to buy loyalty and stay in power, as was explained in the previous chapter, perpetrating crimes may appear to be an appealing option. The dictator essentially faces two choices when the economy starts to deteriorate: he may either increase his rent seeking activities to buy support from the political elite, which may lead to further economic decline and harms any last bit of legitimacy he may have; or he can use repression. Repression targeted to suppress any discontent may entail violence but also diverting food and other resources to loyal groups in society (Bruce Bueno De Mesquita & Smith, 2011, pp. 75-160; Wayne Nafziger & Auvinen, 2002, pp. 154-155). War, economic decline, political instability and atrocity crimes thus go hand in hand and the dictator is able to influence them all.

3.4. THE ROLE OF THE DICTATOR: SETTING UP THE INSTITUTIONS

When these preconditions have been manipulated by dictators to set the scene for mass atrocities, several institutional steps are taken to implement their perpetration. Society and the military apparatus are often restructured to ease the perpetration of atrocities. Creating mass movements can have an enormous appeal and will make it difficult for people to resist and oppose the regime. However, although sometimes the population may be involved in some of the crimes, often specialised units, whether these consist of soldiers that are part of the regular military, elite units or paramilitary organizations, will be trained and required to do the dirty work. Large scale violence seldom spontaneously emerges but usually requires tremendous planning and preparation. Any regime which seeks to execute mass murder is therefore required to alter some institutional structures.

3.4.1. MASS MOVEMENTS

Interest in mass movements soared in the wake of the Second World War when scholars tried to make sense of the participation of so many people in such a destructive phenomenon. Scholars found that while mass movements are highly demanding they are also very appealing (Smeulers & Grünfeld, 2011, pp. 257-261). According to Buechler, 'masses are distinguished by their large size, anonymous nature, loose organization and infrequent interaction. As such, the concept of a mass connotes a group ripe for manipulation and control' (2013, p. 1). People change when they become part of a group, and the change becomes more significant as the control and demands of the group over its members becomes more extreme. In those instances, personal goals are subjugated to those of the group (Staub, 1989, pp. 237-238). Their potential to be destructive was recognized early on and some even saw the process through which the public becomes a mass, as ultimately resulting in totalitarianism (Buechler, 2013, p. 1).

Stemming from the 19th century, LeBon provided the most influential early analysis of groups and crowds arguing that people lost their conscious personality when they became part of a mass and instead adopt a single group mind (Reicher, 1996, p. 535). While his theory had notable shortcomings, it was widely read, including by Mussolini and probably Hitler (Reicher, 1996, p. 538). They used strategies that were deemed important by LeBon. Reicher explains they expressed themselves 'simply, concisely and clearly, they were categorical and unambiguous in their affirmations and they used the same constructions over and over again' (Reicher, 1996, p. 549). In addition, while LeBon's idea that there was a single group mind has come under attack, addressing the crowd in such a manner proved highly effective for Hitler and Mussolini (Reicher, 1996, pp. 539; 549-551).

In the years that followed, many studies were intrigued by the totalitarian movements (Buechler, 2013; Goodwin & Jasper, 2006, p. 612). Numerous theories sought to understand what kind of people were susceptible to fascist and communist movements, but not everyone saw these phenomena as inextricably linked. Hoffer argues that their ideological outlook does not matter, and that all mass movements share similar characteristics. He posits that '[w]hen people are ripe for a mass movement, they are usually ripe for any effective movement, and not solely for one with a particular doctrine or program' (Hoffer, 1951, p. 16).

The presence of a gifted leader is essential to the movement (Hoffer, 1951, p. 113). Frequently, the leader of a mass movement is said to require exceptional qualities and therefore tends to be described as charismatic (Goodwin & Jasper, 2006, p. 613).[27] According to Hoffer, the leader needs to be audacious and should have a 'fanatical faith in a holy cause', while being able to instil devotion into his followers (Hoffer, 1951, p. 115). The mass movement needs 'the iron will, daring

27 See Chapter 2 for a more elaborate explanation of the concept.

and vision of an exceptional leader to concert and mobilize existing attitudes and impulses into the collective drive of a mass movement' (Hoffer, 1951, p. 114). He is able to instill in the masses a willingness to sacrifice oneself and creates true believers from dissatisfied, disenfranchised individuals (Hoffer, 1951, pp. 117-118). Those participating in a mass movement, Hoffer and Fromm argue, release themselves of the burden of freedom and the responsibility of one's own life and failure (Fromm, 1942, p. 3; Hoffer, 1951, p. 118).

Ron Jones, a high school history teacher, created a movement within his class to illustrate to his pupils, who were not aware of the nature of his experiment, why the Nazi party had been so popular in Germany. The movement, called 'The Third Wave' entailed the use of symbolism, discipline, created a sense of community and soon attracted a large following. It quickly got out of hand when dissenting voices where harassed and tensions arose between Wave members and non-Wave members. When he made the link between Nazi Germany and The Wave in a final mass gathering in the auditorium, the pupils were shocked. The Wave had given the pupils a sense of purpose and made them feel like a community (R. Jones, 1972; Smeulers & Grünfeld, 2011, pp. 258-261). Mass movements can be used to bring about and deepen a sense of commitment, to the leader, the regime and the policies, making the latter easier to accept for the entire society (Staub, 1989, pp. 124-125). Despite the earlier literature and the experiences of Jones, subsequent literature established that in fact those who are already actively engaged in society are actually more likely to join these groups than those who are ostracised (Buechler, 2013, p. 2).

Despite the significance and power of mass movements for some regimes and leaders, not all dictators will come to rely on a mass movement. As has been explained in the previous chapter, the extent to which dictators rely on either support or repression is likely to differ. Some have a more narrow support base and rely more on fear than loyalty from the population, to maintain power. Even when the dictator has the organized backing of a powerful movement, however, he will still need professional killers to rid him of his enemies and implement destructive policies. For this purpose, special killing units can be trained.

3.4.2. CREATING SPECIALIZED KILLING UNITS

Although sometimes many civilians may participate in the killings and crimes, destructive regimes and their leaders most often rely on specialised killing units to perpetrate most of the violence. In general citizens do not participate in the actual killings (Valentino, 2000, p. 23). Whether elite units, mercenaries, paramilitary units or death squads, they tend to be instrumental to the reign of terror of the dictator (B. B. Campbell & Brenner, 2002; Kressel, 2002, p. 174). They are part of the larger institutional governmental structure that allows such large-scale crimes to be perpetrated. In some instances, the link between the dictator and the killing units may not be formalized but, as is often the case with death squads and paramilitary units, is rather informal allowing the dictator to kill with deniability (Alvarez, 2006; B. B. Campbell & Brenner, 2002, pp. 506-507; Jamieson & McEvoy, 2005). The members of these units are often explicitly trained to become torturers or killers. The harsh training methods are able to transform ordinary men into obedient instruments of the state (Gibson & Haritos-Fatouros, 1986; Smeulers, 2004) and the conditions in which they find themselves have been qualified as atrocity producing situations. An atrocity producing situation, Lifton explains, is 'one so structured, psychologically and militarily, that ordinary people can readily engage in atrocities' (Lifton, 2004, p. 416)

The macro level justifications of atrocity crimes described above may contribute to the authorization of the crimes for the individual who perpetrates the actual crimes on the ground. The individual comes to believe the crimes are authorized and desired by the state, and by his superiors within the military unit (Kelman, 1993, pp. 23-24; 31; 32-34). Within the military setting, the dominant ideology is echoed during lectures designed to indoctrinate the recruits and to make them believe they are doing the right thing (Crelinsten, 1993; Gibson & Haritos-Fatouros, 1986, p. 56).

Kelman clarifies how the regime is ultimately responsible for ordinary people to become perpetrators of atrocity crimes. He explains it is the state authorities who, on a macro level, define the security threat, define the enemy, and have control over the security apparatus (Kelman, 2005, p. 128). This subsequently provides the justification for the crimes and leads to the exclusion of certain groups from the protection of the state while it creates professional cadres to deal with the threat. Ultimately, at the individual level it causes ordinary people to become perpetrators of mass atrocities as the crimes become authorized and routinized while the victims become dehumanized (see the table below) (Kelman, 2005, p. 128).

The policy context of torture

Conditions conducive to the use of torture as an instrument of policy	**Social processes facilitating torture**	
	At Level of Policy Formation	*At Level of Implementation*
Perception of a Security Threat	Justification of a policy of torture	Authorization of acts of torture
Existence of a Security Apparatus	Development of professional torture cadres	Routinization of torture practices
Presence of Groups Defines as Enemies of the State	Exclusion of target groups from protection of the State	Dehumanization of targets of torture

Source: Kelman, 2005, p. 128

3.5. CONCLUSION

The present chapter has shown that a wide variety of factors put a country at risk for episodes of mass violence. Some of these factors can be created by a dictator once he comes to power. Others are historically determined or otherwise lie outside of the control of the leader. However, even when factors are beyond the reach of the dictator and are not created by him, the leader can use these to turn risk factors into actual situations of mass atrocities. The existing preconditions may make the population susceptible to the perpetration of atrocity crimes but situations will not actually become violent when the dictator does not use his machinery to transform this susceptibility into at least a preparedness to accept their occurrence. Yet, fostering their acceptance through a combination of fear and ideological justifications does not ensure that the crimes are actually committed. In order to ensure the willingness of the population to participate in the crimes, institutions have to be set up. For ordinary citizens such active participation may mean their involvement in a mass movement, and becoming formally affiliated with a certain political party. A soldier may be required to do the dirty work and institutions will often be transformed in such a way that soldiers are prepared to kill out of obedience and loyalty. Overall, it shows how a non-democratic system of government, which can impose one version of the truth on its citizens and can set up institutional arrangements without democratic constraints, is an important facilitator of mass atrocities.

Non-democratic system of government

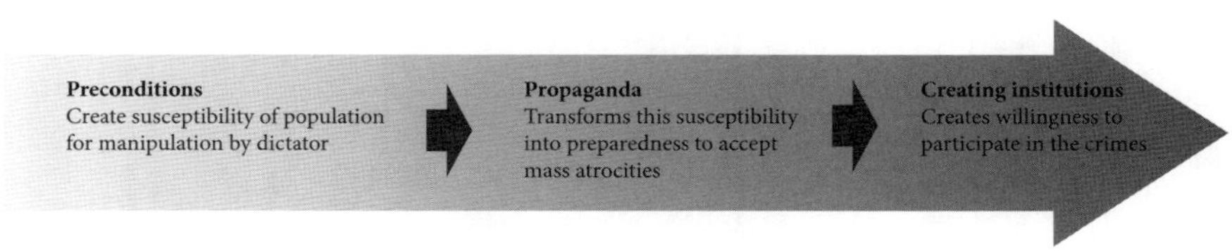

Despite the analytical usefulness of such a model, it should be acknowledged that the process does not always follow this exact chronological order. Although a history of violence and difficult life conditions are likely to precede the propaganda and the creation of institutions, the propaganda will probably continue when the institutions have long been established. In addition, it may be that the leader already started propagating its ideology, generating some followers, and perhaps already perpetrated atrocities on a smaller scale, before coming to power. In addition, not all dictators that are responsible for atrocity crimes create mass movements or oblige people to become part of their political party.

It is sometimes argued that the leaders are more fanatical believers in the ideology than those who actually carry out the killings (Chirot & McCauley, 2010, p. 91). Yet, leaders can push countries further towards situations of mass atrocities in an effort to realize a wide variety of objectives. Some may want to realize a utopian vision dictated by the ideology but others may merely want to centralize power and eliminate any opposition and further their own economic self-interest (Woolf & Hulsizer, 2005, p. 106). Even when leaders themselves do not believe in the ideology they put forward, they are generally able to garner a significant following of individuals who do (Woolf & Hulsizer, 2005, p. 107).

Mass atrocities are more likely to occur in dictatorial regimes, where the leader can create the circumstances in which these crimes can be perpetrated. He should, therefore, be a central focal point in efforts to stop or mitigate atrocities. The next chapter will discuss to what extent the international community has the responsibility or even obligation to try to bring these crimes to a halt.

CHAPTER 4
PREVENTING AND STOPPING MASS ATROCITIES: THE RESPONSIBILITY TO PROTECT

4.1. INTRODUCTION

After WWII, states were determined to prevent similar horrors in the future. In order to realize this, the prevention of interstate conflict, as well as the promotion of human rights and fundamental freedoms, became important goals of the United Nations.[28] Tension, however, emerged between the promotion of human rights through the adoption of the Universal Declaration of Human Rights, which later led to the adoption of the International Covenant on Civil and Political Rights and the International Covenant on Economic, Social and Cultural Rights, and the Convention on the Prevention and Punishment of the Crime of Genocide, for instance, and a strict respect for state sovereignty that meant to ensure international peace and security. State sovereignty, as the foundation for the modern system of states, came to mean they were 'legally equal to each other, not subject to the imposition of supranational authority, and, above all, not intervening in each other's internal affairs' (Evans, 2008, p. 16). The manner in which countries have used sovereignty as an excuse not to intervene when horrendous crimes have been perpetrated or to hide behind it when they have perpetrated the crimes, has increasingly come to be seen as problematic (Cronin, 2007, p. 298).

Although Chapter VII of the UN Charter, authorizes the UN Security Council to intervene in order to 'maintain or restore international peace and security', for a long time this was defined restrictively and the Security Council was hesitant to interfere with state sovereignty. This frequently severely limited the possibilities to protect populations from human rights violations (Askin, 2005, p. 1723; Grünfeld, 1998). Furthermore, during the Cold War, the Security Council was largely deadlocked. The United States and the Soviet Union vetoed an astounding 279 resolutions, and dictators were largely able to act as they pleased within the confines of their own borders for years, often

[28] See Articles 1(1) and 1(3) of the UN Charter.

even while being backed by one of the two superpowers (Ayittey, 2011, pp. 107-108; Boutros-Ghali, 1992). While the Security Council became much more proactive after the end of the Cold War, and increasingly came to see human rights violations as a genuine concern, there was a continuous failure to prevent genocides from happening (Grünfeld, 1998; Österdahl, 2005). The genocides that occurred in Rwanda and Srebrenica in particular, where UN peacekeepers were present but failed to intervene in an effective manner, caused international outcry (LeBor, 2006).

Nations, however, have only quite recently started to organize themselves as sovereign states and sovereignty is not a stark concept but open to reformulation (Shue, 2006, p. 11). Since 2001, when the International Commission on Intervention and State Sovereignty published its report on the responsibility to protect, countries have gradually come to accept that governments have the responsibility to protect their population from mass atrocities and that, when they manifestly fail to do so, this responsibility comes to lie with the international community. Often the so called responsibility to protect (R2P) is described as a break from traditional conceptions of sovereignty but in fact it is only a break from the manner in which sovereignty has been conceptualised over the last 50 years (Glanville, 2010, 2013).

The report dealt with the question 'when, if ever, it is appropriate for states to take coercive – and in particular military – action, against another state for the purpose of protecting people at risk in that other state' (International Commission on Intervention and State Sovereignty, 2001, p. vii). As the report was released shortly after the terrorist attacks on 9/11 which caused the focus of many countries to shift away from protecting populations from atrocities to counter terrorism policies, the report seemed destined to remain unnoticed (Evans, 2008, p. 5). It managed, however, to gain broad support in civil society[29] (Hamilton, 2006, p. 194), and due to a sustained diplomatic effort was unanimously backed at the 2005 World Summit (Evans, 2008, pp. 5-6). The report on the responsibility to protect has been criticized for being too radical, or alternatively as too conservative, but many scholars still consider it the most comprehensive framework to address mass atrocities to date (Hamilton, 2006, pp. 291-292). Although the report and the manner in which it reconceptualized sovereignty, has been challenged along the way, rapid progress has been made and R2P has become an important concept not only in scholarly analysis but also in the international and domestic political arena and civil society.

---

29 Organizations like The Global Centre for the Responsibility to Protect, Asia-Pacific Centre for the Responsibility to Protect, The Canadian Center for the Responsibility to Protect, and the International Coalition for the Responsibility to Protect, continue to play an important role in the development and implementation of the concept and deliver statements in the Informal Interactive Dialogue of the UN General Assembly on the Responsibility to Protect ('Summary of the Seventh Informal Interactive Dialogue on the UN General Assembly on the Responsibility to Protect,' 2015)

It is important to analyse further the extent to which the responsibility to protect has become a widely accepted lens through which sovereignty is now viewed and which duties, if any, it imposes upon the international community. The second paragraph will therefore look at the concept of sovereignty and how it developed over the years, and the extent to which the responsibility to protect really incorporates an alternative conceptualization of sovereignty. Paragraph three will cover the manner in which attempts to protect populations from mass atrocity have developed, particularly within the UN while the fourth paragraph will correspondingly analyse how the duties to do so evolved over time. The fifth paragraph will analyse the emergence and development of the responsibility to protect and will assess to what extent it imposes an obligation to act on the international community. In the sixth paragraph a conclusion will follow.

4.2. SOVEREIGNTY

Usually sovereignty is noted as dating back to the Peace of Westphalia in 1648 which ended the Thirty Years War (e.g. Evans, 2008, p. 15). Within international relations (IR) the Peace of Westphalia has been conceptualized as heralding the start of a new era. A discourse emerged in which IR scholars referred to the 'Westphalian system' or the 'Westphalian order' to signify the international arena as being characterized by sovereign, equal states whose relations are governed by a rule of non-intervention into each other's internal affairs (Schmidt, 2011, pp. 601-602). According to Sørensen, the Peace undermined the power of the church in favour of secular powers, with a corresponding principle that the king shall have the ultimate power within his territory (Sørensen, 1999, p. 591).

The Peace of Westphalia was said to have established the ground rules for the interaction between states, most fundamentally perhaps through the acknowledgement of the integrity and inviolability of each of the country's territories (Axworthy, 2012, p. 3). The sovereign state is 'legally equal to all other states' with 'equal membership of the international society of states, with similar rights and obligations' regardless of any other differences in the extent of their political or economic power (Sørensen, 1999, pp. 592-593). Although admittedly the world did not change overnight it is conceived of as a watershed moment and a 'crucial point in the transition from feudal to modern authority' (Sørensen, 1999, p. 591).

In most IR literature the Peace is less discussed as an actual historical event and has become more of an abstract analytical construct which serves as a benchmark that can be contrasted to more recent developments (Osiander, 2001, p. 251; Schmidt, 2011, p. 602). Westphalian sovereignty encompasses more a 'package of specific ideas' that many scholars use these days to analyse contemporary phenomena, oftentimes by contrasting new developments to this traditional conception of the sovereign relations among states (Schmidt, 2011, p. 615).

Importantly, a debate has emerged to what extent there is continuity in the concept or whether there has been a significant change in recent years (Sørensen, 1999). While some enduring features have been identified, there have been notable changes as well. Sørensen convincingly argues that there are some core features, which he calls constitutive rules, which have remained the same. Sovereign states require territory, people and government, constitutional independence and a unitary supreme authority which is legally equal to all other sovereign states and which interacts with these states in a system, or rather a society, in which there are common rules and institutions (Sørensen, 1999, pp. 592-593). As Sørensen notes, 'the sovereign state remains the preferred form of political organization' and possesses a 'stable core' (Sørensen, 1999, p. 594). Yet the 'rules of sovereignty' are said to vary (Sørensen, 1999, p. 594). These relate to how states interact with regard to war and peace and include the norm of non-intervention and other practices (Sørensen, 1999, pp. 595-596). These, Sørensen notes, have changed remarkably during the last decades (Sørensen, 1999, pp. 596-597). Notably, some now argue that the responsibility to protect 'proposed the most significant adjustment to national sovereignty in 360 years' (Gilbert cited in Axworthy, 2012, p. 3).

This debate has been challenged on a more fundamental basis. In particular, it has been disputed that the rules many scholars attributed to the peace of Westphalia actually were established then and there. It is questioned, for instance, whether sovereignty, as developed in the aftermath of the Peace of Westphalia, truly encompassed the norm of non-intervention, and whether the contemporary conceptualization of sovereignty as responsibility is such a large divergence (Glanville, 2013; Osiander, 2001). Axworthy rightfully notes that sovereignty reflects norms that have been agreed upon within the international community, and as such, it is not a rigid concept (Axworthy, 2012, pp. 4-5). Sovereignty reflects shared understandings and expectations, the content of which have always been evolving over time (Glanville, 2010, p. 5). When looking at the development of the concept, Glanville argues the recent change towards sovereignty as responsibility should not be seen as a deviation of traditional sovereignty but a break from the way the concept was conceived of in the twentieth century (Glanville, 2010, 2013).

The corollary to the supremacy of the sovereign within his country has not always been non-interference, but rather just war, the right to punish those tyrants who negate their duties and defend those suffering unacceptable harm (Glanville, 2013, p. 4). In early modern Europe the idea of absolute sovereign authority already not only encompassed rights but also included the responsibility to uphold laws of God and nature, thus also bestowing on the sovereign the obligation to protect the subjects from harm (Glanville, 2010, pp. 5-7). Although most would deny that the subjects had the right to stand up against a despotic ruler, intervention by another sovereign was more acceptable (Glanville, 2010, pp. 7-8). It was not until the 18th century that statements propounding the sovereign right to non-interference are expressed. It became more common during the 19th century, but the non-intervention principle remained subject to numerous exceptions (Glanville, 2013, pp. 4-5). It is interesting that for a long time a right to wage war was seen as an important element of sovereignty, as in this sense sovereignty is actually limited by the non-intervention norm (Shue, 2006, pp. 14-15). Shue eloquently argues all rights encompass duties, and therefore notes 'if sovereignty is a right, sovereignty is limited' because every right is accompanied by corresponding duties. Shue explains

> 'non-intervention imposes duties that also contain the sovereignty of states that bear the duty. It protects mine by constraining everyone else's and protects everyone else's by constraining mine. This is what rights do. Where there are rights, there are duty imposing rules' (Shue, 2006, p. 15).

Non-interference as a duty-imposing rule became formalized only relatively recently. The Covenant of the League of Nations made some headway in formalizing the right of non-intervention by prohibiting war as a means to conquer territory but war remained a legitimate manner to settle disputes when peaceful measures were deemed insufficient. After WWII the freedom from outside interference became more firmly consolidated (Glanville, 2010, p. 11; 2013, p. 7). The Charter of the UN enshrined what is currently often seen as 'traditional sovereignty' (Glanville, 2010, p. 11).

Therefore, what these days IR scholars associate with Westphalia is 'a product of the ninetheenth- and twentieth-century fixation on the concept of sovereignty' (Osiander, 2001, p. 251). The common perception that the Peace brought forth the principle of non-intervention based on the respect for state sovereignty, actually is not supported by the historical account of the Peace. The peace treaty did not include any provisions of the sort (Osiander, 2001, p. 261). Leo Gross emphasized the importance of the Peace for the interaction between states, but noted that the terms of the settlement do not sufficiently support the notion that these important principles were established by the Peace. The significance of the Peace stems from the implications that the text ended up having (Gross, 1948, p. 26; Osiander, 2001, pp. 264-265). In this manner a convenient narrative was born which has come to underlie the focus within IR (Osiander, 2001, p. 266). As Osiander points out, it is debated as to whether this model is still applicable today, but rarely is it questioned whether it was appropriate in the past (Osiander, 2001, p. 266). It can therefore be argued that the recent development of sovereignty is not breaking away from what it has always been but breaks with how sovereignty has been conceptualized since the 20th century, particularly from the manner in which it was codified in the UN Charter, and actually more closely resembles earlier interpretations of sovereignty.

This 'new' conception of sovereignty, defined sovereignty as responsibility (Evans, 2008, pp. 38-39). The initial report calls it a re-characterization of sovereignty 'from *sovereignty as control* to *sovereignty as responsibility*' (International Commission on Intervention and State Sovereignty, 2001, p. 13). According to the Commission, its significance is threefold. Firstly, the country carries the responsibility to protect its citizens. Secondly, the state is accountable both to its citizens internally as well as to the UN internationally, and thirdly, the agents of the state are accountable for their actions and omissions (International Commission on Intervention and State Sovereignty, 2001, p. 13). The new characterization of sovereignty requires that an abstract entity, the 'international community', is taken more seriously. By viewing nations as bearing responsibility to fulfil their duties, they are set out to be members of a community, to whom they are accountable for their actions (Etzioni, 2006, p. 83). If they do not live up to their responsibilities, the other members in the community may take charge. Certain elements of the manner in which the report has explained the meaning of sovereignty stems back to the pre-charter era whereas other elements have a more recent origin.

Perceiving sovereignty as also entailing responsibility, has quite a long history (Glanville, 2010, p. 8; Luck, 2009, pp. 13-14). However, while the current conceptualisation of sovereignty as something that resides in the individual has some precedents, it was mainly developed more recently as a consequence of the human rights movement (Bellamy, 2009, p. 165). Initially, sovereignty was said to reside in the office of the ruler, until this changed in the 18th century (Glanville, 2010, p. 8). The American Declaration of Independence proclaimed it is the right of the people to topple a destructive government, causing sovereignty to become attached to the people. This was subsequently reinforced with the French Revolution (Glanville, 2010, pp. 8-9). Thereafter, sovereignty came to follow a more nationalist path. Following WWI, legitimacy was derived from the principle of national self-determination (Glanville, 2010, pp. 10-11). Although it was often argued that national self-determination was essential to advancing individual rights, sovereignty did not depend on safeguarding those rights and belonged to the nation (Glanville, 2010, p. 10). Currently, sovereignty is no longer seen as residing in the ruler, not even in the nation; now it is often seen as belonging to the individual.

According to Annan, at the end of the 1990s sovereignty belonged in fact to the individual. Annan argued:

> 'states are now widely understood to be instruments at the service of their peoples, and not vice versa. At the same time individual sovereignty – by which I mean the fundamental freedom of each individual, enshrined in the Charter of the UN and subsequent international treaties – has been enhanced by a renewed and spreading consciousness of individual rights. When we read the Charter today, we are more than ever conscious that its aim is to protect individual human beings, not to protect those who abuse them' (Annan, 1999).

It underlies the idea that individuals have inalienable human rights and protecting those rights is not a violation of sovereignty but promotes the sovereignty of the people (Bellamy, 2009, p. 165). The idea of sovereignty as responsibility stemmed from Francis Deng as special representative on internally displaced people (Bellamy, 2009, pp. 166-167). It is not a contested notion that governments have duties towards their citizens (Bellamy, 2009, p. 167). When considering Shue's argument that all rights are accompanied by corresponding duties, the acceptance that individuals have human rights, causes the idea that states have a corresponding duty not to violate them to logically follow. There is, in this sense, nothing outrageous about the argument that the obligation to protect lies with the state. What is more noteworthy is the idea that there also needs to be a default duty, meaning 'duties that constitute a second-line defence requiring someone to step into the breach when those with the primary duty that is the first-line of defence fail to perform it' (Shue, 2006, p. 16). Despite the fact that it is intuitively entirely logical, there is nothing 'automatic about there being default duties' that should enforce compliance with the primary duty (Shue, 2006, pp. 17-18).

The latter aspect, that these responsibilities are tied to a country's sovereignty, has attracted much criticism. In response to Deng's idea of sovereignty as responsibility, there was criticism from several countries who framed it as an attempt to justify the interference of powerful states in the affairs of weaker ones (Bellamy, 2009, p. 169). The norm of non-interference in a state's domestic affairs provides order and stability in an otherwise anarchic system of states (Cronin, 2007, p. 293) and it provides weaker states with some measure of protection against the influence of more powerful states. Cronin refers to it as the 'single equalizer in a world of great inequality' (Cronin, 2007, p. 294). In 1999, the Algerian president Bouteflika, for instance, responded to a speech of Kofi Annan by stressing that his country

> 'was extremely sensitive to any undermining of our sovereignty, not only because sovereignty is the final defence against the rules of an unjust world, but because we have no active part in the decision-making process in the Security Council nor in monitoring the implementation of decisions … We firmly believe that the interference in internal affairs may take place only with the consent of the state in question' (cited in Bellamy, 2009, p. 178).

These reservations also extend to R2P. Concerns that the R2P would be abused by the stronger countries are understandable, especially for those countries who were once subjected to colonialism. Particularly, since colonial interference was also often based on moral and humanitarian principles (Luck, 2009, p. 17). George W. Bush's policies in the wake of September 11 hampered the process of seeking consensus on the responsibility to protect, as it was argued that countries should not be allowed to hide behind sovereignty when engaging in practices that were detrimental to the safety of the international community overall (Bellamy, 2009, p. 168). When the government relied on humanitarian considerations to justify the war in Iraq when no weapons of mass destruction were found, there was increased awareness of the immense potential for abuse that an intervention that was based on humanitarian reasoning could entail (Evans, 2008, pp. 69-70).

Sovereignty has often also been interpreted as a right not to act (Cronin, p. 296). The more powerful states, according to Luck, see sovereignty as also implying a freedom to choose their own policy. Luck notes they are therefore 'reluctant to accept any interpretation of R2P that implies an automaticity of response' (Luck, 2009, p. 11). Developed countries have been hesitant of formulating any obligation which would limit their sovereign right to choose in which conflicts they should get involved (Luck, 2009, p. 18-20). The US Permanent Representative to the UN at the time, John Bolton, stated unequivocally that 'the Charter has never been interpreted as creating a legal obligation for Security Council members to support enforcement action' and stressed that the US does 'not accept that either the United Nations as a whole, or the Security Council, or individual states, have an obligation to intervene under international law' (cited in Luck, 2009, p. 19). It is the freedom of choice which stronger, developed countries fear losing (Luck, 2009, p. 11).

Many countries have thus held on to the conception of sovereignty as it was enshrined in the Charter for a variety of reasons. Therefore, even though it is often argued that especially developing, less powerful nations, attach particular value to their sovereign rights as they perceive it as a principle that offers protection from other more powerful countries, developed nations, are likewise concerned about losing sovereignty as R2P becomes more influential. The main difference lies in that developing states often fear losing territorial sovereignty, whereas developed states fear losing the sovereign right to choose their own policies (Luck, 2009).

Bellamy has convincingly argued that states have come to accept that they have a responsibility to protect their own populations, as well as those of other states, and that failing to live up to this responsibility should generate criticism (Bellamy, 2015, p. 163). The extent to which its objective is attained, is more disputed (Gallagher & Ralph, 2015, pp. 244-245). A heated debate remains not only on the extent to which it is currently being implemented and how successfully this is done but also how it should be implemented remains contested, as will be explained below. Nevertheless, the development of the responsibility to protect and the way in which sovereignty was defined, has impacted the manner in which policy debates are being framed and the manner in which attempts to end and prevent atrocities have been developed. In order to fully appreciate the progress that has been made and assess which gaps remain, it is important to briefly set out the manner in which states have combated mass atrocities though the UN since WWII and how their own responsibilities to protect human rights have evolved.

4.3. ATROCITY CRIMES AND THE UNITED NATIONS

The Charter of the United Nations formalised the Westphalian system of sovereignty and the norm of non-intervention (Axworthy, 2012, p. 6). Article 2(1) notes that the organization 'is based on the principle of the sovereign equality of all its Members' and prohibits the use of force in Article 2(4). Furthermore, Article 2(7) even explicitly specifies the UN itself must respect the sovereignty of its Member States by noting that

> 'nothing contained in the present Charter shall authorize the UN to intervene in matters which are essentially within the domestic jurisdiction of any state or shall require Members to submit such matters to settlement under the present Charter: but this principle shall not prejudice the application of enforcement measures under Chapter VII'

The United Nations, however, was developed after WWII and set out to prevent interstate conflicts (Axworthy, 2012, p. 6). This created tension when violence perpetrated by a government against its own population increasingly became a concern for the international community (Axworthy, 2012, p. 6). The relationship between protecting human rights and upholding the norm of non-interference became strained.

Although the history of human rights can be traced back centuries, the establishment of the UN can be seen as a seminal moment in the establishment of an international system to protect human rights (Van Genugten, Homan, Schrijver, & De Waart, 2006, p. 40). Influenced by several NGOs, the Charter would eventually accord quite a prominent place to human rights. In the Preamble, the peoples of the United Nations 'reaffirm faith in fundamental human rights' and the focus on human rights is incorporated in several of its Articles.[30] On the basis of these provisions, in combination with the last sentence of Article 2(7) of the Charter in particular, which reads: 'this application shall not prejudice the application of enforcement measures under Chapter VII', it was argued the Charter was not designed to protect governments who grossly violate such rights (Stahn, 2007, p. 112). This, however, created the paradox that while for the first 45 years of its existence the UN was mainly associated with the principle of non-intervention and the prohibition of the use of force, in the post-

[30] Namely Articles 1(3), 13(1), 55 and by extension 56, 62(2), 68 and 76 (Van Genugten *et al.*, 2006, p. 40).

Cold War era it actually became an 'instrument for the use of force' as it leaned more towards an interventionist stance to protect populations from atrocities (Roberts, 2006, p. 71).

In accordance with Article 24 of the UN Charter, the UN Security Council has been tasked with the maintenance of international peace and security 'in order to ensure prompt and effective action by the United Nations'. It may do so either through peaceful means or may rely on Chapter VII when it determines there is a 'threat to the peace, breach of the peace, or act of aggression' as is stipulated in Articles 39 and 41. Article 42 entrusts the Security Council with the power to impose economic sanctions or make use of military force 'in order to maintain or restore international peace and security'. The UN Security Council increasingly came to accept that crimes perpetrated by a government could also threaten international peace and security (Grünfeld, 1998).

In San Francisco, where the Charter was adopted, a French proposal was rejected to include a clause which stipulated an exception to the right of non-intervention when 'the clear violation of essential liberties and of human rights constitutes in itself a threat capable of compromising peace' (Glanville, 2013, p. 8). Likewise, during the Cold War the Security Council was generally unwilling to see human rights violations as falling within the realm of Chapter VII (Wheeler, 2006, p. 33). India argued for instance in 1971 that the ten million refugees which resulted from Pakistan's atrocities threatened the security in the region. The Security Council rejected this line of reasoning and rather suggested this situation fell within the domestic sphere which was protected through Article 2(7) of the Charter (Wheeler, 2006, p. 33).

There are a few exceptions, however, even during the Cold War. In 1966, for instance, the UN Security Council determined that human rights violations allowed them to rely on Article 39 when they determined that the situation in Southern Rhodesia constituted a threat to international peace and security and imposed economic sanctions (RES 232 (1966)). Eleven years later this was repeated with respect to South Africa (Lillich, 1995, p. 5). Both Resolutions refer to the pervasive racial discrimination in the countries. Resolution 232 explicitly '*calls upon* all States not to render financial or other economic aid to the illegal racist regime in Southern Rhodesia'. Resolution 418, concerning South Africa, starts with a strong condemnation of the violence used by the government of South Africa but argues the threat to the peace stemmed from the military build-up in South Africa and its violent policies towards neighbouring countries (RES 418 (1977)). According to Grünfeld, the phrasing of the resolution in this manner 'kept up the appearance that such human rights violations, which were part of the internal oppression, did not constitute a threat to the peace and security' (Grünfeld, 1998, p. 429), implying that at this time human rights violations were not generally accepted as being able to constitute a threat to international peace and security.

A similar reasoning applies to the Security Council's next attempt to stop the perpetration of human rights, through its Resolution of April 5th 1991, in which it sought to halt the oppression of the Kurds in Iraq (Grünfeld, 1998, p. 429). Here too, it seems the consequences of human rights violations, namely the many refugees who fled across borders were said to pose the threat, rather than the human rights violations in and of itself (Grünfeld, 1998, pp. 429-430). The argument previously applied to the situation in Pakistan, namely that these abuses fell within the domestic jurisdiction of the country, was put forward by Cuba, Yemen and Zimbabwe with regard to Iraq but was rejected by the Council (Wheeler, 2006, p. 33). Many states, however, were still weary of setting a precedent that would allow enforcement action on the sole basis of humanitarian concerns (Wheeler, 2006, p. 33). The Resolution, therefore did not explicitly call for enforcement action that would allow military force to be used. The military intervention that followed was nonetheless justified by the alliance on the basis of humanitarian concerns, and it was argued the military actions were in conformity with Resolution 688 (Wheeler, 2006, p. 34). Notably the intervention was not condemned after the fact by the Security Council or General Assembly (Wheeler, 2006, p. 34). While some authors see the Resolution as for the first time having authorized military intervention in order to protect human rights, others noted that this was in fact not the case, as it still referred to the effects the violations caused outside of state boundaries (Lillich, 1995, pp. 6-7). It is probably more reasonable to see it as an important next step in a process that would lead the Council to consider human rights violations solely committed within the borders of the state as threats to international peace and security and necessitating making use of Chapter VII.

The landmark moment came in 1992 when the UN Security Council adopted resolutions on Bosnia-Herzegovina and Somalia. Firstly, it called the situation in Bosnia-Herzegovina a threat to international peace and security and noted that 'the provision of humanitarian assistance in Bosnia-Herzegovina is an important element in the Council's effort to restore international peace and security in the area' (RES 770 (1992)). While generally the council's resolutions dealing with this topic stressed the unique and exceptional nature of the situation at hand (Österdahl, 2005, p. 1), this resolution did not. This may be explained by the fact that the conflict had become internationalized and no longer concerned a purely domestic situation (Österdahl, 2005, p. 3).

The Resolution on Somalia which came thereafter was more typical. The Security Council authorized intervention in Somalia under Chapter VII of the UN Charter and referred to its 'unique' character which required an 'exceptional' response (RES 794 (1992)). The reference was inserted because China and India, who abstained from voting, argued the case was special because there was no longer a government present in Somalia. This eased concerns about sovereignty as it could be argued that the intervention should not be regarded as being against the will of a government since there was none at the time (Wheeler, 2006, pp. 35-36). It nevertheless was groundbreaking, as it signified a willingness to use force because of the human tragedy that unfolded (Lillich, 1995, pp. 7-8; Wheeler, 2006, p. 35). The Resolution makes no mention of the supposed effects of the crisis. In this case the Council unambiguously declared that 'the magnitude of the human tragedy caused by the conflict in Somalia, further exacerbated by the obstacles being created to the distribution of humanitarian assistance, constitutes a threat to international peace and security' (Lillich, 1995, pp. 7-8; RES 794 (1992)).

Subsequently, after the democratically elected President Aristide was overthrown, the Security Council in Resolution 940, authorized all necessary means to ensure a return to democracy (Grünfeld, 1998, p. 437; Lillich, 1995, p. 10). Despite the fact that passing reference was made to the flow of refugees, this is not where the emphasis lay. The Council, rather, stressed the exceptional and unique situation caused by the grave humanitarian situation and emphasized the restoration of democracy (Grünfeld, 1998, pp. 437-438; Lillich, 1995, p. 10). This trend was further reinforced with the interventions in Bosnia and Rwanda (Wheeler, 2006, p. 36). While most situations in the 1990s were still referred to as exceptional, this changed in the years thereafter. Österdahl notes that although there are some exceptions, the Security Council referred to situations less and less as unique and requiring an exceptional response when it noted that humanitarian concerns constituted a threat to international security (Österdahl, 2005). According to Österdahl, labelling each situation unique initially may have been necessary for states to come to an agreement on the resolution and formed an attempt not to set any precedent but it ended up being 'settled practice' to use Chapter VII in situations where human rights were violated (Österdahl, 2005, p. 9).

4.4. EVOLVING DUTIES TO PROTECT HUMAN RIGHTS

Since states have to cooperate, it is beneficial for them to enter into agreements, and states voluntarily limit their discretionary power creating constant tension for states between their own interests and the demands and requirements that are imposed upon them by the international community (Axworthy, 2012, p. 5). The first years after WWII became a crucial period for the development of a framework that set out to protect the rights of individuals (Axworthy, 2012, p. 6). The period after WWII can be seen as a time where 'norm entrepreneurs' tried to increase the involvement of the international community when mass atrocities were perpetrated in a country (Cronin, 2007, p. 297).

The first defining moments came in 1948 with the adoption of the Universal Declaration of Human Rights in 1948 by the UN General Assembly (A/RES/217A), and the UN Convention on the Prevention and Punishment of the Crime of Genocide (henceforth Genocide Convention) by the General Assembly

(A/RES/260(III)A). These were followed by the International Convention on the Elimination of all Forms of Racial Discrimination, which was adopted by the General Assembly in 1965 (A/RES/2106(XX) A), and the International Covenant on Civil and Political Rights and the International Covenant on Social and Political Rights, both adopted by the General Assembly in 1966 (A/RES/2200(XXI)A-C). The Convention against Torture and Other Cruel, Inhuman and Degrading Treatment (CAT) was subsequently adopted by the General Assembly in 1984 (A/RES/39/46).[31]

While important, the impact and reach of the conventions has been debated and criticized. The Genocide Convention in particular is often seen as a rather weak instrument with many limitations (Shue, 2006, p. 19). It explicitly recognized that cooperation among states is necessary 'in order to liberate mankind from such an odious scourge' but this proved difficult to realize in practice. Evans for instance points out that 'it took the major powers years (in the case of the United States, forty years) to ratify it, it was rarely invoked and has never been effectively applied in practice either to prevent or punish actual atrocities' (Evans, 2008, p. 20). Some authors did note, however, that it turned 'the issue of sovereignty on its head by suggesting not only a right to intervene in cases of genocide but a responsibility to do so' (Cronin, 2007, p. 295). A notable development in this regard has been that the ICJ decided in *Bosnia and Herzegovina vs Serbia and Montenegro*

> 'that Serbia has violated the obligation to prevent genocide, under the Convention on the Prevention and Punishment of the Crime of Genocide, in respect of the genocide that occurred in Srebrenica in July 1995' (Bosnia and Herzegovina vs Serbia and Montenegro, ICJ, para. 471(5))

No reparation or damages were assessed because it could not be proven that Serbia could have prevented the genocide if it had tried, but importantly the court argued:

> "the obligation to prevent genocide places a State under a duty to act which is not dependent on the certainty that the action to be taken will succeed in preventing the commission of acts of genocide, or even on the likelihood of that outcome." Bosnia and Herzegovina vs Serbia and Montenegro, ICJ, para. 461)

---

31 For an overview of the most important human rights instruments, see http://www.ohchr.org/EN/ProfessionalInterest/Pages/CoreInstruments.aspx.
These Conventions are an important part of international human rights law and place obligations upon states. Along with the development of international humanitarian law through the Geneva Conventions, the CAT and the Genocide Convention were also important for the development of international criminal law through which individuals can be held accountable when violations of these rights are sufficiently serious to constitute a violation of one of the core crimes (namely genocide, crimes against humanity and war crimes).

The determination above is particularly important because, as Schabas notes, 'here the Court reinforces the "responsibility to protect" set out in the 2005 Outcome Document of the Summit of Heads of State and Government' (Schabas, 2007, pp. 184-185).

Yet between the rapid development of human rights Conventions and Declarations immediately following WWII and the more recent interventionist developments since the 1990s, there was a long period of apathy. Due to tensions among the major powers, the Cold War basically ensured complete inaction regarding humanitarian concerns with the Security Council deadlocked because of their respective veto power and because neither was willing to constrain their allies (Axworthy, 2012, p. 7; Evans, 2008, pp. 21-22). During the Cold War, interventions by India and Vietnam in the 1970s were widely condemned despite the fact they arguably saved many lives (Glanville, 2013, p. 8). The norm of non-intervention had become so dominant at this time that the countries did not even rely on humanitarian reasons to justify their interventions but rather argued they acted in self-defence (Glanville, 2013, p. 8).

After the Cold War, the UN began to be confronted with the inherent tension between the respect for a country's sovereignty which is enshrined in their Charter on the one hand, and the respect for human rights, likewise emphasized in the Charter, on the other (Cronin, 2007, p. 298). Decolonization had reinforced the traditional perspective on sovereignty (Evans, 2008, p. 21), and sovereignty was seen by these new states as an important defence against interference by their former colonisers and the protection of their domestic affairs (Axworthy, 2012, p. 7; Evans, 2008, p. 21).

The end of the Cold War brought forth challenges and opportunities (Cronin, 2007, p. 297). The world powers were no longer deadlocked and the UN Security Council was able to come to agreement on resolutions (Thakur, 2006, pp. 19-20). At the same time, however, the 'decline in superpower support for weak and corrupt governments in the developing world led to conflict and instability' (Cronin, 2007, p. 297). Intrastate conflict and internal violence erupted and with the perpetration of horrendous crimes new hope for an effective security system dissipated (Evans, 2006-2007, p. 706). Especially the failure of the intervention in Somalia and the subsequent tragedies in the Balkans, especially in Srebrenica, and in 1994 in Rwanda, where international forces were present but failed to stop the genocide, resulted in a massive outcry (LeBor, 2006; Power, 2013, p. 146). Many actively called for a more interventionist stance and more forceful policy when confronted with these massive violations of human rights (Evans, 2006-2007, p. 706).

NATO's bombing of Serbia in 1999 became another significant turning point (Bellamy, 2009, p. 163). NATO countries justified their action with humanitarian reasons, but it was done without authorization from the Security Council and condemned by two of its permanent members, Russia and China (Wheeler, 2006, p. 41). Yet the debate that Kosovo sparked became a '*catalyst* for the subsequent development of sovereignty as responsibility' (emphasis in original, Bellamy, 2009, p. 176).

In more recent conflicts we can observe the transformation that has been made since the adoption of the UN Charter and the Cold War period. In many serious contemporary conflicts the question has been less about *whether* the international community should intervene, but *how* they should do so (Bellamy, 2010, p. 155; 2015).[32] An important step into this direction was the development of the responsibility to protect.

4.5. THE RESPONSIBILITY TO PROTECT

In his Millennium Report Secretary General Kofi Annan addressed the tension that had emerged between the felt need to do something about the crimes that were perpetrated within countries and the notion that the sovereignty of each country should be respected. Annan asked the now famous and often reiterated words:

> 'If humanitarian intervention is indeed an unacceptable assault on sovereignty, how should we respond to a Rwanda, to a Srebrenica – to gross and systematic violations of human rights that offend every precept of our common humanity' (Annan, 2000, p. 48).

The Canadian government set out to find an answer to this question. It established a commission, the International Commission of Intervention and State Sovereignty (ICISS), to investigate the question of 'when, if ever, it is appropriate for states to take coercive – and in particular military action, against another state for the purpose of protecting people at risk in that other state' (International Commission on Intervention and State Sovereignty, 2001, p. VII). The report was developed by 15 prominent individuals whom all had very different ideas about the concept of humanitarian intervention (Axworthy, 2012, p. 11; Evans, 2008, pp. 4-5).

The eventual report, however, was not solely about humanitarian intervention. It changed the terms of the debate by letting go of the terminology which referred to a 'right to intervene' or 'the right to humanitarian intervention' towards the responsibilities of states (Evans, 2012, p. 376). As Evans explained, this was important because it allowed the commission to 'find common ground which previously simply did not exist' (Evans, 2012, p. 377). Reframing policy in this fashion was important because it allows politicians to justify a policy which may save lives to their constituencies, making this course of action more likely (Evans, 2012, p. 378).

32 Although it remains a challenge to secure 'close to unanimous understanding of just what kinds of real-world cases the norm is meant to embrace' (Evans, 2012, p. 381).

4.5.1. THE ICISS REPORT

The ICISS report took the 'human security' concept as a starting point (International Commission on Intervention and State Sovereignty, 2001, p. 15). This concept emerged after the Cold War when it became clear that new threats emerged in a globalized world (Axworthy, 2012, p. 8). Axworthy explains that Canada in the 1990s along with several other countries 'recognized that the security of individuals must have commensurate standing as matters of state security. Furthermore, given the nature of threats confronting individuals, it was widely accepted that a broadening of the definition of security was eminent' (Axworthy, 2012, p. 8). Human security was about much more than military threats but incorporated human rights and acknowledged the links between the 'economic development, environmental degradation, and population growth' (Axworthy, 2012, p. 8). The ICISS report noted that it is

> 'the Commission's view that human security is indeed indivisible ... In an interdependent world, in which security depends on a framework of stable sovereign entities, the existence of fragile states, failing states, states who through weakness or ill-will harbour those dangerous to other, or states that can only maintain internal order by means of gross human rights violations, can constitute a risk to people everywhere' (International Commission on Intervention and State Sovereignty, 2001, p. 5).

Furthermore, the Commission has found that 'the emerging concept of human security has created additional demands and expectations' about how states treat their own people (International Commission on Intervention and State Sovereignty, 2001, p. 7).

The Commission subsequently argued that states actually carry the responsibility to protect their people from harm. It thus shifted the debate from the controversial right to intervene, to the notion that the international community has a duty to intervene to help people in peril. The commission borrowed the notion of sovereignty as responsibility from Francis Deng who had originally developed the idea in relation to Internally Displaced Persons (IDPs) (Axworthy, 2012, p. 8). He proposed that states that cannot live up to their responsibilities to their people, lose their sovereign rights (Etzioni, 2006, p. 71). It was argued by the Commission that the relationship between sovereignty and intervention was complementary rather than mutually exclusive (Welsh, Thielking, & MacFarlane, 2001-2002, p. 493). Sovereignty was now conceptualized as being dependent on the respect of human rights and the ability and willingness of the country to protect its population (Welsh *et al.*, 2001-2002, p. 493). The state both carries responsibility towards the international community as well as towards its own citizens; it must respect the sovereignty of other nations but also internally respect the rights of its civilians (International Commission on Intervention and State Sovereignty, 2001, p. 8; Welsh *et al.*, 2001-

2002, p. 493). It builds on the work of Kofi Annan's influential piece on two kinds of sovereignty in which he argued sovereignty resided in the individual, and the Charter of the United Nations was primarily developed to protect individuals, not countries, and should be interpreted as such (Annan, 1999; International Commission on Intervention and State Sovereignty, 2001, p. 13). The focus of the debate in this manner shifted to the victims of violence and their rights, rather than on the state, and the rights of the states. States do not have a 'right to intervene', but people have rights and states have the responsibility to safeguard those rights and protect the population from harm.

Putting sovereignty into this new perspective was a major accomplishment of the Commission, but the broadening of the spectrum of actions and responsibilities was also a major and influential development (Welsh *et al.*, 2001-2002, p. 495). The report held that not only was there a responsibility to react to atrocities, but emphasized that there was likewise a responsibility to prevent and rebuild. Preventative strategies were subdivided into those targeting the root-causes of conflict and those focussing on the immediate triggers for violence (Welsh *et al.*, 2001-2002, p. 495). Three factors were identified on which prevention relies. The first is detailed knowledge of the country and/or region at risk. The second factor is that policymakers have to understand the 'toolbox' potentially available to them on the long and short term in order to prevent outbreak, the continuation or recurrence of conflict. The third is the actual availability of the capability and political will to respond effectively (Evans, 2008, p. 81; International Commission on Intervention and State Sovereignty, 2001, p. 20).

The Commission found that when prevention fails, the international community carries the responsibility to react to protect the population. When necessary, military intervention should be an option according to the Commission but it should fulfil six principles that were identified to guide intervention, namely that it must be executed only when there is a just cause, by the right authority, with the right intention, that it is only used as a last resort, with proportional means and with reasonable prospects for success (International Commission on Intervention and State Sovereignty, 2001, p. 32).

Part of the just cause criteria was the threshold that military intervention was only justified in situations of either 'large scale loss of life, actual or apprehended, with genocidal intent or not, which is the product either of deliberate state action, or state neglect or inability to act, or a failed state situation; or large scale "ethnic cleansing," actual or apprehended, whether carried out by killing, forced expulsion, acts of terror or rape' (International Commission on Intervention and State Sovereignty, 2001, p. 32). Significantly, these conditions could be seen as encompassing a quite broad range of situations including 'state collapse … mass starvation … and overwhelming natural or environmental catastrophes' (International Commission on Intervention and State Sovereignty, 2001, p. 33). Yet it was also very explicit that the situations that would not give rise to a response under the banner of R2P. These were, firstly, systematic racial discrimination and repression of political opponents. Secondly, this would also not include situations where a democratic government is overthrown, and finally, it was pointed out that when states aim to rescue their own nationals or respond to terrorist attacks it suffices to seek recourse to Article 51 of the Charter (International Commission on Intervention and State Sovereignty, 2001, p. 34)

The ICISS determined that the proper body to authorize intervention was principally the UN Security Council, but when it failed, other options that signify legitimacy and widespread support for the intervention should be available (International Commission on Intervention and State Sovereignty, 2001, pp. 48-55). This was perhaps the most controversial aspect of the report (Burke-White, 2012, p. 20). In order to improve effectiveness of the Security Council it was suggested the permanent 5 in the Security Council should refrain from using their veto in R2P situations unless their vital interests were at stake (International Commission on Intervention and State Sovereignty, 2001, p. XIII). When the UN Security Council was in a deadlock but there was widespread support for an intervention, the Commission argued alternatives that reflected broad support and legitimacy may be considered, like the General Assembly or through regional or sub-regional organizations (International Commission on Intervention and State Sovereignty, 2001, p. XIII). Lastly, the commission held that the international community also had the responsibility to rebuild a society when it has been ravaged by atrocities (International Commission on Intervention and State Sovereignty, 2001, pp. 39-45).

The report sparked much academic debate. Its work on military intervention and its related criteria in particular have been subject to criticism. Welsh, Thielking and MacFarlane point out that it might be unwise to insist that states solely act on the basis of a humanitarian motive. They rely on Wheeler's work to note that the focus belongs on the victims and whether they will be rescued through the use of military force, and that some degree of self-interest may be essential to muster domestic support (Welsh *et al.*, 2001-2002, p. 503). A related problem is of course that it is generally impossible to know for certain what would have happened making the 'reasonable prospects for success difficult to assess (Welsh *et al.*, 2001-2002, p. 503). The same goes, one may add for the threshold criteria that R2P should be used to stop 'actual or apprehended' atrocities (Welsh *et al.*, 2001-2002, p. 498). In addition, Welsh, Thielking and MacFarlane point out that the problem with asking the permanent members of the Security Council to negate their use of the veto power unless their vital interests are at stake, raises the problem that each country will interpret it differently and does not preclude the use of the veto when the permanent member is the perpetrating country (Welsh *et al.*, 2001-2002, p. 504).

Feinstein and Slaughter linked the responsibility to protect to what they called a 'duty to prevent', which they argued was 'a corollary principle in the field of global security' (Feinstein & Slaughter, 2004, p. 137). They put forward the idea that the international community has the duty to ensure that dictatorships are not able to acquire and use weapons of mass destruction (Feinstein & Slaughter, 2004). It has proven very controversial. Considering it was linked to Bush' preemption strategy, which they suggested perhaps 'does not go far enough', other scholars have rightfully feared that these kinds of initiatives were threatening the consensus that is being forged around the issue (Evans, 2006-2007, pp. 718-719)

However, despite its critics R2P has become influential in academia as well as in policy (Bellamy & Williams, 2011). The concept has evolved to what some have referred to as 'R2P light' while its development has been praised by others as having taken additional steps to becoming universally accepted and workable (Luck, 2012). Changes in the concept made it more appealing to its critics. Chandler, for instance, was of the opinion that the original report formed a 'powerful normative challenge to the UN's status' but argues the concept has transformed into something which may 'enforce its international authority' (Chandler, 2010, p. 161).

4.5.2. DEVELOPMENT OF R2P

The timing of its release was unfortunate since it came out just after 9/11 (Axworthy, 2012, p. 13). The world was preoccupied with terrorism (Evans, 2008, p. 44) and the debate on humanitarian intervention, which had sparked the ICISS report, gained a new dimension with the invasion of Iraq in 2003. As Louise Arbour explains, the manner in which the US and its allies justified the war in Iraq and relied on the rationale of 'regime change' heightened the concerns for many states and it was almost suffocated at birth (Arbour, 2008, p. 448). Evans explains that the report did not disappear thanks to the appointment of the UN Secretary General's High-level Panel on Threats, Challenges and Change in 2003 (Evans, 2008, p. 5). The Panel was tasked to assess the state of existing policies and institutions to deal with threats to international peace and security (Payandeh, 2010, p. 474). Their report '*A more secure world: Our shared responsibility*' stated:

> 'The Panel endorses the emerging norm that there is a collective international responsibility to protect, exercisable by the Security Council authorizing military intervention as a last resort, in the event of genocide and other large-scale killing, ethnic cleansing or serious violations of humanitarian law which sovereign Governments have proved powerless or unwilling to prevent.' (High-level Panel on Threats Challenges and Change, 2004, p. 66; 106).

The report was tied to institutional reform within the UN and R2P was incorporated in a section which primarily dealt with the use of force and Chapter VII of the UN Charter (High-level Panel on Threats Challenges and Change,

2004, p. p. 65; 106; Stahn, 2007, p. 105). It saw R2P as a means of strengthening its collective security system and related the concept directly to the UN itself. According to the report, the Security Council was the primary actor in the implementation of R2P. The Security Council was characterized as the body which carries the responsibility to protect, and in this light argued the Security Council should adopt guidelines when military intervention is appropriate and 'refrain from the use of the veto in cases of genocide and large-scale human rights abuses' (High-level Panel on Threats Challenges and Change, 2004, p. 66; 82). It seems that right after the US' illegal invasion of Iraq a strong need was felt to reinforce the formal rules guiding intervention (Stahn, 2007, p. 106). It diverged here from the original report by reserving intervention to protect for situations where the Security Council had authorized interventions (Stahn, 2007, p. 106). It noted:

> 'we believe that the Charter of the United Nations, properly understood and applied, is equal to the task: Article 51 needs neither extension nor restriction of its long-understood scope, and Chapter VII fully empowers the Security Council to deal with every kind of threat that States may confront. The task is not to find alternatives to the Security Council as a source of authority but to make it work better than it has.' (High-level Panel on Threats Challenges and Change, 2004, p. 61).

The criteria which they emphasized should guide the use of force were criteria which should guide the UN Security Council, rather than other countries or regional organizations and coalitions, although they requested individual countries, even when not part of the Security Council to adhere to them (High-level Panel on Threats Challenges and Change, 2004, p. 67; Stahn, 2007, pp. 106-107).

The subsequent report of the Secretary General '*In Larger Freedom: Towards Development, Security and Human Rights for All*' also wholeheartedly embraced R2P. It noted

> 'We must also move towards embracing and acting on the "responsibility to protect" potential or actual victims of massive atrocities. The time has come for Governments to be held to account, both to their citizens and to each other, for respect of the dignity of the individual, to which they too often pay only lip service. We must move from an era of legislation to an era of implementation. Our declared principles and our common interests demand no less.' (Annan, 2005, pp. 34-35).

The Secretary General, to this end, urged Member States to

> 'Embrace the "responsibility to protect" as a basis for collective action against genocide, ethnic cleansing and crimes against humanity, and agree to act on this responsibility, recognizing that this responsibility lies first and foremost with each individual State, whose duty it is to protect its population, but that if national authorities are unwilling or unable to protect their citizens, then the responsibility shifts to the international community to use diplomatic, humanitarian and other methods to help protect civilian populations, and that if such methods appear

> insufficient the Security Council may out of necessity decide to take action under the Charter, including enforcement action, if so required' (Annan, 2005, p. 59).

In the report R2P was not directly linked to the use of force but discussed in a section which dealt with the freedom to live in dignity. Stahn interprets this shift as indicating the intention to 'detach the idea of responsibility from an automatic equation of armed force' (Stahn, 2007, p. 107). At the same time, the extent to which this diverges from previous reports should not be exaggerated. The ICISS report was able to further the debate on the protection of people in peril for an important part because it was able to detach protection from military intervention *per se*, focusing on a broader array of possibilities including peaceful means and covering a wider scope by including prevention and rebuilding.

Besides excluding the possibility of acting forcefully without the consent of the Security Council, the original ICISS report and those that came thereafter, did not change as much in substance but it seems slowly the focus came to lie more with peaceful measures and was focused more specifically on international crimes. These developments were an important step to lessen some of the concerns about the use of force in the lead-up to the World Summit.

The 2005 World Summit meeting turned out to be a landmark moment for the responsibility to protect, where R2P gained formal acceptance from the UN Member States. R2P was affirmed in paragraphs 138-140 and adopted by the General Assembly in Resolution 60/1, 2005 (Burke-White, 2012, pp. 21-22). The document limited the type of crimes that may warrant a R2P response. While the original ICISS document followed the broader human security paradigm, the 2005 document only includes genocide, war crimes, crimes against humanity and ethnic cleansing, which have collectively become known as 'mass atrocities' or 'mass atrocity crimes' (Evans, 2008, p. 11). Significantly, this also excludes cases of general repression (Chhabra & Zucker, 2012, p. 60). This was important for reaching consensus because, as Chhabra and Zucker explain, 'potential intervention on claims of a collective Responsibility to Protect against political repression has been and remains the primary source of opposition to the concept' (Chhabra & Zucker, 2012, p. 60). This does not apply to the most serious forms of repression when it may escalate into crimes against humanity, ethnic cleansing or war crimes (when perpetrated within armed conflict), which is the central focus of this research.

Although politically significant, the Outcome Document achieved minimal clarity in comparison to the ICISS report as it ignored the responsibility to rebuild, does not specify what to do when the Security Council is deadlocked, and it does not specify criteria for military action (Burke-White, 2012, p. 27). The phrase that measures under Chapter VII may only be undertaken 'should peaceful means be inadequate' suggests that the last resort requirement (Brunnée & Toope, 2010, p. 192) is the only condition for the use of force, which is still explicitly addressed from the original ICISS report.[33] It turned out to be difficult to find consensus since there were several states that were weary of including the responsibility to protect in the Outcome Document. They argued that the concept was vague and feared that it might be abused (Stahn, 2007, p. 108). Others worried it was incompatible with the Charter which only mandates the UN to safeguard international peace and security and worried it would turn into an obligation to intervene (Stahn, 2007, p. 108).

Responsibility to protect populations from genocide, war crimes, ethnic cleansing and crimes against humanity

138. Each individual State has the responsibility to protect its populations from genocide, war crimes, ethnic cleansing and crimes against humanity. This responsibility entails the prevention of such crimes, including their incitement, through appropriate and necessary means. We accept that responsibility and will act in accordance with it. The international community should, as appropriate, encourage and help States to exercise this responsibility and support the United Nations in establishing an early warning capability.

139. The international community, through the United Nations, also has the responsibility to use appropriate diplomatic, humanitarian and other peaceful means, in accordance with Chapters VI and VIII of the Charter, to help to protect populations from genocide, war crimes, ethnic cleansing and crimes against humanity. In this context, we are prepared to take collective action, in a timely and decisive manner, through the Security Council, in accordance with the Charter, including Chapter VII, on a case-by-case basis and in cooperation with relevant regional organizations as appropriate, should peaceful means be inadequate and national authorities are manifestly failing to protect their populations from genocide, war crimes, ethnic cleansing and crimes against humanity. We stress the need for the General Assembly to continue consideration of the responsibility to protect populations from genocide, war crimes, ethnic cleansing and crimes against humanity and its implications, bearing in mind the principles of the Charter and international law. We also intend to commit ourselves, as necessary and appropriate, to helping States build capacity to protect their populations from genocide, war crimes, ethnic cleansing and crimes against humanity and to assisting those which are under stress before crises and conflicts break out.

140. We fully support the mission of the Special Adviser of the Secretary-General on the Prevention of Genocide.

World Summit Outcome Document (United Nations, 2005).

33 The just cause, and right authority criteria are addressed as well but who may act as the right authority or what constitutes a just cause changed. See Chapter 12 for a more elaborate analysis of this point.

While the General Assembly adopted the World Summit Outcome in Resolution 60/1 (2005), it took longer for the Security Council to adopt it in a Resolution. UN Security Council Resolution 1674, which affirmed the world summit meeting, was preceded by six months of difficult negotiations in the Security Council (Burke-White, 2012, pp. 29-30). Eventually the language was watered down and in the Resolution the Security Council only '*reaffirms* the provisions of paragraphs 138 and 139 of the World Summit Outcome Document' (Burke-White, 2012, p. 30).

In 2009, the Secretary-General's report reformulated R2P as resting on three pillars. The first pillar was concerned with 'the protection responsibilities of the State'. The second pillar referred to international assistance and capacity building and thus is centred around the commitment of the international community to help states to meet their pillar one obligations (Ban, 2009, p. 2; 9). The third pillar is about realising a 'timely and decisive response' and is therefore about the responsibility of the international community to protect the population when the State is 'manifestly failing' to protect (Ban, 2009, p. 9). Ban explained that when implementing R2P, 'the scope should be kept narrow [while] the response ought to be deep, employing the wide array of prevention and protection instruments available to Member States' (Ban, 2009, p. 8), with no particular sequential order being assigned to the different pillars. Ban rather finds 'all three must be ready to be utilized at any point, as there is no set sequence for moving from one to another, especially in a strategy of early and flexible response.' (Ban, 2009, p. 9)

The report was presented at the General Assembly in July 2009 and was followed by a debate (Brunnée & Toope, 2010, p. 200). The debate was preceded by a 'concept note' from Miguel d'Escoto, President of the General Assembly, in which he expressed his doubts about the concept putting forward the argument that '[c]olonialism and interventionism used responsibility to protect arguments' (cited in Brunnée & Toope, 2010, p. 200). However, only a handful of countries, notably Cuba, Nicaragua, Sudan and Venezuela, sought to reopen the debate on the responsibility to protect more generally (Burke-White, 2012, p. 32). The large majority of states nevertheless had a positive attitude towards the concept (Brunnée & Toope, 2010, p. 200) and overall it may be argued that support for the responsibility to protect is growing (Brunnée & Toope, 2010, p. 199).

In September 2009 a resolution followed (RES 63/308) in which the General Assembly took note of the report and '*decides* to continue its consideration of the responsibility to protect' (RES 63/308). The words 'with appreciation' had to be removed in order to come to agreement (Brunnée & Toope, 2010). Its adoption is significant since the report included suggestions on how to implement the responsibility to protect. Burke-White concludes overall that 'states are willing to accept the relatively minimalist construction of the Responsibility to Protect outlined in the World Summit Outcome Document, even when implementation steps are also contemplated' (Burke-White, 2012, p. 33).

The General Assembly has continued to consider the responsibility to protect, as was decided it would in Resolution 63/308 through yearly informal interactive dialogues during which a report, prepared by the Secretary General, is discussed. In 2010, the dialogue concerned *Early Warning, Assessment and the Responsibility to Protect*. During the discussion broad support was voiced for the concept itself and the report, although there continued to be a few states that challenged the R2P concept itself (International Coalition for the Responsibility to Protect, 2010). During the subsequent debate in 2011 on the role of regional and sub-regional arrangements in implementing the responsibility to protect, there were once more a handful of states who challenged the concept itself. However, the majority argued that R2P has in fact been implemented in a variety of situations and was now established as a principle which guided the actions of various actors at national, regional and international levels (International Coalition for the Responsibility to Protect, 2011, p. 1; 3; 8). The 2012 debate on the third pillar was characterized by concern about ongoing atrocity crimes, especially in Syria, while states reiterated that R2P had gained widespread acceptance and could not be renegotiated (International Coalition for the Responsibility to Protect, 2012). Brazil put forward a concept paper in 2011 on 'responsibility while protecting' that received some support from members (UN, 2012). However, overall the third pillar was shown once again to be controversial during this meeting, with some members expressing concern about legitimizing regime change and worried about the application of the pillars. India stated that to argue that there would be no sequence between the pillars is 'wrong and misleading' (UN, 2012). Many States were, however, of the opinion that the international community's response should not be inhibited by fears of misuse of the responsibility to protect and emphasized the third pillar is not limited to the use of force but also encompasses non-violent measures (International Coalition for the Responsibility to Protect; UN, 2012). In 2013, the Secretary General's report that focused predominantly on prevention and the first pillar. From the discussions it became clear that only a very small group of states questioned the extent to which the responsibility to protect had already been fully agreed upon and needed to be refined further before implementation (International Coalition for the Responsibility to Protect, 2013). The year thereafter, the second pillar was explored. Also with regards to the second pillar, the states find consensus on the importance prevention should play in the implementation of R2P (International Coalition for the Responsibility to Protect, 2014). In the informal dialogue of the most recent report in 2015, on the implementation of R2P, it was stressed that the implementation of R2P encompasses much more than military intervention because the possibility of military intervention was still a concern for some states who feared the principle might be abused (International Coalition for the Responsibility to Protect, 2015). In the closing remarks it was observed that a 'real consensus' was developed over the past decade (International Coalition for the Responsibility to Protect, 2015). Therefore, while there is broad acceptance of the norm overall, the use of force especially in the third pillar remains contentious, as is also reflected in the extent to which the different pillars are embedded in international law.

4.5.3. LEGAL STATUS

The strength of R2P is that it built on existing concepts and obligations. Most of the ideas in the original ICISS report have a long history. As mentioned before, the idea of sovereignty as responsibility may be an important break with the conceptions of sovereignty since WWII, but taking into account the history of sovereignty before the UN Charter makes the break from the past seem less dramatic (Glanville, 2010; Stahn, 2007, pp. 111-112). The continuum of prevention, reaction and rebuilding can be traced back, to some extent, to the *agenda for peace* where Boutros Boutros Ghali distinguished between preventive diplomacy, peacemaking and peacekeeping (Boutros-Ghali, 1992; Stahn, 2007, p. 114).[34] And the criteria for intervention, which were in the original report, largely stem from the just war tradition (Stahn, 2007, p. 114).

Legally as well, the report reflected existing obligations. Burke-White explains that the report 'recognizes and embraces existing legal rules', but at the same time also 'questions the adequacy of those rules' (Burke-White, 2012, p. 21). On the one hand, the concept incorporates existing legal provisions but on the other hand also signifies an attempt to extend responsibility beyond the current obligations. In this sense R2P is well grounded in existing international law but should not, at this time, be viewed as an independent rule of law (Burke-White, 2012, p. 17).

According to Stahn, it is not self-evident that states 'intended to create a legal norm' (Stahn, 2007, p. 101), and Strauss even goes so far as to say that the 'history of the Summit Outcome Document revealed that "responsibility" was meant not to include a particular legal obligation, but to rest on existing international law' (Strauss, 2009, p. 314). R2P may, nevertheless, serve as a foundation for further development towards binding law for those elements of the World Summit Outcome which are not already codified in existing international law (Brunnée & Toope, 2010, pp. 211-212; Burke-White, 2012, p. 23). The World Summit Outcome Document derives authority from its adoption by the General Assembly in Resolution 60/1 and because it was reaffirmed by the UN Security Council in Resolution 1674 (Burke-White, 2012, pp. 22; 29-30). Although it appears that even the latter resolution falls short of a decision which members are obliged to implement in accordance with Article 25 of the UN Charter,

[34] Other aspects can furthermore be said to have been developed in other reports, such as the Brahimi report and 'No Exit Without Strategy' (Stahn, 2007, p. 114)

some scholars see this as a step in the 'ongoing process of legalisation' of the responsibility to protect (Burke-White, 2012, p. 30). At the same time, as it stands now, particularly since the Resolution makes no reference to Chapter VII or a threat to international peace and security, as well as considering the Outcome Document itself was already weakly formulated, it certainly imposes no legal obligations on the UN member states (Burke-White, 2012, pp. 30-31).

Consequently, the extent to which R2P can be viewed as a binding international norm is contested. None of the documents that underlie the creation of R2P can be seen as having created binding international law in accordance with the sources of law which are enumerated in Article 38 in the statute of the ICJ (Stahn, 2007, p. 101). The debate mainly centres on the extent to which it may be seen as soft law (Welsh & Banda, 2010), has become a (non-binding) legal norm (Burke-White, 2012), or perhaps is evolving into customary law (Stockburger, 2010; Welsh & Banda, 2010).

According to Welsh and Banda, the Outcome Document is best designated as soft law due to its 'open-ended, malleable language and the fact that their implications have engendered considerable controversy' (2010, p. 230). While not binding at this point in time, they note soft law may become customary law over time and may influence the interpretation of existing laws (Welsh & Banda, 2010, p. 230). Burke-White finds this terminology unhelpful as it is imprecisely defined and notes it may cause the Outcome Document to appear as entailing a binding obligation, which it does not (Burke-White, 2012, p. 23). He argues the responsibility to protect is most usefully seen as a norm, rather than a legal rule (2012, p. 34). Bellamy explains norms are 'shared expectations of appropriate behaviour for actors with a given identity' and finds the common ground in the debate by arguing that while 'there is general consensus that R2P is a norm … [there is] much less agreement on what sort of norm it is' (Bellamy, 2010, p. 160).[35] This is due the fact that different aspects of R2P are more or less specific in the demands they impose on the international community and generate different levels contestation (Bellamy, 2010, p. 161).

Luck points out that summit outcomes can contribute to the development of law but that they are not binding legal obligations (Luck, 2012, p. 86). Scholars differ in the weight that they attach to resolutions, reports from the Secretary General and expert bodies. It is noted occasionally they may be helpful in order to interpret international law or, importantly, may constitute evidence of international custom (Stahn, 2007, p. 101; Strauss, 2009, p. 293; Welsh & Banda, 2010, p. 229) although they do not create customary law (Strauss, 2009, p. 293). Even if one would be able to establish *opinio juris* on the basis of the Outcome Document and resolutions, in order for it to be binding there would also have

---

35 Bellamy explains that while governments tend to see norms as binding, IR scholars 'understand norms as broader social phenomena: shared expectations of appropriate behavior for actors with a given identity' (Bellamy, 2015, p. 162).

to be widespread state practice (Burke-White, 2012, p. 23). State practice does not have to be long term but would have to be 'both extensive and virtually uniform' (North Sea Continental Shelf Case, ICJ, 1969). It has been argued that 'both physical and verbal acts of states may constitute practice' (Stockburger, 2010, p. 389) and inaction when faced with atrocity crimes, or a violation of the presumed rule would not necessarily negate the existence of such a rule. The idea has been put forward that 'where there is overwhelming evidence of state practice in support of a rule, alongside repeated evidence of violations of that rule, such violations do not challenge the existence of the rule in question' (Henckaerts cited in Stockburger, 2010, p. 390). It is, nevertheless, doubtful whether there is state practice and *opinio juris* in the case of R2P. Although Bellamy & Williams (2011) argue a new era of protection is emerging, it would be much too soon, currently, to argue that there is state practice as not only is it still contested but it seems that 'for every invocation of the doctrine in cases like Cote d'Ivoire and Libya, there are failures such as Darfur or Sri Lanka or attempts to misapply the doctrine such as in Georgia and Cyclone Nargis in Myanmar' (Brunnée & Toope, 2010, p. 208; Burke-White, 2012, p. 23; Orchard, 2012, p. 378; Stockburger, 2010, p. 398).

Even if at this point in time it is not possible to qualify the responsibility to protect overall as a binding legal norm, it is certainly not 'devoid of legal content' (Bellamy & Reike, 2010, p. 269). There are elements in the report that were already codified in other legal provisions (Bellamy & Reike, 2010, p. 169; Stahn, 2007, pp. 111-115). It is useful, therefore, to separate R2P into two complementary types of responsibility that correspond with the pillar structure as developed by the secretary general. The first type (pillar one) is that of the state to protect its own population, and the second (pillars two and three) revolve around the responsibility the international community has to react or to prevent mass atrocities in other countries (Bellamy & Reike, 2010, pp. 269-270). It is instructive to look at each of these in turn.

Pillar one is relatively uncontroversial due to the fact that the Outcome Document limited the crimes falling under R2P to genocide, crimes against humanity, ethnic cleansing and war crimes. Genocide and war crimes are codified in their own treaties whereas crimes against humanity are not yet explicitly defined in a specific Convention[36] but, like genocide and war crimes, have been established as a *jus cogens* norm (Bellamy & Reike, 2010, pp. 276-279; Chhabra & Zucker, 2012, pp. 43; 50-51; Strauss, 2009, pp. 315-316).[37] In addition, genocide, crimes against humanity and war crimes are all incorporated into the statutes of the ICTY, ICTR and ICC and jurisprudence has further delineated

---

36 Efforts to create such a Convention are underway however (Sadat, 2011).

37 Although there seems to be more consensus on genocide and crimes against humanity being labeled a *jus cogens* norm since Strauss for one does not mention war crimes as such (Strauss, 2009, pp. 315-316).

the contours of the crimes (Chhabra & Zucker, 2012, p. 42). Ethnic cleansing can generally be seen to fall under one of the other crimes but has no specific legal meaning in itself (Strauss, 2009, p. 315). Due to the fact that these crimes and the corresponding duties of the states towards their own populations are so well established, there are no states that deny having this duty (Glanville, 2012, p. 3).

Pillars two and three are much more controversial and the extent to which states are legally bound to fulfil their duties tends to differ depending on the pillar and the crime. A positive obligation attached to the responsibility to protect would be a rather novel development within international law (Stahn, 2007, p. 115). That the legal nature of pillars two and three was much more contested was already shown during the negotiations of the World Summit in 2005. John Bolton, US Ambassador to the UN, emphasized in communiqués preceding the summit that the responsibility of the state towards its own population was of an entirely different nature than that of the international community. Where the former was a legal obligation the latter was merely a moral obligation (Bellamy & Reike, 2010, pp. 274-275). He managed indeed to water down the agreement to refer to responsibility rather than obligation and only committed to being prepared on a case by case basis to take collective action, thus signifying the voluntary rather than obligatory nature of the provision (Glanville, 2012, pp. 12-13; Stahn, 2007, p. 109). His argument is, nevertheless, much too simplistic and recent developments in the responsibility of both states as well as organizations, may indicate more far reaching obligations are emerging (Bellamy & Reike, 2010, p. 275).

Since there is no specialised Convention on crimes against humanity, there are also no explicit duties listed which extend the responsibility of states beyond the obligation not to commit them. The exceptions are the states which are part of the Rome Statute but they are solely under the duty to investigate crimes against humanity and punish its perpetrators (Bellamy & Reike, 2010, p. 279). For the other two crimes there is a broader responsibility.

International humanitarian law (IHL) includes provisions which oblige states to aid others in fulfilling their duties and there are therefore pillar two and three obligations under IHL (Bellamy & Reike, 2010, p. 277). Article 1 of the Geneva Conventions imposes a duty on states to 'undertake to respect *and to ensure respect* for the present Convention in all circumstances' (emphasis my own). This was interpreted by Pictet to apply 'in the event of a Power failing to fulfil its obligations' and found that in those circumstances the 'other Contracting Parties (neutral, allied or enemy) may, and should, endeavour to bring it back to an attitude of respect for the convention' (Pictet, 1952, p. 26).

The Genocide Convention may also impose pillar two and three obligations. The legal scope of Article 1 of the Genocide Convention in which states commit themselves to prevent and punish has long been uncertain (Bellamy & Reike, 2010, pp. 283-284). The United States for instance, avoided referring to the

Rwandan genocide as an actual genocide in order to avoid an obligation to intervene, yet labelled the situation in Darfur as genocide but argued that this did not bring forth any specific obligation to act. Although there are exceptions, the majority opinion of international legal scholars seems to have agreed with the US that the Convention did not impose such an extensive obligation (Bellamy & Reike, 2010, pp. 283-284). Glanville, for instance, finds that

> 'neither a plain reading of the text nor an analysis of the *travaux préparatoires* provided clear grounds for thinking that it imposed upon states a duty to take action to prevent the occurrence of genocide beyond their borders, other than perhaps an obligation under Article VIII to 'call upon the competent organs of the United Nations' to take "appropriate action"' (Glanville, 2012, pp. 7-8).

A seminal development in this respect has been the ICJ judgment in *Bosnia and Herzegovina vs Serbia and Montenegro* (2007). In its ruling the ICJ found that 'the obligation of States parties is rather to employ all means reasonably available to them, so as to prevent genocide so far as possible.' (Bosnia and Herzegovina vs Serbia and Montenegro, ICJ, para 430).[38] What reasonably available encompasses remains to be seen (Bellamy & Reike, 2010, p. 184) but the court noted the duty extends beyond a referral to the competent UN organs in accordance with Article VIII (Glanville, 2012, p. 16).[39]

The court, furthermore, set out criteria that may guide the assessment of whether a state has met its due diligence obligations which should be assessed '*in concreto*'. According to the court:

> 'The first, which varies greatly from one State to another, is clearly the capacity to influence effectively the action of persons likely to commit, or already committing, genocide. This capacity itself depends, among other things, on the geographical distance of the State concerned from the scene of the events, and on the strength of the political links, as well as links of all other kinds, between the authorities of that State and the main actors in the events. The State's capacity to influence must also be assessed by legal criteria, since it is clear that every state may only act within the limits permitted by international law; seen thus, a State's capacity to influence may

---

38 Glanville notes it is limited in its applicability for pillar two since the judgment offers 'no legal support for the broader notion that the "international community" has an obligation … before the threat of genocide has fully emerged' (Glanville, 2012, p. 25). This, however, is open to interpretation since pillar two also incorporates 'assisting States "under stress before crises and conflicts break out"' (Ban, 2009, p. 15) and it would depend on whether this stress is such that the threat of genocide has materialized whether preventative action may have to be taken to avert the threat under pillar two.

39 The court noted that 'Even if and when these organs have been called upon, this does not mean that the States parties to the Convention are relieved of the obligation to take such action as they can to prevent genocide from occurring, while respecting the United Nations Charter and any decisions that may have been taken by its competent organs.' (Bosnia vs Serbia, ICJ, para 427).

> vary depending on its particular legal position vis-à-vis the situations and persons facing the danger, or the reality, of genocide.' (Bosnia and Herzegovina vs Serbia and Montenegro, ICJ, para 430).

Since the court does not emphasize geographical distance as such but argues that it is the influence which matters, of which geographical proximity is just one determinant, several scholars note this envisages a special role for the UN Security Council's permanent members, although the responsibility seems to fall on all states albeit in different degrees (Arbour, 2008, p. 453; Glanville, 2012, p. 20; Peters, 2011, pp. 21-26). They have the most discretionary powers to act 'within the limits permitted by international law' and are politically powerful actors. Relying on *Bosnia and Herzegovina v. Serbia and Montenegro*, Arbour argues states are 'no longer holders of a discretionary right to intervene, [but] all States are now burdened with the responsibility to take action under the doctrine of responsibility to protect' (Arbour, 2008, p. 449) and that 'because of the power they wield and due to their global reach, the members of the Security Council, particularly the Permanent Five Members (P5) hold and even heavier responsibility than other States to ensure the protection of civilians everywhere' (Arbour, 2008, p. 453). Arbour's argumentation is based, however, on a case dealing with genocide. A duty to prevent or stop violations of the other crimes is – as explained – more difficult to establish, although here as well steps have been taken in this direction.

The ILC draft Articles on state responsibility for example point towards the possibility a broader responsibility may be developing. Article 41 stipulates that:

> '1. States shall cooperate to bring to an end through lawful means any serious breach within the meaning of Article 40.[40]
> 2. No State shall recognize as lawful a situation created by a serious breach within the meaning of Article 40, nor render aid or assistance in maintaining that situation.
> 3. This article is without prejudice to the other consequences referred to in this Part and to such further consequences that a breach to which this chapter applies may entail under international law.'

As Stahn also notes 'the duty of cooperation under Article 41(1) comes close to the idea of collective responsibility under the concept of responsibility to protect', but he states that in some aspects R2P even moves beyond the ILC by modifying

---

40 '*Article 40 Application of this chapter:*
1. This chapter applies to the international responsibility which is entailed by a serious breach by a State of an obligation arising under a peremptory norm of general international law. 2. A breach of such an obligation is serious if it involves a gross or systematic failure by the responsible State to fulfil the obligation.' Responsibility of States for Internationally Wrongful Acts.

an obligation to cooperate to end the breach into the more general responsibility to protect the victims (Stahn, 2007, pp. 115-116).[41] At the same time, the ILC admitted it remained questionable whether the law as it stands prescribes such a positive duty and notes that Article 41(1) 'may reflect the progressive development of international law.'[42] Overall the responsibilities of the international community to prevent and stop all atrocity crimes is not as well established as some of the other responsibilities codified in R2P (Bellamy & Reike, 2010, p. 269). Consequently, a duty for states to cooperate to halt the commission of atrocity crimes remains controversial (Bellamy & Reike, 2010, p. 283).

Furthermore, the ILC has also begun its work on the obligation of international organizations and has found that the UN breached its legal obligations when it failed to prevent the genocide in Rwanda even though it had been in a position to do so. The question to what extent there was a legal failure to prevent the genocide is again contested (Bellamy & Reike, 2010, p. 285) but an important question considering that there is an important role for the UN in implementing R2P.

States referred in the World Summit Outcome Document to the UN Security Council as the only actor who may instigate forceful action against a state who violates its responsibility to protect its own population. This brought forth two questions, firstly, what the UN Security Council may do in order to protect a population from genocide, crimes against humanity, war crimes and ethnic cleansing and, secondly, what the Security Council must do (Peters, 2009, p. 538). Brunée and Toope note there is still uncertainty to what extent the Security Council is obliged by law to intervene when atrocity crimes are committed (Brunnée & Toope, 2010, p. 208). While US Ambassador John Bolton dismissed this idea, and many scholars agree with him, (e.g. Kapur, 2009, p. 562; E. K. White, 2009, pp. 547-549) there are some indications based on, *inter alia*, the *Bosnia and Herzegovina vs Serbia and Montenegro* judgement of the ICJ and the work of the ILC such a responsibility is not unthinkable.

As was explained above, it is now no longer controversial that the Security Council can refer to a humanitarian crisis as a threat to international peace

---

41 Stahn also argues the threshold is modified from, '*serious* breaches of peremptory *norms* of general international law ... to all forms of genocide war crimes, ethnic cleansing and crimes against humanity' (Stahn, 2007, p. 116) but – as earlier explained – there is reason to believe all can be qualified as peremptory norms and it is likely many atrocity crimes when perpetrated can be qualified as 'serious'.

42 Werner emphasizes that states ultimately rejected the inclusion of provisions in the ILC draft articles that might have suggested some form of criminal responsibility for states. At the same time he also argues that in fact some of the institutions that are already in place, most notably the UN Security Council and the international tribunals, already implicate states as guilty actors in the commission of international crimes. States, Werner argues, can be labelled as renegades when they violate core values and can be criminalized 'through the back door' (Werner, 2014, pp. 199-208).

and security in order to make use of its capabilities under Chapter VII.[43] More contentious is whether the Security Council also has a duty to act (Peters, 2009, p. 538). The Secretary General has found that surely the Security Council carries a moral obligation (Peters, 2009, p. 539), but some scholars argue that a legal responsibility may also become relevant for either the institution or its individual members (Arbour, 2008, p. 454; Glanville, 2012, pp. 20-24; Peters, 2009, 2011).

Members of the UN Security Council have been hesitant to compromise their discretion to determine the scope of resolutions. At the initiative of French Foreign Minister Védrine, the original report put forward the idea that the permanent five should commit to refrain from using their veto powers in R2P situations when their national vital interests were not at stake. Eventually, it did not make its way into the final version of the World Summit Outcome Document, amongst others, because of strong resistance from the American representative Bolton (Blätter & Williams, 2011, pp. 314-315). The idea itself, however, has not withered away. It was brought before the General Assembly by five states, Costa Rica, Jordan, Liechtenstein, Switzerland and Singapore (Blätter & Williams, 2011, p. 316), and thereafter it was included in the Secretary General's report '*Implementing the Responsibility to Protect*' to commit to such a strategy (Blätter & Williams, 2011, p. 317).

Despite reluctance by the permanent five to formalize even a code of conduct, some authors go one-step further by ascribing legal responsibility. Relying on the determination by the ICJ that states should 'employ all means reasonably available to them', Glanville finds that 'in those instances where the Security Council authorizes the use of force to prevent genocide, a state would seem to be under an obligation to contribute troops to a military intervention if such measures are "reasonably available" to it. The requirement for Security Council authorisation, in turn, suggests that members of the Council, and perhaps even the institution itself, may bear a particular obligation to facilitate the prevention of genocide' (Glanville, 2012, p. 20). While Glanville recognizes that at the World Summit there was no willingness to commit to any legal obligation, he points to the ILC draft Articles on the responsibility of international organizations which note that organizations, too, are bound by obligations which stem from pre-emptory norms (Glanville, 2012, p. 21). Others find the draft Articles to be premature and there is the problem that since the Security Council is part of the constitutive process of creating international law, it is difficult to comprehend how it may ever be in violation (Glanville, 2012, p. 22).

---

[43] Peters questions whether the Council has unlimited discretion in qualifying situations threats to international peace and security but considering the fact that R2P only covers the most serious human rights abuses, this does not seem immediately relevant (Peters, 2009, p. 538).

Strauss finds that in order to make it a binding obligation, 'agreement on objective criteria for the establishment of manifest failure' and requirements to commence collective action would need to be devised (Strauss, 2009, p. 319). He points out however, that the criteria that the ICISS had developed for this purpose did not end up in the Outcome Document (Strauss, 2009, p. 319). If these problems can be overcome, perhaps it may be conceivable that Security Council resolutions would be subject to judicial review by the ICJ[44] but even if that were to happen, how a failure by the Council to act can be dealt with is even more difficult to conceive (Glanville, 2012, p. 22).

Peters rules out holding the Security Council as an institution responsible but notes its (permanent) members may be held accountable. She advocates interpreting Article 27(7) of the UN Charter, which outlines the voting regulations of the Security Council, in accordance with Article 31(3)(c) of the Vienna Convention on the Law of Treaties which notes that 'any relevant rules of international law applicable in the relations between the parties' shall be taken into account in the interpretation. R2P could then be taken into account as a 'relevant rule of international law' according to Peters (Peters, 2009, p. 540). Peters suggests:

> 'The systematic interpretation would lead to qualifying an illegal or abusive refusal to concur by a P5 either as legally irrelevant or as a mere abstention which, according to established practice, cannot prevent a positive decision of the Council' (Peters, 2009, p. 540).

In addition, she believes 'the legal irrelevance of an abusive veto also flows from the general principle that the United Nations may not invoke internal procedural problems to justify its breach of international law' (Peters, 2009, p. 540). Others argue that to suggest members of the Security Council may issue an 'illegal' veto, misunderstands its nature as a political body (E. K. White, 2009, p. 547). Glanville counters that and states:

> 'all decisions made by states about how to respond to the threat or commission of genocide are political, regardless of whether they are made within or outside of the Security Council, but this does not mean that such decisions cannot also be bound by law. The fact that permanent members have discretion under the UN Charter as to how they exercise their veto does not mean that they cannot also have assumed

44 White emphasizes that 'the International Court of Justice has not yet ruled on the right to review Security Council actions [and] the European Court of Justice (ECJ) in the recent *Kadi* decision found that it had no authority to review Security Council Resolutions in the absence of domestic or Community implementation' (E. K. White, 2009, p. 549). The original ICISS report notes that although in the Lockerbie case affirmed that the Security Council is bound by the Charter, 'there is no provision for judicial review of Security Council decisions, and therefore no way that a dispute over Charter interpretation can be resolved' (International Commission on Intervention and State Sovereignty, 2001, p. 50)

> obligations under other treaties, such as the Genocide Convention, that bound that discretion.' (Glanville, 2012, p. 23).

It seems that, although an interesting thought exercise, Peters' argument seems quite premature, as the legal status of the responsibility to protect for all crimes and all pillars is highly contested and the principle has hardly evolved to established international law. The ideas enshrined in the R2P may evolve over time into customary international law, but we are not there yet. As it stands now R2P should be seen as 'normative principles' which may carry political but no legal weight (Evans, 2012, p. 380). According to Evans, the whole point of the ICISS 'was not to create new legal liability, but to create the conditions for a reflexively *consensual* rather than conflictual response to new internal conflict and atrocity crime situations as they arose in the future' (Evans, 2012, p. 380).

Burke-White advocates embracing the normative impact rather than focussing on its legal status and notes that 'even without legal obligation, RtoP is already having concrete impact … and increased the political and moral costs of inaction in the face of atrocity' (Burke-White, 2012, p. 17). This conclusion seems to be supported by the increased frequency with which the Security Council makes references to the norm (Glanville, 2012, pp. 1-2). Nevertheless, without disregarding the important political influence the concept has already garnered, it might be even more influential, also politically, if it were to become a well-established legal norm. Welsh and Banda highlight three aspects in which legal norms are more likely to generate compliance than moral norms. Firstly, evolution to a legal norm can increase the damage to a state's reputation when the norm is violated. Secondly, they may generate a greater 'compliance pull' because of the legitimacy that these legal norms carry, and finally, 'legal obligations … trigger specific remedies if they are not fulfilled, including, in some cases, the legal liability of the wrongful party' (Welsh & Banda, 2010, p. 228). Therefore, despite the validity in the argument of some scholars that it was lack of will that prevented intervention, rather than the legal possibilities for intervention which were available (Blätter & Williams, 2011, p. 320; Hehir, 2010, p. 229), it is important to realize that the legal status may influence the absence or presence of political will. As a political organ, bringing a veto against a legally binding duty can bring forth political costs for the Security Council and its members as it may lessen its legitimacy. The Security Council's legitimacy is already challenged on several fronts, not least among those its increasingly unrepresentative composition and the occasional unilateral use of force by powerful states and coalitions (Blätter & Williams, 2011, p. 312; Hurd, 2002, pp. 47-48), but legitimacy remains central to the power the UN Security Council as it is mainly reliant on this 'social capital' to ensure the compliance of states (Hurd, 2002, p. 35). Since it relies on its legitimacy to exercise power, the political costs involved in neglecting its responsibility under R2P are likely to influence its decisions.

Overall, R2P is developing fast, but the current status, where it is only legally binding to the extent it reflects already existing obligations, means certain aspects are more developed than others. The first pillar carries more legal weight than the second and third. In addition, within the second and third pillar, the obligations when faced with genocide are better established than that of the other crimes. Yet as it is now increasingly used and accepted, it is not unthinkable that over time the legal obligations become expanded and stronger as it moves to become a legal norm and customary international law.

4.5.4. CHALLENGES FOR IMPLEMENTATION

The non-binding legal status has not prevented the international community from taking slow but certain steps towards the implementation of R2P. Secretary General Ban Ki-moon has been a norm entrepreneur for the responsibility to protect. Through the slogan 'promise less and deliver more', he has urged the UN to start to live up to its rhetoric (Bellamy, 2010, p. 146). In December 2007 he appointed Edward Luck as his Special Adviser on R2P (Bellamy, 2010, p. 146).[45] Luck drew a sharp distinction between the original report and that which states had actually agreed upon at the World Summit in 2005. He was important in establishing the 'narrow but deep' approach to the responsibility to protect, where he focused exclusively on what was agreed upon, while 'utilizing the whole prevention and protection tool kit' (Ban cited in Bellamy, 2010, p. 146). In 2013, Jennifer Welsh was appointed as Special Adviser at the Assistant Secretary General level on the Responsibility to Protect. She has highlighted the importance and challenges of prioritizing the prevention dimension of the responsibility to protect and has argued that there are some examples where prevention seems to have worked, even though it is impossible to ascertain with certainty whether international action under the R2P banner was a crucial determinant in securing a non-violent outcome (Welsh, 2015, p. 12). While ultimately, of course, advocates of R2P seek to bring forth positive change, Luck advocates a broader perspective. He defined implementation as 'the process or act of fulfilment ... It is a matter of advancement rather than attainment' (Luck, 2012, p. 86) and it certainly continues to be an ongoing process. Ban Ki-moon emphasized this point when he argued that the atrocities that are currently being perpetrated and 'the staggering scale of this suffering should compel the international community to frankly assess its failures and redouble its commitment to protect vulnerable populations from the most egregious international crimes' (Ban, 2015, p. 3).

Nevertheless, concrete changes are discernible. Within some states, institutional changes have been made to implement R2P more effectively.

[45] He was succeeded by Jennifer Welsh in July 2013 (UN, 2013).

Examples thereof are the Atrocity Prevention Board in the US and the numerous 'national focal points' for R2P that were set up in many states (Ban, 2015, p. 9; Welsh, 2015, p. 3). In the international arena, in 2015, just ten years after the World Summit, the UN Security Council had adopted 30 resolutions and six presidential statements that deal with R2P, and the Human Rights Council adopted another 13 resolutions that refer to R2P (Ban, 2015, p. 4).

The evolution of R2P has come a long way already in order to make this possible. The Outcome Document lists crimes which make implementation more feasible than the original report (Luck, 2012, p. 91). A human security approach, also applying to natural disaster and under-development would cause tremendous turf problems, for instance, within the UN, but also makes the concept unacceptable to many states fearing undue meddling (Luck, 2012, p. 91). Yet challenges remain. One of the founding fathers of R2P, Gareth Evans, sums up the challenges that remain as follows 'securing close to unanimous understanding of just what kinds of real-world cases the norm is meant to embrace, and what kind of policy responses it actually requires case by case; having in place the institutional capacity to deliver that response; and having the political will to do so' (Evans, 2012, p. 381).

According to Evans, when states are failing to protect their populations under R2P is, on the face of it, an easy question. These are namely 'those where mass atrocity crimes – involving genocide, ethnic cleansing, or other war crimes or crimes against humanity – are actually occurring or imminently about to occur, or where the situation could deteriorate to this extent in the medium or longer term unless appropriate preventative measures are taken' (Evans, 2008, p. 72). Yet in practice opinions on whether a situation fulfils these criteria may differ (Evans, 2008, p. 72). He suggests five factors be looked at to further assess whether a country is at risk and should be a R2P concern. The first one concerns whether a country has a history of atrocity crimes. Secondly, whether tensions that fuelled the violence in the past are still present. Thirdly, a country's coping mechanisms should be assessed for dealing with remaining grievances and tensions. Fourthly, is the matter of how receptive and open a country is to external influence, both positively and negatively, and, importantly the final factor is leadership (Evans, 2008, pp. 74-75).

While Evans acknowledges the leader is important, the role of individuals in implementing the responsibility to protect remained understudied (Luck & Luck, 2016, p. 207). Recently, the individual responsibility to protect (IR2P) was put forward as an approach to study the 'decisions people make before, during, and after atrocity crimes are committed' (Luck & Luck, 2016, p. 208). The concept moves beyond the state as a black box to highlight that those states are 'made up of people whose perceptions, experiences, and biases affect the priorities, decisions and actions of the governments and institutions that employ them' (Luck & Luck, 2016, p. 213). The concept moves beyond the decision-making process of the leaders of the country in which the atrocity takes place and includes vulnerable populations, bystanders, group and community leaders, leaders of foreign influential countries, key officials in international organizations and survivors (Luck & Luck, 2016, p. 214). When intervention is contemplated, the authors argue, the effect that this has on all those groups should be taken into consideration (Luck, Luck, 2016, p. 214).

There remains significant controversy around the intentions of the interveners. History has often shown that humanitarian motives, if they were mentioned at all, have very often been only one of many different reasons to intervene (Cronin, 2007, p. 295). This is why, while some scholars have advocated expanding R2P to also include the prevention of potential security and nuclear disasters, others are apprehensive about such a development since this is likely to only increase fears of neo-colonialist tendencies (Hamilton, 2006). Political consensus does not reach beyond these few crimes and, also in practice, reliance on R2P without a clear violation of these crimes has not been accepted by most countries. Bellamy argues that Russia's invasion in Georgia was not deemed acceptable even though it was couched in R2P terms, and neither was the refusal of the government of Myanmar to allow humanitarian assistance in its country after it was hit by Cyclone Nargis accepted as a case warranting measures under R2P (Bellamy, 2010, pp. 150-152). Therefore, although fears of abuse of the concept raised its head after the US started to use humanitarian reasons for invading Iraq, the latter two situations have shown that R2P does not automatically legitimize any intervention when undertaken for stated humanitarian purposes (Bellamy, 2010, p. 152). At the same time, recent conflicts have shown that the fears the concept might be abused have not abated completely. The intervention in Libya was authorized by the Security Council but the manner in which the coalition provided support to the Libyan rebels until Muammar Al-Gaddafi was killed and the capital was in their hands, while refusing to cooperate with South Africa's mediation efforts, frustrated many. Their actions were widely seen, most prominently by the BRIC (Brazil, Russia, India, China) countries, as violating the terms that were set out by the Security Council (Rotmann, Kurtz, & Brockmeier, 2014, p. 368). Russia subsequently used the Libyan example to justify its vetoes over Syria (Rotmann *et al.*, 2014, p. 368).[46]

The intervention in Libya prompted Brazil to put forward the above mentioned proposal that states should demonstrate responsibility while protecting (Rotmann *et al.*, 2014, p. 368). It enumerated a number of conditions that the international community should observe while intervening. The most important included an emphasis on prevention, restraint with using force and a commitment to only use it a last resort, with care not to do more harm

46 For a more extensive analysis of the intervention in Libya within the R2P framework see Wester (Wester, 2016 – in press).

than good, and only with Security Council authorization. Many conditions reflected discontent with the intervention in Libya as is exemplified by the requirement that 'the scope of military action must abide by the letter and spirit of the mandate conferred by the Security Council' (A66/551; S/2011/701). Brazil retracted the requirement that a rigid sequencing of the pillars was necessary and ceased to be an active advocate of the concept but the proposal sparked a constructive debate among states on the manner in which the third pillar should be implemented (Stuenkel & Tourinho, 2014, pp. 394-395).

Interestingly, there is also concern that R2P may actually be used as a reason not to intervene by hiding behind the notion of complementarity upon which it is built (Stahn, 2007, pp. 116-117). The primary duty lies with the state itself, which may become, what Stahn calls a 'complementarity trap' where 'the argument of states' primary responsibility may be used to constrain, rather than enable, Council involvement' (Stahn, 2007, pp. 116-117).

While Evans, explicitly notes that increasingly there is more consensus on the cases which fall within the realm of R2P (Evans, 2012, p. 381), there remains a strong need to establish criteria to determine when military intervention as a last resort may be warranted (Evans, 2012, p. 384). Several authors refer to the importance of consistency in its application (Ban, 2009, p. 27; Etzioni, 2006, p. 81), and while criteria were incorporated in the original ICISS document, with the exception of using force as a last resort[47], these have largely disappeared from the Outcome Document. Agreement on these criteria would make it more likely that consensus may be reached more easily within the international community about which cases require military intervention (Evans, 2012, pp. 384-385). Although agreement on these issues will not be feasible in the foreseeable future as Evans explains, there remains 'every reason for independent analysts and experts to continue to argue for the salience of the kind of criteria that have emerged, and to evaluate Security Council decision-making by reference to them: by that route, over time, new norms can be established and observed' (Evans, 2012, p. 385).

A neglected problem within the debate, however, is that even if consensus can be found politically, for the implementation, more empirical knowledge is necessary. When have we, for instance, reached the point where military intervention is all that is left as a last resort? Arbour points out:

> 'since the [R2P] doctrine groups different tools along discrete phases, one may be tempted to believe that the available tools for protection come in rigid progression – ranging from the softest to the most muscular options … Although an escalating sequence may make sense in certain cases, it may also leave dangerous protection gaps in others' (Arbour, 2008, p. 457).

---

47 The Outcome Document does not mention 'last resort' as such, but uses the phrase 'should peaceful means be inadequate'.

Concern about these issues has also been reflected in the General Assembly debates where there has been disagreement on whether there is a set sequence in which the pillars should be addressed (UN, 2012). When a point is reached where it is possible to say military intervention should be used as a last resort, is essentially an empirical question that needs to be asked now that progress has been made by scholars and politicians regarding the conceptual debate on the appropriate criteria.

4.6. CONCLUSION

Overall, while some judge positively its ground-breaking nature, and acclaim the very fact that it is well grounded in existing laws while retaining conceptual innovation (Arbour, 2008; Peters, 2011), there are others who find R2P influential but detrimental to the international system, and again others argue it has 'contributed little of substance or prescriptive merit' (Hehir, 2010, p. 218). Uncontested is the responsibility of the states themselves to protect their population from harm and the prerogative of the UN Security Council to intervene when the atrocities threaten international peace and security. It becomes more difficult when the responsibility to protect is interpreted in a manner which assigns the duty upon states and the Security Council to intervene to prevent and react to stop the crimes from occurring.

While a legal duty would perhaps make the compliance greater and would even more strongly pressure states to act in order to prevent and stop atrocity crimes, great strides have been made to have the moral duty now firmly established. Just several decades ago after the Second World War sovereignty seemed an impregnable shield against interference from other countries, it is now seen as entailing responsibilities towards its population. Now that the international community has vocalized its willingness and intention to stop and prevent these crimes from occurring, the difficult task of furthering its implementation remains.

An element thereof is gathering more knowledge. Not only need the factors be identified which lead to conflict and mass atrocities as was done in the previous chapter (Evans, 2008, p. 81), but more knowledge should also be garnered as to when different foreign policy mechanisms are likely to be successful. When contemplating success factors for the implementation of the third pillar, we enter the domain of International Relations (IR) and foreign policy analysis (FPA). Having established that frequently the dictator is important for the perpetration of mass atrocities, the next chapter will analyse what role he plays when foreign policy measures target his regime in order to stop, or mitigate these crimes.

CHAPTER 5
THE INTERACTION BETWEEN STATES AND HEADS OF STATE: THE ROLE OF RATIONALITY

5.1. INTRODUCTION

In previous chapters the characteristics of dictators and dictatorial regimes have been discussed as well as the responsibility of the international community to stop the worst atrocities that are perpetrated by them. When a dictator manifestly fails to protect his population from atrocity crimes or is even complicit in their perpetration, the international community may intervene through the UN Security Council to implement the third pillar of the responsibility to protect. Foreign policy mechanisms that may be used to persuade a dictatorial leader to stop the perpetration of crimes are diverse, and range from diplomacy to sanctions and sometimes even military intervention.[48] These mechanisms are not only intended to emphasize the importance of respect for human rights but also aimed at changing the policies of perpetrating countries (Luard, 1980, p. 579). As Tetlock specifies 'foreign policy is fundamentally social influence: The ultimate objective is to persuade other nations to act in desired ways' (Tetlock, 1983, p. 69). Although often the international community fails to stop the crimes (LeBor, 2006), the domestic policies of dictators might be impacted by the actions of the international community or other states depending on whether the leader will be responsive to the foreign policy mechanisms and modify his tactics that bring about the suffering. In some instances, this means coercing the target state to change its behaviour by threatening the adversary with enough pain that this would outweigh the benefits of resisting the demands for change (Byman & Waxman, 1999, p. 107). That the decision-making process would be done in such a rational manner, however, has been challenged by scholars who pointed to the inability of human beings to live up to the assumptions underlying perfect rationality and has raised issues relating to the level of analysis that is

48 Following Smith *et al*, this research holds that foreign policy can stem from non-state entities. Smith *et al* note that 'although usually linked to the behaviour of a state, [foreign policy] can apply to other actors. Thus it is perfectly possible to speak of companies, regional governments, and non-state actors having foreign policies' (S. Smith *et al.*, 2012a, p. 2).

being investigated (a.o. Stein, 2012). The question becomes whether rationality is attributed to the state or to the individual and what the implications of choosing a particular level of analysis are for examining a state's foreign policy (Carlsnaes, 2012). What determines the reaction of a state to foreign policy measures directed at it, and what is the role of the individual therein?

The role of the individual in determining the outcome of international relations is a contested topic. For a long time, most of the theories were based on the idea that broader power structures determined the policy choices of states and that the leaders of the countries were largely irrelevant for the eventual outcome (Hermann & Hagan, 1998, p. 124). The behaviour of states was often analysed through a rational choice lens that treated states as a black box with similar preferences and objectives (Holsti, 2005; Hudson, 2005, p. 16; Walker, 2011a, p. 7). More recently, foreign policy analysis has stressed the role that individual leaders can play, and advocated more research should focus on them as a unit of analysis (Byman & Pollack, 2001; Hermann & Hagan, 1998). This strand of research complicated the rational choice assumption by highlighting the inability of individuals to make perfectly rational decisions (Mintz & DeRouen, 2010; Renshon & Renshon, 2008; Stein, 2012). Often domestic politics and intra-state dynamics are only analysed to the extent that they are able to help explain the interaction between states. However, it has also been pointed out by some that international factors may also have an impact on domestic politics (Gourevitch, 1978, p. 881).[49] Since the dictator often plays an important part in the perpetration of mass atrocities and, as has been argued in Chapter 3, may initiate what is often a deliberate policy to inflict harm upon a civilian population, it is important to examine his role when attempts are undertaken to bring them to an end. FPA is a useful starting point for analysing the role that dictators play, as the leaders of their country, when the international community uses foreign policy mechanisms to try to bring atrocity crimes to a halt.

Firstly, then, an overview will be given of the most important fields of study when analysing international relations and the primacy accorded to the different levels of analysis within the theories. In addition, it will be assessed to what extent it is reasonable to expect a rational response to foreign policy mechanisms targeted to stop or mitigate the perpetration of mass atrocities on the basis of these theories. Thereafter, it will be argued that FPA provides the most useful and logical point of departure for a subsequent analysis of the individual, and that the position of the dictator warrants such an individualistic approach. However, there are some significant limitations in the existing literature, which should be addressed in order to be able to create a useful differentiation between dictators that signifies their responsiveness to foreign policy measures.

---

49 Gourevitch (1978) mainly mentioned the international distribution of power and economic activity and wealth on domestic state structures rather than efforts to minimize human rights violations and thus had an inherently different focus.

These gaps will be highlighted at the end of this chapter in the conclusion and addressed in subsequent chapters.

5.2. INTERNATIONAL RELATIONS AND FOREIGN POLICY ANALYSIS

Unless overwhelming force is used, and a regime is overthrown, it depends on the reaction of the perpetrating country whether foreign policy mechanisms from other countries will be successful in preventing or minimising mass atrocities. Predicting how another country will respond to foreign policy mechanisms is a notoriously difficult enterprise and international relations theory and foreign policy analysis are the dominant fields of study that have been developed to try to explain the interaction between states.

FPA is generally seen as a sub-field of IR (Hudson, 2005, p. 2; S. Smith *et al.*, 2012a, p. 4; Walker, Malici, & Schafer, 2011, p. 6; B. White, 1999, p. 37), although it remains a contentious issue to what extent the fields converge or should be seen as entirely separate enterprises, each with its own focus (Houghton, 2007; S. Smith, Hadfield, & Dunne, 2012b; Telhami, 2002; Thies & Breuning, 2012). Foreign policy analysis has thus far 'been a kind of free-floating enterprise, logically unconnected to, and disconnected from, the main theories of international relations' (Houghton, 2007, p. 24). Both are ultimately concerned with studying the foreign policy of states, but approach the subject from a different perspective and level of analysis with IR focused on state to state activity and FPA focussing on not only the state itself but also the individuals and groups within them (S. Smith *et al.*, 2012a, p. 5; 7).

The three dominant IR theories are realism, liberalism and constructivism. Realism theorizes states as self-interested entities that compete constantly for power or security. Liberalists hold that these power concerns may be overridden by economic or political considerations (Walt, 1998, p. 38). Constructivism is concerned with how the behaviour of states is affected by collective norms, identities and beliefs (Walt, 1998, p. 38). Neorealism, in particular, has been highly influential. It focused on the system of states and the manner in which states tried to survive given the balance of power among them (Walt, 1998, p. 31). IR therefore has been pre-occupied with an 'international structuralist' approach (B. White, 1999, p. 38) in which scholars explain international relations by looking at the structure of the system and the macropolitical interactions therein (Tanter, 1972, p. 7; Walker *et al.*, 2011, p. 6).

IR generally focuses on the state as the primary unit of analysis which is generally treated as a 'black box', implying that the state can be seen as a single rational unitary actor (Hudson, 2005, p. 2). The system oriented approach tends to discount differences among nations and to assume that the parts of which the system is composed are relatively similar (Singer, 1961, p. 81). The assumption that the state is a unitary actor stems from the idea that its behaviour is not determined by qualms inside the state but is determined by forces external to it (Holsti, 2005, p. 16). States were assumed to have similar primary goals, namely their own security, making them 'functionally equivalent" (Byman & Pollack, 2001, p. 113). The focus of IR scholars thus lay on the anarchical structure of the international arena and interdependence between states. They analysed these structural conditions rather than the leaders operating within them. Often it is reasoned that individuals are left with very little discretionary power when one considers the constraints imposed upon them by the international system and balance of power (Hermann & Hagan, 1998, p. 124; Tetlock, 1983, p. 45). Others argue individuals are unable to impact the major events in world history or that although individuals may occasionally be important they are too individualistic for systematic study (Byman & Pollack, 2001, p. 18; 108). There are also scholars who admit that human idiosyncrasies may influence certain specific interactions between states, but note that since they do not attempt to explain human error and personality they will therefore not be able to explain all variance (Byman & Pollack, 2001, p. 108).

In this manner a theoretical divide emerged separating national, intra-state components and international, interstate components. The prominent neorealist IR scholar Kenneth Waltz for instance held that the national and international arenas are very different at its core. He notes:

> 'national politics is the realm of authority, of administration, and of law. International politics is the realm of power, of struggle, and of accommodation. ... The national realm is variously described as being hierarchic, vertical, centralised, heterogeneous, directed, and contrived; the international realm, as being anarchic, horizontal, decentralised, homogeneous, undirected and mutually adaptive' (2005, p. 70).

Waltz is solely concerned with international politics and 'a theory at one level of generality cannot answer questions about matters at a different level of generality' (Waltz, 2005, p. 77). He therefore warns against expecting his theory to explain particular foreign policy choices of a state. His IR theory, he argues, is for this reason not a theory of foreign policy. He explicitly notes that his work 'makes assumptions about the interests and motives of states, rather than explaining them' (Waltz, 2005, p. 77). According to Waltz, his theory rather explains 'the constraints that confine all states' which 'provide many clues to the expected reactions of states, but by itself the theory cannot explain those reactions. They depend not only on international constraints but also on the characteristics of states' (Waltz, 2005, p. 77). Ultimately, the anarchical structure of the international system is determining the behaviour of states for neorealists, while from the perspective of FPA this system is merely an 'arena for action' (Houghton, 2007, p. 25).

Also within liberalist IR theories the state is the most prominent unit of analysis and when domestic factors are incorporated, the focus lies on the regime type rather than looking inside the state (Houghton, 2007, p. 25; Walt, 1998, p. 32).[50] The focus here lies, as well, largely on structural changes as a determinant for state behaviour (Houghton, 2007, p. 25). Constructivism, on the other hand, is sometimes seen as more closely resembling foreign policy analysis because both deal with how reality is constructed and focus on identity (Houghton, 2007, p. 27; 31).[51] However, important differences remain and relate especially to the level of analysis. As McDermott explains,

> 'constructivism may examine the cultural underpinnings of the norms, ideas and interests that help formulate political action and behaviour, but the individual in such models tends to be shaped and constrained by these larger sociological and cultural forces' (2004b, pp. 7-8).

In this manner constructivist models and psychological models common to FPA provide explanations at different levels of analysis (Houghton, 2007, p. 27; McDermott, 2004b, p. 13). Houghton also admits that there is an element of truth in the notion that many theories stemming from foreign policy analysis have no theory of structure and constructivism does not incorporate a theory about agency (Houghton, p. 41).[52]

Rejecting the more state centric international relations theory, early FPA scholars did not emphasize the importance of states as abstract entities but rather decision makers and their environment (Stern, 2003, p. 184). These decision-making models challenged the unitary actor assumption (Holsti, 2005, p. 24). FPA aims to open up this black box to analyse how these decisions are made and what influences the decision-making process (Hudson & Vore, 1995, p. 210). It explicitly looks at the differences between states (B. White, 1999, p. 38), how they are organized and who makes the decisions (Hermann, 2001, p. 47;

50 The work of Hermann & Kegley (1995) illustrates nicely how a FPA perspective can take on a different, albeit complementary, approach to give further insight into an area usually studied by liberalist IR scholars, namely the democratic peace theory, by making use of political psychology (1995).

51 Walt also noted individuals, especially the elite as the unit of analysis but the focus of constructivism generally lies on collective ideas and norms rather than those of an individual agent (Houghton, 2007, p. 29).
Several scholars who have tried to fit FPA more generally into one of the leading theories seem to be at odds as to where to place it within the IR discipline. Some frame it as a part of liberalism or (neo)realism, but it is more often justifiably contrasted with realist theories in particular (Ripley, 1993; B. White, 1999, p. 24; 42). Others see it as a part of constructivism (e.g.Houghton, 2007) or advocate combining the disciplines through other perspectives (e.g.Thies & Breuning, 2012).

52 What Houghton means by constructivism does include a strong notion of agency but he notes that this is a point of disagreement among constructivist scholars generally (Houghton, 2007, pp. 28-30).

Ripley, 1993, p. 408). Foreign policy analysis starts from the premise that when countries interact with each other in the international arena this is the result of the actions of human decision makers and is thus agent centred (Hudson, 2005, p. 1). Hudson, therefore, points to foreign policy analysis as the 'ground' of IR, or rather its foundation, because ultimately what happens between nations results from the decisions of individuals (Hudson, 2005, p. 1). Foreign policy analysis thus links the 'micro of politics to the macro of the international system' (Groom, 2007, p. 198). It is focused on the individual, the group and the state itself (S. Smith *et al.*, 2012a, p. 7).

Some scholars point to the usefulness of a lower level of analysis when wanting to explain the remaining variation in foreign policy that cannot be explained by, or contradicts with, what one would expect on the basis of systemic variables (Hagan, 2001, p. 10; Hudson, 2005, p. 13). Ikenberry argues it is reasonable to be sceptical about claims that the systematic analysis, focused on the structure of the international system '*determines* foreign policy' (emphasis in original) and that most scholars rather recognize it imposes constraints on foreign policy options (Ikenberry, 2005, p. 4). The system account may shape the general contours of the foreign policy of states but domestic and decision-making variables are required to give more specific and in depth explanations (Ikenberry, 2005, p. 9). Tetlock likewise explains that the overall direction of foreign policy might be dependent on systemic variables but that these theories are unable to explain a nation's response in a particular situation (Tetlock, 1983, p. 46). In addition, he notes there are particular instances during which the individual have more or less freedom to choose. Tetlock explains:

> 'The importance of a level of analysis also depends on the extremity of variables at other levels of analysis. No doubt, systemic pressures are occasionally overwhelming. Policy makers may indeed have no choice but to act in certain ways to prevent devastating domestic or international repercussions' (1983, p. 46).

Yet what Tetlock seems to be neglecting in this instance, is that these constraints are also dependent on how the individual interprets them. Research has shown that during times of crisis power generally becomes concentrated in the hands of the leader (Byman & Pollack, 2001, p. 109; Hermann & Kegley, 1995, p. 515), making his interpretation of the situation essential. What is considered to be 'devastating' is a subjective assessment and dependent on the individuals' priorities and motives. Early work on foreign policy analysis in fact started with the premise that it was the 'definition of the situation' rather than an objective assessment thereof that was determinant for the choice to be made (Snyder *et al* cited in Houghton, 2007, p. 31).

This research therefore challenges the notion that while IR provides useful insight into the structure, FPA rather provides insight into the variability that remains after taking into account the structural conditions (Hudson, 2005,

p. 4). Although FPA may be able to explain what seems illogical when analysed from a systemic perspective, the added value of FPA does not lie solely in the remaining variance that cannot be explained by IR theory. The relationship is better conceptualized by acknowledging that the systemic factors provide a substantial amount of the relevant factors that are subsequently interpreted by the individual decision maker. Indeed, as Ripley observes, '[t]he global system creates constraints and opportunities, but these must be perceived by actors in order to have an effect' (Ripley, 1993, p. 410). In this sense, structural factors certainly have a major influence on foreign policy behaviour as it provides the foundation of what is to be analysed by the decision maker. While Hudson is correct in holding that the interactions between states are the outcome of individual decision makers, making FPA the ground of IR, at the same time, IR is likewise the ground of FPA because the structural variables provide individuals with the 'data' they need to interpret in order to make the decision. From this perspective the concern of Singer that it is only at the systemic level that international relations can be studied as a whole, seems to be unfounded (Singer, 1961). By studying the individual and his interpretation of the situation, indirectly one is incorporating systemic relationships into the analysis to the extent that previous interactions between states and the relationship between them influence the decision makers' interpretation of the situation. As Houghton also argues, the levels of analysis are mutually constituted (Houghton, 2007, p. 41). She explains, 'it is in the cognition and information processing of an actual human agent that all explanatory levels of FPA are in reality integrated' (Hudson, 2005, p. 10).

The debate revolving around the appropriate level of analysis, often referred to as the agent *versus* structure debate, will probably never be completely settled. Singer points out that the appropriate level of analysis depends on the questions the researcher seeks to answer (Singer, 1961). This research seeks to contribute to the analysis of the interaction among states, by bringing a new perspective on how studying the individual and his rationality might be improved and why this is especially important when the focus lies with dictatorial leaders.

5.3. RATIONAL CHOICE

The differences between IR and FPA have played an important role in the rational choice literature. Rationality and power on the one hand, and beliefs, emotions and motivations on the other hand were often seen as the components of two opposing theoretical frameworks. The former relating to rational choice theory in IR and the latter related to behavioural research programmes within FPA, which are often implicitly defined as deviating from rational choice standards (Snidal, 2002, p. 75; Walker, 2011a, p. 7). IR theory, as explained, tends to study the 'states as actors' and the constraints which stem from the international arena.

FPA, on the other hand takes into account all the constraints that are imposed on individual decision makers, including those coming from within the state and constraints stemming from within the individuals themselves (Walker, 2011a, p. 7). Accordingly, while many IR theories have as a logical point of departure the state as a rational unitary actor (Fearon, 1998, p. 298), FPA theories explicitly point out that the individual decision makers within these states are not capable of living up to the standards of perfect rationality. This might be because of either their own cognitive and emotional limitations or because of the manner in which they are influenced by their immediate surroundings and inner circle of advisors (Mintz & DeRouen, 2010; Renshon & Renshon, 2008; Stein, 2012).

As one of the dominant IR theories, realists view the state as a rational unitary actor that searches for security in an anarchical world. Since the Treaty of Westphalia, states are the logical units of analysis and it is argued that the behaviour of states is rational, meaning that their behaviour is determined by '"national interest" usually defined in terms of survival, security, power and relative capabilities' (Holsti, 2005, p. 16). Ripley notes, 'neorealists avoid the thorny theoretical problems associated with subjectively derived "definitions of the situation" by assuming rational behaviour by states. ... Rationality ought to be understood as a "hard core" assumption of neorealism and one of the most important features distinguishing it from FPDM [foreign policy decision-making]' (Ripley, 1993, pp. 407-408). In realist IR theory as well as liberal IR tradition, the crucial goals are subject to instrumental rationality (Forsberg, 2010, p. 38)[53], meaning that 'given their existing preferences, people are expected to engage in an appropriate end-means calculation' (Stein, 2012, p. 132).

When rational actors engage in bargaining, conflicts or negotiation game theory can be used to model their interactions (McDermott, 2004b, p. 47). Deterrence theories are, for instance, often presented in terms of a game theoretical analysis and rely on the notion that states are rational (Berejikian, 2002, pp. 165-169).[54] Game theory is a method that can help to understand decision-making by highlighting the different options states have when dealing with each other (Mintz & DeRouen, 2010, p. 62). Large N studies are often used by rational choice theorists to test their hypotheses, simplifying reality on the basis of explicit assumptions (McDermott, 2004b, p. 53).

The supposed strength of conceptualizing the state as rational unitary actor was that it would allow the researcher to avoid having to be concerned with motives and ideological preferences (Morgenthau cited in Holsti, 2005, p. 16). The assumption was that this unitary actor was able to maximize his goals on the basis of the necessary information. According to Joe Hagan, systemic theories hold

53 Constructivist theories generally offer an alternative to rational choice approaches since they come more from the sociological traditions rather than the economic literature on which rational choice models are usually based (McDermott, 2004b, p. 47).

54 Berejikian (2002) forms an exception and presents a cognitive theory of deterrence.

> 'that decision makers respond more or less directly to the systemic imperatives posed by an anarchic international order. Particularly in international crises, the premise is that the dangers of war are so clear-cut that decision makers recognize the threat and can quickly agree on strategies to deal with it, focus exclusively on the goal of national security, and have the foreign policy authority necessary to commit the state's resources in responding to the threat' (2001, p. 10).

In short, states and their elites were more or less viewed as 'rational actors in pursuit of a few basic goals and interests while overwhelmingly constrained by their structural environment' (Rosati, 2000, p. 48).

The different roles rational choice theory plays in IR and FPA also stems from a discord in their theoretical foundations. While IR tends to rely on rational choice theory which is borrowed from economics, FPA relies more heavily on insights from (social) psychology to understand the limits of rational decision-making (Holsti, 2005, p. 31). Therefore, to the extent that FPA makes use of rational choice, they have done so often in order to show it is rather impossible for people to live up to the expectations imposed by rational choice theory. It is sometimes even argued FPA started because its founding fathers tried to disprove the rational unitary actor assumption in IR (Houghton, 2007). IR thus generally relies on a 'thin' model of rationality in which states respond to rewards and punishments stemming from other states in the international system. In the 'thick' model of rationality, on the other hand, states are also confronted with limitations stemming from within the state and account is taken of the limitations of the individuals' own cognitive and motivational biases (Walker, 2011b, p. 23). When states are presumed to be homogeneous actors, who act on the basis of thin rationality, this may be described as the billiard ball model of IR. States will simply 'collide' with each other like billiard balls on the basis of systemic constraints (Walker, 2011b, p. 23). This contrasts sharply with the 'thick' version of rationality, where behaviour cannot be conceptualized as mere collisions but as actions for which decisions need to be taken (Walker, 2011b, p. 23).

The proposition that individuals may function as rational decision makers imposes stringent requirements on their individual capabilities. In order to behave perfectly rationally the actor must follow the rules specified by the rational actor model (Verba, 1961, p. 106). However, the standards of perfectly rational behaviour are indeed so stringent that it is impossible for an individual to live up to them (Renshon & Renshon, 2008, p. 511). Generally, the characteristics or rules of rational behaviour are that it involves a means-ends analysis, and that the alternative is chosen which maximizes the goal (Verba, 1961, p. 107). It involves purposive, goal-oriented action based on consistent preferences that are ranked and transitive to obtain the most subjective expected utility (MacDonald, 2003, p. 552). Transitivity means that when an individual prefers A to B and B to C, then he must logically also prefer A to C (McDermott, 2004b, p. 52). In addition, dominance and invariance are norms that the individual has to conform to in order for the behaviour to be classified as rational. Dominance means that the decision maker will have to prefer the option that is superior to other options on the relevant characteristics. Invariance means that the order or method in which options are presented does not influence the preference (McDermott, 2004b, p. 52).

When more than one value guides the behaviour, these should be listed in order of importance and the alternatives should be analysed accordingly. They need to be assessed on their merits and all possible alternatives should be considered (Verba, 1961, p. 107). Considering an alternative, on its merits entails that the actor will only consider those values that are affected by the choice for an alternative and thus requires the actor to have all relevant and accurate information to make this decision. In addition, it means that the calculations must be made consciously (Verba, 1961, p. 108). According to Verba, the rational actor model 'allows one to consider all decision makers alike' as long as one knows the other person's goals (Verba, 1961, p. 106). Most rational choice models, however, cannot provide the tools to analyse the nature or origin of the preferences (McDermott, 2004b, p. 14). Snidal contends that rational choice theory can accommodate also goals that are not material but normative or even ideational (Snidal, 2002, p. 73), but there has been 'a strong bias towards material self-interest' (Forsberg, 2010, p. 38; Hechter, 1994, pp. 318-323).

It is readily admitted by Verba that this model is a simplification, both in terms of the individual's own limited capabilities for self-awareness, and computational skills, and because it often concerns group decision-making where different group members might have different goals they hope to obtain (Verba, 1961, pp. 109-112). Assumptions of information certainty and goal maximization do not seem to be realized in actuality, there is often uncertainty regarding the available information, there may be multiple and competing goals, and authority might be dispersed with multiple actors and organizational units having an influence in the decision-making process (Hagan, 2001, pp. 10-11). Insights of FPA thus not only revealed there often is not one unitary actor pulling the strings (Hermann, 2001, p. 47), but also that there are limitations to rational computation that the individual has to deal with while executing their problem solving tasks (Houghton, 2007, p. 25; Mintz & DeRouen, 2010, p. 6).

The decision-making literature therefore points out that only a much more limited kind of rationality can realistically be assumed. As Tanter explains,

> 'as with game-theory, the decision-making scheme assumes rationality, but rationality is a more limited concept than the comprehensive version assumed in game theory. In game theory goals are ranked, all alternatives are specified, consequences are calculated and rational choice consists of selecting the value-maximizing alternative. In the decision-making scheme, however, men are bounded by: (1) the lack of explicit preference ordering; (2) incomplete information on alternatives and (3) inadequate computational skills to calculate the consequences of each option' (Tanter, 1972, p. 10).

In this sense it may be more logical, as Simon did, to identify two kinds of rationality. According to Simon:

> 'If the characteristics of the choosing organism are ignored and we consider only those constraints that arise from the external situation, then we may speak of substantive or objective rationality, that is, behaviour can be adjudged objectively to be optimally adapted to the situation.
>
> On the other hand if we take into account the limitations of knowledge and computing power of the choosing organism, then we may find it incapable of making objectively optimal choices. If, however, it uses methods of choice that are as effective as its decision-making and problem-solving means permit, we may speak of procedural or bounded rationality, that is, behaviour that is adaptive within the constraints imposed *both* by the external situation and by the capabilities of the decision maker' (1985, p. 294).

To asses bounded rational behaviour there is no need to have much information about the objective situation, unless this influences the subjective perspective (Simon, 1985, p. 294). Here again it becomes important to reiterate the decision-making perspective that actors behave in accordance with their 'definition of the situation' rather than relying on the assumption that states operate on objectively rational criteria (Holsti, 2005, p. 24; Ripley, 1993, pp. 407-408). Their definition of the situation and perception of the world will influence their preferences, be influential in what they consider the likely course of events, and will thus determine what is rational behaviour for them.

Whereas with perfect rationality people are expected to maximize utility, bounded rationality rather finds people 'satisficing', meaning that not all options are considered. Bounded rationality acknowledges that people are incapable of this. Rather, people simplify reality and choose the option that is good enough. Once an acceptable alternative is found the individual will not continue to search for better alternatives (Meslin, 1981, p. 199; Mintz & DeRouen, 2010, p. 34).

Miscalculations and other errors do not mean the actor behaved irrationally (McDermott, 2004b, p. 51). An undesirable end result does not even have to be the result of a mistake or stem from irrational behaviour. An event which rightfully was considered unlikely to happen may occur anyway, leading to an undesirable course of events even though the decision-making process was rational (McDermott, 2004b, p. 51). According to Simon it is only irrational when there is no deliberate calculation but may be attributed to passion or impulse without 'the mediation of thought' (1985, p. 301), and even in those situations where behaviour appears to be irrational can those deviations only be analysed in contrast to a 'baseline of rationality' (Snidal, 2002, p. 80).[55] In

[55] It is not argued here, however, that psychology *only* explains emotions and mistakes as deviations from the rational baseline. For a more elaborate discussion on the relationship

order to analyse individual decision makers it therefore becomes important to map what is considered rational decision-making but also all the constraints on the rational decision-making process and to specify when the behaviour is considered irrational.

5.4. THE BOUNDS AND LIMITATIONS OF THE RATIONAL UNITARY ACTOR MODEL

Studying the bounds of individual rational decision-making is a complicated task because, as Renshon and Renshon point out, 'what leaders see is, to a substantial extent, filtered through the multiple, though inconsistent lenses of their own psychologies and beliefs, subject as well to significant cognitive limitations' (2008, p. 509). Factors that hamper rational decision-making stem from within the individual and his immediate surroundings since foreign policy decision-making is often done under time pressure and in highly stressful situations which may contribute to suboptimal decisions (Renshon & Renshon, 2008, p. 513). In order to closely examine the bounds imposed upon rational decision-making, it thus becomes imperative to consider the broader domestic context, surroundings of the decision maker as well as his immediate advisors and the factors that stem from within the individual which may hamper perfectly rational decision-making.

5.4.1. DOMESTIC FACTORS AND FOREIGN POLICY

As Putnam puts forth, more interesting than debating whether domestic politics determine international politics or the other way around, is analysing when and how they influence each other (Putnam, 1988, p. 427). Part of the work that was developed within foreign policy analysis then also looks at national factors which may influence the decision maker and his decision-making process. Some of the national factors that may be influential in foreign policy are related to the characteristics, interests or institutional arrangements within a country and are often related to how the leader deals with these elements. Hermann and Kegley, for instance, use the democratic peace theory which puts forward the notion that democracies do not wage war against each other, to look inside the state by relating it to the leaders' perspectives and leadershipstyles (Hermann & Kegley, 1995). Other scholars, rather, focus on the influence of public opinion and election cycles and how this may impact foreign policy.

between psychology and rational choice and what each can explain in relation to the other see, Mercer (2005).

Leaders may, for instance, want to deflect domestic tensions by shifting attention from the domestic political arena to foreign policy by using force, the influence of the media, public opinion more generally and election cycles have also been researched in this respect (Mintz & DeRouen, 2010, pp. 130-133; 160-162). Economic reasons are also said to influence foreign policy decisions, and states are therefore often accused of having imperialistic motives (Mintz & DeRouen, 2010, p. 130).

Putnam tried to conceptualise the relationship between the different levels of analysis as a two-level game (Putnam, 1988). In the first level, the leader tries to find agreement with other state leaders through international negotiation, but subsequently at the second level, these agreements need to be acceptable for his constituency. The overlap between what is possible at the international level and what is acceptable at a national level is conceptualized as the 'win set' for the country (Putnam, 1988, p. 437). By analysing the two levels it is possible to analyse the role domestic politics play in international negotiation and chances for success of an agreement at the first level (Putnam, 1988, pp. 435-441).

Poliheuristic theory tried to breach the gap between rational and cognitive decision-making theories in a different two-step process (Mintz & DeRouen, 2010, p. 78). In the first step the range of alternatives is reduced through cognitive shortcuts, and subsequently the rational choice approach may explain the option that is eventually chosen (Mintz & DeRouen, 2010, p. 78). In this two-step process domestic politics are viewed as highly important. They are 'the essence of decision' (Mintz & DeRouen, 2010, p. 78). The word itself refers, on the one hand, to the many (poly) heuristics (shortcuts) that play a role in the decision-making process, but at the same time 'poli' is said to refer to the notion that gains and losses are measured in political terms (Mintz & DeRouen, 2010, p. 79). The actor's self-interest and political survival remains paramount which causes domestic politics to have an important impact on foreign policy decision-making (Mintz & DeRouen, 2010, p. 79). The theory states that individuals will first eliminate options which will have negative repercussions on the most important dimension of concern, the domestic political situation (Kinne, 2005, p. 115). The poliheuristic bias may lead to suboptimal decisions as individuals avoid alternatives that may hurt them politically or personally (Mintz & DeRouen, 2010, p. 43). Kinne points out that some actions that may seem wholly irrational when only taking the international setting into account, may make sense from a domestic political context (Kinne, 2005, p. 127). Holsti alternatively emphasized less pragmatic concerns but stressed the importance of how the elite perceived the role of the nation and its place in the international arena with his national role conception theory (Hudson, 2012, p. 25).

5.4.2. THE INFLUENCE OF ORGANIZATIONS AND GROUPS ON DECISION-MAKING

Several theories analyse within the state at the group and organizational level, how rational decision-making may be distorted because of the manner in which organizations work and how groups of individuals interact with each other within these organizations. Irving Janis took a closer look at the influence group dynamics had on the decision-making process. Janis argued 'groupthink' may distort the decision-making process when the desire to maintain group consensus can hamper reaching an optimal outcome (in Hudson, 2012, p. 20). Dissent is stifled or even punished and the group essentially creates a situation of self-censorship (Mintz & DeRouen, 2010, p. 44). It is more likely to occur when there is no impartial leader who tolerates dissent (Mintz & DeRouen, 2010, p. 45). In this situation the search for information is incomplete, alternatives are not sufficiently looked at and as a result groups come to reach decisions that the individuals would not have chosen on their own (Mintz & DeRouen, 2010, p. 45; Moghaddam, 2013, p. 127).

Graham Allison developed a three pronged analysis of the Cuban missile crisis. Firstly, Allison used what he called a rational policy model, thereafter he focused on the organizational process model, and finally, he looked into a bureaucratic-politics model (Allison, 2005, p. 403). Through this study, he showed how decision-making within large organizations can impact the outcome of the decision. The organization in those instances will put its own survival at the top of the list of priorities and will defend its 'turf' in relation to other organizational entities. In addition, standard operating procedures (SOP) may be developed which can hamper other more innovative initiatives of those higher up (Hudson, 2012, p. 21). Both theories have been criticized and refined in subsequent work but have remained highly influential in opening up the black box of the state and analysing more closely the decision-making process (Hudson, 2012, pp. 20-21).[56] Both authors with their work showed the limits of the rational choice paradigm and came up with alternative perspectives from which to explain foreign policy.

The aforementioned Graham Allison was a mentor of Steinbruner and was influential in the latter's work on cybernetic theory of decision-making (Meslin, 1981, p. 195) This theory applies both to the individual as well as to the group level decision-making (Mintz & DeRouen, 2010, p. 70). Cybernetics can be used to analyse very simple decision-making mechanisms (J. D. Steinbruner, 1974, p. 13). In the cybernetic paradigm the individual avoids outcome calculations but rather relies on procedures to process information, and through this process creates outcomes even though 'psychologically he is not engaged in the pursuit of an explicit end result' (J. D. Steinbruner, 1974, p. 66). Steinbruner showed

[56] For a more detailed discussion, see McDermott (2004, p. 239-260).

that individuals often do not maximize expected utility, or make probalistic judgements or assess how to optimally balance competing objectives, rather the individual simplifies the world, working towards one objective (J. Steinbruner, 1976, pp. 235-237). According to Mintz and DeRouen, it takes the 'appearance of a programmed response' (Mintz & DeRouen, 2010, p. 69). What Steinbruner calls 'the cybernetic paradigm' is based on 'selective feedback and programmed operations' (J. D. Steinbruner, 1974, p. 61). In the extreme, behaviour is not 'so much related to the problem at hand as it is to past experience. This decision maker monitors a small set of "critical variables" and his values consist in keeping these variables within tolerable ranges' (J. D. Steinbruner, 1974, p. 63). Steinbruner compares his cybernetic theory to the organizational model of Graham Allison (J. D. Steinbruner, 1974, p. 77). In an organizational subunit, too, the decision makers do not actually attempt to calculate outcomes, but monitor feedback variables and merely take into account the effect of their actions through these variables (J. D. Steinbruner, 1974, p. 73).

This process is largely routine and explains that

> 'as long as acceptable levels of performance are being registered, the organization proceeds routinely, with subunits performing their programmed activities without intervention. The occasion for what we may call a decision (a choice between alternatives) arises when an established performance measure fails to achieve the levels defined as acceptable' (J. D. Steinbruner, 1974, p. 74).

The cybernetic paradigm thus predicts rigidity in large scale decision processes (J. Steinbruner, 1976, p. 239) and a tendency to only make adjustments in the decision-making process 'at the margins' (Mintz & DeRouen, 2010, p. 70). Since presidents rely on organizations, with all their constraints, and require consensus of their advisors, purely rational decisions are not possible (Meslin, 1981, p. 197). Next to these organizational constraints, however, as Steinbruner and others also have pointed out, the decision makers themselves also have limited computational capacities and cognitive restraints (Hudson, 2012; Rosati, 2000; J. D. Steinbruner, 1974, p. 65; 112).

5.4.3. SIMPLIFYING A COMPLEX WORLD

In order to make a decision, a leader has to make a judgement of the situation (McDermott, 2004b, p. 58). These involve an evaluation on the basis of internal values and beliefs and are based 'on a subjective, personal, or idiosyncratic notion' of the likelihood a particular event will occur (McDermott, 2004b, p. 58). The mind of the decision maker is not a '*tabula rasa*' when the decision-making process commences. The individual relies, amongst others, on his beliefs, attitudes, experience, memories, values and his conception of self and the world around him to guide the decision-making process (Hudson, 2012, p. 23). Although beliefs are properties of individuals, they are influenced by, and depend on, the collective, shaped by the time period and generation to which a leader belongs (Hermann & Hagan, 1998, p. 132; Snidal, 2002, p. 75). The underlying assumption of foreign policy analysis is that these beliefs influence behaviour (Rosati, 1995, p. 64).

Due to the nature of foreign policy decision-making, where people act under stress, in a highly uncertain environment decision makers will have to act instinctively, relying on 'basic strategic worldviews, operational codes, heuristics, preferences, leadership strategies and psychological proclivities of the high-level decision makers' (Renshon & Renshon, 2008, p. 514). Decision makers often operate in highly stressful crisis situations and although people vary substantially in their ability to tolerate stress, it often constrains open minded decision-making (Rosati, 2000, p. 70). In this manner, it differs substantially from rational choice. While rational choice tends to assume individuals make decisions consciously and thoughtfully, the cognitive paradigm acknowledges that very often people act automatically and subconsciously (Rosati, 2000, p. 51).

Individuals may use either compensatory patterns to search for relevant information or non-compensatory patterns. In the former pattern, all aspects of an alternative are reviewed and downsides in certain respects may be compensated when the alternative is highly satisfactory in an alternative dimension. The non-compensatory approach relies on shortcuts and heuristics and will discard alternatives that do not meet the requirements of the individual decision maker (Mintz & DeRouen, 2010, p. 34). Alternatives may be discounted in the non-compensatory model because it does not satisfy one facet which is of paramount importance, or several selected dimensions may be chosen against which the alternative is compared (Mintz & DeRouen, 2010, p. 35).

Choosing between competing values is often very difficult for individuals. It is particularly difficult for individuals when they are faced with a 'taboo trade off' involving things of finite value (e.g. money) and of infinite value (e.g. lives of human beings) (Renshon & Renshon, 2008, p. 517). Decision makers may encounter cognitive dissonance when they are faced with having to give up a value that is particularly important to the individual, leading them to rationalize their choice by exaggerating the importance of the chosen value and denigrating any other choices that were available (Renshon & Renshon, 2008, p. 517). Because individuals find it so difficult to compare inherently different values, they simplify their choice by employing different heuristics (Renshon & Renshon, 2008, p. 517).

These heuristics often result in biases that affect foreign policy decision-making in predictable ways. Some are related to the fact that people are just 'not Bayesians: they do not mathematically calculate the odds of future failure based on past experience prior to decision-making' (McDermott, 2004b, p. 59;

68). Rather, people predict likelihood and frequency on the basis of 'initial values that are then insufficiently adjusted to reach new estimates' (McDermott, 2004b, p. 67). This heuristic is referred to as anchoring and adjustment (McDermott, 2004b, p. 67). In addition, people also tend to assume that chance self corrects (law of small numbers) and do not sufficiently take into account that eventually 'a given measurement will revert to the mean', and often tend to assume specific scenarios to be more likely than general ones when the specific scenarios conform to their stereotypes (representativeness heuristic) (McDermott, 2004b, pp. 59-63). People are also influenced by the ease and speed of associations in their memory or imagination although these are not necessarily linked to the objective likelihood of an event occurring (availability heuristic) (McDermott, 2004b, p. 64).[57]

Early work particularly focused on the need of individuals to have cognitive consistency and avoidance of information which does not fit into their belief system (Rosati, 2000, p. 56). Thereafter the decision maker was characterized as a 'cognitive miser' who simplified information, particularly when the environment was uncertain and complex (Rosati, 2000, pp. 56-57). Although functional in the mind of the decision maker, it was contended from the social cognition perspective that different situations evoked different belief systems and that these beliefs might be much less consistent than originally emphasized by cognitive consistency theory (Rosati, 2000, p. 57). Both perspectives seem to carry truth with different people having more or less consistent belief systems, depending, among other things, on the level of expertise and experience (Rosati, 2000, p. 57).

> 'Although individuals may have little difficulty making sense of situations that are relatively stable and familiar in terms of their beliefs, complex and uncertain situations may result in much cognitive inconsistency and confusion, especially if individuals do not have sufficient knowledge and well developed belief systems for providing some degree of understanding' (Rosati, 2000, p. 59).

Rosati suggests that some leaders have grand designs or ideologies, but this is not always the case. Whether they do or they do not however is important for explaining the choices they make (Rosati, 2000, p. 56).

People interpret the world on the basis of a set of beliefs and personal constructs (including 'images' and 'schemas') (Rosati, 2000, p. 52). Images are mental representations that frame a complicated world, essentially allowing us to categorise people and events into stereotypes (Mintz & DeRouen, 2010, p. 101). Common patterns of perception and misperception are, amongst others, rooted in tendencies to categorize and stereotype (Rosati, 2000, p. 59). A leader's

57 McDermott (2004) relies heavily on the work of Kahneman and Tversky who have been criticized in several respects, *inter alia*, because their laboratory experiments would cannot easily be translated into the real world. For an overview of the specific critiques see McDermott, pp. 68-69.

beliefs and belief system may thus have a powerful effect on the decision-making process. The belief system underlies inferences about 'the preferences of both Self and Other regarding policy outcomes' (Walker & Shafer cited in Mintz & DeRouen, 2010, p. 101). One of the most popular methods to analyse a leader's belief system is 'the operational code' which assumes that leaders have a coherent set of beliefs which influences foreign policy (Rosati, 2000, p. 54). Alexander George built upon the 'operational code' concept from Nathan Leites, who, according to George, was referring to 'a set of general beliefs about fundamental issues of history and central questions of politics as these bear, in turn, on the problem of action' (George, 1969, p. 191). Although the operational code does not determine decision-making, it certainly influences it as it underlies the norms, standards, and guidelines which shape the choice of strategy and tactics as well as how he structures and weighs different courses of action (George, 1969, p. 191). Within the operational code, two sets of beliefs are clearly demarcated by George. Philosophical beliefs refer to assumptions and premises about, among others, the 'fundamental nature of politics, the nature of political conflict [and] the role of the individual in history' (George, 1969, p. 199). Instrumental beliefs, on the other hand, rather refer to beliefs about ends-means relationships (George, 1969, p. 199). The operational code was aimed to allow for a more systematic study of ruling groups and individual leaders (George, 1969, p. 220), and has sparked some further interesting studies of foreign policy decision makers (McDermott, 2004b, p. 220; Rosati, 1995, p. 56).

A particularly difficult distinction to make is whether an error is the result of motivated bias or a non-motivated cognitive error. According to Renshon and Renshon, 'a motivated bias is a systematic distortion of information acquisition or appraisal caused by the decision makers' psychological investment in a certain view or understanding regardless of the facts' (2008, p. 512). Non-motivated cognitive errors alternatively are not motivated by any desire to maintain well-being or consistency (Renshon & Renshon, 2008, p. 512). Motivated cognitive errors may be caused by personality needs, or alternatively may be rooted in beliefs (Renshon & Renshon, 2008, p. 512). The more ideological leader will 'interpret the environment through a lens that is structured by their attitudes, beliefs and motives', causing them to have difficulty to change their attitudes and beliefs because 'they selectively perceive information from the environment' (Hermann & Kegley, 1995, p. 521). Biases for this reason often lead to misperception (Mintz & DeRouen, 2010, p. 38).

In addition, people oversimplify causal inferences by over or underestimating one's own importance, and deny responsibility for what goes wrong while claiming credit for positive outcomes, by not recognizing coincidences or actions stemming from unintended consequences but assuming they are planned (Rosati, 2000, pp. 61-62) through pessimism or wishful thinking and through the fundamental attribution error. The latter refers to the tendency to overemphasize situational factors to account for one's own behaviour while overemphasising dispositional causes to explain the behaviour of others. This effect may be exacerbated by the halo effect, where oneself and allies are automatically perceived in a positive light, and the adversaries, in a negative light (Rosati, 2000, p. 61). How a leader perceives his adversary in this manner is likely to impact the policy choice he makes (Renshon & Renshon, 2008, p. 528). Furthermore, leaders tend to be overconfident and overestimate their country's capabilities, underestimate their opponent, while generally focusing more on short term benefits rather than long-term problems (Mintz & DeRouen, 2010, pp. 41-42).

Another method to cope with the complexity of a situation is through the use of historical analogies (Rosati, 2000, p. 63). According to Hagan, 'where there is "uncertainty" ... government's responses will depend upon how leaders perceive and interpret the threats based upon their own belief system' (Hagan, 2001, p. 11). When the decision maker encounters a situation that resembles past experiences, this will often result in intuitive decision-making where the leader will not consider all the information again but will quickly choose an alternative and believe that what was successful in the past will be effective again (Mintz & DeRouen, 2010, p. 27). The decision maker may have preconceived notions of what the best alternative would be, which is sometimes referred to as the preference over preference bias (Mintz, 2004, p. 99). These phenomena may lead to overgeneralizations and the discounting of inconsistent information and alternative possibilities (Mintz & DeRouen, 2010, pp. 27; 39-40). The decision maker may lock on one alternative that had his preference, ignoring other courses of action (Mintz & DeRouen, 2010, p. 40). Several scholars still admit, though that 'reliance on prior beliefs and expectations is not irrational per se ... it becomes irrational only when perseverance and denial dominate openness and flexibility' (Tetlock & McGuire cited in Kahler, 1998, p. 927).

5.4.4. PERCEPTIONS OF LOSSES AND GAINS

Prospect theory deals with decision-making under conditions of risk (McDermott, 2004b, p. 69). The theory was developed by Kahneman and Tversky as an answer to how people tend to view the prospective losses which might be incurred (McDermott, 2004b, p. 69). It has two phases: the editing phase, which deals with how decisions are presented: and the evaluation phase, covering how choices are made (McDermott, 2004b, p. 69).

In the first phase, contrary to what rational choice assumes, it does matter how a choice is presented as it can significantly affect the decisions made. People, for instance, naturally dislike the more extreme options (McDermott, 2004b, p. 70). The order in which information is presented affects the decision and by presenting more extreme options first subsequent options are likely to sound more reasonable (McDermott, 2004b, p. 67; Mintz & DeRouen, 2010, p. 33). The second phase, the evaluation phase, covers the value function and the weighing function (McDermott, 2004b, p. 70). In terms of the value function, it was discovered that people tend to weigh gains and losses relative to a reference point, for example the status quo, rather than in terms of the final outcome, thus contrasting the expected utility model (McDermott, 2004b, p. 70). People tend to be more risk-taking for losses and risk averse for gains, and a loss hurts more than the equivalent gain pleases (McDermott, 2004b, pp. 71-72). In other words, it is more important to avoid loss than it is to secure gain (Mintz & DeRouen, 2010, p. 76). In addition, in relation to the weighing function low probability events are given too much subjective weight relative to medium and high probability events (McDermott, 2004b, p. 72). According to McDermott, '[t]his phenomenon contributes to the certainty effect, where events that are either certain or impossible are given much greater subjective weight in decision-making than would be normatively justified' (McDermott, 2004b, p. 73).

How different decision makers perceive a loss in relation to the gain, however, is not yet sufficiently theorised in foreign policy analysis. Since foreign policy analysis' roots lie with viewing the world from the perspective of the individual decision maker, this is surprising. As will be argued in the chapter that follows, there are profound reasons to believe similar foreign policy measures will be weighted differently between individuals. And although some scholars do note that sanctions are likely to be ineffective with many dictators as they are likely to allow their populations to suffer (Mintz & DeRouen, 2010, p. 137), systematic study of why some dictators attach more weight to some measures than others, is missing.

5.4.5. EMOTIONS AND IRRATIONALITY

Increasingly, the importance of emotions on foreign policy analysis and international relations is recognized (Bleiker & Hutchison, 2008; Crawford, 2000; Lobel & Loewenstein, 2005; McDermott, 2004a, 2004b; Mercer, 2005, 2010; Sasley, 2011; Stein, 2012). So far, however, it has received relatively little attention by IR scholars and remains under-theorized (Bleiker & Hutchison, 2008; Crawford, 2000, p. 118; Sasley, 2011, p. 453). Most of the work that exists on emotions has focused either on the personality of important persons or the manner in which people tend to respond to their environment (Marcus, 2000). In the former, emotion is studied as part of the personality of the individual leader, and with the latter, emotion is rather related to external events and how people respond to them, even deviating from their characteristic dispositions (Marcus, 2000, p. 222). Leaders are frequently studied as case studies where it often argued that childhood experiences have an impact on adult behaviour, hampering rational decision-making and resulting in systematic misperceptions (Marcus, 2000, p. 226). Recently the study of emotions was given a boost by the onset of the 'neurological revolution' (McDermott, 2004a, p. 692)

As McDermott points out (McDermott, 2004a, p. 691) most people assume that behaviour stems from logical and rational decisions. Not surprisingly then, rational choice and the bounds upon rational decision-making through organizational and cognitive processes, has played a dominant role in IR and FPA theorizing. The relationship between emotion and cognition (Crawford, 2000, pp. 123-129; McDermott, 2004a, p. 692) and between emotion and rationality (Mercer, 2005; Simon, 1985, p. 301; Verba, 1961, p. 108) remains subject to debate.

Scholars discussing the role of rationality in political behaviour tended to qualify behaviour that was based on emotions generally as irrational. According to Verba, rational behaviour does not require the individual to experience no emotion, either in relation to the outcome or during the process of deliberation, but the calculations may not be affected by his emotions. However, Verba nuances his statement by noting that:

> 'This problem is more complex than can be gone into here, for an emotional state may change an individual's value hierarchy and thus affect his calculations. Though one can argue that emotion ought not to affect the means selected, it is more difficult to dismiss as irrational the effect of emotion on one's goals' (1961, p. 108).

Simon, speaking of bounded rationality, also argues that there is behaviour that does not even fall within the sphere of bounded rationality. Some behaviour lies outside what is deliberately calculated. According to Simon, sometimes behaviour must be attributed to passion, to 'powerful impulses that do not permit the mediation of thought' (Simon, 1985, p. 301). Although, according to Simon, passion may result in 'radical irrationality' (Simon, 1985, p. 294), the relationship between emotion and rationality is more complex. Simon himself noted, like Verba, that emotions might be directed towards a particular goal and result in rational behaviour. He gives the example of Hitler, whose all-consuming hatred was directed onto the Jews, and who made arguably rational decisions if one assumes the Jews were to be exterminated to satisfy that anger (Simon, 1985, p. 301).

More recent scholars take this argument further by noting that emotions are a necessary prerequisite for rational behaviour (McDermott, 2004b, p. 153; Mercer, 2005, pp. 93-95), and have more precisely mapped out the different relationships emotions and rationality may have towards each other. Existing literature differentiates at least five different ways in which emotions can impact rationality.[58] The first, has already been mentioned, namely that emotion can lead to irrational behaviour when the behaviour is the resultant of uncontrolled impulses (Simon, 1985, p. 301). Although moderate levels of emotions may actually activate processes that are more deliberate by sending the signal

58 McDermott, 2004 mentions 10 ways in which emotion in general can impact decision-making which have here been reduced to five broader categories on the basis of additional literature to illustrate how they specifically relate to rationality.

something is wrong and deliberation is required, very strong emotions may take control over behaviour. (Kaufman, 1999, pp. 136-137; Lobel & Loewenstein, 2005, p. 1050). High anxiety, for instance, may cause individuals to avoid certain information or to shut down completely, blocking out reality (Crawford, 2000, p. 138). In addition, high emotional tension might 'block access to short-term memory, disorganize logical or inferential thought processes, cause loss of control of body parts and functions (e.g. trembling hands, nausea or headaches), block out rational considerations of benefit and cost and promote acts of aggression or violence' (Kaufman, 1999, p. 139). It may cause behaviour to be reduced to impulse and instinct (Kaufman, 1999, p. 139). Moderate levels of fear, on the other hand, may cause individuals to actually look for more information and answers about possible threats (Crawford, 2000, p. 138). Therefore, secondly, emotions may at the same time also enhance rational capabilities by increasing the accuracy of judgement (McDermott, 2004a, p. 700). However, because a concentration of power generally means a concentration of pressure and responsibility, which is likely to enhance anxiety, better decision-making is likely in democracies than in autocracies (Crawford, 2000, p. 139).

Thirdly, it is possible emotions do not enhance rationality or result in radical irrational behaviour, but it may impose limits, or hamper rational behaviour (Lobel & Loewenstein, 2005, p. 1053). Kaufman therefore argues that next to the cognitive constraints, emotions form an additional constraint to rationality. Bounded rationality arises from insufficient or excessive emotions (Kaufman, 1999, p. 135). McDermott notes moods can affect memory, the selection of historical analogies, affect risk perception, and may bias decision makers or their decisions in several ways, all of which may hamper rational behaviour (2004a, pp. p. 699-701) as the cognitive paradigm has shown as well. Emotions will have an impact on the cognitive capacity of decision makers by limiting the number and types of options an individual may consider and may focus the individuals on particular aspects of information (Hanoch, 2002, p. 3; Mintz & DeRouen, 2010, p. 100). Lobel and Loewenstein pointed to several factors that may undermine deliberate processes among which they mention stress and exhaustion, time pressure but also the heat of the moment emotions may lead people to overreact (2005, pp. p. 1051-1056). Emotions may cause a particular option to be more easily chosen because the amount of information that is to be processed per alternative is limited. Emotions may impact the relevancy of the information coming in, thus introducing selective attention (Mintz & DeRouen, 2010, p. 100). In addition, Lobel and Lowenstein note that people tend to have strong emotional reactions to new phenomenon, 'is highly attuned to visual imagery' and emotions are often sensitive to categorizations. People react much more strongly when something happens to 'us' than when it happens to 'them' (Lobel & Loewenstein, 2005, pp. p. 1055-1058). These categorizations also make it more likely that emotions of the other are misperceived. Particularly when the other is viewed as hostile, misperception seems likely (Crawford, 2000, p. 134). Emotional relationships influence this process. As Crawford explains:

> 'Individuals and groups put their relationships to others into emotional categories that influence their perception of the other, especially how ambiguous actions and situations are interpreted. [...] The prior emotional relationship between groups may influence the assignment of reasons and intentions (attributions) to others' behaviour' (Crawford, 2000, p. 134).

Moods may also influence perception and misperception as it influences risk assessment. Negative moods are likely to lead to an overestimation of a negative outcome and positive moods lead to an overestimation of a positive outcome (Crawford, 2000, p. 143). People who experience negative emotions engage in a careful step-by-step analysis that is characterized by logical consistency whereas positive emotions lead to more creative decision-making which is characterized, however, by the use of more simple heuristics (Crawford, 2000, p. 138; McDermott, 2004a, p. 695). In addition, information that is consistent with a person's mood is often more easily noticed and given more attention (McDermott, 2004b, p. 168)

Fourthly, emotions may impact rational decision-making by impacting the preferences of individuals and may even help to understand the foundation of particular preferences (Kaufman, 1999, p. 136; McDermott, 2004a, p. 699). Emotions may be used to cope with multiple, possibly contradictory goals. Emotions may serve to create a hierarchy among those goals by focusing attention on the most vital one and indicate whether to react fast and instinctively or slow and more considerate (Hanoch, 2002, pp. 8-9). McDermott explains that the brain's 'structural makeup requires that emotional information exert an influence before, and sometimes instead of, higher-level cognitive functioning ... rationality, as we understand it, often requires emotional processing first' (2004a, p. 693). A final manner in which emotions may impact rational decision-making is by influencing utility calculations (McDermott, 2004a, p. p. 700). The decision maker may take the expected emotions that will be brought about by a particular decision into account even though people are usually poor estimators of future emotions (McDermott, 2004a, p. 700).

In sum, although some emotions are so powerful as to result in thoughtless, irrational behaviour, other emotions may be seen as part of the bounded rationality paradigm. Bounded rationality may then be conceptualized to include a mixture of cognitive limitations and emotions (Kaufman, 1999; Walker & Schafer cited in Mintz & DeRouen, 2010, p. 102). Since the focus of this research will be on rational behaviour, emotions will only be analysed to the extent that they can form part of bounded rationality. Ultimately, this means thoughtless impulses will be left aside but emotions which impact preferences, utility calculations, or enhance or place further bounds on rational decision-making will be considered in the analysis. This is a complicated and fluid process since individuals are said to feel before they think, and often even act before they think (Stein, 2012, p. 140).

The focus on the individual as decision maker, although complicated because of the many psychological factors that influence the decision-making process, is important as FPA has shown. Rational choice has been an important theoretical framework in explaining international relations and sparked much of the research within foreign policy, which showed the limitations on the rational decision-making process of individuals. Great strides in studying individual rationality, and the role of the individual leader in determining foreign policy, have been made but more needs to be done. The focus on the individual dictator when trying to make foreign policy more effective is important in this respect because while leaders in general may be influential, the influence of the leader in a non-democratic society is even greater as will be shown below.

5.5. THE DICTATOR AS A RATIONAL UNITARY ACTOR?

Because this research seeks to explain how the international community, and countries unilaterally, can make its foreign policy more effective to stop or mitigate the mass atrocities, what is most important is how the target of those foreign policy mechanisms responds to them. Considering the different roles that international and domestic factors, institutional and organizational aspects, and the individual leader may all play in determining foreign policy behaviour, it should be questioned whether it is justified to focus our analysis predominantly on the individual dictatorial leader. Particularly, can we look at the individual dictator as the crucial explanatory factor determining the response to foreign policy mechanisms of other countries or organizations? Smith *et al* warn that scholars must be weary of equating the 'leaders' rationale as the *cause* of a particular action' (emphasis in original S. Smith *et al.*, 2012a, p. 6). One of the primary dilemmas in rational choice as well as psychological models is thus the problem of aggregation (Kahler, 1998, p. 929). It brings us back to the initial debate of finding the appropriate level of analysis.

Much of the literature described above, was developed while studying democracies. Foreign policy theories that focus on domestic factors stress elements like the constraints imposed by their constituency, public opinion and the domestic political situation in general. Ripley, for instance, notes 'decision-makers do not operate in isolation. They rely on organizational and institutionalized procedures in the task of formulating, choosing, and implementing policy options' (Ripley, 1993, p. 408). In general leaders have to manage domestic constraints and domestic opposition may influence foreign policy decision-making (Hermann & Hagan, 1998, pp. 129-133). However, as has been explained in chapter two, these take on a completely different dynamic in dictatorships. Gourevitch notes that although authoritarian regimes cannot easily be seen as unitary states, constraints of institutions and the selectorate within authoritarian regimes take on an entirely different role, and research on democracies cannot simply be transferred onto authoritarian regimes (Gourevitch, 2002, p. 318).

This does not mean, of course, that dictators do not face any domestic constraints. As Frantz and Ezrow note, 'in dictatorships, policies essentially require the tacit support of two actors: the dictator and the dictator's elite support group', whom they need to stay in power (Ezrow & Frantz, 2011, p. 114). Although it should be taken into account that dictators need the support of essential members of the elite, they do have more power to change and shape institutions and have comparatively large discretionary powers (Ezrow & Frantz, 2011, pp. 149-151; Gourevitch, 2002; Kinne, 2005). Post (2004, p. 19 referring to the work of Greenstein) likewise states: 'a totalitarian dictator with near total control over his political environment has a much greater sway of action than a democratically elected president or prime minister in a situation with built-in checks and balances'. As was explained in Chapter 2, the elite, in general, are also less likely to oppose a course of action that the authoritarian leader seeks to follow. In personalist dictatorships particularly, the dictator is able to select the elite whom he feels is most likely to follow his lead and agree with him, or dismiss whomever dares to disagree. (Ezrow & Frantz, 2011, pp. 114-117). This is less so with military or single party dictatorships, with elites in military dictatorships generally being much more in sync than those in single party dictatorships, where there is likely to be more differences of opinion on policy decisions (Ezrow & Frantz, 2011, pp. 114-115). The personality of personal dictators is therefore particularly important when studying its policies because they are not hampered or held back by institutions (Ezrow & Frantz, 2011, p. 235).

A consequence of this inherent tendency towards agreement is that groupthink is more likely. According to Mintz & DeRouen, groupthink becomes particularly likely when the leader does not tolerate dissent (Mintz & DeRouen, 2010, p. 45). This tends to be the case quite often with dictators, especially personalist dictators, who surround themselves with sycophants. In personalist dictatorships, loyalty is often valued more than competence and these dictators are often surrounded by 'yes men' who are likely to provide them with poor intelligence out of fear of upsetting the dictator. This will obviously increase the chances of foreign policy errors (Ezrow & Frantz, 2011, pp. 156-157). According to Moghaddam, while research on groupthink continues to have mixed results,

> 'there is general agreement that groupthink is more likely to come about when a group functions in isolation from expert opinion, is highly cohesive, has a directive

> leader with a preferred solution, and there is a lack of procedures for critical assessment' (2013, p. 129).

While there is some research that suggests that more dedicated members of the inner circle will object when a group drifts to unwise decision-making (Moghaddam, 2013, p. 129), it is doubtful whether this conclusion would hold up in a dictatorship, where members of the inner circle might pay with their lives for taking a different stance (Ezrow & Frantz, 2011, pp. 159-159). Consequently, dictators are cut off from reality and more inclined to make foreign policy mistakes (Ezrow & Frantz, 2011, p. 159). Analysing the policies of Adolf Hitler and Josef Stalin, Chirot argues information flows were impeded. The party could not be questioned and people were too concerned with their own well-being to give honest policy advice (Chirot, 1994, pp. 162-163). 'By the end', Chirot concludes, 'everyone was too afraid to tell the truth' (1994, p. 164).

The focus of an organizational perspective will however be incorporated in this research, solely with a focus on the individual, meaning that the group will be looked at when it is affecting the decisions of the individual. This is warranted as the research will only incorporate case studies of powerful leaders rather than situations in which the decision maker was either a single group or a coalition of autonomous actors (Hermann, 2001; Hermann *et al.*, 2001).

Particularly in those situations where there is one dominant decision maker, the most appropriate level of theoretical explanation revolves around theories that focus upon 'political cognition, political socialisation and leadership' (Hermann & Hagan, 1998, p. 131). Leaders matter, as they are the ones who interpret international and domestic constraints. They are the ones that 'build expectations, plan strategies, and urge actions on their governments that conform with their judgments about what is possible' (Hermann & Hagan, 1998, p. 126).

The notion that the 'beliefs of leaders and the actions of states are *congruent*', meaning that the belief systems 'match' the actions of the state (Walker, 2011a, p. 58) is more likely to be an accurate depiction of reality when one speaks of dictators, than of democratic leaders. In addition, by the time the international community takes decisive steps to stop the perpetration of atrocity crimes, a crisis situation has often materialized or is impending. This is likely to cause power to concentrate more into the highest levels of government, making the leader a crucial determinant of the course of action that is chosen (Hermann & Kegley, 1995, pp. 515-516).

Having put forward the belief that the dictator warrants a closer look at the individual level of analysis it becomes important how to characterize the leader. Whether or not dictators should be conceptualized as rational actors continues to be subject to debate (Etzioni, 2010; Seliktar & Dutter, 2009). The media is not hesitant to characterize them as mad men, and several scholars also question the extent to which dictators are rational (Krauthammer 2005 cited in Malici;

Thornhill and Ward, 2002 cited in Malici; Etzioni 2010; Seliktar & Dutter, 2009). Within this debate the issue is raised as to what the implications for the foreign policy towards those countries might be and what may be expected from these dictatorial leaders (Seliktar & Dutter, 2009; Etzioni, 2010). The underlying fundamental question is whether seemingly erratic behaviour is truly irrational, or whether we merely do not understand their cost benefit appraisal.

5.6. LEADERSHIP AND PERSONALITY OF AUTOCRATIC AND DEMOCRATIC LEADERS

Scholars who have recognized the importance of leaders have tried to differentiate different types of leaders and the corresponding influence on foreign policy behaviour. Although this produced many valuable insights, unfortunately these types dealt more with personal preferences and personality characteristics, and were wholly separate from the issue of how it could be related to the rationality of the individuals.

Early work developed the crusader-pragmatist dichotomy, which was developed by Stoessinger on the basis of case studies of American diplomacy. The crusader was said to possess 'a missionary zeal to make the world better … He sets out to improve the world but all too often manages to leave it in worse shape than it was before' (cited in Wittner, 1981, pp. 118-119). The pragmatist, on the other hand, was said to be guided by facts, common sense and was always flexible (Wittner, 1981, p. 119). Other comparable typologies are the ideologue *vs.* opportunist of Ziller *et al*, directive *vs.* consultative created by Bass and Valenzi, the task oriented *vs.* relations oriented from Fiedler, and transformative *vs.* transactional from, e.g., Burns (Hermann & Kegley, 1995, p. 511). According to Hermann *et al*

> 'these typologies rest on the assumption that the leadership style of one type of leader is guided by a set of ideas, a cause, a problem to be solved, or an ideology, while the leadership style of the other type arises out of the nature of the leadership context or setting in which the leader finds himself or herself' (Hermann *et al.*, 2001, p. 86).

Hermann *et al.* built on this work and have developed a typology of leaders on the basis of their personality that is based on several dimensions. Important for determining the type of leader is whether the leader is responsive to constraints and whether he is open to information. These dimensions result in four categories of leaders: crusader, strategic, pragmatic and opportunistic. The crusader challenges political constraints and is closed to new information, the strategic leader challenges constraints but is open to information, the pragmatist respects constraints but is closed to information, and the opportunist respects constraints and is open to information. When we add a third dimension, the motivation, another more nuanced typology of leadership styles emerges with eight different types. With respect to motivation Hermann *et al* find leaders to be either problem focused or relationship focused. When a crusader is problem focused, he is labelled expansionistic, and when the crusader is relationship focused, he becomes evangelistic. In the former case, the leader's focus is on expanding one's power and influence, and in the latter case, it is on persuading others to accept the message and join his cause. The strategic leader is subdivided into incremental leaders who are problem focused and aim to maintain their manoeuvrability and flexibility, and charismatic leaders, who are relationship focused, who are set on achieving one's agenda by engaging others and persuading them to act. The pragmatic leader is directive when problem focused, and consultative when he is relationship focused. The former guides policy in the direction that is consistent with one's own views while working within the norms and rules of the current position. The latter is actively monitoring whether others will support or actively oppose what he wants to do. Lastly, the opportunistic leader is reactive when problem focused, and accommodative when relationship focused. The reactive leader is focused on assessing what is possible given the nature of the problem and considering what important constituents will allow. The accommodative leader aims to reconcile differences and builds consensus by empowering others and sharing accountability (Hermann *et al.*, 2001, p. 95).

Hermann & Kegley note that there is reason to believe that democracies facilitate the rise to power of leaders who are responsive to their environments and sensitive to popular pressure. This is important, as they will approach foreign policy problems differently. The more responsive leaders will 'seek to tailor their behaviour to fit the demands of the situation, to ascertain where others stand with regard to an issue, and to estimate how other governments are likely to act before making a decision' (Hermann & Kegley, 1995, p. 522). The more responsive leaders are more hesitant to commit the country's resources unless this enjoys the support of their surroundings and are less likely to pursue extreme policies or initiate war, while more ideological leaders will not adapt as easily as their ideological lenses allow only selective information to filter through (Hermann, Kegley, p. 522). Although it is more likely that responsive leaders rise to the top in democracies and ideological leaders in autocracies, there are many exceptions (Hermann & Kegley, 1995, p. 523). When a responsive leader comes to power in an autocracy, he may not be as concerned with the perception of his policies by the wider public but will pay closer attention to those elite that may impact his time in office, and their behaviour during crises will probably be influenced by the interests of those elite (Hermann & Kegley, 1995, pp. 524-525).

Hermann and Kegley believe that ideologically driven leaders see constraints as things to be overcome, rather than as limitations on their behaviour they should accept. In autocracies leaders will select the immediate group of elite with which they are surrounded also on the basis of whether they share basic conceptions about the world and on whether they are loyal. These leaders are least constrained by domestic political pressures (Hermann & Kegley, 1995, pp. 525-526). In addition, as Hermann and Hagan note, 'leaders tend to extrapolate from their own perspectives in solving problems'; they do this especially when there has been little contact with the other side, but also crusader leaders are more prone to 'see what that leader wants to see' (1998, p. 134).

Although useful, these delineations are not easily meshed together with the abundance of literature focused on individual rationality and its bounds. Only incidentally, reference is made to typical biases that belong to a particular category of leaders. This is a pity because it inhibits incorporating lessons derived from one field into the next. An overarching strategy is, therefore, promising as a means of combining the lessons learned.

5.7. CONCLUSION

Since this research is oriented towards explaining the decision-making process of dictators in relation to the foreign policy of other states, the focus will be on the individual as the primary level of analysis. International relations literature will for the most part be left on the sidelines, as the structural conditions will be predominantly studied through the eyes of the decision maker. The interest here goes toward an analysis of the subjective interpretation of the situation by the individual. Foreign policy analysis theory is therefore more appropriate in dealing with the decision-making process, the decision maker himself and his immediate surroundings. However, there remain some important shortcomings in the existing literature.

Literature stemming from the rational choice paradigm has failed to differentiate between individuals and most of the literature that focused on the bounds of rational decision-making has mainly pointed to general biases and limitations common to people in general. The rational choice assumption has meant that elite were considered to be *equally* rational (Razi, 1988, p. 689). This should be nuanced. Etzioni stresses the importance of acknowledging that 'between the completely irrational actor and the perfectly rational one, there are actors with varying degrees of rationality. In other words, rationality is best treated as a continuous and not as a dichotomous variable' (Etzioni, 2010, p. 432).

Razi similarly emphasizes:

> 'the individuals who make up foreign-policy elites are neither exclusively creatures of reason, nor solely a bundle of subconscious impulses and non-intellectual drives but a combination of both, the mix of which is not constant in time, even for the same elite, or across space i.e. for different elites at the same time' (Razi, 1988, p. 690).

Razi thus argues that rationality must be considered a variable rather than a constant and that a distinction should be made between those who are more or less rational (Razi, 1988, p. 690).

Advances in the cognitive and psychological research into individual rationality made some advances in this direction (e.g. Kowert & Hermann, 1997). Rosati acknowledges this, and states that 'we must understand that individual variation in cognitive styles exists. … similar cognitive patterns for individuals do not automatically trigger similar outcomes, and different individuals may not rely on the same cognitive patterns' (Rosati, 2000, p. 71). However, although gradations and nuances in individual rationality are more prominent within the cognitive and psychological theories within FPA, they still rely on that same form of rationality to highlight deviations from it (Forsberg, 2010, p. 34; 38). The work in this field largely 'accepted rational choice as the default position' and focused on specifying its boundaries (Stein, 2012, p. 132). An extensive gap is materializing because these theories do not offer alternative ideas of what rationality is.

Since irrational behaviour is often understood in terms of a rational baseline (Snidal, 2002, p. 80), it becomes very important to have a good conception of rational behaviour for us not to designate any ill understood or *seemingly* illogical or erratic behaviour as irrational. The latter is particularly a considerable hazard with dictators as they are often unjustifiably qualified as irrational. As Malici contends that 'merely asserting that they are crazy or irrational is too simple and indeed wrong' (Malici, 2011, p. 83). Yet, because there are very few alternative ideas of what rationality is, the presumption is that decision makers have an instrumental rational orientation remains firm (Forsberg, 2010, p. 38).[59] This may be resolved by including other forms of rationality into our analysis of foreign policy.

[59] Exceptions can be found in the work of Etzioni (1988), Forsberg (2010) and Heng (2010), and Morris (1999) from a cultural rather than individual rationality standpoint.

CHAPTER 6
DIFFERENT KINDS OF RATIONALITY: THE WORK OF MAX WEBER

6.1. INTRODUCTION

In line with the argument that the state should not be viewed as a black box, Max Weber likewise argued that collective entities need to be opened up to analyse the individuals who constitute them. On the one hand, he noted in his seminal work *Economy and Society*[60] that sometimes it may be necessary for practical reasons to treat social collectivities as if they were individuals (Weber, 1964, p. 101). On the other hand, he argued that 'for the subjective interpretation of action in sociological work [social collectivities such as states, associations and business corporations] must be treated as *solely* the resultants and modes of particular acts of individual persons', adding that 'for sociological purposes there is no such thing as a collective personality which "acts"' (Weber, 1964, pp. 101-102). Although most sociologists tend to view the task of the sociologist as lying with the analysis of what Levine calls '*supra*individual' formations, according to Weber sociology should seek to understand and interpret individual social action (emphasis in original 2005, p. 101). His types of social action have usually been discussed in relation to his work on rationality which has been highly influential (Levine, 2005, p. 102). Some scholars go as far as to designate Weber as an early forbearer of the rational choice approach (Norkus, 2000, p. 259), yet despite the influence he may have had on the development of rational choice, there is much to be gained by incorporating more of Weber's ideas into the contemporary debate on individual rationality.

Rational choice is sometimes said to be a multilevel enterprise with an important focus on macro level outcomes, leaving the analysis of individuals to decision-making theory which highlights the cognitive and psychological factors which influence human action (Hechter & Kanazawa, 1997, p. 192; Kiser & Hechter, 1998, pp. 802-803; Mintz & DeRouen, 2010, pp. 3-6). However, this dichotomy between rational choice and decision-making analysis as mutually exclusive paradigms is unnecessary. It is important to acknowledge that the

---

60 Original title *Wirtschaft und Gesellschaft* and is translated by Henderson & Parsons as The Theory of Social and Economic Organization.

perfectly rational decision maker is an ideal type. Thin models of rational choice make assumptions about individual action rather than examining it in depth, but through the incorporation of decision-making literature and a bounded and thick version of rationality, which pays more attention to values and beliefs (Hechter & Kanazawa, 1997, p. 194)[61], a theoretical framework can be developed which can serve as a useful analytical tool for in depth case studies.

This research acknowledges the great strides that were made by the cognitive approach and takes the more nuanced bounded rationality as a starting point to analyse the manner in which dictators respond to foreign policy decisions of other states or international institutions. Yet even within the more nuanced literature that takes into account the limits of human rationality, there is a serious simplification in the assumption that individual decision makers do not differ in terms of their rationality (Razi, 1988). Literature on bounded rationality can, and should be nuanced by also incorporating a different kind of rationality.[62] Often within the literature on rational choice only attention is paid to the constraints imposed on the individual and not enough attention is devoted to the subjective realm where the actors' utilities originate. Often this is glanced over with the assumption all people are motivated by private and instrumental goods (Hechter, 1994, p. 318). It will be argued here that the work of Max Weber is useful to open up the discussion on rationality by also including other kinds of rationality and acknowledging the diversity in motivations and belief systems that underlie behaviour. Weber's work is particularly suitable for this purpose since his theory can accommodate the role ideology plays in determining an individual's behaviour. Considering the important role ideology plays in the perpetration of atrocity crimes (Alvarez, 2008, pp. 213-214), the relationship between ideology and rationality becomes important when analysing the decision-making process of the dictators who initiate these destructive acts. The differentiation of two kinds of rationality that Max Weber made may serve as a very useful analytical tool for this purpose.

6.2. RATIONALITY IN THE WORK OF WEBER

Max Weber's types of social action, which will be explained in depth below, may be used to nuance the debate on rationality in international relations.

---

61 See section 5.3 for a full explanation of thin models of rational choice in relation to international relations.

62 That different kinds of rationality exist was also recognized by Snellen who identified political rationality, legal rationality, economic rationality and a technical- and social scientific rationality (1987).

They are part of a large and confusing body of work Weber has written on rationality. Rationality was not a unified concept in Weber's work, its meaning changing with the context in which it was used (Swidler, 1973, p. 35), and the concept evolved throughout Weber's writings (G. H. Mueller, 1979, p. 149; Norkus, 2000, p. 272; S. P. Turner, 1983). The concept remained ambiguous and accommodated several, co-existing, forms of rationality (Levine, 1981, p. 10; Segady, 1988, p. 86; Swidler, 1973, p. 35). Although most scholars admit that rationality is of central importance to the work of Weber (Kalberg, 1980; Segady, 1988, p. 85; Swidler, 1973, p. 35; Wallace, 1990, p. 199; Zafirovski, 2005, p. 90) the different manner in which Weber uses the concept throughout his books and essays has caused confusion. Brubaker, for instance, has found over 16 meanings of the word rational (cited in Segady, 1988, p. 86). The ambiguity in Weber's work has resulted in an intense academic debate in which different scholars tried to interpret the uses, concepts and the relationship between the most important concepts related to rationality (Eisen, 1978). Several scholars tried, for instance, to clarify Weber's work by categorizing the different meanings of rationality.

For example, Swidler differentiates between rationalism meaning an 'attitude of pragmatic orientation to the attainment of goals' and rationalisation meaning a process of systematization and rationality as a unique type of social action (Swidler, 1973, pp. 35-36; 38). Another common distinction that is made highlights the difference between subjective and objective rationality (Eisen, 1978, p. 10; Levine, 1981). According to Eisen, Weber used the former when action was believed to be the most efficient and the latter in situations where this was actually so (Eisen, 1978, p. 58). In a similar vein, Levine saw mental processes as the 'locus' of subjective rationality. He, therefore, argued further that both rational forms of social action should be categorized as subjective rationality (Levine, 1981, p. 10). Levine argues that although Weber did not apply this distinction consistently, on the basis of Weber's work subjective rationality should be read as implying 'action that is conscious and deliberate (contrasted with action undertaken for motives that are unconscious or disavowed) and/or action that is oriented to means that are regarded as correct for a given end' (Levine, 1981, p. 10). He continues that objective rationality should be seen as action 'that uses technically correct means in accord with scientific knowledge and/or has been subjected to some process of external systematization' (Levine, 1981, p. 10). Objective rationality Levine associated more with institutionalized norms (Levine, 1981, p. 10). Weber saw objective rationality as empirically valid, verifiable and collectively agreed upon, and saw subjective rationally as dependent on the individual (Wallace, 1990, p. 213).

There are several forms of objective rationality, namely objective instrumental rationality[63], conceptual rationality[64], substantive rationality and formal rationality (Levine, 1981, pp. 12-13). Levine is of the opinion that objective instrumental rationality was explained by Weber as 'the methodical attainment of a particularly given practical end through the increasingly precise calculation of adequate means' (Weber cited in Levine, 1981, p. 12). This may be contrasted with conceptual rationality which pertains more to 'basic cognitive processes of generalization and logical systematization' in order to gain a more theoretical grasp on reality by utilising abstract concepts (Levine, 1981, p. 12). Substantive rationality exists 'as a manifestation of man's inherent capacity for value-rational action' (Kalberg, 1980, p. 1155) but it is important that substantive rationality as related to institutions be separated from value rationality which relates to individuals (Elster, 2000, pp. 23-24). This type of objective rationality, Levine explains, 'accords predominance to ethical imperatives, utilitarian rules, or political maxims' (Levine, 1981, p. 13). It relates to evaluative standards and can be conceived of as establishing 'a valid canon' (Levine, 1981, pp. 12-13) meaning a 'unique "standard" against which reality's flow of unending empirical events may be selected, measured and judged' (Kalberg, 1980, p. 1155). A major difference lies in the notion that while value rational social action by the individual disregards consequences, as is explained below, substantive rationality is guided by the consequences (Elster, 2000, p. 23). Formal rationality relates to procedures to be followed (Elster, 2000, p. 22). It maximizes the predictability through the establishment of rules and procedures in order to minimize personal influence of individuals (Levine, 1981, p. 13). Formal rationality legitimates means-end rationality by relying on 'universally applied rules, laws, or regularities' (Kalberg, 1980, p. 1158).[65]

Weber was largely preoccupied with patterns and regularities in forms of social action that may result in the above mentioned overarching objective forms of rationality. The interest lay mainly in societal wide changes (Kalberg, 1980, p. 1159).[66] Since this research is concerned with understanding and explaining the behaviour of dictators, what is objectively rational is not of central importance here. Therefore, henceforth, attention will be paid to the subjective forms of rationality with a focus on the individual.

---

63 This form of objective instrumental rationality is also referred to as practical rationality (Kalberg, 1980, p. 1151) and should not be confused with the instrumental rationality as social action which belongs to the category of subjective rationality, rather than the particular form of objective rationality meant here.

64 Also referred to as 'theoretical rationality' or 'intellectual rationality' (Kalberg, 1980, p. 1152).

65 Some scholars argue formal rationality corresponds with instrumental rationality and substantive rationality to value rationality (Zafirovski, 2005, p. 92)

66 For a more elaborate explanation of the relationship between the types of rationality and types of social action, see Kalberg (1980) and Levine (1981).

Schematic overview of the different types of rationality that are present in the work of Weber as they are explained by Levine (1981).

Objective rationality: empirically valid	Subjective rationality: from an individual perspective
Subtypes	*Subtypes*
Instrumental rationality	Instrumental rational social action
Conceptual rationality	Value rational social action
Substantive rationality	
Formal rationality	

6.2.1. RATIONAL SOCIAL ACTION: INSTRUMENTAL RATIONALITY AND VALUE RATIONALITY

Max Weber distinguished four different forms of social action that are helpful in understanding the existence of multiple forms of rational and non-rational behaviour. The typology does not refer to all action since not all action is social. Social action requires people to take account of others. Weber specifies 'not every type of contact of human beings has a social character; this is rather confined to cases where the actor's behaviour is *meaningfully oriented to that of others*'. (Weber, 1964, p. 113 emphasis my own). For instance, when overt behaviour is oriented towards inanimate objects, this is not considered social action, and neither is solitary prayer, since in that instance the behaviour is not oriented towards others (Weber, 1964, p. 112). It is important for the present discussion, however, that oriented towards others is not the same as taking the other's reaction, or consequences of one's own actions, into account in the decision-making process. As will be explained below, not all types of social action will take the reaction of others into account when determining their own course of action, even though it may still concern social action.

Since Weber specified it must be 'meaningfully oriented to that of others' a few words on the concept of 'meaning' are required as well. According to Weber, 'meaning' does not 'refer to an objectively "correct" meaning which is "true" in some metaphysical sense.' (Weber, 1964, p. 89). He continues to explain that:

> 'the line between meaningful action and merely reactive behaviour to which no subjective meaning is attached cannot be sharply drawn ... in the case of many psychological processes, meaningful i.e. subjectively understandable, action is not to be found at all; in others it is discernible only by the expert psychologist' (Weber, 1964, p. 90).

Social action, therefore, is distinguished by the meaning the actors attach to their actions, and are 'subjective manifestations of rationality' (Rutgers & Schreurs,

2006, pp. 404-405). Meaning can be understood as a mental construct reliant on action being understood in terms of means ends of which the actor must be consciously aware (Wallace, 1990, p. 205; Weber, 1964, p. 93). In addition, behaviour needs to be purposeful. According to Weber, action is 'devoid of meaning in so far they cannot be related to an intended purpose' (Weber, 1964, p. 93). Motive allows us to understand the meaning of the act (Weber, 1964, p. 95). We thus need to understand the motive of an individual in order to understand why a person behaves in that way (Wallace, 1990, p. 205). Only then do we understand the meaningful act, as we understand why the individual exhibited certain behaviour in order to attain the desired end.

This meaning and the orientation of a particular action underlies his typology of social action. His typology is based on four motives (orientations) which he identified (Rutgers & Schreurs, 2006, p. 405). The first type of social action is oriented towards a system of discrete individual ends. Weber called it *zweckrational*, which is often translated as instrumental rationality (Weber, 1964, p. 115). The second type, involved a 'rational orientation to an absolute value *(wertrational)*' (Weber, 1964, p. 115). The third type of social action Weber referred to, involved an affectual orientation 'especially emotional, determined by the specific affects and states of feeling of the actor' (Weber, 1964, p. 115). Lastly, Weber identified a traditional orientation which stemmed from 'habituation of long practice' (Weber, 1964, p. 115).

His typology of social action thus encompasses two types which he refers to as being rational (Angus, 1983, pp. 144-145).[67] What distinguishes these types from the other two is their conscious or voluntary nature (Eisen, 1978, p. 59; Swidler, 1973, p. 38). Rational action in Weber's typology, according to Eisen, should be seen as 'voluntary, i.e. freely willed' (Eisen, 1978, p. 59). Swidler rather sees the consciousness of the explicit ideas on which the action is based as being the defining feature of rational action in Weber's work (1973, p. 38). Although different authors will use a different terminology, the essence seems to lie in the fact that these acts are not 'unthinking' (Swidler, 1973, p. 38), they require a decision.

The first of the two types of rational social action, instrumental rationality (*zweckrational*) most closely resembles what is commonly understood to constitute rational action. According to Weber instrumental rationality is oriented to a 'system of discrete individual ends' (Weber, 1964, p. 115). The decision maker in this case takes the expectations of the actions of others and possibly changing circumstances into consideration. He weighs the pros and cons of alternative means and the relative importance of different aims in the

67 Zafirovski calls value rationality, traditional and affectual action all non-rational but this is because he is referring to instrumental rationality. It is therefore correct that value rationality is non-rational from an instrumental-economic rational perspective (as Weber also notes himself Weber, 1964, p. 117) but as Zafirovski likewise points out it is non-economically rational (Zafirovski, 2003).

decision-making process (Blokland, 2006, p. 30). According to Weber, in this case the

> 'end, means and the secondary results are all rationally taken into account and weighed.' (Weber, 1964, p. 117).

Alternative means might be considered, as well as the alternative consequences of the means used and the relative importance of different ends (Weber, 1964, p. 117). It allows the decision maker to shift priorities and abandon certain goals when the costs are too high (Varshney, 2003, p. 86). It is consequentialist, meaning that the course of action is pursued that the individual believes is the most effective means to realize the goal considering the situation (Kiser & Hechter, 1998, p. 800). It thus embodies a clear element of '*calculability*' (emphasis in original Eisen, 1978, p. 58). Oakes explains that as an ideal type the instrumental rational actor is 'ruthlessly systematic, acting only on the calculations of all variables germane to their objectives' (Oakes, 2003, p. 39).

Some scholars point out that instrumental rationality may aim to achieve any number of goals, both self-interested as well as altruistic ones (Zafirovski, 2005, p. 91). Many others, however, associate it more with innate self-interest (Angus, 1983, p. 148; Wallace, 1990, p. 208), which seems more in line with Henderson and Parsons translation of Weber's work which formulates *zweckrational* action as being oriented to a 'system of discrete individual ends' (Weber, 1964, p. 117). Mueller as well characterizes purposive, instrumental rationality, as 'marked by material interests in the improvement of social status as its strategic ("ultimate") ends and by calculation and investment as its instrumental corollaries' (1979, p. 166). Also in this research, self-interest is conceived of as underlying instrumental rationality as it most clearly maintains the dichotomy between instrumental rationality and the second type of rationality identified by Weber, value rationality, where the motivation does not stem from self-interest and may even involve self-sacrifice. In contrast to value rationality then in its purest form, instrumental rationality is devoid of values (Starr, 1999, p. 411), and it is presumably the role of values which urge us to help others selflessly.

The second type of rationality that Weber identified is largely neglected in the literature of foreign policy and international relations. When a person acts on the basis of this second type of rationality and thus has a value rational (*wertrational*) orientation, they act out of

> 'a conscious belief in the absolute value of some ethical, aesthetic, religious, or other form of behaviour, entirely for its own sake and independently of any prospects of external success' (Weber, 1964, p. 115).

D'Avray uses Weber's value rationality to also extend to convictions, allowing value rationality to incorporate both 'is' and 'ought' judgements (D'Avray,

2010, pp. 68-69). He notes that convictions that portray a particular sense of what reality is like, what he calls factual convictions, 'seem very similar to values which use adjectives like "good" or "bad"' (D'Avray, 2010, p. 69). For the purposes of the present research, considering the important role ideology plays in the perpetration of mass atrocities (Alvarez, 2008), the conviction often takes the form of an ideology. Ideology can be 'understood in terms of beliefs and belief systems' (Alvarez, 2008, p. 216 citing van Dijk, 1998). Goals and values are often incorporated within this ideology (Alvarez, 2008, p. 216 citing van Dijk, 1998). Like ideology, values and convictions 'tend to be part of a general system of how things are and work', which makes them also difficult to counter (D'Avray, 2010, p. 76). As D'Avray explains, it will seem unlikely that the whole network of ideas is wrong and because it would have such far reaching consequences when people were to be persuaded their beliefs are wrong, people are generally unwilling to be convinced (D'Avray, 2010, p. 75). The conviction also tends to be concrete and therefore more 'vivid' (D'Avray, 2010, p. 90). Nationalism serves as a good example as it draws on symbols like flags, anthems, but also other images and memories of war (D'Avray, 2010, pp. 90-91).

When a person acts out of a value rational orientation his goal is sacred, it does not allow for compromise and is pursued regardless of the consequences (Varshney, 2003, p. 86). Because people who act on the basis of value rationality let their behaviour be determined by their convictions, the act in itself has meaning. According to Weber, 'the meaning of the action does not lie in the achievement of a result ulterior to it, but in carrying out the specific type of action for its own sake' (Weber, 1964, p. 116). The person who acts from a value rational orientation feels obligated to act to fulfil certain 'demands' which he feels are required by 'duty, honour, the pursuit of beauty, a religious call, personal loyalty, or the importance of some "cause" no matter in what it consists' (Weber, 1964, p. 116). It involves a 'consistently planned course of action toward the absolute value' (Angus, 1983, p. 145), and allows the individual to pursue its goal regardless of the chances of success or the high personal costs involved (Varshney, 2003, pp. 86-87; Weber, 1964, p. 116). According to Weber, value rationality is even characterized by a disregard for the consequences of the actions (Weber, 1964, p. 117). Value rationality therefore shows a high degree of commitment to the ultimate value.

The ends for someone acting in a value rational orientation are absolute (Angus, 1983, p. 146). Absolute ends, are ends that have value in and of itself. They are not an intermediary step, a means at the same time, to attain something else (Rutgers & Schreurs, 2006, p. 411). An end is relative on the other hand when it is also a means to attain something else (Rutgers & Schreurs, 2006, p. 412). This would, for instance, be the case if a person aims to obtain wealth (the end) in order to obtain power (making wealth both an end and a means). Relative ends also have an equivalent; they can be replaced by something else with equal value while absolute ends cannot be replaced by something else and do not have such an equivalent (Rutgers & Schreurs, 2006, p. 411). Hechter rather uses the term immanent values, and also points out that '*immanent* values lead to the pursuit of ends that are valued for themselves alone, rather than for their exchange value' (Hechter, 1994, p. 322). Hechter notes that it is precisely the fungibility of instrumental values, that they can be exchanged for whatever that person desires (money is perhaps the quintessential example) that makes them so pervasive in society (Hechter, 1994, p. 322; Hechter & Kanazawa, 1997, p. 194). According to Hechter, the fact that they are so widely shared in societies explains why it has not been considered very important to subject them to further analysis (Hechter, 1994, p. 322). It is, however, important to distinguish them from immanent values which are 'likely to be idiosyncratic', especially when the immanent value cannot be obtained with instrumental rational resources (Hechter, 1994, p. 323). According to Hechter, 'the more salient immanent values are in that situation, the more the resulting behaviour will diverge from that which would be predicted by a theory of instrumental rationality' (Hechter, 1994, p. 323).

Hechter also argues that when immanent values can be attained through instrumental resources 'then their existence would have no behavioural implications at all' (Hechter, 1994, p. 323). On the basis of Weber's work this latter argumentation seems too simplistic. Like Hechter, Weber pointed out that value rationality and instrumental rationality are not mutually exclusive.[68] Weber explained that it is possible, for instance, for a person to try to achieve a value rational goal through instrumental rational means. In this case the

> 'choice between alternative and conflicting ends and results may well be determined by considerations of absolute value. In that case, action is rationally oriented to a system of discrete individual ends only in respect of the choice of means' (Weber, 1964, p. 117).

It is not possible, however, to equate this combination with pure instrumental rational action. Since value rationality carries with it such a profound degree of commitment, the individual is likely to possess much more perseverance in realising value rational goals. Because of the large degree of commitment and the rigidity with which these values are pursued, when value rational goals are pursued by instrumental rational means, this may not be considered as interchangeable with pure instrumental rational action. As Varshney argues, 'the means to achieving these objectives might change, but the objectives themselves would not' (Varshney, 2003, p. 86). Behaving to achieve value rational goals that are pursued through instrumental rational means is therefore a distinct third option next to pure instrumental rational action and pure value rational action.[69]

68 Although Oakes notes Weber intended value and instrumental rationality to be mutually exclusive, Weber was actually quite explicit that in some instances they may coexist to motivate action (Oakes, 2003, pp. 38-39; Weber, 1964, p. 117).

69 Rather than seeing it as a separate option, Angus sees instrumental rationality of being separated in two kinds, one where the ends are decided upon on the basis of values (thus

Although largely neglected by Weber, the reverse would also be possible. People may possess an instrumentally rational goal but may have a value rational orientation in terms of the means on how to achieve it. In this instance, it becomes possible that an individual will utilize certain means to achieve an end that stems from pure self-interest, because of the belief that an alternative course of action is wrong in accordance with some general principle. The value would then pose as a constraint on the means used (D'Avray, 2010, pp. p. 63-64). According to Starr, an individual indeed might 'choose among ends on the basis of instrumental-rational criteria, but invoke value-rational criteria to reject certain means as unacceptable' (Starr, 1999, p. 412).

When there is a conflict between different ends, there are several ways to resolve this dilemma. When there is more than one value, Angus argues that the decision 'on a course of action would have to weigh the loss to one against the benefit to another – decide between the two' (Angus, 1983, p. 146). This plurality of ends means that, when a choice needs to be made between multiple values, the behaviour gradually enters the sphere of instrumental rationality (Angus, 1983, p. 146).

Instrumental rational goals are more flexible. Goals may be abandoned or adjusted when the costs are too high (Angus, 1983, p. 145; Varshney, 2003, p. 86), and 'different possible ends' and their relative importance may be taken into account (Angus, 1983, p. 145; Weber, 1964, p. 117). A choice between different possible ends may also be taken on the basis of self-interest (Angus, 1983, p. 146). In the latter case, a person would take 'them as given subjective wants and arrange them in a scale of consciously assessed relative urgency. He may then orient his actions in such a way that they are satisfied as far as possible in order of urgency, as formulated in the principle of "marginal utility"' (Weber, 1964, p. 117). This situation is more purely instrumental rational. As Angus explains,

> 'the greater the degree to which conflicting ends in instrumental rational action are resolved by reference to an absolute value, the less rational they are from the point of view of instrumental rationality … the other alternative in which discrete ends are not elevated but accepted and related solely with reference to the actor's self-interest is the most rational from the instrumental-rational point of view since there is no reference to an absolute value and, therefore, all consequences of the actor's actions are considered to be relevant' (Angus, 1983, p. 146).

approximating value rationality), the alternative to be decided upon on the basis of self-interest (Angus, 1983, p. 146). The difference lies in the notion that Angus regards the ends still to be ultimately discrete, whereas here it is argued that it constitutes a separate option since the value is now absolute. The latter interpretation seems warranted considering the fact that Weber noted the action was 'rationally oriented to a system of discrete individual ends *only* in respect of the choice of means' (emphasis my own Weber, 1964, p. 117).

Rutgers and Schreurs complicate the distinction further. They interpret Weber's statement that ends can be chosen on the basis of subjective 'wants'[70] and arrange in terms of relative urgency, as being more affectually oriented (Rutgers & Schreurs, 2006, p. 407). More contemporary research – modern neuroscience in particular – indeed indicates that emotions do often influence the ordering of preferences (McDermott, 2004a, p. 699) but it seems unlikely Weber also meant to make a similar argument. Angus, on the other hand, interprets Weber's statement rather as an assessment on the basis of self-interest and instrumental rationality (Angus, 1983, p. 146). It indeed seems to be more plausible Weber was referring with the ordering of preferences to instrumental rationality since Weber continued by saying that from an instrumental rational point of view, absolute values are always irrational:

> 'the more the value to which action is oriented is elevated to the status of an absolute value, the more "irrational" in this sense the corresponding action is. For the more unconditionally the actor devotes himself to this value for its own sake, to pure sentiment or beauty, to absolute goodness or devotion to duty, the less is he influenced by considerations of the consequences of his action' (Weber, 1964, p. 117).

Weber notes a person's behaviour is seldom characterized by only one type of social action (Weber, 1964, p. 117), and next to the two types that deal with conscious, rational decision-making, Weber also has two other types from which he says action originates but which lie on the border of what can be considered 'meaningfully' oriented action (Weber, 1964, p. 116). As will be explained later, action which stems from these types is often uncontrolled and automatic, stemming from emotions and habit. Weber's typology stands in sharp contrast to the contemporary rational choice approach which obviously does not cover the non-rational action types, but also only includes one of Weber's two types of rational action.

6.2.2. WEBER AND RATIONAL CHOICE

Some scholars point to Weber as having developed an early antecedent of rational choice theory and debate has emerged to what extent Weber fits within rational choice sociology (Norkus, 2000, p. 259; Swedberg, 2003, p. 285; 289). As prominent advocates of rational choice theory within sociology, Kiser and Hechter for instance refer to their work as being built upon that of Weber (Kiser & Hechter, 1998, pp. 797-798). They expound their belief that "the core of Weber's approach to historical analysis corresponds to emerging developments in sociological versions of rational choice theory" (Kiser & Hechter, 1998,

70 Rutgers and Schreurs rather use the term 'needs' (Rutgers & Schreurs, 2006, p. 407).

p. 798). Yet although Weber believed scholars should begin their analysis with the assumption that actors had instrumental rational motivations, he became well known for his many types of rationality. Weber explained that

> 'for the purposes of a typological scientific analysis it is convenient to treat all irrational, affectually determined elements of behaviour as factors of deviation from a conceptually pure type of rational action ... it is then possible to introduce the irrational components as accounting for the observed deviations from this hypothetical course ... It is convenient to determine in the first place what would have been a rational course, given the ends of the participants and adequate knowledge of all the circumstances ... The construction of a purely rational course of action in such cases serves the sociologist as a type ("ideal type") which has the merit of clear understandability and lack of ambiguity' (Weber, 1964, p. 92).

He therefore accords primacy to instrumental rationality (Norkus, 2000, pp. 261-262), but Weber's analysis certainly was not limited to instrumental rationality (as is the case for many contemporary rational choice theorists) (Varshney, 2003, p. 87; Zafirovski, 2005, p. 106). Weber acknowledges that sometimes behaviour is dictated by values and frequently action is determined by impulse or habit, and in those situations subjective instrumental rationality solely serves a heuristic function, as a methodological tool. When behaviour is identified as deviating from what is seen as the (instrumental) rational course of action, it becomes important to look at the value rational, traditional or affective types of social action (Norkus, 2000, p. 268).

Weber allows for the existence of misinformation, strategic errors and the like by introducing the notion that one should assess instrumental rationality subjectively (Norkus, 2000, p. 264). Rationality in this manner relates to the reasoning within the mind of the individual, and is not related to the actual outcome (Wallace, 1990, p. 201). Norkus explains that it is possible for the outcome to deviate from what one would objectively find the rational course of action, but still be rational to the individual:

> 'Thus, the observed deviations of the action in its actual course from its objectively rational course are explained by the hypothesis that the action was in fact instrumentally rational, but only in relation to the subjectively, not objectively defined situation' (2000, p. 264).

Behaviour can be instrumentally rational when the 'the motives can be intersubjectively approved', meaning that pure madness cannot be included as instrumentally rational since it involves isolation and disconnect from the other social relations. Collective madness, on the other hand, no longer should be seen as madness but rather as a subculture. Thus, 'subjective rationality can be attributed only to actions that are appropriate with respect to shared definitions of the situation, irrespective of how bizarre and grotesque it may appear to others who don't accept it' (Norkus, 2000, p. 267).

Instrumental rationality is also linked to the thin, objective version of rationality that Weber suggested always be the starting point of any analysis (Kahler, 1998, p. 923; Norkus, 2000, p. 262). However, for the present study the subjective interpretation of instrumental rationality will guide the analysis and account is taken of human limitations. It would be unwise to discount any of the cognitive or psychological limitations described in the previous chapter. An individual may thus exhibit instrumental rational orientation even when the behaviour is extremely bounded by cognitive limitations and miscalculations. The development of models based on bounded rationality have provided 'more realistic definitions of rational behaviour' (Kahler, 1998, p. 939) and the boundedness is here seen as a gradation within instrumental rationality. Forsberg also notes the literature on 'bureaucratic politics and psychological misperceptions still rely on instrumental rationality as the basic form of rationality' (Forsberg, 2010, p. 34). The central differentiation, then, in this study does not originate from the extent to which rationality is bounded, but relates to the different kinds of rationality.

Such a focus on different kind of rationalities is necessary since value systems are neglected even in the more realistic bounded versions of rational choice theories (D'Avray, 2010, p. 31). Contemporary rational choice literature does not really concern itself much with value rationality but conceals it 'in a box marked "preferences"' (D'Avray, 2010, p. 2). In the traditional rational choice framework, the concept preferences is loaded and needs to incorporate convictions, values, 'as well as preferences in the more normal sense' (D'Avray, 2010, p. 29). However, there are good reasons why the two should be distinguished from each other. D'Avray explains,

> 'there are choices made just because one desires the outcome … [and] choices made via reference to a general principle. Call the former preferences and the latter values … *the application of the general principle to unforeseen circumstances might lead to choices cutting right against the gain of preference.*' (emphasis in original D'Avray, 2010, p. 43).

Sometimes behaviour stems not only from the broadest definition of what a person's self-interest entails but also from an examination of what one's interest '*ought to be*' (emphasis my own D'Avray, 2010, p. 46). D'Avray argues overall that value rationality, which he often equates with culture, is immune to counter evidence and appears irrational, but actually shapes the form in which instrumental rationality manifests itself (D'Avray, 2010, pp. 27; 56-59). Society, a collectivity of individuals, may shape the individual as it may create or shape its values and ideas (Wallace, 1990, p. 210). Although not incompatible with the argument made here, D'Avray's argument is more limited. Surely, it is possible that culture will influence the general principles an individual uses to guide himself, and that this will shape instrumental rationality, but this is not always the case. In some instances values will hardly or (as an ideal type) not at all, shape an individual's actions that may stem from innate self-interest.[71] The reverse is also true, that some behaviour will occur because the individual finds it to be good in itself, without instrumental rationality factoring into the situation at all (again in a theoretically pure case). More likely, indeed, behaviour will combine the two rationalities, but will approach one or the other ideal type more or less. Also, when they are combined, individuals might try to achieve its value or instrumental rational goal through instrumental or value rational means to different degrees.

D'Avray's point that culture as a factor shaping instrumental rationality is therefore to be duly taken into account when assessing rationality (D'Avray, 2010, p. 59). Certain instrumental rational behaviour may seem illogical to us as it stems from a different cultural background. However, this does not reduce the analytical usefulness of instrumental and value rationality in isolation of each other when examining where behaviour stems from. Some scholars have noted values differ from one society to the next. Morris, for instance, argued Vietnamese culture manifested itself in a value, rather than an instrumental rational orientation (1999).[72] Value rationality, therefore, has often been analysed on a societal level. Following Hechter, in this research values are rather said to operate within the individual and societal phenomenon are perhaps better qualified as norms (Hechter, p. 321; 330). The individuals will be analysed to see whether they tend more towards a value or instrumental type of rationality. Starr explains the types are 'heuristic devices, developed to help indicate the possible interactions of these two criteria in actual human decisions' (Starr, 1999, p. 412). As ideal types, the extent to which the actor approximates these different types of rationality is the primary concern of this research.

---

71 D'Avray explicitly mentions this point and notes this is not part of what he focuses on in his book. He explains; 'though this book concentrates on the interconnections of values and instrumental rationality, the existence of untrammeled instrumental calculation is in no way denied. It creates "ends" which are unconnected with values and convictions' but mentions that he believes the two are seldom separated (D'Avray, 2010, pp. 63-64). Weber would agree as he states that 'it would be very unusual to find concrete cases of action, which were oriented only in one or another of these ways' (Weber, 1964, p. 117). However, as Weber also contends this does not preclude their usefulness as ideal types 'to which action is more or less closely approximated' (Weber, 1964, p. 117). D'Avray does not deny their ideal typical nature, but his research is explicitly about their interaction rather than as separate concepts influencing behaviour (D'Avray, 2010, pp. 64-65).

72 It should be emphasized that the analysis is based on ideal types (Morris, 1999, 241) and the eventual policy choices of any country tend to be a complex mixture of norms and interests (Middelburg, 2016).

6.2.3. NON-RATIONAL AND IRRATIONAL SOCIAL ACTION: AFFECTIVE AND TRADITIONAL ACTION

Weber also distinguished two types of social action that he considered non-rational. Although intermingled in practice, Weber made the analytical distinction between the non-rational traditional and emotional, also called affectual, types action on the one hand and instrumental and value rationality on the other (D'Avray, 2010, p. 69). The non-rational two types of social action are characterized by the notion that they are 'relatively "unthinking"' (Swidler, 1973, p. 38). The affectual orientation concerns behaviour that is emotional, dictated by the feelings of the actor (Weber, 1964, p. 115). An element which affective rationality has in common with value rationality is that 'the meaning of the action does not lie in the achievement of a result ulterior to it, but in carrying out the specific type of action for its own sake' but is distinguished by 'the clearly self-conscious formulation of the ultimate values' in the case of value rationality (Weber, 1964, p. 116). When behaviour is traditionally oriented it is rather caused by habituation (Weber, 1964, p. 115) and 'necessarily precludes rationality, agency and uncertainty' and concern behaviour which is 'unintentional, unconscious, involuntary and effortless' (Hopf, 2010, p. 539; 541).

Hopf notes habits may evoke an automatic response and may cause the individual to perceive reality on the basis of already existing stereotypes and categorizations which stem from social structures and are acquired through socialisation or cost benefit assessments or imitation (Hopf, 2010, pp. 541-542). It is not disputed that stereotypes are adopted because of social structures and socio-psychological processes, but stereotypes often also become part of an ideology that may be more or less embedded in society (Alvarez, 2008, p. 219; Tindale *et al.*, 2002). When stereotypes stem out of a particular ideology they originate from a reflective value rational process, although the application of a stereotype by a particular individual may be quite automatic. According to Weber traditional action may shade into value rationality when habitual practice is upheld by varying degrees of consciousness (Swidler, 1973, p. 38; Weber, 1964, p. 116). Considering the focus on rationality in this work, stereotypes will here be treated as stemming from either the ideological, value rational, orientation of the individual. Or, when stereotypes are not based on ideology, and are not reflective, we may follow Hopf to come to regard them as part of habit. When stereotypes are seen as a part of habit, it creates a connection between instrumental rationality and habit that is often glanced over. Literature on foreign policy decision-making has documented the manner in which stereotypes can distort (instrumental) rational decision-making (Mintz & DeRouen, 2010, p. 101; Rosati, 2000, p. 59). When action is influenced by past experience, and can be considered habitual, the crucial question is again whether the resulting behaviour is purely reactive. When it is purely reactive and no decision to take the action is even required on the part of the actor, the behaviour would fall outside the scope of the present research. When, however, it merely distorts the decision, it will become relevant as part of the decision-making process. Stereotypes will, therefore, be incorporated in this research to the extent that it places bounds on instrumental rational behaviour by causing misperceptions or is part of an overarching ideology and is part of value rational social action.

Affectual oriented action may also become rationalized when it concerns a conscious release of emotional tension (Weber, 1964, p. 116). According to Swidler therefore, 'it is the degree to which action is controlled by ideas, by conscious choice, which differentiates traditional and affectual action from value rational action', (Swidler, 1973, p. 38). Weber described it as follows:

> 'when affectually determined action occurs in the form of conscious release of emotional tension … it is usually, though not always, well on the road to rationalisation *in one or the other or both* of the above senses' (emphasis my own Weber, 1964, p. 116).

The statement clearly implies emotions can slide into both forms of rational social action (Elster, 2000, p. 36). It may become rationalised when the behaviour becomes conscious, unless this concerns an emotion that is so strong that even though it is conscious, still has to be considered uncontrolled (Eisen, 1978, p. 59).

In certain situations, instrumental rationality may be fully in the service of the affective orientation, without the interference of values, for instance when 'revenge is purely personal rather than embodied in a system of social norms and obligations' (Elster, 2000, p. 36). The emotional person, therefore, may just ignore the costs that are tied to its action while the value rational person may be consciously aware of them while still not letting it affect the decision (Elster, 2000, p. 35). According to Wallace as well, the presence of emotions does not preclude rationality but 'it is only when that emotion closes an unconditioned reflex circuit in the individual's mind between one projected means and one projected end that it departs from rationality' (Wallace, 1990, p. 202).

It is only when it becomes rationalised that the emotive action will fall within the scope of this research, which is solely concerned with the conscious decision-making process of dictators and the role rationality plays therein. As explained in the previous chapter, emotions may impact rationality in different ways. It may enhance rationality, may hamper it or preclude it altogether (Kaufman, 1999, pp. 136-137; Lobel & Loewenstein, 2005, p. 1050; McDermott, 2004a, pp. 699-700). The present work will not focus upon 'automatic reaction' or 'habitual stimuli' that cause affective and traditional action to shift away from rationality (Eisen, 1978, p. 59). Rather, it will focus on the different types of rationality and uncontrolled emotional and habitual responses only become relevant to establish the degree to which rationality is bounded.[73]

It seems clear that Weber determined these two forms of social action as not being rational. Whether these types of social action are best characterized as non-rational or irrational, is a more complicated question. To Weber a particular rational course of action may also be seen as irrational depending on the perspective from which the behaviour is judged (Segady, 1988, p. 93). Behaviour stemming from a value rational orientation will always be irrational when judged from an instrumental rational point of view. As Weber explains from the point of view of instrumental rationality 'the more the value to which action is oriented is elevated to the status of an absolute value, the more "irrational" in this sense the corresponding action is.' (Weber, 1964, p. 117).

Weber was also quite explicit in referring to especially affects as irrational (Wallace, 1990, p. 223; Weber, 1964, p. 92) while Wallace makes a valid point of noting non-rational behaviour would be a more suitable term considering that it is the absence of the conscious, calculating behaviour which is the defining characteristic of affectual and traditional social action (Wallace, 1990, pp. 216; 222-223). Wallace solves the problem by noting that since '"non-rational" subsumes "irrational" [it] is therefore the safer paraphrase' (1990, p. 223). In sum, affective and habitual behaviour are always non-rational due to their automatic, uncontrolled nature but rational social action may be considered irrational when judged from a different rational standpoint.[74]

6.2.4. WEBER AND PSYCHOLOGY

Weber was very sceptical of the role psychology had to play in his work and argued that it is 'erroneous … to regard any type of 'psychology' as the ultimate foundation of the sociological interpretation of action' (Elster, 2000, p. 26; Weber, 1964, p. 108). According to Weber:

> 'The source of error lies in the concept of the "psychic". It is held that everything which is not physical is *ipso facto* psychic, but that the *meaning* of a train of

73 For a different conceptualization of the relationship between emotions and Weber's rational social action types, see Woods who creates the concept of value intuitive rational action in which the instrumental rational, value rational and affectual ideal types of Weber are merged into one category (2001, p. 698).

74 For an alternative perspective, see Ezioni who identifies non-rational actors as those trying to achieve 'out-of-world goals, for which the question of whether or not a given set of means serves well or poorly or not at all cannot be answered' (Etzioni, 2010, p. 435). He gives the example of someone seeking salvation and consequently cannot be deterred (Etzioni, 2010, p. 435). Such a characterization of non-rational, however, negates the inclusion of traditional and affectual action and blurs the distinction with value rationality and is therefore not suitable for the present research.

> mathematical reasoning which a person carries out is not in the relevant sense "psychic". Similarly the rational deliberation of an actor as to whether the results of a given proposed course of action will or will not promote certain specific interests, and the corresponding decision, do not become one bit more understandable by taking "psychological" considerations into account' (Weber, 1964, p. 109).

Elster is right, however, in noting this seems to be misleading (Elster, 2000, p. 26). As was also explained in the previous chapter, the advances in our knowledge on the decision-making process[75] and the distorting factors therein have shown to be quite illuminating (Elster, 2000, p. 26). As the previous chapter noted, emotions tend to influence the end goal as well as the decision-making process itself and decisions are subject to systematic biases and human error, making rationality inherently bounded. It is therefore important that the advances in cognitive and social psychology as well as the research investigating the role of emotion are considered to determine how bounded rationality is, and thus to what extent one of Weber's ideal types is approached.

6.3. THE ETHIC OF CONVICTION AND THE ETHIC OF RESPONSIBILITY

A parallel is often drawn within existing literature between the social action orientations and Weber's distinction between two different kinds of political ethics (Gane, 1997, p. 550). Weber distinguished *Gesinnungsethik,* or the ethic of conviction, and *Verantwortungsethik,* also known as the ethic of responsibility (Starr, 1999, p. 408). It is debatable to what extent they are directly related to the types of social action. Some scholars argue that although Weber did not make the link directly himself 'it is evident we have a perfect parallel with his Wert and Zweck distinction in relation to rationality' and even argue that it is 'likely to conclude that there is not just a parallel but that the two distinctions are identical indeed and yet approach a different perspective' (Rutgers & Schreurs, 2006, p. 413).

Politics inherently strains ethical conduct for Weber as political action may ultimately resort in force, standing in stark opposition to what is ethically good (Gane, 1997, p. 550). In the words of Weber:

> 'no ethics in the world can dodge the fact that in numerous instances the attainment of "good" ends is bound to the fact that one must be willing to pay the price of using morally dubious means or at least dangerous ones – and facing the possibility or even the probability of evil ramifications' (Weber cited in Gane, 1997, p. 550).

75 Elster mentions cognitive psychology and behavioural economics in this regard (Elster, 2000, p. 26).

The ethic of conviction, like value rationality, entails a conviction and commitment that causes disregard for the consequences of the behaviour (Gane, 1997, p. 551; Woods, 2001, p. 692). Gane explains that in such a situation 'the means and consequences of action are subordinated to the demands of the political cause' (Gane, 1997, p. 551). The ethic of responsibility requires rational consideration of means, ends and consequences (Gane, 1997, p. 553). It is, therefore, understandable that a link with value and instrumental rationality is easily made. However, the relationship between the concepts is not as straightforward since pure instrumental rationality as a type of social action is not concerned with any value commitments (Brubaker cited in Gane, 1997, p. 552). Starr agrees but where Brubaker argues both social action rationalities come together in the ethic of responsibility, Starr argues both rational action types are present in each of the ethics (Starr, 1999, p. 407).

It seems overall the concepts cannot be used interchangeably, not least because the types of social action have a broader scope of application and a concern beyond what is or should be considered ethical behaviour. For the present discussion, the interest does not lie in ethical behaviour but in all purposeful behaviour, which is why the social action types will henceforth be the focus.

6.4. VALUE AND INSTRUMENTAL RATIONALITY IN FOREIGN POLICY

This chapter started with the argument that Weber held that for the subjective interpretation of states they should not be solely looked upon as abstract entities. Paradoxically, however, many international relations scholars, most prominently Hans Morgenthau, have used Weber's definition of the state and argued sovereign states were the primary actors in the international arena (Paul, 1999, pp. 225-226). In *Politics as a Vocation* Weber defined the state as 'a human community that (successfully) claims the *monopoly of the legitimate use of physical force* within a given territory' (emphasis in original, cited in Paul, 1999, p. 226). International relations scholars have often translated this with an emphasis of the state as a sovereign unit as the primary actor in international relations (Paul, 1999, p. 226). Morgenthau was influenced by Weber both in terms of methodology as well as substantively (Barkawi, 1998; S. Turner & Mazur, 2009). He used Weber's ideas on the ethic of responsibility but neglected to incorporate many other useful avenues on the basis of Weber's work (Barkawi, 1998, p. 159). Barkawi mentions Weber's sociology of rationalization as well as his ideas on the displacement of cultural values in modern policy-making (Barkawi, 1998, p. 159).

His work on rationality seems to have had less impact on the development of international relations as a discipline. There are, however, some scholars who argue realism and liberalism are based on the premise that actors in the international arena act on the basis of instrumental rationality, whereas constructivism incorporates the idea people behave in accordance with value rationality (Dessler, 1999; P. T. Jackson, 2003, p. 232). A separation thus emerged between theories grounded in instrumental rational behaviour and those sometimes referred to as sociological theorizing that focus on norms, values and identities (Dessler, 1999, p. 133;136; Tannenwald, 2005, pp. 17-18). Yet beyond this general notion that value rationality more closely resembles constructivist reasoning, international relations scholars explicitly using Weber's value rationality are sparse. Sporadically the types of rationality have been incorporated in analysis of EU policy (Toje, 2008, p. 126), the war in Vietnam (Cunningham, 2002, p. 518) and the war between Vietnam and Cambodia (Morris, 1999, p. 241). Often, however, the types are mentioned in passing and are not central, to the overall argumentation.

Overall, value rationality does not seem to hold a very prominent place in the literature on international relations and foreign policy. Particularly also within the foreign policy decision-making literature, the point of departure commonly remains bounded rationality, without distinguishing value rationality from instrumental rationality. The presumption that all decision makers are equally rational dominates in the literature on foreign policy decision-making (Razi, 1988, p. 689). However, differences in rationality are of great consequence for the choices leaders will make as is implicitly acknowledged in the literature. Some scholars have analysed the important distortions strong overarching beliefs systems may have on rational decision-making (Rosati, 2000) and others have explained how this may affect foreign policy decision-making, albeit without explicitly linking it to the rational decision-making literature (e.g. Hermann & Kegley, 1995). Neither has explicitly recognized that leaders may act on the basis of a different kind of rationality, or has acknowledged within foreign policy decision-making the existence of another kind of rationality, existing next to bounded rationality. The difficulty lies in the fact that the literature that does acknowledge a variety of rationalities exists, is largely disengaged from the decision-making literature rather than engaging in their debate. Rare exceptions are Forsberg (2010) and Heng (2010). Forsberg uses Habermas' communicative rationality. For Habermas, communicative action is one out of four modes of rationality[76] and is different from instrumental rationality. Communicative action, Forsberg explains, is not based on interests or motives but relates to the manner in which people coordinate their actions and the way communication can lead to a different choice without any change in costs or benefits (Forsberg,

[76] The others are teological (strategic), normative, and dramaturgical modes of action (cited in Forsberg, 2010, p. 45).

2010, p. 46; 53). Heng uses Weber's types of rationality to build an argument that analyses changes since the Cold War, and especially within the post 9/11 world. According to Heng, the world is becoming less oriented to 'means-end rationality' and now is more 'reflexive' (2010, pp. 19-23). He is focused on individual rationality that changes along with society itself. He links different rationalities to the time-period in which we live and assesses how this influences decision-making. He explains that 'individuals thinking about certain issues at particular times thus can embody a certain type of rationality which ebbs and flows as time, ideas and social circumstances evolve.' (Heng, 2010, p. 20). For the purposes of this research, however, the societal wide changes matter less than the particular individual under scrutiny during periods of mass violence, although to a certain extent they are intertwined.

6.5. VALUE RATIONALITY, INSTRUMENTAL RATIONALITY AND MASS ATROCITIES

Several scholars have pointed out the conventional rational choice paradigm needs to be improved in order to analyse situations in which mass atrocities occur. The willingness to sacrifice oneself for the greater cause has led several scholars to conclude that these acts should be explained on the basis of value rationality rather than instrumental rationality. Varshney, for instance applies the Weberian distinction between value and instrumental rationality to nationalism and ethnic conflict and finds adding value rationality may be helpful to understand national or ethnic conflict fully (Varshney, 2003, p. 89). Kecmanovic uses all of Weber's types of social action to highlight both the rational and irrational elements inherent in nationalism (2005). As another group of people willing to die for a cause, many have argued the motivations of terrorists are also not easily explained through traditional cost-benefit calculations (Tarzi, 2005). To the extent normative beliefs underlie their behaviour, some link it explicitly to Weber's value rational orientation (Tosini, 2010).

According to Mann, Weber's different types of social action are all useful to help explain the occurrence of mass violence (Mann, 2004, p. 26). According to Mann, although instrumental rationality is important to explain human affairs in general, other types may be more important in some circumstances. Regarding habitual action and the other types of social action, Mann explains:

> 'In war we routinely obey an order to kill, even if we bear the victim no hate. Then, as ethnic hostilities escalate, *affectual action* arises. … Finally we may engage in *value-rational action*, committing ourselves to certain goals whatever the costs. This is ideological driven action.' (Mann, p. 26).

Mann subsequently incorporated all of Weber's types of social action into a typology of perpetrators. He, however, neglects to specifically deal with the leader within his typology and most of the types seem to apply to those engaged in the actual killing process rather than the planning and instigating.

Shaw used Weber's different kinds of rationality to analyse the perpetration of genocide and argued that both potentially play an important role. According to Shaw:

> 'Although racist ideologies appear to involve absolute values ... these may often be pursued alongside other more instrumentally rational goals (military, political, economic)' (Shaw, 2007b, p. 89).

Shaw therefore emphasizes that the distinction should solely be used as a heuristic tool which allows scholars to study the complexity of actual cases (Shaw, 2007b, p. 88).

Although not explicitly using Weber's different kinds of rationality, Etzioni on the other hand does focus on the leaders of rogue regimes and argues that rationality 'is best treated as a continues and not as a dichotomous variable' (Etzioni, 2010, p. 432). Similarly, Razi also argues that 'rationality must be treated as a variable rather than a constant', and that it is important to differentiate between more or less rational individuals, rather than differentiating rational and irrational ones (Razi, 1988, p. 690). Razi also focuses on elite rationality and illustrates this with a case study of the Iran-Iraq War and the pivotal roles Khomeini and Saddam played therein (Razi, 1988). When the debate on rationality becomes nuanced, however, and we acknowledge the existence of different kinds of rationality, it becomes important to find out how it is possible to determine the extent to which someone behaves rationally, and more important the kind of rationality that dominates his or her behaviour

6.6. ASSESSING THE TYPE OF RATIONALITY AND PREDICTIVE VALUE

Values or belief systems are relatively resistant to change and immune to counter arguments (D'Avray, 2010, pp. 76-77). It is, therefore, possible to assess whether over a longer period of time an individual lets himself be guided by his values or belief system, or whether his actions are oriented in accordance with discrete individual ends. After describing how it is possible to analyse the type of rationality that dominates the behaviour of the dictator, it is important to evaluate what this means for his foreign policy behaviour.

6.6.1. LOOKING AT THE LIFE OF THE DECISION MAKER

Values differ from person to person, not only to the extent people are guided by strong ideological convictions but naturally also regarding the content of those values. According to Hechter these differences to a large extent can be traced back to the life of the individual. Hechter points out:

> 'the penultimate cause of variation in personal values lies in idiosyncrasies of personal biography, some of which can be explained by individual patterns of group affiliation. Membership in each group may foster particular values' (Hechter, 1994, p. 326).

Values are thus likely to vary because the experiences of people, as well as their role in the social structure which varies because of factors like class, ethnicity and gender (Hechter, 1994, p. 327). The challenge is then to find the way to be able to determine which rationality dominates the behaviour of the dictatorial leader on the basis of his biography and life story.

Fortunately, Weber's theory on social action provides us with some important guidelines. As explained previously, value rationality is characterized by the devotion to values, ideology or a specific conviction. When an individual acts on the basis of value rationality, the end must be absolute, rather than a means to an end at the same time. It is therefore important to ask whether a dictator is affiliated with a particular ideology, but also whether he actually lets himself be guided by the ideology, since sometimes ideology may also be used instrumentally to manipulate the population (Varshney, 2003, p. 86). When the dictator, however, is truly devoted to the greater cause, he will choose to act in a certain manner because the individual believes it is the right thing to do, regardless of the consequences. This disregard for the consequences will result, as Weber explains, in the willingness to sacrifice and perseverance regardless of the chances of success (Weber, 1964, pp. 115-117). This may, for instance, show from an unrelenting commitment and enduring of hardship in a war to be able to impose a political ideology upon the country. The value rational dictator is likely to be loyal to everyone whom he believes is loyal to the fight to implement the ideology as he sees it, but may be ruthless if he feels there are dissenting voices or people undermining the cause. The essential element must surely be that the motivation does not stem from a battle for unlimited power but comes from the belief utopia must be realized.

This is what predominantly separates value rationality from instrumental rationality. Instrumental rational dictators will be calculating and pragmatic weighing costs and benefits to achieve selfish ends. They might be driven to enhance their power. As Mueller explains, instrumental rationality 'is driven by callous, calculating material interest to enhance one's occupational, economic or organizational status, prestige and independence' (G. H. Mueller, 1979, p. 157).

The instrumental rational dictator may instrumentally use ideology as he sees fit to manipulate those around him and the population. He may even change his ideological outlook and will only value those loyal to him, rather than caring about political visions of his advisers.

When a dictator's action's will be oriented towards achieving value rational goals through instrumental rational means, he will be both pragmatic as well as tenacious. In the short term, he will be able to act in a manner that will postpone or even go against obtaining the ultimate ideological goal if he feels it is necessary for its long term attainment. The reverse, a dictator aiming to achieve an instrumental rational goal but taking into account values when it comes to its means, seems unlikely to fall within the scope of this research. Since the present research deals with only those dictators who are responsible for mass atrocities, it seems unlikely that there will be means to achieve self-interested ends that these dictators will not find acceptable on the basis of values.

6.6.2. EXPECTATIONS OF BEHAVIOUR ON THE BASIS OF THE TYPE OF RATIONALITY

When a value rational orientation predominates, the end goal is absolute, it cannot be replaced with an equally valuable alternative and the individual will pursue the goal with a tremendous dedication (Rutgers & Schreurs, 2006, p. 411; Varshney, 2003, p. 86). Striving to attain the goal, will have meaning in itself and will be pursued regardless of possible consequences. As Rutgers and Scheurs explain 'there is no or little reflection on the consequences of the action: only the intrinsic value is taken into consideration' while with instrumental rationality the results are taken into consideration (Rutgers & Schreurs, 2006, p. 407). This unfortunately has the implication that he will not be deterred by costs imposed on him by the international community. Their cost benefit assessment therefore not only diverges as Varshney points out (Varshney, 2003, p. 86) but will actually be absent in any pure case of value rationality. When a leader will try to achieve value rational goals through instrumental rational means the dictator will be more responsive to foreign policy incentives and disincentives stemming from the international community in order to prevent or mitigate the violent policies. These dictators will make a cost-benefit assessment although they will not let go of the ultimate goal. The more value rational the dictator the more risk prone the dictator will be until in the pure value rational case risk will not even be considered but the action will be undertaken that is in line with the value regardless of the consequences.

6.7. CONCLUSION

Rational choice has traditionally been of little use in explaining behaviour that was motivated by altruism and/or ideology (D'Avray, 2010, p. 41), which necessitates changes in order to analyse situations where atrocity crimes are perpetrated. By incorporating value rationality next to instrumental rationality in the theoretical framework used to study the perpetration of mass atrocities, it is possible to differentiate between different kinds of dictators. This makes it possible to do justice to the role that ideology plays and the manner in which belief systems shape the decision-making process.

Although some international relations theorists, most notably Morgenthau, used several concepts of Max Weber's work to analyse international relations, his distinctions between different kinds of rationality remain underutilized and instrumental rationality predominates. Also within foreign policy analysis, which is more suitable for the analysis of individuals, bounded rationality is not sufficiently able to take into account the role ideology plays in changing the cost benefit assessment of individuals.

When the international community seeks to stop or prevent the occurrences of gross human rights violations, it becomes important to assess how responsive the dictator is likely to be when faced with incentives or disincentives. When the goal is to make foreign policy more effective in countering the perpetration of atrocity crimes, it is crucial that the important role ideology may play is taken into account. Max Weber's work provides a unique framework to do so.

In Part II of the book, the theoretical framework that was set out in the previous chapters will be used to study the decision-making process of Pol Pot and Milosevic when they were threatened with military intervention by Vietnam and NATO respectively. Firstly, in Chapter 7, the theoretical framework that was developed in Chapter 3 will be used to analyse the role of Pol Pot in bringing about the mass atrocities in Cambodia. The next chapter, Chapter 8, will use the same theoretical framework to analyse the role that Milosevic played in the atrocities which spread across Yugoslavia in the 1990s. Subsequently, in Chapters 9 and 10, the work of Max Weber will be used to assess which kind of rationality predominated the decision-making process of Pol Pot and Milosevic throughout their lives. In Chapter 11, the extent to which their rationality impacted their decision-making process at the moment they faced the threat of military intervention will be analysed. Finally, in Chapter 12, the implications that this should have for a more effective implementation of the responsibility to protect will be discussed. The book will end with a concluding chapter.

PART II

THE COMPARATIVE CASE STUDY

CHAPTER 7
POL POT AND THE DESTRUCTION OF CAMBODIA

7.1. INTRODUCTION

After Pol Pot rose to power in 1975, his regime inflicted unimaginable horrors on the population in an attempt to transform society in accordance with his communist ideology. Before he was removed from power four years later, his regime had starved, executed and worked to death up to a quarter of the population (Chandler, 1999, p. 4; Kiernan, 2003, p. 587). Throughout its history, Cambodia's fate has been intertwined with that of its neighbours. When the war in Vietnam started in 1960 this had far reaching consequences for Cambodia as well (Becker, 1998, p. xv; 1). Both sides in the war, the communist as well as South Vietnamese and US forces, used Cambodian territory as their battleground (Kiernan, 2002, p. 485). The United States decided to heavily bomb the Cambodian countryside from 1969 to 1973 to target communist sanctuaries, with devastating effects on those living there (Becker, 1998, pp. 16-17; Kiernan, 2002, p. 485; Short, 2004, p. 182; 215). Pol Pot rose to power amidst this chaos, determined to free his country from foreign influence (Becker, 1998, p. 16; K. D. Jackson, 1989, p. 41). Cambodia was frequently seen by its political leaders 'as one of history's great victims' (Becker, 1998, p. xv). After an era of greatness between the 9th and the 15th centuries, Cambodia's territory by the time the Khmer Rouge came to power spanned only a fraction of what it once was and the Khmer Rouge sought to restore the country's former glory (Chandler, 1998, pp. 12-14). Pot changed the name to the country to Democratic Kampuchea, favouring its indigenous pronunciation over the westernised 'Cambodia' (Pina e Cunha, Rego, & Clegg, 2011, p. 272).[77]

While Cambodia has always had the reputation of being a gentle and kind nation, like so many other countries, it has a violent history in which despotic rulers provoked and fought unending wars. When one takes this into consideration the horrors of the Khmer Rouge are hardly an aberration in its history (Becker, 1998, p. xv; A. Jones, 2011, p. 283; Vickery, 1984, pp. 7-9). Its past

[77] For the sake of readability, however, this research will continue to refer to the country as 'Cambodia', neglecting the multiple name changes.

continued to be important for its population and, as will be explained below, the history and corresponding animosities between different groups in the country shaped Pol's genocidal policies. As Peang-Meth explains,

> 'centuries of philosophical-religious influences on Khmer culture and society, and the generalised Khmer characteristics and predispositions that have evolved, have contributed much to the present Khmer tragedy' (Peang-Meth, 1991, p. 455).

When the full extent of the horrors came to light, Cambodia's image as the 'gentle land', characterized by beauty and serenity, where people lived by the peaceful teachings of Buddhist ideology, needed to be revised (A. Jones, 2011, p. 283; Vickery, 1984, pp. 7-9).

The Khmer Rouge operated on the basis of secrecy. Its leaders did not speak out in public, and until 1977, when the Communist Party of Kampuchea (CPK) and its leader Pol Pot revealed itself to the public, it was a mystery who ran the country (Valentino, 2004, pp. 132-133). In the first few years little trustworthy information that detailed exactly what happened inside Cambodia during its reign was available (Kiernan, 2010, pp. 469-472; 475). Concrete facts were hard to come by due to the secrecy and isolation in which the country found itself but there were signs that horrendous atrocities were committed by the Khmer Rouge early on. Often, however, they were deemed unreliable and were nigh impossible to substantiate (Power, 2013, pp. 95-121).

As more information became available, scholars have started to debate the uniqueness and nature of the genocidal violence since only a small fraction of the killings seem to be rooted in hatred towards a national or religious minority. Midlarski, for instance argues that even though some of the killings were directed towards the Vietnamese and were driven by hatred and fear of this eternal enemy, most of the deaths were the result of policies that were meant to realize a utopian Communist society (Midlarsky, 2005, pp. 309-315; 323). Valentino makes a similar point, finding that with the extreme violence perpetrated by communist regimes 'neither pre-existing differences, prejudices, discriminatory practices, nor long histories of conflict between victims and perpetrators are a necessary condition for even the most extreme levels of violence' (Valentino, 2004, p. 92). He points out that in communist regimes many of the victims were hardly distinguishable from the perpetrators, they were often even members of the communist party (Valentino, 2004, p. 92). The extent to which it was nationalism, religious hatred, communism or all of the above that motivated the violence, remains disputed (Beachler, 2009, pp. 229-231). It will be argued here, that whichever ideology served as the primary motivator, there are many similarities with the manner in which other dictatorial regimes orchestrated the perpetration of mass violence. As was explained in Chapter 3, this process starts with creating an enemy based on a reinterpretation of the history of the country, and when the country is susceptible to the message of the dictator, because of difficult life conditions, the dictator can use the country's history to legitimize and justify violence.

In Cambodia, too, 'the other' is created by demonizing those persons the regime believed were not loyal followers of the dominant political elite and their belief system (Valentino, 2004, p. 92). Furthermore, as will be explained below, there were different social schisms in society, which were not only based on ethno-religious differences but on class and differences between the rural and urban populations as well (Edwards, 2004, pp. 59-60; Takei, 1998). While many of the victims and perpetrators in Cambodia were alike, there was extreme hatred and fanaticism 'in the air' (Becker, p. xvi). As Becker argues,

> 'it was no accident that the Khmer Rouge chose the most radical of communist models and tried to revolutionize Cambodia overnight to prove the country's superiority. They were the heirs of the worst in Cambodia's past' (Becker, 1998, p. xvi).

The atrocities of the Khmer Rouge cannot be argued to lie in age old hatreds between different groups but the horrors also cannot be separated from its country's past even though the rise of the Khmer Rouge and the subsequent Cambodian genocide were in no way inevitable because of its history or character (Becker, 1998, p. xv). The fact that it was not inevitable makes it all the more important to investigate how a situation materialized within the country in which such massive violence could be perpetrated. This chapter will use the framework that was developed in Chapter 3 to analyse how the country's history and population were used by Pol Pot to make such extreme violence possible. After discussing previous explanations that have been developed by scholars to explain the horrendous violence more in depth, the history of the country will be briefly introduced as well as the more immediate preconditions present in Cambodian society that made society vulnerable to the murderous regime, while emphasizing the manner in which the Pol Pot was able to take advantage of the desperate state in which the nation found itself to rise to power.

7.2. EXPLANATIONS FOR THE GENOCIDE

In relation to the genocide that swept through Cambodia in the second half of the 1970s, scholars have focused on different causes that potentially explain the horrendous turn of events. Some authors focused on particular preconditions in the recent past, which included war and dictatorial rule that arguably led to the rise of the Khmer Rouge, while others emphasize the inherent characteristics in the Khmer people which stem from their history (Burchett, 1981; Edwards, 2004; Hinton, 1998a, 1998b; Takei, 1998). Vickery, for instance, argues that 'foreign relations and influences are very nearly irrelevant for an understanding of the internal situation' (Vickery, 1984, p. xii).

Several historical and anthropological studies have analysed the different religious and cultural traditions within the country and the extent to which they contributed to the tragedy that unfolded in the second half of the 1970s (e.g. Hinton, 1998a, p. 353; Vickery, 1984, pp. 1-26). Many social schisms divided its people. The Cambodian populace could be divided into three dominant occupational segments before the Khmer Rouge came to power, namely those working in the bureaucracy or public officials, the clergy, and the peasantry. The latter had increased substantially in numbers between 1950 and 1970 (Edwards, 2004, p. 59; Vickery, 1984, p. 12). Social mobility was not always possible causing resentment among the peasant community, which benefitted the Khmer Rouge who recruited new soldiers from the peasant population during the civil war through which the Khmer Rouge rose to power, and received help from them (Edwards, 2004, p. 59; Vickery, 1984, pp. 12-13). Edwards therefore notes that it could be argued that the civil war that raged between the government troops and the Khmer Rouge can be seen as 'an extension of an age-old struggle in Cambodian society between the rural and the urban sectors' and that the 'Khmer Rouge, who gained their support in the rural areas, exacerbated these tensions in order to gain more effective support for their war effort' (Edwards, 2004, pp. 59-60). Vickery confirms that within Cambodian society there were long held tensions between those living in urban centres and those living in the countryside but nuances this further between those who lived nearby cities and those who lived a more isolated existence. He explains,

> 'a more profound division lay between town plus town-related rice and peasantry and those rural groups who, through distance, poverty, ingrained hostility or a conscious preference for autarky, remained on the outside of the Cambodian society which everyone knew and which Phnom Penh considered the only Cambodian society of any importance' (Vickery, 1984, p. 5).

In addition, there are also those who point to the lack of a democratic tradition to explain the hardship that befell Cambodia in the 1970s (Chandler, 1979, pp. 414-416). It has been argued that this tradition, in combination with their belief in Karma, led Cambodians to easily resign in their fate (Chandler, 1979, pp. 415-416). The country also has a history in which violence was relatively normal. Vickery, for instance, argues that violence and danger have been crucial features of Cambodian society for centuries and the violence in the 20th century can be seen as a continuation of such violence (Vickery, 1984, p. 7). Many Cambodians do not seem to have been morally opposed to executing traitors or enemies, although some of the crimes perpetrated by the Khmer Rouge were considered particularly cruel (Vickery, 1984, pp. 7-8).

Hinton notes that there were particular aspects of Cambodian mentality which made the population more accepting of violence in their society and, he argues, the perpetrators more prone to commit it (Hinton, 1998a, 1998b). In his work he argues that although 'culture alone does not "cause" genocide' (Hinton, 1998b, p. 117), the 'Cambodian cultural model of disproportionate revenge (*karsângsoek*) contributed to the genocidal violence that occurred during DK [Democratic Kampuchea]' (Hinton, 1998a, p. 353). The mentality of disproportionate revenge, that stems from a grudge, a *Kum*, is described by Hinton as signifying that an 'eye for an eye' is not the most appropriate form of revenge but that rather that one should take 'a head for an eye' (Hinton, 1998a, p. 353; 355). In addition, it has been argued that Cambodian society is very hierarchical where people are socialized to respect and obey (Hinton, 1998b, p. 99). They also seek to gain such respect and obedience from others and attach much importance to their own honour and how others perceive them (Hinton, 1998b, p. 101). Although the Cambodian society, under the Khmer Rouge, was supposed to be an egalitarian one that had dismantled the traditional divisions in society, it created new ones (Hinton, 1998b, pp. 109-111). This made them more likely to kill those who were designated as enemies of the regime (Hinton, 1998b, p. 115; 117).

The question has also arisen as to whether it was a genuine peasant revolution, but this suggestion can be largely discarded as a proper explanation if only because there also seems to have been much resistance to the revolution among the peasants (Quinn, 1989a, p. 218). Scholars, however, have not reached a consensus regarding the extent to which the Khmer Rouge were supported by the peasant population in Cambodia. Some maintained that the Khmer Rouge had always maintained widespread support among the peasant population, others said initial support quickly dissipated while yet others maintained the people only came to accept the revolution because of the overwhelming force with which it was enacted (Kiernan, 2010, pp. 477-478).

Next to these factors that relate to the situation inside the country, there are also scholars who focus on factors outside of the country (Edwards, 2004) which may have contributed to the popularity of the Khmer Rouge and its rise to power. The domination of the French during the colonial era has been listed as an important factor in that regard. Because of their research into the Ankor Empire and their discovery of the greatness of the Khmer people so many centuries ago, they inadvertently reawakened nationalist sentiments in the population. The French also let several Cambodians study in Paris where they got more acquainted with the Communist ideology which would eventually guide the Khmer Rouge along their destructive path (A. Jones, 2011, pp. 284-285).

It has also been argued that the destabilization of Cambodia due to the massive bombing campaign of the US between 1969 and 1973, was crucial to Pol Pot's rise to power and the subsequent extreme violence they perpetrated thereafter (Edwards, 2004, p. 63). It has been hypothesized, for instance, that the Khmer Rouge had already been brutalized by the civil war which preceded their rise to power (Quinn, 1989a, p. 215). However, because the violence started long before they rose to power and was so systematic and well planned, it may be concluded that in fact the Khmer Rouge were a well-disciplined force carrying out its government's plans, not some out of control, war crazed, brutalized soldiers (Quinn, 1989a, p. 217).

Lastly, the impression emerged that the Cambodian tragedy was the result of the work 'of a few homicidal maniacs' referring to its leaders, Pol Pot, Khieu Samphan and Ieng Sary (K. D. Jackson, 1989, p. 37). However, as Jackson points out, Pol Pot and the other leaders never seemed like 'raving, dishevelled lunatics. In fact, Pol Pot, Khieu Samphan, and Ieng Sary convinced observers that they were serious, thoughtful and intelligent revolutionaries' (K. D. Jackson, 1989, p. 38). In the next few paragraphs, the interaction between the leaders of the Khmer Rouge and the other contributing factors will be explained further.

7.3. HISTORY AND MYTH

One of the most important anchors in Cambodia's history, which is of paramount importance to their identity because it testifies to the great nation it once was, is the legacy of the great kingdom of Ankor. The memory of Ankor which was largely shaped through a colonial lens (Becker, 1998, pp. 28-29; 37-38; Chandler, 2008, p. 2) and gave the country a historic sense of victimization. Becker explains:

> 'By the time Cambodia won its independence this century, its people believed its national pride had been severely wounded, neighbouring Siam and Vietnam had grabbed their territory, nearly always with the aid of a Khmer prince, and the French had declared Cambodians unfit for the modern era' (Becker, 1998, p. 29).

Ankor crumbled eventually partly because of the interference of the surrounding countries. Chandler argues, therefore, that 'key to understanding Cambodian history and the policies of its leaders lies in the country's physical geography and its relations with Thailand and Vietnam' (Chandler, 1998, p. 14). These relationships have formed and been shaped by their interactions throughout centuries. The myths, fears and ideas that eventually led to the horrors of the Khmer Rouge can therefore be seen as being rooted in its history (Becker, 1998, p. 28). As will be explained below, it made the population susceptible to the message of Pol Pot and his Khmer Rouge as a hopeful new alternative to the misery they had known before.

7.3.1. ANKOR

For 600 years between the 9th and 15th centuries the grand Hindu-Buddhist Khmer speaking kingdom of Ankor stretched across a territory that these days consists of Cambodia, Laos, Thailand and Vietnam (Chandler, 1998, p. 12). It was the era of greatness for the Khmer people (Chandler, 2008, p. 35). They made impressive strides in the architectural structures of their buildings and their advances in irrigation engineering (Becker, 1998, p. 29; 31). At the same time, the territorial expansion was accomplished through many wars which took its toll on the population, and the massive temples that were being built were detrimental to the economy, leaving the population dissatisfied (Peang-Meth, 1991, p. 443).

Throughout Ankorean times the king ruled supreme (Chandler, 1998, p. 15). Much of the Ankor culture had been influenced by India. As Indians reached its lands many Khmer accepted the Hindu religion and the idea of a *deva-raj*, or god-king (Becker, 1998, p. 30; Chandler, 2008, pp. 41-42). He had absolute power, but in practice it was limited because of rivalries within the royal family and ambitious regional officials (Chandler, 1998, p. 15).

Early kings ruled in accordance with the Indian religious philosophy Brahamanism (Peang-Meth, 1991, p. 445). Peang-Meth describes how Brahamanism saw life as centred around a

> 'pyramid-like system at the apex of which was the god-king, Devaraja, who acted as an intermediary between the gods and a social order that propounded well defined class/status/rank/role relationships' (1991, p. 445).

This attitude was to have a long lasting impact on society and culture in Cambodia and the notion of the Devaraja which ruled supreme was characteristic for Cambodian life until 1970 (Peang-Meth, 1991, p. 445). At the end of the 12th century Jayavarman VII introduced Theravada Buddhism, although he remained tolerant of Hinduism and did not radically transform the entire Cambodian society (Chandler, 2008, p. 66). Throughout his rule Hinduism and Buddhism have seem to have coexisted alongside each other until in the 13th century when most Cambodians converted to Buddhism (Chandler, 2008, p. 76; 80). The new religion on the one hand provided Cambodians with a somewhat fatalistic outlook on their lives, since karma dictated that whatever came to them in this life was a result of what had been achieved in previous lives (Peang-Meth, 1991, p. 446). On the other hand, however, it also stimulated hard work to improve their future lives (Peang-Meth, 1991, p. 443; 446).

Having god like kings rule the land meant that the country was rigidly divided between the have and the have-nots. Chandler explains:

> 'The population was traditionally divided into those who gave orders *(neak prao)* and those who received them *(neak bomrao)*, between those who exploited others and

> those who paid homage; as the Cambodians graphically put it, between the few who 'possessed' goods and power *(neak mean)* and the larger component of the population who were deprived *(neak kro)*." (Chandler, 1998, p. 15).

During the times when Ankor dominated the region, many peoples in the west and south-east were subjugated to its rule, but as its neighbours grew more powerful and populous its territory shrank rapidly (Chandler, 1998, p. 14).

From the 14th century onwards the Thai and Vietnamese grew more powerful and annexed much of the territory which initially belonged to the Khmer kingdom (Peang-Meth, 1991, p. 443). In order to counteract the Thai influence, the Khmer king decided to marry a princess from the (Vietnamese) Annam Nguyen dynasty in 1620. He allowed her citizens to settle in Cambodia with far-reaching consequences. They established a settlement which would later become Saigon, and in the following years Cambodia's south-eastern provinces (Cochinchina, or Kampuchea Krom) would be ruled by Vietnam (Chandler, 2008, p. 97; 112; Peang-Meth, 1991, p. 443).

The Khmer never saw their loss of land as just, and this episode particularly resulted in widespread resentment among the Khmer population because of the lost territory and numerous Khmer who would now live as a minority in Vietnam (Chandler, 2008, p. 97; 113; Takei, 1998, p. 65). It also had a more immediate impact on the country's internal political dynamics. Political divisions emerged between those that were either pro-Vietnamese or pro-Thai which would last for several centuries (Chandler, 2008, p. 97). These years were marked by the decline of the kingdom, political chaos and numerous invasions of its neighbours (Chandler, 2008, p. 113; Peang-Meth, 1991, p. 443).[78] As the Khmer-speaking kingdom started to fall apart, the region around Phnom Penh became ever more important (Chandler, 2008, p. 94; 96). The invasions of its neighbours became most threatening and destructive in the midst of the 19th century when the kingdom almost disappeared due to continuous invasions by its neighbours (Chandler, 1979, p. 411; 2008, p. 141). Cambodia was invaded by Thailand in 1811, 1833 and 1840 and between 1834 and 1847 lost much of its territory to the Vietnamese after which it returned to the Thai sphere of influence (Chandler, 1979, p. 411). Cambodia, therefore, decided to turn to the French for protection (Peang-Meth, 1991, pp. 443-444).

7.3.2. FRENCH COLONIAL RULE

When King Norodom, the grandfather of Norodom Sihanouk who would come to play an important role in Cambodia's history later on, got into power in 1860, Cambodia covered only a small patch of land in comparison to what it

[78] Chandler objects to the usage of the word 'decline' since Cambodia remained rather strong for some time thereafter (Chandler, 2008, p. 93)

once had been (Becker, 1998, p. 32). He was continuously struggling to maintain his position of power and keep neighbouring countries at bay (Becker, 1998, pp. 32-33). The French offered their protection and he signed a treaty in 1863 and 1864 that allowed France to dictate Cambodia's foreign policy but left Norodom free to rule over his country as he pleased (Becker, 1998, p. 33). Cambodia became part of France's administrative unit Indochina which also included Vietnam and Laos (Burchett, 1981, p. 7).

France, however, soon became dissatisfied with the original arrangement and demanded taxes would be collected and paid to them, ostensibly to cover their costs of protecting the country (Becker, 1998, p. 34). When France still proved to be dissatisfied, Norodom refused to grant France more leeway to infringe upon the country's freedoms (Becker, 1998, p. 34). This obstinacy led France to take more drastic measures and they forced the King by the threat of arms to sign away all Cambodia's freedoms, effectively colonising the country (Becker, 1998, p. 34; Chandler, 2008, p. 175).

The French saw themselves as civilizing Cambodian society, finally bringing progress to a society that had been standing still until that time (Chandler, 2008, p. 14). While under French rule the powers of the king were curtailed, the strict hierarchy which pervaded the entire society remained intact (Chandler, 1998, p. 15). Since the king had accepted the arrangement, resistance against French domination was rare and it was a relatively peaceful time with some segments of the population even benefitting from French rule (Chandler, 1998, p. 15; 2008, p. 168).

Nevertheless, because of their repressive and abusive policies, the French awakened nationalism in the Cambodian population, especially since their work on the nation's mighty past reawakened a sense of pride to be Khmer (A. Jones, 2011, p. 284). French anthropologists extensively studied Ankor, restored the temples and drew parallels between this mythical civilization and the Khmer inhabitants of Cambodia (Straus, 2001, p. 53). The work of the French in Cambodia came to represent to the Khmer the proof that they had been powerful in the past. It pointed out the great disparity with their current size and dependent state, and this was deeply felt and used in the years to come by nationalists. It became a token from which they derived a sense of national identity and which was used to distinguish the Khmer nation from its neighbours (Becker, 1998, p. 38; Chandler, 1998, p. 12; Takei, 1998, pp. 72-73). They rebuilt the temples, and uncovered the advanced irrigation system (Becker, 1998, p. 38). In the region that had been conquered by the Vietnamese but where many Cambodians still lived, Kampuchea Krom, national consciousness was awoken by the French scholar Karpelès. She reminded the inhabitants, the Khmer Krom, that the entire Mekong Delta had once been theirs (Becker, 1998, p. 39).[79] In

[79] Even though in reality this had only been for a very short period, before this time it had been home to the Cham (Becker, 1998, p. 39).

recovering the history of Ankor, according to Takei 'France's historians created a myth which led to Cambodia's fear of extinction' (Takei, 1998, pp. 72-73) although it would be too much to say that they created an artificial fear. Folk poetry also played its part to commemorate especially more recent aspects of their past (Takei, 1998, p. 73) but the knowledge most Cambodians in the 20th century had of their own history, was tainted by all the prejudices and errors that were part and parcel of the French scholarly work on this subject (Becker, 1998, p. 38). In addition, because of the influence of the French, who saw the Vietnamese as more familiar and hardworking than the lazy, strange, Buddhist Khmer, many Vietnamese migrated to Cambodia amongst others to help run the French administration (Becker, 1998, p. 36; Chandler, 2008, p. 185).

Eventually, this cocktail finally led to resentment and by the end of the 19th century resistance towards French rule started to build in 1885. Buddhist monks took the lead as an influential, independent group that sought to protect the values and culture of the nation. It had a profound impact on the country, which became rebellious throughout the next two years (Becker, 1998, pp. 34-35; 40-42). Afterwards, however, resistance continued to simmer underneath the surface (Becker, 1998, pp. 42-43).

7.3.3. WORLD WAR II

When in 1941 the Japanese army made its way into Phnom Penh, France at this time had already surrendered to the Germans and was now ruled by the collaborationist Vichy regime, causing the colonial administration to quickly succumb to requests to cooperate with the Japanese. The Japanese sought to remove European hegemony from the Asian countries and by 1942 dominated much of the region (Becker, 1998, pp. 42-43). Thailand, sensing the fragile state in which the colonial regime found itself, now effectively being dominated by the Japanese, attacked the north-western part of Cambodia. In response, the Japanese decided to seek out a peace agreement and gave two large Cambodian provinces to Thailand (Becker, 1998, p. 43). The elite, realising the French were no longer able to protect them, subsequently joined the resistance which was being spearheaded by the Buddhist community (Becker, 1998, p. 44). Becker notes it was this alliance that 'proved to be the spawning ground for nationalists' from which also Pol Pot, and some of the other Khmer Rouge leaders came (Becker, 1998, p. 44). In the meantime, in the regions that had been conquered by the Thai, a nationalist movement also sprang up. The Thai had encouraged the notion that the Khmer in these provinces were emancipated Khmer, *Khmer Issarka* (Becker, 1998, p. 45). These Issarak forces, as they came to be known, started to fight against the French and the royal government. Consequently, several increasingly violent years between 1946 and 1952 followed as the Issarak forces got hold of more territory through their brutal tactics (Vickery, 1984, pp. 16; 15-16).

In the meantime, King Sisowath Monivong, who had reigned during that time, passed away not long after the attack of the Thai. A successor needed to be found but the French – still present in Cambodia under the watchful eye of the Japanese – decided not to follow the formal line of succession. They rather chose to appoint the 18-year-old Prince Sihanouk (Becker, 1998, p. 43). As the Japanese started to crack down on the colonial rulers and arrested the French population in Cambodia in 1945, Sihanouk decided to dissolve the treaties which were signed with the French in 1863 and 1884 (Becker, 1998, p. 48). Although Sihanouk praised the Japanese for granting them independence, the reality was less glorious than it seemed, since the Japanese now exploited the country and its resources (Becker, 1998, p. 48). In combination with the harsher policies the Thai implemented in the areas under their control, Becker believes 'Cambodia's fierce insistence on neutrality in the next decades had strong roots in this period' (Becker, 1998, p. 48).

7.3.4. INDEPENDENCE

When Sihanouk came to rule the country in 1941 he, according to Becker, 'inherited a country filled with a sense of doom, a people who were taught by colonialists that their race was threatened by ambitious neighbors, and whose culture had reached a zenith centuries earlier' (Becker, 1998, p. 4). Sihanouk took advantage of the country's history, leaned on the legacy of Ankor and the tradition of *deva-raj*, or god-kings, and ruled the country while portraying himself as having such a heavenly mandate (Becker, 1998, p. 5).

As many kings before him had done, Sihanouk chose to appeal to foreign powers to ward of political competitors. After WWII and the defeat of the Japanese, Sihanouk invited the French back to Cambodia in order to avoid a coup against his rule on the condition they compromised some of the power they had in the past (Becker, 1998, pp. 48-49; Chandler, 2008, pp. 210-211).

An electoral act came into effect in 1946 that opened up the country for different parties (Chandler, 2008, p. 212). Two of the most important ones were the Liberal Party, a conservative party that supported the well off, and the very successful Democratic Party. The latter included politicians that wanted independence, preferably peacefully, but also included members that favoured violent resistance through an alliance with the Khmer Issarak or the Communist Viet Minh party that had been established in Vietnam (Becker, 1998, p. 53; Chandler, 2008, pp. 213-214). The latter had been formed by Ho Chi Minh who was trying to stop France from recolonizing the country (Becker, 1998, p. 50). War soon broke out in the North of Vietnam, and the First Indochina War, as it would become known, was to last until 1954 (Becker, 1998, p. 50).

Ho Chi Minh had already created the Indochina Communist Party in 1930 but formally dissolved it in 1945 to hide its association with the resistance war (Becker, 1998, p. 70; Burchett, 1981, p. 7;14). It continued as three separate divisions in the different countries that continued to work closely together. In Vietnam, the Vietminh was active (Vietnamese Independence League), in Laos the Lao Itsala (Free Lao), and in Cambodia there was the Nekhum Issarak Khmer (Khmer Freedom Front) (Burchett, 1981, p. 15). Despite formally separated, Vietnamese soldiers continued to form the core of the fighting units (Burchett, 1981, p. 21). A confused resistance war started in which the nationalists within Cambodia, the Issarak and the communist movement, became partly intertwined but overall formed distinctive fractions both fighting their own battles for independence (Becker, 1998, p. 51; 71). On April 17 1950, the First National Congress of the Khmer Resistance took place where the Unified Issarak Front (also known as the communist Front Issarak Association) was established from the Cambodian ranks of the Communist Indochinese Party (Becker, 1998, p. 70; Chandler, 2008, p. 221).[80] A year later, in 1951, the Cambodians created their own communist party, the Khmer People's Revolutionary Party (KPRP), under the auspices of the Vietnamese communists (Becker, 1998, p. 71; Carney, 1989, p. 16; Chandler, 2008, p. 222).[81] The KPRP members slowly became more prominent in the Issarak Association and took up a leading role (Kiernan, 2002, p. 483).

Sihanouk used the advances made by the Issarak forces as an argument to persuade the French that they should grant Cambodia more independence (Burchett, 1981, p. 19). In 1949 the French decided to compromise their power further by creating what Chandler called 'fictive independent regimes in Indochina' (Chandler, 2008, p. 216). This allowed the US to provide aid to the new countries and to the French themselves, who had been burdened by the increasingly fierce fighting of the First Indochina War (Chandler, 2008, p. 216).

Although the newly established assembly soon became not much more than a rubber stamping body for Sihanouk, the Democrats were influential in Cambodian society (Becker, 1998, p. 53). Sihanouk staged a coup against his own government probably after being pressured to do so by the French since the Democrats had ties to the Issarak (Burchett, 1981, p. 19; Chandler, 2008, pp. 224-225). He promised his people independence as he threw the Democrats out of the assembly and imposed martial law when he was confronted with countless

80 Initially, the nationalist Issarak gained support from Thailand but after a *coup d'etat* there, support ceased to exist from the Thai side of the border and the Issarak's could only rely on the communist Vietnamese for support. Some refused to join the Communists, and henceforth the resistance movement would be split between the communist and non-communist resistance movements (Becker, 1998, p. 70).

81 Although in Vietnam the Indochinese Communist Party morphed into the Vietnam Worker's Party in 1951, it would continue to be known in Cambodia under that name (Becker, 1998, p. 71).

counter demonstrations (Chandler, 2008, pp. 224-225). Not much later, however, in 1953, Sihanouk became a national hero when France granted the country its independence. France at this point in time was faced with the war in Vietnam which was taking its toll, and deterred by the prospect of increased fighting inside Cambodia, finally decided to give in (Chandler, 2008, p. 227). Sihanouk claimed to have been solely responsible for Cambodia's freedom, ignoring the important part that was played by the Communist resistance that was operating under the auspices of the Vietnamese (Chandler, 1998, p. 15).

The Khmer independence fighters lost out on the fruits of the hard won independence at the Geneva Conference on Indochina in 1954 that was convened to bring the First Indochinese War to an end (Burchett, 1981, p. 27). Although they were present, the Khmer Issarak were not allowed to partake in the actual negotiations (Burchett, 1981, p. 28). The conference granted Cambodia military independence and it was decided that Vietminh forces needed to move out of Cambodia, which in actuality meant that the manpower of the Khmer Issarak decreased substantially (Burchett, 1981, p. 42; Chandler, 2008, p. 229). Although some stayed behind, about two thousand Khmer fled to North Vietnam along with the Vietnamese soldiers under the guise of being Vietminh (Carney, 1989, p. 16). Those remaining were largely either appeased by Sihanouk's focus on neutrality and peace, were jailed or were made to disappear (Kiernan, 2002, p. 484).

The Geneva Conference determined that elections needed to take place (Chandler, 2008, p. 229). Sihanouk abdicated his throne and established the Sungkum Reastr Niyum (People's Socialist Community), and the Cambodian communists joined the elections with a political party known as Krom Pracheachon, or the 'Pracheachon Group' (Carney, 1989, p. 17; Chandler, 2008, p. 229). Sihanouk won an overwhelming victory and reclaimed power as an ordinary politician rather than a king but proceeded to rule the country without any regards for democratic standards (Chandler, 1998, pp. 15-16). Although formally a democracy Becker argues Sihanouk ruled Cambodia more as a 'medieval monarch' (1998, p. 8).

Sihanouk valued the agricultural sector above all other, discouraging urbanization and industrialization. (Becker, 1998, p. 6; Vickery, 1984, p. 16). However, rice production, which was its main agricultural product, had never been easy on Cambodian soil. People owned their own land but most found it hard to create a surplus (Vickery, 1984, p. 16). In addition, after WWII there was more demand for rice to be exported, the revenues of which were used to maintain a more luxurious lifestyle in the cities but made it more difficult to feed the growing population (Vickery, 1984, p. 16).

Sihanouk's ideological stance seems to have been confused. On the one hand he used Marxist sounding rhetoric to condemn capitalism, but at the same time presented himself as a staunch anti-communist (Becker, 1998, p. 8; 11). It was not as much capitalism but modernity which Sihanouk seemed to despise (Becker, 1998, p. 8). He emphasized and glorified Cambodia's great Ankor past, which inspired many Cambodians, including the leaders of the Khmer Rouge, that they could overcome vast obstacles (Chandler, 1998, p. 16).

While for a long time social mobility was nearly non-existent in Cambodia (Vickery, 1984, pp. 12-13), after independence hope blossomed as opportunities for higher education increased. Unfortunately, these investments resulted in an increasingly educated population for whom the economy really had no use (Vickery, 1984, pp. 18-19). Rather than stimulating more vocational training that would prepare them for a future as a farmer, most of the educational programmes were modelled to resemble the French educational system (Becker, 1998, pp. 6-7). In essence, they were trained to manage rather than to actually do the manual labour themselves. This not only created class divisions, but also created an entire class of more highly educated people, for whom there was no use in the job market (Becker, 1998, p. 7; Vickery, 1984, pp. 18-19).

There really was no industrial sector requiring a steady flow of educated employees and commerce was dominated by particular families who sent their children to school but no further room opened up in that sector for others (Vickery, 1984, p. 19). Hope for most was vested on attaining a position in the government, but in 1961, Sihanouk announced all government positions had been filled. Sihanouk hoped the unemployed would return to their farms, however with such unprecedented opportunities for upward social mobility, the educated youth did not want to go back to the farms from which they came (Vickery, 1984, p. 19). Education came to be seen as a promise for more status, and most were determined to build a more privileged life for themselves in the cities (Vickery, 1984, pp. 20-21). However, with no more room at a governmental level to absorb the newly educated elite, only a growing economy could have created the opportunities they desired, but unfortunately Cambodia became lodged in a recession after 1963 (Vickery, 1984, p. 23). These factors ultimately increased the traditional tensions between those working in the cities and those in the country (Vickery, 1984, p. 24).

In addition, it also fostered tensions between other groups since different ethnic groups predominated in particular economic sectors (Peang-Meth, 1991, p. 452). The Chinese immigrants mainly worked as businessmen or moneylenders, while Vietnamese inhabitants acted as middlemen and predominated in the service sectors and worked in the colonial regime which always favoured the Vietnamese for administrative positions, leaving the Cambodians as farmers, civil servants and intellectuals (Becker, 1998, p. 8; Locard, 2005, p. 128). The French that lived in Cambodia either owned plantations or facilitated import and export (Becker, 1998). The Khmer thus became 'second-class citizens' which became a source of resentment and animosity, particularly towards the Vietnamese (Locard, 2005, p. 128).

Sihanouk, through his mismanagement, it can be argued, paved the way for Pol Pot to come to power. Chandler for instance argues that

> 'by treating Cambodia as a personal fief, his subjects as children, and his opponents as traitors, Sihanouk did much to set the agenda, unwittingly for the lackadaisical chaos of the Khmer Republic, the horrors of Democratic Kampuchea, and the single-party politics of the post-revolutionary era' (Chandler, 2008, p. 232).

On top of Sihanouk's mistakes, however, more immediate factors contributed to the victory of the Khmer Rouge.

7.4. PRELUDE TO THE GENOCIDE

Between 1952 and 1970 the number of landless peasants increased from 4 to 20 percent of the population, while others were heavily in debt from moneylenders whom charged extremely high interest rates (Hinton, 1998a, pp. 361-362). Overall the poor felt they suffered unduly in comparison to the rich whom they felt profited from their hard work and looked down on them (Hinton, 1998a, pp. 361-362). Particularly, when the war started, the people in the countryside suffered disproportionately in comparison to those living in the city (Vickery, 1984, p. 25). The war and the afore mentioned US bombing between 1969 and 1973 caused many to join the Khmer Rouge motivated by anger over the destruction of their houses and the death of family or friends (Hinton, 1998a, p. 362; Kiernan, 2002, p. 485). Edwards concludes that the communist

> 'leadership took advantage of events that were outside of its control, such as the American bombing, by appealing to Cambodian nationalism, and at its most basic level, to people's desire to survive, in order to recruit members into its army' (Edwards, 2004, p. 64).

The poverty and misery that befell the population during this time thus made them susceptible to the promise of a brighter future which the Khmer Rouge offered.

7.4.1. THE VIETNAM WAR AND THE CIVIL WAR INSIDE CAMBODIA

The Vietnam War, also known as the Second Indochina War, raged from 1960-1975, and spilled over into Cambodia and coincided with a brutal civil war (Becker, 1998, p. 1; Edwards, 2004, p. 63; Locard, 2005, p. 132). Sihanouk had always tried to navigate a neutral course in the highly charged Cold War atmosphere – a policy the Cambodian population stood firmly behind, especially after the Vietnam War started (Becker, 1998, p. 9). Sihanouk had briefly been open to the idea of gaining American protection, but the US was unwilling to give hard guarantees. In addition, Sihanouk was already suspicious of the Americans since he believed, rightly so, that they had been behind a plot to unseat him. These experiences thereafter translated in a firm belief in a neutral foreign policy (Becker, 1998, p. 9).

When in November 1963, two Vietnamese politicians were assassinated with the help of the US, Sihanouk immediately believed the Americans were behind it and further refused all American aid (Becker, 1998, p. 10). At the same time, noticing that domestically unrest started to mount as student demonstrations swept across the country, he placed the blame squarely with the left and forced them to flee. Among those that had to go into hiding, were many who would later form the higher echelons of the Khmer Rouge (Becker, 1998, p. 11). Unfortunately, it had an adverse effect since his crackdown drove many moderates underground into the hands of the more radical KPRP (Kiernan, 2002, p. 484). The situation worsened as the US stepped up its armed struggle in Vietnam and US Special Forces started intruding into Cambodia's territory (Clymer, 1999, pp. 616-631; Kiernan, 2002, p. 484). At the end of the 1960s, the situation rapidly deteriorated. In 1967 the communist resistance, now calling itself Communist Party Kampuchea, started its attack, and in 1969 the US initiated a large bombing raid on Cambodian territory (Kiernan, 2002, p. 484).

Sihanouk would soon start to feel the effects of his principled refusal of American aid. Since the aid was also used to pay for military investments, the army started to turn their back on Sihanouk and right wing opposition slowly started to materialize and get organized, eventually resulting in a pro-American *coup d'état* in 1970 (Becker, 1998, p. 11; 13). The coup brought Prince Sirik Matak and Sihanouk's military and police chief, Lon Nol, to power but it soon became evident that Matak was just a figurehead and Lon Nol led the country as its sole ruler (Becker, 1998, pp. 13-14).

Many Cambodians initially had high hopes of the new leadership, but the coup actually caused Cambodia to further sink away into poverty and despair while the violence continued (Becker, 1998, pp. 13-15; Kiernan, 2002, p. 485). Lon Nol never hid his disdain for the Vietnamese (Becker, 1998, p. 15). His army systematically killed hundreds of ethnic Vietnamese and many others fled across the border in a prelude of what would happen to them during Pol Pot's reign (Kiernan, 2002, p. 485). In addition, since Cambodia was again dependent on US aid, they were dragged further into the Vietnam War (Becker, 1998, pp. 13-15). The American bombing campaign continued in the idle hope that it would lead to negotiations between Lon Nol and the Khmer Rouge (Edwards, 2004, p. 63). The American ground forces had already left Cambodian territory in 1970 but, soldiers from Saigon stayed until 1972, or only withdrew when the Paris Agreement on the Vietnam War was concluded in 1973, and the bombardments continued relentlessly (Kiernan, 2002, p. 485). In May 1973 the US began a massive bombing campaign that brought the war close to home for all Cambodian inhabitants, and about half a million peasants fled to Phnom Penh to escape the violence (Becker, 1998, p. 16). Food became scarce and the population started to suffer incredible hardship (Becker, 1998, pp. 17-18). Phnom Penh increased almost fourfold in terms of its number of inhabitants between 1970 and 1975. Approximately half of the new inhabitants were forced to leave their homes in the countryside because of the bombing raid (Vickery, 1984, p. 17). Some of the bombs were directed towards Khmer Rouge strongholds but many bombing raids were also largely indiscriminate (Edwards, 2004, p. 63). The result was a vehement anti-American and anti-Lon Nol sentiment among the population, and one peasant is documented as having said 'the people were angry with the US and that is why so many of them joined the Khmer communists' (Edwards, 2004, p. 64).

The second reason why the ranks of the Khmer Rouge started to grow rapidly was that Sihanouk had become the front man of the resistance. The former enemies had aligned themselves against the government of Lon Nol. The CPK used Sihanouk as its frontman under the acronym GRUNK (the Royal Government of National Union of Cambodia), which provided them with ever more support, especially from those living in the countryside (Edwards, 2004, p. 57; 60). Because Sihanouk, in the 1950s and 1960s, had strongly opposed communism generally, the Khmer Rouge were not openly calling themselves such but executed their policies in the name of *Ankar*[82], the 'Organization' (Edwards, 2004, p. 62). Next to these foreign communist influences, the Khmer Rouge mixed their ideology with nationalist and traditional Cambodian elements which resonated with the population (Edwards, 2004, p. 62). The idea that the nation should be completely independent from any foreign interference, for instance, was inspired more by 'the centuries-old Khmer fear of foreign invasion rather than from any twentieth-century foreign ideology' (Edwards, 2004, p. 62).

Although initially the interests between the Vietnamese communists and the Khmer Rouge were aligned, the relationship remained strained. Edwards explains 'the ancient traditional hatred and antipathy between the two states and peoples [was] only marginally suppressed. Khmer nationalism – and by extension, anti-Vietnamese feeling – was an important component of the ideology of the guerrilla forces' (Edwards, 2004, p. 62). This also showed in the policies they adopted in areas that were under their control. Kiernan explains how the

> 'Khmer Rouge central leadership attacked its Vietnamese allies as early as 1970, killed a thousand Khmer communist returnees from Hanoi, and in 1973-74, stepped up violence against ethnic Vietnamese civilians, purged and killed ethnic Thai and

82 Anka in (Edwards, 2004).

other minority members of CPK regional committees, banned an allied group of ethnic Cham Muslim revolutionaries, and instigated severe repression of Muslim communities' (Kiernan, 2002, p. 485).

Militarily, the traditionally trained governmental forces had difficulty fighting the Khmer guerrilla forces in the civil war (Edwards, 2004, p. 58) and Lon Nol lost control over most of its countryside (Kiernan, 2002, p. 485). After the US ceased its military engagement in Cambodia, under tremendous pressure from Congress, Lon Nol was left to fight the Khmer Rouge on his own and was doomed to fail (Edwards, 2004, pp. 64-65; Vickery, 1984, p. 14).

7.4.2. ECONOMIC DOWNTURN

There had been long lasting economic difficulties weighing heavily on the country that have been discussed earlier. These included the lack of qualified job opportunities for those who managed to get their degree after the country gained independence and an increased demand for rice to feed the increasingly luxurious lifestyle of the urban population at the expense of the rural population (Vickery, 1984, pp. 16; 18-19). These factors contributed to a growing sense of discontentment and resentment between the different groups in the population (Hinton, 1998a, pp. 361-362; Vickery, 1984, p. 15). Compounding these problems were the debts that many Cambodians needed to repay at exorbitant interest rates (Hinton, 1998a, p. 362). The poorest did not own land but worked for landlords (Hinton, 1998a, p. 362). They were a minority but their numbers increased more than fourfold between 1950-1970, and undoubtedly increased even more in the violent years that followed (Kiernan, 1996, p. 7). Even those who owned land were discontent with the amount they earned for the hard work they needed to put in, believing the rich had a much easier life (Hinton, 1998a, p. 362). According to Vickery, 'exploitation of the peasantry was increasing throughout the 20th century and if it alone did not push them to revolution it was responsible for serious rural-urban antagonisms' (Vickery, 1984, p. 15).

In addition, there was the hardship and hunger brought on by the enduring war and bombardments and years of corrupt, dictatorial rule (Becker, 1998, pp. 16-18). Under Sihanouk the economy suffered tremendously and efforts to counter these adverse effects through nationalization had little effect (Becker, 1998, p. 11). When Lon Nol came into power, the situation unfortunately only worsened. During his reign corruption spiralled out of control and army officials became excessively wealthy. Inflation peaked as well under his rule because Lon Nol decided to print money in order to supplement the aid that got embezzled (Becker, 1998, p. 16).

There were many dissatisfied people in Cambodia that were eager to listen to a message of hope and revolution that the Khmer Rouge offered and the Khmer

Rouge deliberately targeted them, especially the teenage children (Kiernan, 1996, p. 7). People were not necessarily alarmed when the Khmer Rouge reached Phnom Penh. According to Becker, they reasoned: 'The Khmer Rouge were nationalists. Sihanouk was their token leader. Life could not help but improve' (1998, p. 18).

7.5. POL POT, THE KHMER ROUGE AND THE CRIMES

As has been explained before, there were numerous cultural and situational factors, but it is important not to become too deterministic, they did not make the atrocities that ensued inevitable. Regarding the cultural factors, Hinton, for instance, points out that this 'does not guide Cambodian behaviour in a deterministic manner', since there are always a variety of options available to the individual that are equally engrained in national culture and tradition (Hinton, 1998a, p. 353). Genocidal regimes, however, may use these cultural aspects to induce people to commit heinous acts of violence (Hinton, 1998a, p. 353). The Khmer Rouge's ideology redefined the despair of the population, characterizing it as a class struggle (Hinton, 1998a, pp. 362-363). New recruits, for instance, were told that the plight of the poor stemmed from their exploitation by the capitalist class. In this fashion they were thought the proper revolutionary 'consciousness' and were taught to hate the capitalist urban population as a common enemy (Hinton, 1998a, p. 363). It was especially effective with the young cadre who, according to Hinton, 'were described as dedicated and well-disciplined "fanatics"' after they came back from these indoctrination sessions (Hinton, 1998a, p. 363). The Khmer Rouge identified both internal enemies (predominantly the intellectual and urban population) as well as external ones (particularly US imperialism and Vietnam) on whom it could blame all that was wrong with the country (Edwards, 2004, p. 62; Kiernan, 1996, p. 3). In doing so, it used the country's recent history and cultural sensitivities to rise to power and implement its ideological ideas in a manner that would cost so many people their lives. The ideological outlook of the leaders of the Khmer Rouge, with Pol Pot at its head, were instrumental in dictating the course of the disaster (K. D. Jackson, 1989, p. 38). The content of the ideology, and the role Pol Pot played in this destructive process will be detailed below.

7.5.1. THE IDEOLOGY

The stated goal of the Communist Party of Kampuchea was to create a 'socialist revolution' on behalf of the 'peasant worker' (Straus, 2001, p. 50). Its Four Year Plan was focused on establishing self-reliance, autarky and infusing society with revolutionary will (Straus, 2001, p. 50). The ultimate goal was complete independence. Pol Pot believed that even after gaining independence of the French, Cambodia still was not free. At the first congress of the Cambodian Communist Party he said

> '*Cambodia was not independent*, did not enjoy freedom, was in the state of being *half slave and half satellite of imperialism* ... though in form it was independent and neutral, in essence it was not, since its economy was under the blanket of U.S. imperialism' (emphasis in original K. D. Jackson, 1989, p. 39).

In a speech he gave in 1976, he said that he needed people to devote themselves to the goal of attaining independence '[w]e want independence, because we have been the slaves o[f] others for a long time now. But independence always requires a great deal of personal effort' (Chandler, Kiernan, & Boua, 1988, p. 162).

The official rhetoric denied that the victory in the civil war had been achieved largely because of the numerous North Vietnamese forces that contributed to the struggle (K. D. Jackson, 1989, p. 40). Anti-Vietnamese sentiment was pervasive among the leadership, which was not only due to the country's frequent historical subjugation but also because the leadership felt betrayed by their allies at the Paris Peace Accords and had found them to be overly controlling (K. D. Jackson, 1989, p. 41). They therefore feared undue influence of the Vietnamese after the Americans had been defeated and were determined not to be colonised again (K. D. Jackson, 1989, p. 41).

There was already a historical sense of animosity towards the Vietnamese based on their shared history throughout which Cambodia was repeatedly subjected to Vietnamese hegemony. Due to this history of dependence and conflict, Cambodians tended to see their national identity in opposition to the Vietnamese (Chandler, 1979, p. 413). The leadership of the Khmer Rouge were all too familiar with the legacy and the nationalist tradition was highlighted by the Pol Pot regime. It was one of the few traditions which was allowed to remain a prominent feature of Cambodian society (Chandler, 1979, p. 413). Takei explains:

> 'Cambodia represents a clear example of the importance of collective memory; people there perceive a threat from Vietnam that is a continuation of what previous generations have experienced. Pol Pot attempted to destroy much of Cambodia's culture, yet he remained Khmer (Cambodian) because he retained a certain collective memory that an ethnic Vietnamese would not share ... Cambodians are people who share in the collective memory of the former Khmer empire of Ankor and Cambodia's relations with external powers, particularly Vietnam and Thailand' (Takei, 1998, p. 60; 62).

The legacy of the great Ankor Empire was continuously emphasized in what Jones has labelled 'an aggressive nostalgia' (A. Jones, 2011, p. 284). Pol Pot constructed this narrative by turning to the Ankor Empire for strength and inspiration and said in a speech in 1977: 'If our people can build Ankor, they are capable of anything' (Chandler, 2008, p. 298). It brought a desire to maintain the integrity of Cambodia's territory and to regain lost land which had once formed part of the Ankorean Empire (K. D. Jackson, 1989, p. 46; A. Jones, 2011, p. 284). The extreme outlook of the Khmer Rouge was fed by 'a messianic desire to reclaim "lost" Cambodian territories' and was particularly focused on the lands which currently form the southern parts of Vietnam, and have been in Vietnamese hands ever since 1840, that is better known as *Kampuchea Krom* or 'Lower Cambodia' (Chandler, 2008, p. 97; A. Jones, 2011, p. 284). Many of the policies of the Khmer Rouge were driven by this historical desire from greatness and the animosity towards the Vietnamese.

The cities were also emptied partly in response to this fear of foreign influence. Traditionally, the cities were centres where Vietnamese-Khmer and Sino-Khmer minority groups were very prominent (K. D. Jackson, 1989, p. 47). In addition, of course those who were more highly educated lived predominantly in the cities which thus formed a bulwark of those who would later be labelled as enemies of the regime (Vickery, 1984, p. 21). Removing them from the cities also dispersed and disorganized any potential opposition, in the communes on the country side the regime was better able to monitor them (K. D. Jackson, 1989, p. 47). Locard argues that the Khmer Rouge simply did not have the man power to control the cities (Locard, 2005, p. 122). Pol Pot also hinted to the strategic benefits of emptying the cities when he explained that the evacuation of the cities

> 'was decided before victory was won, that is, in February 1975, because we knew that before smashing all sorts of enemy spy organizations, our strength was not strong enough to defend the revolutionary regime' (K. D. Jackson, 1989, p. 47).

Another reason why the cities were emptied is that the regime attached much importance to the cultivation of rice and believed more manpower was needed in the countryside (K. D. Jackson, 1989, p. 48). The agricultural sector and rice production were the most important pillars on which the new society would rest (Straus, 2001, p. 51). The new regime sought to triple rice production as they believed that 'if we have rice, we can have everything' (K. D. Jackson, 1989, p. 48; Straus, 2001, p. 51). They thought that rice had been the key to their success in the past, believing it allowed them to defeat the Americans and Lon Nol in the civil war, and would make them succeed in the future (Straus, 2001, p. 51). Part of the reason why the Khmer Rouge emphasized the production of rice and implemented such horrendous agricultural policies which cost so many people their lives, was the erroneous belief that water management and rice production had underlain the wealth and power of Ankor (Kiernan, 1996, p. 8; Straus, 2001, pp. 54-55). It had been an argument that had been made by the French archaeologists, and Straus found that 'these writings about Ankor inspired the Khmer Rouge's mystical emphasis on rice, irrigation and un-mechanized, organic production' (Straus, 2001, p. 55). The plans of the regime, Pol Pot explained at a meeting of prominent party members, included ambitious goals for the production of rice. They caused many to starve to death because most of its harvest needed to be handed over to the state (Chandler *et al.*, 1988, pp. xiv-xv). Yet for Pol Pot what was important, he explained in the speech, were not the numbers 'but the ideology behind it, and the notion that we must all unite together' (Chandler *et al.*, 1988, p. 121).

The Khmer Rouge did not only make use of the historical legacy of Ankor and the animosity towards the Vietnamese but also took advantage of the already existing schisms between the urban and rural population. The official ideology blamed all the problems that had been pervasive in the country before the revolution on the capitalist urban classes (Edwards, 2004, p. 60). They, for instance, used slogans such as 'trees in the country, fruit in the town' which resonated with the local population due to their already existing resentment of those living in the cities (Hinton, 1998a, p. 363). Pol Pot had been combining the traditions of Cambodian society with revolutionary ideas that were important to him ever since he was a student (Becker, 1998, p. 61), and now old animosities were used to define who did not belong. City people were not to be seen as real Khmer, but rather as enemies that needed to be '"crushed" by "class ardor and fury"' (Hinton, 1998a, p. 363).

During the civil war, Pol Pot and the Khmer Rouge won the support of some of the peasant population with this message and the promise of change. The notion that everyone under the Khmer Rouge was alike, did the same manual labour and received the same meals, was attractive to the disenfranchised peasants (Edwards, 2004, p. 59). Lon Nol's regime was portrayed as a capitalist regime which needed to be defeated by the poor to prevent further exploitation by the rich city people (Hinton, 1998a, p. 363). Throughout their reign the Khmer Rouge would subsequently remind the people of their hatred towards the urban population (Hinton, 1998a, p. 365).

The enemies of the civil war were the first to be killed once the war was over. The Khmer Rouge killed first those who were associated with Lon Nol's regime and the 'new people' from the cities were treated much more harshly (Hinton, 1998a, pp. 364-365; Valentino, 2004, p. 138). They were representative of the capitalist way of life (Valentino, 2004, p. 138). Those living in more isolated rural areas had grown accustomed to the harsh living conditions and were not necessarily less well off. In their minds, they likely did not believe that there was a reason why the new people could not adjust to the same lifestyle, and Vickery explains they 'might easily imagine that failure to adjust was the result of laziness, corruption or factiousness. Of course there must also have been some *schadenfreude* at seeing the pretentious city folk brought down to their level' (Vickery, 1984, p. 5). Due to the longstanding animosities which were further awakened by the Khmer Rouge, the city people, when they arrived in the countryside, were seen as enemies (Hinton, 1998a, pp. 363-364).

In addition, non-Khmer minorities were explicitly targeted for extermination. While some scholars like Kiernan suggest that the racist elements in the ideology of the Khmer Rouge were even more important than those relating to class (Kiernan, 1996, p. 26), others suggest that these are actually intertwined with minority groups being targeted because they were believed to have been resistant to communist policies, and were seen as enemies from communism (Lemarchand, 2003, p. 150; Valentino, 2004, p. 139).[83] A nationalist and communist ideology were combined in the outlook of the Khmer Rouge, and both security considerations and ideological reasoning underlay their policies. In the making of their policies, national security concerns and ideology were actually intertwined since it was the ideology that dictated the dangerous nature of these individuals, which led to them being targeted for destruction to preserve the revolution.

The belief system of Pol Pot and the Khmer Rouge was thus clearly rooted in its own history, but at the same time the foreign influence, particularly of other communist regimes, is clearly discernible. The Khmer Rouge merely tried to improve it (Quinn, 1989a, p. 219). The extreme policies initiated by the Khmer Rouge were meant to allow for a transition to pure communism as soon as possible and were supposed to counteract those elements which prevented the transition in China (Quinn, 1989a, p. 219). Pol Pot's communist doctrine resembled the Chinese model of the Great Leap forward, and he would later admit that 'in the concrete revolutionary struggle of our country, we have creatively and successfully applied Mao Tse-tung's thought' (Quinn, 1989a, p. 220). The influence translated in particular to remarkable similarities with the Cultural Revolution in China (Quinn, 1989a, pp. 224-225). In both revolutions the young were accorded a particularly crucial role (Quinn, 1989a). In Cambodia the young and poor were seen as an impressionable 'blank page on which we can write anything we want', and were valued for their purity (Hinton, 1998a, p. 363; Midlarsky, 2005, p. 316).

In addition, both revolutions sought to uproot those who had been powerful in the society before the revolution (Quinn, 1989a, p. 316). In areas conquered by the communist forces in the first half of the 1970s the existing leaders were purged and replaced with new young communists that were to head the newly established communes which were also closely made to resemble the Chinese variant (Midlarsky, 2005, p. 317; Quinn, 1989a, p. 227). In both communist regimes, a favourable political outlook was a much more valued characteristic for the new young leaders than expertise (Midlarsky, 2005, pp. 317-318; Quinn, 1989a, pp. 227-228). Mao believed the intellectuals had always formed an obstacle on the road to communism. The Khmer Rouge had learned from the Chinese experience (Quinn, 1989a, p. 228). In China the intellectuals were only sent to the countryside after they appeared to pose an impediment to the revolution, but

83 For a more elaborate overview of this discussion, see Beachler (2009, pp. 229-231).

in Cambodia the cities were immediately emptied and in the following two years the intellectuals were subjected to harsh punishment and executions (Midlarsky, 2005, p. 318; Quinn, 1989a, p. 228).

Both revolutions had an anti-urban and anti-Western orientation with a corresponding focus on independence and self-reliance (Quinn, 1989a, p. 229). The Cambodian revolutionaries also drew inspiration from the Chinese model on how to provide collective incentives to the people and Pol Pot received advice from Chinese officials of the manner in which they had garnered particular successes (Midlarsky, 2005, p. 319). The desire of the Khmer Rouge to make a 'Super Great Leap Forward', in this sense, clearly resembles Mao's plans for a Great Leap Forward (Straus, 2001, p. 50). Ultimately, it seems, however, that Pol Pot and the Khmer Rouge were much more extreme in the manner in which they implemented the revolution (Midlarsky, 2005, p. 319).

There are also many similarities with Stalin's policies. Remarkable, in this respect, are the swiftness with which the agricultural sector was collectivized, the manner in which both regimes had a very narrowly defined in-group and the level and scope of violence which their regimes employed, including the many purges of the party (Quinn, 1989a, pp. 234-235). In both countries extensive confessions were extorted from the victims of these political purges before their executions (Quinn, 1989a, p. 235). In short, Pol Pot adhered to Mao's plan with Stalin's methods, but was determined to do so faster and more thoroughly than had been tried in either China or the USSR (Quinn, 1989a, p. 236; Valentino, 2004, p. 133).

7.5.2. USING THE IDEOLOGY TO LEGITIMIZE ITS CRIMES

Refugees have testified that after 1977 public officials became more open about the necessity of killing its enemies and became less concerned with who witnessed the murderous violence (Quinn, 1989b, p. 201). In the rhetoric used by the regime, we find neutralization techniques that legitimize the crimes.[84] Sykes and Matza identified five neutralization techniques: the denial of responsibility, the denial of injury, the denial of the victim, the condemnation of the condemners, and the appeal to higher loyalties (Sykes & Matza, 1957).

With the denial of responsibility the person believes that the act was caused 'by forces outside of the individual and beyond his control', and Sykes and Matza emphasize that 'interpretations of responsibility are cultural constructs and not merely idiosyncratic beliefs' (Sykes & Matza, 1957, p. 667). The denial of injury is predicated on the belief that the act does not bring forth any harm while the denial of the victim posits that even though there is harm, the harm was deserved (Sykes & Matza, 1957, p. 668). By condemning the condemners,

[84] For a further explanation on neutralization techniques, see Chapter 8.

the attention of the act is shifted from one's own acts to past behaviour of those who are criticizing the behaviour in the first place (Sykes & Matza, 1957, p. 668). Lastly, when an individual appeals to higher loyalties, he gives precedence to certain obligations or norms even when this requires him to violate others (Sykes & Matza, 1957, p. 669). While initially developed in a study on juvenile delinquency, the techniques have also been deemed useful to explain mass atrocities (Alvarez, 2001; Neubacher, 2006; Smeulers & Van Niekerk, 2009; Weerdesteijn & Smeulers, 2011).[85] In Cambodia as well, these neutralization techniques were embedded in the institutions and Pol Pot's message.

The denial of responsibility is predominantly present on an institutional level, to make individual perpetrators feel less responsible for their acts. The responsibility could be shifted to a higher authority that demanded the behaviour. At times, refusing to obey an order could lead to the death of the perpetrator leaving many to feel like they did not have a choice. Hinton, for instance, interviewed a perpetrator who told him: 'I couldn't refuse ... I was afraid they would suspect me until they saw me kill with their own eyes' (Hinton, 1998b, p. 113).

Euphemisms were used that allowed all involved to deny the true harm that was inflicted on its victims. Denial of injury, in this sense, was brought about by conveying the necessity to take out the root in order to eradicate the weed, meaning that individuals needed to be killed in order to remove the entire social class from society. In addition, people were told that 'we must burn the old grass and the new will grow', thus making the killings into something beautiful and transformative (Quinn, 1989b, pp. 200-201). In a speech Pol Pot similarly spoke of enemies in the party in terms of an 'illness' that needed to be 'examined' (Chandler, 2008, p. 267).

Those killed were denied their status as victims by designating them as enemies that brought their fate onto themselves. Radio broadcasts urged that 'the enemy must be utterly crushed' (Quinn, 1989b, p. 185). The Khmer Rouge conveyed the message that once an individual was labelled an enemy, one was expected to no longer have any emotions that related to the manner in which the person was treated (Hinton, 1998b, p. 113). They were often dehumanized, and Pol Pot is known to have referred to his enemies as 'evil microbes' (Chandler, 2008, p. 267). In addition, people were often equated with animals and referred to as such: 'Comrade Ox never refused to work. Comrade Ox was obedient. Comrade Ox did not complain. Comrade Ox did not object when his family was killed' (cited in Hinton, 1998b, pp. 365-366). These enemies were responsible for whatever went wrong in the country. When the communes were unable to meet the unrealistic targets set by the regime, these failings would be attributed to class enemies that sabotaged their plans (Valentino, 2004, p. 137). The security

[85] For an in depth analysis of different forms of denial in relation to mass atrocity, see also (S. Cohen, 2001)

forces were instructed to presume that 'wherever there are catastrophes or under-achievements in terms of building the country, defending the country or sorting out popular living standards, enemies exist in those places' (cited in Valentino, 2004, p. 137). Even children were encouraged to report traitors of the revolution through the propaganda of the regime (Hinton, 1998b, p. 111; Valentino, 2004, p. 137).

The higher loyalties were tied to the creation of a new, idealistic, socialist society that could be realized, according to Pol Pot, 'as long as we believe in the party, believe in the people, and as long as we love the nation' (Chandler *et al.*, 1988, p. 162). It was this revolution which needed to be protected against its enemies (Hinton, 1998b, p. 113). The rationale behind the killings was that 'it is better to arrest ten people by mistake than to let one guilty person go free' (Power, 2013, p. 120). The underlying message was that it was crucial to safeguard the revolution and all measures were warranted to safeguard that goal.

The regime also condemned those that accused them of horrendous human rights violations. When the British expressed their concern over the human rights situation in Cambodia, the Khmer Rouge denounced them for doing so. It countered that the British only had the right to become a slave, thief, prostitute or to be unemployed and in a letter to the UN, Ieng Sary rejected the criticism by arguing it came from the 'propaganda machine of the imperialists, the expansionists, annexationists', and suggested the regime would never kill as many people as it was accused of (Power, 2013, p. 126).

7.5.3. POL POT'S HOLD OVER THE REVOLUTION AND RESISTANCE

While the Khmer Rouge seem to have received some popular support during the civil war (Abuza, 1993, p. 1013), as time progressed it seems that fear predominantly dictated how the population behaved. Quinn describes, for instance, how 'an atmosphere of terror' was created in the communes 'in which families feared to speak even in their own homes or in front of their children for fear of being taken away and never being heard of again' (Quinn, 1989b, p. 193). The Khmer Rouge had little support among the population and it seems they were aware of it. Opposition also tended to grow as the policies became more radical causing the Khmer Rouge to increase the level of violence to force the population into compliance (Valentino, 2004, pp. 135-136). The Khmer Rouge saw resistance as being tied to the social class of a particular person leading to whole classes of people needing to be destroyed (Valentino, 2004, pp. 137-138).

Collectivization, in this sense, was not only important from an ideological standpoint but also became crucial to tighten the grip of the regime over its population (Valentino, 2004, pp. 135-137). The communes were the hub where propaganda would be communicated to the masses, where children particularly were indoctrinated, and people were coerced to tell on others who had failed to live by the regime's rules (Valentino, 2004, p. 137). While resistance from the population was made extremely difficult, within the communist party there were, from the very beginning, those that did not agree with the extreme policies that were enacted by Pol Pot. While Pol Pot equated debate with treason (Chandler, 1998, p. 17), many communist officials seem to have questioned the necessity of having the changes be so far reaching and of implementing them so quickly (Valentino, 2004, p. 133). Dissatisfaction among his ranks started to grow and this led to two coup attempts from disaffected members of the elite. The first most likely occurred in 1976[86], and the second foiled coup occurred in 1978 (Quinn, 1989b, pp. 194-207). The first stemmed wholly from dissatisfied military and party leaders who resented the extreme violence that had taken hold of the society. After the Minister of the Interior and Cooperation was executed, because he had been unhappy with the rapid and brutal manner in which the communization had taken place, other dissatisfied leaders started to plot to kill Pol Pot (Quinn, 1989b, pp. 194-195). The plan had been to poison Pol Pot, but it failed when a guard tasted his meal and died on the spot (Quinn, 1989b, p. 195). The second coup was encouraged by the Vietnamese, who reached out to Cambodian party officials in the hopes that they could organize an uprising (Quinn, 1989b, p. 194; 205). It sought to either bring the regime to an end or at least to wrestle the Eastern region out of Pol Pot's hands (Quinn, 1989b, p. 205). The plan was prevented from materializing any further, however, in May 1978 (Quinn, 1989b, p. 205).

In both instances, the coups were followed by massive purges. From late 1976 onwards the regime sought to eliminate anyone who may have been complicit in the plot, and thereafter started to target anyone who may be suspect for any reason imaginable (Quinn, 1989b, pp. 197-198). Most of them were brought to Tuol Sleng, where they would be tortured, forced to make false confessions and subsequently killed (Quinn, 1989b, p. 198). In many areas party officials were also replaced, often simply disappearing and later found dead in mass graves (Quinn, 1989b, p. 199). A few months later the policy would spread beyond the politically active cadre to include anyone who was suspect, and their families (Quinn, 1989b, pp. 200-202). The second coup led to purges that were predominantly targeted at anyone who could possibly collaborate with, or be sympathetic to, the Vietnamese (Quinn, 1989b, p. 205). Therefore, after 1978, according to Quinn, 'the country was basically entirely run by Pol Pot, Ieng Sary and their wives' (Quinn, 1989b, p. 206). Ultimately, resistance within the party was never able to unseat him without outside help from the Vietnamese. Quinn explains that after surviving the first attempt on his life, 'Pol Pot's political plan

86 For a discussion on why the most likely date of the coup fell in 1976 rather than 1970, as the Khmer Rouge would later claim, see Quinn (1989b, pp. 194-197). Chandler *et al.* note that information about the unsuccessful coup remains very unclear (Chandler *et al.*, 1988).

had largely achieved its goals inside Cambodia. He had destroyed virtually all of his potential and real opposition' (1989b, p. 208).

7.5.4. INSTITUTIONS AND PERPETRATORS

The Khmer Rouge placed many poor and young in prominent positions as they were more likely to have the right ideological mind-set and hate the urban population while remaining loyal to the regime to which they owed their new position of power (Hinton, 1998a, p. 365; 1998b, p. 110). The propaganda of the Khmer Rouge ensured that this attitude did not dissipate and constantly reminded them of the injustice that was done to them by the city people (Hinton, 1998a, p. 365). The Khmer Rouge deliberately targeted mainly the young and disenfranchised, since they already tended to be resentful towards the old society (Quinn, 1989a, pp. 236-237). They also recruited from particular minorities for the same reason, they had particular grievances that could be exploited (Quinn, 1989a, p. 236). Pol Pot, talking about his support base in the Northeast region reportedly said:

> 'I know perfectly these national minorities. They were miserable ... completely illiterate people who did not have even the slightest idea of cities, automobiles and Parliament [but who] dared to fight under the guidance of the The Party' (Quinn, 1989a, p. 236).

Brisse also noted how the Khmer Rouge had been 'cleverly playing on old historical grudges' (cited in Quinn, 1989a, p. 237). Their method of recruitment that included a shrewd propaganda campaign, their use of children that generally started their training at the age of 12, and the manner in which they trained them, namely in a particularly brutal fashion where they were desensitized by having to kill and torment animals and even people, was effective in creating a brutal and loyal force (Quinn, 1989a, pp. 237-239). Quinn notes, the young cadres were most ruthless, and were at times forced to kill even their loved ones to prove their loyalty (1989a, p. 239).

Many of the horrors were inflicted upon the population within the communes in which they lived, but others met their deaths in places such as Tuol Sleng prison. Much of the violence was perpetrated to destroy the old society by forcing people to flee the city, for instance, and build a communist society in its place (Quinn, 1989b, p. 180). The regime also used extensive violence, on the one hand, to counter threats they believed stemmed from the Vietnamese and their collaborators, and on the other hand, from treachery within the party (Quinn, 1989b, p. 180). For the latter purpose they used the confessions that were given by its victims while they were tortured, to purge his cadres (Quinn, 1989a, p. 235). These victims would go to extermination centres, the most notorious being Tuol Sleng prison, where the training and indoctrination of the perpetrators was reinforced even more (Hinton, 1998b, p. 113). Each victim that would enter Tuol Sleng prison because they were a suspected traitor would be photographed, given a number, interrogated, tortured until they confessed their crimes, before being killed (Fawthrop, 2005, p. 78). In this sense it resembled more an extermination centre rather than a prison, since there are only 7 known survivors of those 14,000 people who were arrested and killed (Fawthrop, 2005, p. 78).[87] The director of Tuol Sleng, nicknamed Duch, ensured that confessions ended up with the higher echelons, thus further fuelling Pol Pot's belief that the unfolding economic disaster could be attributed to enemies that were sabotaging the revolution (Fawthrop, 2005, p. 80).

7.6. THE INTERNATIONAL COMMUNITY AND CAMBODIA

Throughout Pol Pot's rise to power and subsequent reign, the world was dominated by the power structures of the Cold War that divided the world between communist and capitalist countries. As was to be expected, this dynamic is reflected in the allies the Khmer Rouge chose to maintain, but what is more surprising is that the capitalist countries were not more outspoken in condemning the horrors of the Khmer Rouge. As will be further explained in this paragraph, however, part of the answer to the latter enigma is to be found in the extreme secrecy in which the Khmer Rouge operated and the particular recent and the traumatic history of the US in this region.

During the 1950s, the US provided Cambodia with economic aid. Cold War logic dictated that Cambodian neutrality was preferable to a potential alliance the country may forge with either North Vietnam or communist China (Clymer, 1999, p. 613). However, the traditional suspicions of Cambodia towards its neighbours, Thailand and Vietnam, strained its relationship with the US, since both were valued allies of the US (Clymer, 1999, p. 613). In addition, Sihanouk's belief (which was largely correct) that the US secretly sought to undermine him and his regime damaged relations between the countries even further (Clymer, 1999, pp. 613-614). Overall, however, throughout the Kennedy period the countries had a relatively friendly relationship. This would change soon thereafter (Clymer, 1999, p. 614).

In the years preceding the Khmer Rouge's rise to power, the US predominant role was one that destabilized the country and facilitated the ultimate victory of the Khmer Rouge. As explained above, the constant heavy American

[87] 14,000 records have been preserved, the actual number of people killed may be higher (Fawthrop, 2005, p. 78). Power notes there are 5 known survivors out of 16,000 who entered the facility (Power, 2013, p. 143)

bombardments had the adverse effect of strengthening the Khmer Rouge militarily (Lemarchand, 2003, pp. 151-152). After coming to power, the only diplomatic contact which Democratic Kampuchea maintained was with China and North Korea (Midlarsky, 2005, p. 319). The lack of foreign observers initially muddied the assessments of many countries on how grave the situation inside Cambodia had become, and political interests coloured assessments of the brutal nature of the regime (Beachler, 2009; Power, 2013, p. 90). When government officials and scholars did express concern, these were received with scepticism, as people were inclined to believe the statements were motivated by the government's anti-communist stance (Beachler, 2009, p. 223; Power, 2013, p. 103). Even as the depth of the tragedy slowly became clear, however, the US held on to its policy which was, according to Power, characterized by 'non-engagement, non-condemnation and non-interest' (Power, 2013, p. 90). The US thereafter had become extremely reluctant to get involved in the region again after its involvement in the Vietnam War and early bombing of the Cambodian countryside. These memories caused many to be steadfast in their opposition to any US involvement. Power explains that even those that were concerned about the situation in Cambodia understood that

> 'drawing attention to the slaughter in Cambodia would have reminded America of its past sins, reopened wounds that had not yet healed at home, and invited questions about what the United States planned to do to curb the terror' (Power, 2013, p. 122).

People no longer wanted to have anything to do with that region and the horrors were not even condemned (Power, 2013, pp. 122-123).

For a long time, the situation in Cambodia was also not raised at the United Nations as a problem that needed to be addressed. Israel was the first to express its concern and warn of 'auto-genocide' in 1977, and a year later Britain brought the subject to the attention of the UN Commission on Human Rights, arguing a special human rights rapporteur should be appointed to investigate the situation (Power, 2013, p. 125; 542). The Soviet Union, Yugoslavia and Syria, however, lent their support to Democratic Kampuchea and blocked this route (Power, 2013, p. 125). The United Nations Security Council also remained passive. It never found that the situation in Cambodia amounted to a threat to international peace and security (Delbrück, 1991-1992, p. 898). The Security Council at this time still held a rather strict definition of what warrants such a situation and was deadlocked due to the Cold War (Evans, 2008, pp. 21-22; Grünfeld, 1998, pp. 429-430; Wheeler, 2006, p. 33).

Initially, the Khmer Rouge received substantial support from the Vietnamese. According to Womack 'the Vietnamese were the most important ally of the Khmer Rouge until victory in April 1975' (Womack, 2003, p. 113). Their common goals and belief system weighed more heavily than historical animosities, but the alliance soon disappeared as the Khmer Rouge became more powerful (Lemarchand, 2003, p. 151).

Thailand largely maintained a good relationship with the Khmer Rouge even though it was anti-communist, since both regimes sought to contain Vietnamese hegemonic aspirations for the region (Power, 2013, p. 126).[88] China continued to be a very important ally to Pol Pot, and provided the Khmer Rouge with military equipment and support throughout its reign, and both countries continued to do so even after they were removed from power (Power, 2013, p. 126; 147; Solarz, 1990, p. 102). After the fall of the regime, many countries joined China and Thailand and decided to stand behind the deposed Khmer Rouge regime (Solarz, 1990, pp. 102-103). After Vietnam invaded Cambodia in 1978 and removed Pol Pot from power, most countries denounced the intervention of the Vietnamese, which was widely seen as a gross violation of the country's sovereignty (Hanlon, 2006b, pp. 60-61).[89] Vietnam immediately started to display the signs of the horrendous violence that had pervaded Cambodia's society, but although the brutal nature of the regime became difficult to deny, arguments that genocide was committed were relegated to the realm of fiction by some and seen as a 'tool of Hanoi propaganda' (Fawthrop, 2005, p. 81; Power, 2013, pp. 142-145).

7.7. CONCLUSION

Cambodia's history of foreign invasion, their lost empire, the years under the yoke of colonialism, the dictatorships that followed and the years of civil war, made them particularly vulnerable to a group of nationalists that proclaimed they wanted to build a new and equal society with the help of their former king Sihanouk. The Khmer Rouge managed to win the civil war partly because of the support they were given by the people on the ground, who could not even imagine that their victory would bring about horrors that far exceeded those of the civil war. In the midst of this political upheaval, backed by important sections of the rural population, from which they recruited their soldiers, the Khmer Rouge rose to power (Edwards, 2004, pp. 64-65).

The message and ideology that Pol Pot and the Khmer Rouge propagated, tied into this history; it built on long held sensitivities and animosities that were inherent in Cambodian culture. The schisms, history and culture of the country did not make violence inevitable, but made the population more susceptible to the violent and hate filled ideology of the Khmer Rouge. Hinton explains how the Khmer Rouge tried to use the resentment that was felt by those living in the countryside towards those living in the city, and the 'goal was often not difficult to achieve given the initial resentment many of the poor felt toward rich

88 Although there were also some so cross border skirmishes, see Chapter 11 for details.

89 See Chapter 11 for more details.

city people who allegedly looked down upon them, enjoyed a much easier life and supported Lon Nol, who was responsible for the overthrowing of Sihanouk and the carpet bombing of the countryside' (Hinton, 1998a, p. 363). There had always been tensions between the rural and urban populations, but the recent war, which disproportionately affected the rural population, the unemployment of the newly educated and the economic downturn caused, among others, by the civil war exacerbated these animosities even further (Vickery, 1984, pp. 15-26).

In addition, Pol Pot and the Khmer Rouge used the historical resentment much of the population felt against the Vietnamese whom also became enemies of the state that needed to be eliminated. Historically, Cambodians tend to have an image of Vietnam as a threatening neighbour continuously seeking to expand southward, and many Cambodians perceive this past as relevant for the present and see much continuity between the two (Takei, 1998, p. 62). Chandler explains how in the past

> 'the presence of rival patrons to the west and east set in motion a whipsaw between Thai and Vietnamese influence … [which] lasted until the 1860s, and arguably was revived under Democratic Kampuchea, where eastern-zone cadres were accused by Pol Pot and his colleagues of having "Cambodian bodies and Vietnamese minds"' (Chandler, 2008, p. 97).

Because of their historical background, the collective memories of the Vietnamese and Cambodians are diametrically juxtaposed to each other. For Vietnam, the southern conquests are a sign of their greatness, while Cambodians see it as a tragedy (Takei, 1998, p. 65). Considering the violent history between the countries, Chandler explains it is not surprising Cambodians came to 'associate periods of powerlessness with periods of Vietnamese control, and periods of nationalist unrest … with killing Vietnamese' (Chandler, 1979, p. 411). Vietnam's conquest of the southern parts of Cambodia have been equated with 'eating silkworms' where land is steadily absorbed, a seemingly slow process but one that will ultimately destroy the leaves and plants rapidly. Takei argues this left its mark, and left Cambodia largely resistant to any compromise (Takei, 1998, p. 74). Many people, and particularly the communist elite, were scared of the intentions of the ethnic Vietnamese residents within Cambodia that continued to have an important role in society after they were favoured for particular jobs by the French colonial regime (Chandler, 1998, p. 4; Locard, 2005, p. 128). The Vietnamese where traditionally an important 'other' for the Cambodian nation. Early texts emphasized both the docility of the Cambodian people as well as their violent history in which they killed numerous Vietnamese, a seemingly contradictory narrative that was rectified with the presumption that different rules applied to the Vietnamese, as they were non-Buddhist and wholly different from the Cambodian nation (Chandler, 1979, p. 413).

The new people and the minorities living within Cambodia, groups which actually overlapped since the minorities lived overwhelmingly in the city centres before the revolution, became the main enemies of the regime (Kiernan, 2010, p. 478; Peang-Meth, 1991, p. 452). The failings of the regime were in fact scapegoated onto them and they were to be destroyed. From the very start, the policies initiated by the Khmer Rouge in the captured areas were brutal, and when they violently emptied the cities and rapidly, without regard for the consequences of the population, set in motion the collectivist efforts, opposition in the party ranks started to build. The opposition that emerged as a consequence of his brutal policies led Pol Pot to violently turn against many in his own party (Valentino, 2004, pp. 99-100).

The Khmer Rouge did not thrive because of the widespread support given to them by the population. They had installed a system that brutally repressed them and kept them in a state of terror. Resistance was made extremely difficult. People were merely trying to survive, and it was made particularly difficult to trust fellow Cambodians preventing large scale opposition from being coordinated. This, does not mean, however, that propaganda or their communist and nationalist message have not played a role at all. The regime did try to legitimize their crimes, making it easier for the perpetrators to reconcile the crimes they perpetrated with their own character and morals and the propaganda of the regime, which indoctrinated children even to keep an eye on their parents, facilitated the paranoia in society even within the family.

In sum, it is fair to say that many of the long term pre-conditions that can potentially lead to mass murder which have been identified in the literature and were elaborately discussed in Chapter 3, were present in society long before Pol Pot rose to power. Pol Pot and the Khmer Rouge contributed to the emergence of new more immediate preconditions such as the horrendous civil war and economic and political unrest that followed. They subsequently took advantage of these factors as they rose to power and used the susceptibility of the population that stemmed from these preconditions, their suspicion to the urban population and the Vietnamese, in their communist and nationalist message to legitimize their violence.

CHAPTER 8
MILOSEVIC AND THE DISSOLUTION OF YUGOSLAVIA

8.1. INTRODUCTION

In the 1990s, the horrible violence that took hold over the Balkans shocked the world. The communist dictator Josip Broz Tito had promoted 'brotherhood and unity' among the peoples living in Yugoslavia since he came to power after World War II, but after he died in 1980, the federation would soon unravel (Fine, 2006, p. 277; Kollander, 2004, pp. 7-8).[90] In the years that followed, Yugoslavia's economy started to falter. These problems were exacerbated by the end of the Cold War, which caused the country to lose some of its strategic importance and international prestige (Woodward, 1995, pp. 15-16). The rising nationalism that subsequently swept through the region would soon lead to the dissolution of the country. After Slovenia declared independence in the summer of 1991, a ten-day war followed in which 50 people lost their lives. Slovenia was relatively homogeneous in its ethnic composition[91], and it was apparent that it had a strong national guard ready to protect the country (Kollander, 2004, p. 7; 10). In Croatia, on the other hand, about 12 % of the population was Serb (Kollander, 2004, p. 10), and in Bosnia, matters were even more complicated. About 40 % of the population were Bosnian Muslims, or Bosniaks, and the country furthermore was home to large Serbian and Croatian minorities (Kollander, 2004, p. 11).[92] With their declarations of independence, war between these parties was imminent as the Croat and Serb minorities had been seeking to unite with their 'mother country' and the Bosnian Muslims also feared remaining in a Serb dominated Yugoslavia (Kollander, 2004, p. 11; LeBor, 2006, p. 26).

A long and brutal war followed, especially in Bosnia, where towns were cleansed of their minority populations. It entailed brutal campaigns of killings, intimidation, rape and other brutal acts (Kollander, 2004, p. 12). After peace was

---

[90] For the sake of readability, the territory that has existed under different names between 1918-1991 will be referred to throughout as Yugoslavia.

[91] An estimated 90% of the population consisted of ethnic Slovenes (Bugajski, 1993, p. 95).

[92] Bosnian Muslims, or Bosniaks, formed 43% of the population, the largest minority were the Serbs constituting 31.4% of the population while Croats constituted 17.3% of the population (Kollander, 2004, p. 11).

established between the former republics of Yugoslavia, violence also erupted in Kosovo. As will be more extensively covered in Chapter 11, the violence caused NATO to take collective action, hoping to force Milosevic to refrain from using further violence. An 11 week bombing campaign ensued, during which NATO demanded that Serbia withdrew its forces and commit to a ceasefire while agreeing to the deployment of an international force to the region, allowed refugees to return, and grand humanitarian agencies unimpeded access (Roberts, 1999, pp. 102-103). While Milosevic eventually relented, Kosovo's population continues to live in limbo as their independence was recognized by some states but not by others (Judah, 2008, p. 148).[93]

Throughout the wars, the horrors were portrayed by the respective regimes as legitimate. In order to prepare the population for war and legitimize the brutal acts that accompanied the war, Milosevic used a sophisticated propaganda campaign that gave renewed, contemporary meaning to historic events. While he portrayed himself and the Serbs as victims and defenders of the unity of Yugoslavia, he actually played an important part in Yugoslavia's dissolution (Brosse, 2003; LeBor, 2003, p. 133; Morus, 2007a, 2007b). Many commentators immediately started laying the blame with the region's burdensome past, while others recognized the troubling role that the leaders played in inciting the violence (Majstorovic, 1997). However, rather than looking at which factor – ethnic hatred or elite manipulation – was the most important cause of the wars, in the former Yugoslavia, it seems more fruitful to assess how all relevant factors – as were set out in chapter 3 – interacted with each other.

The present chapter serves to establish the role Milosevic played in bringing about the crimes in the former Yugoslavia. In addition, when analysing the primary case study of the war in Kosovo, and Milosevic decisions therein, it is crucial to realize that neither Milosevic's, nor NATO's, decisions happened in a vacuum. The memories of the wars, during the early 1990s, were still lodged into the minds of all the different actors and influenced the choices they made four years later in 1999 when violence broke out again.

The theoretical framework that was set out in Chapter 3 will be applied to the Yugoslav case in the present chapter. In this manner, the more general risk-factors for mass atrocities as they have been developed in the literature will be combined with the specific theories and literature on the Yugoslav conflict. The first section will elaborate on the different theories that are said to explain the outbreak of the secessionist wars that tend to focus on either the region's troublesome past or the role of the elite. Subsequently the history of the region will be analysed in more detail and thereafter, the role Milosevic played in its demise will be investigated by looking at the manner in which he used the past to incite and legitimize the

93 A major step was taken, however, in 2010 when the ICJ ruled in its advisory opinion that Kosovo's declaration of independence did not constitute a breach of international law (ICJ, 2010, http://www.icj-cij.org/docket/files/141/16010.pdf). Currently 91 states have recognized Kosovo's independence (State Portal of the Republic of Kosova).

crimes and his role in creating the necessary institutional set up. In addition, thereafter, the role of the international community in trying to stop the violence during the 1990-1995 wars will be detailed as this is likely to have shaped the expectations Milosevic had of intervention by the international community when violence broke out again in 1999.

8.2. EXPLANATIONS FOR THE WAR

Theories abound that are said to explain the dissolution of Yugoslavia, and it is rare for any author to look at any one particular explanatory variable. Usually multiple causes are factored in, although scholars differ as to which cause they contribute more significance (Ramet, 2005, p. 55). Two dominant approaches can be discerned, however, that seek to explain ethnic conflict more generally and the Yugoslav conflict specifically; the primordial and the constructivist or instrumentalists (Hanlon, 2006a; Majstorovic, 1997). These theories differ in the role that ethnic hatred played in bringing forth the violence and the role that the elite played in inciting the conflict.

Primordialism is perhaps the most controversial one. Hanlon explains primordialism as the belief that ethnicity involves 'an exceptionally strong affiliation which is often linked to ancient conflicts, age-old hatreds and past atrocities' (Hanlon, 2006a, p. 97). This perspective is often seen as problematic because it frequently leads to the presumption that the differences between different ethnic groups are insurmountable and violence is inevitable (Hanlon, 2006a, p. 97). Constructivists and instrumentalists do not take the mere existence of these conflictual attitudes for granted, but argue that identity is constructed, or at the very least shaped by social systems, leaders and circumstance (Hanlon, 2006a, p. 98). Hanlon explains that 'because of this, constructivists focus on elites and the way they manipulate ethnic, religious or class identity' (Hanlon, 2006a, p. 98). While Hanlon treats constructivism and instrumentalism as one category that counters the conclusions of primordial scholars, others point to the more subtle differences between them. Sékulić, Massey and Hodson point to the rational choice focus that underlies instrumentalism causing it to focus on the 'political entrepreneurs [who] cultivate fear, and pursue ethno-nationalist goals in order to advance their own political (and material) interests' and the ethno nationalist groups that equally seek to safeguard their own interests, for land or jobs for instance, through ethnic hatred and violence (Sekulić, Massey, & Hodson, 2006, pp. 798-799).

Importantly, Hanlon points out that these different approaches have important policy implications as well. Constructivists will advocate trying to remove the points of contention and conflict whilst keeping the groups together, and primordialists will want to separate the groups from each other in order to prevent further violence (Hanlon, 2006a, p. 99; Majstorovic, 1997, pp. 170-171). However, which perspective one adheres to not only affects where the groups should live, whether interventionist policies should try to keep the groups together or separate them, it also influences the choice of who to direct the policies to. The primordial perspective suggests that the problem lies with the population, while the elite variant of instrumentalism and constructivist theories suggest that the elite are at fault. Adhering to the latter theories would therefore also imply that any interventionist policy instrument should be aimed at the leaders of the warring groups. These different perspectives will first be discussed in the context of Yugoslavia's demise before turning to other factors that have been identified in the literature which are said to explain the war and the atrocities that went along with it.

8.2.1. ANCIENT HATREDS AND ELITE MANIPULATION

Arguments that point to ancient hatreds have been very influential. Often the Yugoslav conflict was explained through what Zakosek calls 'a "civilizational" or cultural argument and points at ethno-cultural or even anthropological factors in order to explain the traits of Balkan nationalisms' (Zakosek, 2007, p. 33). These arguments were primarily voiced in non-academic circles and focused upon the ethnic hatreds that were passed down from time immemorial (Jovic, 2001, p. 103). Controversially, Kaplan wrote about the Balkans:

> 'Twentieth century history came from the Balkans. Here men have been isolated by poverty and ethnic rivalry, dooming them to hate' (Kaplan, 2005, p. li).

It is often referred to as the 'ancient hatreds' debate, although most versions hardly refer back to 'ancient times' but trace the origin of the ethnic tensions to the end of the Ottoman Empire and the rise of nationalism (Hagen, 1999, p. 52). Godina came to the conclusion that considering the violent past of the different nations, 'what is surprising is not the present outburst of nationalism, but the lengthy non-nationalistic period in the past' (Godina, 1998, p. 411). According to this perspective, the existing hatreds and nationalist tendencies were suppressed during communist rule but after the death of Tito, these are said to have risen to the surface (Kaldor, 2006, p. 36; Kaplan, 2005, p. xi; Sekulić *et al.*, 2006, p. 800).

This perspective was popularised in different media outlets and ultimately reached politicians at which point it influenced their policy choices. While Kaplan argues he has been an adamant advocate of military intervention, ironically his book seems to have given Bill Clinton the excuse not to act (Kaplan, 2005, pp. x-xi). While the debate gained more traction in none academic circles, it has influenced academic work as well. Even when acknowledging that it is not unique for the Balkan region to have historical narratives which are important for their national identity, Zakosek for instance still argues, that 'it seems that the obsession with the past is typical for East European nationalisms' (Zakosek, 2007, pp. 32-35). Even though he says he disagrees with any attempt to explain the war in cultural terms, by referring to such an 'obsession', Zakosek nevertheless seems to essentialize Balkan identity as one that is inherently conflict prone. Therefore, even when formally denouncing the primordial perspective, the influence of the theory still leaves its mark on contemporary scholarly discourse.

This is troubling for two reasons. Firstly, and most importantly, as Sekulic *et al* point out, the theory lacks empirical support (Sekulić *et al.*, 2006, p. 800). While there is undoubtedly a violent history between the groups, which gives intuitive credibility to the theory, in fact, Serbs and Croats had not fought each other before the 20th century, intermarried, and the most recent polls before the war showed high levels of tolerance (Gagnon, 1994, pp. 133-134). While nationalism was present among the different groups, there was no hostility or intolerance (Sekulić *et al.*, 2006, p. 801). In addition, if nationalist tendencies and ethnic schisms were pervasive in the Tito's Yugoslavia, more than anything it would show that nationalism does not need to become violent.

It has frequently been argued, therefore, that the different nationalist leaders that emerged after the death of Tito are the real cause of the violence. They have been said to have 'activated and directed' collective memories and translated them into ethno-nationalist political goals (Sekulić *et al.*, 2006, p. 801). Elites sought to make ethnic identity the only salient one as it served their own political goals (Gagnon, 1994, p. 132). According to Gagnon,

> 'the Serbian leadership from 1987 onward actively created rather than responded to threats by Serbs by purposefully provoking and fostering the outbreak of conflict along ethnic lines, especially in regions of Yugoslavia with good inter-ethnic relations' (Gagnon, 1994, p. 132).

The middle ground is sought by those who argue that identity is flexible and open to be shaped and influenced but also acknowledge that it is constrained by existing myths and memories (Majstorovic, 1997, p. 171). This perspective stresses therefore that anything that is constructed needs to be embedded in the existing memories and myths and cannot be created "out of thin air" (Majstorovic, 1997, p. 172). As Majstorovic points out,

> 'historical memory constraints the options that leaders exercise in conflict creation and in peacemaking. Ethnic identity in the former Yugoslavia, however, has also been and will continue to be somewhat adaptive but only within a framework that does not threaten the constraints imposed by myth and memory' (Majstorovic, 1997, p. 171).

Sekulic, Massey and Hodson phrase it slightly differently as an interactive process between leaders, intellectuals, journalists and other opinion makers and the public (Sekulić *et al.*, 2006, p. 820). They specify the interactionist element by arguing:

> 'political entrepreneurs and opinion leaders are limited in how far the definition of an ethnic other can be construed as a threat to personal and public safety, and even the degree of ambiguity they can introduce in order to generate fear of the other' (Sekulić *et al.*, 2006, p. 820).

War further facilitated the reinterpretation of the others as dangerous and untrustworthy (Sekulić *et al.*, 2006, p. 821). Oberschall explains this process in terms of different 'cognitive frames', one that was operative in times of peace, and another one which dominated in times of crisis (Oberschall, 2000). A cognitive frame according to Oberschall, is a 'mental structure which situates and connects events, people and groups into a meaningful narrative in which the social world that one inhabits makes sense and can be communicated and shared with others' (Oberschall, 2000, p. 989). The leaders, Oberschall points out, activated the crisis frame but did not invent it, as it was already shaped by memories of past wars (Oberschall, 2000, p. 989).

Conceptions of the other are much more effective when framed within already existing cultural sensitivities as was also explained in Chapter 3. There certainly were sufficient pre-existing cultural schisms between different groups, an important pre-condition for mass violence, to allow for the reinterpretation of the relationship between the groups. Majstorovic therefore argues it would be desirable to view the process of primordialization as a continuous process in which ethnic identity is shaped and reformulated (Majstorovic, 1997, p. 171). When looked upon in this fashion it also becomes clear that 'the debate between the primordialist notion of ethnonational identity and the argument that this identity is socially constructed is a needlessly constructed dichotomy in itself' (Majstorovic, 1997, p. 171). Yet the extent to which the history constrained the elite remains to be debated and while Majstorovic believes – especially for Serbia – the influence of the elite to be 'not as significant as one would think' (1997, p. 178), it is maintained here that the role played by Milosevic was actually very important in giving renewed contemporary relevance to historical events. The sections below will analyse the existing memories and myths within the former Yugoslavia and how the elite reformulated them and gave them a renewed meaning.

8.2.2. OTHER FACTORS

Besides these two dominant strands of research that pit historical ethnic hatred against elite influence, several other factors have been identified in the literature. The economic situation in particular and the role international politics played is frequently mentioned as having contributed to the demise of multi-ethnic

Yugoslavia (Jovic, 2001, p. 101; Woodward, 1995).[94] An economic crisis in the 1970s had a tremendous impact on the country, but Woodward believes the story might have ended very differently if it was not followed by the end of the Cold War which eroded Yugoslavia's strategic position internationally (Woodward, 1995, p. 16). With the fall of the Berlin Wall, Yugoslavia lost its ability to attract economic and political support from the West (Jovic, 2001, pp. 110-111)

In addition, the inability of Tito to truly unify the different nations into one community with a common identity, is mentioned by several scholars as a factor that facilitated its disintegration (Ramet, 2005, p. 63; Sekulic, Massey, & Hodson, 1994; Zakosek, 2007, p. 36). It has also been argued that the disintegration of Yugoslavia was caused by the institutional makeup of Tito's communist state. In this scenario it is argued that the socialist institutions 'became increasingly dysfunctional' and it is believed that while they were first used to 'channel ethnic politics' in the end they ended up being 'tools in the hands of the ethnic political elites' (Zakosek, 2007, p. 34).

Lastly, it has been suggested that it is the anarchy, which manifests itself as a great sense of insecurity when there is state breakdown that causes ethnic violence to break out (Oberschall, 2000, pp. 983-984). However, although this certainly played a role, Oberschall rightfully wonders why the insecurity would result in fear when day-to-day personal experience actually shows there is nothing to be scared of (Oberschall, 2000, p. 984). One may wonder to what extent this factor is not only a cause but also a consequence of the conflict, not able to explain its origin but able to explain its escalation.

A major problem however with the literature more generally is that it often assigns too much responsibility to a general cause and that rather all causes should be assessed in a single framework (Jovic, 2001, p. 101). The current chapter will integrate these perspectives into one coherent whole, suggesting one should look at the interplay of factors.

8.3. HISTORY AND MYTHS

Many nations have a violent history – the nations that made up the former Yugoslavia are no exception. Some scholars maintain that indeed the history

94 Jovic actually identifies 7 factors: 1. the economic argument, 2. the 'ancient hatred' argument, 3. the nationalism argument, 4. the cultural argument, 5. the 'international politics' argument, 6. the 'role of personality' argument and 7. the 'fall of empires' argument (Jovic, 2001). All these theories will be incorporated in the present chapter, but not as separate arguments, since it seems that there is considerable overlap between these different factors. Nationalism and culture are important for the 'ancient hatred' debate as well as the elite manipulation debate. The role the personality of Tito played in maintaining peace (and the manner in which this is linked to an empire style reign where supra-national interests prevailed), as well as the role that Milosevic played with promoting violence, will be extensively covered by highlighting how they chose to deal with the other factors that were present.

of Yugoslavia is not characterized by hostilities which are inherently different from those that have scarred the rest of Europe (Ramet, 2005, p. 3). However, considering the allegations that ancient hatreds form the cause of the wars, and keeping in mind that scholarly literature in general identified schisms between different groups as an important, even though not sufficient, precondition for the onset of atrocities, it is worthwhile examining Yugoslavia's past.

Religion and language are the two dominant factors that separate the different groups in the former Yugoslavia from each other. When people spoke a different language, it was the language barrier which separated them from each other, when they spoke the same language it was religion (Judah, 2009, p. 43). While several different languages are spoken in the republics of the former Yugoslavia, Croatian, Bosnian and Serb inhabitants largely spoke the same language, although Serb areas use the Cyrillic script, while in Bosnia and Croatia the Latin alphabet was used (Hagen, 1999, p. 53; Judah, 2009, p. 44). The difference in their written language reflected their religious differences. Most Serbs had an Orthodox Christian heritage while most Croats had a Catholic background, and in Bosnia a substantial part of the population was Muslim (Hagen, 1999, p. 53; Judah, 2009, pp. 43-44).[95] The Albanian speaking population was also divided religiously although most of them were Muslim (Hagen, 1999, p. 53). To complicate matters further, most of the republics were not ethnically homogeneous. In Croatia about 12% of the population was Serb and Bosnia was divided among the different ethnic groups with 44% being Muslim, 31% Serbs and 17% Croat (Woodward, 1995, p. 33). In this manner, schisms thus had a connection to written and spoken language, religion as well as territory.

For the Serbian population tensions were rooted in a complex composition of myth and fact that together formed the collective legacy of the Serbs as a nation. The key events that were important in forming the collective memory up and until the outbreak of the war in Yugoslavia will be covered but it remains a contentious issue to select the moment to start the narrative that is to explain the disintegration of Yugoslavia. While some would start with the rise to power of several of the most vocal nationalist leaders not long before the wars started, others would go back centuries to emphasize the historic roots of the ethnic tensions. Since the purpose of the present chapter is to analyse the role Milosevic played, the narrative will begin at the moment many Serbian nationalists would start their story, with the start of what came to be known as their era under 'agelong Turkish slavery' (Križan, 1994, p. 47).

95 While the traditionally Muslim part of the Bosnian citizens these days prefers to be called Bosniaks, the present book will also continue to designate them as 'Bosnian Muslims' since this is how they were identified during the time of the conflict. In doing so the present work does not refer to their religious beliefs *per se* but includes all those belonging to this 'ethnic group' which in its broadest sense is taken to mean any group of people 'who collectively and publicly identify themselves as a distinct group based on various cultural features such as shared ancestry and common origin, language, customs and religious beliefs' (Haviland, Prins, Walrath, & McBride, 2008, p. 313).

8.3.1. THE OTTOMAN EMPIRE

In the 14th century the 200-year-old kingdom of Nemanja, that had brought the Serbs together as a nation, disintegrated with the death of Tsar Dusan and the Ottoman conquests that followed (Judah, 2009, p. 9). This period has been crucial for the nation building process of the Serbian people, and the memory to this glorious period remains important until this day.

The dynasty was founded by Stefan Nemanja and by the end of his reign his realm included much of what today is central Serbia and Kosovo, and stretched from Montenegro, to Hercegovina (Judah, 2008, p. 19). His son Rastko, today better known as St Sava, was the founder of the Serbian Orthodox Church and he has been described as having 'founded Serbian statehood and national identity' as he portrayed the Serbs as chosen people meant to rule over their land (Judah, 2008, p. 19; 2009, p. 20). He centred the Church in Pec, Kosovo which Serbs came to see as the 'cradle of their civilization' (Judah, 2008, p. 18; 2009, p. 20). The sanctification of Sava and the Nemanja's thereafter provided the Serbian nation with heavenly protectors that watched over them (Judah, 2009, p. 20). It was the only genuinely Serbian institution while they were subjected to Ottoman domination (Judah, p. 17), and throughout this time, the memory of their great dynasty was kept alive through folk poetry and through the church (Judah, 2008, p. 21; 2009, p. 17; Križan, 1994, p. 48). It allowed myths about their national history to be passed on for generations. These myths have become more important than the actual historical events. The one that is perhaps the most famous, narrates the events that took place in Kosovo on June 28, 1389 (Judah, 2008, pp. 20-21).

The battle at Kosovo Polje came to signify the end of the medieval Serbian Empire and is of mythical significance to the Serbian people (Bieber, 2002, p. 95; Križan, 1994, pp. 47-48; Mikula, 2002, p. 64). It refers to a battle that was fought by Christian forces, under the leadership of the Serbian Knez Lazar Hrebeljanovic, against the Ottoman forces that were led by Sultan Murad (Bieber, 2002, p. 96). In the story, Knez Lazar is offered a choice on the eve of the battle, between a kingdom on earth or in heaven. Prince Lazar chose the heavenly kingdom and the next day the Serbs were defeated on the battlefield (Bieber, 2002, p. 96). While the battle was said to have been lost militarily, it is portrayed as a moral and spiritual victory as it explains how defeat was voluntarily accepted in order to protect Christian Europe from Muslim aggressors (Bieber, 2002, p. 96; Križan, 1994, p. 48). The Sultan was killed after the battle, or so the myth goes, by a knight that pretended to surrender to the enemy in order to gain access to the Sultan (Bieber, 2002, p. 96; Judah, 2008, p. 20). The myth also mentions how Vuc Brankovic betrayed the Serbian army before the battle and therefore enabled its defeat (Bieber, 2002, p. 97).

In reality, it had not been the first important battle against the Ottoman Empire (Judah, 2009, p. 9), and the battle at Kosovo Polje most likely ended in a stalemate, rather than an outright defeat (Bieber, 2002, p. 96). It actually took the Ottoman forces almost another century to conquer the remnants of the medieval Serbian state (Bieber, 2002, p. 96). In addition, the knight that killed the sultan, most probably never existed, but was celebrated as a martyr (and while Vuc Brankovic was real, he probably did not betray the Serbs) (Bieber, 2002, pp. 96-97). Sharing folk myths and clinging to their Orthodox Christian religion became important ways for the Serbs to cling to their national identity throughout the time that they were ruled by the Ottoman Empire (Judah, 2008, p. 21; Križan, 1994, p. 48). The value of the myth, therefore, does not stem from its historical accuracy but from the manner in which it provided a historical foundation on which national rhetoric and territorial claims with respect to Kosovo could be built, regardless of the fact that Serbs would come to constitute a minority in the region (Bieber, 2002, pp. 95-96).

In the centuries that followed Serbian forces resisted Ottoman rule on multiple occasions, and were forced to flee or left voluntarily in search of a better life (Hagen, 1999, pp. 56-57; Judah, 2008, pp. 32-33; 2009, pp. 52-53; Sell, 2002, pp. 73-74). The number of Serbs which fled from Kosovo was so large that it left the Albanians as the majority in the region (Hagen, 1999, pp. 56-57). Serbia would only regain full independence and recognition at the Congress of Berlin in 1878 (Judah, 2009, p. 56), but Kosovo remained in Ottoman hands (Judah, 2008, p. 23). While it was not part of the nation state, it was crucial to the nation. In 1889, at the 500th anniversary of the battle, Serbia's foreign minister proclaimed:

> 'The new history of Serbia begins with Kosovo – a history of valiant efforts, long suffering, endless wars and unquenchable glory... We bless Kosovo because the memory of the Kosovo heroes upheld us, encouraged us, taught us and guided us' (cited in Judah, 2008, p. 23).

In the 19th century the nationalist ideology was articulated in earnest by the Serbian politician, Ilija Garasanin (Judah, 2009, p. 56). He argued that lost territories (most notably Macedonia, Kosovo and the Sandzak) needed to be reclaimed (Judah, 2008, p. 37). The text in essence was a 'secret strategy for the establishment of a Greater Serbia at the expense of the crumbling Ottoman Empire' (Sell, 2002, p. 72). Hopes of reclaiming lost territory, especially Bosnia Hercegovina, were dashed when the Habsburg monarchy annexed it in 1908, but Serbia did not give up its campaign to recover lost lands completely (Farley, 2006, p. 56). Belgrade started expanding southward and, eventually, the Serbs reclaimed much of Kosovo during the Balkan war of 1912 (Judah, 2008, pp. xix; 37-38; Sell, 2002, p. 72).

By the time Serbia regained control over Kosovo, Serbs were a minority but the conquest was nevertheless viewed as noble act which had liberated the population (Judah, 2008, p. 39). Many Orthodox Slavs indeed saw the Serbian forces as liberators from Ottoman repression but it brought death and destruction for the Albanian Kosovars (Stefanović, 2005, p. 475). Albanian resistance was crushed and several horrific massacres took place (Judah, 2008, p. 39). It has been estimated that about 80% of the Muslim villages had been burnt and that the onslaught had caused about 25,000 refugees to pour into northern Albania (Stefanović, 2005, pp. 474-475). By 1915, the tide was turning and Serbia was invaded by the Austro-Hungarians, along with Bulgaria and Germany, causing many – Serbs this time – to flee across Kosovo. Thousands died, after being captured by the invading army, but also in reprisal attacks that the Albanian population unleashed upon the fleeing Serbs in retaliation for the violence that had been done to them in the years before (Judah, 2008, pp. 40-41). The Serbs returned in 1918 with the help of the French and Italians and the Kingdom of Serbs, Croats and Slovenes was declared (Judah, 2008, p. 41).

8.3.2. THE FIRST YUGOSLAVIA, 1918-1941

Before 1918 only Serbia and Montenegro formed independent countries; the other nationalities were part of the larger Ottoman or Austro-Hungarian empires (Kollander, 2004, p. 4). Even though the unification of these countries could not have been foreseen, visions of how unity among the South Slav peoples could be advanced had been around for several years (Farley, 2006, pp. 60-61). At the end of WWI, after weeks of negotiations, the Serbs proved willing to give up their own state to forge a unity with the other nations (Farley, 2006, pp. 63-65). Conflict arose, however, when it needed to be decided how this new country should be organized. While the Serbs decided on a centralist state, headed by King Aleksander Karadjordjevic, most Croats desired more autonomy (Djokić, 2012, pp. 80-81; Farley, 2006, pp. 66-67; Kollander, 2004, p. 5).

In addition, violent resistance from the Kosovar Albanians to their incorporation into the kingdom lasted until 1924 (Judah, 2008, p. 42). According to Sell, the manner in which the Serbs ruled over Kosovo throughout the inter-war years can be described as 'internal colonization' (2002, p. 74). They dominated within the elite, the educational system was Serbian and they tried to change the ethnic balance in the region by confiscating land from the Kosovar Albanians and promoting Serbian and Montenegrin settlers to move there (Sell, 2002, p. 74; Stefanović, 2005, p. 480). Despite these efforts the changes were marginal and by the 1930s only about a third of the inhabitants of Kosovo reported having a Slavic mother tongue compared with 60% speaking the Albanian language (Stefanović, 2005, p. 480).

When the problems seemed unsurmountable, the king Aleksander Karadjordjevic decided to abolish the constitution and impose a dictatorship (Djokić, 2012, pp. 82-83; Farley, 2006, pp. 67-72). In doing so the king proclaimed 'we are no longer Serbs, Croats and so on but Yugoslavs' and renamed the country Yugoslavia (Fine, 2006, p. 276). A ban was imposed on all political or ethnocentric activity which actually hit the Croats harder than the Serbs (Farley, 2006, pp. 72-74). The Serbs already saw their heritage reflected in the presence of the king and saw their flags due to its affiliation with the Orthodox Church but the Croats lost all opportunities to display their national symbols and all their influence in the state (Farley, 2006, pp. 74-75). This led to the insurrection of several opposition movements (Farley, 2006, p. 75). One of them, the Ustashe movement, adopted violent tactics and by 1931 the king decided to compromise and adopt a new constitution (Farley, 2006, pp. 75-78). It was too little, too late as no real power was transferred. Before Aleksander, who seemed to have had a change of heart in the final months, was able to implement real changes he, was assassinated by a man whom had ties to the Ustashe movement (Farley, 2006, pp. 78-83; Kollander, 2004, p. 5). In 1939 a new compromise was reached but it was not to last due to the advent of WWII (Kollander, 2004, p. 5).

8.3.3. WORLD WAR II AND THE CIVIL WAR, 1941-1945

The Second World War ushered in a new chapter of Yugoslav history and it would be a bloody one. After Yugoslavia was invaded, the country was partitioned. Italy ruled over Dalmatia, Montenegro, western Macedonia and Kosovo. Due to the fact that most citizens from the latter two areas were Albanian, these two regions were united with Albania which had been occupied by Italy since 1939 (Fine, 2006, p. 273). Serbia was occupied by the Germans and in Croatia a puppet state was set up that also ruled over Bosnia Hercegovina. It was headed by the Ustashe, which declared independence and founded the Independent State of Croatia (NDH) (Fine, 2006, p. 273; Kollander, 2004, p. 5). Next to targeting Jews, Roma and anti-Ustashe Croats, the regime also explicitly persecuted Serbs with the aim of 'killing one third, expelling another third, and converting the remaining third to Catholicism' (Djokić, 2012, p. 72; Fine, 2006, p. 273). Thousands were locked in concentration camps, tortured and killed as the Ustashe leader Ante Pavelic tried to establish an ethnically pure Croatian state (Cox, 2006, pp. 224-226). This was done in a particularly gruesome manner. According to Cox 'the Ustaše shocked even the Nazis by their cruelty and persistence with which they went after the Serbian civilians' (2006, p. 225).

Armed resistance movements sprung up. The Serbian royalists, the Chetniks, were led by Dragoljub Mihailovic and the communist resistance movement was led by Josip Broz, better known as Tito (Kollander, 2004, p. 5). They fought against the German and Italian forces, and the Ustashe, but to make matters worse, also fought against each other (Kollander, 2004, p. 5). In retaliation of the anti-Serb policies of the Ustashe, the predominantly Serb Chetniks attacked Croatian villages in the Krajina region of Croatia and rural Bosnia, and because of these policies the liberation war became preoccupied with inter-ethnic strife (Fine, 2006, pp. 275-276).

Tito explicitly denounced the inter-ethnic violence and promised a multi-ethnic socialist state (Fine, 2006, pp. 276-277). The idea of an overarching Yugoslav identity had lost sway after the royal dictatorship, where the term was used to hide Serb domination (Fine, 2006, pp. 276-277). Tito therefore envisioned having the different ethnic groups living together in 'brotherhood and unity' rather than trying to establish one new overarching Yugoslav identity (Fine, 2006, p. 277). Serbs were, nevertheless, still the largest ethnic group among the Partisans because it operated mainly in Serb areas and most of the violence was also directed at the Serbs. At the same time, however, most Partisan fighters seemed to adhere to the multi-ethnic ideology (Fine, 2006, p. 277). He governed the liberated areas and when the war was over he controlled much of Yugoslavia's territory. After he won the war with the help of the Red Army, he established a republic (Fine, 2006, p. 279).

He met resistance from the Kosovar Albanians as the Partisans tried to reclaim its territory. They were never very resistant to the Italian occupation and a Kosovo Albanian SS Division had participated in the Holocaust (Petrović & Stefanović, 2010, p. 1082). They were inherently sceptical of the prospect of creating a new Yugoslavia. Since they had become part of Greater Albania after the occupation, the sentiment was that the fascists had given them more than Yugoslavia ever had (Petrović & Stefanović, 2010, p. 1083). After the Nazis occupied Albania after Mussolini's demise, the Kosovars were encouraged by the Nazis to fight against the Serbs and Tito's forces and the Partisans therefore came to see the region as counter revolutionary and anti-Yugoslavia (Fine, 2006, p. 282; Hagen, 1999, p. 58). After the war, the Kosovar Albanians continued to fight for about another year against its reincorporation in the Yugoslav state (Hagen, 1999, p. 58). Formally, however, even Kosovo voted to become part of Tito's Yugoslavia as he ensured loyalty by positioning predominantly Serbs and Montenegrins within the governmental institutions (Fine, 2006, p. 282).

8.3.4. TITO'S YUGOSLAVIA

After the war, several atrocities were perpetrated to get rid of any opposition. Large numbers of defeated fascists were shot, and ethnic Germans and Italians were forcefully removed from the country (Carmichael, 2010, p. 1046). Fine estimates that as many as 15,000 individuals were summarily executed. Some of these were war criminals, but others had merely been guilty by association (Fine, 2006, p. 283). And while the death of many of those who had likely opposed Tito's plans to create a socialist or multi-ethnic state could have made the challenge of building a peaceful multi-ethnic state easier, resistance continued to pose a problem in the first few years, and it was not before 1951 that the last Chetnik guerrillas were defeated (Fine, 2006, p. 283).

In these early years, repression was most serious (Flere & Klanjšek, 2014, p. 7). However, the first few post war years were also characterized by rapid modernization and beneficial policies which included free education, the promotion of gender equality, improved infrastructure and investments in health care and social insurance (Carmichael, 2010, p. 1045). In doing so he implemented his own version of socialism (Carmichael, 2010, p. 1045). From the 1960s onwards Yugoslavs were able to travel freely, work abroad and own land (Carmichael, 2010, p. 1046). As time progressed the security organs also became less overbearing, which meant that in the late 1950s and 1960s Yugoslavia was actually a pleasant place to live (Fine, 2006, p. 293).

Tito sought to conceptually separate the new country from interwar Yugoslavia, which was seen as bourgeois (Jović, 2004a, pp. 281-282). Whereas the pre-war kingdom had been dominated by the Serbian monarchy, the new Yugoslavia needed to be founded on the equality of the Yugoslav peoples (Petrović & Stefanović, 2010, p. 1080). The different ethnic groups did not have to give up their old identities and come together as one new nation, but rather envisioned all the different nations cohabiting peacefully in one federation consisting of six republics and two autonomous provinces. This approach was enshrined in the new creed 'brotherhood and unity' (Godina, 1998, p. 413; Jović, 2004a, p. 283; Kollander, 2004, p. 6).

The national identity was preserved, but elements of a new supranational identity, which was to take priority, were added (Godina, 1998, p. 416).[96] Differences were not denied but were deemed unimportant (Lindstrom, 2006, p. 234). The particular history, identity and myths of the different Yugoslav nations were de-emphasized under Tito (Sell, 2002, p. 72). As Sekulic *et al* point out, 'to identify as a Yugoslav was to condemn the forces that betrayed the memory of the war and to identify with the efforts of the Partisans to create a progressive, socialist society' (Sekulic *et al.*, 1994, p. 85). In order to maintain friendly relations among the different groups, Tito did not come to terms with the horrible crimes the Croatian Ustashe had perpetrated, but focused the narrative of WWII on the struggles of the Partisan resistance (Morus, 2007a, p. 153).

Tito became the embodiment of the Yugoslav identity. He did not represent any particular nation – he had a Croatian father and a Slovenian mother, and an incredible personality cult was developed around him (Carmichael, 2010, p. 1045; Djilas, 1995, p. 117). However, Tito was not the sole mastermind behind the ideology. Edvard Kardelj was crucial in developing the official ideology (Jović, 2004a, p. 277). Kardelj tried to construct a Yugoslav identity not only on the basis of the inclusive prescription that relations among the different ethnic

[96] Some authors, e.g. Jovic, find argue that Tito did not try to 'create a Yugoslav nation' an argument that is built on the premise that the existing nations were never meant to disappear (2004a, p. 284). While the latter aspect is agreed with, it is maintained here, following Godina (1998), that the supranational identity co-existed next to the older ethnic identities.

groups should be guided by brotherhood and unity but also incorporated exclusive elements that allowed 'the other' to be created (Jović, 2004a, p. 277). They were to unite against enemies, both internal and external.

Internally, enemies were all those who did not toe the exact party line. The enemies had a uniting force; in the face of the (imaginary) enemy the differences between the republics seemed insignificant (Godina, 1998, p. 415). Nationalism became the most important internal enemy and as such Yugoslavia 'needed nationalism and nationalists to maintain its own integration' (Godina, 1998, p. 415) and 'bourgeois nationalism' was frequently attacked in the communist propaganda (Sekulic, Massey, Hodson, p. 801).

External enemies were to be found in capitalism generally, and, after Tito broke with Stalin in 1948, also Stalin and his Soviet style communism (Godina, 1998, p. 414; Jović, 2004a, p. 285). The main point of disagreement concerned the role of the state. While Yugoslavia's federal structure was originally modelled on that of the Soviet Union, the latter had strengthened the state apparatus, and Tito's Yugoslavia aimed at far going decentralisation of the state as an important step towards a 'self-governing' society (Jović, 2004a, pp. 284-286; Petrović & Stefanović, 2010, p. 1080). Tito felt very strongly in the sanctity of the socialist notion that state functions should be minimized (Jović, 2004a, p. 286).

Within the federation the different republics were given quite some autonomy to accommodate any desires for self-determination (Petrović & Stefanović, 2010, p. 1080). The centralized communist party kept all political and economic control but each republic had its own legislative assembly, government, judiciary, anthem, coat of arms and flag (Petrović & Stefanović, 2010, p. 1080). Tito balanced the different groups within Yugoslavia, trying to keep them satisfied while preventing any group of gaining the upper hand (Hagen, 1999, p. 55). In doing so a distinction was made between those groups that already had ethnic homelands outside of the Yugoslav territory (this would include the Albanians for instance) and those who relied solely on Yugoslavia to provide them a homeland (e.g. Slovenes, Croats and the Serbs) (Petrović & Stefanović, 2010, p. 1085). Each nation was meant to receive its own republic, and one multinational republic was to be established but several disputed areas created a problem (Fine, 2006, p. 281; Petrović & Stefanović, 2010, p. 1080). Eventually, it was decided that the solution was to make Kosovo and Vojvodina autonomous regions (Fine, 2006, p. 281).

Kosovo, which had been so rebellious during WWII, and the Albanian majority that lived there, were seen as largely counter revolutionary (Fine, 2006, pp. 281-282). However, despite the strained history, Tito did not openly vilify the Albanian Kosovar population for their intransigence during WWII. In 1945 he said:

> 'We know you joined the German Army, that you fought against us, but we will not hold you responsible for that. We know that you were manipulated. We don't want

> Kosovo Šiptars [a common term for Kosovo Albanians at the time, MW] to be second or third class citizens. We want you to have your rights, equality, your language, your teachers, to feel *as if* you were in your own country' (emphasis in original Petrović & Stefanović, 2010, p. 1084).

On the one hand, the statement is problematic since Tito here implicitly argues Yugoslavia is in fact not their country. On the other hand, the statement reflected a pacifying tone that was forward looking and rejected any need for vengeance. Regardless of Tito's conciliatory words, it is noted by Petrovic and Stefanovic that because 'Kosovo Albanians consistently and *en masse* supported anti-communist forces, … [there was] a deep suspicion that they – as a people – were not loyal to the revolutionary regime and thus did not deserve equal status in the new country' (Petrović & Stefanović, 2010, p. 1085).

Because of this deep seated suspicion, Kosovo was dominated by Serbian officials until the 1960s (Judah, 2008, pp. 51-53). The Serbian secret police chief, Alexandar Rankovic, implemented a largely anti-Albanian policy until 1966 when he was dismissed (Judah, 2008, p. 51; Petrović & Stefanović, 2010, pp. 1089-1090; 1096). After the centralist Rankovic was removed from power, and spurred on further in 1968 by student demonstrations, Tito eventually granted Kosovo far reaching autonomy (Hagen, 1999, p. 58; Petrović & Stefanović, 2010, pp. 1089-1096; 1099). Petrovic and Stefanovic argue that the Albanian population soon started to assert their autonomy at the expense of the Serbs. According to these authors, 'what started as a movement for equal treatment of Kosovo Albanians slowly but surely became a push for Albanian domination and marginalisation of Kosovo Serbs' (Petrović & Stefanović, 2010, p. 1096). Thus, grievances remained and frustrations on both sides mounted. Kosovar Albanians again held massive demonstrations in 1981 because they wanted to become a full republic, while Serbs felt that they were disadvantaged in comparison to the other republics (Mikula, 2002, pp. 67-68; Petrović & Stefanović, 2010, pp. 1100-1103).

Although Yugoslavia throughout the years became increasingly decentralized, Tito remained 'almost unchallenged' as the leader of the Yugoslav communist movement (Carmichael, 2010, p. 1045). He tried to position himself as the only truly important decision maker and according to Jovic, 'identified the state with himself, and concentrated all real power in his own hands' (Jovic, 2001, p. 112). It is sometimes argued that when Tito died, Yugoslavia died along with him (Jovic, 2001, p. 112). However, this, of course, is an oversimplification and other factors certainly exacerbated the problems Yugoslavia faced after Tito's death.

8.4. PRELUDE TO WAR

In the years leading up to the war, several factors compounded Yugoslavia's problem, while the country lost effective ways of dealing with them. After

Tito's death, the constitution provided for a collective presidency with eight representatives from the different republics that required them to reach consensus. Each had a veto power on the major issues, and it became increasingly clear that the republics had conflicting interests, making it impossible to find appropriate solutions for the most important problems (Fine, 2006, p. 309). The mounting economic difficulties and the end of the Cold War had particularly far-reaching effects on the country and its eventual demise. As happened in countless other states (Woolf & Hulsizer, 2005, p. 105), economic and political upheaval pushed the country further down the path of mass atrocities.

8.4.1. ECONOMIC BREAKDOWN

During his reign Tito improved the living standard significantly, but did so with borrowed money that was not always invested in the economy but was also spent on public services like schools and health facilities (Fine, 2006, pp. 294-297). At the same time, however, there had been little corruption and Yugoslavia was not a complete economic failure which was bound to collapse (Fine, 2006, p. 294; Jovic, 2001, p. 103). In fact, it had been one of the most advanced states of the region (Jovic, 2001, p. 103).

There was nevertheless much discontent with several crucial policies of Tito. The government, for instance, redistributed money from the richer towards the poorer regions but could not prevent the income gap between its richest republics and its poorest provinces continuing to grow (Fine, 2006, pp. 296-298; Jovic, 2001, pp. 101-102). The richest republics, Slovenia and Croatia were dissatisfied with that situation as they saw their money disappear to inefficiently run businesses in the south, but the Serbs were not happy either (Fine, 2006, p. 298). Krizan explains that the Serbs saw the widening of the gap as a 'result of anti-Serb orientation of the Western Republics' (Križan, 1994, p. 55).

Unemployment started to rise in the 1970s after reforms started to liberalize the market (Fine, 2006, p. 302). The economic crisis sparked a constitutional crisis which eventually led to the new constitution being adopted in 1974 (Fine, 2006, p. 303; Jovic, 2001, p. 102) In the early 1980s, Yugoslavia sought assistance from the IMF (Kaldor, 2006, pp. 39-40; Sekulić *et al.*, 2006, p. 804). The subsequent austerity measures that were imposed meant 'disaster' in the poorer republics which experienced even higher unemployment and more political instability (Fine, 2006, p. 310). Competition between the republics intensified and as money kept being printed inflation started to rise (Kaldor, 2006, pp. 39-40).

The economic crisis, however, would not have had such a destructive impact had the crisis not been used 'to destroy the constitutive concept of Yugoslav socialism' (Jovic, 2001, p. 102). Political debate between politicians advocating further decentralization and those favouring recentralization became heated. The latter approach was strongly advocated by the Serbs, who sought to reduce the autonomy of the autonomous provinces (Sekulić *et al.*, 2006, p. 804). Slovenia and Croatia on the other hand wanted more decentralization (Sekulić *et al.*, 2006, p. 804).

Slowly but surely the different sides came to believe it was no longer in their interest to remain part of Yugoslavia (Jovic, 2001, p. 102). The richest republics believed that being part of Yugoslavia was hampering their further development while Yugoslavia's poorest region, Kosovo, also came to this conclusion when it became frustrated that its GDP, although increasing in absolute terms, was falling when calculated per head of the population (Jovic, 2001, p. 102).

Yet its eventual disintegration emerged at a time when the economic situation within Yugoslavia was improving and inflation had been dropping in the final months of 1989 and early 1990 (Jovic, 2001, p. 102). By this time, the nationalist rhetoric had taken its own momentum. As Jovic argues, 'economic factors were not important per se for the disintegration of Yugoslavia, but in the context they provided for political leaders, who used them to argue that their ethnic and/or political group was disadvantaged in Yugoslavia' (Jovic, 2001, p. 103).

8.4.2. END OF THE COLD WAR

During the Cold War Yugoslavia was in an extraordinary position as a communist country that had broken away from the Soviet sphere of influence. After 1948 the Soviet Union discontinued all financial aid and loans and for a moment Yugoslavia seemed to be in a dire situation. Fine explains how, just a few years after the devastation of WWII, Yugoslavia 'now found itself isolated, facing economic disaster and the possibility of Soviet intervention' (Fine, 2006, p. 290). However, the outbreak of the Korean War staved off a possible invasion and Tito's refusal to pledge allegiance to the capitalist West, actually made Yugoslavia relatively powerful as it allowed Tito to become the leader of the non-aligned movement (Fine, 2006, pp. 290-291). With the Cold War coming to an end, this unique position lost in favour (Jovic, 2001, p. 110). Woodward explains the far-reaching consequences this had for Yugoslavia. She argued that since the 1960s Yugoslavia had depended on access to foreign capital that was granted because of Yugoslavia's strategic position. However, the end of the Cold War according to Woodward,

> 'challenged and undermined that strategic significance, the role of the Yugoslav army, and the country's alternative markets in the East and the in the third world without providing any new bases for security and domestic political and economic viability' (Woodward, 1995, p. 16).

As a consequence, it became unable to attract the necessary political and economic aid from the West when its economy took a turn for the worst (Jovic,

2001, pp. 110-111). The West, believing liberalization was necessary for further assistance, caused instability and created conditions that were potentially 'explosive' (Woodward, 1995).

Jovic, however, cautions that the impact of the Cold War can be overstated since *perestroika* and *glasnost* and the rapprochement between East and West, were generally welcomed by the Yugoslav communist leadership. In addition, these leaders did not feel threatened by the reforms, but also did not always implement the reforms that the IMF or other foreign creditors demanded. In fact, with the downfall of the Soviet Union it saw one of its main threats dissipate and Yugoslavia started taking steps to strengthen their ties with the European Community (EC) (Jovic, 2001, p. 111). It may be the case of course that the Yugoslav elite merely could not oversee the dramatic consequences the change in the bi-polar world system would have for their country, but Jovic has a point that it would be undesirable to neglect the role domestic processes played in Yugoslavia's dissolution during this time (Jovic, 2001, pp. 111-112).

8.4.3. SERBIAN SOCIETY AFTER TITO: REINTERPRETING HISTORY

The death of Tito and the end of the Cold War also meant the end of the official narrative with which Tito had tried to construct a collective identity, and space opened up for new interpretations of the past (Jović, 2004b, p. 101). Morus puts forth the idea that authority entails the capability to have people accept your interpretation of reality. She explains:

> 'the mark of authority is the ability to name and define … when those people also define the "people" who make up a nation, and hence those that are outside of that nation, those people then also have political authority. Still, if a people are happy with their social and economic condition, have jobs, a good standard of living and are generally hopeful about the future then an attempt to reconstitute their primary identity will largely be unsuccessful.' (Morus, 2007a, p. 145).

When the country however, is suffering from upheaval, as also explained in Chapter 3, the population becomes more susceptible to the influence of leaders. In this case, the recent economic downturn, the death of Tito and the loss of prestige internationally, caused Yugoslavia to embrace a new interpretation of its present and future.

The foundational myth for the Serbs had receded somewhat into the background of the political life in Serbia until after the death of Tito (Bieber, 2002, p. 99). Nationalist narratives like the Kosovo myth never really disappeared but were pushed to the background and made way for other 'more contemporary foundational myths, such as the numerous tales surrounding the wartime communist partisans' (Bieber, 2002, p. 99). After Albanian protests in Kosovo in 1981, the Orthodox Church, writers and the elite started to refocus their attention on the position of the Serbs in Kosovo (Bieber, 2002, pp. 99-100).

Obviously, the reinterpretation of history was a process that did not occur at one particular moment in time, but there were crucial moments in this process. The release of the Serbian Academy of Arts and Sciences (SANU) memorandum was such a moment. It was leaked to the press and the Academy expressed discontent over the publication of the material but did not rescind the content (Križan, 1994, p. 59; Vetlesen, 2005, p. 149). Morus calls it 'retrospectively as the precipitating event that awakened Serbian national consciousness' (Morus, 2007a, p. 142). Others have referred to it as a 'political earthquake' (Vetlesen, 2005, p. 149).

The memorandum vilified Tito for weakening Serbia by hampering its economic growth and for giving autonomy to two of its regions, which meant that, unlike the other republics, Serbia was not able to have complete control over its entire territory (Guzina, 2003, p. 101; Kollander, 2004, p. 8). All the while, according to the memorandum, Serbians that were living outside of Serbia in the other republics were not able to make use of their own language and culture and Serbian minorities in Kosovo were being brutally repressed (Guzina, 2003, p. 101; Kollander, 2004, p. 8). The document even spoke of a genocide against the Serbian people, arguing that

> 'the physical, political, juridical and cultural genocide of the Serbian population of Kosovo and Metohija is the heaviest defeat in the history of Serbian liberation struggles' (cited in Križan, 1994, p. 58).

The SANU Memorandum contributed to a Serbian national identity that was built on the portrayal of the Serbs as historic victims who were under constant threat of extremist Muslims (Morus, 2007a, pp. 147-149). Within the memorandum the myth of the battle at Kosovo was given renewed relevance for the Serbian nation, which was awaiting its redemption, awaiting its kingdom in heaven (Morus, 2007a, p. 149). History was traced from its mythical defeat at Kosovo, to its victimization of WWII and the wrongs that were being currently inflicted on the Serb nation by the Kosovo Albanians (Morus, 2007a, pp. 149-152). Memories of WWII were used to enflame tensions between the different groups by portraying the present troubles as a mere continuation of Serb victimization during WWII (Morus, 2007a, p. 150). The Albanian Kosovars were equated with the Nazis and the memorandum argued that the Serbs in Croatia were currently facing dangers that were reminiscent of their fate under the Ustashe regime (Morus, 2007a, pp. 152-153). The rhetoric focussed on the Jasenovac camp as a symbol of Croat aggression and Serb victimization, tapping into painful memories that did not get a public forum in Titoist Yugoslavia (Morus, 2007a, pp. 151-153)

Although the memorandum did not advocate dissolving Yugoslavia *per se*, it argued Serbia should only remain in Yugoslavia on its own terms, with a new constitution to replace the one from 1974, with measures in place that would bring an end to the genocide in Kosovo, with the reintegration of the Vojvodina region within Serbia, with a greater say in all matters relating to the Serbs in the other republics, and only if the anti-Serbian conspiracy would be brought to an end (Guzina, 2003, p. 102). Otherwise, it argued, the existence of the socialist state was indeed at stake (Guzina, 2003, p. 101).

There is some reason to believe that the memorandum was created in collusion with some of the nationalist political elite within Serbia who could then use it as a pretext to move forward with the plan of creating a Greater Serbia (Brosse, 2003, pp. 37-38). The idea of Greater Serbia the nationalists sought to achieve was based on the lands that medieval Serbia encompassed right before they became subjected to Ottoman rule (Mikula, 2002, p. 66). As Milosevic adopted the nationalist discourse that was set out in the memorandum, the myth about the battle of Kosovo regained in prominence.

In 1987, in a now famous speech, Milosevic was sent to Kosovo where he got the opportunity to address a crowd that had gathered. Some allege the whole incident was set up and pre-planned with the local police (Brosse, 2003, p. 39), but whether this was the case or not, it certainly turned out to be a pivotal moment in Milosevic's career. When one of the police officers beat one of the protestors, Milosevic told the Serbian minority 'no one has the right to beat the people'. It was the leading story in the press and aired repeatedly on TV in the days thereafter (Brosse, 2003, pp. 39-40). According to De la Brosse this moment sealed 'Milosevic's image as the saviour and unifier of the Serbian people and consolidate[d] his power within the Party' (Brosse, 2003, p. 40; Morus, 2007b, p. 9).

In 1989, Milosevic again gave a speech when the 600th anniversary of the battle of Kosovo was commemorated (Zakosek, 2007, p. 30). During the speech he is reported to have said:

> 'today six centuries later, we are once again in battles, and facing battles. They are not armed battles, although the possibility of those cannot be excluded' (cited in Zakosek, 2007, p. 30).

Bieber explains that the 600th anniversary actually posed the 'ideal opportunity to adjust the myth to its contemporary needs' (Bieber, 2002, p. 100). By this time Milosevic had gained enough political traction to reverse the autonomy of Kosovo and the constitutional amendments with which this was accomplished were now seen as 'late justice' for those who sacrificed themselves 600 years earlier (Bieber, 2002, pp. 101-102). During Milosevic's reign, remembering historical events served contemporary political goals and aspirations. Milosevic spoke of the necessity of unity among the Serbs. A lack of unity had caused hardship in the past and emphasized the need for Serbs to create and maintain unity now. While on the surface an innocent appeal, Morus explains that the 'unity' Milosevic spoke of, meant a unity of all Serbs, meant uniting all Serbs in one nation, and meant uniting all lands traditionally Serbian (Morus, 2007b, p. 13) – a feat the Serbs tried to accomplish a few years later through brutal ethnic cleansing campaigns.

8.5. MILOSEVIC AND PUBLIC OPINION: INCITING AND LEGITIMIZING ATROCITIES

The history and myths set out above are part of the society in which Milosevic was socialized and the problems the Serbian nation faced after the death of Tito, were the problems Milosevic faced as a young politician. Milosevic could use the history and the nation's qualms because he understood them. Staub rightfully points out, it is important to understand the society a leader comes from, as the leader, too, 'is affected by social conditions' (Staub, 2010, p. 174). However, it is equally important to understand what he did with these societal conditions, as will be further explicated below. History, myths, society and problems are malleable and open to interpretation. While Tito used the past to emphasize a common heritage and culture, Milosevic used them to create unity among Serbs while alienating the other nations.

It is often debated to what extent populations support dictatorial leaders that are responsible for atrocities (Valentino, 2000, pp. 21-25). Very often a violent leader does not enjoy the support of the entire population nor do they have to (Valentino, 2000, p. 21). While problems may arise if the public actively opposes violent policies (Staub, 1989, p. 123), powerlessness or silent acquiescence from the majority of the population is sufficient to perpetrate mass atrocities (Valentino, 2000, p. 25). No leader is able to rule alone and when there is too much opposition, his position of power may become untenable but as long as active support is maintained from a powerful few, passivity among the majority is sufficient (Ezrow & Frantz, 2011, pp. 55-57; 82). Passivity is perhaps best ensured through the use of repression whilst creating tacit support for the crimes. The latter means that it is necessary to rationalize and legitimize the crimes. This is, mostly done through propaganda. In Yugoslavia it was predominantly the nationalist sentiment which justified the crimes. The nationalist rhetoric relied on the historical schisms that were present, but gave them new meaning. History was reinterpreted in such a way that these historical moments were given new impetus and contemporary historical meaning.

8.5.1. AUTHORITARIAN NATURE OF MILOSEVIC'S REGIME

Milosevic's regime has been described as being characterized by '"soft" authoritarianism' (Sell, 2002, p. 193), although Milosevic' reign in Kosovo was much harsher. In Kosovo police brutality was much more common and many were imprisoned for political reasons (Sell, 2002). Levitsky and Way argue that some regimes, like the one of Milosevic during the 1990s, which combine democratic institutions with authoritarian governance, should be seen as 'competitive authoritarian regimes' (Levitsky & Way, 2002, pp. 51-52).[97] This term reflects that even though there are democratic processes in these countries, which 'are widely seen as the principle means of obtaining and exercising authority', in reality politicians violate them so often that these regimes are best 'described as a (diminished) form of authoritarianism' (Levitsky & Way, 2002, p. 52). Considering the fine line between the dictatorships and democracies it becomes important to analyse what Milosevic's sources of power were and how he was able to garner enough influence to dominate the political system.

The origins of Milosevic's power should be traced back to the end of the 1980s when he was discovering the power of nationalist sentiment during his 1987 speech in Kosovo. Throughout 1988 and early 1989 popular rallies were held in different parts of the country that would further consolidate Milosevic's position of power. These 'rallies for truth' were meant to seem like spontaneous expressions of public opinion but in reality were carefully orchestrated by Milosevic's regime (LeBor, 2003, p. 107). He used these demonstrations to remove the leadership of Vojvodina, Kosovo and Montenegro (Sell, 2002, pp. 54-55) and filled the positions with more 'appropriate' and 'national' individuals (Bieber, 2002, p. 102). According to Morus, by 1989 Milosevic was the undisputed leader of the Serbian people (Morus, 2007b, p. 11).

In 1990, Serbia subsequently adopted a new constitution that gave its President wide ranging powers that could be pushed through without it needing to be ratified by government or parliament, and which fell outside the purview of the constitutional court (L. J. Cohen, 2006, p. 451). Under the new constitution the President, once elected, basically could not be held accountable by any other institution or the public, ensuring Milosevic's '*de facto* authoritarian and personal control' (L. J. Cohen, 2006, p. 451).[98] In addition, he refused to delegate any of his decisions. He kept potential threats to his leadership at bay by regularly reshuffling his staff and maintained full control over the decisions that needed to be taken (L. J. Cohen, 2006, p. 452). One of his former advisors is reported to have said that 'he practically does not need advisers ... for in the end everything ends up as what he orders' (L. J. Cohen, 2006, p. 452).

97 See Chapter 2 for more explanation on the most important authoritarian regime types.

98 It was possible to recall him but this required the vote of more than half of the entire electorate, while he could be voted into power with just half of the votes cast (L. J. Cohen, 2006, p. 451).

When Milosevic formally broke with the communist legacy in July 1990, and the League of Communists (SKS) was formally dissolved to form the Socialist Party of Serbia (SPS), the country supposedly became a multi-party democracy (L. J. Cohen, 2006, pp. 455-456). In reality, however, another major party SK-PJ (later JUL), was dominated by Milosevic's wife Mira Markovic, and his own party was actually a mere continuation of the old (L. J. Cohen, 2006, pp. 455-457). Milosevic maintained the existing power structures, allowing him to control the police, army, economy and the media (L. J. Cohen, 2006, pp. 455-456).

As will be explained in more detail in section 8.6, Milosevic built a large and reliable police force early on (L. J. Cohen, 2006, p. 467) but he did not only rely on a strong internal security apparatus to maintain his rule. Equally important, however, was his influence over societal institutions. The judicial system was hardly independent. As in communist times, judges were partly appointed on the basis of their political orientation and budget cuts created such insecurity within the judiciary that it became even more subject to political influence (L. J. Cohen, 2006, p. 469). In addition, Milosevic had far-reaching control over the economy. Not only was he in control of much of the formal economic and financial sector by making access to powerful positions and privileges conditional on absolute loyalty to his regime (L. J. Cohen, 2006, p. 464), but at the same time a large informal sector also appeared. The sanctions, inflation and eventual decline in the economy caused the emergence of a large black market dominated by individuals who owed their new found wealth to Milosevic and had vested interests in his political survival (Sell, 2002, pp. 192-193; Sorensen, 2003, p. 67; 75).

However, one of the most important tools for him to maintain control was the media (L. J. Cohen, 2006, p. 436). Journalism, like most other aspects of Serbian society, also became infused with nationalism, and these forms of 'patriotic journalism' led to a loss of ethics and the falsifying of information (Oberschall, 2000, p. 993). Each journalist did not want their own nationality to be disadvantaged and therefore joined in 'a competitive spiral of propaganda' (Oberschall, 2000, p. 993). Anyone that did not cooperate enthusiastically in propagating the nationalist stance was coerced into doing so by the regime. According to De la Brosse (2003), Milosevic personally ensured that the press freedom was restricted and a uniform message was conveyed.

He appointed the editors in chief and ensured that recalcitrant journalists were demoted, condemned, dismissed and sometimes even attacked, arrested, convicted or otherwise mistreated, while those loyal to the regime could count on a promotion (Brosse, 2003, pp. 5-6). Fines, licenses and permits were used to control the press and ensure that only loyalists could air their message (Brosse, 2003, p. 6). During the war in Kosovo, soldiers were reportedly even stationed in different media outlets in order to ensure that any outgoing news bulletins matched the official party line (Brosse, 2003, p. 86). Milosevic used them to tie into the existing historical myths and schisms between the different groups and gave the past renewed contemporary relevance. It used the region's loaded history to further antagonisms against the other groups. Mikula, for instance, explains that 'Milosevic's propaganda machine incessantly used images from the real Croatian genocide against the Serbs during World War II to portray every contemporary Croat as a latter-day fascist ready to follow in the footsteps of his or her predecessors' (Mikula, 2002, p. 65). These references to 'Ustasha fascists' were made to conjure up the memories of WWII and in effect 'hijack and manipulate History [sic] in order to mobilise Serbian opinion' (Brosse, 2003, pp. 30-32). A sense of orientalism was likewise targeted towards both the Bosnian Muslims and Kosovar Albanians as parallels with the Ottoman era were drawn (Mikula, 2002, p. 65). The Bosnian Muslims were called 'Mujahedin' and were closely associated with the memory of the Ottoman subjugation (Brosse, 2003, p. 63). Throughout Milosevic's rule, the media emphasized Serbian historical heroism, victimization and a sense of fatalism that blended history and contemporary events and functioned to prepare the public for war (Brosse, 2003, p. 4; Mikula, 2002, p. 65).

Some independent media existed, but only within bounds. While Milosevic ensured that most of the media outlets were firmly in his own hands, he tolerated some dissent and free speech to portray Serbia as a democratic nation for the international community (Brosse, 2003, p. 81). Allowing such media to exist only had limited impact anyway since their information did not reach most of the people (Brosse, 2003, p. 92).

Milosevic thus used most of the tools that have been described in Chapter 2. He made people economically dependent on his continued rule, used sophisticated methods to secure legitimacy, and used repression to secure his position of power. That being said, in comparison to the Cambodian case, Milosevic relied much more on securing limited support for his regime and spent more time on creating a façade of legitimacy than Pol Pot did. Whereas the latter relied heavily on executions and terror to force compliance with his continued rule

8.5.2. PROPAGANDA AND THE LEGITIMIZATION OF THE CRIMES

The media primarily functioned to deny, legitimize and rationalize the crimes while strengthening its own support base. Many stories covering the wars were based on flat out lies; these included stories of Croats and Muslims who were accused of brutally murdering 41 children and babies in 1991, reports that Serbian babies were fed too zoo animals in Sarajevo, and claims that Albanian men were raping Serbian women *en masse* (Brosse, 2003, pp. 6-8; 50; 77-78).

In a damning report that was compiled at the request of the Prosecutor of the ICTY, De la Brosse found:

> 'Slobodan Milosevic knowingly used and controlled the media in Serbia to impose the themes of nationalist propaganda to justify to the citizen the creation of a state – which would be home to all Serbian people – and also to strengthen his authority' (2003, p. 5).

The propaganda was phrased in such a way that it allowed the population to view the violence as legitimate and it allowed them to neutralize any feelings of guilt.

In the classical criminological study of Sykes and Matza five neutralization techniques were identified that allow the individual to rationalize behaviour and protect the individual from self-blame (Sykes & Matza, 1957, pp. 666-667). As explained previously, the five techniques that Sykes and Matza identified are the denial of responsibility, the denial of injury, the denial of the victim, the condemnation of the condemners, and the appeal to higher loyalties (Sykes & Matza, 1957, pp. 667-669). The dominant discourse that was put forward by Milosevic's regime encompassed these neutralization techniques.

The denial of the victim was primarily promoted through two reinforcing processes. One was the dehumanization of the victim, the other was through the belief that they deserved their fate. While Alvarez sees dehumanization as a separate category that extends the neutralization techniques of Sykes and Matza, it is maintained here that when the humanity of the person is taken from them, it also becomes impossible to view them as a victim since the obligations towards the person are taken away. The person is placed outside of the 'universe of moral obligation' (Fein, 1993, p. 82). The manner in which the enemy was dehumanized, was reflected, for instance, in the manner in which Serbs at times equated Muslims with diseases or animals (Alvarez, 2001, p. 126). Karadzic, for instance, is reported as having said that the Serbs were merely trying to ensure that 'Islamic fundamentalism doesn't *infect* Europe from the south' (emphasis my own) (Alvarez, 2001, p. 126).

By making the Bosnian Muslims and Croats into vicious enemies that need to be stopped (Brosse, 2003, pp. 59-63), the violence inflicted against them was wholly justified and an act of self-defence. As Alvarez explains, the 'Serbs' status as a victimized people transformed their violence from aggression to self-defense' (Alvarez, 2001, p. 65). Protecting the Serbian state against the enemies also served as the higher purpose that warranted the brutal acts (Alvarez, p. 125). The idea that they were defending Serbia and the rest of Europe against Muslim fundamentalism overshadowed any other values, like the prohibition against killing. As Alvarez explains, murder was 'elevated from a criminal act into an almost sacred obligation' (Alvarez, 2001, p. 125).

The denial of responsibility came from the sanctioned nature of the acts. The state demanded that they be carried out and the individual merely followed orders. While this was perhaps most strongly felt on the ground, where Serbian soldiers were threatened with death if they did not follow orders (Alvarez, 2001, p. 116), propaganda also frequently stressed the necessity of the battle as great harm would befall upon their nation if nothing was done (Cigar, 1995, p. 82; Judah, 2009, p. 171). This not only gave them a higher purpose but could also make the Serbs feel like they had little choice or agency in the matter. In an interview with Seierstad, an elderly Serbian man told her that the 'Serbs never started a war. We were attacked, first by the Slovenes, then by the Croats and then by the Muslims, and of course we had to defend ourselves' (2004, p. 20). Many Serbs believed they merely did what had to be done, that they were doing their patriotic and religious duty to prevent any harm to their nation and this absolved them from personal responsibility (Cigar, 1995, p. 82).

Injury can be denied by using euphemistic language (Alvarez, 2001, pp. 117-118). Violence was not explained in terms that carried with it a disproving connotation, but was given a positive twist. The term ethnic cleansing made it seem as though it was a 'correction of an assumed, impure, unnatural and demeaning state' (Cigar, 1995, p. 71) and the term thus hid the gruesome, bloody reality that the process actually entailed.

In addition, anyone inside or outside of the country who dared to criticize the acts of the Serbs or the Milosevic regime, was likely to face condemnation themselves. They were castigated as a traitor and possibly even harassed (Cigar, 1995, p. 84; Sudetic, 1991). Much criticism also stemmed from the international community which Serbs skilfully countered by pointing out serious human rights violations that had been perpetrated in the past by those critical countries (Alvarez, 2001, p. 123; Cigar, 1995, p. 95). Serbia's parliament, for instance, voted to send a fact finding mission to the US to investigate human rights violations which occurred during riots that had broken out in Los Angeles in 1992 (Cigar, 1995, p. 95). Similarly, a Yugoslav representative at the UN, in a session to discuss Serb atrocities in detention camps, demanded that US crimes in Vietnam be investigated instead (Cigar, 1995, p. 95).

Ultimately, criminal activities and violence became normalized in Serbian society during the 1990s (Dimitrijevic, 2008, p. 8). Arkan, the leader of one of the most feared paramilitary units – the Tigers – became a national hero, and even the pop culture in Serbia, reflected a glorification of violence (Weerdesteijn & Smeulers, 2011). This was also beneficial to Milosevic's regime. Kronja explains that the 'entertainment industry spread a problematic system of values, lifestyle and emotional sensibility which was systematically and manipulatively used to break up the morality and civil order of Serbian society for the sake of the Milošević regime's power' (Kronja, 2004, p. 5).

8.6. INSTITUTIONS AND PERPETRATORS

An institutional foundation had already been set up by Tito which facilitated the arming of the different republics militarily as Tito had decided to set up Territorial Defence Units (TOs) next to the national army (Carmichael, 2010,

p. 1046; Kaldor, 2006, p. 41). After the Soviet Union invaded Czechoslovakia in 1968, Tito had made the decision to change Yugoslavia's defence system and developed TOs that were composed of reservists and answerable to the local communist parties (Judah, 2009, p. 170; Kaldor, 2006, p. 41). When the country started to fall apart in the early 1990s, these TOs were used by the Serb leadership to arm the Serbs outside of Serbia, through a small group of loyal Serb officers who together formed the so-called *Vojna Linija*, or Military Line (Judah, 2009, pp. 169-171; LeBor, 2003, pp. 142-143). Their now infamous plan was called RAM, and detailed the contours of a Greater Serbia which included land from Bosnia and Croatia where weapons and ammunition should be distributed to arm Serbs outside of Serbia (Judah, 2009, p. 170; LeBor, 2003, p. 143; Sell, 2002, p. 123)

Yugoslavia also had a national army (JNA), which traditionally had been dominated by Serbs (Križan, 1994, p. 53). Milosevic initially established friendly relations with the military but many remained too committed to an independent Yugoslav stance, causing Milosevic to be very apprehensive about trusting the national army. He therefore created a strong and loyal police force within Serbia, but by 1991 Milosevic increasingly managed to use the Yugoslav army to defend Serb interests as well (L. J. Cohen, 2006, pp. 467-468; Kaldor, 2006, p. 41). However, because he had dismissed numerous officers and cut back significantly on spending, in combination with the loss in status that the army had to endure, the military became demoralized, and consequently the Yugoslav army fell somewhat apart in the early months of the war (L. J. Cohen, 2006, pp. 468-469; J. Mueller, 2000, p. 43). Mutiny and desertion were quite common, and many avoided the draft and never even reported for duty (J. Mueller, 2000, p. 48).

Paramilitary units were formed to supplement the ordinary forces but there are indications that the morale actually worsened in the JNA because of the presence of the thugs who were preoccupied with looting the conquered territory (J. Mueller, 2000, p. 49). Mueller describes these groups, who perpetrated much of the violence, as a 'group of well-armed thugs and bullies' (J. Mueller, 2000, p. 43). Many individuals who formed the core of these paramilitary units indeed had criminal backgrounds but it would be a simplification to argue that they are all marauding bandits.[99] Many joined because of a toxic mix of peer pressure and fear. They were not only fearful of the enemy but also of other Serbs who were more fanatical and feared being seen as a traitor (Oberschall, 2000, p. 997). Some were also forced to join the war effort at gun point even when they personally did not care about the war at all while again others did see it as a sacred obligation (Alvarez, 2001, p. 125; Stewart, 2007, pp. 172-192).

The paramilitary units provided Milosevic with 'plausible deniability' (Ron, 2000, p. 293) while Milosevic was clearly pulling the strings (Alvarez, 2006,

99 Nikolic-Ristanovic estimated that about one in five had committed a serious crime before joining the war effort (Nikolic-Ristanovic, 1998, p. 465).

pp. 18-20). Vojislav Seselj, one of the most notorious paramilitary leaders, reportedly once said:

> 'Milosevic organized everything. We gathered the volunteers and he gave us special barracks at Bubanj Potok, all our uniforms, arms, military technology and buses. All our units were always under the command of ... the Yugoslav army' (Alvarez, 2001, p. 82).

Milosevic always denied being involved in the conflict in Bosnia (Stewart, 2007, p. 194). Formally, the JNA had withdrawn its forces from Croatia in 1991 and had not been a part of the Bosnian conflict since 1992, but they had left Serbs from Bosnia behind, as well as any volunteers and their equipment and supplies (S/1994/674, p. 30). While Milosevic might not have unlimited control over the Serbs in the other republics, it is clear he did have far reaching influence over them as they could count on weapons, personnel and financial help from the leadership in Belgrade (Cigar, 1995, pp. 87-88; Sell, 2002, pp. 370-371). In Kosovo, Serbian forces were present in the region, according to Milosevic to fight the Albanian terrorists (Sell, 2002, pp. 372-373), but similar tactics as those employed in Bosnia were used during the conflict in Kosovo. A brutal paramilitary force which had been active during the Bosnian war, Arkan's Tigers, also unleashed its reign of terror in Kosovo (Stewart, 2007, pp. 259-261). As the region was ethnically cleansed of the Kosovar Albanian population, horrific massacres were perpetrated that were reminiscent of the previous conflicts (Stewart, 2007, p. 260).

8.7. ROLE OF THE INTERNATIONAL COMMUNITY

The actions of Milosevic during the Kosovo crisis need to be placed in the context of the experiences he had with policies of the international community during the earlier wars. In order to understand his decision-making process during the Kosovo war we need to look at the manner in which he engaged with the international community in the years pre-ceding the conflict, during the wars that tore Yugoslavia apart in the first half of the 1990s.

The actions of the UN, US, Russia and the European Community (EC) have been heavily criticized. According to many scholars, the impartial stance which had been guiding their actors often amounted to complicity (Betts, 1994; K. J. Campbell, 2001; LeBor, 2006; Power, 2013; Sells, 1998). Overall, it seems fair to say that the attitude of the international community towards these wars was marked by indecision, divisions and broken promises in which ultimately the political will to intervene was lacking. It has been pointed out by British observers that 'there was a real unwillingness to address the war and its causes. The prevailing attitude, with the exception of a few colleagues, was that this was a terrible war and all parties were to blame, and we had to manage it as best we could' (LeBor, 2006, p. 48).

National interests seemed to play as much of a role as humanitarian concern. Russia had long been an ally to the Serbs and was worried about setting an example for its own problems with Chechnya, while China had similar concerns regarding Tibet (LeBor, 2006, p. 49). The European Community was eager to show it could manage the crisis. At the beginning of the crisis Jacques Poos, proclaimed, on behalf of a high level mediation team that was sent to Yugoslavia by the European Community, that: 'This is the hour of Europe' (Riding, 1991, pp. 441-442; D. Smith, 2002). He added, 'it is not the hour of the Americans', verbalizing the EC's determination to show independence from the US. However, in those first crucial years, it failed in showcasing its independence and it failed to manage the crisis (D. Smith, 2002, p. 443). The US initially took the position that, in the words of Secretary of State James Baker, 'we don't have a dog in this fight' (A. Jones, 2011, p. 325). Especially after the debacle in Somalia later on, where a US military intervention resulted in the deaths of 18 American soldiers whose bodies were dragged through the streets of Mogadishu, any willingness to consider more forceful actions evaporated (LeBor, 2006, p. 50). David Owen, the European envoy to former Yugoslavia, came to the conclusion that 'the Serbs always knew that the United States was not committed. As long as that was the case, they would call their bluff' (LeBor, 2006, p. 57).

8.7.1. BROKEN PROMISES AND FAILED EFFORTS FOR PEACE

The international community struggled to agree on a policy. Even within Europe, divisions among the Member States of the EC dictated the decision-making process. It was initially Germany that took a strong stance. The war in Croatia had been raging for six months, when in January 1992 the EC decided to recognize its independence after much persistent lobbying from Germany (LeBor, 2006, pp. 26-27). This gave Bosnia little other choice but to follow in its footsteps or be left in what was left of Yugoslavia which was dominated by the Serbs (LeBor, 2006, p. 26). The German stance has been heavily criticized by some authors. Hodge, for instance, argues that the German policy was committed to the principle of self-determination without considering the consequences thereof in the Balkans (Hodge, 1998, p. 6). Hodge believes 'Bonn's actions stampeded the European Community [and] broke Western unity' (Hodge, 1998, p. 14). In addition, their own violent history in the Balkans, as well as constitutional provisions, formed a respectable reason why they were unable to contribute to any military efforts to intervene, allowing them to avoid responsibility for the consequences of their policy (Hodge, 1998, p. 5; 11).[100]

On April 6th 1992, the EC decided to recognize Bosnia, as well, as an independent country (LeBor, 2006, p. 28), and a very destructive war ensued. As a response the United Nations decided to impose sanctions which prevented the sale of arms to these countries. However, while this hardly impacted the Bosnian Serbs, who received supplies and support from the former Yugoslav army, it made it harder for the Muslim population to defend themselves (Kollander, 2004, p. 12). In addition, UN decided to send a peacekeeping force, UNPROFOR, to the region with the consent of all parties. They were not to take sides in the conflict (Kaldor, 2006, pp. 61-65).

The misconception that was underlying much of the misguided policies was the idea that the problem at hand required policies that sought to re-establish peace, rather than stop atrocities. It was conceived as a problem between warring factions rather than as one where there was a victim and perpetrator (K. J. Campbell, 2001; Kaldor, 2006, p. 61). This led to the situation where humanitarian assistance was emphasized to deliver food to people that were waiting to be slaughtered (K. J. Campbell, 2001, p. 65).

After President Clinton succeeded George H.W. Bush, he initially sought to implement more forceful policy. In May 1993, he wanted to implement a 'lift and strike' tactic which entailed the lifting of the arms embargo that prevented the Bosnians from defending themselves while threatening the Bosnian Serbs with airstrikes (Chollet, 2005, p. 4). The Europeans, however, rejected the plan and the US soon backed down (Chollet, 2005, p. 5).

Throughout the war the Europeans were reluctant to lift the embargo, fearing that this may hamper the safety of their troops on the ground (Chollet, 2005, p. 7; Lane, 1996, p. 145). Betts argues, therefore, that for some time the presence of the UN forces actually hindered a more forceful reaction because the troops on the ground were vulnerable to retaliation (Betts, 1994, p. 25), but the US was no more willing to take risks. Clinton explained:

> 'I was reluctant [to unilaterally lift] the arms embargo, for fear of weakening the United Nations. I also didn't want to divide the NATO alliance by unilaterally bombing Serb military positions ... And I didn't want to send American troops there, putting them in harm's way under a UN mandate I thought was bound to fail.' (cited in Chollet, 2005, p. 5).

It was not the mere fact that he did not have faith in the UN mandate that made Clinton unwilling to put boots on the ground. Richard Holbrooke, the US

---

100 Only after their constitutional court ruled in 1994 that the constitution does not prevent a military contribution, Germany decided to send troops to the region under UN auspices (Hodge, 1998, p. 16).

Special Envoy to the Balkans, explained that the disaster in Somalia also had a tremendous effect. According to Holbrooke,

> 'The administration was burned and traumatized by what happened in Somalia. Congress was up in arms, and the United States was reeling. This was a very critical point. History is continuous, and you are always affected by what has just happened. Somalia took out all the will for action, both in Rwanda and Bosnia' (LeBor, 2006, p. 50).

In combination with the (occasionally) strong rhetoric, the hollowness of US policy became painfully obvious (Callahan, 1998, p. 143).

Numerous measures that aimed to stop the parties from fighting were suggested or tried, but nearly all of them were poorly enforced or ineffective. The Security Council had, for instance, decided that humanitarian aid needed to be able to reach the people without hindrance, but these convoys were nevertheless constantly obstructed. The No Fly Zone and the arms embargo that were put in place were violated repeatedly. The safe areas that had been created by the UN were overrun, causing a horrific massacre at Srebrenica to take place. Indeed, the last few months of the war saw some of the worst violations of international criminal law, despite the creation of the International Criminal Tribunal for the former Yugoslavia (ICTY) (Kaldor, 2006, pp. 65-66). In the meantime, the parties rejected numerous peace plans between 1991 and 1995 (Kaldor, 2006, pp. 62-66). According to Richard Holbrooke 'there were over 30 ceasefires and agreements in Bosnia prior to the Dayton Peace Accords' which were eventually to bring peace to the region (Holbrooke in Chollet, 2005, p. ix) .

8.7.2. TOO LITTLE, TOO LATE

Some of the most gruesome crimes became turning points in the war. The bombing of civilians at a market place in Sarajevo in 1994 was such a turning point (Chollet, 2005, pp. 5-6; Kollander, 2004, p. 14). The attack, which had been captured on camera, caused a tougher policy to be initiated. NATO threatened with airstrikes, possibly also to protect the UN forces in the area, if the Bosnian Serbs did not retreat somewhat and the US started a new diplomatic offensive (Chollet, 2005, p. 6; Kollander, 2004, p. 14). The US decided to arrange a new agreement between the Croats and Muslims that envisioned a combining of forces that would enable them to fight their common enemy, the Bosnian Serbs, together (Chollet, 2005, p. 6). An agreement was reached that provided for a Muslim-Croat Federation thus ending the fighting between them (Sell, 2002, p. 215). In addition, the US started to secretly train the Croatian army and hinted that they would not oppose the strategy of having Iran covertly supplying weapons to the Bosnians (LeBor, 2006, p. 78; Sell, 2002, p. 215).

Internationally, meanwhile the US also sought to strengthen unity among the countries involved and established the Contact Group, comprising the US, Russia, Great Britain and France, who developed a plan that entailed a division of Bosnia, but the Serbs refused to sign (Chollet, 2005, p. 6; Sell, 2002). The agreement's division of Bosnia, however, would serve as the basis of the eventual peace agreement at Dayton (Kollander, 2004, p. 16).

At the end of 1994, and again in the spring of 1995, fighting intensified. In November 1994 the UN safe area Bihac came under assault and as a reaction NATO initiated limited 'pin prick' airstrikes. France and Britain, fearing retaliatory attacks against their forces, insisted that further military force would not ensue (Chollet, 2005, p. 7). In May 1995, a similar scenario repeated itself. After NATO again initiated airstrikes against the Bosnian Serb forces for shelling Sarajevo, the latter took hundreds of UN peacekeepers hostage and as the international community backed down, the Europeans began discussing whether to withdraw their forces (Chollet, 2005, p. 8; Sell, 2002, pp. 226-227).

Not long after, the Bosnian Serbs overran Srebrenica, killing over 6000 men while Dutch peacekeepers stood by (LeBor, 2006, pp. 93-114; Sell, 2002, p. 232). After the horrors of the massacre at Srebrenica became apparent, the international community was again shocked into action. After another attack on the central market in Sarajevo, NATO finally started a major bombing campaign (LeBor, 2006, pp. 114-132; Sell, 2002, pp. 246-247).

By this point, the Serbs were losing territory fast because of the new military might of the US trained Croatian and Bosnian alliance, and in Serbia the economic sanctions were beginning to be felt causing a willingness to come to a peace agreement to grow (Kollander, 2004, pp. 15-16). This eventually led to an agreement being reached at Dayton that allowed Milosevic to walk away as the 'great "peacemaker"' (K. J. Campbell, 2001, p. 67).

8.8. CONCLUSION

While it is certainly not the case that ethnic tensions were the sole, or even most important cause, of the wars in Yugoslavia, schisms between different parts of the population had been present among the population. Milosevic grew up and was socialized in Yugoslavia as part of the Serbian community, and would build his support base upon nationalist tensions that were brewing among the population. It is therefore essential to set Milosevic as a leader in the context of the country which he led.

There were many pre-conditions that forewarned that Yugoslavia was at risk of mass atrocities. Coinciding with Tito's death was the loss of its position as the leader of the non-aligned movement due to the end of the Cold War. Within Serbia, dissatisfaction with the elite was redirected and the misfortune was scapegoated on 'others'. However, the 'others' of Tito's Yugoslavia, the so-called 'class enemies', were no longer salient after the Cold War and new others needed to be created (Jovic, 2001, p. 104). This was done through a reinterpretation of history. The idea was put forward that an anti-Serbian attitude had been present in Yugoslavia and this created the foundations for the Serbian nationalist politicians to generate their support base. These new versions of history were crucial, for 'without (if needed – forceful) forgetting of peaceful coexistence between neighbours who belonged to different ethnic groups, there could be no success for new, separatist doctrines' (Jović, 2004b, p. 102). What had been forgotten was remembered anew and who had been a victim in history and who a villain was reassessed (Jović, 2004b, p. 102).

The wars of succession which followed were not the direct consequence of ancient ethnic hatreds, but Milosevic made use of the existing environment. As De la Brosse points out as well, 'conditions in the country … were exceptionally favourable' for the nationalist propaganda at the end of the 1980s (2003, p. 91). The susceptibility of the Yugoslav population stems from a strenuous past that created schisms among different parts of the population. It did not in any way make the war inevitable but created a fertile ground for hate sowing politicians. It is impossible to know what would have happened had any other leader been at the helm of Serbia. However, it was Milosevic who took the reins, replaced those most important to his rule with his own loyalists and made himself so powerful that his choices could be, and were, instrumental in steering the country to disaster.

He was able to legitimise the atrocities through his control over the media, and he set up the institutions that actually perpetrated the atrocities. Milosevic ensured that some of the most brutal forces, the paramilitary units were created, and provided the necessary military aid to the Bosnian Serbs. The wars of succession provided a pretext for some of the most gruesome crimes which were portrayed as merely being a consequence of the war, and this actually was a rather successful strategy. The ethnic cleansing campaigns were mistakenly seen by the international community as a side effect of the war, rather than its actual goal (Kaldor, 2006, p. 61).

When the international community tried to intervene again in Kosovo, a track record had been set of broken promises and empty threats. Kosovo, which was seen as the cradle of Serbian society even though the majority of the population was now Albanian, was an important catalyst for the violence that spread across the Balkans but was not resolved at Dayton. Milosevic's role in causing the atrocities in Kosovo will be more extensively dealt with in Chapter 11 but the conflict in Kosovo cannot be analysed in isolation to the earlier conflicts.

CHAPTER 9
THE RATIONALITY OF POL POT

9.1. INTRODUCTION

That ideology played an important role in shaping the events in Cambodia seems beyond doubt. Many people suffered a horrendous death because of the imposition of policies that were meant to bring forth a communist utopian society. The real question is whether Pol Pot used this ideology instrumentally because it suited his personal goals and ambitions, or whether there was a genuine belief in the righteousness of the revolution that propelled these developments. Scholars differ somewhat of opinion on this manner. Some scholars are convinced a lust for power lay at the root of these atrocities while others belief it was the uncompromising commitment to the ideology that is to blame. Chindawongse, for instance, believes that power was Pol Pot's predominant overarching goal and that the desire to change society was only necessary and desirable to obtain and maintain control over the country (Chindawongse, 1991, p. 127). According to Chindawongse,

> 'the Pol Pot leadership regarded ideology as an instrument of policy rather than an idealized blueprint of objective to be achieved. Its ultimate objective was to create conditions within the CPK and to restructure social and economic relationships in Cambodia to foster the achievement and perpetuation of a political power monopoly' (1991, p. 132).

Jackson, on the other hand found that the most important motive for the elite was the desire to create an egalitarian society in combination with utter disgust for the old regime (K. D. Jackson, 1989, pp. 54-56). Chandler does not see how one option should negate the others and is convinced that it was a 'courageous, doomed attempt by a group of utopian thinkers', while at the same time it was also the result of an extreme 'thirst for power' (Chandler, 1999, p. 3).

Other scholars are not convinced a rational explanation for the violence can be found because, they argue, Pol Pot was crazy. Polin described Pol Pot as 'a madman who takes himself for an avenging deity' (Polin, 1980, p. 45). Valentino, on the other hand, sees Pol Pot's paranoid psychological mindset as being intimately linked to his ideological outlook. According to Valentino, the paranoia communist leaders often suffer from is attached to the extreme

Marxist outlook that they have and should not be seen as solely something which stems from 'their personal psychological aberrations' (Valentino, 2004, p. 100). Valentino believes Pol Pot was not just preoccupied with maintaining power, but was concerned about the threat counterrevolutionaries formed to his belief system (Valentino, 2004, p. 100). Quinn counters these claims and argues that while many thought the killings were the result of madness, they in fact had a clear purpose namely 'destroying every root, every vestige of individualist thought' in order to build a society which consists of people that are 'totally dedicated to, and knowing only, a collectivist regimen' (Quinn, 1989b, p. 193).

The purpose of this chapter is to probe the question of whether Pol Pot acted rationally, and if so, what type of rationality dominated his behaviour. In order to do so, Weber's theory on rationality will be applied to the life of Pol Pot to ascertain which form of social action he was predominantly oriented towards. The analysis, however, is complicated by the fact that Pol Pot was incredibly secretive throughout his reign.

At the start of the revolution in particular, not much was known about the leader of the country who called himself Pol Pot. It was only in September 1977, probably because he was pressured to come out into the open by the Chinese and was photographed on an official state visit to that country, that he was identified as Saloth Sar (Chandler, 1998, p. 13; 1999, p. 2). He had used numerous aliases throughout his life and once reportedly told his secretaries 'It is good to change your name ... the more often you change your name the better. It confuses the enemy' (Short, 2004, p. 5). He believed secrecy had helped to secure victory and maintained it as long as he could (Chandler, 1998, p. 13). Throughout his rise to power and subsequent reign he lived in accordance with the belief that 'if you preserve secrecy, half the battle is already won' (Short, 2004, p. 5). His rule was so secretive that some thought Khieu Samphan was the mastermind behind it, and that the brutality within the country was due to his mental state, his 'personal neuroses and sexual impotency [and that he] was the virtually "insane" architect of these policies' (Quinn, 1989a, p. 218). While in the first years of his rule Pol Pot remained somewhat of a mystery, as he gave few interviews and held few speeches (Becker, 1998, p. 168), slowly but surely more information has been gathered by a variety of scholars (most notably by Chandler, 1999; Short, 2004) which will be brought together and analysed in the present chapter.

Since Pol Pot did not rule alone, the role his inner circle played will be more closely examined at the end of this chapter. Ultimately, however, Pol Pot was in control over the country and its policies, and predominantly determined the course of the country (Heder, n.d., p. 1). It is therefore important to examine the extent to which one of the two types of rationality, which were identified by Max Weber, dominated his behaviour in order to explain the choices that were made by him later on, when Vietnam invaded and put an end to his reign.

9.2. YOUNGER YEARS

Pol Pot would later claim he was a peasant and plantation worker (Chirot, 1994, p. 218), but he actually came from quite a prosperous family. The man who would become known as Pol Pot, was born as Saloth Sar in the small town Prek Sbauv, whose inhabitants were described by a French official as 'the most deeply Cambodian and the least susceptible to our influence' (Kiernan, 2004, pp. 25-26). He was born on May 25th 1925[101] to a well off farmer's family with connections to the royal palace (Chandler, 1999, pp. 7-8; Short, 2004, p. 15). Sar had eight siblings, five of whom survived into the 1990s (Chandler, 1999, p. 8).[102] His family had extensive royal connections as his aunt was part of the household staff of the king, and her daughter, Sar's causin Meak, danced in the royal ballet, was a royal concubine and gave birth to a son of Prince Sisowath Minivong who became king in 1927 (Chandler, 1999, p. 8; Short, 2004, pp. 16-17). She held a prominent place in the royal household as the 'lady in charge of the women' (Chandler, 1999, p. 8). Sar's sister, Roeung, who was better known as Saroeun, also became a consort to the king when she was 16 years old and stayed by his side until the latter's death (Chandler, 1999, p. 8; Short, 2004, p. 17). In addition, a brother of Saloth Sar worked at the palace and ended up marrying one of the dancers of the royal ballet that his sisters were also part of (Chandler, 1999, p. 8).

When Sar was nine or ten years old, he and his older brother went to live with Saroeun and Meak, which was not an uncommon feature of traditional Cambodian life (Chandler, 1999, p. 8). His parents sent him there to allow Sar to attend primary school but decided that before doing so, he needed to spend a year in a Buddhist monastery. There he learned the importance of strict discipline and traditional poetry that allowed him to appeal to the peasant masses later on, using words to simplify 'social life to the extreme' (Polin, 1980, pp. 43-44; Short, 2004, pp. 20-21).

In 1978, Saloth Sar described his upbringing to Yugoslav journalists in the following terms:

> 'I am from a peasant family; during my childhood, I lived with my parents and helped them in the agricultural work. But after, according to custom, I lived in a pagoda to learn how to read and write. I spent six years in a pagoda and was a monk for two years' (Kiernan, 2004, p. 27).

His brothers dispute this account and claim Sar never had to work the fields, leaving home to go to the monastery at the age of six (Kiernan, 2004, p. 27).

---

101 There is some confusion about his date of birth because Pol Pot always insisted it was 1925, but French colonial records point to 1928 (Chandler, 1999, pp. 7-8).

102 There is also some confusion about the number of brothers and sisters Sar had, since Kiernan mentions he came from a family of seven children (Kiernan, 2004, p. 25) while Short mentions nine children but states three died at a very young age (Short, 2004, p. 16).

After leaving the monastery when he was eight he attended a Catholic primary school, chosen for its good reputation, where he was remembered as someone who was 'very charming' (Chandler, 1999, pp. 16-17; Kiernan, 2004, p. 27; Short, 2004, p. 23). There, he would spend the next six years (Kiernan, 2004, p. 27). Sar was not a gifted student and probably was held back two years because he was unable to keep up with the rest of the class (Short, 2004, p. 28; 31). He is also likely to have failed an entrance exam to a school in Phnom Penh causing him to divert the continuation of his education to Kompong Cham city, where he would attend Norodom Sihanouk High School (Kiernan, 2004, p. 27). The French had established the school in honour of Prince Norodom Sihanouk and chose twenty boys from different provinces to enrol in the first class, and among these twenty was Saloth Sar (Chandler, 1999, p. 17). Here, too, he is remembered fondly. A contemporary has said that 'his manner was straightforward, pleasant, and very polite' and he has been said to have 'thought a lot, but said very little' (Chandler, 1999, p. 19). He was only a mediocre student and, according to Chandler, 'seemed to have had no clear ambitions' (Chandler, 1999, p. 19).

Becker describes him during his school going years as a 'striving, ambitious young man who at an early age decided, consciously or not, to play a greater role than his farming father had' (Becker, 1998, p. 52), but there is actually not much that suggests he was ambitious in this stage of his life; that seemed to have come much later after he started to dedicate himself to the liberation struggle. He is, rather, remembered by his brother as a 'kind, pleasant and unremarkable young man during this period; studious, serious, not a troublemaker and not political' (Becker, 1998, p. 51).

In 1947 Sar was allowed to go to the Lycée Sisowath where he met Ieng Sary who was in a class above him (Short, 2004, p. 36). Sar does not seem to have been very politically engaged at this time, although there are reports he contributed to the campaign of the most important opposition party in Cambodia, the Democratic Party. Ieng Sary was certainly active for them and was even arrested for organizing a demonstration (Chandler, 1999, p. 23; Short, 2004, p. 38; 42). Sary was the more academically distinguished, the more politically aware and made a bigger impression than Sar did at this point in time, but the two struck up a strong friendship that would last a lifetime (Chandler, 1999, p. 22; Erken, 2010, pp. 119-120).

In 1948 Sar failed the examinations that would have allowed him to get a baccalaureate, and therefore Sar enrolled at the Russey Keo Technical School to study carpentry (Chandler, 1999, p. 21; Kiernan, 2004, p. 29; Short, 2004, p. 42). A year later he was awarded a scholarship to study in Paris (Kiernan, 2004, p. 29). It is unclear why he was given a scholarship to pursue his education in Paris in 1949 but it might be because of his connections to the Democratic Party (Chandler, 1999, p. 24). Becker notes that the privilege of being allowed to study in Paris made Sar feel special, or 'chosen' (Becker, 1998, p. 55) but it seems in actuality it was not a major accomplishment, given the small amount of students who applied for the grand (Short, 2004, p. 43)

In Paris, Sar would find his calling and become a dedicated communist, but the first steps along this path seem somewhat disingenuous since Sar became a communist 'when it was the popular thing to do' (Chandler, 1999, p. 25). The communist party in France had never been more popular, Stalin's personality cult was at its height, the communists were victorious in China, and the war in Korea had just started (Chandler, 1999, p. 25).

Not all aspects of his life were completely dominated by politics during this time. Although Sar remembers he was quite motivated in the first year of his studies, many of his friends saw Sar as a '*bon vivant*' who mainly just wanted to have a good time (Chandler, 1999, p. 26; Short, 2004, p. 49). His decision to go to Yugoslavia in 1950 as a manual labourer, for instance, seems to have been more motivated by a desire to have fun than by political considerations. In an interview in 1997 he remembered 'I went [to Yugoslavia] because it was vacation time and I had no money ... we went just for pleasure' (cited in Chandler, 1999, p. 28). At the same time, the collective projects and mass mobilization of the people probably made an impression on Sar (Chirot, 1994, p. 219), and Kiernan argues Sar is likely to have sympathized with Yugoslavia's independent stance from the Soviet Union (Kiernan, 2004, p. 120).

The most important friendships during this time were with politically engaged fellow students, many of whom would later hold important positions in the Khmer Rouge or were otherwise important for determining the fate of Cambodia later on. Among these newfound friends were Thiounn Mum and his three brothers. Mumm arrived in Paris a few years before Sar in 1946 and became a member of the French Communist Party in 1951, probably introducing Sar to the party the year thereafter (Becker, 1998, pp. 55-56; Chandler, 1999, pp. 26-27; Short, 2004, p. 458). More importantly perhaps, he was the long-time member of the *Cercle Marxiste*, a study group which discussed predominantly communists texts and nationalist issues, along with Keng Vannsak, who was a major source of inspiration for Saloth Sar during this time (Chandler, 1999, pp. 27; 33-37; Short, 2004, p. 52; 452; 458). Vannsak was, first and foremost, a nationalist and anti-royalist who would come to lead the Democratic Party in the 1950s (Chandler, 1999, p. 27; Short, 2004, p. 452). Ieng Sary, who came to Paris the year after Saloth Sar, introduced Sar to Keng Vannsak (Chandler, 1999, p. 26; 31), and by 1951 they started to meet regularly and hold political discussions in Vannsak's home (Chandler, 1999, p. 33).[103]

Some remember Sar hardly ever contributed to the discussions and did not always show up, while others rather held that Sar during this time 'was the most intelligent, the most convinced, the most intransigent. It was he who animated

103 Becker believes the Thiounn brothers first became friends with Sar and Sary and brought them into the study sessions (Becker, 1998, p. 56)

the debates and most impressed the newcomers', but there is reason to believe the latter description was actually the result of a case of mistaken identity and actually referred to another participant (Chandler, 1999, pp. 33-34). Whether it happened immediately or was a gradual process that happened throughout the next year, the discussions eventually shaped Sar's outlook and belief system. They talked about a range of issues, especially the future of Cambodia which by now got caught up in the Vietnam War (Short, 2004, p. 52). Sar particularly remembered feeling 'patriotic and against French colonialism', viewing the war merely as a part of the anti-colonial struggle (Short, 2004, p. 52). His national identity became increasingly important, being so far away from his land and people (Chandler, 1999, pp. 27-28).

The predominant focus of the group of friends was national liberation more so than any particular type of ideological orientation (Short, 2004, p. 58). From these informal discussions, however, the *Cercle Marxiste* was formed. It was a secret organization of different cells of a handful of people, one of which was always in contact with the leadership but no one knew the entire organizational structure (Short, 2004, p. 63).

The discussions among the students were often too difficult for him to grasp completely, and Sar would later confess he never understood Marx' books when he read them (Short, 2004, pp. 65-66) but he came to view the communist ideology merely as a way in which good was to overcome evil and it gave him a sense of purpose (Short, 2004, p. 65). Those who had been part of the discussions were more nationalist, and anti-royalist than necessarily communist (Kiernan, 2004, p. 121). They drew most of their inspiration not from the example set by their Vietnamese neighbours but looked towards the former Ankor Empire (Chirot, 1994, p. 218).

Sar got enthralled in the possibilities the communist movement offered. Chandler explains that

> 'by 1951, if not before, he was caught up in a wave of optimism about the potentialities of the Communist movement. Unlike many of his contemporaries, Saloth Sar never abandoned communism or regretted his decision. Instead he made a lifelong commitment to the cause' (Chandler, 1999, p. 27).

Soon after joining the *Cercle*, Sar also decided to join the French communist party (Short, 2004, p. 66). He slowly became more politically active, but throughout this time took a backseat to Ieng Sary. It was said both of them 'ate and slept revolution' but Sary took the lead (Short, 2004, p. 68). Sar still did not appear overly ambitious or power hungry; he wanted his success to have been the cause of external factors, and in service of what circumstances required from him. Chandler explains 'he wanted his rise inside the movement to be seen as a response to historical imperatives, patriotism, and the wishes of others rather than to a strategic plan or calculated moves on his part' (Chandler, 1999, p. 40).

Sar's task during this time included for instance helping out with the secret journal of the *Cercle* along with Sary, a process through which he met his future wife, Khieu Ponnary who was the sister of Sary's fiancée, Thirith (Short, 2004, p. 68). The eventual marriage seems to have been based on mutual respect and dedication to the cause. Both needed a spouse they could trust completely and Khieu seems to have been dedicated as much to the political beliefs as Sar was (Becker, 1998, p. 58).

Slowly but surely he got more caught up in the movement and its ideology. A friend at the time remembers how on one occasion

> 'there was an internal discussion and we were asked to decide and declare whether we were prepared to dedicate our lives to the revolution. Saloth Sar was one who said that he was' (Chandler, 1999, p. 39).

As he became more enticed by his political activities, he started to neglect his studies more and more (Chandler, 1999, p. 38). He often failed his examinations and his academic career never seemed to have been a priority for him (Chandler, 1999, p. 26). Then, in 1952 at the start of the new academic year, the group of friends that had formed the *Cercle* gathered for another meeting, to discuss how to further the resistance effort and whether members of the *Cercle* should return to Cambodia to engage in the struggle there (Short, 2004, p. 81). It was decided that it was necessary someone would return to assess the situation there. Sar remembered someone needed

> 'to carry out a reconnaissance ... and make an assessment of the different resistance organizations. [then we would] take a decision over which movement we should support – and which organization we should join" (Short, 2004, p. 82).

In addition, the leadership of the circle wanted this individual to investigate whether the different organizations could be united. Sar offered to go (Short, 2004, p. 82). By this time, he had his scholarship revoked because he did not manage to pass the required exams at his Radio-Electricity School. This had not prevented others from hanging around in Paris but Sar now believed he was needed at home. Leaving Paris, therefore, seems to have been a conscious choice (Kiernan, 2004, p. 122; Short, 2004, p. 82). He left Paris in December 1952, became a member of the Indochina Communist Party and joined the communist resistance against the French which was mostly organized and dominated by the Vietnamese (Chandler, 1999, p. 26). Ponnary also lost her scholarship due to the political activities she was engaged in and returned with Sar to her homeland (Becker, 1998, p. 62).

Whether it was peer pressure and conformity or the *Zeitgeist* which led him to embrace communism, once he became a communist, he did so wholeheartedly. As Becker notes 'the years in France established a mind-set in

Sar that would never alter significantly' (1998, p. 60). Quinn even goes as far as to argue that the education the Khmer Rouge leadership received in France should be seen as a contributing factor that caused the genocide since it was in France that they were exposed to communist thought for the first time (Quinn, 1989a, p. 231). While it certainly should not be seen as the only or even primary cause of the violence that occurred in the country in the years that followed, the time Saloth Sar spent in Paris certainly made a big impression on him, and influenced the path he chose to follow.

The man that would grow to become the most important and influential leader of the communist movement in Cambodia, at this point in time did not seem to possess many of the qualities one would expect from someone that would leave such an important mark on the future of his country. Because Sar was a rather mediocre student and not very ambitious, Cunha *et al* argue he 'ascended to leadership in spite and not because of personal characteristics' (Pina e Cunha *et al.*, 2011, p. 275). They argue that

> "charisma and power grew from position. Sar was the man at the centre of the movement. Dispositions and circumstances, local and global co-created a powerful leader from someone in whom, originally, there appeared to be little apparent leadership potential" (Pina e Cunha *et al.*, 2011, p. 283).

Charisma, from this perspective, in Sar's case is actually partly constructed because of circumstances and context (Pina e Cunha *et al.*, 2011, p. 283). At the same time, however, as a personality trait his perseverance and determination to contribute to the liberation of his country should not be discounted. While it is true that Sar became so powerful because of who he was in conjunction with local and global forces (Pina e Cunha *et al.*, 2011, p. 278), leadership potential can be found already in these early years in his amicable personality. People liked him and were willing to listen to him. Due to his diverse background he easily connected with a great variety of people and hid all his true intentions behind a smile (Short, 2004, p. 44). As will be explained below, this skill turned out to be very useful as he rose to the top of the organization and persuaded others of the righteousness of the movement and the communist principles upon which they would build a new Cambodia.

9.3. RISE TO POWER

Saloth Sar may not have been an exceptional child or student, but once he found his calling in Paris, all the pieces seemed to fall into place. He became dedicated to the ideology that gave his life a sense of meaning and purpose and, in the years that were to come he would be willing to make sacrifices and endure hardships in order to advance the revolutionary goals.

9.3.1. RETURNING TO CAMBODIA

As he came back from France he realized that his country was at war and when he returned to his home village, he spoke to many relatives who lost everything. Sar would later explain how he saw that 'the Cambodian countryside was being pauperized. Having lived in Europe, seeing these things hurt my heart' (Short, 2004, pp. 85-86). He saw colonialism as the underlying problem and knew that his country needed to be independent (Short, 2004, p. 86). His new-found passion for politics soon became apparent to his family, and as an explanation for this change of heart, Sar told his brother 'I think about the people' (Chandler, 1999, p. 41). He used the fact that he was a member of the French communist party to be introduced to the Indochina Communist Party (ICP) in order to join the armed struggle (Burchett, 1981, p. 53; Chandler, 1999, p. 41). In 1953 Sar joined up with Rath Samoeun, whom he knew from the *Cercle* in Paris, to go to the Viet Minh Eastern Zone Headquarters (Short, 2004, p. 90; 96). While there, they were disappointed and frustrated with the marginal roles that were designated to Cambodian contributors. Sar would later recall the experience:

> 'As I had just come back from abroad ... they didn't trust me. [Almost every-one] was Vietnamese – there were just a handful of Cambodians – and everyone spoke Vietnamese. ... All I was allowed to do was cultivate cassava. After a while, they let me work ... in the canteen. I was the deputy mess officer. The mess officer himself was Vietnamese. ... even the messengers were Vietnamese. The Cambodians were there in name only' (Short, 2004, p. 96).

The man who introduced him to the Vietnamese dominated resistance, Pham Van Ba, described Sar as a 'young man of average ability but with a clear desire for power' (Burchett, 1981, p. 54), which may be explained by Sar's desire to uncouple his own revolution from Vietnamese patronage. It should be noted, however, that Sar at this point was not vehemently anti-Vietnamese. He would later state that

> '[although] I saw that the Cambodian movement was completely controlled by [them] ... it did not shape my thinking to be anti-Vietnamese ... I thought we should have a good relationship with Vietnam. I just wanted to make our movement independent' (Short, 2004, p. 98).

Sar's usefulness in either case was soon recognised by the ICP as they started to realize he was ideally placed to bridge gaps among the different groups because he was well connected to the Cambodian elite, the democrats and the French communist party (Chandler, 1999, pp. 42-43). He went to work at the headquarters, working at the propaganda section and furthered his political education under the guidance of Tou Samouth (Burchett, 1981, p. 54; Chandler, 1999, pp. 42-43).

In 1954 it was decided Saloth Sar should return to Phnom Penh to further the Communist cause from within the city (Burchett, 1981, p. 54). During these first few years back in the capital, Sar fulfilled several roles at once. He for instance worked with the Democrats to help prepare for the 1955 election and aimed to bend the party's affiliation more to the left while hiding his affiliation with the resistance (Chandler, 1999, p. 45). In the city he could also mobilize students to aid the revolutionary cause (Burchett, 1981, p. 54). Burchett, however, notes that Sar also used this new position to 'recruit a nucleus of students around which to build his own faction within the party' (Burchett, 1981, p. 54). As more and more members of the Paris *Cercle* returned to Cambodia, a rift had started to emerge within the party and a struggle for power ensued (Burchett, 1981, pp. 54-55). Sar and his friends, Ieng Sary and Son Sen formed the 'hard line' believing armed struggle against Sihanouk needed to be waged while others saw room to cooperate with him in a fight against what they saw as the biggest threat, namely US imperialism (Burchett, 1981, p. 55; Etcheson, 1984, p. 57).

While 'total supremacy' was not achieved until 1977, Sar's faction soon became very powerful within the communist party (Etcheson, 1984, p. 46). His position to engage in both open and hidden party work put him in an important position as much of the communication between different fractions went through him (Short, 2004, p. 116). Keng Vannsak, who also had returned to Cambodia from Paris and was now working for the Democratic Party, started to see Sar in a new light during this time. Vannsak was working with Sar and Khieu Ponnary and was impressed by Sar's 'measured and intelligent' appearance, that Vannsak had never noticed before in Paris (Chandler, 1999, p. 46; Short, 2004, p. 108). Throughout this campaign, Sar's friendship with Khieu Ponnary also grew stronger (Chandler, 1999, p. 49).

Sar married Khieu Ponnary in 1956, perhaps on the rebound. His feelings for another woman did not materialize into an actual relationship because she cut their love affair short when he did not acquire a politically prestigious position fast enough (Chandler, 1999, p. 49; Short, 2004, p. 117). Khieu was in her mid-thirties and, for Cambodian standards, was an older woman. She had been working as a schoolteacher for several years when she got married and was respected by her students but made others uncomfortable because of her focus on politics, her career and her sober appearance. They would call her derogatorily 'the old virgin' (Chandler, 1999, pp. 49-50). They were an odd couple in many ways. On the one hand, because Khieu was older than Sar which was quite uncommon in Cambodia, and on the other hand, because few women from Khieu's standing would settle for a man whom had as little prospects for the future as Sar did at the time (Chandler, 1999, p. 50). Chandler, therefore, hypothesises that it could have been Sar's charm which made Khieu fall for him or 'perhaps she and Saloth Sar were drawn together by their shared commitment to utopian politics' (1999, p. 50).

During this time Sar also started a career as a teacher (Chandler, 1999, p. 50). Although his academic track record was always rather poor he seems to have been well-liked and respected as a teacher (Chandler, 1999, p. 51; Short, 2004, p. 120). The school where he was teaching provided a platform for his political ideas and a façade behind which he could engage in his secret party work. Chandler believes that Sar's 'decision to become a teacher at Chamraon Vichea seemed to owe more to drift and circumstance than to ambition or choice' and the opportunities it provided for his political involvement carried much weight in determining his path (Chandler, 1999, pp. 51-52). At the same time, however, he was not espousing many radical ideas in his teachings. This was in line with the spirit of the times where the term communism was not necessarily associated with strictly Marxist ideas but, according to Chandler, was used to describe anyone 'who had simple tastes, a good education and a hatred for corruption' (Chandler, 1999, p. 53) and these values did come to the fore in his interaction with students. One of Khieu's students who met him described how he could 'explain things in such a way that you came to love justice and honesty and hate corruption' (Chandler, 1999, p. 51).

Sar, who became known as Pol in revolutionary circles around this time, also arranged his private life largely in conformity to those virtues. He lived in a house that he shared with Ieng Sary and his wife Thirith. Many were surprised at their refusal, because of ideological grounds, to hire servants, but Sar had always lived a relatively modest life, except for the fact that he drove a for Cambodian standards luxurious car which had been a hand down from his sister Roeung (Chandler, 1999, p. 53; Short, 2004, p. 116).

9.3.2. AGAINST ALL ODDS

By the end of the 1950s, the revolutionary struggle seemed an eternal uphill battle and one that they simply could not win. Sihanouk had cracked down hard on the communists and their ranks were shrinking rather than growing (Becker, 1998, p. 89; Short, 2004, p. 120). Pol would later explain '90 percent of our revolutionary forces in the countryside' had left the revolutionary movement, had died or had been arrested by 1959 and some high profile party members had defected (Chandler, 1999, p. 56; Short, 2004, p. 124). By this time there was no strategy, and they were left more or less to their own devices (Chandler, 1983, p. 292).

Twenty-one members met in Phnom Penh in secret to discuss the blows the movement had to endure and to set out its future. They needed to develop a strategy, further crystallize the ideology they were to adhere to and develop the organization further so they could attract support both within the country and elsewhere (Chandler, 1983, p. 292; Etcheson, 1984, p. 57). The name of the party was changed to 'Worker's Party of Kampuchea' and drew up new statutes, signalling that they were now on equal footing to its Vietnamese counterpart although in practice it remained reliant on Vietnamese supervision (Chandler, 1983, p. 292; 1999, p. 60; Kiernan, 2004, p. 190; Morris, 1999, p. 37).[104] They also selected their central committee with Tou Samouth as Party Secretary, Nuon Chea – who would later become known as Brother Number Two – became his right hand man, Pol was third in the hierarchy and Ieng Sary was elected as the fifth[105] most important party member (Kiernan, 2004, p. 190). Those who had been educated in France, and now took up high positions in the Central Committee held more radical ideas, being relentlessly opposed to Sihanouk and his policies, while other party members continued to recognize the popularity he still enjoyed throughout much of the countryside and credited him for maintaining the neutrality of their country (Kiernan, 2004, p. 191). Pol would later recall:

> 'at that time, Cambodia was a satellite of imperialism, of US imperialism in particular. This means that Cambodia was not independent ... This was one analysis. Did this analysis generate any conflicting opinion? Yes, it did. There were a number of factions which thought that Cambodia was independent. ... However, through our analysis we found that Cambodia was not independent' (Kiernan, 2004, p. 191).

They also stressed the importance of initiating an armed struggle (Etcheson, 1984, pp. 58-59) even though this went against the wishes of the Vietnamese (Chandler, 1999, p. 60). In 1960 this was still the minority position and Samouth expressed the most commonly held position that the Vietnamese should not be antagonised and Sihanouk's neutral policy not jeopardized (Etcheson, 1984, p. 58).

Repression by Sihanouk continued and in 1962 Tou Samouth disappeared (Etcheson, 1984, p. 59; Short, 2004, pp. 140-141). While Pol was later blamed for his death, possibly because the Samouth had been too pro-Vietnamese, this remains highly uncertain and it seems more likely that government forces were behind his disappearance (Chandler, 1999, p. 61; Frings, 1997, p. 830; Kiernan, 2004, p. 198). Although he was more radical than many others, Pot Pot still was not completely anti-Vietnamese. He may have resented their tutelage, but he seems to have been realistic about the fact that at that point in time collaborating with them remained a necessity. Pol, for instance, had told a former class mate a few years earlier that 'the wheel of history' ensured that Cambodia should entertain a friendly relationship with Vietnam 'which is so much stronger' (Chandler, 1999, p. 45). When the bonds with the Vietnamese started to loosen, however, Pol believed this was a positive development since 'it gave us the chance to be independent and to develop our movement ourselves' (Short, 2004, p. 121). Pol Pot, and his clique, overall remained suspicious of Vietnamese patronage and

[104] Short believes the name change only occurred three years later when Pol Pot took over the leadership of the party (Short, 2004, p. 142)

[105] Short rather mentions Ieng Sary was elected fourth in the hierarchy (Short, 2004, p. 138)

influence. According to Chindawongse, they 'distrusted Vietnamese motives and exhibited hatred toward the Vietnamese as an ethnic group' (Chindawongse, 1991, p. 129).

After Samouth's disappearance, Pol became secretary of the party's Central Committee. In doing so he bypassed Nuon Chea about whom rumours, possibly spread by Pol, had been circulating which questioned his loyalty (Chandler, 1999, pp. 61-64; Short, 2004, p. 141). At this point, the former students from Paris held 5 of the 12 most important positions in the party (Etcheson, 1984, p. 60). Pol would later declare that the day that he became Secretary General should go down in history as the moment the party was founded. He explained that it was necessary to 'rearrange the history of the Party into something clean and perfect, in line with our policies of independence and self-mastery' (Womack, 2003, p. 113). He would henceforth frequently try to make reality conform to his ideological vision of what it should be.

In 1963 Sihanouk started to target the left and a list of people that were considered to have communist leanings was composed by the government which included Ieng Sary and Pol Pot causing them to flee to the Vietnamese border where they started to take steps to eventually commence the armed struggle (Burchett, 1981, pp. 57-58; Chandler, 1999, p. 63). Sihanouk probably did not know yet they were also a member of the forbidden Communist Party's Central Committee and they were probably only included on the list because they worked for leftist schools. Pol, however, presumed Sihanouk had this knowledge and was not about to take any chances (Chandler, 1999, pp. 63-64; 2008, pp. 241-242). Pol later said:

> 'In 1963, I could not stay any more in Phnom Penh. I had to join the maquis. I was not very well known to the public. But Lon Nol's [who would later overthrow Sihanouk in a coup d'état] police followed my activities. They knew me but they did not know exactly who I was. In Phnom Penh I was the general responsible [for] the movement in the capital; I was also in charge of liaison with the countryside' (Chandler, 1999, p. 64; Short, 2004, p. 454).

From this moment onwards he disappeared from public life altogether (Etcheson, 1984, p. 59). Short describes life at the Vietnamese base as 'spartan'. It was remote, sunlight hardly penetrated through the thick jungle in which they lived and it took a toll on their health (Short, 2004, p. 145). A year later, Pol convinced the Vietnamese to let them set up their own base 'to avoid political complications and build the revolution step by step ourselves' (Short, 2004, p. 146). While they remained under Vietnamese control (Short, 2004, p. 146), there were increasingly signs that the Cambodian communists and the Vietnamese had divergent interests and goals. In the autumn of 1964 they held a meeting of the central committee and decided all forms of struggle, including military, were justified against Sihanouk and throughout this process stressed 'self-reliance', which was perceived to be synonymous with independence from the Vietnamese (Short, 2004, p. 146).

Throughout the next seven years the leadership lived completely isolated and this time which they spent surrounded with likeminded revolutionaries influenced Pol tremendously. He was inspired by the problems he saw in the countryside and the isolation likely strengthened his paranoia and sense of destiny (Chandler, 1999, p. 65; Short, 2004, p. 147). In these first few years, the movement did not manage to make much progress and Pol was completely dependent on the Vietnamese. It must have been a dark period for him personally (Chandler, 1999, p. 67).

9.3.3. TENSIONS WITH THE VIETNAMESE

Pol's only time away from the jungle environment in the next seven years occurred in 1965-1966 when he spent several months in Vietnam and China (Chandler, 1999, p. 65). This was the moment that Pol supplanted Vietnamese patronage finally with that of the Chinese (Chandler, 2008, p. 247). He walked the Ho Chi Minh trail for two and a half months and upon arrival met with senior officials but could not secure Vietnamese support for a violent struggle against Sihanouk (Short, 2004, pp. 156-157). Vietnam was focusing on its own war, and since Sihanouk had a strained relationship with the US and had broken off all diplomatic ties with them. He had consequently become an ally as they shared a mutual enemy, the US (Short, 2004, p. 157). Sihanouk even allowed Vietnamese troops to make use of Cambodian territory and a good bond with Sihanouk had become important to the Vietnamese (Short, 2004, p. 157). The Vietnamese therefore felt that the Cambodian communists needed to wait until Vietnam had waged its struggle and were displeased by all the talk of self-reliance (Short, 2004, p. 157).

Pol Pot[106] documented his visit to Vietnam 12 years after the fact in a text that sought to justify the ongoing war with Vietnam. As such it is biased in the manner in which it is written but not necessarily factually incorrect (Chandler, 1999, p. 70). In it he describes how the Cambodians sought to steer their own political course which clashed with the Vietnamese desire to maintain control (Chandler, 1999, p. 70). It was a source of resentment and this sentiment was reinforced when Pol was reviewing the party's history from the point of view of the Vietnamese:

> 'I found that from 1930 … to 1965, all the Vietnamese Communist Party documents depicted the Cambodian … and Lao People's revolutionary Parties as branches of the Vietnamese party … Both [Parties] implemented the rules, the political line and

[106] Pol Pot is at least the most likely author of the document (Chandler, 1999, p. 70).

> the strategy of the Vietnamese Party. Until I read these documents myself, I trusted and believed the Vietnamese. But after reading them I didn't trust them any more. I realized that they had set up Party organizations in our countries solely to achieve their aim of the Indochinese Federation. They were making one integrated party to represent a single, integrated territory' (Short, 2004, p. 158).

It seems to have been a pivotal moment for Pol, who lost what little faith he had in the Vietnamese (Short, 2004, p. 159). How open or outspoken the conflict was at that time, however, is questionable, and Pol probably hid his discontent (Chandler, 1999, p. 71; Short, 2004, p. 158).

The Vietnamese continuously refused to help Cambodia launch a military struggle but the two countries were nevertheless forced to rely on each other because of the importance of the Ho Chi Minh trail for the Vietnamese and because they relied on Cambodian territory to provide them with cover for their military bases and sanctuaries. The Cambodian communists at the same time were not strong enough to go completely without Vietnamese support (Short, 2004, pp. 170-171).

According to Morris, throughout the 1960s Pol's communist values were more important to him than his traditional Cambodian values which dictated a hostile attitude towards the Vietnamese (Morris, 1999, p. 38). The Vietnamese collaboration at this point was an important aspect of the means with which the overarching goal, a communist utopia, was to be attained. Pol was still pragmatic about those means as long as they would lead him closer to his goal.

From Vietnam Pol made his way into China where he arrived at the end of December and found their belief system to correspond better with his own (Short, 2004, pp. 159-160). The Chinese believed, as did Pol, that the most important divide was between the people that were being oppressed and the imperialists who exploited them, rather than between capitalism and communism *per se*, as the Vietnamese believed (Short, 2004, p. 160). It was the beginning of a long alliance that Pol would see as being the solution to their ability to break free from Vietnamese influence (Short, 2004, p. 161).

Tensions between the Cambodian communists and the Vietnames became more palpable in the years that followed. In 1966 the leadership decided to change their name, without informing Hanoi, to the Communist Party of Kampuchea. Although seemingly insignificant, the move probably gave Pol the feeling he was in control (Chandler, 1999, p. 75).[107] They also moved the location of their base to a more remote location on Cambodian soil to escape the constant oversight of the Vietnamese (Short, 2004, p. 162). He set up a new headquarters in isolated area, and in the years that followed 'lost touch with everyday Cambodian life, polished his Utopian ideas, nourished his hatreds, and thought about seizing power' (Chandler, 2008, p. 247).

---

107 Etcheson believed the name change already occurred in 1963 while Becker thinks the name change took place in 1971 (Becker, 1998, p. 93; Etcheson, 1984, p. 59).

By 1967 it was deemed impossible to survive while waging only a political struggle but the resources and manpower were lacking for a full blown military struggle and Vietnam still refused to help (Chandler, 1999, p. 79; 81; Short, 2004, p. 170). They therefore decided to use military tactics to protect the leadership and continue the political effort to increase their forces (Chandler, 1999, p. 79). Short believes the guerrilla war was basically forced upon him. He explains that 'in a deeply corrupt state, ruled by an autocrat and racked by social and economic injustice, armed rebellion had become not just the natural but inevitable choice of any idealistic young man' (Short, 2004, p. 190). Pol emphasized the virtuous nature of fighting a war without the proper resources, seeing it in light of the purity of being self-sufficient (Becker, 1998, p. 107). They started to clash militarily with Sihanouk's forces from 1968 onwards (Chandler, 1999, p. 80) and the tide soon started to turn, their ranks doubled between 1968 and 1970 due to the harsh repression and the start of American bombing raids (Chandler, 1999, p. 83).

Despite the successes in garnering more and more support for their movement, life as a revolutionary continued to be harsh. The base had to move regularly along the Vietnamese border, and at times Pol had to walk for weeks, while falling ill, being struck by malaria, to get to the next encampment (Chandler, 1999, p. 67; 74; Short, 2004, p. 172). Soon, however, at least the struggle became more hopeful.

Towards the end of the 1960s Pol Pot travelled to Hanoi and Beijing again and was there when Sihanouk arrived there as well after being deposed by Lon Nol (Chandler, 1999, p. 83; 85). The fact that Sihanouk was now deposed by the pro-American Lon Nol also meant that Pol had the full support and backing of the Vietnamese against the new ruler of Cambodia (Chandler, 1999, p. 85). Pol knew that the Vietnamese would not let Sihanouk return to power and, for the first time, the prospects that Pol would seize power became realistic and he decided to form an alliance with Sihanouk in order to shore up international support for their movement (Chandler, 1999, p. 85). In addition, since Sihanouk became the official front of the organization, they did not seem very radical or extreme to the Cambodian people but seemed more like a variation of what the population already was accustomed to (Becker, 1998, p. 3).

Becker described the level headed pragmatism with which Pol approached the situation. According to Becker:

> 'Saloth Sar had formed his wartime alliances with sophisticated pragmatism ... Sar did not covet the spotlight but was content to wait out his rivals and use his enemies of yesterday as expedient allies of the moment' (Becker, 1998, pp. 138-139).

By 1970 Pol's forces held large swathes of land but the military odds were still favourable to Sihanouk (Chandler, 1999, p. 81; 2008, p. 247). Initially the Vietnamese organized much of the resistance and in the first few years their support was essential to fight the government forces, but by 1971 resentment among the Cambodian communists started to grow (Chandler, 1999, pp. 88-90). While the Khmer Rouge mainly wanted weapons that would allow them to wage their own war, Vietnam predominantly sent troops. Ultimately, the Khmer Rouge leadership came to resent the Vietnamese influence over those areas of Cambodia which they had 'liberated' and were now within their control (Short, 2004, pp. 204-205).

Despite this undercurrent of animosity, even Pol acknowledged that they still needed the Vietnamese and was in favour of continuing to work closely together with them 'because we are fighting a common enemy' (Short, 2004, p. 226). However, from this time onwards, slowly but surely the Khmer Rouge started to become more confident that they could hold their own and the movement started to become more independent (Short, 2004, pp. 236-237).

In 1972 Pol travelled through the areas his forces had established control over and proclaimed the message that they should work towards 'independence mastery' and 'self-sufficiency', and came to the conclusion that the revolution was not progressing fast enough (Short, 2004, pp. 227-228). It became a crucial moment in the revolution (Short, 2004, p. 228). Until then the policies in the areas under their control had been relatively moderate but that was all about to change, with collectivization efforts underway and religious practices abolished, life for the Cambodian population under the control of the Khmer Rouge was to change drastically. Still, many people, especially the very poor peasants, continued to benefit from the policies and for many others the sacrifices seemed to be manageable (Short, 2004, pp. 229-232).

Increasingly, ideological zeal started to dominate the decisions of the leadership and shape the policy choices that were being made. In 1973, they launched a doomed military attack on Phnom Penh in the midst of the intensive American bombing campaign. Morris argues this decision by the Khmer Rouge leadership can hardly be explained because of military rationality. It rather was motivated by a desire to humble the US and 'a fanatical ideological zeal, whereby they imagined that they would be proving the virtue of Khmer communism and their ability to outshine the Vietnamese communists' (Morris, 1999, p. 59; 68). In addition, they also started to attack their Vietnamese allies, even before they had defeated the Cambodian government forces, putting themselves at serious risk (Morris, 1999, p. 68).

In 1973 the Vietnamese and the Americans, after years of negotiating, reached an agreement over the implementation of a ceasefire throughout the region (Chandler, 1999, pp. 94-95). The Vietnamese urged Pol Pot to honour this agreement and the US did the same with Lon Nol, but while Lon Nol acquiesced, Pol Pot refused to do so. Pol not only saw strategic objections to such an agreement, being unwilling to revert back to only a political struggle without the Vietnamese to protect them and was by now probably convinced they could now win the war themselves, but also saw the agreement as a betrayal (Chandler, 1999, p. 95). Pol Pot later said he believed that had they accepted a ceasefire in 1973 'we would have become slaves of the Vietnamese, and the Kampuchean [Cambodian] race would have entirely lost its identity' (Takei, 1998, p. 72). Instead they sought to expand the area under their control and started to implement the communist policies that would later wreck the country once they got into power (Chandler, 1999, p. 96).

The changes that were implemented from 1973 onwards were drastic and coincided with an increase in the influence of Pol Pot's fraction within the party as they set in motion purges of all those who had favoured a more moderate stance or rapprochement with the Vietnamese (Quinn, 1989a, p. 227; Valentino, 2004, p. 136). Throughout these early years, glimpses of the brutality that the regime would exhibit later on occasionally raised its ugly head as executions were the fate that awaited those who resisted (Short, 2004, p. 230; 249). The Khmer Rouge started to implement more radical agricultural policies and the areas under their control became collectivized (Valentino, 2004, p. 136). Before 1973, there were some land distribution initiatives, but overall private property was not abolished and the peasant lifestyle overall was not threatened. During this time peasant support was also forthcoming but as the policies became more radical opposition to them started to mount (Valentino, 2004, p. 136). Strict control was exercised by the Khmer Rouge by confining everyone to cooperatives, which bound the people in one place, safeguarded the harvest and kept enemies out. They cut off contact with the outside world and abolished the use of money, making illegal trade useless. All the resources of the cooperatives would be used for the revolution (Becker, 1998, p. 148). Pol Pot explained the logic behind it as follows:

> '[Before cooperatives] the landowners and merchants gathered all the rice to sell to the Lon Nol clique and to the Vietnamese. The poor strata ran out of rice ... the Revolutionary Army of Kampuchea who were fighting at the front, they were running out of rice and fed with rice soup at every meal ... that is why in 1973, the Central Committee of our Party decided to create cooperatives' (Becker, 1998, p. 148).

To a large extent Pol Pot lived by the rules he imposed on his population. All the party cadre needed to eat meagerly, live without too many material luxury items and even Pol dressed in 'black peasant clothes, with a red-and-white *karma* around the neck and sandals cut from car tyres' (Short, 2004, p. 236). Pol Pot and Nuon Chea were, however, exempt from the self-criticism sessions (Short, 2004, p. 235).

In Phnom Penh the living conditions also worsened rapidly and Lon Nol fled the city in March 1975 (Chandler, 2008, p. 254; Short, 2004, p. 264). The Khmer Rouge eventually took the city on April 17 1975 but Pol stayed clear of the scene as its inhabitants were being evacuated and only arrived in secret several days later (Chandler, 1999, pp. 103-104; Short, 2004, p. 286). That summer, he gave a speech in the deserted city, in which he glorified his movement and their achievements (Becker, 1998, p. 26). He said:

> 'in the whole world, since the advent of the revolutionary war and since the birth of U.S. imperialism, no people and no army has been able to drive the imperialists out to the last man and to score total victory over them ... In our 2000 year history, we have never before liberated our country and achieved full independence like this' (Becker, 1998, p. 26).

Of course, the troops would not have been able to do it without the help from the Vietnamese and the Chinese, but Pol Pot made no secret of proclaiming the supremacy and independence of his movement (Becker, 1998, p. 27).

While the leadership seems to have believed that the evacuation was a success, and that the thousands who had died were a necessary and minor price to pay for advancing the revolution, Pol felt the need to justify it to the world outside (Short, 2004, p. 287). Towards the West the message was that none of it had been planned but was done because of the 'realisation that a food shortage was immanent ... and that there was a plan by US lackeys to attack us that prompted [it]' (Short, 2004, p. 287). Chinese journalists, however, were given another explanation in which security reasons were emphasized:

> 'until we had smashed all kinds of enemy spy organisations, we did not have enough strength to defend the revolutionary regime' (Short, 2004, p. 287).

The evacuation of course had been pre-planned and was motivated by a complex mix of security and ideological considerations (Short, 2004, p. 287).

Pol worked day and night, paperwork and priorities needed to be sorted out and they were still fearful of their enemies (Chandler, 1999, p. 105). A contemporary remembers, 'the whole day was full of work ... Generally at night it went on until eleven or twelve, and sometimes until one in the morning' (Chandler, 1999, p. 105). Thiounn Mumm described Pol at this time by referring back to Axelrod's description of Lenin: 'he was a revolutionary twenty four hours a day, and when he slept, he dreamt about revolution' (Chandler, 1999, p. 107). During these first few days after their victory, there is no sign that Pol made an effort to inquire about his family that had lived in the city; they seemed to have stopped to matter to him in the years leading up to victory. One of his brothers had died on the road during the evacuation like so many others (Chandler, 1999, p. 104). Pol's wife Khieu Ponnary was diagnosed with paranoid schizophrenia and was deeply disturbed by the time the war came to an end (Becker, 1998, p. 171; Short, 2004, pp. 210-211). His family fell apart as the revolution started to pick up pace.

There is no sign that this was distracting Pol from attaining his goals. He always placed the revolution first. He placed it above his own well-being and that of his family. He occasionally had to make some sacrifices along the way, especially when he left for the maquis to try to realize the utopian vision of an independent, communist Cambodia and he did so, initially, even though the prospects of success seemed bleak. Throughout these early years he seems to have been relatively pragmatic regarding the means with which success was to be achieved, forging alliances with people who he perceived to be enemies and viewed with distrust out of sheer necessity. Being willing to sacrifice his well-being, forging ahead regardless of the chances of success to realize his utopian vision but exhibiting a pragmatic attitude in the way to go about this, it seems that throughout this time of his life Pol seems to have been willing to achieve his value rational goal through instrumental rational means.

9.4. HIS REIGN

Now that Pol's forces had seized control over the country, he was finally able to transform his utopian vision of what the country should be into concrete policies and soon all of Cambodia would be subjected to the radical measures the Khmer Rouge had already started to implement in the regions under their control. Pol Pot described his eight main goals in a meeting he held with several military and civilian officers a month after their victory on May 20th 1975. He emphasized he wanted to empty all the towns, markets needed to become a distant memory, as well as any form of currency that was in existence at this point. Buddhist monks needed to be defrocked, all the leaders of the previous Lon Nol regime needed to be executed, cooperatives needed to be established in which communal dinners became the norm, the Vietnamese minority that was still living in the country needed to be expelled and troops needed to be sent to border areas, particularly to the border between Cambodia and Vietnam (Midlarsky, 2005, p. 311). By this time, some of these goals were already under way to being realized. Overnight the traditional way of life seized to exist through these efforts of the new regime that aimed to shift the loyalty of the population from the family unit to the regime (Haenen, 2014, pp. 88-91; Valentino, 2004, p. 137). Rather than favouring the rights of the collective over those of the individual, the rights of the individual were simply abolished altogether (Short, 2004, p. 11).

The agricultural sector was collectivized in the hopes that with the labour force pooled together, the production could move beyond the subsistence level on which it had been functioning. Surpluses needed to be realized as forests were cleared and more land needed to be tended (Valentino, 2004, p. 134). The profits could then be used by the state to invest in industry and defense (Valentino, 2004, p. 135). Valentino explains how 'Pol Pot's faction was convinced that collectivization was the most efficient means to attain the economic and military independence that they believed was necessary to free Cambodia from the continues ravages of foreign powers' (Valentino, 2004, p. 134). The Khmer Rouge refused to accept foreign aid except from China, even though Ieng Sary and Pol Pot realized when they toured around the city for the first time, that the war had hit the city much harder than they expected and they did not find the abundance of goods they hoped to find (Becker, 1998, pp. 168-170). The official position was that production levels needed to be tripled, securing three tons per hectare. According to an official report, 'striving for three tons has a very profound meaning. Three tons means national defense' (Valentino, 2004, p. 135).

It was also believed collectivization allowed the regime to exercise more control over its own population (Valentino, 2004, p. 135). On the one hand, they hoped that collectivization would increase the standard of living and thus their support base, but it also allowed them to monitor and possibly eliminate those who remained resistant (Valentino, 2004, p. 135).

Pol Pot believed that in order to survive, the changes had to be implemented speedily and thoroughly. A year after their victory Pol Pot explained:

> 'why must we move so swiftly? Because enemies attack and torment us. From the east and the west they persist in pounding and worrying us ... There is no time to wait for another occasion; waiting until 1977 ... would be very slow. We won't wait. We must do it [now] even though we have only just emerged from war' (Valentino, 2004, pp. 136-137).

These enemies not only resided inside the country but the danger posed by external enemies was also a prime motivator to act quickly. Midlarsky explains that 'haste was also required to place the revolution on a firm footing prior to the eventual confrontation with Vietnam ... the Khmer Rouge fully expected such a way of domination to take place shortly after their victory over the Lon Nol forces' (Midlarsky, 2005, p. 318). Pol Pot expressed these feelings to the Standing Committee when we said 'if we run really fast Vietnam won't be able to catch us' (Short, 2004, p. 293). Ultimately, however, collectivization was also a goal in and of itself, a step towards realising their utopian vision, and there do not seem to have been any attempts to increase agricultural productivity in any other way (Valentino, 2004, p. 135). Midlarsky argued that Pol Pot must have reached the conclusion that Chinese restraint caused their revolution to fail and was not about to make the same mistake (Midlarsky, 2005, p. 320). Pol Pot was vocal in his criticism towards other communist countries for their moderate stance towards eliminating all traces of individualism and for failing to permanently eliminate all forms of private property (Valentino, 2004, p. 135). Despite the scepticism of other high ranking officials of implementing the revolutionary changes so speedily and drastically, to Pol Pot and those who supported him, these policies were the key to realising their ideological goals (Valentino, 2004, p. 133).

Although Pol stood undisputedly at the head of the movement, in practice his armed forces were highly fragmented. The country was effectively divided into six zones and each had their own armed forces (Becker, 1998, p. 173). Out of sheer necessity, these regional leaders had acted quite autonomously throughout the war and were given orders and directives but were given quite a lot of freedom in the manner in which they executed these orders (Becker, 1998, p. 174). Pol Pot thus stood for the enormous task of consolidating their hold on power. Communication in the war torn country proved to be difficult but the central leadership used this to their advantage. They ensured that the zones were not able to communicate directly with each other but needed to do so through Phnom Penh. They also ensured they were completely in charge with the distribution of goods; it was highly inefficient but provided them with the control and power they needed (Becker, 1998, pp. 170-171).

A party document from March 1976 formally recognized that 'Comrade Pol' was the country's Prime Minister and it was around this time that Saloth Sar completely let go of his old identity and henceforth became only known as Pol Pot (Chandler, 1999, p. 111; 2008, p. 261). The pseudonym probably served to hide his true identity but also marked a rite of passage (Chandler, 1999, p. 111). To emphasize the collective nature of the revolution he also became known as Brother Number One (Chandler, 1999, p. 113).

In 1976-1977 Pol's focus was on the 'Four Year Plan to Build Socialism in All Fields' and the continuous necessity to purge enemies who were blamed for the plan's failings (Chandler, 1999, p. 114). Pol Pot perceived the plan as an essential component to keep Vietnamese dominance at bay (Chandler, 1999, p. 114). Overall, according to Chandler, the plan reflected a 'blind faith in revolutionary zeal' (Chandler, 1999, p. 118). After a visit to the South-West of the country, Pol noticed that the lack of food was weakening his labour force and decided that the best way to remedy this problem was yet another redistribution of people throughout the country. After Phnom Penh was emptied, citizens rather randomly ended up around the country and Pol believed it was time to send them wherever their labour was needed most (Short, 2004, p. 308). The timing, however, proved disastrous. It was too late in the season for the newcomers to actually help grow the crops and the areas they were sent to were unable to provide all the newcomers with food (Short, 2004, p. 309).

According to Short, the starvation that spread across the country was incomprehensible to Pol, but this is questionable. Short argues Pol believed the country was on its way to reaching utopia and proclaimed the revolution a success (Short, 2004, p. 353). While it may be true that Pol was convinced of the eventual righteousness of his path and sternly held the hardships were merely intermediate steps towards a prosperous and righteous society, it does not mean he lacked understanding of the serious condition his country was in. The fact that he proclaimed success, may have been a façade, a way to keep up appearances. This is supported by the fact that in private circles he acknowledged food shortages existed (Short, 2004, p. 353). He concluded that the problem lay within the party, rather than the policies (Short, 2004, p. 353).

> 'This is our fault ... [our] revolutionary stance and consciousness are not yet strong ... there are people in charge ... who question the stance of independence mastery and self-reliance ... this is a shortcoming ... if we solve ... this problem everywhere, we will be able to advance' (Short, 2004, p. 353).

The answer, according to Pol, was staying even truer to the ideology. It required perseverance and persistence.

In 1976 Pol Pot became increasingly concerned about enemies within the party as the testimonies of those presumed to be traitors were piling up at the torture and interrogation facility that was given the codename S21 (Chandler, 1999, p. 3; 129). In a speech, Pol referred to the endless search for enemies even within their own ranks. He saw it as a 'sickness' that was pervasive in the party and feared that 'they will rot us from within' (Chandler, 1999, p. 129). The party for this reason needed to be cleansed. It needed to be done by stressing the virtues of the collective living arrangements, by examining life histories and rearranging cadre in different zones (Chandler, 1999, p. 130).

No mercy was to be shown to anyone Pol Pot believed was unable or unwilling to devote himself fully and unconditionally to the revolution. Violence in this sense formed an integral part of the revolution. Pol Pot stated that similar to waging war, in order to build socialism 'the Party leadership must exercise its leading role by the use of cutting-edge violence ... This is the most important factor, the decisive factor, which is the power that drives things forward' (Short, 2004, p. 294). Violence would secure the success of the revolution. The party was guided by the reasoning that 'one hand is for production, the other for beating the enemy' (Valentino, 2004, p. 137).

Pol Pot not only feared enemies were undermining his revolution but also worried about conspiracies against him and the search for enemies extended to those he feared might be plotting against him (Chandler, 1999, p. 113). Pol Pot started to purge some of his long-time friends in September 1976 (Chandler, 1999, p. 127). Their friendship stretched back to the 1950s, and especially Keo Maas' loyalty to the leader seems to have been genuine (Chandler, 1999, pp. 127-128). Pol Pot's suspicions, however, were not entirely without merit, and in the first year of his rule there was still resistance to his radical policies within the party which even resulted in a coup attempt in 1976 when several military and other senior party members tried to poison Pol and another one in 1978 at the instigation of Vietnam (Midlarsky, 2005, p. 322; Quinn, 1989b).[108]

---

[108] Short raises some doubts as to whether these coup attempts actually occurred. He states that Ieng Sary actually admitted that 'there were no coup attempts ... it was all greatly

In response to the perceived threats in 1976, secrecy was anxiously maintained and elaborate ruses were set up to confuse the enemy. In September 1976, for instance, Pol Pot officially resigned because of his ill health but he resumed his work in October and it is likely that his resignation was staged (Chandler, 1999, p. 122). It was probably meant to confuse his enemies and he likely hoped they would step forward so they could be eliminated (Chandler, 1999, p. 122).

In early 1977 the purges picked up pace, S21 became busier than ever and a number of cadre members who had worked closely alongside Pol Pot were purged (Chandler, 1999, p. 131; Quinn, 1989b, p. 197). Although perhaps initially sparked by the coup attempt, the purge soon expanded to anyone who appeared to have been pro-Vietnamese or whose loyalty was questioned (Quinn, 1989b, p. 197). Pol Pot probably worked long hours to review the numerous files that stemmed from S21 (Chandler, 1999, p. 132), and it became policy that 'it is better to arrest ten people by mistake than to let one guilty person go free' (Valentino, 2004, p. 142). Pol Pot felt the party's mantra should be 'Purify the Party! Purify the army! Purify the cadres!' (Short, 2004, p. 284).

Some argue Pol became paranoid, trusting no one and fearful of being killed (Chandler, 1999, p. 132; Pina e Cunha *et al.*, 2011). Yet Short believes Pol was not so foolish as to believe all the confessions that were extracted under torture at Tuol Sleng (Short, 2004, p. 358). As a general rule it only became suspicious if someone had been accused three times (later five as the number of people in Tuol Sleng rose), showing that certain value was attached to the confessions that were extracted but there have also been cases where even eight accusations were not deemed reason for concern (Short, 2004, p. 358). The confessions were predominantly useful as proof when a purge which was deemed desirable anyway would be carried out (Short, 2004, p. 359).

According to Valentino, such destructive force would not have been necessary to maintain power. He argues this feat could have also been accomplished by reaching a compromise with the more moderate politicians. The violence of most communist leaders within their own party stemmed not only from a desire to maintain power but also genuinely to protect their revolution. Valentino explains: 'it is not possible to understand why these communist leaders reacted so violently to the prospect of political opposition without appreciating that they believed it threatened not merely their personal leadership, but their most deeply held goals' (Valentino, 2004, p. 100). Valentino concludes that

> 'these purges appear to have been part of an effort by Pol Pot and perhaps a few other like-minded Khmer Rouge leaders to protect the achievements of the revolution from what they perceived to be powerful and omnipresent enemies' (Valentino, 2004, p. 140).

---

exaggerated. In Pol's mind, there were serious incidents. But in fact they were a pretext – a pretext for a crack-down' (Short, 2004, p. 360).

This violence was not only directed towards these internal enemies, but also towards enemies that came from outside of the country, especially the Vietnamese. Pol ordered communist cadres that had been trained in Hanoi to be killed (Short, 2004, p. 250), and as time progressed the schism between those that were even moderately pro-Vietnamese and Pol Pot and his inner circle grew. One of the ways in which this came to the fore was through a dispute over the founding date of the party, with the Pol Pot clique preferring the 1960 date, which implicitly dismissed the help they received from the Vietnamese in these early years. It meant even having knowledge of the arguments in favour of the earlier date was enough to get you killed (Chandler, 1983; Frings, 1997, p. 807; 825).

In the years that followed these purges and wanton killings extended to large parts of the population that was suspected of hampering the revolutionary progress. Pol Pot explained in an address:

> 'Contradictions do exist within the ranks of our people. These contradictions stem from the differences in the nature of the remaining class vestiges. It is understandable that each person can not easily shed the vestiges of the class to which he belonged for generations and which he has just recently renounced for the proletarian nature of the revolution' (Quinn, 1989b, p. 203)

He publicly declared education and self-criticism should be the preferred solution for this problem, while only 'isolating and eradicating only the smallest number' but in practice mass murder and terror seem to have been the preferred option (Quinn, 1989b, p. 204).

In 1978 he finally recognized that a large part of the population still was not fed properly and slowly worked towards greater freedoms as foraging became permitted again, one day was given off every ten days, and family life was given new leeway (Short, 2004, p. 382). In addition, the arbitrary killings lessoned – although purges of those accused of having 'Vietnamese heads in Khmer bodies' actually only seemed to get worse (Short, 2004, pp. 382-383). In the autumn the reintroduction of money was even considered (Short, 2004, p. 383). How much more moderate the regime would actually have become, is impossible to determine as just a few months later Vietnam would put an end to Pol Pot's reign. There does not seem to be much evidence, however, that Pol Pot changed his mind about the desirability of a communist utopia altogether and perhaps these changes, although radical in comparison to the policies beforehand, should be seen as a process in which the details of the revolution's execution were tweaked while the overarching vision remained intact. These changes were perceived and justified because the measures they had originally implemented actually had the side effect of infringing on their independence. The decision to abolish money, for instance, meant that diplomats needed to travel abroad with suitcases of US dollars, the prime symbol of imperialism and the dismal state the country was in meant they had to rely on Chinese experts (Short, 2004, p. 383). Throughout his reign Pol Pot oversaw one of the most extreme and brutal communist revolutions known to man and throughout struggled tirelessly to overcome the obstacles he saw as impeding the transformation of his country.

Pol does not seem to have suffered as many hardships as he had to endure while climbing to power. On the photographs that are available of him at the time he seems well fed and his health was infinitely better than that of the people he ruled. However, at the same time he continued to live a relatively sober life, in which in some general sense he abided by similar rules as he imposed on the rest of the population and continued to work hard to do what he thought was necessary. Overall throughout his reign Pol Pot continues to be committed to the ideology, and while many of his closest aides eventually had to face their death in the purges, he also stayed true to a select few that would remain with him throughout the decades.

9.5. INNER CIRCLE

Pol Pot not only displayed an exceptional certitude in the righteousness of his own policies but also gathered people around him who felt the same way or at least never voiced any disagreement. More moderate politicians would fall victim to Pol's purges as he considered them traitors (Short, 2004, p. 360). In doing so, he removed everyone who may have exercised a more moderate influence on his policies. Throughout the country, there was nothing that required a more restrained approach from the central leadership and because Cambodia is a relatively small state, the leadership was soon able to implement their policies throughout the country. There was no place to hide (Midlarsky, 2005, p. 320).

The most important people that formed Pol Pot's inner circle during these crucial years, had been with him for decades. This section will delve further into the most important individuals that may have influenced Pol Pot's policy and explain how they would have been unlikely to have tempered or restrained his ideological zeal. The role of four individuals will be examined more closely because of the role they played, and influence they possibly had over Pol Pot's decisions.

First, the key role that was played by the man who was second in command, Nuon Chea, will be analysed, and thereafter the influence of the two individuals who could exercise the most influence over Pol Pot's foreign policy, Ieng Sary and Son Sen, will be scrutinized. Lastly, more details will be provided about Khieu Samphan, who was Cambodia's head of state. It is striking that this core of loyalists all survived throughout the duration of the regime. Only Son Sen was killed, but not until after Pol Pot's regime was forced into exile (Short, 2004, pp. 452-458). The role of Pol's wife, Khieu Ponnary, will not be further analysed because she was disturbed, suffering from paranoid schizophrenia by the time Pol Pot got into power and she seemed to be sidelined from that moment onwards. During the times when she was really ill, Pol and Khieu did not even sleep together so she would not keep him awake with her rants about the enemies she believed surrounded them (Becker, 1998, p. 171; Short, 2004, pp. 210-211).

Pol Pot's right hand man was Nuon Chea. He became known as 'Brother Number Two'[109] and was responsible for various aspects of the functioning of the regime which included propaganda, the training and discipline of cadres and was involved when there were internal or external security questions ("ECCC Trial Chamber Judgement 002/01," 2014, p. 158, para. 303-305). He was born as Lao Kim Lorn and came from a prosperous family in the Battambang Province but was educated in Thailand where he joined the Communist Party of Thailand before he returned to Cambodia to help the communist resistance effort from his home country (Chirot, 1994, p. 226, para. 305-306; "ECCC Trial Chamber Judgement 002/01," 2014; Short, 2004, pp. 119-120). His activism intensified in the years that followed and he received a few years of training in Vietnam before he finally settled down in Phnom Penh in 1955 where he was introduced to Pol Pot and started to work with him ("ECCC Trial Chamber Judgement 002/01," 2014, pp. 159-160, para. 307-308). When Pol Pot fled with Ieng Sary to the maquis, Nuon Chea visited them from time to time to inform them about the situation in the capital until he too had to leave ("ECCC Trial Chamber Judgement 002/01," 2014, pp. 160-162, para. 309-311). He became deputy Secretary of the Party in 1960 and has retained that position for the duration of the regime ("ECCC Trial Chamber Judgement 002/01," 2014, p. 164, para. 313). On the basis of the early involvement of Nuon Chea with the various communist parties, the ECCC Trial Chamber in its judgement concludes that 'NUON Chea was a strong proponent of waging "class struggle" and argued that he "supported the view that revolution should rely on peasants of the lowest classes in order to impose on Cambodia the dictatorship of the proletariat' ("ECCC Trial Chamber Judgement 002/01," 2014, p. 492, para. 840). He thus seems to have been loyal, not only to his friend Pol Pot but also stood behind the policies that were enacted throughout the country.

Ieng Sary would become known to the world as Brother Number Three and had a long and personal bond with Pol Pot ("Ieng Sary," 2013). He was born in Kampuchea Krom and had always been distrustful of the Vietnamese (Midlarsky, 2005, p. 314). He was born as Kim Tran but later changed it into Ieng Sary because it sounded more Khmer (Becker, 1998, p. 53). He had moved to Cambodia as a child and became politically active in high school when he

[109] Nuon Chea denies being called 'Brother Number Two' but claims he was rather known under several other aliases that include 'Brother Nuon', 'Uncle Nuon', 'Grand Uncle Nuon', 'Comrade Deputy Secretary' or just 'Brother' ("ECCC Trial Chamber Judgement 002/01," 2014, p. 163, para. 312).

headed a group called 'Liberation of Cambodia from French Colonialism' (Becker, 1998, p. 53).

He met Pol at Sisowath High School and then studied with him in Paris where he, like Pol Pot and Khieu Samphan, became a member of the French Communist Party ("ECCC Closing Order," 2010, p. 251, para. 994-995). He was one of the founders of the Marxist *Cercle* and became Pol Pot's brother-in-law when they married sisters (Becker, 1998, p. 199; "ECCC Closing Order," 2010, p. 251, para. 995). In Paris, Sary was known to be serious and demanding, with some even quitting the *Cercle* because they could not, or did not want to, live up to Sary's stringent demands (Short, 2004, p. 64).

He returned to Phnom Penh in 1957 and soon started to climb in the hierarchy of the communist party there. By 1960 he was the fourth most influential party member and by 1963 became a full member of the standing committee ("ECCC Closing Order," 2010, p. 251, para. 996-997). That same year he also fled to the Vietnamese border where he joined Pol Pot and Son Sen ("ECCC Closing Order," 2010, p. 251, para. 998). In 1970 he travelled to Hanoi and then to Beijing, where he managed the party's relations with Norodom Sihanouk ("ECCC Closing Order," 2010, pp. 251-252, para. 999). He went back to Cambodia in April 1975 and was in a position to 'discuss and join in the decision-making' of all policies ("ECCC Closing Order," 2010, p. 252, para. 999-1001). He was given the official role of Deputy Prime Minister of Foreign Affairs in 1975, although it seems his appointment was only formalized in 1976 ("ECCC Closing Order," 2010, pp. 253-254, para. 1008).

Becker argues Sary was one of the few people that was actually allowed to disagree and argue with Pol about the policy that should be adopted, but at the same time would always accept any duties and commands imposed on him once Pol had taken a decision (Becker, 1998, pp. 199-200). Pol Pot trusted Sary, but only to a limited extent and members of the *Cercle* remember how Pol worried that Sary might be too stubborn and possibly could even fail to take orders from the top. Therefore, as Becker explains,

> 'Sary was the one man Pol Pot trusted to put forward the true face of revolutionary Cambodia to the outside world but apparently not to command troops or take charge of major domestic duties that would give him a base to challenge Pol Pot's power' (Becker, 1998, p. 199)

Ieng Sary consequently was highly influential but all the crucial decisions were taken by the entire Standing Committee and not Ieng Sary individually ("ECCC Closing Order," 2010, p. 225, para. 1014). Even though Sary seems to have been genuinely committed to the cause for which he worked tirelessly ever since high school and seems to have truly loyal to Pol Pot, throughout the latter's reign, Pol Pot always remained in charge.

Khieu Samphan was formally the head of state but widely regarded as a mere figurehead (Chirot, 1994, p. 226). He, too, has a long history with Pol Pot. He first met him at the junior high school he attended and then also studied at Sisowath high school, after which he, too, spent some time in Paris and joined the *Cercle*, becoming its leader when Ieng Sary left ("ECCC Trial Chamber Judgement 002/01," 2014, pp. 182-184, para. 351-353). In Paris he pursued a doctorate in economics ("ECCC Trial Chamber Judgement 002/01," 2014, p. 184, para. 353). In his dissertation he critiqued the state the Cambodian economy was in, arguing that the elites in the city were unproductive and advocated creating cooperatives in the agricultural sectors while stressing the nation needed to become more independent since foreign aid was distorting their economy (Chirot, 1994, p. 219; "ECCC Trial Chamber Judgement 002/01," 2014, pp. 184-185, para. 354; Tan, 1979, p. 3). It was not particularly radical and was not a model for the policies that would later be adopted when Pol seized power (Chirot, 1994, p. 219; "ECCC Trial Chamber Judgement 002/01," 2014, p. 185, para. 355).

When he returned to Cambodia, the idealistic Khieu established a newspaper which was critical of Sihanouk's regime leading him to be harassed and detained while his newspaper was shut down ("ECCC Trial Chamber Judgement 002/01," 2014, pp. 185-186, para. 356; Short, 2004, pp. 132-133). He nevertheless joined Norodom Sihanouk's political party and in 1962 became his Secretary of State for Commerce (Becker, 1998, p. 96; "ECCC Trial Chamber Judgement 002/01," 2014, p. 186, para. 357). Sihanouk wanted to use him to co-opt the left and make use of their expertise. Khieu, according to Becker, was mostly just naïve and genuinely tried to make a difference (1998, pp. 96-97). A few years later in 1967, Sihanouk turned on him and Khieu was forced to flee from Phnom Penh to the countryside where he formally joined the communists two years later ("ECCC Trial Chamber Judgement 002/01," 2014, pp. 187-188, para. 361-362).

In the early 1970s, Khieu was formally Commander in Chief but in reality had very little influence over the armed forces, which was a task Pol kept for himself ("ECCC Trial Chamber Judgement 002/01," 2014, p. 189, para. 365). In 1976 he became the head of state, but Khieu's role as such was 'largely symbolic' ("ECCC Trial Chamber Judgement 002/01," 2014, p. 196, para. 381). He made speeches in support of the revolution that were dictated by Pol Pot and although he admitted he agreed with most of it, secretly he disagreed with some of the choices that were made. While disagreeing with the decision to abolish money, for instance ("ECCC Trial Chamber Judgement 002/01," 2014, p. p. 197, para. 383), according to the trial chamber of the ECCC 'he believed … that human rights were a concern secondary to the pressing issue of independence of Cambodia. The well-being of the people and the need to seek their consent to sacrifice and suffer for the policies of the Khmer Rouge could wait. Indeed, KHIEU Samphan was convinced that coercion was necessary to collectivise society' ("ECCC Trial Chamber Judgement 002/01," 2014, p. 536, para. 946).

According to Short, '[Pol] placed growing trust in him. He appreciated his patience and perseverance, and the fact that when he was given a task, he would carry it out to the letter, doing neither more nor less than he was asked' (Short, 2004, p. 336). Samphan has been described in this sense as a loyal and docile minion, upon whose loyalty Pol Pot could rely (Heder, n.d., p. 1). Ultimately, Samphan was trusted and kept informed but his decision-making powers were much more limited than his formal title would suggest ("ECCC Trial Chamber Judgement 002/01," 2014, p. 209, para. 408-409).

Son Sen also studied in Paris and was a member of the *Cercle Marxiste* (Becker, 1998, p. 198). He came back to Cambodia in 1955 to dedicate himself to the revolution and ended up on Sihanouk's list of suspected subversives which meant he needed to flee (Becker, 1998, p. 200). He was put in charge of military tasks even though Pol Pot had some doubts about how courageous and dedicated Son Sen truly was. In the years that followed, Son mounted an incredibly successful guerrilla war (Becker, 1998, p. 200). On this basis, it was only logical that he became the ministry of defence after the Khmer Rouge were victorious. Even though eventually he was not really up for the task, as his lack of knowledge caught up with him, he managed to keep his position by accusing potential competitors for the position of treason (Becker, 1998, p. 201).

These four men shared a long history with Pol Pot and became loyal trustees who survived for the duration of his reign. Not all close associates of Pol Pot, regardless of how loyal they may have been, were so lucky, however. Neither loyalty to Pol nor a shared history that went back to his days in Paris were enough to shield anyone from being executed (Chandler, 1999, p. 33; 127). The small circle of people Pol Pot trusted enough to have them remain at his side for so many years, however, enabled him to rule unopposed and impose his will on the decisions that were taken.

Most of the inner circle were not merely loyal out of fear of what may happen when they dissented, although this of course may also have played a part, but were to a large extent, in agreement over the path that needed to be followed. According to Quinn, for instance, a picture emerges in which 'a small, totally dedicated group of intellectuals, alienated and driven by their perception of an unjust society, [possess the] belief that a new, just social system can be formed only by an enormous act of violence' (1989a, p. 234).

Regardless of the opinions of the others, however, in the end, it was Pol Pot who had the final decision, especially when from 1976 onwards, he had drawn all power to himself. Khieu Samphan explains how Pol Pot

> 'would listen impassively and with immense patience to detailed reports from lower-level officials … He liked to hear the views of many different people … The more information the better. He would retain whatever was relevant to the problem at hand, and work out an initial hypothesis, which he would keep to himself. When he had refined it and reached a conclusion which satisfied him, he would make his

> decision, which then became irrevocable. Afterwards he would call a meeting [of members of the standing committee], explaining the problem before them in such a way that, without anyone realising it, the discussion was oriented towards the result he desired … After everyone had spoken, he would make the summing up – selecting points from their speeches which buttressed his position. … Then he would announce his decision, making it appear that everyone contributed to its formulation. There was no vote. It was stated: "The collectivity has decided"' (Short, 2004, p. 340).

Differences of opinion were not tolerated and it made those surrounding him careful in their interactions with him (Pina e Cunha *et al.*, 2011, p. 277). Ultimately, Midlarsky is correct to argue that 'the unprecedented use of violence were tactics chosen by a united Khmer leadership' (Midlarsky, 2005, p. 320) if only because Pol purged all who had a propensity to disagree with him and never tolerated dissent.

9.6. CONCLUSION

Saloth Sar, who would become known as Pol Pot, found his calling while studying in Paris. He showed remarkably little ambition before this time and was not an exceptionally brilliant or motivated student. Back then, however, he was known for his kind demeanour and charm which caused him to be able to interact with a wide variety of people, characteristics that would serve him and the revolution well in later years. It may be questioned in these early years how genuine his devotion to communism as such was. He may not have fully grasped all the intricacies of the ideology as such and interpreted it more broadly as a manner in which good could triumph and provide a solution for the injustice that was persevering in his own country. Whether his mind-set at this time was best explained as nationalist or communist, his dedication to this cause, what he saw to be just, was genuine and long lasting. It gave him a sense of purpose in life and henceforth he would dedicate his life towards furthering that cause, liberating his country from foreign domination and war, and create a communist utopia in its wake.

When he returned to Cambodia and worked as a liaison between different opposition movements and as a teacher, his strategic position between the groups and his likeability and charm ensured that he soon would become an influential figure in the revolutionary movement. By the end of the 1950s, however, the prospects for the movement seemed bleak as Sihanouk clamped down on subversive activities and party membership was dropping. Pol Pot's climb in the hierarchy of the party was fast until he had to flee when it appeared Sihanouk was on to him and some of the other party officials.

It marked the start of a dark period in Pol's life, in which the chances of success seemed nearly nil and he had to make great personal sacrifices to keep the revolution going. He was suffering under the harsh living conditions in the jungle and frequently falling ill. Pol Pot thus pursued his goals 'regardless of personal cost to themselves' as Weber believes is characteristic of people who act on the basis of value rationality and 'independently of any prospects of success' (Weber, 1964, p. 115)

At the same time, his value rational outlook at this point in time was only limited to the end goal and did not encompass the choice of means yet. He was pragmatic, collaborating closely with the Vietnamese, and later Sihanouk, even though antagonisms between the Cambodian and Vietnamese communists started to grow. Pol Pot was trying to attain his value rational goal, with instrumental rational means. He was still relatively practical about whatever means the revolution required. Even though working with the Vietnamese went against much of what he believed in, he was willing to indulge them, as long as it would lead to his victory and would allow him to establish the independent communist country he longed for.

As they became more powerful, ideological considerations started to play a bigger role in determining the manner in all the decisions that were taken, also with regard to the means with which the war was waged. The Khmer Rouge actively sought to outdo the Vietnamese communists and took pride in what they saw as their efforts to singlehandedly defeat the American army. They started collectivising efforts, implementing more extreme policies in the areas under their control, and Pol became less compromising. After the Khmer Rouge seized power, Pol's faction was still the most radical. In the years that followed, he eliminated all moderate elements as he worked hard to implement the communist policies that he believed could make the country great again. He became increasingly anti-Vietnamese and changed the history of the party to mask any contribution the Vietnamese made to their struggle. He tried to change reality to what he wanted it to be, to conform to his beliefs. He exhibited the same attitude when it came to the policies that he implemented, refusing to see the policies themselves as flawed, and blaming disappointing results on enemies that were undermining his efforts. As Chandler explains in relation to the four-year plan:

> 'Pol Pot saw the document as the means by which Cambodia could accelerate toward socialism. The unreality and sloppiness of most of its proposals reveal a blind faith in the possibilities of success' (Chandler, 1999, p. 115).

They continued to export rice when their own population was starving and refused to amend their policies, or moderate or change the pace in which the revolution was realized in order to stave off hunger (Valentino, 2004, p. 140). It is unlikely that the famine was deliberately created by the Khmer Rouge, but rather than ameliorating it, their policies frequently made it worse and they specifically redirected its consequences to particular groups that were seen as treacherous from their ideological stance (Valentino, 2004, pp. 139-140). Overall some have concluded: '[Pol] demanded a radical, intransigent application of the principles adopted' (Kaonn cited in Short, 2004, p. 339). He pursued the goal 'entirely for its own sake' (Weber, 1964, p. 115) because he believed them to be right.

He believed that as long as the people's beliefs were in conformity with the ideology, the rest would work itself out (Short, 2004, pp. 350-351). His goal had become sacred to him and no longer allowed for compromise, showing that his value rational orientation had started to dominate his decision-making process (Varshney, 2003, p. 86). He now followed a 'consistently planned course of action towards the absolute value' as his ideology required from him (Angus, 1983, p. 145).

In some ways, Pol Pot was utterly dishonest about many aspects of the revolution and his personal life. As a former teacher he actually belonged to the group of people he consistently targeted throughout his rule and invented a biography to hide it (Pina e Cunha *et al.*, 2011, p. 277). At the same time, however, his dedication to the cause seems to have been genuine. As Short explained, 'Pol did believe he was acting for the common good and that sooner or later everyone would recognize that' (2004, p. 296). He even incorporated some of the elements of the ideology in his own life by generally maintaining a rather modest life style, even though of course he was in no way deprived of basic necessities as the population under his rule had been. For Pol, as Short again emphasizes 'ideology was primary. Everything else took second place' and merely following the dictates of the ideology would lead to success (Short, 2004, p. 351). The revolution was even more important than his family. His family was not completely sheltered from the violence that befell the rest of the population and one of his brothers died during the evacuation of Phnom Penh like so many others.

Pol Pot was willing to sacrifice his own personal welfare, and that of others, even though the chances that he would ever obtain a position of power for a long time seemed minor. For the duration of his reign, he continued to be determined to achieve his goals and make his country great again. He remained convinced, until the final year – when he recognized certain means needed to be amended to reach the end successfully – convinced of the righteousness of his own policies. The violence that was inflicted by Pol Pot and his Khmer Rouge was extreme and stemmed from a fanatical belief in a different society but it was not irrational. As Becker explains,

> 'one of the most frightening aspects of the Khmer Rouge is the intent behind their madness. Much of the destruction of their revolution was done in name of the future' (Becker, 1998, p. xvi).

CHAPTER 10
THE RATIONALITY OF MILOSEVIC

10.1. INTRODUCTION

Ironically, the names of the couple that led the country into political and economic chaos referred to freedom and peace. Slobodan signifies freedom and Milosevic would become known as 'Sloba-Sloboda' no longer merely referring to the name, but relating it to the concept itself. His wife Mirjana, who would later also become a prominent figure in Serbian politics, carries a name which is a derivative from *Mir* (peace) (Stevanovic, 2004, p. 1; 5). Their legacy could not have been more different. As Chapter 8 argued, Milosevic was influential in orchestrating Yugoslavia's demise and the bloodshed that came along with it.

Milosevic in the past has been labelled a cold apparatchik, referred to as 'the slickest con man in the Balkans', has been called the 'devil of Dedinje' and eventually would be known as 'the butcher of the Balkans' (Post, 2004, p. 179; Stevanovic, 2004, p. 1). In those scenarios Milosevic is often portrayed as a 'dangerous mad man' (translated from Detrez, 2002, p. 7) and has been described as 'neurotic' (Stevanovic, 2004, p. 2). However, there are no indications Milosevic was actually mad and conclusions that a leader suffers from mental disorders need to be handled with care. As Detrez points out, any policy – especially those coming from the international community – is not served by the perception of the other as crazy (Detrez, 2002, pp. 7-8). While strong indications of a particular psychological disorder may be very telling and can be taken into account when devising foreign policy, (e.g. Glad, 2002) if this is merely an assumption that has no basis, as appears to have been the case with Milosevic, it can be very counterproductive. It is also questionable to what extent this was merely an image painted of Milosevic in the popular media or whether it actually impacted diplomats and other politicians. Anecdotal evidence seems to indicate that they did not perceive Milosevic as crazy or suffering from serious mental disorders. Quite the opposite, at least by 1993 Milosevic was seen by foreign diplomats as someone with whom it was possible to negotiate and reach an understanding (Doder & Branson, 1999, p. 89). The present chapter will use the work of Max Weber to assess the extent to which either of the two types of rationality, dominated the decision-making process of Milosevic throughout his life.

While it is clear Milosevic was an important factor in bringing forth Yugoslavia's dissolution[110], the question remains why Milosevic acted the way he did. This question needs to be addressed and answered in order to understand the type of rationality that was most pervasive in shaping his behaviour. Several scholars still differ as to what seems to have motivated Milosevic. Gagnon believes that the war in Yugoslavia in general was in the interests of its leaders and served to expand the ethnic hatreds that were present. He argues that

> 'by constructing individual interest in terms of the threat to the group, endangered elites can fend off domestic challengers who seek to mobilize the population against the status quo, and can better position themselves to deal with future challenges' (Gagnon, 1994, p. 132).

This would imply an instrumental use of the violence to attain his selfish goals. Djilas on the other hand is of the opinion that Milosevic believed in the nationalist goals. According to Djilas,

> 'Milosevic's sympathy for the plight of the Serbs in Kosovo was genuine. He is not simply a monster only interested in power, as many of his opponents characterize him' (Djilas, 1993, p. 87).

The present chapter will, therefore, analyse Milosevic' life story on the basis of several of the most prominent biographies that have been written about him and will, subsequently, try to flesh out the points of consensus. It will use both the analysis of these scholars, as well as more importantly, the manner in which Milosevic has behaved throughout his life to come to an understanding of his rationality.

10.2. YOUNGER YEARS

Milosevic was born on 20 August 1941 in Pozarevac, Serbia, which is situated in an area that has a rich history. The first uprising against the Turks began there and is described as the centre of peasant culture (Sell, 2002, pp. 11-12). It was also historically important as the region where the Chetnik resistance movement during WWII originated from (Sell, 2002, p. 12). There is no evidence, however, that Milosevic was particularly moved by this legacy and according to Sell, he never seems to have 'displayed much interest in Serb national traditions' (Sell, 2002, p. 72).

His parents came from Montenegro and moved to Serbia just before Milosevic was born (Doder & Branson, 1999, p. 14). His father, Svetozar, was a religious man and initially worked as an Orthodox priest (Stevanovic, 2004,

110 See Chapter 8.

p. 3). He studied Russian and theology and became a professor of Russian at the Theological Academy of the Serbian Orthodox Church (Sell, 2002, p. 11). His mother, Stanislava, was a firm believer in the Communist ideology and worked as a primary school teacher (LeBor, 2003, p. 1; Sell, 2002, p. 11). Both of his parents seem to have held partisan sympathies during WWII. Stanislava was part of an underground movement, hid people in the family's house and passed messages through to others in the resistance but Milosevic' parents never fought themselves (LeBor, 2003, p. 6). Stanislava's brother, however, was a partisan war hero, who committed suicide when Tito broke with Stalin (Doder & Branson, 1999, pp. 15-16). The suicide brought shame on the family and was traumatic for Milosevic as his uncle had been someone he looked up to (Doder & Branson, 1999, p. 16).

Stanislava remained a dedicated communist even when her husband, as a religious, highly educated man, started to have doubts about the movement (LeBor, 2003, pp. 7-8). In the end, Milosevic' parents were bound to separate but it was not the political differences that would tear the couple apart, but Svetosar's inability to settle in Pozarevac. He returned to Montenegro in 1947 (LeBor, 2003, p. 8).[111] Slobodan was henceforth raised by his mother, who sought to desperately hide their destitute state (Doder & Branson, 1999, p. 16). Milosevic' brother remembers how their childhood was marked by poverty and deprivation:

> 'we spent the war and all our childhood in Pozarevac. They were very miserable times. We were always hungry. It was very hard to find something to eat and my mother had to sell everything to survive' (cited in LeBor, 2003, p. 2).

Stanislava, whose life revolved around her sons, has been described as ambitious, protective and dominant (Doder & Branson, 1999, p. 16; LeBor, 2003, p. 13). Milosevic reportedly dreaded returning home and face his mother's condemnation if he let his grades slide (Stevanovic, 2004, p. 3). She pushed him to excel at school and remain at the top of his class (Windgassen, 2002, p. 237). Every day she would ensure Slobodan could go to school 'in a fresh white shirt, like a junior version of the Communist official she hoped he would be' (LeBor, 2003, p. 13). She therefore not only passed on her ideas about communism (Doder & Branson, 1999, p. 16) but also taught them the importance of trying to become successful. Being serious and not allowed to play sports, 'in case he sweated and caught a cold', Slobodan did not have many friends growing up (LeBor, 2003, p. 13).

He threw himself on his studies and his activities for the Communist youth organization (LeBor, 2003, pp. 13-14). He was serious, determined and well-mannered, which won him the respect of his teachers (Djukić, 2002, p. 26; Sell,

111 There are contradictory stories whether Slobodan's brother Borislav stayed with his mother or accompanied his father when he left, but scholars agree Slobodan stayed with his mother (Stevanovic, 2004, p. 3; 214).

2002, p. 15).[112] A childhood friend remembers 'Slobodan was his own person … He was an excellent student. Even at that time it was clear to me that he was absolutely devoted to his personal ambitions' (LeBor, 2003, p. 14).

While in high school Slobodan met the other woman that would have such a tremendous influence over his life: his future wife Mira Markovic (Sell, 2002, p. 16). Mira came from a prominent family with ties to the Communist regime. Her uncle served as Prime Minister of Serbia, her aunt was Tito's secretary and mistress and her father became a minister in Tito's government (LeBor, 2003, p. 16; Sell, 2002, p. 17). Both of her parents had joined the partisans during WWII. Her father, Moma Markovic, became a national hero while her mother was executed by the end of the war. Her father, in his memoires, accused her mother of having betrayed her fellow partisans but Mira never believed her mum betrayed anyone (Doder & Branson, 1999, p. 19; Sell, 2002, p. 17).[113] She was raised in Posarevac by her grandparents (Djukić, 2002, p. 25) where she also met Milosevic. The two undoubtedly loved each other but Mira's connections and those of her father also gave it a functional element. A school friend explained:

> 'she was the only person in Pozarevac with such a prominent revolutionary background. That was my impression from the beginning, although I don't deny they developed a special relationship. He relied on his mother and Mira, and I think she is the only person he trusts' (cited in LeBor, 2003, p. 21).

They also had many things in common, neither for instance, had much contact with their fathers. Mira's father started a new family after the death of her mother and Milosevic also did not have much contact with his father after the latter had left the family. In 1962 his father committed suicide (LeBor, 2003, pp. 17; 26-27). Milosevic, on a student trip to Russia at the time, did not attend the funeral and just ten years later his mother killed herself as well, some say because of a conflict with Mira (Sell, 2002, p. 16). Slobodan and Mira got married in the meantime, in 1965, and several months later their daughter Marija was born, followed nine years later by their son Marko (Stevanovic, 2004, p. 12)

After high school Milosevic went to Belgrade University where he studied law (LeBor, 2003, p. 22). He stood out because of his 'buttoned down seriousness' and became enthusiastic for politics when he became the head of the law faculty's Communist Party organization (Sell, 2002, p. 19). He turned out to be a 'genius for party politics' and did everything efficiently and with zeal (Sell, 2002, p. 19). A fellow student remembers how he and Milosevic shared their disdain for other

112 Djukic is known to be well informed as well as an author with Serbian nationalist sympathies (for a more detailed analysis of Djukuc's nationalist tendencies, see Ramet (2005, pp. 170-172) but because of his pendency to uncover many interesting facts and details about Milosevic's and Markovic's life, his work will be used albeit with caution.

113 Controversy regarding the actual circumstances surrounding her mother's death remain unclear until this day (Stevanovic, 2004, p. 5).

students who would try to get in good favours with prominent party leaders, but while it was reason enough for his fellow student representative to take a step back, Milosevic realized it was all part of the game (Doder & Branson, 1999, p. 22). A game he eventually mastered and he is remembered as frequently currying favours from those above him while being a bully to those lower in the pecking order (Sell, 2002, p. 20). During his studies he again did not have many friends but struck up a very close friendship with Ivan Stambolic (LeBor, 2003, p. 23). The two came from similar backgrounds but had very different personalities. As LeBor explains: 'While Milosevic wanted top marks in every subject, Stambolic was just happy to pass. ... Milosevic was somewhat distant, and always seemed to be calculating how to best exploit events for himself. Stambolic was much more popular, a warm and genuine person with a wide circle of friends' (LeBor, 2003, p. 23).

Milosevic made his mark on high party politics for the first time when there were meetings with prominent politicians throughout the country to discuss the new constitution. When they visited Belgrade University, Milosevic suggested changing the proposed name for the country from the Federal Socialist Republic of Yugoslavia to the Socialist Federal Republic of Yugoslavia to emphasize its socialist orientation (LeBor, 2003, p. 29; Sell, 2002, p. 20). The proposal was readily accepted (Doder & Branson, 1999, p. 22; Sell, 2002, p. 20). Milosevic graduated with generally high marks, were it not for the mandatory courses that required more physical activity, like 'pre-military education' (Doder & Branson, 1999, p. 24; LeBor, 2003, p. 31). Similarly, thereafter when he was drafted into the JNA, he scored high for the theoretical courses, but remained lacking in courses that tested his military skills and required physical agility (Djukić, 2002, p. 32; Doder & Branson, 1999, p. 25).

He started his career with a job at the city government at the information department where he got a true sense of the importance of the media in wielding power (Doder & Branson, 1999, p. 25). Thereafter, Milosevic climbed the ladder of party politics rapidly by continuously following in the footsteps of Ivan Stambolic. Between 1968 and 1978 he worked for the energy company Technogas, eventually replacing Stambolic as its director in 1970 (Doder & Branson, 1999, p. 25; Sell, 2002, p. 24; Stevanovic, 2004, p. 10). Assessments of Milosevic performance during this time vary. While Stevanovic points out Milosevic's work seems to 'have been undistinguished at best and divisive at worst', LeBor found that although Milosevic initially knew little of economics, he learned fast and listened to the advice of others (LeBor, 2003, p. 40; Stevanovic, 2004, p. 10). When Stambolic became Prime Minister of Serbia, he ensured Milosevic became the president of Beobanka (Doder & Branson, 1999, pp. 25-26), where he managed to make great strides in transforming the bank into one which was more Western and could compete with other banks in capitalist societies (LeBor, 2003, pp. 49-50). On the one hand, LeBor considers this career path to be a rather curious choice for someone seeking to rise to the highest ranks of politics but Judah disagrees, and found that these functions provided him with the prestige he needed to enter the political arena (Judah, 2009, p. 161; LeBor, 2003, pp. 40-44). When he returned to party politics he advanced rapidly, thanks to Stambolic's tutelage. Stambolic came to head the committee of the Belgrade League of Communists and ensured Milosevic a part time position as chief of one of the district committees in 1982 (Sell, 2002, p. 25; Stevanovic, 2004, p. 24). Most politicians either disappeared from the political landscape all together after having worked in the committee, or they moved up to the real centre of power (Stevanovic, 2004, p. 24). Within Yugoslavia, terms were brief and no one was elected twice to the same position, it was a make or break moment (Stevanovic, 2004, pp. 25-26). Because of his friendship with Stambolic, Milosevic was able to move up. In 1984, Milosevic took on Stambolic's position, leading the Belgrade Communist Party, as the latter moved up to become the president of the Serbian League of Communists (LeBor, 2003, p. 58; Sell, 2002, p. 25).

The formative years of Milosevic life paint a picture of a man who was ambitious, and focused. He did not see the necessity to apply himself to obtaining and maintaining a social life. He did not have many friends but a very select group of people that he cared for, most notable among those his wife Mira. His mother firstly, and later Mira, pushed him to do better, be successful and he sought to live up to their expectations. In addition, in the few relationships he had at that moment, particularly those with Ivan Stambolic but also initially with Mira, there was next to an emotional component, also a functional element that made them appealing.

10.3. RISE TO POWER

During his years at the bank he had been progressive (LeBor, 2003, pp. 43-50), and as a politician Milosevic was part of the Kreigher commission that called for some economic reforms prompting accusations that he was revisionist (LeBor, 2003, p. 57). Overall, however, he sought to maintain the reputation of being conservative, loyal to Tito's memory and legacy (LeBor, 2003, p. 57). In doing so he tried to keep everybody happy by having a different message, depending on the audience (LeBor, 2003, p. 66). To one group which consisted out of reform minded Yugoslav politicians and when dealing with diplomats and external audiences coming from the West, he portrayed himself as a modernizer, who thanks to his time as a banker understood the market economy and portrayed himself as the right person to lead the reforms (LeBor, 2003, pp. 67-68). At the same time, however, he also sought to maintain support from the conservatives by continuing to honour the legacy of Tito (LeBor, 2003, pp. 66-69). He showed a socialist orthodox orientation that fought to retain a heavy influence of Marxism in the different aspects of Yugoslav society (Doder & Branson, 1999, p. 33; Sell, 2002, p. 30). Consequently, the older generation saw him as the right candidate to get the country back on the right communist track (Stevanovic, 2004, p. 25). Throughout this time, Sell explains, he 'displayed a devotion to socialist orthodoxy that had not been apparent when his primary focus was on economic affairs' and he manoeuvred to the top of the party hierarchy strictly toeing the communist party line (Doder & Branson, 1999, p. 32; Sell, 2002, p. 30).

In 1985, for instance, the question arose as to whether compulsory classes in Marxist education needed to be continued at Belgrade University. Several liberal politicians, among whom Stambolic, felt the classes should be abandoned, but Milosevic and his wife Markovic were among several hardliners who eventually ensured the classes stayed (LeBor, 2003, p. 69). Similarly, when the work of, the anti-communist writer Slobodan Jovanovic – whom Tito had denounced as a nationalist and sentenced to death in 1947 – was going to be published in Belgrade, Milosevic rose up against it and called Jovanovic a 'war criminal' (LeBor, 2003, p. 69; Stevanovic, 2004, p. 24). Just five years later Milosevic ostensibly changed his mind and hailed the publication of his life work as an important cultural event and honoured it with a prestigious award (Doder & Branson, 1999, p. 32).

Two years after becoming the head of the Belgrade Communist Party, Milosevic again followed in Stambolic's footsteps and became the head of the Serbian Communist Party. It was not an easy election though, since Milosevic at this time did not enjoy much standing within the communist party (Sell, 2002, p. 31). He only managed to win because Stambolic threw his weight behind his protégé (Stevanovic, 2004, p. 26). The two friends fell out over the decision of who should be elected as Milosevic' successor as head of the Belgrade party and Milosevic unsuccessfully tried to block Dragisa Pavlovic from being appointed (Sell, 2002, p. 32; Vladisavljević, 2004, p. 193). He believed Pavlovic in the past had tried to limit Milosevic's access to Stambolic and proposed other candidates but lost out (LeBor, 2003, pp. 73-74; Sell, 2002, p. 32). Milosevic then tried to place his own loyalists in the Serbian League of Communists which Stambolic prevented, so Milosevic placed them as heads of different party commissions (Sell, 2002, p. 33). Milosevic proceeded to make these commissions more powerful by having the media report heavily on their meetings, generating a large support base for them among the population (Sell, 2002, p. 33).

Throughout his political career he is described as being 'arrogant towards his subordinates, very cruel and disrespectful but he was very forthcoming, pliant and even subservient to those above him in the party hierarchy' (Sell, 2002, p. 30). He was also called 'power hungry' by a fellow prominent political personality during this time, constantly trying to impress audiences to realize his ambitions but never being forthright about what he wanted or intended to do (Sell, 2002, p. 30). The latter was reflected as well in the manner in which he dealt with the SANU memorandum.[114] When it came to light, Milosevic had been presenting himself as a true communist, and he could have condemned the document to strengthen this position, but he decided otherwise (Djukić, 2002, p. 40). Rather, he decided to ride the wave of nationalism but do so initially quite conspicuously. While Stambolic outright rejected the memorandum, Milosevic's strategy was much less outspoken (Guzina, 2003, p. 103). Milosevic would denounce the memorandum before the party in closed meetings but refrained from doing so publicly, and ensured both the nationalists and conservatives thought Milosevic was an ally (Doder & Branson, 1999, p. 42). According to LeBor, he started to 'exploit rising nationalism within the framework of Titoist orthodoxy' (LeBor, 2003, p. 79). While he would always argue that he wanted to maintain a federal Yugoslavia, he also started to repeat the idea from the memorandum that the federation was unable to solve Serbian grievances (Guzina, 2003, p. 103). Milosevic saw clear advantages of the rhetoric that was adopted in the memorandum. As Guzina explains, 'being a conservative communist and staunch antiliberal, he recognized in the memorandum the arguments that would not only legitimize his rise to power but also provide him with a political agenda that would look reformist to the communists and patriotic to the nationalists' (2003, p. 103). The nationalist sentiment of Milosevic included elements of communism or socialism along with nationalist and democratic discourse which were all centred around the concept of the nation (Shigeno, 2004, pp. 142; 144-145). Democracy was significant only to the extent that it applied to the liberty and equality of the Serbs and spoke to the need to secure the democratic rights of the Serbian people (Shigeno, 2004, p. 145). Serbs were also portrayed as the victims of the nationalism of the other nations, drawing a continuity of communist times where nationalists were conceived of as some of the most important enemies (Shigeno, 2004, p. 154). The nation became the new point of reference and served a similar function to the one the workers served during the communist era (Shigeno, 2004, p. 155).

Initially, these familiar sounding ideas of the Memorandum were predominantly debated in elite circles (Morus, 2007a, p. 146) and Milosevic was able to use it to his advantage. The fact that Ivan Stambolic strongly denounced the nationalist memorandum had made him look passive and weak in the eyes of much of the Serbian population (Shigeno, 2004, pp. 142-143). Milosevic decided to use this changing political landscape, which had weakened his friend and mentor Stambolic, by pulling the rug from underneath him to advance his own position.

In the spring of 1987, Stambolic asked Milosevic to go to Kosovo Polje and talk to a group of Kosovar Albanian politicians to try and calm the nationalist tensions that had been building in the region (Djukić, 2002, p. 41; LeBor,

114 See Chapter 8. The memorandum was drafted by the Serbian Academy of Arts and Sciences and was influential in forming and spreading nationalism throughout society (Morus, 2007a).

2003, p. 78). Milosevic, who had never shown much interest in Kosovo, is said to have been 'taken aback by the depth of the feeling in Kosovo and the sheer passion and fury of the local Serbs', and promised to return a few days later to discuss what more could be done for the plight of the Kosovars (LeBor, 2003, p. 79). Being a Serb himself, Milosevic must have understood how important Kosovo was for his nation, but this was the first time he had experienced such a violent and emotionally laden atmosphere, and he initially appeared to be in shock (LeBor, 2003, p. 79; Sell, 2002, p. 1). He seemed dazed and nervous when he was asked to calm the crowd (LeBor, 2003, p. 80; Sell, 2002, p. 1). It may be that the scale and power of the nationalist sentiment had shocked him, but there are indications he had been involved in the staging of his appearance that day (Brosse, 2003, pp. 39-40).[115] Azem Vllasi, the Albanian chief of the League of Communists of Kosovo, strongly felt that Milosevic had been part of its organization because Milosevic initially agreed to meet the leadership before heading to the crowd at Kosovo Polje, but Milosevic had delayed his arrival and went immediately to the demonstration (LeBor, 2003, pp. 79-80; Sell, 2002, p. 3). Most of Milosevic's speech conformed to the party line but he ended his speech by saying 'this is your country; your homes, fields and memories are here' and added that 'Yugoslavia cannot exist without Kosovo. Yugoslavia and Serbia will not give up Kosovo' (Sell, 2002, p. 3). The sentence that would stick with the Serbian population the most was his creed that the police were no longer to beat the Serbian people again. It gave him popularity as the politician who stood up against the police and was loyal to his people (Sell, 2002, pp. 1-2). The whole episode was disconcerting to Stambolic who warned Milosevic.

> 'I asked him, 'if you go on like this what will become of our country?' I saw we were totally opposed in our methods. We had two different policies on Kosovo. The distance between us began to grow' (cited in LeBor, 2003, p. 83).

Stambolic never openly spoke out against Milosevic but was stunned his opinion was so easily ignored by his friend (Vladisavljević, 2004, p. 195).

Milosevic, in the meantime, made sure to point out – in closed circles – that nationalism could never be tolerated (Djukić, 2002, p. 42; Doder & Branson, 1999, p. 42; Judah, 2009, p. 160). Judah reports Milosevic having said in an unpublicised speech in front of policemen and party officials that

> 'the appearance of the Memorandum of the Serbian Academy of Arts and Sciences represents nothing else but the darkest nationalism. It means the liquidation of the current socialist system of our country, that is the disintegration after which there is no survival for any nation or nationality ... Tito's policy for brotherhood and unity ... is the only basis on which Yugoslavia's survival can be secured' (Judah, 2009, p. 160).

---

115 Although Stevanovic (Stevanovic, 2004, p. 29) seems to believe it was more spontaneous.

According to Judah, 'it goes to show that he was an opportunist telling different audiences different things in order to garner their support' (Judah, 2009, p. 160). This strategy immediately gave him the support of the intellectual nationalists and provided him with the opportunity to start to manipulate and use the discontent of the people (LeBor, 2003, pp. 83-85).

Incidents that were not about nationalist strife were given a nationalist connotation. There was, for instance, the incident where a Kosovar Albanian recruit killed four fellow soldiers and wounded six others. One of them was Serb but the rest were of different nationalities (Judah, 2009, p. 162; Vladisavljević, 2004, p. 195). Even though it was clear that there had not been any nationalist motivation for his acts, an anti-Albanian media barrage followed. Journalists that were loyal to Milosevic heavily criticized the Kosovar Albanian leadership, accusing them from failing to reel in nationalist sentiment which they argued had ultimately caused such horrible acts (Judah, 2009, p. 162; Vladisavljević, 2004, p. 195). In the end 10,000 people attended the funeral (Judah, 2009, p. 162).

Pavlovic tried to defuse the situation and warned such reporting could only backfire and make matters worse (Vladisavljević, 2004, p. 195). In a speech he said 'We must criticize Serbian nationalism today because, among other things, Serbian nationalists imagine themselves as saviours of the Serbian cause in Kosovo, without in fact being able to solve a single social problem, and especially without being able to improve inter-nationality events' (LeBor, 2003, p. 87). It was an obvious attempt to undermine Milosevic (LeBor, 2003, p. 87), who retaliated soon thereafter. He ensured that the press started to attack Pavlovic, and by association, Stambolic. Rather than claiming responsibility for the message they put forward, Milosevic used a journalist, Dragoljub Milanovic, under whose name an article written by Mira was published that undermined Palovic's message and wrote it off as a consequence of conflict within the communist party between those who were in favour of the Serb cause and those who were traitors (Doder & Branson, 1999, p. 48; LeBor, 2003, p. 88).

The final blow was dealt at the eighth session of the Serbian Communist Party. Pavlovic had tried to strengthen his position by building on the support of Stambolic and had a letter that attested to that fact. However, Pavlovic's letter was not well received and four sympathizers agreed to sign another letter in which they stated that they felt undue pressure was placed on the committee (Doder & Branson, 1999, p. 49; LeBor, 2003, p. 90; Vladisavljević, 2004, p. 196). At the start of the eighth session Milosevic made his move and accused Pavlovic of being against Tito and Yugoslavia (LeBor, 2003, p. 92; Stevanovic, 2004, p. 30). The charge itself was irrelevant. There was opposition from a minority of liberal politicians but when the time came to vote, Pavlovic was expelled from the party presidency (LeBor, 2003, pp. 93-94). The whole affair had taken a toll on Stambolic's standing as well and pressurized by a smear campaign in the press, he agreed to resign in December 1987 (LeBor, 2003, p. 94; Vladisavljević, 2004, p. 196).

After Stambolic's removal from power, thousands officials were fired and replaced by individuals who were more loyal to Milosevic (LeBor, 2003, p. 101). Milosevic then launched his 'anti-bureaucratic revolution' which was targeted against the bureaucracy of the league of communists of Serbia that had supposedly always been reluctant to stand up against the Albanian separatists, and was targeted against the leadership of the other nations and autonomous provinces, particularly those of Kosovo (Shigeno, 2004, p. 143). Bureaucracy became a catch all phrase for their enemies, enemies which were defined through a nationalist lens (Shigeno, 2004, pp. 143-144). The revolution involved mass rallies, called 'Meetings of Truth' that were being organized throughout the country (Judah, 2009, p. 163). Milosevic never attended the meetings but they were clearly organized from the top. Transportation was often arranged and they at times received police escorts (Sell, 2002, pp. 56-57). The protestors successfully called for the political leadership in those towns to step down and consequently the leadership in Montenegro and Vojvodina indeed decided to step down at the end of 1988 and early 1989 (Gagnon, 1994, p. 150).

In November 1988, the leadership in Kosovo also caved and under Serb pressure the Kosovar Albanian leader Azem Vllasi also resigned (Sell, 2002, pp. 81-82). Some note that earlier in their careers Milosevic and Vllasi were friends, but the latter soon realized that they had incompatible goals and Milosevic could not be trusted (Sell, 2002, pp. 67; 81-82). In response to these events, miners started a strike to demand the reinstatement of their leader, but Milosevic organized a counter demonstration in Belgrade. Fearful that the violent crowd would wreck the capital and knowing that only Milosevic could calm them, the army decided to acquiesce to Milosevic' demands and send in the army to subdue the strike in Kosovo. Martial law was declared in Kosovo and Vllasi was arrested and sent to prison (LeBor, 2003, pp. 108; 116-119). It was a pivotal moment because it was the first incident in which the JNA was used as an instrument in service of Milosevic (LeBor, 2003, p. 119). Vllasi was imprisoned and Kosovo's autonomy was officially abolished in March 1989 in a round of voting that had been full of fraud and manipulation (Gagnon, 1994, p. 150). Not only were Serbian officials present to monitor how the Albanian delegates voted, sometimes they voted themselves and those who courageously refused to conform, lost their jobs and were threatened with criminal prosecution (Sell, 2002, p. 87). Similar tactics were used to gain influence in Serb areas in Croatia and Bosnia. In Slovenia, as well, the plan was to arrest dissidents while the army was supposed to keep any demonstrations in check. It caused a backlash that led to reformists in those regions gaining more widespread support from the populations (Gagnon, 1994, pp. 150-152).

It is highly unlikely Milosevic wanted Yugoslavia to break up at this point. Rather, he sought to dominate the existing institutions, and increase Serbian influence (LeBor, 2003, p. 85; Sell, 2002, p. 95). However, his policies ended up greatly contributing to its downfall. The election results in 1990 in the other republics, where parties won that favoured more decentralisation, can be viewed as a backlash to Milosevic' strong nationalist stance (Gagnon, 1994, pp. 150-153).

All he ever wanted was power and nationalism was a mere instrument to attain it. As was described in the previous section, even though he grew up in an area that was important for Serbia's past there is no evidence this past was ever important for him. He did not seem very concerned with his national heritage. He was never a devoted nationalist or communist. He used a different ideological stance for different audiences, at one moment calling for revisions, the other moment presenting a more conservative attitude. He was a 'one time Communist apparatchik [who] reinvented himself as a charismatic nationalist' (Sell, 2002, p. 3) but it was hardly a smooth transition which reflected a change of heart. As he rose to power, he seemed to be at one time a reformist, while at other moments a conservative socialist who was determined to honour Tito's legacy, and importantly, for some time, appeared to be both. While first a socialist and only then a nationalist, there was no clear demarcation line that separated these eras and political orientations from each other. Which ideology he adhered to, depended on the audience to which he spoke. As LeBor phrases it: 'Milosevic's relationship to nationalism is similar to his relationship to communism. He understood the political power that both bestow, and exploited both for his own advantage' (LeBor, 2003, p. 182). Already in this phase of his life it became evident that, in the words of one former associate, Milosevic 'decides first what is expedient for him to believe and then he believes it' (cited in L. J. Cohen, 2006, p. 439).

Judah explains that Milosevic had a great organizational talent which allowed him to place individuals in prominent positions whose dominant personal characteristic was loyalty to Milosevic and his regime (2009, p. 162). He, however, was not loyal to those who helped him build his career. He was the godfather of Stambolic's children (Sell, 2002, p. 20) and he had been the best man at his wedding (LeBor, 2003, p. 31), but there was a very large utility element to his friendship and when he was no longer useful for his career, he needed to be removed. His career took priority over his personal relationships. There is a long list of people who Milosevic betrayed, and Post goes so far as to call him a 'master of betrayal' (Post, 2004, p. 182).

10.4. HIS REIGN

During his reign Milosevic was eager to expand his power and sphere of influence and was unconcerned whether this meant he needed to wage war or make peace. His self-interest prevailed over any other concerns.

10.4.1. WAGING WAR

Dominating Serbia, Montenegro, Vojvodina and Kosovo, it was now widely believed Milosevic wanted to take over and rule the whole of Yugoslavia (Sell, 2002, p. 95). Milosevic's speech in Kosovo in 1989 was a perfect opportunity to celebrate his own rise to power and his success in abolishing the autonomy of the province (LeBor, 2003, p. 120; Sell, 2002, p. 88). He spoke passionately about the region and its continued importance for the Serbs as a nation (LeBor, 2003, p. 122). After this speech, however, Milosevic would not visit the region for another six years (Sell, 2002, p. 94). He had hoped to become Yugoslavia's next Tito, but his attempts to dominate the country failed as Yugoslavia started to fall apart because Milosevic' nationalist rhetoric increased anxieties over living in a Yugoslavia that was dominated by the Serbs and sparked nationalism and desires for self-determination in the other republics (Sell, 2002, pp. 95-107).[116]

When the Slovenes walked out on the last meeting of the League of Communists, and the Croats followed, as the latter held the Yugoslav Party without the Slovenes was not an option, Milosevic was visibly angry and upset (LeBor, 2003, p. 134; Sell, 2002, pp. 104-105). With its demise, Milosevic realized, every effort to dominate Yugoslavia dissipated (Sell, 2002, p. 105). Milosevic, however quickly modified his goals at this point; if he could not be Tito's successor in a unified Yugoslavia, he would extend Serbia and at least dominate most of the old territory (Doder & Branson, 1999, p. 63). He developed a new strategy with which he sought to unite all Serbs in one state (Sell, 2002, p. 108). Milosevic realized at this point that Slovenia's exit from Yugoslavia would actually make it easier for him to include the parts of Croatia where a large number of Serbs lived and subsume them in Serbia (Sell, 2002, p. 115). Milosevic initiated a heavy handed military and political policy, ostensibly aimed at preventing Slovenia from seceding, but they had mutual interests (LeBor, 2003, pp. 132-133). Milosevic knew that his tactics would further drive Slovenian calls for independence, but this actually created the opportunity for Milosevic to present himself as the defender of Yugoslavia (LeBor, 2003, pp. 132-133). Slovenia's leader, Milan Kucan, explained;

> 'At a certain point of time Slovenia and Serbia had a common interest for reforming the society, but obviously based on completely different principles. This created the 'community of interests' in that Milosevic's Yugoslavia had no room for Slovenia and Slovenia did not want to be in Milosevic's Yugoslavia' (cited in LeBor, 2003, p. 135).

When the JNA intervened in Slovenia a dangerous precedent was set, the army would intervene in order to prevent countries from leaving Yugoslavia, which

---

116 As explained earlier in Chapter 8, Yugoslavia under Tito was a federation that consisted of six republics and two autonomous provinces.

Milosevic was able to exploit when the other republics, which had a substantial Serbian minority within their borders, tried to secede (LeBor, 2003, p. 137). The war in Slovenia, however, was meant to be brief. As a close associate to Milosvic explained:

> 'We didn't want a war with Slovenia. Serbia had no territorial claims there. It was an ethnically pure republic – no Serbs. We couldn't care less if they left Yugoslavia … We would have been overstretched' (cited in LeBor, 2003, p. 138).

Milosevic was unwilling to let Croatia go in its entirety (Doder & Branson, 1999, p. 77; LeBor, 2003, p. 135). Milosevic and Tudjman, the leader of Croatia, for this reason, had conflicting interests when it came to Croatian territory, but the two men both saw advantages in dividing up Bosnia between them (Sell, 2002, p. 119). A brutal war followed but the hardship that befell Yugoslavia because of these policies did not seem to concern Milosevic at this point in time. LeBor points out 'Milosevic showed no concern for the human cost of his policies. The equation was simple enough: war ensured political power; political power demanded war' (LeBor, 2003, p. 146). He needed crises to deflect attention from the problems and hardship that were caused by his own leadership (Post, 2004, p. 185). Post believed that for Milosevic 'peace would be the greatest and most dangerous crisis of all' (Post, 2004, p. 185). Milosevic, however, was unable to completely prevent unrest from arising among the population and the looming wars sparked counter demonstrations. In March 1991, for instance, students headed to the streets and were soon joined by countless others (Doder & Branson, 1999, p. 77). The police brutally supressed the demonstrations by sending tanks into the streets of Belgrade which only further enraged the demonstrators (Doder & Branson, 1999, p. 78). When Milosevic met with student representatives they demanded the release of the imprisoned protest organizer Draskovic, called for the dismissal of Dusan Mitevic, who was responsible for Milosevic' propaganda campaign, and of the Minister of the Interior Radmilo Bagdanovic (Doder & Branson, 1999, p. 78). As demonstrations started to spread across Serbia, Milosevic became worried and willing to acquiesce to some of these demands to appease the crowd (LeBor, 2003, p. 161). He released Draskovic from jail, and Mitevic and Bagdanovic agreed to step down but in practice were merely reassigned and continued to be close to Milosevic (Doder & Branson, 1999, p. 79).

Similar protests would follow in 1992 and 1993. Early in 1992, the economic situation in Serbia was dire, inflation soared and discontent among the population rose (Doder & Branson, 1999, p. 123). The elite, like the nationalist Dobrica Cosic, started to distance themselves from Milosevic (Doder & Branson, 1999, pp. 126-127; LeBor, 2003, p. 196). Milosevic responded to this new threat by co-opting Cosic who became the federal president of Yugoslavia.[117] Upon

[117] He was ousted from power in June 1993 (Doder & Branson, 1999, p. 190).

accepting the function Cosic demanded real changes but realized all too soon that they were not forthcoming and that his new position did not wield him much power (Doder & Branson, 1999, pp. 130-132; Sell, 2002, p. 199). In addition, Milosevic met with the opposition leaders, becoming 'the very picture of calm and tolerance, and eager to make concessions' (Doder & Branson, 1999, p. 135). On top of that, Milosevic ensured that Milan Panic, a wealthy Serb-American businessman, took up the position of Prime Minister which finally secured an end to the protests (Doder & Branson, 1999, pp. 133-137).

Milosevic sank into a depression as Panic proved to be a difficult adversary and even before he officially started, demanded from Milosevic that the latter would resign (Doder & Branson, 1999, pp. 137-140; 145-148), Milosevic initially acquiesced, but later denied he made such an arrangement, possibly after being influenced to do so by his wife (Doder & Branson, 1999, pp. 150-156; Sell, 2002, p. 201). Some claim, he was never planning to leave although those present at the meeting believed he was serious (Doder & Branson, 1999, p. 148). At this point Mira became more actively involved in Serbian politics and saved Milosevic from the depression to which he was succumbing (Doder & Branson, 1999, pp. 139-140). She had established her own political party in 1990 and became a more prominent figure in the political landscape by the summer of 1992 (Doder & Branson, 1999, pp. 139-140).

After a fist fight in parliament between a member of the opposition and an ally of Milosevic, demonstrations broke out again in June 1993 (Doder & Branson, 1999, p. 190). Riot police intervened once more and the opposition leader Draskovic was savagely beaten. After spending three weeks in prison he decided he would go on a hunger strike, causing several demonstrators and members of parliament from the opposition to follow his lead as an act of solidarity. As calls for mass protests grew stronger as well, Milosevic feared the situation could get out of hand and possibly threaten his hold on power, and he consequently quickly decided to issue a presidential pardon for Draskovic (Doder & Branson, 1999, pp. 191-193).

Milosevic continuously proved willing to compromise when he believed this to be necessary to guarantee his hold on power. This attitude is reflected as well in the manner in which he decided it would be opportune for him to transform himself from 'warmonger to peacemaker' (Doder & Branson, 1999, pp. 188-189). An important factor in Milosevic's decision to work towards a negotiated peace agreement was his desire to lift the sanctions that were imposed on Serbia (LeBor, 2003, pp. 119-220). When they were enacted, it took a while before they had the intended effect. LeBor explains that the initial reaction of the Serbian population was to adopt a 'Balkan version of the "Blitz-spirit" of wartime Londeners. They dug for victory, and grew their own food' and created an extensive grey and black shadow economy (LeBor, 2003, p. 210). Milosevic blamed the sanctions for the economic downturn and portrayed them as the necessary price they needed to pay for supporting the Serbs in the other republics (Andreas, 2009, p. 108; LeBor, 2003, p. 210). However, as the sanctions increasingly had a detrimental impact on the Serbian economy unrest in Serbia's society grew, which Milosevic rightfully saw as a destabilizing factor for his power base (Doder & Branson, 1999, p. 176; LeBor, 2003, p. 220).[118]

10.4.2. MAKING PEACE

In order to lift the sanctions, he had come to the realisation that a peace agreement needed to be reached, but the Serb leadership in Croatia and Bosnia was obstinate. (Doder & Branson, 1999, pp. 175-189; LeBor, 2003, p. 220; Sell, 2002, pp. 208-209). In the years that followed, Milosevic abandoned the Serbs in both republics. Doder and Branson believe that at this point 'Milosevic showed his true colors, abandoning the national dream that had once stirred his people when he realized that it was an impediment to his rule' (1999, p. 212). According to Sell, 'Milosevic badly wanted an agreement and was prepared to sacrifice the interests of the Bosnian Serbs to get one' (Sell, 2002, p. 228).

In 1993, and again in May of 1995, Croatian forces attacked the Serb held areas in Croatia and Milosevic did not respond. In 1993 Croatia succumbed to the pressure of the international community to allow for the return of peacekeepers, but in 1995 the international community deliberately turned a blind eye when they took back territory. They had fostered a peace agreement between Croatia and Bosnia and had trained Croatian forces so they would be more apt to combat the Serbs together with the Bosnian forces (Chollet, 2005, p. 6; LeBor, 2003, pp. 225-229; Stevanovic, 2004, p. 102). The Krajina region was recaptured in a large scale ethnic cleansing campaign that sent between 150,000 and 200,000 Serbs on the run (LeBor, 2003, p. 229). Coming to the aid of the Serbs in Croatia would have further challenged the international community and although Milosevic, realizing supporting the Krajina Serbs no longer was in his best interests, appears to have been emotionally shaken by the onslaught, he decided not to act (Ashbrook & Bakich, 2010, p. 544; LeBor, 2003, pp. 220; 228-230; Sell, 2002, pp. 242-243). It could have been predicted days in advance that numerous refugees would make their way into Serbia, but no precautions had been taken to accommodate the thousands of refugees that fled across their border (Sell, 2002, p. 242). The media in Belgrade would not even report on what happened in the region and in the little news that was provided, Karadzic and the Serbian Croatian leadership was blamed. It allowed him to deflect blame whilst not harming the chances of a negotiated peace deal with Croatia (Doder & Branson, 1999, pp. 212; 219-220).

118 It must be noted that for a while the sanctions regime actually strengthened Milosevic's regime because of its hold over the profitable black market that emerged (Andreas, 2009, pp. 110-111).

Perhaps the abandonment of the Krajina Serbs was not wholly surprising considering that Belgrade never cared as much for their fellow Serbs in Croatia as they did for those in Bosnia. Close associate to Milosevic, Borislav Jovic, reportedly said:

> 'We are not interested in the Serbs in Croatia. [...] We are exclusively interested in Bosnia Herzegovina, which was, and will be Serbian' (LeBor, 2003, p. 230).

Milosevic, however, proved unwilling to come to their aid as well, prioritizing the lifting of the sanctions regime that had been imposed on Serbia by the UN. After the Bosnian Serb leadership repeatedly failed to accept proposed peace plans, the media in Belgrade started to demonize them and Milosevic broke off political and military relations (Doder & Branson, 1999, p. 199; LeBor, 2003, pp. 232-234). Thereafter, when NATO started to bomb the Bosnian Serbs that surrounded Sarajevo, Milosevic drank heavily and seemed undone but remained utterly passive (LeBor, 2003, pp. 238-243). It had been possible to break the alliance between Milosevic and the Bosnian Serbs because, according to Kollander, 'Milosevic was ultimately convinced that it was in his best interest to abandon the Bosnian Serbs' (Kollander, 2004, p. 15).

His attempts to forge the peace agreement according to Sell 'dramatically changed his relationship with the international community' (Sell, 2002, p. 209). Slowly but surely Milosevic started to position himself towards the international community as the great peacemaker, a man that was part of the solution rather than the problem (Doder & Branson, 1999, p. 189). As the Bosnian Serbs were being beaten back, Milosevic needed a peace agreement badly (Sell, 2002, p. 245). He could not allow the Croatian and Bosnian offensive to sweep through Bosnia and take all of the Serb held territory. The defeat and the resulting large amount of refugees could have further destabilised Serbia and according to Sell 'might have fatally weakened Milosevic' (Sell, 2002, p. 245).

As the Bosnian Serbs were losing territory fast, Karadzic succumbed to Milosevic's demands and allowed him to negotiate on behalf of all Serbs at Dayton (Doder & Branson, 1999, pp. 221-222; Sell, 2002, p. 245). Formally the agreement kept Bosnia intact as a single state but the country would be divided into two entities, the Croat-Muslim federation and the Serb republic, each with its own armies, police force, political structures and judiciary although these would function under the authority of a multinational government (Kollander, 2004, p. 16; LeBor, 2003, p. 247). The final agreement essentially legitimized the brutal ethnic cleansing campaign of the Serbs and the Muslim-Croat federation would cover 51% of its territory while the Serb republic would spread across the other 49% (LeBor, 2003, p. 247). The Bosnian Serb delegation, however, only signed the agreement reluctantly and under severe pressure from Milosevic (Sell, 2002, p. 254). Milosevic later told diplomats that he was only able to secure their signatures by threatening to arrest all of them (Sell, 2002, p. 254). Throughout the negotiations they had been kept completely out of the loop by Milosevic, who was in full control over the peace negotiations (Sell, 2002, p. 251). According to the British diplomat David Austin:

> 'Serbia was ruled by one man. Milosevic gave the impression that he had nothing else to do but talk to us. He had an intellectual arrogance that nobody else in the country could do it. He knew the subject intimately. He took decisions, made concessions, and he never had to consult anybody. He just did it' (LeBor, p. 240).

Milosevic was lonely and depressed at Dayton, and distressed from being separated from his wife for such a long time, but those emotions never became apparent during the negotiations (Sell, 2002, p. 255). However, he would complain a lot about the refusal of the Bosnian Serbs to listen to him and his inability to control them. He reportedly said: 'They are like children. You know what it is like Mr Austin, trying to control children', and would mock them and call them bastards (LeBor, 2003, p. 240). At the same time, however, he had significant influence over them, and this would occasionally show as Milosevic sought to re-establish his dominance over them. He told Holbrooke, for instance, to 'pay no attention to those guys … I'll make sure they accept the final agreement' (Doder & Branson, 1999, p. 223). According to Sell, 'the most striking feature of the Dayton negotiations was the utter contempt with which Milosevic treated the Bosnian Serbs' and Austin remembers how Milosevic 'humiliated them' and he hardly allowed them to provide input for the final agreement (LeBor, 2003, p. 250).

In the agreement many of the most important elements for the Serbs were secured, including the continuation of their name *Republika Srpska* (LeBor, 2003, p. 247; Sell, 2002, pp. 249-254). However, Milosevic had also been willing to compromise on some crucial issues (Sell, 2002, p. 253). Karadzic had sought to divide Sarajevo, but Milosevic willingly gave up the city, telling the Bosnian Muslim delegation: 'You deserve Sarajevo because you fought for it and those cowards killed you from the hills' (LeBor, 2003, p. 251). He also compromised on Brcko when the town almost became a deal breaker (Doder & Branson, 1999, p. 225). The Bosnian Serbs were very discontent with the final agreement but Milosevic was hailed in his propaganda as the great peacemaker (Doder & Branson, 1999, p. 226; Sell, 2002, p. 254).

From his time at Dayton, and his behaviour throughout his reign, it becomes apparent Milosevic was primarily concerned with increasing and maintaining his hold on power. Sell believes Milosevic initial goal was to dominate Yugoslavia as the leader of the Serbs, which backfired because his own use of nationalism provoked nationalism in the other republics. As the other republics started to secede, Milosevic came to realize his initial goal was untenable and found an alternative that required him to change strategies. He did not mind Yugoslavia falling apart violently, but sought to use the wars to increase his power by creating a greater Serbia (Sell, 2002, p. 5). Sell in this regard pointed out that 'Milosevic with no firm beliefs, was ever the artful improviser' (Sell, 2002, p. 119).

Doder & Branson believe that trying to get the Vance Owen plan accepted, was seen by Milosevic as a small set back that was necessary for the greater good (Doder & Branson, 1999, p. 179), but it is highly questionable how attached he was to this greater good in the first place. Throughout his time in power, Milosevic showed little actual concern for the creation of this nationalist goal, the realization of a greater Serbia was only his secondary goal when succeeding Tito fell through. He never visited Kosovo again after he celebrated the anniversary of its famous battle in 1989 and he never attempted to improve the living conditions there, not even for its Serbian inhabitants (Sell, 2002, p. 269). In addition, he abandoned the Serbian cause when NATO started bombing Serb military targets and when the Serbs in the Krajina region were violently expelled. He turned his back on them in order to secure a peace agreement which he considered essential to maintain his hold on power at Dayton, and Milosevic's desire to come to an agreement caused him to make far-reaching compromises which he knew went beyond what the Bosnian Serbs deemed acceptable. According to LeBor, the 'willingness to abandon Serbs who have been on the front line fighting for Serbdom is an absolute characteristic of Milosevic' (LeBor, 2003, pp. 251-252).

Milosevic had always been willing to adjust his goals if the costs turned out to be too high. When demonstrations threatened his rule in 1991 and 1992, he sought to appease the population. For a brief moment, he even appears to have been pragmatic enough to consider stepping down in order to secure a safe and secure position abroad, but was able to hold onto power by making lesser concessions. In 1991, this meant he needed to sacrifice some of his closest advisors, although one should be critical of the extent to which this should be seen as a genuine sacrifice since they remained important members of his inner circle albeit in different functions. In a similar fashion, the decision to install Panic and Cosic in 1992 is questionable as a compromise because it seemed he had hoped they would have been harmless while it looked good (Doder & Branson, 1999, pp. 131-137; LeBor, 2003, pp. 196-199; Sell, 2002, p. 199). He was, however, also willing to pardon Draskovic and with the compromises made at Dayton, showed himself to be pragmatic and calculating.

10.5. AFTER DAYTON

In the first months after Dayton he was the important man whom everyone thanked, but disappointment in Serbia soon followed as not all sanctions were removed by the international community. The 'outer wall of sanctions' remained intact as they were tied to the situation in Kosovo, which gained renewed diplomatic attention after the conflict in Bosnia was resolved. Milosevic felt betrayed by Holbrooke whom he believed had broken his promise to have all the sanctions lifted (Doder & Branson, 1999, p. 227; LeBor, 2003, p. 257; Sell, 2002, pp. 257-258). According to Sell, this had two effects: he stopped trusting the international community and became more apathetic and less involved in running the country (Sell, 2002, pp. 257-258). Throughout this time, he became more disheartened, isolated, detached from reality, and perhaps even paranoid (LeBor, 2003, p. 257; Sell, 2002, p. 257). He furthermore purged some of his closest associates from his inner circle of advisers, possibly due to the influence of his wife, but there are also indications some had opposed Milosevic's policy concerning Dayton (Doder & Branson, 1999, p. 227; LeBor, 2003, pp. 257-258; Sell, 2002, pp. 257-258). Mira and Milosevic seemed to be turning Serbia away from the international community towards isolation and back to its communist roots (Doder & Branson, 1999, pp. 227-228). Milosevic's Socialist Party of Serbia became less influential and he started to rely more on his wife's political party (LeBor, 2003, pp. 257-258; Sell, 2002, pp. 256-257). Mira had become the founder, advocate and spokesperson of *Jugoslovenska Udruzena Levica* (United Left Wing of Yugoslavia), better known as JUL (Stevanovic, 2004, p. 121). Conflicts between prominent members of organized crime networks became more frequent, and a prominent aspect of Serbian society and assassinations became more common (Stevanovic, 2004, p. 117). Stevanovic explained that after the wars 'the only part of the economy that was still functioning was the illegal plunder that enriched the presidential family and its supporters' (Stevanovic, 2004, p. 120). Particularly those associated with Mira Markovic would acquire vast amounts of wealth fast (Stevanovic, 2004, p. 117).

Milosevic' regime upped his propaganda media storm to present their president as the great peacemaker but was not entirely successful and the majority of the Serbs saw Dayton as a defeat for the Serbian nation (Doder & Branson, 1999, pp. 226-227). His grip on power seemed to be slipping as resistance towards his rule was once again mounting. Feeling victorious after Dayton, Milosevic moved to call for elections in 1996. In the federal parliamentary election Milosevic won overwhelmingly, but in the municipal election which were held simultaneously, the opposition won (Doder & Branson, 1999, p. 232; Stevanovic, 2004, p. 126). Unrest and demonstrations followed as Milosevic moved to annul the elections (Sell, 2002, pp. 259-260; Stevanovic, 2004, pp. 126-127). It was a desperate time for Milosevic, who relied on his wife and her associates to confirm that he still had the support of the passive majority, and they decided to call them into action again by organizing counter-demonstrations (Doder & Branson, 1999, pp. 233-235). Powerful businessmen who made up the core of JUL, shut down their factories and told their employees to take part in Milosevic's counterdemonstrations (Doder & Branson, 1999, p. 235). However, the strategy that had worked so well when he rose to power, had overtly lost its lustre and the demonstrations were passionless (Stevanovic,

2004, pp. 127-128). In addition, there seemed to be sympathies among some of the security services and among former loyalists of Milosevic for the opposition (Sell, 2002, p. 260). Milosevic appeared to be losing political support as opposition grew and gained momentum (Stevanovic, 2004, p. 128).

However, although opposition leaders enjoyed tremendous success in mobilizing the masses, they failed to articulate more far-reaching demands beyond acknowledgement of the original election results. Milosevic, recognizing the seriousness of the situation, acquiesced to these limited demands in February 1997 (Stevanovic, 2004, p. 129). In November, Milosevic agreed to comply with the election results of the previous year thus showing, according to Sell, that 'one element of Milosevic's genius for retaining power was his ability when under pressure to make tactical concessions that over the long run act to defeat his enemies' (Sell, 2002, p. 260). Throughout these gloomy months Milosevic again showed he 'was pragmatic when he had to be and ready to cooperate when forced to' (Stevanovic, 2004, p. 129).

Thereafter, in 1997 Milosevic had himself elected as President of Yugoslavia. He needed to move to the federal presidency because the constitution did not allow him to serve another term as president of the republic of Serbia (LeBor, 2003, p. 273). He ensured that a trusted ally succeeded him as the president of Serbia, but in practice, he took the power he had with him to his new position. Although formally Milosevic was much less powerful in his new position, informally he retained much of his influence. Until Milosevic's move to the federal presidency Serbia had always been more powerful than the federation, but the situation reversed the moment Milosevic changed his function (Sekelj, 2000, pp. 59; 71-72). It became evident, however, that slowly but surely some of his power was slipping away as public support started to disappear (Sekelj, 2000, p. 72).

10.6. THE INFLUENCE OF MIRA MARKOVIC

Milosevic and his wife seem to have had an extraordinarily close relationship that did not always conform to what was conventional among his generation in Serbia (Stevanovic, 2004, pp. 123-124). He was never with any other woman besides Mira, which was quite unusual in the macho Balkan culture, and seemed to be a loving and devoted father (LeBor, 2003, p. 30; Sell, 2002, p. 16; 26). In their private life, Mira seemed to have been somewhat domineering. Friends of the couple have explained that they did not fight very often but when they did, she would finally get whatever it was she wanted by feigning an illness and staying in bed until Milosevic caved (Orizio, 2004, p. 174).

However, it was not only behind closed doors that Mira managed to influence her husband. Mira became particularly important in post-Dayton Yugoslavia but from the beginning exerted a tremendous influence over her husband. It has been said she was the one who encouraged him to enter politics (Orizio, 2004, p. 172). One former advisor of Milosevic once said: 'Mira gave him the love for power and the ambition. She made him what he is' (LeBor, 2003, p. 22) and according to a friend of Mira, he would 'utter her thoughts and assessments as his own unaware of where she ends and he begins' (Doder & Branson, 1999, p. 20).

A well-known story, which has always been denied by Mira, depicts her walking past a shop window with a cousin[119] and telling her companion 'that's where my Slobodan's picture will be one day' (Djukić, 2002, p. 33; LeBor, 2003, pp. 31-32; Sell, 2002, p. 18). According to Djukic, she encouraged him to be even more ambitious, she wrote his speeches and she pushed him away from Stambolic (Djukić, 2002, p. 39). Mira always denied she had such a far-reaching influence on her husband:

> 'I do have an influence, and he has an influence on me. But what does that mean, 'having influence'? Communication between people means having influence. If we had lunch three times you would have some influence on me, and I would have some influence on you. This is communication. If I tell you about the books I have been reading and you keep that in mind, that is an influence' (LeBor, 2003, p. 114).

However, most observers have been convinced her influence has been more significant. She is said to have been his most trusted advisor, although she denied this as well (LeBor, 2003, pp. 158; 184-185). Some even believe, Milosevic would not have been as powerful as he ended up being were it not for his wife and it has even been suggested by some that without her, Milosevic would have been no more than a provincial functionary (Windgassen, 2002, pp. 134-135). This, however, seems to be an exaggeration since it was also primarily Milosevic's mentor and friend, Stambolic, who propelled him to a position of power. Windgassen, however, argues that Mira had many long conversations with Slobodan and Ivan Stambolic to decide on the future course Milosevic' career should take (Windgassen, 2002, pp. 238-239) and as Milosevic's most trusted advisor she undoubtedly had an enormous impact not only on him but also on his rise to power.

Already in 1990 Mira established her own political party, the League of Communists – Movement for Yugoslavia (LC-MY) (which was later re-launched as JUL) (LeBor, 2003, p. 156;159). It was a small group, with a very limited membership but because those who were involved were influential, the party itself was of significance as well (LeBor, 2003, p. 156). Many influential individuals from the business world were party members and many were accused of greatly benefitting from the war and the illegal practices that emerged after

119 Sell says it was a school friend (2002, p. 18).

sanctions were imposed (Windgassen, 2002, p. 244). After Dayton Mira further eroded the influence of Milosevic closest advisors, allowing her own political organization to gain in strength (Sell, 2002, pp. 256-257).

Like Milosevic, she has been described as ambitious, and without moral scruples (Windgassen, 2002, p. 235), but others have believed her to be genuinely more ideological, socialist and anti-nationalist, than her husband (LeBor, 2003, p. 182). Most scholars seem to agree that Milosevic's prime motivation was staying in power (Ramet, 2005, p. 160), but it was his friend and mentor Stambolic who perhaps phrased it most eloquently:

> 'Milosevic in essence does not have convictions. He is prepared to accept a new ideology every day. He changes opinion and allies frequently. He uses everyone, before discarding them. But Mira acts out of conviction. She wants a Greater Serbia, at any cost' (translated by author from Windgassen, 2002, p. 245).

She attested to this and has said 'Ideology has never meant as much to my husband as it does to me ... he would never say, "I'll die for socialism, I'll die for internationalism" like I would' (Doder & Branson, 1999, p. 138). Mira saw herself as an ideologue, feminist and socialist (Orizio, 2004, p. 190; Post, 2004, p. 180). Mira explained:

> 'I believe in a new kind of Socialism based on the best models, theoretical and practical, of Socialism as we have known it up to now and of capitalism. ... What matters is that in this society people should be happy, live well, have equal rights. As for nationalism that's another lie about us: we are patriotic not nationalistic' (Orizio, 2004, p. 190).

Many believe Mira's staunch belief in socialism stems from her mum's history (Sell, 2002, p. 17) and had said that 'communism is in my genes' (Doder & Branson, 1999, p. 20). Mira was not a nationalist, she had always stood firmly by the communist ideology and it remains difficult to understand how Mira's anti-nationalist sentiment fitted within their lives (LeBor, p. 182). While one political advisor believed that 'she poured all her left-wing ideology into him, and he accepted it' (LeBor, 2003, p. 22), it seems questionable to what extent either was committed to their preferred ideology, nationalist, left wing or otherwise. Orizio found that it was Mira's idea to use nationalism rather than her beloved communist ideology in the political arena, understanding it would be much more popular among the people (2004, pp. 174-175).

Considering the influence she held over her husband, her role should be taken into account when analysing his decision-making process. Ultimately, the question then becomes to what extent she changed or influenced the choices he would otherwise make. It seems at times she may have hampered his ability to compromise somewhat. Some believe it was actually Mira who did not want

Milosevic to give up power when requested to do so by Panic. Also, her more principled stance may have had this effect, but although she likes to present herself as a very principled person, it seems she, like her husband, was pragmatic above all else.

10.7. CONCLUSION

Milosevic acted predominantly out of an instrumental rational orientation. His behaviour was oriented to obtain discrete individual ends (Weber, 1964, p. 117), namely to obtain and maintain power. The desire to obtain power and success was something Milosevic grew up with. Its importance was first emphasized by his mother and after he met Mira, she further stimulated his ambitions. He was focused and serious as a child and young man, more interested in his doing well in school than to attain popularity among his peers. This focus also dominated throughout his career. His personal relationships, even when there was a sincere emotional bond, always also had an instrumental element in them. Mira and Stambolic both had connections that must have been attractive to the young Milosevic. Milosevic's relationship with Mira genuinely seems to be based primarily on love and devotion, but in relation to Stambolic self-interest soon prevailed. He showed he was willing to betray his best friend when this served his best interest. He understood the weaknesses of others, used them and got rid of those people when he saw them as forming a threat, when they got too close or when he did not need them anymore (Doder & Branson, 1999, p. 133; 142; Sell, 2002, p. 175).

He was serious and ambitious but this alone does not answer the question of what he sought to attain. Some believe the nationalist goals were important for Milosevic (Djilas, 1993, p. 87). Doder and Branson, for instance, seem to suggest that Milosevic was committed to the nationalist cause. They argue that 'the few known remarks about his desire to restore Serbia to the glory of its medieval empire reveal[ed] the grip of mythology and folklore on his psyche' (Doder & Branson, 1999, p. 64), but in fact the mythology and folklore had always been important to the Serbs as a nation, and Milosevic, being a Serb himself, of course knew this. There is no reason to assume he believed in it, or that it had a substantial impact on his psyche, it was a tool to manipulate the masses and Milosevic used it as such.

Milosevic changed the focus of his ideology frequently. At the start of his career, he appeared to be a reform minded communist, while later on to a different audience he rather presented himself as a conservative communist, committed to safeguarding Tito's legacy. Then, as he was climbing the political ladder in communist Yugoslavia, nationalism became more popular and just as easily as he was willing to betray his friend to get ahead, he was willing to betray the communist ideology when he realized there were more opportunities for personal glory if he capitalized on the rising nationalism.

There are no signs, however, that he was dedicated to any of the ideologies he put forward. According to LeBor: 'Milosevic was not an idealistic believer in class struggle' (2003, p. 62). As a school friend explained: 'power was his only ideology and he didn't care about anything else' (LeBor, 2003, p. 62). Eventually, Doder and Branson also come to the conclusion that 'Milosevic was driven solely by power' (p. 82). Similarly, Djilas who also found Milosevic to be genuinely concerned with the plight of his people also, refers to Milosevic as an opportunistic politician who 'had no difficulty changing his political stripes from communism to nationalism' (Djilas, 1993, p. 94).

LeBor believes the first wars seem to have been motivated by his hunger for power, but he also notes, Kosovo aroused more passion in him than the earlier wars of the 1990s (LeBor, 2003, p. 146; 184). At the same time, one would expect if this were the case, he would have been more involved in the plight of the Serbs in Kosovo throughout his time in power (Sell, 2002, p. 269). Ultimately, throughout his time in power, when the nationalist ideology started to inhibit attaining or maintaining power, he was willing to make compromises and betray any nationalist goals.

He was never very loyal to the Serbian people. According to Sell, 'he consistently betrayed the interests and lives of the Serbian people' (Sell, 2002, p. 176). This is reflected in his apathy when NATO started its bombing campaign against the Bosnian Serbs and when entire Serbian villages were brutally cleansed in the Krajina region. In addition, he humiliated the Bosnian Serbs at Dayton while giving away Sarajevo, a compromise he must have known was unacceptable to them (LeBor, 2003, pp. 251-252). As he sought to be seen as a peacemaker, he decided to abandon the nationalist goals in the first half of the 1990s (Sell, 2002, p. 170). He manipulated the international community who were indecisive on whether to see him as the key to a solution or the root of the problem (Sell, p. 4).

As Sell explains, Milosevic's 'true objectives ... were to gain, expand and finally, simply hang onto power' (Sell, 2002, p. 4). As President of Serbia, he formally had to tolerate others above him but the federal presidency was largely a ceremonial function, and according to Doder & Branson 'Milosevic was not interested in titles or pomp: his only interest was the real thing – power' (1999, p. 131; 144). He cared for having power, for the sake of having it. Sell explains:

> 'Milosevic did not seem intent on using power for any of the conventional purposes. He was not interested in what he could do with power for his country. Nor, at least until the end, was he concerned with using power to destroy his opponents. Unlike his wife, Milosevic did not seem to be vindictive toward vanquished political foes or even, judging by his friendly behaviour toward Tudjman at Dayton, particularly resentful toward those who bested him. Milosevic, in fact, was not very good at using power for anything other than keeping it' (Sell, 2002, pp. 169-170).

Milosevic thus sought to attain discrete individual ends, in his case power, and acted on the basis of instrumental rationality. According to Weber, when an individual acts on the basis of instrumental rationality, the expectations of others and the changing circumstances will be taken into account. In addition, the relative importance of the different aims is considered, allowing the individual to shift priorities when costs become too high (Varshney, 2003, p. 86). Milosevic was able to recognize that circumstances were changing after he rose to power. He had hoped to be able to dominate Yugoslavia and rule as a second Tito, but he came to realize after Slovenia walked out of the 14th and last session of the League of Communists, that any hope of attaining this goal had evaporated when the representatives of the other republics refused to continue. He then adjusted his goals and strategies, to no longer dominate Yugoslavia in its entirety but to rule over a Greater Serbia, and calculated this feat was actually more easily achieved without Slovenia in Yugoslavia. Milosevic was able to skilfully adapt to short term changing circumstances although he only poorly oversaw the consequences of his actions in the long term. Sell, therefore describes him as a 'brilliant tactician but a disastrous strategist' (Sell, 2002, p. 4).

Throughout his career, Milosevic took into account how he expected others would behave and was willing to shift priorities and abandon certain goals when the costs got too high. This was particularly evident in the manner in which he reacted towards the demonstrations that were frequently being held in opposition to his regime where he would firstly try to subdue them or counteract them, and only if this proved to be impossible sought to appease the crowd. When in 1988 there was a strike of Albanians demanding the reinstatement of Vllasi, Milosevic acted calculatingly, organized a counter demonstration, forcing the army to step in on his behalf to reinstall order. When such a counter attack proved impossible, he was always willing to compromise when the costs got dangerously high, as was the case with the demonstrations of 1991, 1992, 1993 and 1996 – instances in which he eventually acquiesced to the demands of the crowd. When the unrest in the population started to erode his existing power base, he weighed the pros and cons and decided peace was necessary. Milosevic, again taking the changing circumstances into account, decided to transform himself into a peacemaker.

Milosevic did not let any of the ideologies he outwardly seemed to adhere to, truly determine his behaviour. He rather used them selectively when they suited him. Throughout his career, he was willing to sacrifice friends and important nationalist goals in order to stay in power. He strived for discrete individual ends, set out to realize these in a calculating manner and was always willing to compromise and negotiate when he believed he had no other choice.

There are thus elements in Milosevic's life which indicate that instrumental rationality dominated his decision-making throughout most of his life and career. His friends and personal relationships had a functional element and when Milosevic did not need them anymore, he eliminated them. In addition, he changed his ideology frequently, initially being more progressively socialist, then a true conservative, while becoming more nationalist in its discourse towards the population. He never adhered to one ideology but shifted between different ones, depending on the time, place and audience for which he spoke. He subsequently was not loyal to nationalism either when he remained passive as fellow Serbs were being cleansed and bombed and when he humiliated them at Dayton whilst making compromises he knew would be unacceptable to them.

When these factors are also present in the lives of other dictators, they may be indicators that hint that a leader's behaviour is dominated by instrumental rationality. However, these are just indicators which emerged while studying Milosevic. It would be too simplistic to make a list of conditions which each dictator needs to live up to in order to qualify him as an instrumental rational leader. Each dictator requires anew an in-depth analysis in which it is assessed whether ideology or selfish reasons drive his choices. Essentially, each case requires an analysis to assess whether the goal that the dictator seeks to attain is absolute, as was the case with Pol Pot. In the case of Milosevic these factors were clear signs he was never truly committed to the Serb cause but with other leaders, a slightly different picture may emerge.

Milosevic, for instance, was not overspending or living extremely luxurious in the early years and he never excessively enriched himself (LeBor, 2003, p. 65; 213). Even though he and his family gathered a large fortune during his time in office, Milosevic's own lifestyle was relatively modest. He enjoyed expensive cigars and Scotch and started to use some of Tito's luxurious villas as his own but the latter were mainly used as a place to get away and for official purposes (Sell, 2002, p. 171). He never became too corruptible or greedy (Doder & Branson, 1999, pp. 34-229). However, when acquiring wealth and a life of luxury is the primary motivation of a dictator, this too would also be a clear sign of an instrumental rational orientation.

Having identified power as Milosevic's prime motivation begs the question whether his desire for power was absolute, did it become a thing to strive for similar to beauty or honour, did it become an absolute value (Weber, 1964, p. 116). In other words, did power as a goal take on a value rational connotation? Stevanovic believed that 'all he was interested in was power, at any cost' (Stevanovic, 2004, p. 114), suggesting indeed that Milosevic pursued power as a goal regardless of the chances of success or any personal costs it may entail (Varshney, 2003, pp. 86-87; Weber, 1964, p. 116). However, if one would believe those present at the meeting where Milosevic seriously considered leaving power, it becomes apparent that power was not absolute as a goal, but that Milosevic was potentially willing to give it up under extreme circumstances.

The mere fact that value rationality did not predominated Milosevic' decision-making process, does not mean value rationality did not play an important role in the conflicts. Sell seems to suggest as much by arguing that 'without any core beliefs or values other than his own political survival, Milosevic was simply incapable of arousing lasting conviction or sustained sacrifice on the part of others' (Sell, 2002, pp. 151-152). While it is true that there was resistance towards his regime, and often the wars appeared to be deeply unpopular, this statement seems too simplistic. There were certainly those who believed in the greater cause even though Milosevic himself did not. He was an instrumental rational dictator but that does not mean he was not able to arouse value rational sentiments in others (Varshney, 2003). It needs to be remembered Milosevic did not develop the ideology, he 'merely' spread it, and for years after the wars the discourse of the Milosevic regime still lingered among the population (Dimitrijevic, 2008).

As has been discussed in Chapter 5, there are always limitations to the extent to which a person can act perfectly rational; rationality in this sense is always bounded by factors within the person as well as factors related to the institutional environment in which the decisions are taken. Milosevic tended to make most of the decisions on his own (LeBor, 2003, pp. 157-158), but especially after the wars in the first half of the 1990s, his inner circle may have further hampered rational decision-making. He would not easily have gotten a critical question or answer since, according to Sell, Milosevic 'preferred to surround himself with yes men and does not deal easily with criticism' (Sell, 2002, p. 172), thus increasing the chances that groupthink occurs and, as was explained in Chapter 5, this will increase the chances that errors in the decision-making process are made (Mintz & DeRouen, 2010, p. 45). In addition, his emotions may have gotten in the way of perfectly rational decision-making when Milosevic found himself to be frequently distressed emotionally, started to drink and become more recluse (Doder & Branson, 1999, p. 233). Over time, it became clear Milosevic was losing some of his support but he was not ready to relinquish power. The new propaganda message that was put forward by the regime was that Serbia was wrongly blamed for the horrors of the war and the crimes committed throughout the wars were denied (Stevanovic, 2004, p. 119; 124). In addition, Milosevic created crises which he would then resolve, to try to foster admiration in the eyes of his followers (Stevanovic, 2004, p. 115). As Stevanovic pointed out 'if everything ran smoothly, the peacemaker would become insignificant' (Stevanovic, 2004, p. 115). Throughout his career Milosevic had thrived on the politics of fear and needed war to produce the fear that moved the Serbs to rally behind him (Djilas, 1993, p. 88). Luckily for him, unrest was brewing in Kosovo which had been entirely neglected at Dayton.

CHAPTER 11
MILITARY INTERVENTION: LESSONS LEARNED FROM THE WARS WITH NATO AND VIETNAM

11.1. INTRODUCTION

In 1979, Pol Pot was confronted with the threat of military intervention when its border conflict with Vietnam spiralled out of control. Twenty years later Milosevic's survival in power was also at stake when NATO was prepared to bomb Milosevic back to the negotiating table. Each of the leaders had to consider whether they were willing to halt their violent policies in the contested areas and whether they were willing to negotiate a more peaceful resolution to the conflicts. Both of the interventions are likely to have saved the lives of numerous individuals but were highly controversial. To a certain extent, both episodes reflected the time in which they were fought; while Vietnam became an international outcast, NATO's intervention was seen as 'illegal but legitimate' by the Independent International Commission on Kosovo. The Commission argued: 'the intervention was justified because all diplomatic avenues had been exhausted and because the intervention had the effect of liberating the majority population of Kosovo from a long period of oppression under Serbian rule' (The Independent International Commission on Kosovo, 2000, p. 4). In the 1970s, the perpetration of atrocities was never a good reason to infringe upon the sovereign rights of any country, but by the end of the 1990s the international community was torn between the injustice of intervening and the injustice of standing by while innocent civilians are slaughtered. The intervention in Kosovo therefore raised questions about the rightfulness of military intervention for humanitarian purposes and eventually led to the report of the International Commission on Intervention and State Sovereignty in which the responsibility to protect was conceptualised.

Many problems plague military intervention by foreign powers when a regime perpetrates unimaginable atrocities. The dilemma of whether there is a will to intervene, as well as the question whether military intervention should even be considered an option, is discussed extensively elsewhere (e.g. Chomsky,

2012; Power, 2013; Wheeler, 2000).[120] The intention of this chapter is merely to provide an assessment of the possible ways in which different leaders may respond to the threat of, and the actual use of, military force. Scholars have debated the extent to which the decisions of both Milosevic and Pol Pot can be considered rational, considering the military might of the intervening powers and the balance of powers in the international arena.

Samantha Power for instance believes the West in relation to Kosovo was 'failing to imagine evil and was presuming they were dealing with rational actors, even as they demonized Milosevic as a Balkan Hitler' (Power, 2013, p. 451). According to Power, they assumed Milosevic was a rational actor, whose aim was not Greater Serbia but only cared about himself and who would therefore soon buckle under pressure (Power, 2013, pp. 451-452). They assumed he would use the guise of NATO airpower to reach a compromise and cling to power (Power, 2013, p. 452). Her assessment raises the question whether the fact that it took Milosevic much longer than expected to make his way to the negotiation table, necessarily means he is not a rational actor.

As for Cambodia, Jackson notes many wondered whether Cambodia was run by rational individuals because of its continuous cross border skirmishes (K. D. Jackson, 1989, p. 45). Morris for instance stated that 'the behaviour of Cambodia's leaders makes no sense from the perspective of any theory that incorporates a "rational actor" assumption' (Morris, 1999, p. 16). Becker seeks an explanation in the character and state of mind of the leadership. She describes Pol Pot and the Khmer Rouge leadership as emotional, impulsive and unintelligent actors. According to her:

> 'from the end of 1977 through 1978 the Khmer Rouge, through miscalculation and stupidity, transformed what they hoped would be a useful limited border dispute with Vietnam into a full war, in part by saying only total war would fend off the Vietnamese threat ... they proved themselves too mad to control the war' (Becker, 1998, p. 293).

Leighton, too, recognizes that many may perceive the idea of 'little Cambodia challenging its more powerful neighbour' as bizarre or inexplicable (Leighton, 1978, p. 450). Jackson, Leighton and Morris all nevertheless state that the unspeakable fear the Cambodians felt towards the Vietnamese and their revolutionary ideology goes a long way towards explaining the hostilities (K. D. Jackson, 1989, p. 46; Leighton, 1978, p. 450; Morris, 1999, p. 17). Short similarly cites the following explanation:

> 'Cambodia's hostile, if not aggressive, behaviour towards Vietnam and Thailand is not entirely irrational. Cambodia has tried various means [over the centuries] to

---

120 See also Chapter 4.

> fend off its enemies. Nothing has worked well. What is left is ...seemingly irrational behaviour ... The rule, as it is for a small dog surrounded by bigger, stronger dogs, is to bristle, assuming an aggressive posture and so fearfully troublesome, so indifferent to consequences, as to convince others to leave well alone' (Short, 2004, p. 373).

However, while it may explain why a dog would bark, it does not explain why it would continuously bite and actually provoke the occupation of their country, the exact outcome they had feared most of all.

The present chapter investigates the decision-making process of Pol Pot and Milosevic throughout the military intervention by NATO and Vietnam. It will not merely analyse to whether the decision-making process of Pol Pot and Milosevic made sense to an objective observer, but will analyse how the situation they were in was interpreted by the leaders and the extent to which their different kinds of rationality influenced the decisions they made. In order to make a direct comparison between the situations, they will both be discussed in the present chapter.

After a reflection on whether the two cases can be usefully compared to each other in a most similar comparative case study design, the situations leading up to the wars will be investigated. Thereafter, the atrocities that were perpetrated will be discussed as well as the response this provoked internationally. Subsequently, the final attempts to a negotiated peaceful solution to the conflicts will be scrutinised before turning to the interventions and the decision-making process of Pol Pot and Milosevic about whether to come to a negotiated resolution to the conflict.

11.2. MOST SIMILAR COMPARATIVE CASE STUDY

Even though Pol Pot and Milosevic found themselves in remarkably similar situations when they faced the threat of military intervention, they made very different choices. Pol Pot throughout the years had repeatedly refused to come to negotiated resolution of the conflict and was eventually removed from power, while Milosevic's decision to reach a compromise with NATO meant that he was able to rule his country a while longer. The two situations will be compared with each other in a most similar case study design[121], and it is therefore important to analyse to what extent these situations are actually alike and identify differences which may potentially be of importance. It will always be impossible to find two cases that are similar in every single way, and real world occurrences such as these cannot possibly live up to the standards of a lab experiment where all variables can be controlled. The cases under scrutiny here are in no way identical,

---

121 See Chapter 1 for a more elaborate explanation of the most similar case study design methodology as well as its advantages and disadvantages.

but it will be argued that the factors which are most relevant to the present study are nevertheless comparable. As will be explained below, in both situations there was one powerful individual who ultimately had the power to determine the course of action and both of these leaders were confronted with the threat of military intervention because they were perpetrating atrocious crimes in a contested border region. In addition, both of these leaders faced interventions by forces that were much stronger than they were and they were both offered peace deals. Conventional wisdom would therefore dictate that each would do well to consider the peace deal and negotiate a peaceful outcome of the conflict at hand. Yet neither leader seemed to be willing to seriously negotiate, at least not in the beginning.

Before analysing the cases and the decision-making process of Pol Pot and Milosevic in a more detailed manner, it is important to have a more in depth understanding of the similarities and differences of these cases to assess whether they can actually be usefully analysed in a most similar research design.

11.2.1. SIMILARITIES

As was argued in previous chapters, both countries were ruled by non-democratic leaders with a great amount of power. At the same time, when conceptualizing democracy and dictatorship on a scale[122], the degree to which each country can be classified as dictatorial differs. Cambodia in this sense was much more extreme than Serbia with Pol Pot facing less institutional constraints, but as was stated in Chapter 8, Milosevic always played a critical role in the decision-making process. It can furthermore be argued, that his control over the atrocities in Kosovo was even greater than his influence had been during 1990-1995 wars. As Daalder and O'Hanlon explain:

> 'Whereas Milosevic had relied primarily on local Serb surrogates in the Croatian and Bosnian wars, the violence in Kosovo was directly controlled by him and involved land within Serbia itself that was of great historical, cultural, and religious importance to all Serbs' (Daalder & O'Hanlon, 2000, p. vii).

As president of Yugoslavia he was formally the supreme commander and also used this authority to make all the important decisions himself (LeBor, 2003, p. 282). In addition, according to LeBor, 'Milosevic appears to have taken a much greater role in micro-managing the Kosovo war than in Bosnia or Croatia' (LeBor, 2003, p. 282).

Because Kosovo was seen as an autonomous province of Serbia, rather than a fully-fledged republic during Tito's reign, and because the calls for independence

---

122 See Chapter 2 for a full explanation on how dictatorship and democracy are usually no longer seen as mutually excluding categories but as either ends of a spectrum.

had remained peaceful, the region had been neglected during the Dayton Accords. Kosovo was of tremendous importance to the Serbs which made it all the more troubling that they were now seeking independence. The violence that was used to subdue the Kosovar Albanian calls for independence escalated to the point where mass atrocities were perpetrated, causing many refugees to spill across borders into neighbouring countries (Power, 2013, pp. 449-450). Pol Pot, too, faced the threat of military intervention because of horrendous atrocities his troops were perpetrating in a contested border region. There had been a long lasting border dispute between Vietnam and Cambodia, with the latter believing they had historic rights to what used to be Cochinchina, which had fallen into Vietnamese hands. In addition, both countries claimed rights over a few islands in the gulf of Siam and an area along the seacoast that was deemed to be of economic importance due to the supposed presence of oil (Pouvatchy, 1986, pp. 441-442; Short, 2004, p. 357).

In both situations, the army that threatened to invade was much bigger and more powerful than their own. NATO estimated that the Serbs had dispatched some 15,000 army troops and another 14,000 heavily armed police to Kosovo. The Serb government had a defence budget of about 1,5 billion US dollar annually, and in total 110,000 active duty personnel, excluding the thousands of heavily armed police units. While substantial, it does not compare with NATO's 4,000,000 active duty military personnel or their combined defence budget of 450 billion US dollar (Daalder & O'Hanlon, 2000, p. 103). The Vietnamese were also much stronger than their Cambodian counterpart was. For their final offensive, the Vietnamese sent over 100,000 troops across the border, which were supported by another 20,000 Cambodian fighters and a number of planes that flew forty to fifty sorties per day (Power, 2013, p. 142). They had helicopters, aircrafts and heavy artillery at their disposal (Chandler, 1999, p. 155). Pol Pot's forces consisted of about 30,000 armed men and women which were joined by another 100,000 villagers and conscripts (Chandler, 1999, p. 157). Overall, while Cambodia had no more than 70,000 troops at its disposal, for the Vietnamese this was estimated at 615,000 in 1977 (Morris, 1999, p. 103). Next to the disparity in troop size, and the quality of the weaponry, the population in Vietnam was much larger. Vietnam had a population of 50 million, while there were only about 7 million people living in Cambodia and on top of that, the Vietnamese population was in a better condition since most Cambodians were weak and exhausted from the years of repression (Morris, 1999, p. 103).

While both interventions were largely justified in humanitarian terms, in both cases strategic and security interests were also on the line, and for Vietnam its territorial integrity played an important role as well as possibly its imperial ambitions (Bazyler, 1987, p. 608; Chandler, 1999, p. 133; Etcheson, 1984, pp. 193-194; Morris, 1999, p. 16; Power, 2013, p. 448). Both parties were also offered peace deals on numerous occasions, suggesting that for both leaders there potentially was a way out of their predicament. Although, as will be discussed in more detail below, the peace agreements that were proposed in relation to the conflict with Pol Pot were very broad and mere requests to start a dialogue, while in the Serbian case they were generally much more elaborate.

11.2.2. DIFFERENCES

Before turning to an analysis of the manner in which each of the two leaders reached the decision of whether or not to negotiate a peaceful solution, it is important to delineate which factors differed in the case studies and the extent to which this may have influenced their decision. Perhaps the most evident difference is the era in which each of the dictators operated. Pol Pot reigned in the midst of the Cold War while the conflict over Kosovo escalated only in the 1990s, after the Cold War had come to an end. International power relations, as was explained in Chapter 5, are often seen as an important explanatory factor within international relations, particularly within theories that discount the influence of the individual leader. The extent to which the foreign policy of a particular state is determined by the 'system of states' or rather by the individuals who rule them, is already addressed in a theoretical sense in Chapter 5. It is argued that while certainly these macro influences should not be neglected, ultimately decisions are made by individuals who process, value and interpret these factors. Beyond the theoretical argument, however, it is important to analyse how this played out in this particular case study.

The question therefore becomes, how important the influence of the Great Powers and the Cold War competition for regional influence was on the conflict in Cambodia. It should be acknowledged that this was significant. Zbigniew Brzezinski, who was US National Security Advisor at the time, even argued that the conflict between Cambodia and Vietnam was a 'proxy war' between its great power patrons, China and the Soviet Union (Leighton, 1978, p. 450). In this proxy war Vietnam was backed by the Soviet Union while Cambodia received aid from China (Short, 2004, pp. 373-374). The struggle for power and influence over Cambodia was globalized because of Vietnam's choice to alienate China and align itself with the Soviet Union, which according to Morris 'convinced Beijing that Hanoi's actions in Cambodia were in Moscow's interests, at Moscow's behest, and threatening to Chinese security' (Morris, 1999, p. 6). In this sense Vietnam's tendencies to expand its power and sphere of influence, which were reflected in the history of the region[123], was an important factor that dominated the relationship between China and Cambodia as well. The Chinese viewed Vietnam as a risk because it could spread Soviet influence throughout the region, and since the communists in Laos were too weak to form any sort of barrier to

123 See Chapter 7.

Vietnamese influence, the Chinese had cast their hopes on Cambodia (Short, 2004, pp. 300-301). The relationship between the two was mutually beneficial, Cambodia posed an opportunity for China to contain the Vietnamese influence in the region by keeping Cambodia strong, and in turn Cambodia received military and economic aid and training (Short, 2004, p. 301).

Burchett also notes that especially China seems to have had an enormous influence on the decisions made by Pol Pot on behalf of his country. According to Burchett, China was determining the foreign policy of Cambodia:

> 'By then Peking was running Khmer Rouge affairs. ... Whereas Vietnam had stubbornly refused to be placed in China's pocket, Pol Pot had jumped into it himself. China has been charged on many occasions with being interested in fighting the United States to the last Vietnamese and was certainly no less averse to fighting Vietnam to the last Kampuchean' (Burchett, 1981, p. 149).

Burchett argues Cambodia was only willing to take on the Vietnamese, because they believed they had the backing of China and because there were 7,000-8,000 military 'advisers' from China on the ground already and the country had been providing extensive material military to Cambodia (Burchett, 1981, pp. 149; 165-170). In addition, Burchett notes that the Vietnamese proposal to have a UN mission present on the ground was blocked by China and the same fate befell the plan to have a non-aligned good offices mission (Burchett, 1981, p. 161). On this basis, it may be argued that Pol Pot's actions were objectively rational because he may have believed the Chinese would come in to save them, but, as will be explained later, the Chinese had in fact clearly limited their support and had actually refused to send troops or 'volunteers'. Ultimately, neither China nor the Soviet Union actually promoted the violence between the countries, nor did they benefit from it (Leighton, 1978, p. 450). China actually seems to have discouraged Pol Pot from continuing further along this aggressive path (Ciorciari, 2014, p. 232) and was therefore actually more of a moderating influence than is acknowledged by some scholars. China seems to have feared, more so than the Cambodians themselves, that the policies of Pol Pot would ultimately cause the country to self-destruct (Morris, 1999, p. 85). In addition, as Morris pointed out, the Soviet Union which was supporting Vietnam was more powerful than China during this time (Morris, 1999, p. 5). The influence of Russia and China in the Cold War context therefore still makes Pol Pot's decision to continue to fight difficult to reconcile in particular with realist and liberalist theories of IR which assume that a state acts rationally in pursuit of increasing or maintaining power and/or economic prosperity.[124] Cambodia, nevertheless, continued to provoke war with its neighbour, and while China influenced the decisions of the Khmer

124 See Chapter 5 for more information on the state of the art of IR theories, the role that rationality plays therein and the remaining gaps in the research.

Rouge leadership, it could not determine their policy in its entirety (Morris, 1999, p. 84).

Of course influential allies did not seize to play a role after the Cold War ended and Russia in this respect was very important for Serbia. However, like China had done in the case of Cambodia, Russia had made it very clear to Serbia that its support was limited. It ensured that no UN Security Council resolutions were passed that explicitly approved armed military intervention, but would not back up Milosevic' regime in any military sense in case conflict broke out (Hosmer, 2001, pp. 42-47; Vrieze, 2000, p. 45). The differences in this respect are therefore not as big is they initially appear to be.

When Russia indicated towards Milosevic that it planned to withdraw its support, as will be explained more in depth later, this was an important factor which caused Milosevic to reach a compromise with NATO (Hosmer, 2001, p. xiii). Yet China's words of moderation seemed to have had little impact on Pol Pot, even though one would expect the influence of powerful patrons to have been much bigger during the Cold War. It seems that the influence of other powerful countries did not pre-determine a particular outcome in either of the case studies, and it is therefore worthwhile investigating the role the individual played and analyse how the individual leaders perceived and interpreted the relevant domestic and international factors that played a role.

11.3. BEFORE THE WARS

Neither of the two conflicts materialized overnight. There was a long history of animosity between the warring parties, which was discussed in more detail in Chapters 7 and 8. This cultural baggage influenced the manner in which the leaders interpreted the events that unfolded at the end of the 1970s and 1990s. As Staub notes, leaders cannot be insulated from the society from which they stem (Staub, 2010, p. 174) and the history of a country, when kept alive through stories and myths, is part of the history of the leader who grew up hearing them. He will know what is important for the national identity of his country, even when it is not important to him personally. This needs to be kept in mind while the more immediate history of the conflicts is narrated below.

11.3.1. THE DISPUTE WITH VIETNAM

As was explained in previous chapters, Cambodia and Vietnam have a long history of subjugation and domination and the border dispute between the countries pre-date Pol Pot's rise to power. When the French ruled over Cambodia from 1863 until 1953 they redrew the borders of the country. In relation to Thailand, the changes turned out rather favourably, but in the east, large swathes of Cambodian territory were designated to be under the control of the Vietnamese (Chandler, 2008, pp. 167-168; Morris, 1999, p. 32). The French did so without prior consent of the Cambodian king. Most prominently, Cochin-china region (or Kampuchea Krom), which encompassed the region surrounding Saigon, was designated as being Vietnamese in 1948 through the Along Bay agreement (Morris, 1999, p. 32;91).

After Cambodia gained independence in 1953, the border issues flared up (Amer, 1997, p. 80). While Sihanouk admitted he desired to reclaim some of the lost land, he acted cautiously (Morris, p. 39). He requested the Vietnamese to respect the 'existing borders' of Cambodia and the Communist Democratic Republic of Vietnam and its National Liberation Front were forthcoming with such a promise. The government of the Republic of Vietnam in Saigon, at the same time, would not make the same commitment (Amer, 1997, p. 80). Consequently, Sihanouk became more supportive of Hanoi while its relations with Saigon became strained. It was not until Sihanouk was overthrown and Lon Nol entered the picture that they improved (Amer, 1997, p. 80). Eventually the communist forces were victorious in both countries. After the victories the promise of the Vietnamese communists to respect Cambodian borders proved to be an empty one and the old border disputes boiled up again (Becker, 1998, p. 300).

At the start of Pol's reign, many Cambodians still felt the humiliation of having the Kampuchea Krom region taken away from them, and still glowing from their victory at home, the Khmer Rouge were determined to recapture the region (Morris, 1999, p. 92). Immediately there were military encounters along the borders and over islands in the Gulf of Thailand (Amer, 1997, p. 80; Morris, 1999, p. 92). There had been several meetings to resolve the border dispute even before the conflict escalated. In the first two years of Pol Pot's rule, the leadership of the two countries tried to negotiate a solution but failed time and again. To the Khmer Rouge it seemed like Vietnam was unwilling to uphold the agreement that was made with Sihanouk in 1967 when it recognized Cambodia's borders (Becker, 1998, p. 300).

The first meeting was arranged in Hanoi in June 1975 which resulted in relatively peaceful coexistence for the rest of the year and for most of 1976 (Amer, 1997, p. 80). In May 1976, talks were held in Phnom Penh to prepare for a subsequent summit in Hanoi when a border treaty was meant to come to fruition. While the Cambodians were not seeking an immediate escalation of the conflict, tension noticeably started to build up (Short, 2004, p. 356). The Cambodians had been willing to make some concessions and expressed the preparedness to recognize *de jure* Vietnamese ownership of the islands, but now started to wonder whether their stand had not been a futile policy of appeasement (Short, 2004, p. 357). The Vietnamese in turn disregarded a flagrant attempt by the Cambodian delegation to falsify the map that was to be used to commence negotiations, and were even willing to cede the area (Burchett, 1981, p. 146). More problems arose when they discussed the maritime border.

The Vietnamese claimed an additional stretch which they believed to contain oil, and according to Short, the Khmer Rouge leadership felt Vietnam was behaving as a 'neighbourhood bully' (Short, 2004, p. 357). The negotiations were suddenly suspended by the Cambodian delegation that refused to hear the Vietnamese proposal on how to settle the maritime border (Burchett, 1981, p. 146). In the end, the two sides could only agree on a three-pronged pledge that 'all conflicts must be settled in a spirit of solidarity, friendship, and mutual respect and that the liaison committees of the two sides must investigate and meet to settle them' (Burchett, 1981, p. 146).

While outwardly relations remained cordial, a speech made by Pol Pot in June showed that tensions were building. According to Pol,

> 'there is a continuous, non-stop struggle between revolution and counterrevolution. We must keep to the standpoint that there will be enemies 10 years, 20 years, 30 years into the future. Are [these enemies] strong or not? That does not depend on them. It depends on us. If we constantly take absolute measures, they will be scattered and smashed to bits' (Short, 2004, p. 357)

The Party and the country needed to maintain and build up its strength, in order to face their enemies that were present inside, but also outside of the country. According to Pol Pot 'outside enemies are just waiting to crush us … enemies of all kinds want to have small countries as their servants' (Short, 2004, p. 358). It was an unambiguous reference to Vietnam (Short, 2004, p. 358).

In July Pol decided that the country needed to start preparing for war with Thailand and Vietnam (Short, 2004, p. 359). A few months later in December 1976, Defence Minister Son Sen described the changing relationship with the Vietnamese:

> 'before Vietnam was our friend, but 'a friend with a conflict'. Now it has become our real enemy' (Short, 2004, p. 363).

Pol Pot, by this time, was describing the relationship between Cambodia and Vietnam to the Central Committee as a 'constant, antagonistic contradiction' (Short, 2004, p. 363) but not everyone in the party felt so strongly. The party was divided and Pol Pot devised a rouse to identify everyone who was likely to disagree with him. He changed the date the party was ostensibly created, not only to assert its independence and dissociate from the help they received in the beginning from the Vietnamese communists, but also to see who would protest. This move not only rearranged the history of the party but also undermined the authority of senior members of the party (Becker, 1998, p. 301). Thiounn Mumm explains:

> 'In 1977 there was a violent fight between the patriots who said that Kampuchea must be independent of Vietnam and those who said Kampuchea must be close friends with Vietnam. This battle continued until the middle of 1978' (Becker, 1998, p. 300).

Spurred on by the confessions that were gathered at Tuol Sleng, purges within the party picked up pace (Becker, 1998, p. 301; Short, 2004, pp. 359-360). Pol Pot and Duch had become convinced that the Vietnamese were interfering with their policies, and according to Becker, 'all soon discovered there was no choice but to agree with Pol Pot or die' (Becker, 1998, pp. 301-302). The story that was created was that by taking on Vietnam, they were also fighting the Soviet Union, which Becker believes 'suited Pol Pot's psychological and political purposes. … Just as he and the party claimed to have defeated the United States in the earlier war, now they claimed to be beset by the other superpower' (Becker, 1998, p. 304).

Pol's hatred and distrust of the Vietnamese partly explains why his regime was so incredibly brutal and forms an integral part of his communist vision of the world. One of the reasons Pol Pot felt that the revolution should be completed very soon was because he believed that Cambodia's neighbours formed a constant threat to the nation. In 1976 he said:

> 'Why must we move so swiftly? Because enemies attack and torment us. From the east and the west they persist in pounding and worrying us; this is their strategy … If we are slow and weak, the contemptible people to the west will mistreat us also. If, on the other hand, we are strong and courageous for one, two, three, or four years, the contemptible people to the east and the contemptible people to the west will be unable to do anything to us' (Morris, 1999, p. 72).

The revolution would make the country stronger and would allow them to counter and cope with enemies more easily (Morris, 1999, p. 72). The final years of Pol Pot's reign therefore saw the simultaneous escalation of the hatred towards the Vietnamese, brutal suppression of the influence Pol Pot believed they had inside the country, and the border war.

11.3.2. THE DISPUTE OVER KOSOVO

The historical significance of Kosovo to the Serbs as a nation has been narrated already in Chapter 8 but to fully understand the conflict in 1999, it is important to get a deeper understanding of the last few decades before the war broke out. It may be recalled from Chapter 8 that the more recent foundation of the Kosovo conflict can be traced back to its status as an autonomous region, rather than a republic, in Yugoslavia (Calic, 2000, p. 21; The Independent International Commission on Kosovo, 2000, pp. 34-35). Kosovo Albanians had been subjected to maltreatment by Tito's administration ever since WWII, and while the 1974 constitution was a notable improvement as it allowed the region to govern itself to quite a large extent, its status as an autonomous region formed an impediment to independence later on (Calic, 2000, p. 21; The Independent International Commission on Kosovo, 2000, pp. 34-35). As an autonomous region, Kosovo would not get the same rights as a republic and the inhabitants were considered a nationality (*naradnost*) and not a nation (*narad*). The idea behind the distinction was that the Albanians – as did the Hungarians in Vojvodina – already had a homeland to turn to (The Independent International Commission on Kosovo, 2000, pp. 35-36). The international community would later follow this line of reasoning, making it much more difficult for Kosovo to claim independence (Sell, 2002, p. 262). Consequently, in Kosovo, the issue for the international community was never one of self-determination or independence, it centred on protecting minorities and human rights (Daalder & O'Hanlon, 2000, p. 9).

For several years, independence was also not the immediate aim for the Kosovar Albanians. In the early 1980s, the goal was to change its status in society. Even though the Kosovar Albanians suffered discriminatory measures, most Albanians did not actually want independence as such. The student demonstrations of 1981, for instance, were not necessarily sparked by the desire to be independent, but by a dissatisfaction with feeling like they were second-rate citizens (The Independent International Commission on Kosovo, 2000, p. 36). The demonstrations were put down immediately and many people were arrested, imprisoned and a state of emergency was declared (The Independent International Commission on Kosovo, 2000, p. 36). Academic staff in the universities were fired and Albanian textbooks were no longer available to students (The Independent International Commission on Kosovo, 2000, p. 37). In addition, there was widespread despair over the economic condition the region was in, it had been lagging behind the rest of Yugoslavia for several decades and many people believed that Kosovo would be able to remedy the inequality if it had more control over their economy (The Independent International Commission on Kosovo, 2000, pp. 37-38).

While there were also many Serbs who generally feared for their personal safety and suffered from harassment and discrimination, the media in Belgrade exaggerated the extent to which they were in danger (The Independent International Commission on Kosovo, 2000, pp. 38-39). Rumours were plentiful. The most notorious incident involved the farmer Djordje Martinovic who made the news because he had a bottle inserted in his anus, which some scholars said was reminiscent to the old Turkish practice of impalement (Judah, 2009, p. 156). While it is highly doubtful whether his injuries were the result of an act of aggression (LeBor, 2003, pp. 77-78), it testifies to the climate of fear and suspicion.

Further intensifying fears, was the disparate birth rate between the Albanian and Serb population in the region which, combined with the decision of many Serbs to leave the region, slowly changed the ethnic balance, making the Serbs an increasingly marginal minority (Power, 2013, p. 445). Policies were enacted to turn the trend around: Serbs and Montenegrins were stimulated to return while there were incentives for Albanians to go and work in other parts of Yugoslavia. In addition, there were restrictions on selling property to Albanians and family planning was encouraged for the Albanian community (The Independent International Commission on Kosovo, 2000, p. 41).

Nationalists from the Serbian Academy of Arts and Sciences gave a voice to the dissatisfied Serbs. The memorandum which was leaked to the press charged that genocide was in fact perpetrated against the Serb population and further stimulated anti-Albanian sentiment (Power, 2013, p. 445). The manner in which Milosevic stimulated this development and built a career by riding this wave of nationalism has already been covered in Chapter 8. Milosevic' rise to power enabled him to revoke Kosovo's autonomous status and thereafter discrimination and human rights violations against the Kosovar Albanian population became much more prevalent (The Independent International Commission on Kosovo, 2000, p. 41). Many were harassed, shop owners were subjected to different fiscal measures and there was even plunder (Doder & Branson, 1999, p. 240). In addition, there were also discriminatory language policies, Albanian cultural and media institutions were closed and importantly, the school system was required to teach a Serbian curriculum (The Independent International Commission on Kosovo, 2000, p. 41). Many people lost their jobs, arrests became more arbitrary and frequently people were detained without a trial (The Independent International Commission on Kosovo, 2000, p. 42).

While Milosevic was gathering power in Serbia and as the living conditions in Kosovo worsened, the Democratic League of Kosovo (LDK) was established in December 1989 (Judah, 2008, p. 69). They set up a parallel state system with a parallel school system, health care services and Ibrahim Rugova was elected as its President (Judah, 2009, p. 314). Taxes were paid on a voluntary basis but hardly anyone chose to opt out from paying them, even though the additional tax was crippling for many (The Independent International Commission on Kosovo, 2000, pp. 46-48). Soon the informal economy made up 70 % of the total economic activity and provided many new job opportunities (The Independent International Commission on Kosovo, 2000, p. 47). While to some extent it was tolerated that the Kosovar Albanians set up their parallel state, beatings, arrests and intimidation remained rife (Sell, 2002, p. 269). By 1993 the living conditions were so horrendous, ethnic Albanians started to leave the region, a process some have referred to as 'silent cleansing' (Sell, 2002, p. 270). Milosevic, in the meantime, upped the military presence in the region when the wars in the rest of Yugoslavia broke out and distributed arms to the Serbian population, hoping this would deter the Kosovar Albanians from initiating another violent conflict (Sell, 2002, p. 269).

11.4. THE ATROCITIES AND THE INTERNATIONAL RESPONSE

The conflicts had been brewing for years and when the conflicts finally turned violent, the ferocity with which the wars were fought proved disastrous for the civilian population living in the area. While the conflict in Kosovo received much more media attention and was better documented, there were witnesses in both countries who expressed being horrified by the atrocities that were perpetrated.

11.4.1. THE ATROCITIES IN VIETNAM AND THE INTERNATIONAL RESPONSE

Ever since 1973, Cambodian forces had been occasionally engaged in armed attacks against the Vietnamese, mostly within their own country but at times across the Vietnamese border (Morris, 1999, p. 95). At the time of their victory in 1975, the Khmer Rouge had control over approximately 55,000-60,000 troops and was no match for the Vietnamese army which encompassed 685,000 troops, and was technologically more advanced (Morris, 1999, p. 92). Nevertheless, this did not withhold the Khmer Rouge from attacking islands in the Gulf of Thailand a few weeks later in early May (Morris, 1999, p. 92). Like the Kampuchea Krom region, the islands had been assigned to Vietnam by the French colonialists and the Khmer Rouge decided they would reclaim them (Morris, 1999, p. 92).

First on May 4, the Phu Cuoc island was invaded, after initially refusing to withdraw their troops after the Vietnamese emphasized they were trespassing on their territory, the Cambodian army eventually withdrew after 'a demonstration of force' by Vietnam (Burchett, 1981, p. 145). Just days later, Cambodian forces occupied the Vietnamese island Tho Chu (Poulo Panjang), killing many of the island's inhabitants. On May 25th Vietnam decided to initiate a counterattack, and when Cambodian forces retreated, they took 515 civilians from the island who were presumably killed (Burchett, 1981, p. 145). The Vietnamese decided to take a stand and retaliated in early June by seizing the Cambodian island Hon Troc (Poulo Wai) (Burchett, 1981, p. 145; Morris, 1999, p. 92). In less than a month the Vietnamese recaptured not only the islands but also captured several hundred Cambodian soldiers which were returned after the Vietnamese were given assurances no more attacks would follow (Burchett, 1981, p. 145; Morris, 1999, p. 92). Afterwards an attempt was made to restore the relationship between the countries. That summer Pol Pot welcomed representatives of Vietnam and dismissed the incident as mistaken geography by lower level cadre (Morris, 1999, p. 92). In addition, Pol Pot and Nuon Chea travelled to Vietnam to commence negotiations on the border dispute. An effort was made to portray the relationship between the countries as cordial (Morris, 1999, pp. 92-93).

In May 1976, the preparations for further negotiations between Vietnam and Cambodia took place in Phnom Penh. While the Cambodians hoped they could contain the situation, they were also clear that they would guard their territorial integrity (Burchett, 1981, pp. 145-146; Short, 2004, p. 356). As explained above, the negotiations failed and while friendly relations were maintained on the outside, the inner circle in Cambodia started to question whether they should continue the present strategy (Short, 2004, p. 357). The situation nevertheless remained relatively peaceful for another year with public displays of affection that showcased their warm relationship. Radio Phnom Penh, for instance, broadcasted a commentary which was entitled: 'Militant Solidarity and Friendship Between Peoples of Democratic Cambodia and the SRV Grow Constantly Greener and Sturdier', and Vietnam publicly voiced its admiration for Cambodia's achievements (Morris, 1999, pp. 93-94). The open displays of affection concealed the true animosity that was still overwhelmingly present (Morris, 1999, p. 95). On occasion Pol Pot alluded to tensions between the countries and in July 1976 hinted that problems could arise but that Cambodia would always continue to take a principled stance. According to Pol, the friendship between the Vietnamese and Cambodia was a 'strategic question and a sacred sentiment … only when this friendship and solidarity is strong can the revolution of the two countries develop satisfactorily', but continued 'obstacles and difficulties' could emerge and that Cambodia would always 'stand firmly on this position' (Morris, 1999, p. 94). By the end of 1976 he argued that the country needed to prepare itself to take up arms against the Vietnamese because he thought they were 'lying in wait, looking for opportunities to make trouble … Every day they are making plans to destroy us' (Short, 2004, p. 359; 363).

In April 1977, on the two-year anniversary of their victories, the gloves came off. While the Vietnamese elaborately congratulated their neighbour on the landmark, Pol Pot did not respond in kind. The Cambodians chose the second anniversary of Vietnam's victory to attack several villages in the South of the country, leaving hundreds of civilians dead (Morris, 1999, p. 98). Throughout the next few months, systematic attacks followed. The Vietnamese chose to retaliate but also proposed to find a more peaceful solution, an offer which was rejected outright by the Khmer Rouge (Morris, 1999, pp. 98-99).

The border attacks were extremely vicious. A Vietnamese official remembered that the 'most barbarous crimes were committed. Women were raped, then disembowelled, [and] children cut in two. Pagodas and schools were burnt down' (Short, 2004, p. 372). Chanda narrates the massacre of hundreds of civilians in the Tay Ninh province of Vietnam, which was witnessed by the Hungarian journalist Gyori, who was taken to a village which had been attacked by the Khmer Rouge two days earlier (Chanda, 1986, p. 193).

> 'In house after house bloated, rotting bodies of men, women and children lay strewn about. Some were beheaded, some had their bellies ripped open, some were missing limbs, others eyes' (Chanda, 1986, p. 194).

The Khmer Rouge murdered entire families, with the occasional survivor only being able to tell the tale because she pretended to be dead, hiding under a pile of bodies (Chanda, 1986, p. 220). Several days later, the Vietnamese congratulated Pol Pot when he announced the existence of the Kampuchean Communist Party, which had been shrouded in mystery until that time. Vietnam continued to hope that an all-out war could be avoided (Morris, 1999, p. 99). They soon started to believe, however, that the situation had become untenable and started to contemplate removing Pol Pot from power (Morris, 1999, p. 101). From October 1977 onwards, Vietnam started to organize Cambodian refugees to build up a resistance movement and the Tay Ninh massacre sparked the defection of Khmer officials who would become important players in the downfall of the regime (Chanda, 1986, p. 197; Morris, 1999, p. 101). Fearing the consequences of an openly hostile attitude towards Cambodia for their relationship with China, Vietnam decided to act cautiously (Morris, 1999, p. 100). Early diplomatic efforts in the summer of 1977, however, failed when Cambodia refused to meet Vietnamese representatives and Vietnam refused to acquiesce to Cambodia's demand to withdraw its forces a kilometre from the border (Becker, 1998, pp. 309-310; Short, 2004, p. 373).

In September 1977 Pol Pot expressed his gloomy vision on the conflict during a meeting with the Chinese Chairman Hua.

> 'The Vietnamese have an expansionist policy towards South-East Asia. We tried to negotiate with them, but it was useless … From a strategic point of view, only the development of the revolutionary movement in South-East Asia will really solve this problem. Otherwise the difficulties between Cambodia and Vietnam will go on for who knows how many centuries' (Short, 2004, p. 376).

The Chinese found this far-fetched and urged a peaceful settlement (Short, 2004, p. 376). China hosted a visit of Pol Pot and Vietnam's chief negotiator in October but the talks amounted to no more than an endless stream of accusations back and forth (Chanda, 1986, p. 199; Short, 2004, p. 376). Pol Pot confessed at a news conference he was concerned that there was an 'enemy' which was 'trying to strike [Cambodia] from within and without' (Short, 2004, p. 376).

In December a Chinese Politbureau member flew to Cambodia for a ten day visit (Chanda, 1986, p. 203). While not making direct references to the conflict, he expressed China's support for Cambodia and explicitly stated that 'no force can stand in the way of friendly relations between China and Cambodia, which will be comrades forever' (Chanda, 1986, p. 203). A few days later, the Lao President tried to bring about a negotiated solution, a final attempt which Pol

Pot immediately indicated was absolutely pointless. He refused to listen 'and he just kept on saying all sorts of bad things about Vietnam', according to one Lao official (Chanda, 1986, pp. 204-205). Pol Pot rather made use of the opportunity to urge Laos to take on a more independent stance *vis a vis* the Vietnamese as well (Chanda, 1986, p. 205).

Vietnam eventually launched its first substantive attack on Cambodian soil in October 1977 (Chanda, 1986, p. 196). They inflicted numerous casualties on the Khmer forces but the latter was not deterred (Chanda, p. 196). By December 1977 the border war was escalating, and Vietnam sent 20,000 men into Cambodia's 'Parrot's Beak' province, Svay Rieng (Morris, 1999, p. 101). Pol Pot, and the other party leaders, had not anticipated such a violent and large scale military campaign, and were unprepared for the limited opposition that their forces were able to muster (Chanda, 1986, pp. 206-207). The Cambodian's were outnumbered two to one (Becker, 1998, p. 310) and Pol Pot's domestic policies had made the tragedy all the greater. Most of the doctors had been sent to the countryside for hard labour and there was very little medical assistance to those soldiers who were brought back wounded. The hospitals were now filled with peasant boys who were assigned the role of 'revolutionary doctor', with disastrous consequences (Chanda, 1986, p. 206).

The Khmer Rouge leadership opted for a political as well as military response. They decided to send additional troops to the Eastern Zone to fight the Vietnamese, but more importantly they chose to denounce Vietnamese aggression before the world and severe all diplomatic ties with their powerful neighbour (Chanda, 1986, p. 207; Morris, 1999, p. 102). The statement that was made on behalf of the Cambodian government was, according to Burchett, 'a virulent tirade against Vietnam' (Burchett, 1981, p. 150). Pol Pot explained they needed to 'firmly stir up national hatred and class hatred for the aggressive Vietnamese enemy' and wanted his forces to 'kill the enemy at will, and the contemptible Vietnamese (*a-yuon*) will surely shriek like monkeys screeching all over the forest.' They needed to 'smash them so that they are completely gone from our beloved land' with just 'piles of the enemy's bones' left (Kiernan, 1996, pp. 386-387).

The Vietnamese withdrew in January 1978, which was celebrated as 'an even greater victory than April 17 1975' for Khmer forces, even though they had suffered many losses (Chanda, 1986, p. 213; 298; Morris, 1999, p. 102). Their military setback seemed minor compared to the embarrassment which they managed to inflict on the Vietnamese (Chanda, 1986, p. 207). The Vietnamese in fact, it seems could have easily taken the capital already at this point in time, but doing so was not politically expedient from a Vietnamese perspective and they merely hoped to sway Pol Pot from using violence any further (Morris, 1999, p. 102). In this objective they utterly failed. On behalf of the Cambodian leadership the following statement was issued

> 'Our 6 January victory over the annexationist, expansionist, Vietnamese aggressor enemy has given all of us greater confidence in the forces of our people and nation, in our KCP [Kampuchean Communist Party] and our Cambodian Revolutionary Army and in our Party's line of people's war' (Morris, 1999, p. 103).

They backed up these words with military means and continued their cross-border attacks (Morris, 1999, p. 103).

While it is impossible to know with certainty whether Pol Pot had Peking's blessing or informed them beforehand of their plans, it is plausible that the political move was also aimed to force China to choose sides and more unequivocally declare their support to Cambodia and deliver on its promises of military aid (Chanda, 1986, p. 209). China was unhappy with the move, and arranged for another meeting to work out a political solution (Chanda, 1986, p. 210). China, determined to keep the Soviet Union which backed Vietnam, at bay, and prevent further escalation, sent a Chinese representative to Cambodia to further the road to peace. Pol Pot, however, denied their request to meet with Sihanouk, and in addition, refused to contemplate further negotiations (Chanda, 1986, p. 210). The country's independence was again stressed and they further insulted China by emphasizing they would only accept friends who treated them as equals (Chanda, 1986, p. 211). Cambodia's radio announced: 'we distinguish between good and bad friends. We respect and love friends who are good to us, who respect the independence, sovereignty, and territorial integrity of Cambodia, and who deal with us on an equal footing. But our friend making criterion is not based on whether this or that friend can provide material aid' (Chanda, 1986, p. 211). Chanda argues that 'Pol Pot's defiance narrowed Peking's options' (Chanda, 1986, p. 211), especially since Vietnam by this time was accusing China of using Cambodia to attack their country (Chanda, 1986, p. 212). It might have been this provocation by the Vietnamese, or Pol Pot's stance that they were not going to bend to accommodate Peking's wishes, but China decided to let go of its hope for a political solution and its policy of outward neutrality, and provide Pol Pot with material aid (Chanda, 1986, p. 212).

After the retreat of Vietnam's soldiers from the Eastern Zone, a new round of purges began since Pol Pot reasoned that the only explanation for the losses which they suffered must have been that there remained traitors in their ranks (Chanda, 1986, p. 213; Morris, 1999, p. 106). Pol Pot believed during this time he was infallible and stronger than ever, but while he was given records that showed the production of rice was improving, the documents were overly optimistic (Becker, 1998, pp. 293-294). As domestic policies started to flounder, the Khmer Rouge leadership needed to place the blame elsewhere (Becker, 1998, p. 291). They started targeting numerous zone secretaries, especially those who had had previous contacts with the Vietnamese (Becker, 1998, p. 291). Pol was convinced that there had been several traitors that needed to be dealt with immediately (Becker, 1998, p. 310). The Eastern Zone was then cleansed from numerous individuals in the leadership as well as ordinary people (Becker, 1998, p. 311). Becker explains that 'Phnom Penh was preparing for a border war with Vietnam and wanted no traitors in positions of importance' (Becker, 1998, p. 296).

The Vietnamese in the meantime chose to change course, building an armed opposition force of the numerous Khmer that were now residing in their country after they had fled Pol Pot's brutal regime (Chanda, 1986, pp. 214-215). Those who fled from the Eastern zone, were used to build up a force that was prepared to counter Pol Pot (Becker, 1998, pp. 312-313).

While the attacks on Vietnam would have the most detrimental consequences for the Khmer Rouge, and will be the main focus of this chapter, the attacks on Thailand are equally puzzling. It is difficult to comprehend why the Khmer Rouge would want to create two fronts and perpetrate continuous attacks against Thai villages while the latter seems to have been adamant to retain amicable relations with the Khmer Rouge (Morris, 1999, pp. 78-79).

The violence against the Thai population living in the border region was brutal (Becker, 1998, p. 291). The Thai government communicated that witnesses to the attack were shocked by the 'unprecedented savagery' but overall the atrocities on Thai territory were minor in comparison to those that befell the villages along the border with Vietnam (Burchett, 1981, pp. 153-155). Despite the occasional warning that military retaliation would follow, overall the Thai prioritised keeping the relationship between the countries as good as possible. Some of the Thai leaders even believed that the attacks were not coordinated by the higher echelons of the Khmer Rouge but were the work of renegade soldiers (Morris, 1999, p. 78). While evidence cumulated that these were coordinated attacks which supported Thai communist insurgents, and even though this knowledge also spread within the Thai government, some wishful thinking that this was not the work of the Khmer Rouge leadership remained until the spring of 1978 (Morris, 1999, pp. 78-81). The skirmishes lasted until the summer of 1978, when the Chinese interfered and ensured Ieng Sary travelled to Thailand (Morris, 1999, p. 82). Sary embarrassed the host government by fiercely denouncing Vietnam during the press-conference, but the visit did signal more peaceful relations between the two countries (Morris, 1999, pp. 82-83).

The attacks on its other neighbour can be explained by Pol's fear that Thailand, too, could form a potential threat or by the desire to further the communist cause in the neighbouring country (Morris, 1999, p. 82; 86). In either case, it is important to acknowledge that the relationship with Thailand was never as tense as it was with Vietnam, due to historical reasons. They had never tried to interfere with their Communist policies, nor did Thailand pose the same threat because militarily it was not as strong (Becker, 1998, p. 292).

After Pol Pot came to a tacit understanding with Thailand that peace should be maintained, and as the border conflict with Vietnam started to escalate, Cambodia and Vietnam started to compete for diplomatic support from

ASEAN. Some ideological compromises were made since countries that were either pro-American or anti-Chinese were visited as well, but this was considered justified by the need to awaken sympathy for their country that was about to be swallowed by their dangerous neighbour (Morris, 1999, pp. 83-84).

11.4.2. THE FIRST ATROCITIES IN KOSOVO AND THE INTERNATIONAL RESPONSE

Considering the repression and animosity that existed in the region, some have argued it is surprising Kosovo remained relatively peaceful throughout most of the 1990s (The Independent International Commission on Kosovo, 2000, p. 34). This relative peace turned out to be a blessing and a curse because the situation in Kosovo hardly received attention while there were brutal and bloody wars waging in the other republics (Judah, 2008, p. 68; Sell, 2002, p. 264). There had been some half-hearted attempts to resolve the conflict but, Kosovo was never truly the priority. Bellamy, in this respect, argues that 'not only did the West fail to prevent the conflict it failed to even attempt to prevent the conflict' (Bellamy, 2002, p. 2). In The Hague in 1991, Lord Carrington, for instance, tried to negotiate more autonomy for the province but needed to let go of this goal in an effort to persuade Milosevic to negotiate a peaceful settlement for the other wars (Sell, 2002, p. 262). The year thereafter at the 1992 London conference, the Kosovar delegation was invited to watch, but not participate (Bellamy, 2002, p. 29). A CSCE (Conference for Security and Co-operation in Europe) observer mission was sent into Kosovo and a special working group was established (Sell, 2002, p. 263; Weller, 1999, p. 218). Unfortunately, it would not last for more than a year. In 1993 Belgrade terminated the observer mission which had been very effective in reporting on the numerous human rights violations that had been perpetrated by Milosevic' regime after its membership of the organization had been revoked because of its role in the war in Bosnia (Sell, 2002, p. 270; Vrieze, 2000, p. 15).

That there was growing concern about the situation in Kosovo is exemplified by the Christmas warning on December 24 1992. President Bush' message was clear: 'In the event of conflict caused by Serbian actions, the United States will be prepared to employ a military force against Serbians in Kosovo and in Serbia proper' (cited in Doder & Branson, 1999, p. 244). In addition, the US made sure to let the Albanians know that if they initiated the violence the warning would not apply. Rugova acknowledged that he did not have complete control over all opposition forces but he stressed he was committed to avoiding violence because he was well aware that this would result in a bloodbath (Sell, 2002, p. 265). The warning was repeated by Clinton's administration in 1993 and again in 1998 (Doder & Branson, 1999, p. 244). At the same time, the European countries emphasized that the independence of Kosovo would never be recognized. It was envisioned that the region would regain a large degree of autonomy but Serbia's borders were to be respected (Vrieze, 2000, p. 11).

The involvement of the international community was nevertheless key to the strategy of the Kosovar Albanians to obtain independence (Vrieze, 2000, p. 4). They tried to use peaceful diplomatic means to delegitimize the Serbian regime and provoke international sympathy and concern for their cause (Schnabel & Thakur, 2000, p. 4; The Independent International Commission on Kosovo, 2000, p. 48; Vrieze, 2000, pp. 4-5). The non-violent strategy was mainly a pragmatic one and did not necessarily arise out of a principled stand. Rugova, the most prominent face of the opposition movement as the leader of the LDK (Democratic League of Kosova), explained: 'The Serbs only wait for a pretext to attack the Albanian population and wipe it out. We believe that it is better to do nothing and stay alive than be massacred' (The Independent International Commission on Kosovo, 2000, p. 43). Ultimately, the strategy failed them and when the other wars came to an end at Dayton, Kosovo was still part of what was left of Yugoslavia along with Serbia and Montenegro (Schnabel & Thakur, 2000, p. 4). Most believed it to be ill-advised to risk a chance at peace in Bosnia in order to improve the human rights situation in Kosovo and the conflict was once more pushed to the sidelines (Bellamy, 2002, p. 52).

In 1993 an opposition movement that favoured a more violent approach, the KLA (Kosovo Liberation Army) was created. In the first few years the KLA occasionally killed a police officer, but for quite some time, it remained a rather marginal force because it was difficult to get the weapons it needed (Judah, 2009, p. 319). The disillusionment with Rugova's strategy when Kosovo was neglected at the Dayton accords, resulted in more support for the KLA (Judah, 2008, p. 79).

In 1996, Milosevic struck a deal with Rugova to reopen the schools in Kosovo, but he never lived up to its terms. When western politicians confronted Milosevic with this, he merely told them that their information was incorrect and that all that mattered was that he restored order. As long as they minded their own business, the situation would continue to be under control (Doder & Branson, 1999, p. 238). Tensions rose further when anti-government demonstrations became more frequent, both in Serbia proper as well as in Kosovo. In the winter of 1996-1997 there were demonstrations against Milosevic and his regime in Serbia which gave an impulse to the ethnic Albanians and resulted in numerous student protests in Kosovo (Doder & Branson, 1999, p. 238).

In the summer of 1997, Milosevic ensured he was elected as president of Yugoslavia after the disorganized opposition boycotted the parliamentary session (Doder & Branson, 1999, p. 236). The subsequent elections in Montenegro and Serbia did not go as planned for Milosevic. It cost him utmost difficulty to manipulate the elections in Serbia and get his front man elected and unsurprisingly, according to the officials of OSCE, the elections were 'fundamentally flawed' (Doder & Branson, 1999, pp. 239-240).

Albania, in the meantime, descended into a state of anarchy in the spring of 1997. Financial pyramid schemes, the so-called 'Ponzi' schemes, collapsed and the state imploded causing weapons to become more freely available (Judah, 2008, p. 80; 2009, p. 320). Consequently, that winter Kosovo's conflict became more violent. The KLA started attacking police patrols and Milosevic responded with violent retributions (Doder & Branson, 1999, p. 241). When Robert Gelbard, the US Special \envoy, described the KLA as a terrorist organization, Milosevic is likely to have interpreted it as a sign that it was time to act (Judah, 2008, p. 81; LeBor, 2003, p. 278; Sell, 2002, p. 280). His retaliations become increasingly violent and brutal and support for the KLA in the meantime soared, making it much easier for them to attract recruits (LeBor, 2003, p. 278; Power, 2013, p. 445). In March, a brutal encounter occurred when the KLA tried to fight of the arrest of Adem Jashari. This resulted in a massacre of 51 individuals, including Jashari and 20 people of his family (Judah, 2008, p. 81; LeBor, 2003, p. 278). That spring and summer the war escalated leaving numerous people dead or on the run (Daalder & O'Hanlon, 2000, pp. 27-28; 40)

More moderate voices in Milosevic' government and military started to speak up and there were rumours a coup might be impending (LeBor, 2003, p. 279). At the same time, however, Kosovo continued to be important to many Serbs and pressure was also placed on Milosevic to act decisively. It seems Milosevic was also personally not unaffected by these emotions. He seemed to believe in the importance of Kosovo for Serbia and was as passionate about the region as many of his citizens (LeBor, 2003, p. 280). According to NATO General Klaus Naumann:

> 'It seemed to me that Bosnia did not concern him as much as Kosovo. He regarded Kosovo as Serbia's heartland. He told us that Kosovo is an integral part of Serbian history and culture, and he could not give it up' (LeBor, 2003, p. 280).

At times he became emotional when speaking about the region, demonising its Albanian population (LeBor, 2003, p. 280), p. 280). At the same time, underlying this sentiment was also the knowledge that his position of power was dependent on how he dealt with the region. He knew that any leader who gave up the region would inevitably lose power (LeBor, 2003, p. 280). As Daalder & O'Hanlon explain 'Milosevic's stake in Kosovo was much greater than in Bosnia' (2000, p. 85).

Serbia's aggressive policies sparked renewed political involvement from the West (Judah, 2009, p. 321). The countries which made up the Contact Group (France, Germany, Great Britain, Italy, Russia and the US), that had monitored the Bosnian War, condemned the violence and threatened with sanctions if Milosevic would not stop his violent tactics and let humanitarian aid into the region (Daalder & O'Hanlon, 2000, p. 24; 28). The UN Security Council referred approvingly to the Contact Group's demands and imposed an arms embargo by adopting Resolution 1160 in March 1998 under Chapter VII (Weller, 1999, p. 219). While it reaffirmed Serbia's basic claims that Kosovo was a part of Serbia and that the KLA were terrorists, for the first time it also recognized that the conflict was not merely an internal matter but formed a threat to international peace and security (Bellamy, 2002, pp. 76-77).

Additional sanctions were agreed on by most of the Contact Group (except for Russia) in April and early May (Daalder & O'Hanlon, 2000, p. 29). Just a few days later, however, Richard Holbrooke convinced the Contact Group to weaken some of these sanctions in exchange for a meeting between Milosevic and Rugova (Sell, 2002, p. 283). Milosevic did not seem serious about negotiating anything with Rugova and the meeting tarnished the latter's standing with the Kosovar Albanian population (Sell, 2002, pp. 283-284). The month thereafter Milosevic met with Yeltsin in Moscow. He had high hopes for the meeting but did not receive the support he desired. Rather, Yeltsin used the meeting to persuade Milosevic to allow an observer mission (the Kosovo Diplomatic Observer Mission – KDOM) into the region and noted that Milosevic should not count on Russia's support if it did not heed their advice (Sell, 2002, pp. 285-286). For Milosevic the move made sense; make small compromises to prevent more intrusive measures from materialising (Sell, 2002, p. 286).

In the meantime, NATO started to discuss the option of using military force (Daalder & O'Hanlon, 2000, p. 32). They held a military exercise in June 1998 that meant to show NATO's prowess. According to Sell: 'NATO had three guiding principles: avoid casualties to its own forces, avoid collateral damage to Serb forces and civilians and bring any conflict to a quick end' (Sell, 2002, p. 288). The intention was never to defeat Serbia but to change Milosevic' mind (Sell, 2002, p. 288). By July, the US was actually putting the message out there that intervention was unlikely in the near future and ruled out groundforces (Daalder & O'Hanlon, 2000, p. 35; 53). General Naumann believed, however, that Milosevic at this point 'rightly concluded that the NATO threat was a bluff ... and finished his summer offensive' (Daalder & O'Hanlon, 2000, pp. 32-33; Sell, 2002, p. 287).

The UN Security Council adopted Resolution 1199 in September under Chapter VII of the UN Charter in which it was again demanded that there would be an end to all hostilities and unimpeded access of humanitarian aid. Russia was dead set against specifying how compliance with the resolution would be ensured but NATO was already taking steps that brought it closer to military intervention. Their military options were spelled out and on September 24 the 'activation warning' for an air campaign was discussed. In order to forge consensus among the NATO states, Holbrooke was sent to negotiate with Milosevic one final time (Daalder & O'Hanlon, 2000, pp. 42-45). When the two men met, Milosevic asked NATO General Short, who formed part of Holbrooke's team, on their first meeting 'So are you the man who is going to bomb me' (Sell, 2002, p. 289). Milosevic also openly wondered when he spoke with Holbrooke: 'are you crazy enough to bomb us over these issues we're talking about in that lousy little Kosovo?' (Sell, 2002, p. 289). Holbrooke ultimately felt Milosevic was not taking them seriously (Sell, 2002, p. 289). Then on October 10, NATO approved the 'activation orders' which enabled them to commence bombing (Sell, 2002, p. 289). Milosevic then proceeded to plead with Holbrooke to have the order lifted and when NATO refused, this infuriated him and left him feeling betrayed (Doder & Branson, 1999, p. 247). The threat, it seems, finally became credible and on October 13 Milosevic agreed to withdraw forces and allow monitors into the region (Sell, 2002, p. 289). Milosevic also believed he was in a position to make some concessions because he was convinced that the KLA had been mostly defeated and he reasoned he would rather have an unarmed OSCE verification mission than having to accept an armed UN or NATO force (Bellamy, 2002, p. 99).

The October agreement eased some of the immediate concerns as humanitarian organizations could now enter the region and the Kosovo Verification Mission (KVM) which was deployed gave the refugees some sense of security, allowing some of them to return home (Daalder & O'Hanlon, 2000, p. 49). The agreement, however, also had some major flaws. It was vague and lacked enforcement mechanisms (Sell, 2002, p. 289). More importantly, nothing was resolved regarding the eventual status of the region and the Albanians were not included in the negotiations (Daalder & O'Hanlon, 2000, p. 50; Sell, 2002, p. 290). After agreeing to the conditions, Secretary General Solana, along with Generals Clark and Naumann, went to Milosevic to make it official but found him to be defiant. He even denied that there were Serbian troops present in Kosovo (Sell, 2002, p. 290). After he finally admitted having them there, he promised they would be withdrawn but still tried to stall actually having to do it (Sell, 2002, p. 290). Clark then threatened: 'Get real. You have to pull out your forces and if you don't there is an activation order. And if they tell me to bomb you, I'm going to bomb you good. You don't want to get bombed so get those forces out' (Sell, 2002, p. 290). Eventually Milosevic conceded (Sell, 2002, pp. 290-291).

The October agreement was important for the KLA who were able to recuperate after having suffered extensive losses in the preceding months and in this sense the agreement was seen as lifesaving for the organization (Sell, 2002, p. 293). It began to unravel as the KLA started to make use of the lull in fighting and the violent incidents slowly became more horrendous and frequent (Judah, 2008, p. 84). In Serbia, Milosevic, too, used the agreement to prepare for more hostilities. According to Sell, he 'used the atmosphere of crisis to put the country on a war footing, consolidate his own internal position through a sweeping crackdown on the independent media, and purge politicians and leaders of the army and police who questioned his hard-line stance on Kosovo' (Sell, 2002, p. 291). He fired the head of his secret police, Jovica Stanisic and the head of the army, Momcilo Perisic, and put hardliners he could trust in their place (Daalder & O'Hanlon, 2000, p. 58). In addition, he started to develop a plan – operation horseshoe – which allowed him to cleanse a region, shaped like a horseshoe, from its Albanian inhabitants (Daalder & O'Hanlon, 2000, pp. 58-59).

While US Special Envoy to Kosovo, Christopher Hill, continued to search for a solution to the conflict, by the end of the year, a deadlock seemed to have been reached (Daalder & O'Hanlon, 2000, pp. 60-61; Weller, 1999, p. 220). The next year there was no more restraint and 45 Albanians were killed at the village of Racak. The chief of the OSCE monitoring mission, William Walker, referred to it as an 'unspeakable atrocity' (Sell, 2002, p. 294). This was reason enough for Milosevic to ban him from the country and Clark and Naumann were sent to negotiate with Milosevic one last time (Sell, 2002, p. 294). They found him to be 'extremely stubborn' and unwilling to yield to their demands to allow Walker to stay, allow Arbour to investigate and to reduce his forces (Sell, 2002, p. 294), p. 294). Instead, Milosevic maintained 'This was not a massacre. This was staged. These people are terrorists' (Sell, 2002, p. 294), p. 294). He tried to evade having to make any meaningful commitments. He eventually expressed the willingness to allow Arbour to come but posed such elaborate terms and conditions that her visit would be insignificant. He believed he could string NATO along, and while he may have been genuinely angry, it was also part of the manner in which he chose to manipulate the alliance. According to Clark Milosevic 'got angry at us because he thought he could kick the sh- out of us without any serious penalty' (Sell, 2002, p. 295).

The massacre at Racak was a seminal moment that would change the course the war would take. In the spring of 1999 there was one more attempt to reach a peaceful solution (Judah, 2008, p. 84). The US and European allies changed tactics and set an ultimatum: Milosevic needed to accept the agreement as it was presented to him and, if he did not, military intervention would follow.

11.5. PEACE NEGOTIATIONS

There are some inherent difficulties in comparing the peace agreements that were offered to the Milosevic and Pol Pot. The proposal presented to Milosevic at Rambouillet was much more detailed and further advanced than the final attempt by Vietnam to resolve the border conflict with Cambodia peacefully. Initially both leaders failed to seriously consider the proposals. The question why this was so will be addressed in the remainder of the chapter after a more in depth discussion of the final attempts to come to a peaceful solution.

11.5.1. A FINAL FUTILE PEACE PLAN AND THE PREPARATIONS FOR WAR

A final attempt by the Vietnamese to reach a peaceful proposal to their border conflict with Pol Pot came on February 5th 1978. It encompassed three basic elements. They proposed that:

> '1) An immediate end shall be put to all hostile military activities in the border region; the armed forces of each side shall be stationed within their respective territories, five kilometres from the border.
> 2) The two sides shall meet at once in Hanoi, or Phnom Penh, or at a place on the border, to discuss and conclude a treaty on mutual respect and a border treaty between the two countries.
> 3) The two sides shall reach an agreement on an appropriate form of international guarantee and supervision' (Burchett, 1981, p. 160).

Copies of the proposal were sent to the UN and the non-aligned movement but there was no reply from Pol Pot. Combodia, nonetheless, sent a clear message just days after the proposal was put forward by shelling the Tay Ninh capital in Vietnam and three district centres in the Mekong Delta were attacked (Burchett, 1981, pp. 160-161).

The Vietnamese were, rightfully, under no impression that their offer was acceptable to Pol Pot: 'we knew ... that the Khmer Rouge would never accept that proposal, but at least the blame of rejection would be on them' (Chanda, 1986, p. 216). It seems by this time, the Vietnamese were already making preparations to invade Cambodia before the year's end (Becker, 1998, p. 314). The proposal was not genuine. It was merely a gesture to the international community to signal that they had at least tried to work out another remedy.

In May, the Vietnamese turned directly to the UN, hoping they were willing to appoint a mission to mediate the dispute between the countries, but China prevented the initiative from going forward (Burchett, 1981, p. 161). Then again, in July a similar request was placed at a meeting of the non-aligned countries in Belgrade. While many looked favourably upon the proposal of a 'good offices' mission, China here too exerted diplomatic pressure and had Yugoslavia, the host country, oppose the initiative on the basis that this would be 'divisive' because Cambodia was not behind the initiative. The representative of Yugoslavia reasoned, that accepting such a proposal would mean that they would be 'interfering in the internal affairs' of Cambodia (Burchett, 1981, p. 161). At this point, a negotiated solution was already a far-fetched possibility but Pol Pot had never been willing to negotiate. It was a mere continuation of the road that they had chosen to embark on earlier. Thereafter, for both sides, the veil of diplomacy was left behind and each prepared themselves for further escalation.

In the spring of 1978 when the Vietnamese village Ha Tien was attacked, the Vietnamese tried to put Cambodia's aggression on display and showed foreign journalists the atrociousness with which the Cambodian attacks were executed. Men, women and children were hacked to pieces, some beheaded, others disembowelled. A truly horrendous attack where all living things, including the livestock had been killed (Chanda, 1986, pp. 219-224). There was a Khmer phrase: 'This is our country' written in charcoal on one of the doors (Chanda, 1986, p. 224).

In the meantime in Cambodia, Pol Pot's variant of a media campaign was launched as well. He received several Yugoslav journalists to whom he simply explained: 'If Vietnam is truly friendly toward us ... there will be no difficulty in immediately solving the problem' (Chanda, 1986, pp. 224-225). Four Communist journalists from the US followed and thereafter representatives from Belgium and Sweden (Becker, 1998, pp. 315-316). A propaganda offensive for foreign consumption had started in which Pol Pot expressed the grand achievements he had brought about in the country and countered the horror stories the refugees had brought into the world (Becker, 1998, p. 316). In October Sary even invited UN Secretary Waldheim to come and visit the country, hoping it would stall a Vietnamese invasion, but the latter refused as long as he was unable to make a simultaneous trip to Vietnam (Becker, 1998, pp. 322-323). Then in November, as a final move in the communication strategy, they invited some members of the international press, two American journalists and a British scholar who was assassinated before the end of the trip (Becker, 1998, p. 323; 429).

In addition, more young men, who barely received any training, were drafted into the army as the distinction between 'old' and 'new' people was removed to mobilize the whole population (Becker, 1998, pp. 317-318). Only minorities were not drafted, because they were not trusted (Becker, 1998, p. 318). Rather than being preoccupied with finding a peaceful solution, Pol Pot by this time was focussing his attention to prepare for the war, which was now inevitably going to come.

11.5.2. THE PEACE NEGOTIATIONS AT RAMBOUILLET

While the NATO countries had been shocked by the massacre at Racak, and decided more urgent measures needed to be taken, few could agree already on military force. A final diplomatic solution needed to be tried first (Daalder & O'Hanlon, 2000, pp. 64-65). The last diplomatic attempt to forge an agreement was initiated at a castle in the French village Rambouillet (Daalder & O'Hanlon, 2000, p. 65). It essentially entailed an ultimatum: either the parties were to accept an interim agreement or face the consequences (Daalder & O'Hanlon, 2000, p. 71). For the Serbs this meant that failing to sign would result in an air campaign, for the Albanians a failure to sign would mean that the international community would leave them to their own devices (Daalder & O'Hanlon, 2000, p. 77). Albright explained in a speech that:

> 'Three outcomes are possible. If President Milosevic refuses to accept the Contact Group proposals, or has allowed repression in Kosovo to continue, he can expect NATO air strikes. If the Kosovo Albanians obstruct progress at Rambouillet or

> on the ground, they cannot expect the NATO and the international community to bail them out. Decisions on air strikes and international support will be affected, and we will find additional ways of bringing pressure to bear. If the two sides do reach agreement, we will need to concentrate our effort on making sure that it is successfully implemented' (Daalder & O'Hanlon, 2000, p. 77).

According to Sell, 'the basic U.S. game plan at Rambouillet was to pressure the Albanians into accepting the draft agreement, then use the threat of NATO airstrikes to compel Milosevic to sign' (Sell, 2002, p. 297). They thus wanted to increase the costs of continuing the war effort for Milosevic, persuading him to comply.

At the start, they were provided with a framework agreement, an annex on the constitution of Kosovo and two additional annexes which dealt with elections and the proposed ombudsman (Weller, 1999, p. 228). Both parties were then asked to comment on the draft (Weller, 1999, p. 228). The core principles at Rambouillet were non-negotiable and changes could only be made if both parties agreed with them. The mere participation at Rambouillet was to imply broad agreement with the basic principles of the proposed text (Daalder & O'Hanlon, 2000, p. 78; Weller, 1999, p. 226). In the draft agreement the territorial integrity of the FRY was emphasized but Kosovo would be given extensive autonomy and would be able to govern itself through its own institutions (Sell, 2002, p. 296).

Milosevic did not attend the conference, possibly because he feared arrest should there be a sealed indictment against him at the ICTY, but he may also already have decided that there was no chance that an agreement could ever be reached. He sent a low-level delegation in his place who hardly seemed interested in negotiating (Daalder & O'Hanlon, 2000, p. 79; LeBor, 2003, p. 287; Sell, 2002, p. 297). They barely participated in most of the initial negotiations, but were pre-occupied with drinking heavily, strolling in the gardens and singing nationalist songs (Daalder & O'Hanlon, 2000, p. 79; Sell, 2002, p. 297). Even if they would have wanted to engage in the discussions in a meaningful way, they would not have been able to, considering the fact that these officials were not influential enough (Daalder & O'Hanlon, 2000, p. 79).

The Albanian delegation included individuals from a broad subsection of the political landscape and they decided to appoint Hashim Thaci to head it, bypassing President Rugova (Daalder & O'Hanlon, 2000, p. 79; Weller, 1999, p. 227). The first order of business was getting the highly divided Albanians to sign, and only then did attention turn towards the Serbs (Sell, 2002, pp. 297-298). The Kosovar delegation prepared its comments thoroughly and left the annexes as well as unnegotiable principles untouched (Weller, 1999, p. 228), but the Serbian delegation refused to constructively engage with the negotiators. More than a week after the start of the conference, the Serbian delegation had not provided any constructive comments (Weller, 1999, p. 229). In the second week, however, the Serbs started to negotiate more seriously when Serb President

Milutinovic joined, and after Hill spoke with Milosevic in Belgrade (Daalder & O'Hanlon, 2000, p. 81; Weller, 1999, p. 229). The Kosovar Albanians had objected to the visit since the parties had agreed on total isolation (Weller, 1999, p. 229).

Shortly afterwards, the Serbian delegation presented a lengthy commentary on the proposed agreement but quite a lot of it was going against the non-negotiable principles (Daalder & O'Hanlon, 2000, p. 81; Weller, 1999, p. 229). Violating their own ground rules, the negotiators produced a new draft on the basis of the concerns expressed by Belgrade while leaving the comments of the Albanian delegation unanswered. The new version was highly unfavourable in the eyes of the Kosovar delegation and they felt their trust had been breached (Bellamy, 2002, pp. 137-138; Daalder & O'Hanlon, 2000, p. 81; Weller, 1999, pp. 230-231). To make matters worse, the Serbs believed the changes were not far reaching enough, and when Hill travelled back to Belgrade for another meeting, Milosevic refused to meet with him (Daalder & O'Hanlon, 2000, p. 81).

Annex B of the Rambouillet agreement, which granted NATO access to the entire country, is sometimes blamed for the failure at Rambouillet, and is seen by some as a truly unacceptable provision (Bellamy, 2001, p. 36; 48). Doder and Branson, for instance, argue that Milosevic was willing to grant Kosovo its autonomy but would not allow foreign troops to enter his country (Doder & Branson, 1999, p. 251). Yet Serb negotiators never raised it as a problem. It was inserted because NATO believed it possibly wanted to supply its troops through FRY territory (Sell, 2002, p. 301). Milosevic was even provided with the opportunity to rewrite it, but he declined to do so (Bellamy, 2001, p. 49). The perception among one of the conference organizers was that 'Milosevic had clearly instructed Milutinovic not to conclude this or any other deal' (Sell, 2002, p. 299).

A day before the deadline, both sides continued to demand significant changes and many important elements had not even been discussed (Weller, 1999, pp. 231-232). With some of the annexes only just having been presented to the parties, once more the deadline was extended, this time to the 23rd February (Weller, 1999, pp. 231-232). Negotiations then started to pick up pace and the concerns of the Kosovar delegation were now more deliberately taken into account as well (Weller, 1999, p. 232). At the end of the talks the Kosovar delegations expressed support for the agreement but wanted to consult its constituents before it signed (Weller, 1999, p. 233) and voiced a willingness to sign at a later date when the parties would meet again in Paris on the 15th of March (Daalder & O'Hanlon, 2000, p. 65; 83). The Serbian delegation wanted to continue the discussions (Weller, 1999, p. 233).

During the negotiations in February and March the Serbs actually had become more active in Kosovo (Webber, 2009, p. 450). It seems the Serbs sought to achieve two goals, namely to expel many Kosovar Albanians from the region while at the same time discouraging NATO from launching a ground offensive

(Webber, 2009, p. 450). Milosevic was becoming isolated and only listened to loyal hardliners, who convinced him they could defeat the KLA and that the US should not be trusted (Daalder & O'Hanlon, 2000, p. 94). According to Sell, Milosevic had developed a 'bunker mentality' (Sell, 2002, p. 299). His aides possibly painted a rosier picture than reality warranted and Milosevic lost touch with reality, only believing what he wanted to believe (Sell, 2002, p. 300). He continued his policy of firing all those who would not see eye to eye with his policies, this time sacking General Aleksander Dimitrijevic, the head of military intelligence who had counselled a more cautious approach (LeBor, 2003, p. 288). Holbrooke was dispatched several days before the meeting in Paris to meet with Milosevic. Despite meeting for hours, and warnings from Holbrooke that 'we might be on a collision course between Yugoslavia and the Western authorities, including NATO', Milosevic would not give in (Daalder & O'Hanlon, 2000, p. 83). He issued a statement in which he explained that 'attempts to condition a political agreement on our country's acceptance of foreign troops … are unacceptable' (Daalder & O'Hanlon, 2000, p. 83). As expected, in Paris, the Kosovar delegation expressed its willingness to sign and were committed to talk about the manner in which the agreement was to be implemented. The Serbs, however, presented a new draft which would have basically started the discussions all over (Weller, 1999, p. 234).

In mid-March Holbrooke visited Milosevic once more, and on the visit he told Chris Hill: 'you are a superpower. You can do what you want. If you say Sunday is Wednesday, you can, it is up to you' (LeBor, 2003, p. 288). The final attempt to reach a peaceful solution came on March 22nd when Richard Holbrooke travelled to Belgrade to get Serbia to cease its offensive and sign the Rambouillet interim agreement, but the following day the Serbian parliament formally voted against it (Weller, 1999, p. 236). While, when the October agreement was forged, Milosevic seemed distressed about the prospect of NATO bombing, now in March he seemed 'cool and almost contemptuous' about the prospect of bombing according to Holbrooke (Sell, 2002, p. 299). Even though Holbrooke explained the bombing would be 'swift, severe and sustained' Milosevic responded 'go ahead and bomb us' and explicitly acknowledged he understood it would start soon after Holbrooke left (Sell, 2002, p. 299). Milosevic had resigned himself with the prospect of bombing and said to Holbrooke: 'No more engagement, no more negotiations, I understand that, you will bomb us. You are a great and powerful country, there is nothing we can do about it' (LeBor, 2003, p. 288). Two days later the war started.

Holbrooke never believed Milosevic was being either paranoid or irrational in rejecting Rambouillet (Sell, 2002, p. 300). There were actually three reasons that he believed played a role in Milosevic's decision-making process. Firstly, he believed Milosevic looked at the American bombing campaign a few months earlier in Iraq, which lasted only a few days and believed he could withstand a similar ordeal. Secondly, he believed there may have been a leak in NATO's intelligence and that Milosevic possibly had access to the bombing list which was still light at the time and finally, according to Holbrooke, Milosevic did not believe he could reach an acceptable compromise at this point and believed he could get a better deal later on (Sell, 2002, p. 300).

The NATO alliance hinted repeatedly that they were not prepared for a long lasting military operation and openly ruled out ground forces (Sell, 2002, p. 302). NATO had expected that the bombing would never last as long or would eventually include so many targets (Sell, 2002, p. 303). Milosevic at this time did not seem to take the threat of military intervention very seriously (LeBor, 2003, p. 286). He expected the bombing, if there was any, to be 'polite' and would only cause his country to rally behind the flag and increase his support domestically (LeBor, 2003, p. 287). In addition, he knew that behind NATO's determined façade there were much internal divisions among its constitutive countries (LeBor, 2003, p. 287). According to NATO general Naumann, 'He thought NATO was not cohesive, and he did not believe that there would be any bombing. That was a tragic mistake on his part. It was also a big mistake on the part of certain NATO countries, who gave him hints that no bombing would happen' (LeBor, 2003, p. 287). Mutual miscalculation led to a tragic war that would soon become much more comprehensive than either side had expected it to.

11.6. THE INTERVENTION

When it became clear that peaceful solutions were no longer feasible, NATO and Vietnam started to plan their military interventions. NATO's offensive started out somewhat hesitantly, they never expected the intervention would last so long or would require such far reaching military action. While NATO's goal of bringing Milosevic back to the negotiating table had not changed, NATO never had its heart set on regime change, it seems Vietnam by now was determined to remove Pol Pot from power and planned its intervention accordingly.

11.6.1. THE FINAL VIETNAMESE OFFENSIVE

In preparing the intervention, the Vietnamese decided to rely heavily on former Cambodian communist cadre that had fled their country, predominantly during the purge of the Eastern Zone. By the end of the spring, the Vietnamese were giving aerial support by flying as much as thirty bombing missions on a daily basis to support the Cambodian 'liberation army' whose leadership was in the hands of former Cambodian cadre (Morris, 1999, p. 107). Pol Pot's brutal policies had ensured numerous individuals were receptive to Vietnamese calls to offer resistance. When the executions picked up pace in May, several members of the local leadership fled into the jungle with a substantial number of forces. They managed to briefly offer resistance to Pol Pot's forces but after the fighting died down in July, revenge killings engulfed the region (Chanda, p. 253-254). As Chanda explained, 'In the eyes of Pol Pot and his friends, the people of the Eastern Zone had shown their colors – they were "Khmer bodies with Vietnamese minds" and had to be crushed' (Chanda, 1986, p. 254). Not only the fighters themselves were killed, but the entire villages in which they were found (Chanda, 1986, p. 254). Those who managed to stay alive in the jungle soon started to contemplate defecting to Vietnam, which had begun calling for a Khmer uprising in June (Chanda, 1986, pp. 254-255). In September, when the Vietnamese again infiltrated Cambodian territory, contact was established between the Vietnamese and the surviving Eastern Zone cadres (Chanda, 1986, p. 255). They trained the soldiers and broadcasted appeals for the Cambodians to desert, come to Vietnam and join the resistance movement (Morris, 1999, pp. 109-110). Leaflets were also thrown out of airplanes which promoted an uprising against Pol Pot and presented their plans to return a sense of normalcy of everyday life by reintroducing family life, religion, markets and money after the war had ended (Chanda, 1986, p. 340).

When Cambodia's Minister of Defence, Son Sen, asked the Chinese for military support in their conflict with Vietnam in July 1978, he got lectured on the virtues of self-reliance (Chanda, 1986, p. 261). China decided not to get militarily involved in Cambodia for numerous political, economic, ideological and practical reasons but agreed to increase its weapons supply and send a large number of military advisors, an estimated 5000 in total (Chanda, 1986, pp. 260-262). In addition, China decided to punish Vietnam for its aggressive and obstinate behaviour (Chanda, 1986, pp. 260-261).

On December 3, Hanoi announced that a 'Kampuchean United Front for National Salvation' was established in a part of Cambodia that had already been 'liberated'. A Central Committee was formed, according to the Vietnamese, which was composed of 200 representatives of the people with Heng Samrin at its head (Morris, 1999, p. 110). It was the basis of the puppet government that they wanted to set up after capturing Phnom Penh to hide behind and make the intervention appear more legitimate (Morris, 1999, p. 111).

The move towards Phnom Penh started out slowly in the first two weeks of December when parts of the two Vietnamese divisions moved into the south-eastern part of the country. The start of the final offensive coincided with Christmas with thirteen divisions, or 150,000 troops (Morris, 1999, p. 111), and by January first they had already captured several provincial capitals (Chanda, 1986, pp. 341-342). The United Front seemed to be enjoying some popular support. They would disband communal kitchens and reinsure the population through the presence of monks in the areas they captured (Kiernan, 1996, p. 442).

The Vietnamese then started to bomb Khmer Rouge positions. Pol Pot had foolishly gathered thirty thousand troops in the border area that could now be targeted by the Vietnamese airpower and artillery (Burchett, 1981, p. 207; Chanda, 1986, p. 342). While the Chinese advisors were immediately pulled out of the war zone, they left a largely untrained force who knew how to use a machete but was no match for the modern Vietnamese army (Chanda, 1986, p. 342). On January 4, when seven provinces were under their control, the Vietnamese made the final decision to steam ahead towards Phnom Penh (Chanda, 1986, p. 343). After a brief pause in the fighting, which Pol Pot mistakenly interpreted as a hopeful sign that victory was still within their reach, the Vietnamese made their way to the edges of the city by January 7 (Chanda, 1986, pp. 343-344).

The Khmer Rouge had placed several arms caches in the Cardamom Mountains in case they needed to retreat from the capital but outwardly Pol Pot remained confident (Chanda, p. 344). Just a few weeks earlier, on December 11 Pol had said that the Khmer Rouge were ready for a 'protracted war' and even the day before Pol Pot was forced to flee, he seemed certain in a conversation with Sihanouk, that they would be able to 'liquidate' the Vietnamese in two months (Chanda, 1986, p. 344; Chandler, 1999, p. 156). Pol Pot possibly had not been as certain about his victory as he portrayed himself to be, given his contingency plans, but he still seems to have been taken aback by the speed at which Cambodia's defences failed (Chanda, 1986, p. 344).

Chanda describes the scene as follows:

> 'By the time Pol Pot realized that there was no victory around the corner, it was too late. Within less than twenty-four hours the capital had to be abandoned, leaving behind not only unfinished meals and tons of rotting fish but also mountains of weapons and ammunition and a self-incriminating archive at Tuol Sleng' (Chanda, 1986, p. 345).

The speed with which they had to leave thus suggests that at the very least Pol Pot had not foreseen events moving this quickly. On January 7th helicopters flew Pol Pot and some close allies to safety to an encampment along the Thai-Cambodian border (Chandler, 1999, pp. 156-157).

11.6.2. THE KOSOVO WAR

The war began on March 24 1999. When NATO decided to commence their military operations, they never aimed to defeat the Serbs but 'merely' sought to bomb Milosevic back to the negotiating table (Daalder & O'Hanlon, 2000, pp. 2-3). They wanted Milosevic to consent to several conditions which they had set, namely: a cessation of the fighting, withdrawal of all Serbian forces that were active in the region, the presence of an international force, the return of refugees with unimpeded access for humanitarian aid, and a political framework that was based on the Rambouillet Accords (Roberts, 1999, p. 103). Ultimately, the bombing raids were to weaken Serbia militarily and were meant to pressurise Milosevic to change his policies (Roberts, 1999, p. 111). In other words, they sought to make the decision to continue with the atrocities so costly, he would decide to change his policy.

The war can be divided into three phases. In the first phase, NATO targeted anti-aircraft defences and command bunkers (Power, 2013, p. 456). In the second phase, which was initiated on March 29th 1999, it more than doubled the amount of planes and started targeting the infrastructure south of Belgrade and the economy more generally (Power, 2013, p. 456; Stevanovic, 2004, p. 156). From April 3rd onwards, phase three commenced, during which Belgrade itself was targeted (Power, 2013, p. 456). Eventually the intervention had tripled the number of planes over time before Milosevic would eventually change his mind (Daalder & O'Hanlon, 2000, p. 103).

When the war started Milosevic took charge, as the supreme commander (Stevanovic, 2004, p. 152) and considered his options. If an attack would occur, he figured there were several options available to him, he could return to Bosnia to wreak havoc or could spread the conflict in Macedonia (Doder & Branson, 1999, p. 254). There is reason to believe he tried to destabilize Bosnia but failed (Bellamy, 2002, pp. 162-163). He eventually chose another option; he decided to increase the violence in Kosovo. Villages were burnt to the ground and cultural and religious sights destroyed as people were killed and women sexually assaulted (LeBor, 2003, p. 290). Paramilitary and the Special Operations Unit (JSO), the praetorian guard of Serbian Intelligence Services, did the ugliest and violent work. The paramilitary forces were also used as a scapegoat and blamed by Milosevic for any excesses that occurred during battle (Doder & Branson, 1999, p. 261; LeBor, 2003, pp. 290-291). Milosevic maintained that in any war bad things were bound to happen but that at least in Kosovo it was not as bad as it had been in Vietnam, for instance. According to Milosevic some houses were burned, yes, but certainly not entire villages (Power, 2013, p. 453). According to Milosevic, citizens fled because the terrorists spread the wrong information, causing people to leave in fear (Doder & Branson, 1999, p. 261).

Milosevic military campaign which included widespread ethnic cleansing and had become known under as *Potkovica* (Horseshoe), now became even more widespread and violent (Stevanovic, 2004, p. 152). Daalder & O'Hanlon explain Milosevic's decision to increase the ethnic cleansing of the Albanian population as follows: 'Before the bombs began to fall, he had an incentive to keep NATO from attacking him. Once the attack was under way, however, he no longer had the same reason to hold back' (Daalder & O'Hanlon, 2000, p. 107). By March 1999, before the violence escalated, it was estimated there were already 260,000 internally displaced persons, another 100,000 were seeking refuge in the region and a similar amount of people was displaced elsewhere (Roberts, 1999, p. 113).

Some estimates indicate that an astounding 90% of the Kosovar Albanian population left their homes at one point during the war (Webber, 2009, p. 451).

The NATO allies believed they would only need to bomb for a few days before Milosevic would relent, and Milosevic in turn believed that NATO would never have the unity it needed to launch a decisive offensive or put boots on the ground (Stevanovic, 2004, pp. 150-151). According to Daalder & O'Hanlon, Milosevic strategy was to 'hunker down, tolerate the bombing, and wait for Russian pressure or NATO internal dissension to weaken the alliance's resolve' (Daalder & O'Hanlon, 2000, p. 106). Milosevic's expectation of NATO was coloured by his experience during the earlier wars which caused him to see 'them all as bureaucrats who delayed finding solutions to problems until it was too late, or until after their next elections' (Stevanovic, 2004, p. 151). He even told the German Foreign Minister Joschka Fischer 'I can stand death – lots of it – but you can't' (Sell, 2002, p. 301). Milosevic's violent response, however, had some undesirable and unexpected consequences for him because it actually increased NATO's determination to win the war and strengthened their alliance (Doder & Branson, 1999, p. 260; Hosmer, 2001, p. xiii).

In the NATO countries there was some amazement that the Serbian population did not call their leader into account but this line of reasoning failed to take the autocratic nature of the Milosevic regime into consideration (Stevanovic, 2004, pp. 162-163). As the conflict unfolded, the independent press had been removed completely from the political landscape (Stevanovic, 2004, p. 146) and political opposition had also been restricted further (Stevanovic, 2004, pp. 136-137). News agencies could only report on information that was released by the government news agency and propaganda increased the fear and panic among the population as the Western politicians were equated with Hitler and Nazism (Stevanovic, 2004, p. 153). Military and communications installations were bombed as patriotism swept through the country and people tried to form human shields on bridges (LeBor, 2003, pp. 288-289). Concerts were organized and the attendees wore t-shirts on which the word 'target' was defiantly written (Stevanovic, 2004, p. 155). Encouraged by the state run propaganda, Serbs united behind their country and their leader (Doder & Branson, 1999, p. 260). Throughout the war the prevailing attitude had been that anyone who collaborates with foreigners is a traitor, and in the state run media politicians vied for favour by arguing who was most nationalistic (Stevanovic, 2004, pp. 147-148). While in Belgrade life continued, albeit in fear, in the provinces it largely came to a halt. There was no money and the supply of water and electricity was interrupted (Stevanovic, 2004, p. 155). The suffering of the population increased significantly as NATO became more determined and started to disrupt transportation, water and electricity (Power, 2013, pp. 456-457). In addition, as if the truth was not horrible enough, rumours were spread that atomic bombs would be used and the water had been poisoned (Stevanovic, 2004, p. 153).

There were few victories for Milosevic to boast about but on March 31st three US soldiers were captured and subsequently released a few weeks later after several religious and political leaders from the US convinced Milosevic this would be advantageous to him in the media war that was being waged against him (Doder & Branson, 1999, p. 265; Sell, 2002, p. 307). The many mistakes that were made by the NATO allies also played into Milosevic's hands and fed into the regime's propaganda (LeBor, 2003, p. 292). They bombed a bridge on April 12th killing numerous individuals because a passenger train was just passing by, and two days later struck a group of Albanian refugees who were mistakenly identified as a military convoy (Daalder & O'Hanlon, 2000, p. 122). They also accidentally bombed the Chinese embassy, killing three and injuring eighteen, apparently because an outdated street map was used (Daalder & O'Hanlon, 2000, p. 147; Doder & Branson, 1999, p. 266).

In late March and throughout April, NATO increased the pressure it brought to bear on Milosevic's regime. They had increased the number of targets and more precisely articulated the conditions with which Milosevic needed to comply in order to bring the war to an end. They also began to discuss a naval blockade, and signalled their intention to hold the Serbian top leaders criminally responsible for their actions in Kosovo (Daalder & O'Hanlon, 2000, p. 139). In addition, at the NATO summit at the end of April, NATO signalled that it intended to win this war, at all cost (Daalder & O'Hanlon, 2000, p. 138). Yet while some of its members discussed the option of putting boots on the ground, others, including the US, continued to insist that this was not an option (Daalder & O'Hanlon, 2000, pp. 138-139; 163). Early May, the possibility began to be looked at more thoroughly and on May 18 Clinton asserted that NATO 'will not take any option of the table' (Daalder & O'Hanlon, 2000, pp. 156-157; Power, 2013, pp. 458-459). Not long thereafter, the threat became more concrete. On May 27 Arbour issues a warrant for Milosevics's arrest and NATO's troop size at Kosovo's border grew considerably (Daalder & O'Hanlon, 2000, p. 157; Doder & Branson, 1999, p. 272; Power, 2013, p. 458). While the war did not have a tremendous impact on Serbia's military capabilities, it was detrimental to its economy and infrastructure (Doder & Branson, 1999, p. 271). People grew tired of the war and the demonstrators now turned against Milosevic (Daalder & O'Hanlon, 2000, p. 159; Doder & Branson, 1999, pp. 267-268). Even Milosevic's cronies felt the impact and the opposition became more vocal (Daalder & O'Hanlon, 2000, p. 159). In addition, many in the military deserted and hid in the countryside (Stevanovic, 2004, p. 156). By the end of the 1990s Milosevic's hold on power was questioned domestically and differences over Kosovo thus took the form of a 'final reckoning' between Milosevic who needed to maintain control over the region and the NATO countries who wanted to make up for their failings in the earlier wars (Webber, 2009, p. 454).

With the pressure on Milosevic mounting and the war escalating, a dialogue was initiated between Clinton and Yeltsin (Daalder & O'Hanlon, 2000, p. 167).

On May 6th the G8 made a statement on the basis of which negotiations could commence, but which slightly weakened NATO's initial demands, and Milosevic indicated a willingness to do so (Daalder & O'Hanlon, 2000, p. 168). It indicated Russia would not throw its whole weight behind the Serbian cause, and Milosevic knew it (Doder & Branson, 1999, pp. 269-270). The NATO countries, Russia and the European Union set out to formulate the specific demands with which Milosevic needed to comply. They quickly forged agreement on several important elements: there was to be an interim administration which was headed by the UN with an international military force, refugees needed to be allowed to return, he needed to allow humanitarian agencies access to the region and in return Yugoslavia's territorial integrity would not be questioned (Daalder & O'Hanlon, 2000, pp. 169-170). More contentious was the demand that Milosevic would withdraw all his troops, and there was disagreement over the moment NATO would seize their bombing campaign, after Milosevic started to withdraw his forces or already after agreement was forged. There was also disagreement over the command structure and contributing countries to the peacekeeping mission that was to be deployed (Daalder & O'Hanlon, 2000, pp. 168-171). The Russian representative Chernomyrdin realized the others had an unwavering commitment to these terms and went to see Milosevic in May, urging him to accept the main conditions, stressing the fact that he believed ground forces would otherwise be deployed (Daalder & O'Hanlon, 2000, p. 171). Milosevic, however, objected over who would head the forces and refused to accept troops from countries who bombed Serbia in Kosovo, and rejected NATO troops in the North of Kosovo outright. In addition, he wanted part of the troops to be under UN command (Daalder & O'Hanlon, 2000, p. 171). It was first up to Europe, Russia and the US to agree on the details of what needed to be accepted by Milosevic. It was decided that eventually a small number of Serbian forces were allowed to return to Kosovo but that Milosevic first needed to withdraw all his troops. In relation to the composition and command of the peacekeeping force it was emphasized that NATO's presence therein would be 'substantial' (Daalder & O'Hanlon, 2000, p. 172).

Finally, on June 2nd their demands became final and were presented as unchangeable to Milosevic (Daalder & O'Hanlon, 2000, p. 173). Milosevic then turned to Chernomyrdin and asked: 'Is this what I have to do to get the bombing stopped?', who then answered in the affirmative. The Finnish, European representative Ahtisaari confirmed 'this is the best you can get. It's only going to get worse for you'. Milosevic relented and agreed he would advise parliament to agree to the conditions which it dutifully did on June 3rd (Daalder & O'Hanlon, 2000, p. 174). In the final agreement minor, 'cosmetic' changes were made to the Rambouillet terms that allowed Milosevic to save face but in reality he gained little while tremendous damage had been inflicted on his country (Doder & Branson, 1999, pp. 171-172). Things moved quickly thereafter. Serb forces withdrew in the time frame they were given and Resolution 1244 was adopted by the Security Council, placing Kosovo under UN administration and authorising an international security presence (Bellamy, 2002, pp. 200-202).

11.7. THE RESPONSIVENESS OF POL POT AND MILOSEVIC

It should be acknowledged that once the final offensive was under way the prospects of negotiating a favourable outcome were much more realistic for Milosevic than they were for Pol Pot. Yet this does not explain why Pol Pot actually initiated and provoked the conflict with the much stronger army and was unwilling to even seriously consider negotiations. It was not until the fall of 1977 that Vietnam started to even plan for his overthrow (Morris, 1999, pp. 98-101), before that time as was explained, they were seeking a peaceful solution to their conflict through various diplomatic initiatives and generally acted with restraint. It is therefore important to consider why these leaders made such different choices, even though both knew that their armies were unable to stand up to the invading armies in the long run.

11.7.1. WHY POL POT CONTINUED TO FIGHT

The question remains to what extent Pol Pot's value rational orientation influenced his decision-making process when he was confronted with the threat of military intervention. Of course, the entire conflict cannot be reduced to the ideology of one man. Underlying the border conflict was not merely Cambodia's contested history with Vietnam and Pol Pot's suspicion of Vietnams intentions. An important part of the conflict centred on a disputed area at sea where it was believed that a plenitude of petroleum could be found (Chandler, 1999, p. 133). At the same time, however, the goal to guard their territory ferociously was linked with the hatred of the Vietnamese that was an integral part of the ideology of Pol Pot (K. D. Jackson, 1989, p. 46). Pol Pot had always devoted his life to the dictates of the ideology, and as Short observed, 'the Khmer Rouge policy, right up to the last hours, remained wholly consistent with everything that had gone before' (Short, 2004, p. 399). Consequently, his ideology and the hostile manner in which he interpreted the behaviour of the Vietnamese, eternally suspicious of their intentions, distorted his decision-making process and led to the misperception that Vietnam was a threat to his country and movement long after this ceased to be the case (Morris, 1999, p. 111).[125]

---

[125] See Chapter 5, most notably 5.4.3 for a more elaborate explanation of how ideology distorts the decision-making process.

Pol Pot said in a 1978 speech that if they had accepted a ceasefire from the Vietnamese in 1973 'we would have become slaves of the Vietnamese, and the Kampuchean race would have entirely lost its identity' (Takei, 1998, p. 72). Pol Pot perceived the conflict with the Vietnamese as being all or nothing, life or death and he believed all was lost anyway if he would not defeat the Vietnamese. He had always been suspicious of Vietnamese influence and it was this suspicion that influenced his decisions regarding Cambodia's foreign policy but also had an impact on the choices he made domestically. It would be wrong to try to separate Pol Pot's policies inside his own country from those he adopted towards his powerful neighbour. Both were greatly influenced by the fear that emanated from Cambodia's relationship with Vietnam and it was this fear that caused so many people to die, within the country and in the border region. It motivated the destructive speed with which the revolution was pushed through (Morris, 1999, p. 72).

Cambodia's foreign policy was anchored in paranoia (Morris, 1999, p. 74). Pol Pot believed there were always enemies hidden in their ranks:

> 'In our new Cambodian society, life and death conflicts still exist, as enemies in the form of various spy rings working for imperialism and international reactionaries are still planted among us to carry out subversive activities against our revolution' (Morris, 1999, p. 98).

While at the start of his reign, there may have been reason for Pol Pot to be weary of the potential of Vietnam to subjugate Cambodia and make it a satellite state, such a danger realistically disappeared already in 1975 after internal purges in the party (Morris, 1999, p. 111; 114). Pol Pot and his inner circle, according to Morris, were delusional in thinking that the Vietnamese posed an immediate threat to them. The entire leadership was 'saturated with a culture of paranoia' (Morris, 1999, p. 114). When combined with the powerful belief that the revolution needed to be drastic and fast, a dangerous outlook was formed which contributed to the destruction of their regime (Morris, 1999, p. 114).

Did Pol Pot believe he could intimidate his stronger neighbour? Or even actually win the war (Morris, 1999, p. 5)? The Khmer Rouge leadership believed they had defeated the United States which had bombed their country to counteract the Vietnamese communists, and they believed that since the Vietnamese certainly were not as powerful as the US, there was no reason why they would not be able to defeat the Vietnamese as well (Morris, 1999, p. 98). According to Sihanouk, the Radio broadcast of May 10 reflected Pol Pot's mind-set and inability to deal with reality (Chanda, 1986, p. 298). The broadcast discussed the retreat of the Vietnamese forces and linked it to an overarching strategy that would allow them to defeat their stronger neighbour:

> 'We were small in number and we had to attack a larger force. Therefore, we had to preserve our forces to the maximum. and [sic] try to kill as many of the enemy as possible. This was our slogan. In terms of numbers, one of us had to kill 30 Vietnamese. If we could implement that plan, we would certainly win. We would defeat Vietnam, regardless of its size … So far, we have succeeded in implementing this slogan of 1 against 30 … our losses are one-thirtieth of those of the Vietnamese … Using these figures, 1 Kampuchean soldier is equal to 30 Vietnamese soldiers … If we have 2 million troops, there should be 60 Vietnamese. For this reason, 2 million troops should be more than enough to fight the Vietnamese, because Vietnam only has 50 million inhabitants. We do not need 8 million people. We need only 2 million troops to crush the 50 million Vietnamese; and we still would have 6 million people left. We must formulate our combat line in this manner in order to achieve victory' (Morris, 1999, p. 104).

The argument was of course completely unrealistic, but says a lot about Pol Pot's views on the topic. In particular, it shows the manner in which Pol Pot sought to attain an extreme goal, namely the entire destruction of the Vietnamese people and was unconcerned with the costs of such a victory. Two million people were a very reasonable sacrifice, since the country would still have six million people left. People in general were hardly perceived as a cost and survivors remember that the phrase 'Keeping [you] is no gain. Losing [you] is no loss' became common (Chandler, 1999, p. 117).

Within the overarching Maoist ideology of Pol Pot, the belief was embedded that will power would prevail over material capabilities and this belief may explain to some extent the conviction that eventually Vietnam would be defeated (Morris, 1999, p. 74; 87). Even in the final days, on the morning of January 2nd when Pol Pot met with the Yugoslav ambassador, he seemed confident they would eventually be victorious (Chanda, 1986, p. 315). On January 5th, as the Vietnamese were approaching Phnom Penh, Sihanouk was summoned to meet with Pol Pot who asked him to acquire support for their country at the United Nations. Even then Pol seemed to be optimistic about Cambodia's future in his meeting with Sihanouk: 'Within two months we will wipe out the Vietnamese' Pol said (Chanda, 1986, pp. 302-303). Yet these statements were meant for a specific audience, Cambodia's citizens, a foreign ambassador and Sihanouk, whose support and help he sought. There are also strong indications that he actually was not as confident as he pretended to be. He was already concerned in the summer of 1977, that he might lose the border war (Becker, 1998, p. 306). In addition, hours after the visit of the Yugoslav ambassador for instance, whom he confidently told that the Vietnamese would be defeated, the decision was taken to evacuate most of the diplomatic staff from the capital (Chanda, 1986, p. 315), signalling that perhaps Pol Pot was not as certain of his army's ability to fight off the Vietnamese as he seemed to be.

The speed with which the Vietnamese invasion engulfed the country, most likely still took him by surprise (Becker, 1998, p. 433), and perhaps he hoped that through another guerrilla war he would eventually regain control over his country. At the same time, however, the decision to be uncompromising towards the Vietnamese regardless of the costs to his country, his own position of power or the chances of actually winning the war, seem to have been greatly influenced by his dedication to the ideology that guided him along the path he considered righteous.

11.7.2. WHY MILOSEVIC STRUCK A DEAL

Was Milosevic's behaviour during the war in Kosovo also consistent with his earlier decision-making process analysed in Chapter 10? Throughout his life, Milosevic had shown himself to be calculating, ambitious and mainly concerned with safeguarding his own interests. Therefore, the question arises, why he did not settle immediately at Rambouillet but commenced a war that he knew he probably could not win. There had been a general expectation on the basis of his behaviour at Dayton that Milosevic would cave after only a few days of bombing (Daalder & O'Hanlon, 2000, p. 101; Roberts, 1999, p. 110; Sell, 2002, p. 302). Was Kosovo different for Milosevic?

It is striking that Milosevic decided to micromanage the conflict in Kosovo even more than he had done in the earlier wars and removed any institutional restraints to his decision-making capabilities along the way (Doder & Branson, 1999, p. 253; LeBor, 2003, p. 282). Perisic, who was fired for disagreeing with Milosevic's hard-line approach, described him as being reckless and having no sense of reality, while rejecting 'competent opinions and proposals from others (Doder & Branson, 1999, p. 253; LeBor, 2003, p. 283). According to Perisic, his inner circle was composed of loyalists 'without sufficient personal integrity' and included 'those who hold no office or position but who know, and, unfortunately, can do everything' with whom he meant, Mira and her entourage (Doder & Branson, 1999, p. 253). While of course Perisic is likely to have some grievances towards Milosevic, and his word should not be accepted at face value, the fact that Milosevic had fired those who tended to disagree with him, is likely to have hampered his ability to assess the situation from an objectively rational perspective.[126] He may still have acted in accordance with subjective instrumental rationality, as rational as the situation and personal limitations allowed him to be, but there are indications that Milosevic also became more emotional which may have hampered a rational decision-making process.

Throughout the war he showed signs of stress (Sell, 2002, p. 306) and as the thread of force increased, Milosevic started to drink (LeBor, 2003, p. 281).

126 See for instance the work on Janis which was also explained in Chapter 5.

From time to time Milosevic seems to have behaved quite emotionally when it came to Kosovo. US ambassador Warren Zimmerman described Milosevic as 'unyielding, emotional, pugnacious and full of invective for its Albanian inhabitants' when Kosovo was discussed, and Lord Owen, the European envoy, likewise observed that 'over Kosovo the polite mask sometimes broke and we would be in an ugly confrontation' (Sell, 2002, p. 267). There were thus moments where he was unreflective about his response, acting from his emotions, which Weber would characterize as affective social action. These may have been linked to value rationality as Milosevic believed that Kosovo was an integral and important part of Serbia. General Naumann explains Milosevic's reaction:

> 'as soon as you mentioned Kosovo in a way which may have triggered the thought in his mind that he may lose Kosovo one day, he got very emotional. He told us, I don't know how often, that Kosovo is really the cradle of Serb culture and religion' (Sell, 2002, p. 267).

NATO's supreme commander Clark likewise found Milosevic to be 'excessively emotional about the Albanians.' According to Clark, Milosevic would always talk 'about how bad these people were … It was dehumanization of another group. It's a straight incitement to ethnic cleansing' (Sell, 2002, p. 267). Milosevic would at times emotionally revert back to the myth of Prince Lazar and explain to visitors how he was fighting 'life and death issue of national honor and sovereignty' (Doder & Branson, 1999, p. 263). Although talking to Milosevic may on occasion have seemed, in the words of Clark, 'like watching a Nuremberg rally', according to Sell, in the end 'there is little proof that he actually cared much for the province' (Sell, 2002, p. 269). He visited the region only once after his famous speeches there and never tried to improve the living conditions in Kosovo, not even for its Serb population (Sell, 2002, p. 269). In the end, Doder and Branson seem to think as well his ultimate goal was survival in power and, having misused the old myths for political ends, it would have been unthinkable to have given up Kosovo (Doder & Branson, 1999, p. 273). 'Kosovo is not Bosnia. Kosovo is my head' Milosevic is reported to have said to a US diplomat in 1998 (Sell, 2002, p. 281). Hosmer also explains his initial refusal to accept Rambouillet in these terms:

> 'Milosevic might have endangered his continued rule had he accepted Rambouillet's terms without a fight or a prior consensus to yield on the part of the Serbian populace' (Hosmer, 2001, p. xii).

The perception on his part, therefore, at the time of the Rambouillet negotiations is that compromising on Kosovo carried great risks, while he believed that the consequences of not negotiating probably would not be as bad as NATO presented them. On the basis of his experience during the earlier wars in

Yugoslavia, he became convinced that NATO's threats would not amount to much (Sell, 2002, p. 301). There had been so many empty threats already, and in Rambouillet they let two deadlines pass only to provide him with extensions (Daalder & O'Hanlon, 2000, pp. 94-95). Milosevic is also likely to have concluded from Iraq's experience with Desert Fox that the bombing would most likely be short and there were still many countries opposing a bombing campaign, also within NATO (Bellamy, 2002, p. 150; Daalder & O'Hanlon, 2000, p. 95). Strengthening Milosevic's sentiment that NATO was not very determined was the fact that ground forces had been repeatedly ruled out (Bellamy, 2002, p. 150; Daalder & O'Hanlon, 2000, p. 96). In addition, he believed that if he could show that the air campaign was actually counterproductive and worsened the fate of the Albanian citizens, by enhancing the scale and gruesomeness of the ethnic cleansing campaign, the alliance would not hold (Hosmer, 2001, p. xii).

For Milosevic, there were also some positive side effects once the air campaign commenced. He was able to blame NATO for the poor state of the economy and through a sophisticated media campaign caused the Serbian population, which had grown weary of Milosevic's mismanagement, to rally around the flag and their leader (Doder & Branson, 1999, p. 278; Hosmer, 2001, p. xiii; Post, 2004, pp. 183-184), Branson, p. 278). He does not seem to have believed he could defeat NATO, an obviously much stronger force. When he met with an American scholar and journalist he explained that: 'We have never thought that we could defeat NATO, an alliance of some 700 million people armed with the most advanced and sophisticated weaponry in the world' but he believed that if he could only survive an attack of the most powerful force in the world, that should be considered a victory in and of itself (Doder & Branson, 1999, p. 263; 273).

However, as was explained earlier, once the bombing campaign progressed some of his previously held expectations did not materialize. Milosevic was surprised by how well the alliance held up and stood firm behind their demands and when Milosevic increased the ethnic cleansing campaign this actually strengthened NATO's resolve. In the meantime, the bombing campaign had increased in strength and became more effective, while Serbia's army had been able to do little damage to the NATO coalition, downing only two airplanes (Hosmer, 2001, p. xiii; Sell, 2002, pp. 306-307). While Milosevic's military capabilities were only marginally diminished because of the bombing, NATO had inflicted serious damage on Serbia proper (Roberts, 1999, pp. 117-118). The population had grown weary of the hardship. After enduring a month of bombing the mood in the country started to change and the environment became more accommodating to compromise (Hosmer, 2001, pp. xiii-xiv). The political elite also started to suffer the consequences of the war and grew concerned about the economic devastation that was caused by the bombing and the sanctions (Hosmer, 2001, pp. xiv-xv). Milosevic calculated he was probably able to make concessions that would have cost him his hold on power before (Hosmer, 2001, p. xiv).

In the meantime, the KLA was growing in strength, but it is questionable whether this was a decisive factor for Milosevic since he continued to receive highly positive reports from his commanders (Hosmer, 2001, p. xvi; Sell, 2002, p. 312). The threat of more comprehensive intervention, meaning unconstrained air raids with the possibility of boots on the ground, however weighed heavily on Milosevic' decision to settle (Sell, 2002, pp. 311-312). According to Hosmer, Milosevic knew that unconstrained bombing was potentially detrimental to his position in power and that his best chances of surviving in power were to not let his country unravel into chaos (Hosmer, 2001, p. xviii).

The impact of the indictment that the ICTY issued in May 1999 on Milosevic's decisions is not entirely clear. While some have said it actually induced him to come to terms with NATO, others believe it rather made him more determined. Fearing, it would complicate negotiations, US officials tried to forestall the indictment and Chernomyrdin too was reportedly unhappy the indictment was issued (Sell, 2002, p. 313).

Milosevic also believed that he could count on the unwavering support of Russia, and when he saw that its commitment was dwindling, this became an important indicator the time to settle was ripe. By the end of April Milosevic started to prepare for peace when he released the US soldiers the Serbian army had captured, ensured that the refugee problem lessoned and withdrew some of its forces (Sell, 2002, p. 307). He also indicated he was willing to consider the return of refugees when they were citizens of the FRY. While on face value it made Milosevic seem cooperative, for most of the refugees it did not provide any solace since most had been forced to give their identity cards to Serb soldiers, making it impossible for them to return (Sell, 2002, p. 308).

Milosevic was presented with an ultimatum on June 2nd and he soon relents, publicly defending his choice to accept the deal while admitting that there really had been no choice as the nation would have been destroyed otherwise (Sell, 2002, pp. 308-310). The decision was accepted as a victory because Serbia's territorial integrity had been maintained and they had defended the honour of the UN. The regime turned it into a celebration, fireworks included (Stevanovic, 2004, p. 165). NATO had compromised on some of its terms, most significantly, that the UN would have an important hand in how Kosovo would be administered, Russia would play a greater role in the troops that were to be stationed there and NATO forces were not granted unhindered access throughout the FRY. Milosevic, however, also needed to compromise and conceded to 'substantial autonomy' for Kosovo (Roberts, 1999, p. 117). The eventual deal that was struck on June 10, in some respects was even less favourable than the original plan at Rambouillet, but they provided Milosevic with enough political cover to concede while maintaining his credibility (Hosmer, 2001, p. xix).

As Sell explains: 'Despite his boast to General Clark before the war that "Kosovo is more important than my head" Milosevic decided to try to cut his losses and go for the best deal he could get' (Sell, 2002, p. 311). Stevanovic similarly concludes, 'Milosevic's surrender lay outside the sphere of politics and beyond any concern for the country he led or for the people who followed him. The explanation lies in his "unusual personality" and his adamant determination to act according to his own interests' (Stevanovic, 2004, p. 166). For Milosevic, his primary motivation had not changed since the earlier wars in the Balkans, he still predominantly cared only about his own position of power.

11.8. CONCLUSION

The choices that were made by Pol Pot and Milosevic seemed at face value to be irrational. They created a situation in which a much more powerful force threatened to intervene militarily to stop the horrendous crimes they were perpetrating and then refused to consider any form of rapprochement. The reasons they had for their refusal to find a negotiated solution differed remarkably, and Milosevic was eventually willing to come to an agreement. While the behaviour of both leaders seemed to be irrational at the time, neither of the two leaders actually was irrational. Both of the decisions were rational from the point of view of the leader. The fact that Milosevic was eventually willing to come to an agreement but Pol Pot was not, can be partly attributed to the different kinds of rationality that dominated their behaviour.

Pol Pot had long been distrustful of the Vietnamese with whom his country had such an antagonistic history in which Cambodia repeatedly had to accept being subjugated to their powerful neighbour. This conviction contributed to a brutal domestic policy in which they needed to push the revolution forward aggressively at all cost in order to stay ahead of the Vietnamese and needed to rely solely on themselves and maintain absolute independence. At the same time, the fear of the Vietnamese also informed a dangerous and risky foreign policy in which Pol Pot provoked the border war over land that had once belonged to Cambodia. His ideology led him to view the situation through a fatalist lens and he believed all was lost anyway when they would allow Vietnam to dominate them. The war became an all-important sacred goal that did not allow for compromise.

Milosevic, on the other hand, was much more calculating and his behaviour continued to be dominated by instrumental rationality. He nevertheless seemed to care much more about Kosovo, and was more emotionally invested in this conflict, when compared to the conflicts of the first half of the 1990s. While he was never willing to invest actual time or money into the region, he got emotional about the idea of having to give it up. The attachment to the region was not necessarily related to the nationalist ideology, but he believed his fate was intertwined with that of Kosovo. He knew how important Kosovo was for the Serbian people and feared losing control over his position of power if he lost control over the region. When Milosevic was presented with the Rambouillet accords, there was a lot at stake for him personally. He calculated that chances were high he could not survive politically in office if he settled. He believed that considering the fragile nature of the NATO alliance, the empty threats that had gone before and the fact that they were overtly ruling out ground forces, the intervention would be mild and he would be able to withstand it. His plan was to show the allies that intervention would not be beneficial to the plight of the Kosovar Albanians by increasing the atrocities that were perpetrated against them, and undermine NATO's determination to bomb him to the negotiating table. Milosevic, however, was badly mistaken. The brutal ethnic cleansing campaign only strengthened the resolve of NATO and when Milosevic realized this, he displayed a willingness to change course. Therefore, from the end of April onwards, he started to pave the way for a peace agreement. He was eventually willing to come to an agreement when he believed this was politically tenable for him and would allow him to stay in power.

CHAPTER 12
LESSONS LEARNED FOR THE IMPLEMENTATION OF THE RESPONSIBILITY TO PROTECT

12.1. INTRODUCTION

While the previous chapter investigated two case studies that played out before the responsibility to protect was developed and adopted by states, overarching lessons about the manner in which the ideology of a non-democratic leader influences his decision-making process, can be relevant for the future implementation of the responsibility to protect.

As was explained in Chapter 4, the third pillar of the responsibility to protect expressed the preparedness of states to intervene, under Chapter VII of the UN Charter if need be, to protect the population from genocide, war crimes, crimes against humanity and ethnic cleansing when the state in which the crimes occurs is unwilling or unable to do so. Frequently, as we have seen in previous chapters, when mass atrocities have occurred in non-democratic regimes, the dictator actually has orchestrated the violence. He has incited the crimes, legitimized them and formed the institutions that perpetrated the crimes. Under those circumstances, when the dictator plays such a crucial role, intervening under the third pillar often means that the international community needs to persuade the dictator to stop the perpetration of atrocities.

Within the framework of the responsibility to protect and Chapter VII of the UN Charter, peaceful measures are preferred over force in order to achieve the objective, but military intervention should be considered as a last resort. What are the lessons that can be drawn from the interventions in Cambodia and Kosovo for the manner in which the responsibility to protect should be implemented and what implications does it have for the manner in which we study dictators and their rationality? Are these interventions success stories? These are the questions that will be asked and answered in the present chapter.

Firstly, the different choices each of the dictators made will be explained from the perspective of Weber's two types of rationality. Secondly, the rationality of the decision will be differentiated from that of the dictator who took the decision and it will be analysed what role mistakes and misperceptions played in the decision-making process. Thirdly, lessons will be drawn for the implementation of the responsibility to protect by looking at the role the rationality can play in determining whether the last resort requirement that is integral to the third pillar of the responsibility to protect, as well as Chapter VII of the UN Charter, has been fulfilled. Finally, it will be assessed to what extent the interventions of NATO and Vietnam can be considered success stories.

12.2. RATIONALITY AND RESPONSIVENESS

On the basis of the previous chapter it becomes clear that Pol Pot did not only let his value rational orientation influence his decision-making process regarding his domestic policy but this was also an important determinant for the manner in which he interacted with his more powerful neighbour, Vietnam. The historical animosity fuelled his dedication to create a communist utopia inside Cambodia that was to make the country so powerful and independent, Vietnam would never be able to subjugate it again (Morris, 1999, p. 72). In addition, it provided him with a sense that the war he was fighting was a holy war, which needed to be fought. He developed a zero-sum conception of the relationship with Vietnam and he perceived it as all-important that Cambodia would be victorious. His dedication to the cause meant that he was not concerned with the consequences of his actions but predominantly followed the path that he considered righteous and in accordance with the ideology. Consequently, when Vietnam threatened to intervene because of the atrocities he perpetrated in the border region, Pol Pot was not swayed to cease his aggressive policies. As we saw in Chapter 7, when Pol Pot rose to power, he for some time collaborated with the Vietnamese and seemed to have combined his value rational outlook with a more instrumental rational utilization of the means. In relation to the border conflict, there had been attempts early on in his reign to have come to some sort of negotiated solution but the willingness to talk dissipated in the years that followed. From the moment he started to provoke war, he was unwilling to even consider a dialogue and followed his chosen path unwaveringly.

Milosevic on the other hand, seems to have been predominantly guided by instrumental rationality. Milosevic seemed to care more about Kosovo than he did about Bosnia and at times had difficulties keeping his emotions in check, but these emotions can largely be traced back to the fact that to a large extent his position of power was tied to the outcome of the Kosovo war. Ultimately, he seems to have been concerned with safeguarding his own future more so than protecting Serbia's cradle of civilization. What he did to the best of his capabilities was to calculate what was in his own best interest to do. In doing so, he tried to take the response of others and the secondary consequences into account, as Weber says is characteristic of someone acting on the basis of instrumental rationality. He made many mistakes in doing so, but when he realized the error in his ways, when he realised that the alliance would hold up, that Russia was not standing by the Serbian cause unconditionally and that the more forceful action was actually immanent, he was willing to negotiate.

The present case study therefore suggests that value rational leaders, because of an unwillingness to take the consequences of their actions into account and view the overarching goal as so important, are highly unresponsive to either incentives or threats that are to change their chosen path. Instrumental rational leaders on the other hand, seek to attain goals that are self-interested. Since they act calculating and take the consequences of their actions into consideration, they will, *cetarus paribus*, actually be much more responsive than the value rational leader.

Unfortunately, this does not mean that these leaders are easily deterred from perpetrating atrocity crimes, it merely means that changing the policies of value rational leaders is even more difficult. It also means that much of the literature that was discussed in Chapter 2 which seeks to explain the behaviour of dictators and their decision-making process, is not necessarily applicable to value rational leaders. Most of the literature either assumes that they are completely irrational or will actually assume instrumental rationality guides their behaviour. As was explained in Chapter 2, it usually assumes that the dictator's main goal is maintaining power, an inherently instrumental rational goal. Most of the literature in the field of foreign policy analysis is subject to the same pitfall. It is, therefore, important to realize that this literature is actually only applicable to a subsection of the dictators. The other dictators, who are utterly unresponsive, do not necessarily have to be crazy, they are not irrational, they are merely unresponsive.

There may be many other reasons, unrelated to changing the behaviour of the dictator's policies, which cause a country, or regional- or international organization to initiate a particular policy. They may just want to signal intolerance of the behaviour that is exhibited or it may be necessitated by domestic political considerations, but it is important that there should not be a mistaken presumption about the difficulty of influencing ideological leaders of changing their chosen course. Cooperating with these regimes, or appeasing their leaders may have detrimental consequences but a much more challenging task lies in researching which policies should be resorted to.

12.3. THE RATIONALITY OF THE DECISION AND THE DECISION MAKER: MISTAKES AND MISPERCEPTIONS

It should be recognized that the responsiveness of a dictator does not rest solely on the type of rationality that predominates. Even when a leader acts mainly on the basis of instrumental rationality, this is certainly no guarantee that he will bow to the demands of the international community. While a complete overview of relevant factors that would make a favourable end result more likely, falls outside of the scope of the present research which is only focused on the decision-making process of the dictatorial leader, there are some lessons that can be learned from the present case study.

In relation to the war in Kosovo, a major problem was that the US only decided what it was willing to do reluctantly and slowly. This incremental and reactive approach was troubling (Daalder & O'Hanlon, 2000, p. 17). The diplomatic effort lacked clarity and the mixed signals that were sent aggravated the situation (The Independent International Commission on Kosovo, 2000, pp. 3-4). Daalder & O'Hanlon even argue that, although difficult, the war could possibly have even been prevented had there been a 'much more robust and credible threat' that included putting boots on the ground before the conflict escalated (Daalder & O'Hanlon, 2000, pp. 182-183). The continuous indecisiveness and wavering of the NATO allies caused Milosevic to miscalculate that he could withstand the bombing campaign because it would not last long, and be very restrained (LeBor, 2003, p. 287). NATO had not followed through on threats on multiple occasions and had ruled out ground forces, giving Milosevic plenty of reason to think that he did not have to fear decisive action (Daalder & O'Hanlon, 2000, p. 189; Hosmer, 2001, p. 24). In addition, he mistakenly believed that the alliance would fall apart if he could show that bombing would only worsen the plight of the Kosovar Albanians (Hosmer, 2001, pp. 26-29). It actually strengthened the alliance and incrementally increased NATO's commitment and preparedness to resort to war. Milosevic miscalculated, but NATO had given him sufficient reason to do so before and during the war in Kosovo.

Even when a particular policy is clearly articulated, however, and the objectively rational decision would have been to accommodate the wishes of an intervening force, there may be personal and situational circumstances which might dictate a different outcome. When a dictator acts largely on the basis of instrumental rationality this does not necessarily mean that he will choose an outcome which is objectively rational. He will merely act calculating to the extent possible considering the situation in which he finds himself and as far as possible considering human limitations in this respect.

As was shown in Chapter 2, cronies may distort the decision-making process. In Serbia there were initially some officials in the government who dared to disagree with Milosevic. After the war several high officials claimed 'we told him he could be a wise coward or a foolish hero [but] he would not listen' (Doder & Branson, 1999, p. 283). Milosevic seems to have gone through great lengths to silence any opposition against his decisions. The fact that he fired the head of his secret police, Jovica Stanisic, and the head of the army, Momcilo Perisic, and replaced them with more likeminded individuals (Daalder & O'Hanlon, 2000,

p. 58) probably created an environment in which the decision-making process was hampered in the sense that an objectively rational outcome was much less likely.[127]

With both instrumental rational and value rational leaders the extent to which the decision conforms to standards of objective rationality should be differentiated from the rationality of the decision maker. Value rational leaders are not irrational. They make the conscious choice to follow a path they perceive to be righteous and when they do so regardless of the consequences of their actions or the chances of success, from an objectively rational standpoint, the decision may be irrational. The decision maker, deliberately dedicating himself to the sacred goal, merely acts from a different kind of rationality. While the instrumental rational leader will do his best to weigh costs and benefits and take the reaction of others and consequences of his behaviour in account, the leader may miscalculate or misconstrue the situation. This may be caused by biases or errors stemming from his own capabilities of rational calculation and might stem from mixed messages coming from the intervening force. While the latter should be prevented, the eventual decision can always be irrational from an outsider's perspective, even when the decision maker is not.

12.4. MILITARY INTERVENTION AND THE RESPONSIBILITY TO PROTECT

While some dictators and their choices at times may appear irrational this does not have to be the case when it is acknowledged that not only are the chances that dictators miscalculate substantial and that there are actually different kinds of rationality that can influence their decision-making process. The question remains what effect the acknowledgement that there are different types of rationality should have on the implementation of R2P, especially in its most controversial form, when military intervention is considered in order to stop mass atrocities.

The original report contained elaborate directives as to when military intervention is justifiably and appropriately used. When R2P was eventually adopted at the world summit in 2005, the criteria for military intervention were less explicitly mentioned and hardly elaborated on. Pattison argues that the criteria which have already been developed in the Just War tradition, and from which the original report heavily borrowed, are still part and parcel of R2P (Pattison, 2014, p. 28). Some of the criteria that are mentioned by Pattison are explicitly mentioned in the World Summit Outcome Document, others derive

[127] Irving Janis argued that seeking to always uphold group consensus increases the chances that the outcome is sub-optimal (see Chapter 5).

from other legal obligations states are subjected to and it is instrumental to discuss them in turn.

Pattison rightfully points out that the just cause principle is reflected in the requirement that R2P only deals with situations in which genocide, war crimes, crimes against humanity and ethnic cleansing are perpetrated (Pattison, 2014, p. 28). Interventions that are enacted within the R2P framework, according to Pattison, will also fulfil the legitimate or right authority criterion because the Outcome Document clearly states that intervention should be coordinated within the UN and that coercive intervention should be authorized by the UN Security Council on the basis of Chapter VII (Pattison, 2014, p. 28). In addition, Pattison seems to agree with the analysis that was put forth in Chapter 4, that the phrase that force may be used 'should peaceful means be inadequate' should be understood to mean that the last resort requirement is still present in R2P as it was adopted in 2005 (Pattison, 2014, p. 28).

Similar to the manner in which the right authority is crucial to R2P, the right intention, according to Pattison, is ensured by the fact that interventions need to be approved by the UN Security Council (Pattison, 2014, p. 28). Even though the original ICISS report made a comparable statement and argued that 'one way of helping ensure that the "right intention" criterion is satisfied is to have military intervention always take place on a collective or multilateral rather than single-country basis' (International Commission on Intervention and State Sovereignty, 2001, p. 36), it would nevertheless seem presumptuous to argue that all UN Security Council Resolutions are motivated by the right intention. Forsythe concludes, in this respect, that the Security Council is essentially above all a political organ whose decisions are first and foremost dictated by the national interest of its members, most notably, of course, of its five permanent members (Forsythe, 2012). This in fact was also recognized in the original report as it stated:

> 'It may not always be the case that the humanitarian motive is the *only* one moving the intervening state or states, even within the framework of Security Council-authorized intervention. Complete disinterestedness – the absence of any narrow self-interest at all – may be an ideal, but it is not likely always to be a reality: mixed motives, in international relations as everywhere else, are a fact of life' (emphasis in original, International Commission on Intervention and State Sovereignty, 2001, p. 36).

While Security Council authorisation was a sufficient safeguard to ensure the right intent for those who drafted the initial report, it is not self-evident that the countries who eventually adopted R2P at the World Summit Outcome Document subscribed to the reasoning above.

Pattison also argues that *jus in bello* is ensured within the R2P framework because countries are bound by international humanitarian law. In a similar vein he argues that 'proportionality in the resort to force (as an *ad bellum* matter) is a central principle of international law' and therefore also binds states when they intervene in a country under the R2P framework (Pattison, 2014, pp. 28-29). While he is correct in noting that the intervening country would be bound by international (humanitarian) law, the Outcome Document is silent on *jus in bello* and *ad bellum* and conflating the different origins of state obligations and political commitments (note that R2P's legal grounding is still contentious)[128] risks conceptual confusion. In sum, the latter three requirements cannot be directly deduced from Paragraphs 138-140 of the World Summit Outcome, and seeing them as an integral part of R2P is less than obvious.

This leaves the first three criteria, namely just cause, right authority and last resort, as directly forming part and parcel of R2P and in need of further investigation in light of the present research. The first two criteria are relatively straight forward. This research has only dealt with dictators who perpetrated mass atrocities, or ensured mass atrocities were perpetrated on their behalf. With regards to the second criterion it is important to keep in mind that the interventions in the present chapter were not authorized by the UN Security Council. For the third criterion, it will be argued that the decision-making process of the dictatorial leaders could help with the interpretation and implementation of the last resort requirement.

Before explaining this argument more in depth, it is important to set out what exactly is meant with 'last resort'. Aloyo summarizes the research to date and reasons there are currently four broad interpretations of the last resort requirement.[129] Firstly, there is the 'strict last resort' requirement (Aloyo, 2015, p. 190). It is characterized by two elements, the first is that peaceful alternatives should always be preferred over violent alternatives and the second is the idea that all alternatives must have been tried (Aloyo, 2015, p. 190). This conception of the last resort requirement is, however, problematic because there is never a definite end to other peaceful means that could potentially be tried, while very often the measures that are left are unlikely to work (Aloyo, 2015, pp. 190-191).

The second manner in which the last resort requirement can be interpreted is called the 'necessity last resort'. As formulated by Aloyo, it 'holds that last resort means that war is permissible only if it is necessary to achieve a just cause' (Aloyo, 2015, p. 191). All non-violent means need to be exhausted if they have some chance of success, even when they are unlikely to be effective (Aloyo, 2015, p. 192). Not only is it difficult to know how big the chances of success actually are, an additional problem with this conceptualization of the last resort requirement is that it would require the implementation of peaceful measures even when

128 See Chapter 4 for an analysis of the legal grounding of R2P.

129 Pattison divided the different ideas about what the last resort should entail into three categories: 'literal account', 'reasonable chance account', and the 'least awful account' (Pattison, 2015, p. 16). Because there are based on the work of Aloyo and overlap with his categories they will not be discussed separately.

these may potentially result in more deaths than a military intervention would have (Aloyo, 2015, p. 192).

The 'reasonable chance last resort' requires that all peaceful measures that have a reasonable chance of being effective are tried before resorting to military intervention (Aloyo, 2015, p. 192). While it solves some of the previous difficulties and only requires peaceful measures that are likely to work to be given 'a reasonable amount of time', there is still the problem that perhaps war would have resulted in less harm than some peaceful measures and in addition that sometimes earlier war could have potentially saved lives (Aloyo, 2015, p. 193).

The last interpretation of last resort is therefore preferable, according to Aloyo. The 'reasonable last resort' merely requires that 'every reasonable peaceful alternative should be exhausted' (Aloyo, 2015, p. 194). This latter interpretation has the added benefit that it does not require the use of peaceful means, if military intervention will save more lives (Aloyo, 2015, p. 194).[130] A critique is therefore that it actually does not require military intervention to be used as a last option (Aloyo, 2015, p. 196). Pattison builds on this conceptualization to add a comparative element between the policy instruments to come to what he calls the 'Presumptive Last Resort' (Pattison, 2015). According to Pattison it holds that:

> '*(i) war should (generally) be the last feasible option; and (ii) the comparatively best non-violent, feasible option(s) should be tried first*' (emphasis in original Pattison, 2015, p. 17)

The comparative element rests on the idea 'that *doing* harm should generally be avoided' and presumes that war is usually the worse option and that other options do not require interveners to do as much harm, 'even if they may *allow* for more harm overall' (emphasis in original Pattison, 2015, pp. 17-18). It entails a presumption against going to war but this may not apply when the harm that would otherwise occur is much greater than the harm inflicted by war, or when peaceful alternatives, such as economic sanctions, inflict more harm than war (Pattison, 2015, p. 18). Since the presumption is not absolute, it seems Pattison's conceptualization does not differ in essence from the reasonable last resort requirement but re-emphasizes that war should presumably come last in a series of options, unless there are strong reasons that override this. It thus also opens the debate on what reasonableness is, opening up the question how much harm should be allowed to occur in order to avoid inflicting harm. The second requirement of comparing non-violent options also usefully starts the debate on which non-violent options should be favoured (Pattison, 2015, p. 18).

---

130 Ultimately Aloyo (2015) argues that the last resort requirement is unnecessary and can be subsumed under the proportionality principle of the just war tradition. Since proportionality is not explicitly mentioned in R2P, the present research will only focus on the last resort requirement.

The manner in which the last resort requirement is phrased in Paragraph 139 of the World Summit Outcome Document, lends itself to be interpreted as requiring that all reasonable measures should be attempted. Paragraph 139 expresses a willingness of the international community to take collective action under Chapter VII of the UN Charter, 'should peaceful means be inadequate'. While this clearly signals that peaceful means are preferred, it does not stipulate they need to be exhausted. A few states maintain that the three pillars of R2P[131] need to be implemented in a sequential manner but most see them as mutually reinforcing and deny that their sequential implementation is desirable or necessary as was also explicitly argued by the Secretary General in his 2009 report (Ban, 2009; International Coalition for the Responsibility to Protect, 2015). In addition, the Outcome Document does not specify how big the chances of success of peaceful measures should be, but merely states that when these are no longer sufficient to protect the population, forceful measures should be considered, leaving much discretionary room for policy makers to determine the reasonableness of the peaceful measures.

Besides the fact that there is no guidance in the formulation of R2P regarding the chances of success of peaceful means, there is another element that complicates an analysis of the last resort requirement in the R2P framework. A detailed reading of Paragraph 139 of the Outcome Document leaves some confusion about whether the phrase, 'should peaceful means be inadequate' refers to all measures within Chapter VII which can be used once Chapters VI and VIII no longer suffice, or whether it refers to military intervention under Article 42 when the non-military measures in Article 41 of the UN Charter are inadequate. Therefore, while most discussions of the last resort requirement discuss military intervention as a last resort when other measures, such as sanctions, no longer suffice, Chapter VII to which Paragraph 139 refers, deals with the option of military intervention as well as sanctions.

The reference to 'peaceful means' seems to indicate that a distinction is made between war as opposed to non-violent measures, thus also differentiating between Articles 41 and 42. Looking at the entire paragraph, however, this differentiation does not seem to be enough. Analysing the paragraph in full it can be argued that the last resort requirement in the R2P framework should be seen to consist of multiple steps. The entire paragraph stipulates that:

> 'The international community, through the United Nations, also has the responsibility to use appropriate diplomatic, humanitarian and other peaceful means, in accordance with Chapters VI and VIII of the Charter, to help protect populations from genocide, war crimes, ethnic cleansing and crimes against humanity. In this context, we are prepared to take collective action, in a timely and decisive manner, through the Security Council, in accordance with the Charter,

131 See Chapter 4 for a more elaborate explanation on the pillars.

> including Chapter VII, on a case-by-case basis and in cooperation with relevant regional organizations as appropriate, should peaceful means be inadequate and national authorities manifestly fail to protect their populations from genocide, war crimes, ethnic cleansing and crimes against humanity' (World Summit Outcome Document paragraph 139).

First, the Outcome Document mentions peaceful means that can be initiated under Chapters VI and VIII of the UN Charter. While it is not entirely clear whether these need to be exhausted first, the fact that the paragraph starts with enumerating these peaceful means, suggests they should be contemplated first. Only after having discussed these peaceful means, do the countries express a willingness to resort to take collective action under chapter VII.

Within Chapter VII of the UN Charter, Article 42 states that first, the measures under Article 41 should be considered and only when these (nonviolent) means are deemed 'inadequate' can the UN Security Council resort to military intervention. The last resort requirement in R2P therefore seems to be layered. First, there is the idea that action under Chapters VI and VIII should be considered before measures under Chapter VII can be resorted to and thereafter within Chapter VII there is a second layer in the last resort requirement. Within measures taken under Chapter VII first measures under Article 41 like sanctions or the interruption of economic or diplomatic relations should be considered, and only when these are deemed 'inadequate' can military intervention become an option. The last resort requirement within R2P requires policy makers to first determine whether measures under Chapters VI and VIII will suffice and then whether measures under Article 41 are adequate or whether they need to resort to Article 42.

Because of the manner in which the last resort requirement is formulated in Paragraph 139 of the World Summit Outcome Document, it also forms a useful starting point in the discussion started by Pattison on how to weigh the 'comparatively best non-violent option(s)' that should be tried first (Pattison, 2015). According to Paragraph 139, this should entail first those measures that can be employed under Chapters VI and VIII of the UN Charter and only thereafter those that can be imposed through Chapter VII.

The remaining problem is how one knows which measures are likely to work and what measures will be inadequate. This is primarily an empirical question that is incredibly difficult to answer. Within the specific focus of the present research, the question becomes, which measures can possibly persuade the dictator to stop perpetrating mass atrocities? When the dictator is ideologically motivated, as was the case with Pol Pot, the case study suggests peaceful dispute resolution (the domain of Chapter VI) is unlikely to work, as would any regional arrangements under Chapter VIII. Vietnam tried to enlist the help of the UN as well as from the non-aligned movement in order to resolve the conflict, but Pol Pot expressed a clear unwillingness to even consider negotiations which has been explained, largely stemmed from his value rational orientation which led to a disregard of the consequences of his actions and a determination to pursue the overarching value rational goal. For similar reasons, measures under Article 41 of the UN Charter will unlikely be persuasive for the value rational dictator, leaving solely military intervention. Under which circumstances this would be appropriate depends on many factors, specific to each case and goes beyond the scope of the present research.

As for the instrumental rational leader, most of the literature that has been done on the effectiveness of particular foreign policy tools assumes instrumental rationality on the part of the actors and is therefore applicable to these leaders.[132] It should be emphasized again, however, that the circumstances surrounding non-democratic leaders are such that their rationality tends to be much more bounded than that of democratic leaders. Most notably, the fact that they are frequently surrounded by sycophants and act on the basis of miss-information makes them more likely to act on mistaken presumptions.

Ultimately it should be concluded that, unfortunately it remains extremely difficult to bring atrocities to a halt and the promise of 'never again' is likely to be frequently broken in the time to come. The fact that it is never easy, however, does not mean that we should not differentiate between different non-democratic leaders that are pressured to stop perpetrating mass atrocities. Considering the reduced responsiveness of value rational leaders, the rationality of the dictatorial leader should be a piece in the puzzle in determining whether only military intervention is left as a last resort and all other measures are likely to have failed.

12.5. THE INTERVENTION IN KOSOVO AND CAMBODIA: SUCCESS STORIES?

Military intervention frequently has detrimental effects on a country and society and this certainly should not be resorted to lightly. Intervening in any situation in which mass atrocities are perpetrated is highly problematic, it is not always just, and peace and democracy do not automatically follow. The present study's focus on military intervention in this sense should in no way be confused with an argument in favour of military intervention in situations where atrocities are perpetrated. Nor should the present research be misconstrued as presenting the interventions that are analysed in the comparative case studies as models of how R2P should work in practice.

It should be kept in mind that R2P was created partly in response to the war in Kosovo, which was deemed by many countries as unacceptable since it was not explicitly authorized by the UN Security Council. The present interventions,

132 See chapter 3 for an overview of the literature.

even though arguably the interventions by NATO and especially the intervention by Vietnam are likely to have saved many lives (Hanlon, 2006b, pp. 60-61; Power, 2013, p. 472), are questionable as success stories of how atrocities should be brought to a halt. Neither Vietnam nor NATO can be said to have had predominantly humanitarian motives (Bazyler, 1987, p. 608; Power, 2013, p. 448), and both powers invaded without authorization of the UN Security Council. The fact that countries in 2005 made military intervention conditional on the authorization of the UN Security Council, indicates that even when atrocities are perpetrated, countries continue to view military intervention without Security Council authorization as highly problematic. During the Cold War, as was explained in Chapter 4, intervening out of humanitarian concerns was largely seen as undesirable altogether.

In addition, especially the manner in which NATO chose to fight the war in Kosovo has been highly criticized. They chose to rely solely on an air campaign and flew at high altitudes because there was a general unwillingness to risk the lives of the soldiers of the invading countries (Power, 2013, p. 450; Roberts, 1999, p. 110). Had they been more accepting of this risk, this could have possibly saved many lives on both the Kosovar Albanian as well as the Serbian side (Webber, 2009, p. 456) because the height increased the risk of unnecessary civilian deaths (Daalder & O'Hanlon, 2000, p. 123). There was a lot of collateral damage, targets were at times wrongly identified and the focus was on immovable targets which necessarily had more impact on civilians than on moving military targets (Roberts, 1999, p. 115). The war cost an estimated 500 civilians their lives, and between 576 and 5,000 Serbian soldiers were killed. In addition, the bombing not only had crippling effects on Serbia's production of arms, but also electricity, and it incapacitated the country's oil refinery capabilities (Webber, 2009, p. 451). NATO disrupted the lives of Serbia's population because their targets included bridges, power plants, communication and media facilities and political headquarters. Therefore, while the stated goal was to disrupt the command and control structure, they also victimized the wider population (Power, 2013, p. 458). More could have been done to prevent serious harm to the population as is evidenced by the use of cluster bombs and the depleted-uranium tipped armor-piercing shells and missiles that caused environmental damage (The Independent International Commission on Kosovo, 2000, p. 5). The means which were used did not match any of the purported humanitarian goals (Roberts, 1999, p. 110). The Independent International Commission on Kosovo which had been tasked with investigating the crisis in Kosovo called it a success and a failure, and argued a higher standard to protect civilians should be upheld in future endeavours (The Independent International Commission on Kosovo, 2000, p. 5). Daalder & O'Hanlon conclude that the 'story of the Kosovo crisis is largely a saga of NATO and its major international partners doing the right thing in the wrong way' (Daalder & O'Hanlon, 2000, p. 16). NATO's intervention, therefore, warrants more reflection about the means that are chosen, highlighting the importance of initiatives like 'the responsibility while protecting' that was put forward by Brazil.[133]

While it may be the case that in the end the intervention saved lives, in the short term there were some perverse results. As stated earlier, Milosevic first decided to dramatically increase the atrocities against the Albanian population (Power, 2013, p. 461) and later when the Albanian refugees returned they subsequently expelled 100,000 Serbs from their homes and killed 1,500 (Power, 2013, p. 463). According to Power 'although the bombing campaign paid sizable dividends for the majority of ethnic Albanians, its execution and aftermath have been used to confirm the futility, perversity, and jeopardy of acting to stop atrocity' (Power, 2013, p. 451).

In Cambodia's case, Vietnam's intervention resulted in a protracted civil war, foreign domination and the international community played a shameful part in which they continued to support the Khmer Rouge. After the Khmer Rouge fled to the Thai border[134], China supplied them with weapons and the US provided covert assistance worth up to 12 million US dollars a year (Power, 2013, p. 147; 153). According to Power:

> 'The KR tactics changed little. KR soldiers captured and executed foreign tourists and inflicted terror upon those Cambodians who had the misfortune to live under KR control' (Power, 2013, p. 153).

The idea of independence mastery thus had to be severely compromised, but according to Chandler this was not particularly problematic for Pol 'since the main objective – throwing the Vietnamese out of Cambodia – was shared by his major patrons' (Chandler, 1999, p. 159).

After the deposed regime of Pol Pot and the new government which had been put in place by the Vietnamese, both requested to represent Cambodia at the UN, the UN Credentials Committee had to determine which of the two regimes should be given this formal recognition. The representative of the US convinced six of the nine committee members that the manner in which a government treated their own citizens should not be taken into account and the committee recommended the Khmer Rouge were to be recognized as the legitimate government (Power, 2013, pp. 149-152). The issue was then taken up by the General Assembly, where a heated debate followed in which Pol Pot and

133 See Chapter 4, and 4.5.4 in particular, for a more detailed explanation.

134 Although Cambodia had its own strained history with Thailand, both of the countries shared a mutual animosity towards Vietnam which contributed in a willingness to cooperate. Perhaps even more important for the Thai government was that China was prepared to stop its support for the Thai communist movement if the government would shelter the Khmer Rouge (Chandler, 1999, p. 159).

the Khmer Rouge were condemned for the many atrocities they inflicted on their population (Power, 2013, p. 151). Most, however, still felt the illegal invasion of Vietnam should not be dignified with Cambodia's seat at the UN, no matter how brutal the old regime was (Power, 2013, pp. 151-152).

Support for the old regime only abated with the end of the Cold War in sight (Power, 2013, p. 154). Pol Pot continued to try to keep a hold over the country, and blocked any attempt to bring about peace until well into the 1990s (Chandler, 1999, p. 173; Kiernan, 2002, pp. 489-490). Many of the high level cadre would eventually defect to the government or tried to otherwise escape prosecution when the establishment of the Extraordinary Chambers in the Courts of Cambodia neared (Kiernan, 2002, pp. 491-492). Pol Pot was sentenced to death in absentia by the new government in August 1979. In 1981 the party was officially absolved, although in practice nothing changed, and this should therefore be seen as predominantly a political ploy (Chandler, 1999, pp. 160-161). Officially a coalition was formed, but one that was still dominated by the Khmer Rouge leadership (Chandler, 1999, p. 161). Pol Pot's forces also did most of the fighting against the Vietnamese and their puppet government (Chandler, 1999, p. 162). In 1995, Pol Pot suffered a stroke and two years later he was removed from power because he made the fatal decision to assassinate Son Sen (Chandler, 1999, pp. 180-181). He was subjected to a show trial in the final year of his life and died in his sleep in April 1998 (Chandler, 1999, p. 181; Kiernan, 2002, p. 492). Reflecting on Pol's life, Chandler finds that:

> 'he never stepped from the path he chose to follow in the 1950s and never spoke in detail about the price the Cambodian people paid to be subordinated to his vision of Cambodia and, after 1977, his abiding hostility toward Vietnam. Altering or abandoning his vision was impossible to Pol Pot' (Chandler, 1999, p. 187)

Milosevic was removed from power on October 5 2000 after there was a general uprising against him and his regime. He was arrested on 31 March 2001 and was accused of abusing his position of power (LeBor, 2003, p. 315). Despite promises he would not be handed over to The Hague, he was transferred to the ICTY on June 28 2001 (LeBor, 2003, p. 317). He died in his cell from natural causes on March 11 2006 ('Milosevic "died of natural causes"' 2006).

12.6. CONCLUSION

Pol Pot was guided throughout his reign predominantly by his value rational orientation while Milosevic acted overwhelmingly on the basis of instrumental rationality. This was true for the choices they made both domestically as well as internationally. While the instrumental rational leader is more responsive and takes the consequences of his actions into account, anticipating the reaction of others, this does not mean that there will be an objectively rational outcome, or the desired outcome. Miscalculations and misperceptions may inhibit any rational assessment of the situation. The cause of such mistakes may sometimes lie partly with the intervening force, as was the case with NATO. However, it may also originate in the domestic circumstances in which the leader finds himself, for instance, when he is surrounded by cronies, or may stem from his own personal limitations and biases. In this sense, a distinction should be made between the subjective rationality of the decision maker and the objective rationality of the outcome.

The difference in the extent to which instrumental and value rational leaders can be influenced by intervening forces, can be helpful in determining whether peaceful measures should be deemed inadequate. The responsibility to protect requires policy makers to first assess whether measures under Chapter VI or VIII of the UN Charter might be adequate to address the atrocities. Only when this is not the case, can measures under Chapter VII be considered and then first peaceful measures under Article 41 need to be examined, and only when they are not sufficient to bring about an end to the crimes, can military intervention become an option. The unresponsiveness of the value rational leader would be a useful indicator in this assessment that peaceful measures may not work.

Even when military intervention is likely to have saved the lives of many people, this does not necessarily mean that the interventions should immediately be considered a success. Both of the interventions that have been analysed in the present research displayed serious flaws on account of the international community. The most flagrant and problematic aspect is of course both occurred without the approval of the UN Security Council but there are other problematic aspects. In the case of the intervention in Cambodia, the unwavering support for the Khmer Rouge in the years after Pol Pot was deposed is reprehensible considering that the evidence of the horrors the Cambodian population had suffered during the reign of Pol Pot surfaced almost immediately. It should be acknowledged that it reflects the *Zeitgeist* during which mass atrocities, especially when they occurred within the borders of the country, were not deemed to be a concern for the international community, which was primarily concerned with safeguarding state sovereignty. In 1999, there were proponents of the idea that mass atrocities should not be allowed to happen without question. There was still much criticism because it occurred without explicit UN Security Council approval but an initiative to condemn the intervention also did not garner enough support. What most have agreed upon, however, is that the manner in which NATO intervened was unacceptable because it risked and cost too many civilians their lives.

Influencing dictators to change course will always be difficult, especially with unresponsive value rational leaders, but dealing with an instrumental rational leader is no guarantee for success either. The unresponsiveness of value rational leaders in particular should, however, be kept in mind when devising a particular policy and taken into account when assessing the decision-making process of these leaders. All too often both policy as well as scholarly research is still grounded in the assumption that the primary goal of any dictator is to retain power while this does not necessarily have to be the case.

CHAPTER 13
CONCLUSION: A PIECE OF THE PUZZLE

13.1. INTRODUCTION: TIMES HAVE CHANGED

Dictators are shrouded in mystery and therefore inherently difficult to study, but this difficulty is matched by its importance as dictators continue to subject their population to horrible crimes. While they differ tremendously in the degree to which they plunge their country into a life of poverty and death, the worst forms of violence, genocide, crimes against humanity, war crimes and ethnic cleansing, occur more often in non-democratic regimes. Frequently, in those situations the dictator is not only unable to prevent them, but actually creates the circumstances in which lower level cadre feel compelled to perpetrate the crimes. The dictator can incite and legitimize the atrocities by propagating an exclusionary ideology. In addition, he is able to create the institutions in which perpetrators will feel duty-bound to perpetrate the horrible acts. Because there are often very few institutional provisions that constrain the power of the dictator and he can exert enormous influence over his regime's policies, studying him, his motivation and rationality are essential in order to bring these crimes to a halt.

After World War II, countries pledged 'to save succeeding generations from the scourage of war' and reaffirmed their 'faith in fundamental human rights' (Preamble of the UN Charter). In the years that followed, however, the focus on preventing war between countries, by respecting the sovereignty of each nation, restricted efforts to prevent or stop the perpetration of mass atrocities within states. For years, sovereignty was conceptualized in such a way that it prevented other countries or the international community from intervening in the domestic policies of a dictator who perpetrated atrocities in his own country. After the horrendous events in Rwanda and the former Yugoslavia, this idea was increasingly seen as problematic. Failing to intervene effectively to stop those horrendous crimes, as well as intervening without the authorization of the UN Security Council, as happened in 1999 in Kosovo, were both deemed unacceptable. It led Kofi Annan to ask his famous question what should be done in those instances (Annan, 2000, p. 48).

The Canadian government then brought a group of experts together to answer this important question. In 2001 they published their groundbreaking report in which they introduced 'the responsibility to protect'. The report changed the way that sovereignty had been interpreted since WWII. It argued that sovereignty entailed the responsibility to protect the population. When countries convened at the World Summit in 2005 and endorsed the responsibility to protect, although in a more limited form than was originally envisioned in the report, this was a watershed moment. Countries made the political commitment to protect their population from genocide, war crimes, ethnic cleansing and crimes against humanity, help other countries protect their population when they are unable to do so, and voiced a preparedness to act, through the UN Security Council, if need be, under Chapter VII, and intervene when a state manifestly fails to protect its own population.

Unfortunately, its implementation leaves much to be desired. When mass atrocities are perpetrated in dictatorial regimes, and the dictator is the instigator, the extent to which measures directed at mitigating or stopping mass atrocities are successful, depends largely on the responsiveness of the dictator. Whether he is willing to change his policies becomes a crucial variable in whether mass atrocities can be brought to a halt. The present research has therefore sought to answer the question of why and to what extent dictatorial leaders will differ in their responsiveness to measures from third countries and the international community that are aimed to stop them from committing mass atrocities. It furthermore set out to analyse what consequences this has for the implementation of the responsibility to protect.

In answering this question, it was first deemed necessary to analyse how the dictator brings forth mass atrocities, how the dictator created the necessary circumstances, and how he relates to other risk factors and preconditions for mass atrocities that are considered important in the literature. After having established his role in the perpetration of mass atrocities, the decision-making process and rationality of the dictator was scrutinized. Through a comparative case study of Pol Pot and Milosevic the extent to which the type of rationality influenced their decision-making process was assessed and subsequently the implications that the findings had for theory as well as the implementation of the responsibility to protect have been investigated.

13.2. THE ROLE OF THE DICTATOR IN MASS ATROCITIES

While most scholars agree that the dictator can be very important for the process through which mass atrocities are perpetrated, how he facilitates the perpetration of these crimes remained understudied. Whether atrocity crimes are perpetrated, certainly does not only depend on a non-democratic regime, or its leader, and he is not always the instigator of atrocities. They can, amongst others, be perpetrated in an armed conflict, by rebel groups, by a political rival or can occur when there is inter-communal violence (Welsh, 2015, p. 8), and are associated with numerous risk factors, of which a non-democratic regime is just one. The risk factors include a history of violence and conflict, schisms in society and difficult life conditions caused by economic or political crises, or war. It is therefore important to analyse how the dictator interacts and relates to these other factors and how a dictator can use the factors that put a country at risk, but often also has the power to create additional risk factors, in order to to incite and facilitate the perpetration of atrocity crimes.

When a country has a history of violence, and there are schisms in society, the dictator is able to give these historical occurrences contemporary relevance by reinterpreting the history of the country. In doing so he can use pre-existing schisms to further polarize society and can legitimize the violence through an exclusionary ideology. The content of the ideology will differ but it generally justifies the violence and portrays the victims of the crimes as enemies who are deserving of their fate. Difficult life conditions, whether due to circumstance or due to the dictator's policy, can make the population more susceptible to the dictator's message that is usually spread through the media in a propaganda campaign.

In addition, the dictator will need to create the institutions that allow the regime to perpetrate atrocities. He may facilitate mass participation by creating a mass movement and he can create specialised killing units that will perpetrate the most gruesome crimes. These specialised killing units can facilitate broader participation in the violence by taking the lead in the killing process, they may form an important part of the security apparatus that carries out the crimes behind closed doors, they can be a paramilitary organization with only loose ties to the regime to provide for plausible deniability or a combination of the above. The individual is often explicitly trained to carry out such a gruesome task and he relies on the authorization that is provided by the regime, through the ideology that is propagated, as well as on the institutional hierarchy that commands the perpetration of the crimes to be able to perpetrate the violence.

13.3. THE DICTATOR AS A RATIONAL ACTOR

When the dictator initiates and facilitates the perpetration of mass atrocities, he is likely to also be an important determinant for the success or failure of foreign policy measures to mitigate or stop the crimes. As was explained in Chapter 2, dictators are unable to rule singlehandedly but they are generally much more important for any policy decision than leaders of democratic regimes. Therefore, if the responsibility to protect is to be implemented effectively in situations where the dictator deliberately fosters a conducive climate for their perpetration, other countries, or the international community, needs to convince the dictator to change his policy of perpetrating atrocities. Most of the literature that has analysed the impact of foreign policy measures assumes that this will happen when costs outweigh the benefits. International relations theory does this while assuming states are the primary actors, which strive to attain particular goals and as such seek to attain an objectively rational outcome. Foreign policy analysis acknowledges that the individual is important and scholars have emphasized the human limitations in calculating the objectively rational outcome. In dictatorships these limitations are likely to be even more extensive due to the limited access the leader has to information because of the presence of sycophants and because there is a greater risk of groupthink.

While the latter strand of research made great strides in analysing the role and bounds of rationality in the decision-making process of leaders, there is an important shortcoming that is especially troubling when studying mass atrocities. It is highly problematic that the research is unable to accommodate the role that ideology potentially plays in the decision-making process. While it is sometimes argued that ideology can be seen as a preference, this line of reasoning is insufficient because ideology can make people act in a manner that goes against their preferences. Although not all dictators will be genuinely committed to the ideology, some are, and their devotion to the ideology is likely to influence their decision-making process. The influence of ideology is likely to make them seem irrational when their behaviour is analysed in accordance with the dominant approaches in foreign policy analysis and international relations because those approaches assume a particular kind of rationality. Weber calls this type of rationality, instrumental rationality. It entails a calculation of the costs and benefits to obtain a self-interested end while considering possible different alternatives and the potential reactions of others. He also identified a second type of rationality, value rationality, which entails the conscious decision to be devoted to some cause, no matter of what it consists, regardless of the chances of success. It is therefore important to assess which type of rationality dominates the decision-making process of dictators, by analysing the choices they made throughout their lives.

13.4. RATIONALITY AND THE DECISION-MAKING PROCESS OF POL POT AND SLOBODAN MILOSEVIC

The decisions of Pol Pot and Milosevic when they were threatened with military intervention by a much stronger force in response to the atrocities that their forces were perpetrating in a contested border region, can be explained in this light. Both of the dictatorial leaders created the circumstances in society without which these crimes would not have been possible. Both of the leaders were able to exercise much influence over the policy choices that were made within their respective countries, but they were guided by different kinds of rationality.

Both dictators used the preconditions in society that were already there, a history of violence and war, schisms in society, difficult life conditions and created additional pre-conditions and risk factors by creating a non-democratic system of government and by aggravating the difficult life conditions, to foster a climate that was conducive to mass violence.

Although Vietnam did not pose a threat to Cambodia, or to Pol Pot's continued rule, by the time Pol Pot initiated the border dispute, Cambodia's history was tainted by the constant threat of invasions from its more powerful neighbours, Vietnam especially. The lingering distrust would be of great importance to Pol Pot and the choices he made. In addition, the pre-existing schism between Cambodia's urban and rural population is important to understand his rise to power and subsequent reign. Pol Pot rose to power in a brutal civil war while the country was being destroyed by endless bombing campaigns by the US. The countryside had suffered disproportionately, aggravating already existing tensions between the city and the countryside. Pol Pot and his Khmer Rouge used these antagonistic feelings of the rural population in particular to rise to power and prominence. The history of the country was used to legitimize his rule, and old traditions were incorporated into his new revolutionary movement. Resentment towards the city population and the Vietnamese was, moreover, used to legitimize the crimes that especially targeted these groups. Pol Pot, in addition, created the institutions that made these crimes possible. People were trained to become torturers and soldiers. Many people were tortured to death and countless individuals were executed by the communist cadre that defended the brutal regime.

Milosevic, likewise, used existing preconditions, and created new ones, to foster a situation in which these crimes could be perpetrated. He rose to power in the wake of Tito's death while the country found itself facing difficult times. Yugoslavia was confronted with a dramatic economic downturn while the end of the Cold War eroded the country's prestige internationally. Noticing the power of nationalist rhetoric, he started using the pre-existing schisms between the different groups in Yugoslavia to generate more power. Through an elaborate propaganda campaign, he spread nationalism and hatred. The rhetoric created fear in the other republics and Milosevic's nationalist stance contributed to the disintegration of the country, generating another important risk factor for the perpetration of mass atrocities. While he ensured he had control over the national army to fight his battle, he set up additional institutions that facilitated the perpetration of the crimes. The paramilitary units that were used next to the national army perpetrated the most horrendous crimes while providing Milosevic with plausible deniability regarding his own involvement.

Using Max Weber's theory on rationality to analyse the biographies of these two leaders, it becomes clear that the two dictators acted on the basis of different kinds of rationality. Pol Pot found his calling while studying in Paris. He was pre-occupied with his activities in a small circle of students who were passionate about the prospects of communism for their country and whom were determined to bring forth its liberation of the colonial yoke. He never cared much for his studies and when he returned to Cambodia he dedicated himself to the revolution and fought a war of independence even though it seemed unlikely he would ever win. When his forces conquered Phnom Penh, his communist ideals were implemented immediately. Cities were evacuated and family life came to a halt in favour of collectivization. He never wavered from the path he saw as just and pursued it with incredible perseverance and determination.

Milosevic on the other hand, was not committed to a particular ideology but used socialism and nationalism for different audiences at different times to garner support and power. When he saw how his nationalist stance resonated with the population, this became his dominant strategy. He tried to gain control over as much of Yugoslavia as he could, hoping to establish himself as the new Tito, but when the country started to unravel because of the climate of ethnic hatred and fear that he had helped to establish, he decided he would rule over as much of it as he could. Brutal wars followed in Croatia and Bosnia but when it became more useful for him personally to establish peace, he abandoned them. He stood by as the Krajina region was cleansed and humiliated the Bosnian Serbs at Dayton, making more concessions than the Bosnian Serbs were willing to accept. He proved to be pragmatic, abandoning certain goals when necessary, and compromising when costs became too high.

These different rationalities caused the two leaders to make wholly different choices when they found themselves facing foreign intervention by a much larger force. In 1979 Vietnam had enough of Pol Pot's aggressive border incursions during which his forces massacred numerous villages. Before establishing an army of the refugees that had fled Pol Pot's murderous regime, Vietnam tried to reach out diplomatically several times in the hopes of working out a more peaceful solution but Pol Pot rejected every attempt outright. Staying true to what he saw was the righteous path, Pol Pot was eventually forced to flee as Vietnamese forces entered the capital. His ideological outlook prevented him from being able to compromise; he wanted to fight off the Vietnamese enemy, regardless of cost or consequence.

Milosevic faced military intervention by NATO in 1999 after he failed to sign the Rambouillet peace accords. When the bombing campaign commenced on March 24, Milosevic increased the violence in Kosovo, hoping to show NATO that their air raids were counterproductive. After the international community had failed to act decisively during the wars of the first half of the 1990s, and they had broken ultimatums and had frequently wavered in relation to the conflict in Kosovo, Milosevic did not expect the bombing to last long and anticipated it would be mild. In addition, he did not expect the alliance to hold up. He miscalculated. The horrendous violence that his troops inflicted on the Kosovar Albanian population enhanced the determination of NATO. The bombing raids became more extensive and after initially rallying around the flag, eventually the population as well as his cronies started to become dissatisfied with Milosevic's rule. Milosevic decides to compromise and reached an agreement with NATO in June. Milosevic now believed he was in a position to make concessions that would have cost him his power beforehand. In addition, Russia also started to put pressure on him to settle and he started to realize that NATO was determined to win the war and feared they would actually put boots on the ground. Milosevic therefore was highly pragmatic and calculating in his decision to settle.

13.5. IMPLICATIONS FOR THEORY AND THE RESPONSIBILITY TO PROTECT

Most of the theories on dictatorships assume that the leader's primary purpose is staying in power. However, this assumption does not always hold true for all dictators. Much of the existing literature on dictators and dictatorships is therefore only applicable to those instances where instrumental rationality dominates a dictator's decision-making process. In international relations and foreign policy analysis literature the focus lies on this particular type of rationality, which can cause value rational dictators to be perceived as irrational even though they are not. They can act rationally and make a conscious choice, but do so on the basis of a different kind of rationality.

The ideology that motivates some decision makers, can make a particular goal so important that the dictator will pursue it regardless of costs to himself, dedicate himself to its attainment and will do so regardless of chances of success. These value rational leaders will no longer be concerned with the consequences of their actions, and consequently, they will be harder to influence with foreign policy measures. This should be taken into account when deciding whether force should be used as a last resort. The last resort requirement that is embedded in the responsibility to protect necessitates an assessment whether measures under Chapters VI or VIII of the UN Charter are likely to suffice to protect populations from mass atrocity. If measures under Chapter VII are necessary, the latter chapter specifies that peaceful measures should be tried first before resorting to military intervention when there is a threat to international peace and security. The last resort requirement of the responsibility to protect is thus two pronged: first between Chapters, favouring Chapters VI and VIII, and subsequently within Chapter VII. Deciding which measures are likely to work, is an extremely difficult assessment and the type of rationality which dominates the decision-making process of the leader is an important piece of the puzzle because ideological, value rational dictators, will *cetarus paribus*, be less responsive than instrumental rational dictators.

Even when the dictator acts overwhelmingly on the basis of instrumental rationality, and tends to be more easily swayed through foreign policy mechanisms, this of course does not mean they will always be successful. A distinction should be made in this regard between the rationality of the decision maker and the extent to which his choices are objectively rational. The advances that have been made in foreign policy analysis, which specify the limits of people to reach an objectively rational outcome, should be taken into account. At the same time, it should also be noted that limits to an objectively rational outcome do not only come from the individual, they can also be inherent in his surroundings. The manner in which a dictatorial regime functions often inhibits a dictator from reaching an optimal decision. In particular, that he will favour less competent and therefore also less threatening individuals, and generally does not tolerate dissent or disagreement, means that the supply of information as well as the policy advice he receives, is inherently of lesser quality and less reliable. This likely played a role for Milosevic, who fired anyone opposing a confrontational approach during the crisis in Kosovo. Cronies tend to fear for their jobs, livelihoods and even lives when expressing disagreement or opposition to the dictators, making groupthink a more likely scenario and hampering the decision-making process.

It is not only the characteristics of dictatorial regimes that can lead to a suboptimal outcome. Limitations to an objectively rational outcome can also stem from the international community and the policy choices that are made by those trying to influence the dictator. The policies of the international community during the wars in Yugoslavia in the first half of the 1990s had been characterized by indecisiveness and lack of determination. This was probably in the back of Milosevic's mind when the conflict in Kosovo escalated. When NATO subsequently failed to send a unison message and the US continued to rule out ground forces, Milosevic assumed any force used would not last long or be intense, especially because the alliance seemed to be divided internally. He was wrong and miscalculated. The failure to send a clear message that ethnic cleansing would have severe repercussions, may have hampered an earlier negotiated solution to the problem.

While both of the interventions are likely to have saved thousands of lives, neither should be considered unquestionably a success story. Both did not have sufficient legal authorization of the Security Council. In addition, the intervention in Cambodia did not immediately bring peace to the country, and its population continued to suffer for many years. In the case of Kosovo, the manner in which the intervention was executed resulted in unnecessary civilian deaths, because NATO was unwilling to risk the lives of their own soldiers. The findings of this research should therefore not be confused with an argument that favours military intervention but argues that unfortunately, some dictators will be highly unresponsive to foreign policy measures.

13.6. CONCLUSION

Dictators differ in the extent to which they are responsive to foreign policy mechanisms from other countries or the international community, and a key variable that contributes to this difference is the degree to which the dictator actually believes in the ideology he propagates. Ideological dictators, who perceive the goal that they strive for as sacred, will be less likely to compromise this stance and change their domestic policies that are usually closely tied to the ideology.

The ideological commitment some of these dictators have, sits uncomfortably in the rational choice paradigm that continues to dominate the debate among international relations scholars who generally continue to focus on states rather than individuals, and where the focus is still on what objectively the most favourable outcome is, given the costs and benefits involved. Foreign policy analysis focused on the individual and the limitations of people to behave rationally, but still presumed a more limited form of instrumental rationality predominates the choices of decision makers. Neither is able to accommodate the role that ideology plays in the decision-making process because it can cause people to act against their preferences and may cause self-destructive behaviour. Rather than seeing these actors as irrational, it would be more sensible to see these actors not as behaving with a complete lack of rationality but to acknowledge that they act on the basis of a different kind of rationality. This finding is potentially highly relevant to the wider discipline. Although this research focused on non-democratic leaders, there is little reason to assume that the conclusions would be different for other leaders. The findings are not restricted to the domain of dictatorial leaders, but the implications that the type of rationality has for the final policy decisions, are much greater for non-democratic regimes where the influence of the leader is more extensive.

The conclusions of this research should have implications for both theory and practice. The extensive body of work that has been done under the assumption that the primary objective of leaders is maintaining their position of power is very insightful when it comes to dictators who are, in the words of Max Weber, instrumentally rational, like Slobodan Milosevic. For dictators who are utterly devoted to the ideology, however, this research is less useful. These leaders, like Pol Pot will, no matter what the costs, or the chances of success, pursue their ideological goals. This does not make them irrational, but less responsive to pressure from outside of their country. These differences between different dictators should be taken into account when trying to prevent or mitigate atrocity crimes and are therefore important to further a more effective implementation of the responsibility to protect. It should carry implications in particular for how the last resort criterion is assessed with ideological leaders not being as responsive as instrumental rational leaders. This does not mean that military intervention is the best or preferred option, not even with value rational leaders. The two cases analysed in this research are both questionable success stories, but it is important to realize that in some situations, lesser measures are unlikely to work.

In the end there are no easy answers, and it is impossible to know with certainty which measures will undoubtedly be successful in any given situation. The picture is not complete yet. For years scholars have focused on the instrumental rational dictator and tried to analyse his decision-making process and valuable insights have been generated by those efforts but it is important that a similar effort is made in relation to the value rational dictators. Part of this research should explicitly focus on the question of which measures could potentially be effective in influencing value rational dictators.

This research was only able to present a piece of the puzzle but it is important that the effort to obtain the complete picture continues, and this needs to be done through an interdisciplinary lens. Attempts to further the implementation of the responsibility to protect should focus on the topic at hand, not any particular discipline. This research has shown that concepts like rationality, which are used in a different manner in different disciplines, can be usefully combined and integrated in one research if only the distinctions are clearly understood and taken into account. In addition, doing so can fill the gaps in theoretical frameworks that have been developed with one particular disciplinary lens. It is time international relations and foreign policy analysis take into account different kinds of rationality[135], and the research on dictators needs to take into consideration that not all dictators have maintaining their position of power as their primary goal and motivation. Especially, with regard to mass atrocities, which have been researched from a multitude of perspectives, it is important that the fields of study consciously but carefully learn from each other. Concepts need to be closely scrutinised for their meaning within the framework of the discipline at hand, and might not be easily transferrable but, as this research has shown, such an undertaking is worthwhile. It can lead to significant advantages in further developing and refining the theory, and can contribute to a better understanding of the manner in which mass atrocities can be brought to a halt.[136]

---

135 As Morris (1999) also argued by in relation to the culture of the elite, this research argues is also necessary with regard to the decision-making process.

136 Some of the findings of the present research have previously been published (Weerdesteijn, 2015, 2016 – in press).

REFERENCES

Abuza, Z. (1993). The Khmer Rouge Quest for Economic Independence. *Asian Survey, 33*(10), 1010-1021.

Adair-Toteff, C. (2005). Max Weber's Charisma. *Journal of Classical Sociology, 5*(2), 189-204.

Adesnik, D., & McFaul, M. (2006). Engaging autocratic allies to promote democracy. *The Washington Quarterly, 29*(2), 5-26.

Allison, G. T. (2005). Conceptual Models and the Cuban Missile Crisis. In G. J. Ikenberry (Ed.), *American Foreign Policy* (pp. 402-446). New York: Pearson Longman.

Aloyo, E. (2015). Just War Theory and the Last of Last Resort. *Ethics & International Affairs, 29*(02), 187-201.

Alvarez, A. (2001). *Governments, Citizens and Genocide: A Comparative Interdisciplinary Approach* Bloomington: Indiana University Press.

Alvarez, A. (2006). Militias and Genocide. *War Crimes, Genocide & Crimes Against Humanity, 2*, 1-33.

Alvarez, A. (2008). Destructive Beliefs: Genocide and the Role of Ideology. In A. Smeulers & R. Haveman (Eds.), *Supranational Criminology: Towards a Criminology of International Crimes* (Vol. 6, pp. 213-232). Antwerp: Intersentia.

Amer, R. (1997). Border Conflicts between Cambodia and Vietnam. *IBRU Boundary and Security Bulletin, 5*(2), 80-97.

Andreas, P. (2009). Criminaliserende gevolgen van internationale economische sancties. *Justitiele verkenningen, 35*(3), 100-126.

Angus, I. (1983). Disenchantment and modernity: The mirror of technique. *Human Studies, 6*(1), 141-166.

Annan, K. (1999). Two concepts of sovereignty. *The Economist*. Retrieved from http://www.economist.com/node/324795

Annan, K. (2000). "We the Peoples" The Role of the United Nations in the 21st Century. New York: United Nations.

Annan, K. (2005). In larger freedom: towards development, security and human rights for all: United Nations.

Arato, A. (2016). *Post Sovereign Constitution Making*. Oxford: Oxford University Press.

Arbour, L. (2008). The responsibility to protect as a duty of care in international law and practice. *Review of International Studies, 34*(03), 445-458.

Arendt, H. (1962). *The Origins of Totalitarianism*. Cleveland: Meridian Books, The World Publishing Company.

Arendt, H. (1963). *Eichmann in Jerusalem: A Report on the Banality of Evil*. New York: Penguin Books.

Ashbrook, J., & Bakich, S. D. (2010). Storming to partition: Croatia, the United States, and Krajina in the Yugoslav War. *Small Wars & Insurgencies, 21*(4), 537-560.

Askin, K. D. (2005). Never Again Promise Broken Again-Again-and Again. *Cardozo L. Rev., 27*, 1723-1729.

Axworthy, L. (2012). RtoP and the Evolution of State Sovereignty. In J. Genser & I. Cotler (Eds.), *The Responsibilty to Protect: The Promise of Stopping Mass Atrocities in Our Time*. New York: Oxford University Press.

Ayittey, G. B. N. (2011). *Defeating Dictators: Fighting tyranny in Africa and around the world* New York: Palgrave Macmillan.

Baehr, P. R. (2009). Foreign Policy. In D. P. Forsyth (Ed.), Encyclopedia of Human Rights: Oxford University Press.

Bailey, K. D. (1994). *Typologies and Taxonomies: An Introduction to Classification Techniques*. Thousand Oaks: Sage Publications.

Ban, K.-m. (2009). Implementing the responsibility to protect: United Nations.

Ban, K.-m. (2015). A vital and enduring commitment: implementing the responsibility to protect: United Nations.

Bandura, A. (1999). Moral Disengagement in the Perpetration of Inhumanities. *Personality and Social Psychology, 3*(3), 193-209.

Bar-Tal, D., Halperin, E., & De Rivera, J. (2007). Collective Emotions in Conflict Situations: Societal Implications. *Journal of Social Issues, 63*(2), 441-460.

Barkawi, T. (1998). Strategy as a vocation: Weber, Morgenthau and modern strategic studies. *Review of International Studies, 24*(02), 159-184. doi: doi:null

Baron, R. S., & Kerr, N. L. (2003). *Group process, group decision, group action*. Buckingham: Open University Press.

Baumeister, R. F. (2001). *Evil: Inside Human Violence and Cruelty*. New York: A.W.H. Freeman/Holt Paperback.

Bazyler, M. J. (1987). Reexamining the Doctrine of Humanitarian Intervention in Light of the Atrocities in Kampuchea and Ethiopia. *Stanford Journal of International Law., 23*(2), 578-620.

Beachler, D. W. (2009). Arguing about Cambodia: Genocide and Political Interest. *Holocaust and Genocide Studies, 23*(2), 214-238.

Becker, E. (1998). *When the War was Over: Cambodia and the Khmer Rouge Revolution*. New York: Public Affairs.

Bellamy, A. J. (2001). Reconsidering Rambouillet. *Contemporary Security Policy, 22*(1), 31-56.

Bellamy, A. J. (2002). *Kosovo and International Society*. New York: Palgrave Macmillan.

Bellamy, A. J. (2009). Kosovo and the Advent of Sovereignty as Responsibility. *Journal of Intervention and Statebuilding, 3*(2), 163-184.

Bellamy, A. J. (2010). The Responsibility to Protect—Five Years On. *Ethics & International Affairs, 24*(2), 143-169.

Bellamy, A. J. (2015). The Responsibility to Protect Turns Ten. *Ethics & International Affairs, 29*(02), 161-185.

Bellamy, A. J., & McLoughlin, S. (2009). Preventing Genocide and Mass Atrocities: Causes and Paths of Escalation. St Lucia: Asia-Pacific Centre for the Responisbility to Protect.

Bellamy, A. J., & Reike, R. (2010). The Responsibility to Protect and International Law. *Global Responsibility to Protect, 2*(3), 267-286.

Bellamy, A. J., & Williams, P. D. (2011). The new politics of protection? Côte d'Ivoire, Libya and the responsibility to protect. *International Affairs, 87*(4), 825-850.

Berejikian, J. D. (2002). A Cognitive Theory of Deterrence. *Journal of Peace Research, 39*(2), 165-183.

Betts, R. K. (1994). The delusion of impartial intervention. *Foreign Affairs*, 20-33.

Bieber, F. (2002). Nationalist Mobilization and Stories of Serb Suffering: The Kosovo myth from 600th anniversary to the present. *Rethinking History, 6*(1), 95-110.

Blätter, A., & Williams, P. D. (2011). The Responsibility Not To Veto. *Global Responsibility to Protect, 3*(3), 301-322.

Bleiker, R., & Hutchison, E. (2008). Fear no more: emotions and world politics. *Review of International Studies, 34*(Supplement S1), 115-135.

Blokland, H. T. (2006). *Modernization and its Political Consequences: Weber, Mannheim and Shumpeter* New Haven: Yale University Press.

Boesche, R. (1996). *Theories of Tyranny from Plato to Arendt*. University Park: The Pennsylvania State University.

Bogaards, M. (2009). How to classify hybrid regimes? Defective democracy and electoral authoritarianism. *Democratization, 16*(2), 399-423.

Botte, A. (2015). Redefining the responsibility to protect concept as a response to international crimes. *The International Journal of Human Rights, 19*(8), 1029-1043.

Boutros-Ghali, B. (1992). An Agenda for Peace: Preventive diplomacy, peacemaking and peace-keeping: United Nations.

Bratton, M., & Masunungure, E. (2008). Zimbabwe's Long Agony. *Journal of Democracy, 19*(4), 41-55.

Brooker, P. (2014). *Non-Democratic Regimes*. Basingstoke: Palgrave Macmilan.

Brosse, R. d. l. (2003). Political Propaganda and the Plan to Create 'A State For All Serbs:' Consequences of using media for ultra-nationalist ends *ICTY Expert Reports*: ICTY.

Browning, C. R. (1992). *Ordinary Men: Reserve Police Battalion 101 and the Final Solution in Poland*. New York: Aaron Asher Books.

Bruce Bueno De Mesquita, & Smith, A. (2011). *The Dictator's Handbook: Why Bad Behaviour is Almost Always Good Politics* New York: Public Affairs.

Brunnée, J., & Toope, S. J. (2010). The Responsibility to Protect and the Use of Force: Building Legality? *Global Responsibility to Protect, 2*(3), 191-212.

Buechler, S. M. (2013). Mass Society Theory. In D. A. Snow, D. d. Porta, B. Klandermans & D. McAdam (Eds.), The Wiley-Blackwell Encyclopedia of Social and Political Movements: Blackwell Publishing Ltd.

Bugajski, J. (1993). The fate of Minorities in Eastern Europe. *Journal of Democracy, 4*(4), 85-99.

Burchett, W. (1981). *The China Cambodia Vietnam Triangle*. Chicago: Vanguard Books.

Burke-White, W. W. (2012). Adoption of the Responsibility to Protect. In J. Genser & I. Cotler (Eds.), *The Responsibility to Protect: The Promise of Stopping Mass Atrocities in Our Time*. Oxford: Oxford University Press.

Burnell, P. (2006). Autocratic opening to democracy: why legitimacy matters. *Third World Quarterly, 27*(4), 545-562.

Byman, D. L., & Pollack, K. M. (2001). Let Us Now Praise Great Men: Bringing the Statesman Back In. *International Security, 25*(4), 107-146.

Byman, D. L., & Waxman, M. (1999). Defeating US coercion. *Survival, 41*(2), 107-120.
Calic, M.-J. (2000). Kosovo in the twentieth century: A historical account. In R. T. Albrecht Schnabel (Ed.), *Kosovo: and the Challenge of Humanitarian Intervention.* Tokyo: The United Nations University.
Callahan, D. (1998). *Unwinnable Wars: American Power and Ethnic Conflict.* New York: Hill and Wang.
Campbell, B. B., & Brenner, A. D. (Eds.). (2002). *Death Squads in Global Perspective: Murder with Denialbility.* New York: Palgrave Macmillan.
Campbell, K. J. (2001). *Genocide and the Global Village.* New York: Palgrave.
Carlsnaes, W. (2012). Actors, structures and foreign policy analysis. In S. Smith, A. Hadfield & T. Dunne (Eds.), *Foreign Policy: Theories, Actors, Cases* (pp. 113-129). Oxford: Oxford University Press.
Carmichael, C. (2010). Introduction: The Yugoslav Communist Legacy. *Europe-Asia Studies, 62*(7), 1045-1050.
Carney, T. (1989). The Unexpected Victory. In K. D. Jackson (Ed.), *Cambodia 1975-1978: Rendezvous with Death* (pp. 13-35). Princeton: Princeton University Press.
Chanda, N. (1986). *Brother Enemy: The War after the War.* San Diego: Harcourt Brace Jovanovich Publishers.
Chandler, D. (1979). The Tragedy of Cambodian History. *Pacific Affairs, 52*(3), 410-419.
Chandler, D. (1983). Revising the Past in Democratic Kampuchea: When Was the Birthday of the Party?: Notes and Comments. *Pacific Affairs, 56*(2), 288-300.
Chandler, D. (1998). Cambodia's Historical Legacy. *Accord, 5*, 12-19.
Chandler, D. (1999). *Brother Number One: A Political Biography of Pol Pot.* Bankok: Silkworm Books.
Chandler, D. (2008). *A History of Cambodia.* Boulder: Westview Press.
Chandler, D. (2010). R2P or Not R2P? More Statebuilding, Less Responsibility. *Global Responsibility to Protect, 2*(1-2), 161-166.
Chandler, D., Kiernan, B., & Boua, C. (1988). *Pol Pot Plans the Future: Confidential Leadership Documents from Democratic Kampuchea, 1976-1977.* New Haven: Yale university Southeast Asia Studies.
Chhabra, T., & Zucker, J. B. (2012). Defining the Crimes. In J. Genser & I. Cotler (Eds.), *The Responsibility to Protect: The Promise of Stopping Mass Atrocities in Our Time.* Oxford: Oxford University Press.
Chindawongse, S. (1991). Pol Pot's Strategy of Survival. *The Fletcher Forum, 15*(Winter 1991), 127-145.
Chirot, D. (1994). *Modern Tyrants: The Power and Prevalence of Evil in Our Age* New York: The Free Press.
Chirot, D., & McCauley, C. (2010). *Why Not Kill Them All? The Logic and Prevention of Mass Political Murder* Princeton: Princeton University Press.
Chollet, D. (2005). *The Road to the Dayton Accords: A Study of American Statecraft.* New York: Palgrave Macmillan.
Chomsky, N. (2012). *A New Generation Draws the Line: Humanitarian Intervention and the "Responsibility to Protect" Today.* Boulder: Paradigm Publishers.
Cigar, N. (1995). *Genocide in Bosnia: The Policy of "Ethnic Cleansing".* Texas: A&M University Press.
Ciorciari, J. D. (2014). China and the Pol Pot regime. *Cold War History, 14*(2), 215-235.

Clymer, K. J. (1999). The Perils of Neutrality: The Break in U.S.-Cambodian Relations, 1965. *Diplomatic History, 23*(4), 609-631.

Cohen, L. J. (2006). The Milosevic Dictatorship: Institutionalising Power and Ethno-Populaism in Serbia. In B. J. Fischer (Ed.), *Balkan Strongmen: Dictators and Authoritarian Rulers of South Eastern Europe* (pp. 425-478). London: Hurst Company.

Cohen, S. (1996). Government Responses to Human Rights Reports: Claims, Denials, and Counterclaims. *Human Rights Quarterly, 18*(3), 517-543.

Cohen, S. (2001). *States of Denial: Knowing about atrocities and suffering.* Cambridge: Polity Press.

Cox, J. K. (2006). Ante Pavelić and the Ustaša State in Croatia. In B. J. Fischer (Ed.), *Balkan Strongmen: Dictators and Authoritarian Rulers of Southeast Europe* (pp. 199-238). London: Hurst & Company.

Craig, G. A., & George, A. L. (1995). *Force and Statecraft: Diplomatic problems of our time.* New York: Oxford University Press.

Crawford, N. C. (2000). The Passion of World Politics: Propositions on Emotion and Emotional Relationships. *International Security, 24*(4), 116-156.

Crelinsten, R. D. (1993). In Their Own Words: The World of the Torturer. In R. D. Crelinston & A. P. Schmid (Eds.), *The Politics of Pain: Torturers and their Masters* (pp. 39-72). Leiden: COMT.

Cronin, B. (2007). The Tension Between Sovereignty and Intervention in the Prevention of Genocide. *Human Rights Review, 8*(4), 293-305.

Cunningham, K. (2002). A Critical Theory of the "Rationality" of US Foreign Policy: The Case of the American War in Vietnam. *New Political Science, 24*(4), 509-523.

D'Avray, D. L. (2010). *Rationalities in History: A Weberian Essay in Comparison* Cambridge: Cambridge University Press.

Daalder, I. H., & O'Hanlon, M. E. (2000). *Winning Ugly: NATO's War to Save Kosovo.* Washington D.C.: Brookings Institution Press.

Davenport, C. (1999). Human Rights and the Democratic Proposition. *Journal of Conflict Resolution, 43*(1), 92-116.

Day, L. E., & Vandiver, M. (2000). Criminology and genocide studies: Notes on what might have been and what still could be. *Crime, Law and Social Change, 34*(1), 43-59.

Decalo, S. (1989). *Psychoses of Power: African Personal Dictatorships.* Boulder: Westview Press.

Delbrück, J. (1991-1992). A Fresh Look at Humanitarian Intervention Under the Authority of the United Nations. *Indiana Law Journal, 67,* 887-901.

DeMeritt, J. H. R. (2012). International Organizations and Government Killing: Does Naming and Shaming Save Lives? *International Interactions, 38*(5), 597-621.

Desai, R. M., Olofsgård, A., & Yousef, T. M. (2009). The Logic of Authoritarian Bargains. *Economics & Politics, 21*(1), 93-125.

Dessler, D. (1999). Constructivism within a positivist social science. *Review of International Studies, 25*(01), 123-137.

Detrez, R. (2002). Inleiding (R. Dokter, Trans.) *Milosevic & Markovic of het einde van het Servische sprookje* (pp. 7-23). Antwerpen: Manteau.

Dimitrijevic, N. (2008). Serbia After the Criminal Past: What Went Wrong and What Should be Done. *The International Journal of Transitional Justice, 2*, 5-22.

Djilas, A. (1993). A profile of Slobodan Milosevic. *Foreign Affairs, 72*(3), 81-96.

Djilas, A. (1995). Tito's Last Secret: How Did He Keep the Yugoslavs Together? *Foreign Affairs*, 116-122.

Djokić, D. (2012). Nationalism, Myth and Reinterpretation of History: The Neglected Case of Interwar Yugoslavia. *European History Quarterly, 42*(1), 71-95.

Djukić, S. (2002). *Milošević & Marković of het einde van het Servische sprookje* (R. Dokter, Trans.). Antwerpen: Standaard UItgeverij.

Dobson, W. J. (2013). *The Dictator's Learning Curve: tyranny and democracy in the modern world.*

Doder, D., & Branson, L. (1999). *Milosevic: Portrait of a Tyrant.* New York: The Free Press.

Donnelly, J. (2003). *Universal Human Rights in Theory & Practice.* Ithaca: Cornell University Press.

Drezner, D. W. (2011). Sanctions Sometimes Smart: Targeted Sanctions in Theory and Practice. *International Studies Review, 13*(1), 96-108.

ECCC Closing Order, No. 002/19-09-2007-ECCC-OCIJ (Extraordinary Chambers in the Courts of Cambodia 2010).

ECCC Trial Chamber Judgement 002/01, No. 002/19-09-2007/ECCC/TC (Extraordinary Chambers in the Courts of Cambodia 2014).

Edwards, M. (2004). The rise of the Khmer Rouge in Cambodia: internal or external origins? *Asian Affairs, 35*(1), 56-67.

Eisen, A. (1978). The Meanings and Confusions of Weberian 'Rationality'. *The British Journal of Sociology, 29*(1), 57-70.

Elster, J. (2000). Rationality, economy and society. In S. Turner (Ed.), *The Cambridge Companion to Weber* (pp. 21-41). New York: Cambridge University Press.

Erken, R. (2010). Cambodia Under the Pol Pot Regime (1975–1979). An Example of a Totalitarian Communist Regime? *Revista de Historia Actual, 4*(4), 107-130.

Escribà-Folch, A. (2012). Authoritarian Responses to Foreign Pressure: Spending, Repression, and Sanctions. *Comparative Political Studies, 45*(6), 683-713.

Escribà-Folch, A., & Wright, J. (2010). Dealing with Tyranny: International Sanctions and the Survival of Authoritarian Rulers. *International Studies Quarterly, 54*(2), 335-359.

Etcheson, C. (1984). *The Rise and Demise of Democratic Kampuchea.* Boulder: Westview Press.

Etzioni, A. (1988). Normative-Affective Factors: Towards a New Decion-Making Model. *Journal of Economic Psychology, 9*, 125-150.

Etzioni, A. (2006). Sovereignty as Responsibility. *Orbis, 50*(1), 71-85.

Etzioni, A. (2010). Rational Actors: Neither Mad nor M.A.D.: The Meanings of Rationality, Rogue States and Terrorists. *Defense & Security Analysis, 26*(4), 431-438.

Evans, G. (2006-2007). From Humanitarian Intervention to the Responsibility to Protect. *Wis. Int'l L.J., 24* (703), 703-722.

Evans, G. (2008). *The Responsibility to Protect: Ending Mass Atrocity Crimes Once and for All.* Washington, D.C.: Brookings Institution Press.

Evans, G. (2012). Lessons and Challenges. In J. Genser & I. Cotler (Eds.), *The Responsibility to Protect: The Promise of Stopping Mass Atrocities in Our Time.* Oxford: Oxford University Press.

Ezrow, N., & Frantz, E. (2011). *Dictators and Dictatorships: Understanding Authoritarian Regimes and their Leaders* New York: Continuum.

Farley, B. (2006). Aleksandar Karadjordjević and the Royal Dictatorship in Yugoslavia. In B. J. Fischer (Ed.), *Balkan Strongmen: Dictators and Authoritarian Rulers of Southeast Europe* (pp. 50-86). London: Hurst & Company.

Fawthrop, T. (2005). The Secrets of S21. *Index on Censorship, 34*(1), 78-81.

Fearon, J. D. (1998). Domestic Politics, Foreign Policy, and Theories of International Relations *Annual Review of Political Science, 1*(1), 289-313.

Fein, H. (1993). Accounting for genocide after 1945: Theories and some findings. *International Journal on Minority and Group Rights, 1*(2), 79-106.

Fein, H. (1995). More Murder in the Middle: Life-Integrity Violations and Democracy in the World, 1987. *Human Rights Quarterly, 17*, 170-191.

Fein, H. (2000). Civil wars and genocide: Paths and circles. *Human Rights Review, 1*(3), 49-61.

Feinstein, L., & Slaughter, A.-M. (2004). A Duty to Prevent. *Foreign Affairs, 84*(1), 136-150.

Fine, J. V. A. (2006). Strongmen can be beneficial: the exceptional case of Josip Broz Tito. In B. J. Fischer (Ed.), *Balkan Strongmen: Dictators and Authoritarian Rulers of Southeast Europe* (pp. 269-317). London: Hurst & Company.

Flere, S., & Klanjšek, R. (2014). Was Tito's Yugoslavia totalitarian? *Communist and Post-Communist Studies, 47*(2), 237-245.

Forsberg, T. (2010). Rational Choice and Psychology in Crisis Decision-Making. In H. Kurkeinen (Ed.), *Strategic Decision-Making in crisis and War* (Vol. 42, pp. 33-63). Helsinki: National Defence University.

Forsythe, D. P. (2012). The UN Security Council and Response to Atrocities: International Criminal Law and the P-5. *Human Rights Quarterly, 34*, 840-863.

François, M., & Sud, I. (2006). Promoting Stability and Development in Fragile and Failed States. *Development Policy Review, 24*(2), 141-160.

Franklin, J. C. (2008). Shame on You: The Impact of Human Rights Criticism on Political Repression in Latin America. *International Studies Quarterly, 52*(1), 187-211.

Friedrich, C. J. (1961). Political Leadership and the Problem of the Charismatic Power. *The Journal of Politics, 23*(1), 3-24.

Friedrich, C. J., & Brzezinski, Z. K. (1965). *Totalitarian Dictatorship and Autocracy.* Cambridge: Harvard UP.

Frings, K. V. (1997). Rewriting Cambodian History to 'Adapt' It to a New Political Context: The Kampuchean People's Revolutionary Party's Historiography (1979-1991). *Modern Asian Studies, 31*(4), 807-846.

Fromm, E. (1942). *The Fear of Freedom.* London: Routledge.

Gagnon, V. P., Jr. (1994). Ethnic Nationalism and International Conflict: The Case of Serbia. *International Security, 19*(3), 130-166.

Gallagher, A., & Ralph, J. (2015). The Responsibility to Protect at Ten. *Global Responsibility to Protect, 7*(3-4), 239-253.

Gandhi, J., & Przeworski, A. (2007). Authoritarian Institutions and the Survival of Autocrats. *Comparative Political Studies, 40*(11), 1279-1301.

Gane, N. (1997). Max Weber on the Ethical Irrationality of Political Leadership. *Sociology, 31*(3), 549-564.

Gartner, S. S., & Regan, P. M. (1996). Threat and Repression: The Non-Linear Relationship between Government and Opposition Violence. *Journal of Peace Research, 33*(3), 273-287.

Geddes, B. (1999). What do we know about democratisation after twenty years? *Annual Review of Political Science, 2*(1), 115-144.

Van Genugten, W., Homan, K., Schrijver, N., & De Waart, P. (2006). *The United Nations of the Future: Globalization with a Human Face*. Amsterdam: KIT Publishers.

George, A. L. (1969). The "Operational Code": A Neglected Approach to the Study of Political Leaders and Decision-Making. *International Studies Quarterly, 13*(2), 190-222.

Gibson, J. T., & Haritos-Fatouros, M. (1986). The Education of a Torturer: there is a cruel method in the madness of teaching people to torture. Almost anyone can learn it. *Psychology Today*(November), 50-58.

Glad, B. (2002). Why Tyrants Go Too Far: Malignant Narcissism and Absolute Power. *Political Psychology, 23*(1), 1-2.

Glanville, L. (2010). The antecedents of 'sovereignty as responsibility'. *European Journal of International Relations, 17*(2), 233-255.

Glanville, L. (2012). The Responsibility to Protect Beyond Borders. *Human Rights Law Review, 12*(1), 1-32.

Glanville, L. (2013). The Myth of "Traditional" Sovereignty. *International Studies Quarterly, 57*(1), 79-90.

Godina, V. V. (1998). The Outbreak of Nationalism on Former Yugoslav Territory: A Historical Perspective on the Problem of Supranational Identity. *Nations and Nationalism, 4*(3), 409-422.

Goodwin, J., & Jasper, J. M. (2006). Emotions and Social Movements. In J. E. Stets & J. H. Turner (Eds.), Handbook of the Sociology of Emotions (pp. 611-635). New York: Springer.

Gourevitch, P. (1978). The Second Image Reversed: The International Sources of Domestic Politics. *International Organization, 32*(4), 881-912.

Gourevitch, P. (2002). Domestic Politics and International Relations. In W. Carlsnaes, T. Risse & B. A. Simmons (Eds.), *Handbook of International Relations* (pp. 309-329). London: Sage Publications.

Graham, V. (2006). How firm is the handshake? South Africa's use of quiet diplomacy in Zimbabwe from 1999 to 2006. *African Security Review, 15*(4), 113-127.

Gregory, P. R., Schröder, P. J. H., & Sonin, K. (2011). Rational dictators and the killing of innocents: Data from Stalin's archives. *Journal of Comparative Economics, 39*(1), 34-42.

Groenhuijsen, M. S. (2011). De Arabische lente, internationaal strafrecht en het Internationaal Strafhof. *Delikt en Delinkwent, 41*(9), 1005-1016.

Groom, A. J. R. (2007). Foreign Policy Analysis. *International Studies, 44*(3), 195-215.

Gross, L. (1948). The Peace of Westphalia, 1648-1948. *The American Journal of International Law, 42*(1), 20-41.

Grünfeld, F. (1998). Human rights violations: a threat to international peace and security. In M. v. Castermans-Holleman, F. v. Hoof & J. Smith (Eds.), *The role of the nation-state in the 21 century* (pp. 427-441). The Hague: Kluwer International.

Grünfeld, F. (1999). The Effectiveness of United Nations Economic Sanctions. In W. M. J. v. Genugten & G. A. d. Groot (Eds.), *United Nations Sanctions: Effectiveness and effects, especially in the field of human rights*. Antwerp: Intersentia.

Guliyev, F. (2011). Personal rule, neopatrimonialism, and regime typologies: integrating Dahlian and Weberian approaches to regime studies. *Democratization, 18*(3), 575-601.

Guzina, D. (2003). Socialist Serbia's Narratives: From Yugoslavia to a Greater Serbia. *International Journal of Politics, Culture, and Society, 17*(1), 91-111.

Haber, S. (2014). Authoritarian government. In D. A. Wittman & B. R. Weingast (Eds.), *Oxford Handbooks Online*: Oxford University Press.

Hadenius, A., & Teorell, J. (2007). Pathways From Authoritarianism. *Journal of Democracy, 18*(1), 143-157.

Haenen, I. (2014). *Force & Marriage: The criminalisation of forced marriage in Dutch, English and international criminal law*. Cambridge: Intersentia.

Hafner-Burton, E. M. (2008). Sticks and Stones: Naming and Shaming the Human Rights Enforcement Problem. *International Organization, 62*(04), 689-716.

Hagan, J. D. (2001). Does Decision Making Matter? *International Studies Review, 3*(2), 5-46.

Hagen, W. W. (1999). The Balkans' Lethal Nationalisms. *Foreign Affairs, 78*(4), 52-64.

Hamilton, R. J. (2006). Responsibility to Protect: From Document to Doctrine – But What of Implemlentation. *Harv. Hum Rts. J., 19* 289-297.

Hanlon, J. (2006a). Ethnicity and Identity. In H. Yanacopulos & J. Hanlon (Eds.), *Civil War, Civil Peace*. Milton Keynes: The Open University.

Hanlon, J. (2006b). Intervention. In H. Yanacopulos & J. Hanlon (Eds.), *Civil War, Civil Peace* (pp. 49-71). Milton Keynes: The Open University.

Hanoch, Y. (2002). "Neither an angel nor an ant": Emotion as an aid to bounded rationality. *Journal of Economic Psychology, 23*(1), 1-25.

Harff, B. (2003). No Lessons Learned from the Holocaust? Assessing Risks of Genocide and Political Mass Murder since 1955. *The American Political Science Review, 97*(1), 57-73.

Havel, V., & Tutu, D. (2012). Introduction. In J. Genser & I. Cotler (Eds.), *The Responsibility to Protect: The Promise of Stopping Mass Atrocities in Our Time* Oxford: Oxford University Press.

Haveman, R., & Smeulers, A. (2008). Criminology in a state of denial – towards a criminology of international crimes: supranational criminology. In A. Smeulers & R. Haveman (Eds.), *Supranational Criminology: Towards a Criminology of International Crimes* (pp. 3-26). Antwerp: Intersentia.

Haveman, R., Smeulers, A., Parmentier, S., & Poot, C. d. (2011). De staat van de criminologie van internationale misdrijven. *Tijdschrift voor Criminologie, 53*(4), 287-309.

Haviland, W. A., Prins, H. E. L., Walrath, D., & McBride, B. (2008). *Anthropology: The Human Challenge* (12 ed.). Belmond, CA: Thomson Higher Education.

Hechter, M. (1994). The Role of Values in Rational Choice Theory. *Rationality and Society, 6*(3), 318-333.

Hechter, M., & Kanazawa, S. (1997). Sociological Rational Choice Theory. *Annual Review of Sociology, 23*, 191-214.

Heder, S. R. (n.d.). *Khieu Samphan and Pol Pot: Moloch's Poodle*. Australian National University. Retrieved from http://repository.forcedmigration.org/pdf/?pid=fmo:51

Hegre, H., Ellingsen, T., Gates, S., & Gleditsch, N. P. (2001). Toward a Democratic Civil Peace? Democracy, Political Change, and Civil War, 1816-1992. *The American Political Science Review, 95*(1), 33-48.

Hehir, A. (2010). The Responsibility to Protect: 'Sound and Fury Signifying Nothing'? *International Relations, 24*(2), 218-239.

Hendrix, C. S., & Wong, W. H. (2013). When Is the Pen Truly Mighty? Regime Type and the Efficacy of Naming and Shaming in Curbing Human Rights Abuses. *British Journal of Political Science, 43*(03), 651-672.

Heng, Y. K. (2010). Reflexive Rationality and the Implications for Decision-Making. In H. Kurkeinen (Ed.), *Strategic Decision-Making in crisis and War* (Vol. 42, pp. 19-32). Helsinki: National Defence University.

Hermann, M. G. (2001). How Decision Units Shape Foreign Policy: A Theoretical Framework. *International Studies Review, 3*(2), 47-81.

Hermann, M. G., & Hagan, J. D. (1998). International decision making: Leadership matters. *Foreign Policy, 110*, 124-137.

Hermann, M. G., & Kegley, C. W., Jr. (1995). Rethinking Democracy and International Peace: Perspectives from Political Psychology. *International Studies Quarterly, 39*(4), 511-533.

Hermann, M. G., Preston, T., Korany, B., & Shaw, T. M. (2001). Who Leads Matters: The Effects of Powerful Individuals. *International Studies Review, 3*(2), 83-131.

Hiebert, M. S. (2011). MARO as the Partial Operationalization of R2P. *Genocide Studies and Prevention, 6*(1), 52-58.

High-level Panel on Threats Challenges and Change. (2004). A more secure world: Our shared responsibility: United Nations.

Hinton, A. L. (1998a). A Head for an Eye: Revenge in the Cambodian Genocide. *American Ethnologist, 25*(3), 352-377.

Hinton, A. L. (1998b). Why Did You Kill?: The Cambodian Genocide and the Dark Side of Face and Honor. *The Journal of Asian Studies, 57*(1), 93-122.

Hodge, C. C. (1998). Botching the Balkans: Germany's Recognition of Slovenia and Croatia. *Ethics & International Affairs, 12*(1), 1-18.

Hoefnagels, M. (1977). *Political violence and peace research*. Amsterdam: Swets & Zeitlinger.

Hoffer, E. (1951). *The True Believer*. New York: Harper Perennial.

Holsti, O. R. (2005). Models of International Relations and Foreign Policy. In G. J. Inkenberry (Ed.), *American Foreign Policy: Theoretical Essays* (pp. 14-40). New York: Pearson Longman.

Hopf, T. (2010). The logic of habit in International Relations. *European Journal of International Relations, 16*(4), 539-561.

Hosmer, S. T. (2001). *The Conflict over Kosovo: Why Milosevic decided to settle when he did*. Santa Monica, CA: RAND Corporation.

Houghton, D. P. (2007). Reinvigorating the Study of Foreign Policy Decision Making: Toward a Constructivist Approach. *Foreign Policy Analysis, 3*(1), 24-45.

Hudson, V. M. (2005). Foreign Policy Analysis: Actor-Specific Theory and the Ground of International Relations. *Foreign Policy Analysis, 1*(1), 1-30.

Hudson, V. M. (2012). The history and evolution of foreign policy analysis. In S. Smith, A. Hadfield & T. Dunne (Eds.), *Foreign Policy: Theories, Actors, Cases* (pp. 13-34). Oxford: Oxford University Press.

Hudson, V. M., & Vore, C. S. (1995). Foreign Policy Analysis Yesterday, Today, and Tomorrow. *Mershon International Studies Review, 39*(2), 209-238.

Huntington, S. P. (1991). How Countries Democratize. *Political Science Quarterly, 106*(4), 579-616.

Hurd, I. (2002). Legitimacy, Power, and the Symbolic Life of the UN Security Council. *Global Governance 8*, 35-51.

Ieng Sary. (2013). *The Economist.* Retrieved from http://www.economist.com/news/obituary/21575742-ieng-sary-foreign-minister-and-brother-no-3-cambodias-khmer-rouge-regime-died-march

Ikenberry, G. J. (2005). Introduction. In G. J. Ikenberry (Ed.), *American Foreign Policy: Theoretical Essays* (pp. 1-12). New York: Pearson Longman.

International Coalition for the Responsibility to Protect. (2010). GA dialogue on Early Warning, Assessment and the Responsibility to Protect. Retrieved 21 June, 2016, from http://www.responsibilitytoprotect.org/ICRtoP%20Report%20of%20EW%20dialogue%20on%209 %20August%202010 %20FINAL.pdf

International Coalition for the Responsibility to Protect. (2011). Interactive dialogue of the General Assembly on the role of regional and sub-regional arrangements in implementing the Responsibility to Protect. Retrieved 21 June, 2016, from http://www.responsibilitytoprotect.org/ICRtoP%20Report%20on%20RIGO%20GA%20dialogue%20on%20RtoP%20FINAL(1).pdf

International Coalition for the Responsibility to Protect. (2012). UN General Assembly Dialogue on the Responsibility to Protect: Timely and decisive response. Retrieved 25 July 2013, from http://responsibilitytoprotect.org/index.php/component/content/article/35-r2pcs-topics/4331-un-general-assembly-dialogue-on-the-report-of-the-secretary-general-on-the-responsibility-to-protect-timely-and-decisive-response

International Coalition for the Responsibility to Protect. (2013). United Nations General Assembly holds fifth informal, interactive dialogue on the Responsibility to Protect focusing on the theme of state responsibility and prevention. Retrieved 2 May, 2016, from http://www.responsibilitytoprotect.org/index.php/component/content/article/35-r2pcs-topics/5004-united-nations-general-assembly-holds-fifth-informal-interactive-dialogue-on-the-responsibility-to-protect

International Coalition for the Responsibility to Protect. (2014). United Nations General Assembly holds sixth informal, interactive dialogue on the Responsibility to Protect, focusing on collective responsibility and international assistance. Retrieved 2 May, 2016, from http://www.responsibilitytoprotect.org/index.php/component/content/article/136-latest-news/5597-icrtops-summary-of-the-general-assemblys-sixth-informal-interactive-dialogue-on-rtop

International Coalition for the Responsibility to Protect. (2015). Summary of the seventh General Assembly dialogue on the responsibility to protect. Retrieved

21 June, 2016, from http://responsibilitytoprotect.org/General%20Assembly%20 Dialogue%20Summary%202015 %20Final.pdf

International Commission on Intervention and State Sovereignty. (2001). The Responsibility to Protect. Ottawa: International Commission on Intervention and State Sovereignty.

Jackson, K. D. (1989). The Ideology of Total Revolution. In K. D. Jackson (Ed.), *Cambodia 1975-1978: Rendezvous with Death* (pp. 37-78). Princeton: Princeton University Press.

Jackson, P. T. (2003). Defending the West: Occidentalism and the Formation of NATO. *Journal of Political Philosophy, 11*(3), 223-252.

Jackson, R. H., & Rosberg, C. G. (1982). *Personal Rule in Black Africa: Prince Autocrat, Prophet, Tyrant*. London: University of Califormia Press, Ltd.

Jakobsen, P.V. (2011). Pushing the Limits of Military Coercion Theory. *International Studies Perspectives. 12*, 153-170.

Jamieson, R., & McEvoy, K. (2005). State Crime by Proxy and Juridical Othering. *British Journal of Criminology, 45*(4), 504-527.

Jentleson, B. (1996). Preventive diplomacy and ethnic conflict: possible, difficult, necessary *Policy Papers* (Vol. 27): Institute on Global Conflict and Cooperation, University of California.

Jones, A. (2011). *Genocide: A Comprehensive Introduction* (2nd ed.). Abingdon, Oxon: Routledge.

Jones, R. (1972). The Third Wave – 1967, an account. Retrieved 10 January 2014, 2014, from http://libcom.org/history/the-third-wave-1967-account-ron-jones

Jovic, D. (2001). The Disintegration of Yugoslavia: A Critical Review of Explanatory Approaches. *European Journal of Social Theory, 4*(1), 101-120.

Jović, D. (2004a). Communist Yugoslavia and its "Others". In J. R. Lampe & M. Mazower (Eds.), *Ideologies and National Idenitities: The Case of Twentieth-century Southeastern Europe* (pp. 277-302). New York: Central European University Press.

Jović, D. (2004b). 'Official memories' in post-authoritarianism: an analytical framework. *Journal of Southern Europe and the Balkans Online, 6*(2), 97-108.

Judah, T. (2008). *Kosovo: what everyone needs to know*. New York: Oxford University Press.

Judah, T. (2009). *The Serbs: History, Myth and the Destruction of Yugoslavia* (3rd ed.). New Haven: Yale University Press.

Kahler, M. (1998). Rationality in International Relations. *International Organization, 52*(04), 919-941.

Kailitz, S. (2013). Classifying political regimes revisited: legitimation and durability. *Democratization, 20*(1), 39-60.

Kalberg, S. (1980). Max Weber's Types of Rationality: Cornerstones for the Analysis of Rationalization Processes in History. *American Journal of Sociology, 85*(5), 1145-1179.

Kaldor, M. (2006). *New & Old Wars: Organized Violence in a Global Era* (2nd ed.). Cambridge: Polity Press.

Kalyvas, A. (2007). The Tyranny of Dictatorship: When the Greek Tyrant Met the Roman Dictator. *Political Theory, 35*(4), 412-442.

Kaplan, R. D. (1991). History's Cauldron. *The Atlantic Monthly, 6*, 92-104.

Kaplan, R. D. (2005). *Balkan Ghosts: A Journey Rhrough History*. New York: Picador.

Kapur, A. (2009). Humanity as the A and Ω of Sovereignty: Four Replies to Anne Peters. *European Journal of International Law, 20*(3), 560-567.

Kaufman, B. E. (1999). Emotional arousal as a source of bounded rationality. *Journal of Economic Behavior & Organization, 38*(2), 135-144.

Kelder, J. (2010). Een beschermde diersoort? In M. Blankesteijn & I. d. Zwaan (Eds.), *De Grote Dictator Tour*. Houten: Spectrum.

Kellerman, B. (2004). *Bad Leadership: What It Is, How It Happens, Why It Matters*. Boston: Harvard Business School Press.

Kelman, H. C. (1993). The Social Context of Torture: Policy Process and Authority Structure. In R. D. Crelinston & A. P. Schmid (Eds.), *The Politics of Pain: Torturers and their masters* (pp. 21-38). Leiden: COMT.

Kelman, H. C. (2005). The policy context of torture: A social-psychoioqical analysis. *International Review of the Red Cross, 87*(857), 123-134.

Kiernan, B. (1996). *The Pol Pot Regime. Race, Power and Genocide in Cambodia under the Khmer Rouge, 1975-79*. New Haven: Yale University Press.

Kiernan, B. (2002). Introduction Conflict in Cambodia, 1945-2002. *Critical Asian Studies, 34*(4), 483-495.

Kiernan, B. (2003). The Demography of Genocide in Southeast Asia: The Death Tolls in Cambodia, 1975-79, and East Timor, 1975-80. *Critical Asian Studies, 35*(4), 585-597.

Kiernan, B. (2004). *How Pol Pot Came to Power: Colonialism, Nationalism and Communism in Cambodia, 1930-1975*. New Haven: Yale University Press.

Kiernan, B. (2010). The Historiography of the Cambodian Genocide. In D. Stone (Ed.), *The Historiography of Genocide* (pp. 468-486). New York: Palgrave Macmillan.

Kinne, B. J. (2005). Decision Making in Autocratic Regimes: A Poliheuristic Perspective. *International Studies Perspectives, 6*(1), 114-128.

Kirkpatrick, J. (1979). Dictatorships and Double Standards. *Commentary, 68*(5).

Kiser, E., & Hechter, M. (1998). The Debate on Historical Sociology: Rational Choice Theory and Its Critics. *American Journal of Sociology, 104*(3), 785-816.

Kollander, P. (2004). The Civil War in the Former Yugoslavia and the International Intervention. In J. S. Morton, R. C. Nation, P. Forage & S. Bianchini (Eds.), *Reflections on the Balkan Wars: Ten Years After teh Break Up of Yugoslavia*. New York: Palgrave MacMillan.

Kooijmans, T. (2011). *Dit is mijn zaak!* Tilburg: Tilburg University.

Kowert, P. A., & Hermann, M. G. (1997). Who Takes Risk: Daring and Caution in Foreign Policy Making. *Journal of Conflict Resolution, 41*, 611-637.

Krain, M. (1997). State-Sponsored Mass Murder: The Onset and Severity of Genocides and Politicides. *Journal of Conflict Resolution, 41*(3), 331-360.

Krain, M. (2000). Democracy, internal war, and state-sponsored mass murder. *Human Rights Review, 1*(3), 40-48.

Krain, M. (2012). J'accuse! Does Naming and Shaming Perpetrators Reduce the Severity of Genocides or Politicides? *International Studies Quarterly, 56*(3), 574-589.

Krain, M. (2014). The effects of diplomatic sanctions and engagement on the severity of ongoing genocides or politicides. *Journal of Genocide Research, 16*(1), 25-53.

Kressel, N. J. (2002). *Mass Hate: The Global Rise of Genocide and Terror.* Cambridge: Westview Press.

Kreutz, J. (2006). The Nexus of Democracy, Conflict and the Targeting of Civilians, 1989-2005. In L. Harbom (Ed.), *States in Armed Conflict 2005.* Uppsala: Department of Peace and conflict research.

Križan, M. (1994). New Serbian nationalism and the Third Balkan War. *Studies in East European Thought, 46*(1), 47-68.

Kronja, I. (2004). Politics, Nationalism, Music, and Popular Culture in 1990s Serbia. *Slovo, 16*(1), 5-15.

Kuperman, A. J. (2011). Mass Atrocity Response Operations: Doctrine in Search of Strategy. *Genocide Studies and Prevention, 6*(1), 59-65.

Kyemba, H. (1997). *A State of Blood.* Kampala: Fountain Publishers Ltd.

Lane, C. (1996). Call to Arms. In N. Mousavizadeh & L. Wieseltier (Eds.), *The Black Book of Bosnia: the consequences of appeasement* (pp. 143-146). New York: Basic Books.

LeBor, A. (2003). *Milosevic: A Biography.* London: Bloomsbury Publishing.

LeBor, A. (2006). *"Complicity with Evil" The United Nations in thr Age of Genocide.* New Haven: Yale University Press.

Leighton, M. K. (1978). Perspectives on the Vietnam-Cambodia Border Conflict. *Asian Survey, 18*(5), 448-457.

Lemarchand, R. (2003). Comparing the Killing Fields: Rwanda, Cambodia and Bosnia. In S. L. B. Jensen (Ed.), *Genocide: Cases, Comparisons and Contemporary Debates* (pp. 141-173). Copenhagen: The Danish Center for Holocaust and Genocide Studies.

Levine, D. N. (1981). Rationality and Freedom: Weber and Beyond. *Sociological Inquiry, 51*(1), 5-25.

Levine, D. N. (2005). The Continuuing Challenge of Weber's Theory of Rational Action. In C. Camic, P. S. Gorski & D. M. Trubek (Eds.), *Max Weber's "Economy and Society": A critical companion.* Stanford: Stanford University Press.

Levitsky, S., & Way, L. (2002). The rise of competitive authoritarianism. *Journal of Democracy, 13*(2), 51-65.

Lidén, G. (2014). Theories of Dictatorships: Sub-Types and Explanations. *Studies of Transition States and Societies, Vol 6*(No 1), 50-67.

Lifton, R. J. (2004). Doctors and Torture. *New England Journal of Medicine, 351*(5), 415-416.

Lillich, R. B. (1995). The Role of the UN Security Council in Protecting Human Rights in Crisis Situtations: UN Humanitarian Intervention in the Post-Cold War World. *Tulane Journal of International & Comparative Law, 3*(1), 1-17.

Lindstrom, N. (2006). Yugonostalgia: Restorative and reflective nostalgia in former Yugoslavia. *East Central Europe/L'Europe du Centre Est/Eine wissenschaftliche Zeitschrift, 32*(1-2), 231-242.

Linz, J. J. (2000). *Totalitarian and Authoritarian Regimes.* Boulder: Lynne Rienner Publishers.

Linz, J. J., & Stepan, A. (2004). Modern Nondemocratic Regimes. In P. O'Neil & R. Rogowski (Eds.), *Essential Readings in Comparative Politics* (pp. 154-165). New York: Norton.

Lobel, J., & Loewenstein, G. (2005). Emote Control: The Substitution of Symbol for Substance in Foreign Policy and International Law. *Chicago-Kent Law Review, 80*, 1045-1090.

Locard, H. (2005). State Violence in Democratic Kampuchea (1975–1979) and Retribution (1979–2004). *European Review of History: Revue européenne d'histoire, 12*(1), 121-143.

Luard, E. (1980). Human Rights and Foreign Policy. *International Affairs, 56*(4), 579-606.

Luck, E. C. (2009). Sovereignty, Choice, and the Responsibility to Protect. *Global Responsibility to Protect, 1*(1), 10-21.

Luck, E. C. (2012). From Promise to Practice: Implementing the Responsibility to Protect. In J. Genser & I. Cotler (Eds.), *The Responsibility to Protect: The Promise of Stopping Mass Atrocities in Our Time* Oxford: Oxford University Press.

Luck, E. C. & Luck, D. Z. (2016). The Individual Responsibility to Protect. In S. P. Rosenberg, T. Galis & A. Zucker (Eds.), *Reconstructing Atrocity Prevention* New York: Cambridge University Press.

MacDonald, P. K. (2003). Useful Fiction or Miracle Maker: The Competing Epistemological Foundations of Rational Choice Theory. *American Political Science Review, 97*(04), 551-565.

Majstorovic, S. (1997). Ancient Hatreds or Elite Manipulation? Memory and Politics in the Former Yugoslavia. *World Affairs, 159*(4), 170-182.

Malici, A. (2011). The United States and Rogue Leaders. In S. G. Walker, A. Malici & M. Schafer (Eds.), *Rethinking Foreign Policy Analysis: States, Leaders, and the Microfoundations of Behavioural International Relations* (pp. 83-96). New York: Routledge.

Mandel, D. R. (2002). Instigators of Genocide: Examining Hitler From a Social-Psychological Perspective. In L. S. Newman & R. Erber (Eds.), *Understanding Genocide: The Social Psychology of the Holocaust*. Oxford: Oxford University Press.

Mann, M. (2005). *The Dark Side of Democracy*. Cambridge: Cambridge University Press.

Marcus, G. E. (2000). Emotions in Politics. *Annual Review of Political Science, 3*(1), 221-250.

Maynard, J. L. (2015). Preventing Mass Atrocities: Ideological Strategies and Interventions. *Politics and Governance, 3*(3), 67-84.

McDermott, R. (2004a). The Feeling of Rationality: The Meaning of Neuroscientific Advances for Political Science. *Perspectives on Politics, 2*(04), 691-706.

McDermott, R. (2004b). *Political Psychology in International Relations* Ann Arbor: University of Michigan Press.

McLoughlin, S. (2014). *The Structural Prevention of Mass Atrocities: Understanding Risk and Resilience* London: Routledge.

McLoughlin, S., & Weerdesteijn, M. (2016). Eliminating Rivals, Managing Rivalries: a Comparison of Robert Mugabe and Kenneth Kaunda. *Genocide Studies and Prevention: An International Journal, 9*(3), 116-136.

Mercer, J. (2005). Rationality and Psychology in International Politics. *International Organization, 59*(01), 77-106.

Mercer, J. (2010). Emotional Beliefs. *International Organization, 64*(01), 1-31.

Merriam, S. (1995). What Can You Tell From An N of l?: Issues of validity and reliability in qualitative research. *PAACE Journal of Lifelong Learning, 4*, 50-60.

Meslin, B. M. (1981). Cognitive Decision-Making and Crisis Management: The Iranian Crisis. *Fletcher Forum, 191*, 191-221.

Middelburg, A. (2016). *Empty Promises? Compliance with the Human Rights Framework in relation to Female Genital Mutilation/Cutting in Senegal.* Tilburg: PrismaPrint.

Midlarsky, M. I. (2005). *The Killing Trap: Genocide in the Twentieth Century.* Cambridge: Cambridge University Press.

Mikula, M. (2002). Nationalism and the Rhetoric of Exclusion. *Southeast European Politics, 3*(1), 62-70.

Milgram, S. (1974). *Obedience to Authority.* New York: Harper and Row.

Milosevic 'died of natural causes'. (2006). *CNN.* Retrieved 28 June, 2016, from http://edition.cnn.com/2006/WORLD/europe/04/05/milosevic.death/

Mintz, A. (2004). Foreign Policy Decision Making in Familiar and Unfamiliar Settings: An Experimental Study of High-Ranking Military Officers. *The Journal of Conflict Resolution, 48*(1), 91-104.

Mintz, A., & DeRouen, K. (2010). *Understanding Foreign Policy Decision Making* Cambridge: Cambridge University Press.

Moghaddam, F. I. (2013). *The Psychology of Dictatorship* Washington, DC: American Psychological Association.

Morris, S. J. (1999). *Why Vietnam Invaded Cambodia: Political Culture and the Causes of War* Stanford: Stanford University Press.

Morus, C. (2007a). The SANU Memorandum: Intellectual Authority and the Constitution of an Exclusive Serbian "People". *Communication and Critical/Cultural Studies, 4*, 142-165.

Morus, C. (2007b). Slobo the Redeemer: The Rhetoric of Slobodan Milosevic and the Construction of the Serbian "People". *Southern Communication Journal, 72*(1), 1-19.

Moshman, D. (2007). Us and Them: Identity and Genocide. *Journal of Theory and Research, 7*(2), 115-135.

Mueller, G. H. (1979). The notion of rationality in the work of Max Weber. *European Journal of Sociology, 20*(01), 149-171.

Mueller, J. (2000). The Banality of "Ethnic War". *International Security, 25*(1), 42-70.

Neubacher, F. (2006). How Can it Happen that Horrendous State Crimes are Perpetrated? *Journal of International Criminal Justice, 4*(4), 787-799.

Nikolic-Ristanovic, V. (1998). War and Crime in the Former Yugoslavia. In Vincenzo Ruggiero, N. South & I. Taylor (Eds.), *The New European Criminology: crime and social order in Europe* (pp. 462-479). London: Routledge.

Nincic, M. (2006). The Logic of Positive Engagement: Dealing with Renegade Regimes. *International Studies Perspectives, 7*(4), 321-341.

Norkus, Z. (2000). Max Weber's Interpretive Sociology and Rational Choice Approach. *Rationality and Society, 12*(3), 259-282.

Oakes, G. (2003). Max Weber on Value Rationality and Value Spheres: Critical Remarks. *Journal of Classical Sociology, 3*(1), 27-45.

Oberschall, A. (2000). The manipulation of ethnicity: from ethnic cooperation to violence and war in Yugoslavia. *Ethnic and Racial Studies, 23*(6), 982-1001.

Odell, J. S. (2001). Case Study Methods in International Political Economy. *International Studies Perspectives, 2*(2), 161-176.

Orchard, P. (2012). The evolution of the responsibility to protect: at a crossroads? *International Affairs, 88*(2), 377-386.

Orizio, R. (2004). *Talk of the Devil: Encounters with Seven Dictators* (A. Bardoni, Trans.). London: Vintage.

Osiander, A. (2001). Sovereignty, International Relations, and the Westphalian Myth. *International Organization, 55*(02), 251-287.

Österdahl, I. (2005). The Exception as the Rule: Lawmaking on Force and Human Rights by the UN Security Council. *Journal of Conflict and Security Law, 10*(1), 1-20.

Overy, R. (2004). *Dictators: Hitler's Duitsland, Stalin's Rusland.* Amsterdam: De Bezige Bij.

Padilla, A., Hogan, R., & Kaiser, R. B. (2007). The toxic triangle: Destructive leaders, susceptible followers, and conducive environments. *The Leadership Quarterly, 18*(3), 176-194.

Parmentier, S. (2013). Van Mechelen naar Kigali en Srebrenica. *Panopticon, 34*(1), 001-004.

Pattison, J. (2014). The Case for Criteria: Moving R2P Forward after the Arab Spring. In R. W. Murray & A. McKay (Eds.), *Into the Eleventh Hour: R2P, Syria and Humanitarianism in Crisis.* Bristol: E-International Relations.

Pattison, J. (2015). The ethics of diplomatic criticism: The Responsibility to Protect, Just War Theory and Presumptive Last Resort. *European Journal of International Relations, 21*(4), 935-957.

Paul, D. E. (1999). Sovereignty, survival and the Westphalian blind alley in International Relations. *Review of International Studies, 25*(02), 217-231.

Payandeh, M. (2010). With Great Power Comes Great Responsibility – The Concept of the Responsibility to Protect within the Process of International Lawmaking. *The Yale Journal of International Law, 35*, 469-516.

Peang-Meth, A. (1991). Understanding the Khmer: Sociological-Cultural Observations. *Asian Survey, 31*(5), 442-455.

Peceny, M., Beer, C. C., & Shannon, S.-T. (2002). Dictatorial Peace? *The American Political Science Review, 96*(1), 15-26.

Peters, A. (2009). Humanity as the A and Ω of Sovereignty. *European Journal of International Law, 20*(3), 513-544.

Peters, A. (2011). The security Council's Responsibility to Protect. *International Organizations Law Review, 8*(1), 15-54.

Petrović, A., & Stefanović, Đ. (2010). Kosovo, 1944–1981: The Rise and the Fall of a Communist 'Nested Homeland'. *Europe-Asia Studies, 62*(7), 1073-1106.

Pictet, J. S. (1952). *Commentary published under the general editorship of Jean S. Pictet* (Vol. I): International Committee of the Red Cross.

Pina e Cunha, M., Rego, A., & Clegg, S. (2011). Pot, alias Brother Number One: Leaders as instruments of history. *Management & Organizational History, 6*(3), 268-286.

Pinker, S. (2011). *The Better Angels of Our Nature: Why Violence has Declined.* London: Viking.

Polin, S. (1980). Pol Pot's diabolical sweetness. *Index on Censorship, 9*(5), 43-45.

Post, J. M. (2004). *Leaders and their followers in a dangerous world: The psychology of political behaviour* Ithaca: Cornell University Press.

Pouvatchy, J. R. (1986). Cambodian-Vietnamese Relations. *Asian Survey, 26*(4), 440-451.

Power, S. (2013). *A Problem from Hell: America and the Age of Genocide* New York: Basic Books.

Putnam, R. D. (1988). Diplomacy and domestic politics: the logic of two-level games. *International Organization, 42*(03), 427-460.

Quinn, K. (1989a). Explaining the Terror. In K. D. Jackson (Ed.), *Cambodia 1975-1978: Rendezvous with Death* (pp. 215-240). Princeton: Princeton University Press.

Quinn, K. (1989b). The Pattern and Scope of Violence. In K. D. Jackson (Ed.), *Cambodia 1975-178: Rendezvous with Death* (pp. 179-208). Princeton: Princeton University Press.

Rajkovic, N. (2016). *The transformation of international legal rule and the challenge of interdisciplinarity.* Tilburg: Tilburg University.

Ramet, S. P. (2005). *Thinking about Yugoslavia: Scholarly Debates about the Yugoslav Breakup and the Wars in Bosnia and Kosovo.* Cambridge: Cambridge University Press.

Razi, G. H. (1988). An Alternative Paradigm to State Rationality in Foreign Policy: The Iran-Iraq War. *The Western Political Quarterly, 41*(4), 689-723.

Regan, P. M., & Henderson, E. A. (2002). Democracy, threats and political repression in developing countries: Are democracies internally less violent? *Third World Quarterly, 23*(1), 119-136.

Reicher, S. (1996). 'The Crowd' century: Reconciling practical success with theoretical failure. *British Journal of Social Psychology, 35*, 535-553.

Renshon, J., & Renshon, S. A. (2008). The Theory and Practice of Foreign Policy Decision Making. *Political Psychology, 29*(4), 509-536.

Resnick, E. (2001). Defining Engagement. *Journal of International Affairs, 54*(2), 551.

Richter, M. (2005). A Family of Political Concepts. *European Journal of Political Theory, 4*(3), 221-248.

Richter, M. (2007). The Concept of Despotism and l'abus des mots. *Contributions to the History of Concepts, 3*(1), 5-22.

Riding, A. (1991). Conflict in Yugoslavia; Europeans send High-Level Team. *The New York Times.* Retrieved from http://www.nytimes.com/1991/06/29/world/conflict-in-yugoslavia-europeans-send-high-level-team.html

Ripley, B. (1993). Psychology, Foreign Policy, and International Relations Theory. *Political Psychology, 14*(3), 403-416.

Roberts, A. (1999). NATO's 'humanitarian war' over Kosovo. *Survival, 41*, 102-123.

Roberts, A. (2006). The United Nations and Humanitarian Intervention. In J. M. Welsh (Ed.), *Humanitarian Intervention and International Relations* (pp. 71-97). Oxford: Oxford University Press.

Ron, J. (2000). Territoriality and Plausible Deniability: Serbian Paramilitaries in the Bosnian War. In B. B. Campbell & A. D. Brenner (Eds.), *Death Squads in Global Perspective: Murder with Deniability* (pp. 287-312). New York: Palgrave MacMillan.

Rosati, J. A. (1995). A Cognitive Approach to the Study of Foreign Policy. In L. Neack, P. J. Haney & J. A. K. Hey (Eds.), *Foreign Policy Analysis: Continuity and Change in Its Second Generation* (pp. 49-70). Englewood Cliffs, N.J.: Prentice-Hall.

Rosati, J. A. (2000). The Power of Human Cognition in the Study of World Politics. *International Studies Review, 2*(3), 45-75.

Roth, G. (1968). Personal Rulership, Patrimonialism, and Empire-Building in the New States. *World Politics, 20*(02), 194-206.

Rotmann, P., Kurtz, G., & Brockmeier, S. (2014). Major powers and the contested evolution of a responsibility to protect. *Conflict, Security & Development, 14*(4), 355-377.

Rummel, R. J. (1994). Power, Genocide and Mass Murder. *Journal of Peace Research, 31*(1), 1-10.

Rutgers, M. R., & Schreurs, P. (2006). The Morality of Value- and Purpose-Rationality: The Kantian Roots of Weber's Foundational Distinction. *Administration & Society, 38*(4), 403-421.

Sadat, L. N. (Ed.). (2011). *Forging a Convention for Crimes Against Humanity* Cambridge: Cambridge University Press.

Sasley, B. E. (2011). Theorizing States' Emotions. *International Studies Review, 13*(3), 452-476.

SC/6659. (1999). Security Council Rejects Demand For Cessation Of Use Of Force Against Federal Republic Of Yugoslavia [Press release]. Retrieved from http://www.un.org/press/en/1999/19990326.sc6659.html

Schabas, W. A. (2007). Whither genocide? The International Court of Justice finally pronounces. *Journal of Genocide Research, 9*(2), 183-192.

Schmidt, S. (2011). To Order the Minds of Scholars: The Discourse of the Peace of Westphalia in International Relations Literature. *International Studies Quarterly, 55*(3), 601-623.

Schnabel, A., & Thakur, R. (2000). Kosovo, the changing contours of world politics, and the challenge of world order. In R. T. Albrecht Schnabel (Ed.), *Kosovo and the Challenge of Humanitarian Intervention: Selective Indignation, Collective Action and International Citizenship*. Tokyo: United Nations University Press.

Scobell, A. (2005). Making Sense of North Korea: Pyongyang and Comparative Communism. *Asian Security, 1*(3), 245-266.

Segady, T. W. (1988). Rationality and irrationality: New directions in Weberian theory, critique, and research. *Sociological Spectrum, 8*(1), 85-100.

Seierstad, A. (2004). *Met de rug naar de wereld: Portretten uit Servië*. Breda: De Geus.

Sekelj, L. (2000). Parties and Elections: The Federal Republic of Yugoslavia. Change without Transformation. *Europe-Asia Studies, 52*(1), 57-75.

Sekulic, D., Massey, G., & Hodson, R. (1994). Who Were the Yugoslavs? Failed Sources of a Common Identity in the Former Yugoslavia. *American Sociological Review, 59*(1), 83-97.

Sekulić, D., Massey, G., & Hodson, R. (2006). Ethnic intolerance and ethnic conflict in the dissolution of Yugoslavia. *Ethnic and Racial Studies, 29*(5), 797-827.

Seliktar, O., & Dutter, L. E. (2009). Assessing the Rationality of Autocrats: The Case of Saddam Hussein. *International Journal of Intelligence and CounterIntelligence, 22*(2), 275-297.

Sell, L. (2002). *Slobodan Milosevic and the Destruction of Yugoslavia*. Durham: Duke University Press.

Sells, M. A. (1998). *The Bridge Betrayed: Religion and Genocide in Bosnia*. Berkeley: University of California Press.

Sémelin, J. (2003). Toward a vocabulary of massacre and genocide. *Journal of Genocide Research, 5*(2), 193-210.

Shaw, M. (2007a). The general hybridity of war and genocide. *Journal of Genocide Research, 9*(3), 461-473.

Shaw, M. (2007b). *What is Genocide?* Cambridge: Polity Press.

Shigeno, R. (2004). Nationalism and Serbian Intellectuals. *Perspectives on European Politics and Society, 5*(1), 135-159.

Short, P. (2004). *Pol Pot: The History of a Nightmare*. London: Murray Publishers.

Shue, H. (2006). Limiting Sovereignty. In J. M. Welsh (Ed.), *Humanitarian Intervention and International Relations* (pp. 11-28). New York: Oxford University Press.

Simon, H. A. (1985). Human Nature in Politics: The Dialogue of Psychology with Political Science. *The American Political Science Review, 79*(2), 293-304.

Singer, D. J. (1961). The Level-of-Analysis Problem in International Relations. *World Politics, 14*(01), 77-92.

Smeulers, A. (2004). What transforms ordinary people into gross human hights violators? In S. Carey & S. Poe (Eds.), *Understanding human rights violations: new systematic studies*. Alderschot: Ashgate Publishing.

Smeulers, A., & Grünfeld, F. (2011). *International Crimes and Other Gross Human Rights Violations: A Multi- and Interdisciplinary Textbook* Leiden: Martinus Nijhoff Publishers.

Smeulers, A., & Van Niekerk, S. (2009). Abu Ghraib and the War on Terror—a case against Donald Rumsfeld? *Crime, Law and Social Change, 51*(3-4), 327-349.

Smeulers, A., & Werner, W. (2010). The Banality of Evil on Trial. In C. Stahn & L. Van den Herik (Eds.), *Future Perspectives on International Criminal Justice*. The Hague: TMC Asser Press.

Smith, D. (2002). Europe's Peacebuilding Hour? Past Failures, Future Challenges. *Journal of International Affairs, 55*(2), 441-460.

Smith, M. G. (2016). Review of the UN High-Level Independent Panel on Peace Operations, Uniting Our Strengths for Peace: Politics, Partnership and People. *Global Governance: A Review of Multilateralism and International Organizations, 22*(2), 179-187.

Smith, S., Hadfield, A., & Dunne, T. (2012a). Introduction. In S. Smith, A. Hadfield & T. Dunne (Eds.), *Foreign Policy: Theories, Actors, Cases* (pp. 1-9). Oxford: Oxford University Press.

Smith, S., Hadfield, A., & Dunne, T. (Eds.). (2012b). *Foreign Policy: Theories, Actors, Cases*. Oxford: Oxford University Press.

Snellen, I.T.H.M. (1987). *Boeiend en Geboeid: Ambivalenties en ambities in de bestuurskunde*. Alphen aan den Rijn: Samsom Uitgeverij.

Snidal, D. (2002). Rational Choice and International Relations. In W. Carlsnaes, T. Risse & B. A. Simmons (Eds.), *Handbook of International Relations* (pp. 73-95). London: Sage Publications.

Sofer, S. (2001). Being a 'pathetic hero' in international politics: The diplomat as a historical actor. *Diplomacy & Statecraft, 12*(1), 107-112.

Solarz, S. J. (1990). Cambodia and the International Community. *Foreign Affairs, 69*(2), 99-115.

Sondrol, P. C. (1991). Totalitarian and Authoritarian Dictators: A Comparison of Fidel Castro and Alfredo Stroessner. *Journal of Latin American Studies, 23*(3), 599-620.

Sørensen, G. (1999). Sovereignty: Change and Continuity in a Fundamental Institution. *Political Studies, 47*(3), 590-604.

Sorensen, J. S. (2003). War as social transformation: Wealth, class, power and an illiberal economy in Serbia. *Civil Wars, 6*(4), 55 – 82.

Stahn, C. (2007). Responsibility to Protect: Political Rhetoric or Emerging Legal Norm? *The American Journal of International Law, 101*(1), 99-120.

Starr, B. E. (1999). The Structure of Max Weber's Ethic of Responsibility. *Journal of Religious Ethics, 27*(3), 407-434.

State Portal of the Republic of Kosova. Retrieved 10 May 2016, 2016, from https://www.rks-gov.net/sq-AL/Pages/ShtetKaneNjohurKosoven.aspx

Staub, E. (1989). *The Roots of Evil: The Origins of Genocide and Other Group Violence.* Cambridge Cambridge University Press.

Staub, E. (2000). Genocide and Mass Killing: Origins, Prevention, Healing and Reconciliation. *Political Psychology, 21*(2), 367-382.

Staub, E. (2010). *Overcoming Evil* Oxford: Oxford University Press.

Stefanović, D. (2005). Seeing the Albanians through Serbian Eyes: The Inventors of the Tradition of Intolerance and Their Critics, 1804-1939. *European History Quarterly, 35*(3), 465-492.

Stein, J. G. (2012). Foreign policy decision making: rational, psychological and neurological models. In S. Smith, A. Hadfield & T. Dunne (Eds.), *Foreign Policy: Theories, Actors, Cases* (pp. 130-146). Oxford: Oxford University Press.

Steinbruner, J. (1976). Beyond Rational Deterrence: The Struggle For New Conceptions. *World Politics, 28*(2), 223-245.

Steinbruner, J. D. (1974). *The Cybernetic Theory of Decision.* Princeton Princeton University Press.

Stern, E. K. (2003). Crisis Studies and Foreign Policy Analysis: Insights, Synergies, and Challenges. *International Studies Review, 5*(2), 155-202.

Sternberg, R. J. (2003). A duplex theory of hate: Development and application to terrorism, massacres, and genocide. *Review of General Psychology, 7*(3), 299-328.

Stevanovic, V. (2004). *Milosevic: The People's Tyrant* (Z. Filipovic, Trans. T. Johansson Ed.). London: I.B. Tauris.

Stewart, C. S. (2007). *Hunting the Tiger: The Fast Life and Violent Death of the Balkans' Most Dangerous Man.* New York: Thomas Dunne Books/St. Martin's Press.

Stockburger, P. (2010). The Responsibility to Protect Doctrine: Customary International Law, an Emerging Legal Norm, or Just Wishful Thinking. *Intercultural Human Rights Law Review, 5*, 365-406.

Straus, S. (2001). Organic purity and the role of anthropology in Cambodia and Rwanda. *Patterns of Prejudice, 35*(2), 47-62.

Straus, S. (2015). Triggers of Mass Atrocities. *Politics and Governance, 3*(3), 5-15.

Strauss, E. (2009). A Bird in the Hand is Worth Two in the Bush On the Assumed Legal Nature of the Responsibility to Protect. *Global Responsibility to Protect, 1*(3), 291-323.

Stuenkel, O., & Tourinho, M. (2014). Regulating intervention: Brazil and the responsibility to protect. *Conflict, Security & Development, 14*(4), 379-402.

Sudetic, C. (1991). In Zagreb and Belgrade, the War Is Taking Its Toll. *The New York Times*. Retrieved from http://www.nytimes.com/1991/10/10/world/in-zagreb-and-belgrade-the-war-is-taking-its-toll.html?pagewanted=3&src=pm

. Summary of the Seventh Informal Interactive Dialogue on the UN General Assembly on the Responsibility to Protect. (2015). New York: Global Centre for the Responsibility to Protect.

Swedberg, R. (2003). The Changing Picture of Max Weber's Sociology. *Annual Review of Sociology, 29*, 283-306.

Swidler, A. (1973). The Concept of Rationality in the Work of Max Weber. *Sociological Inquiry, 43*(1), 35-42.

Sykes, G. M., & Matza, D. (1957). Techniques of Neutralization: A Theory of Delinquency. *American Sociological Review, 22*(6), 664-670.

Takei, M. (1998). Collective memory as the key to national and ethnic identity: The case of Cambodia. *Nationalism and Ethnic Politics, 4*(3), 59-78.

Tan, L. H. (1979). Cambodia's Total Revolution. *Index on Censorship, 8*(1), 3-10.

Tannenwald, N. (2005). Ideas and Explanation: Advancing the Theoretical Agenda *Journal of Cold War Studies 7*(2), 13-42.

Tanter, R. (1972). International System and Foreign Policy Approaches: Implications for Conflict Modelling and Management. *World Politics, 24*, 7-39.

Tarrow, S. (2010). The Strategy of Paired Comparison: Toward a Theory of Practice. *Comparative Political Studies, 43*(2), 230-259.

Telhami, S. (2002). Kenneth Waltz, Neorealism, and Foreign Policy. *Security Studies, 11*(3), 158-170.

Tetlock, P. E. (1983). Psychological research on foreign policy: A methodological overview. In L. Wheeler (Ed.), *Review of personality and social psychology* (Vol. 4, pp. 45-79). Beverly Hills: Sage.

Thakur, R. (2006). *The United Nations, Peace and Security*. Cambridge: Cambridge University Press.

The Independent International Commission on Kosovo. (2000). The Kosovo Report: Conflict, International Response, Lessons Learned. Oxford: Oxford

Thies, C. G., & Breuning, M. (2012). Integrating Foreign Policy Analysis and International Relations through Role Theory. *Foreign Policy Analysis, 8*(1), 1-4.

Tindale, R. S., Munier, C., Wasserman, M., & Smith, C. M. (2002). Group Processes and the Holocaust. In L. S. Newman & R. Erber (Eds.), *Understanding genocide: the social psychology of the Holocaust*. Oxford: Oxford University Press.

Toje, A. (2008). The Consensus—Expectations Gap: Explaining Europe's Ineffective Foreign Policy. *Security Dialogue, 39*(1), 121-141.

Tucker, R. C. (1965). The Dictator and Totalitarianism. *World Politics, 17*(04), 555-583.

Tullock, G. (1987). *Autocracy*. Dordrecht: Martinus Nijhoff Publishers.

Turchetti, M. (2008). 'Despotism' and 'Tyranny' Unmasking a Tenacious Confusion. *European Journal of Political Theory, 7*(2), 159-182.

Turner, J. C., Brown, R. J., & Tajfel, H. (1979). Social comparison and group interest in ingroup favouritism. *European Journal of Social Psychology, 9*(2), 187-204.

Turner, S., & Mazur, G. (2009). Morgenthau as a Weberian Methodologist. *European Journal of International Relations, 15*(3), 477-504.

Turner, S. P. (1983). Weber on Action. *American Sociological Review, 48*(4), 506-519.

UN. (2012, 5 September 2012). World not fulfilling "never again" vow, Secretary-General tells General Assembly meeting on Responsibility to Protect. Retrieved 24 July 2013, 2013, from http://www.un.org/News/Press/docs/2012/ga11270.doc.htm

UN. (2013). New special UN adviser to focus on responsibility to protect. Retrieved 24 July, 2013, from http://un.org.au/2013/07/16/new-special-un-adviser-to-focus-on-responsibility-to-protect/

United Nations. (2005). 2005 World Summit Outcome: United Nations: General Assembly.

Valentino, B. (2000). Final solutions: the causes of mass killing and genocide. *Security Studies, 9*(3), 1-59.

Valentino, B. (2004). *Final Solutions: Mass Killing and Genocide in the Twentieth Century*. Ithaca: Cornell University Press.

Varshney, A. (2003). Nationalism, Ethnic Conflict, and Rationality. *Perspectives on Politics, 1*(1), 85-99.

Verba, S. (1961). Assumptions of Rationality and Non-Rationality in Models of the International System. *World Politics, 14*(1), 93-117.

Vetlesen, A. J. (2005). *Evil and Human Agency: Understanding Collective Evildoing*. Cambridge: Cambridge University Press.

Vickery, M. (1984). *Cambodia: 1975-1982*. Sydney: South End Press.

Vladisavljević, N. (2004). Institutional power and the rise of Milošević. *Nationalities papers, 32*(1), 183-205.

Vrieze, F. d. (2000). *De Kosovo-Diplomatie: Waarom de voorspelde oorlog niet werd voorkomen*. Berchem: De Wrikker.

Walker, S. G. (2011a). Foreign Policy Analysis and Behavioural International Relations. In S. G. Walker, A. Malici & M. Schafer (Eds.), *Rethinking Foreign Policy Analysis: States, Leaders and the Microfoundations of Behavioural International Relations* (pp. 3-20). New York: Routledge.

Walker, S. G. (2011b). Macropolitics and Foreign Policy Decisions: The Billiard Ball Model of IR. In S. G. Walker, A. Malici & M. Schafer (Eds.), *Rethinking Foreign Policy Analysis: States, Leaders and the Microfoundatoins of Behavioural Intrenational Relations* (pp. 21-43). New York: Routledge.

Walker, S. G., Malici, A., & Schafer, M. (Eds.). (2011). *Rethinking Foreign Policy Analysis: States, Leaders and the Microfoundations of Behavioural International Relations*. New York: Routledge.

Wallace, W. (1990). Rationality, human nature, and society in Weber's theory. *Theory and Society, 19*(2), 199-223.

Waller, J. E. (2010). The Ordinariness of Extraordinary Evil: The Making of Perpetrators of Collective Violence. In A. Smeulers (Ed.), *Collective Violence and International Criminal Justice: An Interdisciplinary Approach* (pp. 19-37). Antwerpen: Intersentia.

Walt, S. M. (1998). International Relations: One World, Many Theories. *Foreign Policy, 110*(Spring), 29-46.

Waltz, K. (2005). Anarchic Orders and Balances of Power. In G. J. Ikenberry (Ed.), *American Foreign Polic: Theoretical Essays* (pp. 60-83). New York: Pearson Longman.

Wayne Nafziger, E., & Auvinen, J. (2002). Economic Development, Inequality, War, and State Violence. *World Development, 30*(2), 153-163.

Webber, M. (2009). The Kosovo war: a recapitulation. *International Affairs, 85*(3), 447-459.

Weber, M. (1964). *The Theory of Social and Economic Organization* (T.P.A.M. Henderson, Trans.). New York: The Free Press.

Weerdesteijn, M. (2015). Stopping Mass Atrocities: Targeting the Dictator. *Politics and Governance, 3*(3), 53-66.

Weerdesteijn, M. (2016 – in press). Dealing with Dictators: the importance of interdisciplinary research when addressing complex criminality. In D. B. Abels, D., Peeters, S., Vriend, K, Van der Wilt, H. (Ed.), *Complex Criminality.* The Hague: Boom/Eleven international publishing.

Weerdesteijn, M., & Smeulers, A. (2011). Propaganda en Paramilitairen: De normalisatie van geweld in het Servië van de jaren negentig. *Tijdschrift voor Criminologie, 53*(4), 328-344.

Weller, M. (1999). The Rambouillet Conference on Kosovo. *International Affairs, 75*(2), 211-251.

Welsh, J. (2015). The responsibility to prevent: Assessing the gap between rhetoric and reality. *Cooperation and Conflict.*

Welsh, J., & Banda, M. (2010). International Law and the Responsibility to Protect: Clarifying or Expanding States' Responsibilities? *Global Responsibility to Protect, 2*(3), 213-231.

Welsh, J., Thielking, C., & MacFarlane, S. N. (2001-2002). Responsibility to Protect – Assessing the Report of the International Commission on Intervention and State Sovereignty. *International Journal 57*, 489-512.

Werner, W. (2014). International Law and Renegade Regimes. In W. Wagner, W. Werner & M. Onderco (Eds.), *Deviance in International Relations: 'Rogue States' and International Security* (pp. 193-213). New York: Palgrave Macmillan.

Wester, K. (2016 – in press). *Promise and Pitfalls of the Responsibility to Protect and Lessons to be Learned from the Case of Libya.* Amsterdam: University of Amsterdam.

Wheeler, N. J. (2000). *Saving Strangers: Humanitarian Intervention in International Society.* Oxford: Oxford University Press.

Wheeler, N. J. (2006). The Humanitarian Responsibilities of Sovereignty: Explaining the Development of a New Norm of Military Intervention for Humanitarian Purposes in International Society. In J. M. Welsh (Ed.), *Humanitarian Intervention and International Relations* (pp. 29-51). Oxford: Oxford University Press.

White, B. (1999). The European Challenge to Foreign Policy Analysis. *European Journal of International Relations, 5*(1), 37-66.

White, E. K. (2009). Humanity as the A and Ω of Sovereignty: Four Replies to Anne Peters. *European Journal of International Law, 20*(3), 545-549.

Windgassen, A. (2002). *Vrouwen van dictators: Heulen met de macht* (R. v. d. Veen, Trans.). 's-Graveland: Fontaine Uitgevers bv.

Wintrobe, R. (1990). The Tinpot and the Totalitarian: An Economic Theory of Dictatorship. *The American Political Science Review, 84*(3), 849-872.

Wintrobe, R. (2009). Dictatorship: Analytical Approaches. In C. Boix & S. C. Stokes (Eds.), *The Oxford Handbook of Comparative Politics*: Oxford Handbooks Online.

Witteveen, W. J. (2011). Brutus over tirannicide en het risico van wederkerige wetteloosheid. *RegelMaat, 26*(6), 351-356.

Wittner, L. S. (1981). How Realistic is American Diplomacy? *Reviews in American History, 9*(1), 118-123.

Womack, B. (2003). Asymmetry and systemic misperception: China, Vietnam and Cambodia during the 1970s. *Journal of Strategic Studies, 26*(2), 92-119.

Woods, P. A. (2001). Values-intuitive rational action: the dynamic relationship of instrumental rationality and values insights as a form of social action. *The British Journal of Sociology, 52*(4), 687-706.

Woodward, S. L. (1995). *Balkan Tragedy: Chaos and Dissolution After the Cold War.* Washington D.C.: The Brookings Institution.

Woolf, L. M., & Hulsizer, M. R. (2005). Psychosocial roots of genocide: risk, prevention, and intervention. *Journal of Genocide Research, 7*(1), 101-128.

Zafirovski, M. (2003). Human Rational Behaviour and Economic Rationality. *Electronic Journal of Sociology, 7*(2).

Zafirovski, M. (2005). Is sociology the science of the irrational? Conceptions of rationality in sociological theory. *The American Sociologist, 36*(1), 85-110.

Zakosek, N. (2007). The Heavy Burden of History: Political Uses of the Past in the Yugoslav Successor States. *Politicka misao, XLIV*(5), 29-43.